Economics for today

2nd Edition

For

Monica, Caleb and Lilly-Anne

and

Veronica, Chloe, Thomas and Nicola

Economics for today

2nd Edition

Allan Layton
Tim Robinson
Irvin B. Tucker

THOMSON

Australia · Canada · Mexico · Singapore · Spain · United Kingdom · United States

Level 7, 80 Dorcas St
South Melbourne, Victoria, 3205

Email: highereducation@thomsonlearning.com.au
Website: www.thomsonlearning.com.au

First published in 2002. Second edition published 2005.
10 9 8 7 6 5 4 3 2
08 07 06

National Library of Australia
Cataloguing-in-Publication data

Layton, Allan P.

2nd ed.
Bibliography.
ISBN 0 17 012264 6.

1. Macroeconomics. I. Tucker, Irvin B. II. Robinson, T. J. C. (Tim J. C.), 1945 – . III. Title.

330

Editor: Frances Wade
Project editor: Tony Davidson
Developmental editor: Nigel Chin
Publishing manager: Michael Tully
Indexer: Russell Brooks
Text designer: Rachael Harris
Cover designer: Rachael Harris
Cover image from Getty Images
Typeset in Bembo 10.5/14 pt by Linda Hamley
Production controller: Jodie Tamblyn
Printed in China by China Translation and Printing Services Ltd.

This title is published under the imprint of Thomson.
Nelson Australia Pty Limited ACN 058 280 149 (incorporated in Victoria) trading as Thomson Learning Australia.

The URLs contained in this publication were checked for currency during the production process. Note, however, that the publisher cannot vouch for the ongoing currency of URLs.

Brief contents

Contents

About the authors

Professor Allan Layton, BEcon. (Hons), MEcon., PhD, received his doctorate from the University of Queensland in 1982. Since then he has held academic posts at La Trobe University, Griffith University, Macquarie University, the University of Queensland and the Queensland University of Technology in Australia, and at Columbia University in the USA. He is currently Professor of Economics and Head of the School of Economics and Finance at the Queensland University of Technology. His research and teaching interests span international business-cycle analysis, financial and monetary economics, macroeconomic policy, and applied econometrics. He is the author of *Modern Australian Macroeconomics* and has published widely in international academic journals. He has also acted as consultant to a number of private- and public-sector organisations in Australia and in the USA.

Associate Professor Tim Robinson, BEcon. (Hons), PhD, worked in the private sector for seven years prior to embarking upon an academic career. Part of his time in the private sector was spent running his own small business. He is currently Associate Professor of Economics in the School of Economics and Finance at Queensland University of Technology, where he has taught introductory and intermediate economics for many years. He has taught at a number of universities and has published in the areas of environmental economics, applied welfare economics, the history of economic thought, the teaching of economics, and the new economy. Books he has authored or co-authored include *Economic Theories of Exhaustible Resources*, *Macroeconomics: a Contemporary Introduction* and *Microeconomics: a Contemporary Introduction*. He has also undertaken economic consulting work in the areas of curriculum development, financial investment, taxation and the environment.

Dr Irvin B. Tucker, BS, SC, PhD, has taught introductory economics at the University of North Carolina at Charlotte and the University of South Carolina. He is former Director of the Center for Economic Education at the University of North Carolina at Charlotte and long-time member of the National Council on Economic Education. He has published widely in professional journals, and is author of *Survey of Economics*.

Preface to the second edition

This new edition of *Economics for Today* follows on from the success of the first edition, which has been adopted for one-semester courses at both undergraduate and postgraduate levels across Australia and in New Zealand. It retains the 'student friendly' approach and the many boxed features of the first edition. There has been revision of the text with supporting diagrams where necessary to improve flow and clarity, and the real-world examples have been brought up to date. All relevant data have also been completely updated.

A new appendix to Chapter 14 briefly explains the 'Keynesian Cross' approach to macro modelling as well as directing the interested student to the publisher's website where further material, sourced from the authors, introduces the IS LM BP (Mundell Fleming) model.

An interesting new feature is the introduction of material relating to economics and ethics. Ethical considerations have been recently brought to the fore, as far as modern business practice is concerned, following a spate of highly publicised corporate scandals in 2002–04 in various countries, including Australia. This new material, which is included in a number of chapters in the text, should help fulfil the requirements of international accrediting bodies, which are increasingly requiring the integration of ethical issues into business units.

Most important, in making the revisions for this second edition, the authors owe a debt of gratitude to the many adopters and potential adopters who have provided feedback on the first edition.

Preface to the first edition

Text with a mission

The purpose of *Economics for Today* is to teach, in an engaging style, the basic principles of microeconomics and macroeconomics to students who will take a one-semester course in economics. With the growth of business studies in areas outside economics, including the increasingly popular MBA, there has been a huge increase in the number of students studying introductory economics as a terminal course. This book is aimed at these students. It also provides a firm foundation for students who will progress to further studies in economics.

Rather than taking an encyclopaedic approach to economic concepts, *Economics for Today* focuses on some of the most important tools in economics, such as supply and demand analysis, and applies them to clearly explain real-world economic issues.

Every effort has been made to make *Economics for Today* the most 'student friendly' text on the market. This book was written to simplify the often confusing array of economic analyses that forces some students simply to memorise in order to pass. Instead, it presents a straightforward and balanced approach that effectively teaches the application of basic economic principles. After reading this book, the student should be able to say 'the economics stuff in the news finally makes sense'.

How it fits together

The text presents the core principles of microeconomics and macroeconomics in an international context. The first ten chapters introduce the logic of economic analysis and develop the core of microeconomics. Here students learn the role of demand and supply in determining prices in markets characterised by varying degrees of competition. This part of the book explores issues such as minimum wage laws, market failure, economies and diseconomies of scale, competition policy and aspects of microeconomic reform. The next eight chapters develop the macroeconomics part of the text. Using the modern aggregate demand and aggregate supply model, the text develops a clear and workable understanding of the determinants of changes in the price level, national output and employment in the economy. The study of macroeconomics also includes a discussion of a nation's monetary system, explaining how the supply of, and demand for, money influence the economy. It also introduces the student to important issues relating to the conduct of modern monetary and fiscal policy. Throughout the book, the significance of international influences on national economies is recognised, and to further underline the great importance of international considerations in understanding modern macroeconomics, the final chapter is devoted to international matters. For example, students will learn how the supply of and demand for currencies determine exchange rates, and what the implications are of a high or low value for the dollar.

Text flexibility

Economics for Today is easily adapted to lecturers' preferences for the sequencing of microeconomics and macroeconomics topics. The text can be used in a macroeconomic–microeconomic sequence by teaching the first four chapters and then Chapters 11 to 18. The microeconomics content can then be covered with Chapters 5 to 10. This approach allows students to identify with macro issues – which tend often to be in the news – before studying microeconomics.

The book has eighteen chapters and will allow students to easily cover approximately one and a half chapters each week over twelve teaching weeks. Alternatively, some chapters and some parts of chapters can be omitted at the discretion of the lecturer. Some proposals along these lines are included in the Instructor's Manual.

An alternative placement for Chapter 18, 'International trade and finance', is also possible. As well as incorporating international issues throughout, *Economics for Today* explicitly addresses international influences on national economies in Chapter 18. Some instructors may prefer to cover Chapter 18 earlier – immediately after Part 4, for example.

Special features

Each chapter contains a number of current real-world exercises and topics for discussion:

- **Online exercises** at the end of each chapter guide students to websites to use as a basis for problem-solving exercises.
- **Internet margin notes** throughout the text provide Internet addresses of sites relevant to the topics being discussed, and encourage students to visit the sites for more information.
- **You make the call** sections in each chapter ask students to answer a simple question related to the topic being discussed. Answers are provided at the end of the chapter.
- **International focus** sections in each chapter highlight chapter topics in a global context.
- **Analyse the issue** sections in each chapter provide a brief case study for students to analyse.
- The **summary** at the end of each chapter includes graphs and causation chains to refresh students' memories of the chapter topics.

Resources guide

FOR THE STUDENT

As you read this text you will find a wealth of features in every chapter and part to enhance your study of economics and help you understand how it is applied in the real world.

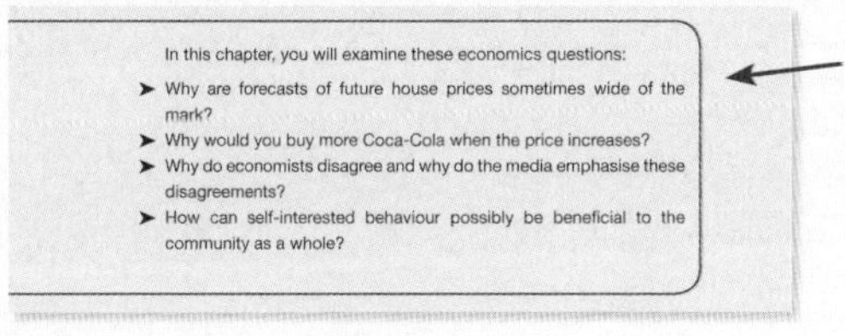

Economics questions are listed at the start of each chapter to give you a clear sense of what economic concepts will be covered.

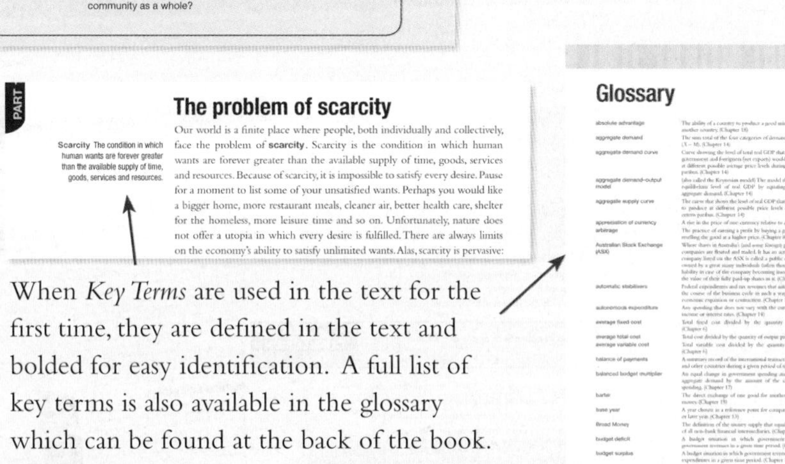

When *Key Terms* are used in the text for the first time, they are defined in the text and bolded for easy identification. A full list of key terms is also available in the glossary which can be found at the back of the book.

Analyse the issue topics present a brief case study so that you can apply the ideas explained in each chapter.

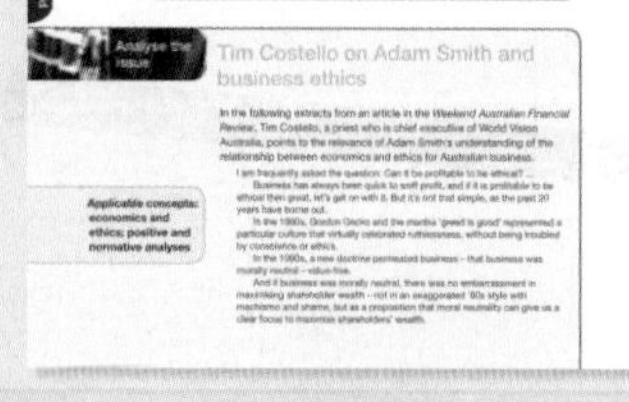

You make the call sections in each chapter ask what you would do in a hypothetical situation, giving you the chance to apply what you've just learned. Answers are given at the end of the chapter.

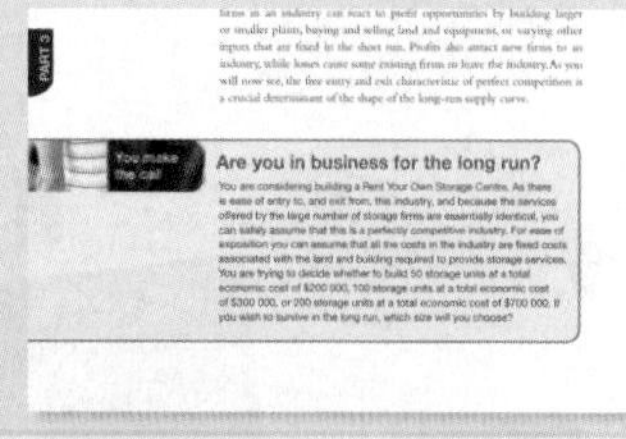

International focus sections explore global influences on economics, showing the way in which international phenomena affect the chapter topic.

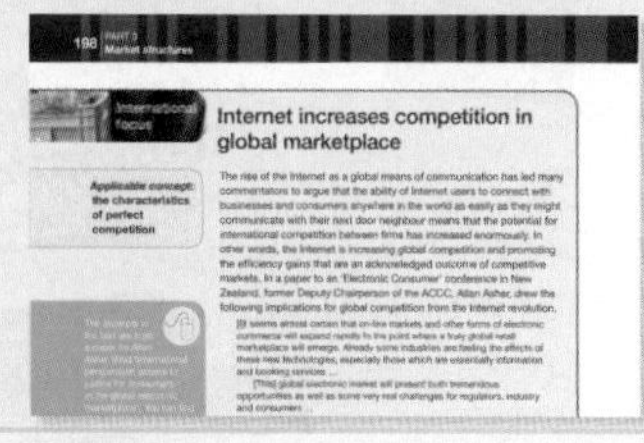

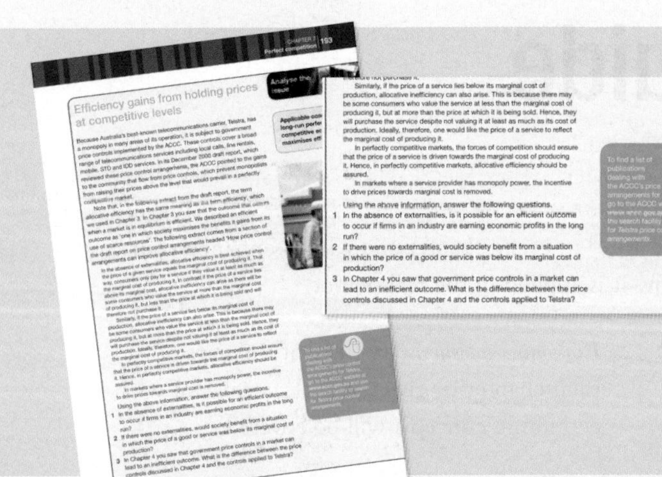
CHAPTER 7 153 Perfect competition

Efficiency gains from holding prices at competitive levels

Analyse the issue

...ore not purchase it.

Similarly, if the price of a service lies below its marginal cost of production, allocative inefficiency can also arise. This is because there may be some consumers who value the service at less than the marginal cost of producing it, but at more than the price at which it is being sold. Hence, they will purchase the service despite not valuing it at least as much as its cost of production. Ideally, therefore, one would like the price of a service to reflect the marginal cost of producing it.

In perfectly competitive markets, the forces of competition should ensure that the price of a service is driven towards the marginal cost of producing it. Hence, in perfectly competitive markets, allocative efficiency should be assured.

In markets where a service provider has monopoly power, the incentive to drive prices towards marginal cost is removed.

Using the above information, answer the following questions.

1 In the absence of externalities, is it possible for an efficient outcome to occur if firms in an industry are earning economic profits in the long run?
2 If there were no externalities, would society benefit from a situation in which the price of a good or service was below its marginal cost of production?
3 In Chapter 4 you saw that government price controls in a market can lead to an inefficient outcome. What is the difference between the price controls discussed in Chapter 4 and the controls applied to Telstra?

To find a list of publications dealing with the ACCC's price control arrangements for Telstra, go to the ACCC website at www.accc.gov.au and use the search facility to search for Telstra price control arrangements.

Internet links in the margins throughout each chapter help you use the web for further research.

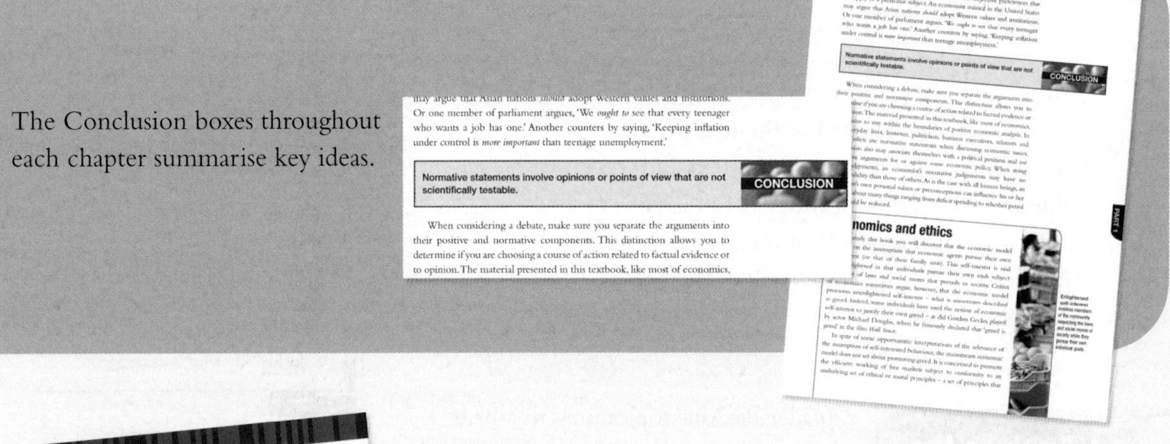
CHAPTER 1 Introducing the economic way of thinking 15

may argue that Asian nations *should* adopt Western values and institutions. Or one member of parliament argues, 'We *ought* to see that every teenager who wants a job has one.' Another counters by saying, 'Keeping inflation under control is *more important* than teenage unemployment.'

Normative statements involve opinions or points of view that are not scientifically testable. CONCLUSION

When considering a debate, make sure you separate the arguments into their positive and normative components. This distinction allows you to determine if you are choosing a course of action related to factual evidence or to opinion. The material presented in this textbook, like most of economics,

The Conclusion boxes throughout each chapter summarise key ideas.

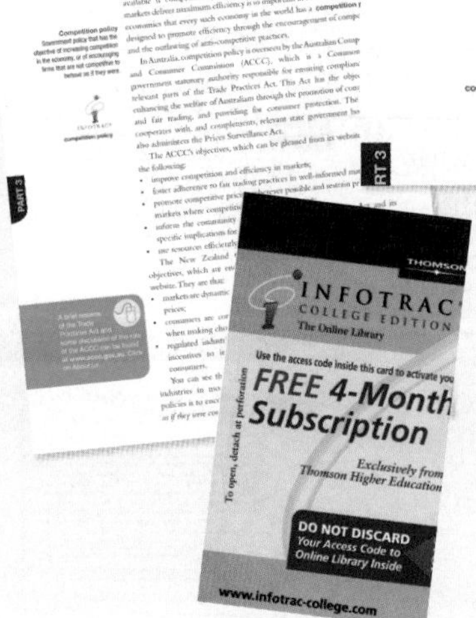
176 PART 3 Market structures

...firms that are not competitive to behave as if they were.

INFOTRAC® competition policy

In Australia, competition policy is overseen by the Australian Competition and Consumer Commission (ACCC), which is a Commonwealth government statutory authority responsible for ensuring compliance with relevant parts of the Trade Practices Act. This Act has the objective of enhancing the welfare of Australians through the promotion of competition and fair trading, and providing for consumer protection. The ACCC cooperates with, and complements, relevant state government bodies and also administers the Prices Surveillance Act.

The ACCC's objectives, which can be gleaned from its website, include the following:

- improve competition and efficiency in markets;

Infotrac® search terms are also available throughout each chapter. Included with this text is a passcode that gives you a FREE four-month subscription to InfoTrac College Edition. This online library will provide you with access to full-text articles from thousands of scholarly and popular periodicals. Don't restrict yourself to the search terms provided throughout the book, think of your own search terms and expand your general economics knowledge.

At the end of each chapter you'll find several learning tools to help you to not only review the chapter and key concepts but also to help you extend your learning.

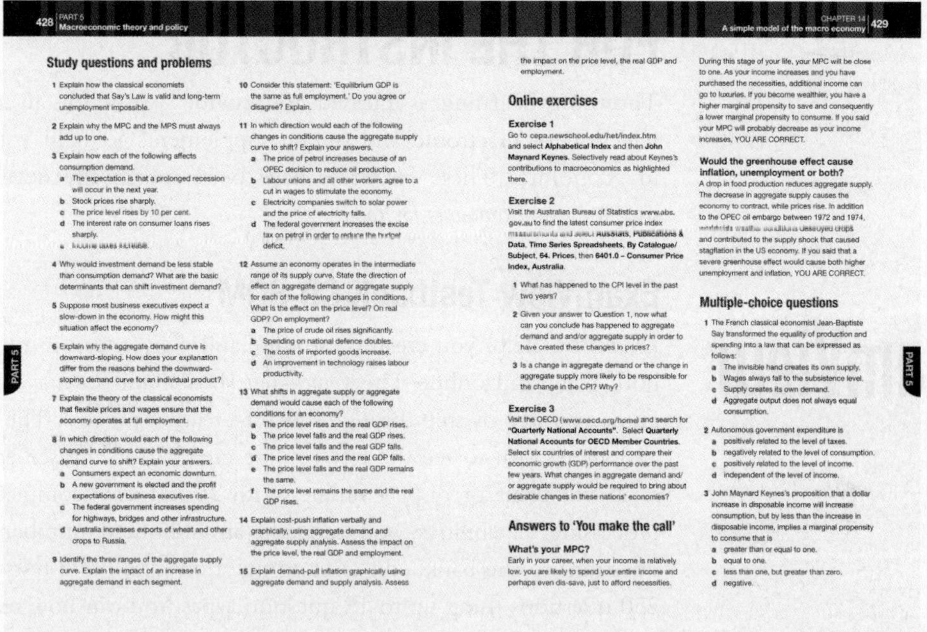

428 PART 5 Macroeconomic theory and policy

Study questions and problems

1 Explain how the classical economists concluded that Say's Law is valid and long-term unemployment impossible.

2 Explain why the MPC and the MPS must always add up to one.

3 Explain how each of the following affects consumption demand.
   a The expectation is that a prolonged recession will occur in the next year.
   b Stock prices rise sharply.
   c The price level rises by 10 per cent.
   d The interest rate on consumer loans rises sharply.
   e Income taxes increase.

4 Why would investment demand be less stable than consumption demand? What are the basic determinants that can shift investment demand?

5 Suppose most business executives expect a slow-down in the economy. How might this situation affect the economy?

6 Explain why the aggregate demand curve is downward-sloping. How does your explanation differ from the reasons behind the downward-sloping demand curve for an individual product?

7 Explain the theory of the classical economists that flexible prices and wages ensure that the economy operates at full employment.

8 In which direction would each of the following changes in conditions cause the aggregate demand curve to shift? Explain your answers.
   a Consumers expect an economic downturn.
   b A new government is elected and the profit expectations of business executives rise.
   c The federal government increases spending for highways, bridges and other infrastructure.
   d Australia increases exports of wheat and other crops to Russia.

9 Identify the three ranges of the aggregate supply curve. Explain the impact of an increase in aggregate demand in each segment.

10 Consider this statement: 'Equilibrium GDP is the same as full employment.' Do you agree or disagree? Explain.

11 In which direction would each of the following changes in conditions cause the aggregate supply curve to shift? Explain your answers.
   a The price of petrol increases because of an OPEC decision to reduce oil production.
   b Labour unions and all other workers agree to a cut in wages to stimulate the economy.
   c Electricity companies switch to solar power and the price of electricity falls.
   d The federal government increases the excise tax on petrol in order to reduce the budget deficit.

12 Assume an economy operates in the intermediate range of its supply curve. State the direction of effect on aggregate demand or aggregate supply for each of the following changes in conditions. What is the effect on the price level? On real GDP? On employment?
   a The price of crude oil rises significantly.
   b Spending on national defence doubles.
   c The costs of imported goods increase.
   d An improvement in technology raises labour productivity.

13 What shifts in aggregate supply or aggregate demand would cause each of the following conditions for an economy?
   a The price level rises and the real GDP rises.
   b The price level falls and the real GDP rises.
   c The price level falls and the real GDP falls.
   d The price level rises and the real GDP falls.
   e The price level falls and the real GDP remains the same.
   f The price level remains the same and the real GDP rises.

14 Explain cost-push inflation verbally and graphically, using aggregate demand and aggregate supply analysis. Assess the impact on the price level, the real GDP and employment.

15 Explain demand-pull inflation graphically using aggregate demand and supply analysis. Assess the impact on the price level, the real GDP and employment.

Online exercises

Exercise 1
Go to cepa.newschool.edu/het/index.htm and select **Alphabetical Index** and then **John Maynard Keynes**. Selectively read about Keynes's contributions to macroeconomics as highlighted there.

Exercise 2
Visit the Australian Bureau of Statistics www.abs.gov.au to find the latest consumer price index measurements and select **AusStats, Publications & Data, Time Series Spreadsheets, By Catalogue/Subject, 64. Prices**, then **6401.0 – Consumer Price Index, Australia**.

1 What has happened to the CPI level in the past two years?

2 Given your answer to Question 1, now what can you conclude has happened to aggregate demand and and/or aggregate supply in order to have created these changes in prices?

3 Is a change in aggregate demand or the change in aggregate supply more likely to be responsible for the change in the CPI? Why?

Exercise 3
Visit the OECD (www.oecd.org/home) and search for **"Quarterly National Accounts"**. Select **Quarterly National Accounts for OECD Member Countries**. Select six countries of interest and compare their economic growth (GDP) performance over the past few years. What changes in aggregate demand and/or aggregate supply would be required to bring about desirable changes in these nations' economies?

Answers to 'You make the call'

What's your MPC?
Early in your career, when your income is relatively low, you are likely to spend your entire income and perhaps even dis-save, just to afford necessities. During this stage of your life, your MPC will be close to one. As your income increases and you have purchased the necessities, additional income can go to luxuries. If you become wealthier, you have a higher marginal propensity to save and consequently a lower marginal propensity to consume. If you said your MPC will probably decrease as your income increases, YOU ARE CORRECT.

Would the greenhouse effect cause inflation, unemployment or both?
A drop in food production reduces aggregate supply. The decrease in aggregate supply causes the economy to contract, while prices rise. In addition to the OPEC oil embargo between 1972 and 1974, worldwide weather conditions destroyed crops and contributed to the supply shock that caused stagflation in the US economy. If you said that a severe greenhouse effect would cause both higher unemployment and inflation, YOU ARE CORRECT.

Multiple-choice questions

1 The French classical economist Jean-Baptiste Say transformed the equality of production and spending into a law that can be expressed as follows:
   a The invisible hand creates its own supply.
   b Wages always fall to the subsistence level.
   c Supply creates its own demand.
   d Aggregate output does not always equal consumption.

2 Autonomous government expenditure is
   a positively related to the level of taxes.
   b negatively related to the level of consumption.
   c positively related to the level of income.
   d independent of the level of income.

3 John Maynard Keynes's proposition that a dollar increase in disposable income will increase consumption, but by less than the increase in disposable income, implies a marginal propensity to consume that is
   a greater than or equal to one.
   b equal to one.
   c less than one, but greater than zero.
   d negative.

CHAPTER 14 A simple model of the macro economy 429

- The *Key concepts* box lists the main ideas covered in the chapter.
- The end of chapter *Summary* provides you with key points from the chapter, giving you a snapshot of the chapter's content.
- *Study questions and problems* and *Multiple-choice questions* enable you to apply the theory you have learnt, which you can test in the real world using the *Online exercises*.

For updates and news relating to *Economics for Today*, please go to the companion website. At www.thomsonlearning.com.au/higher/economics/layton/2e

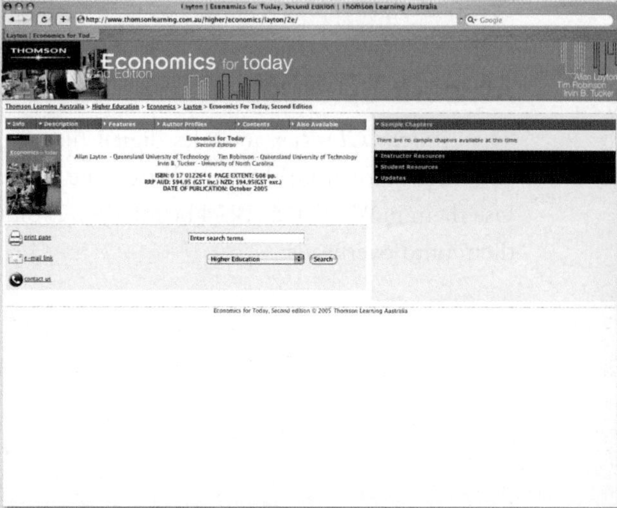

FOR THE INSTRUCTOR

Thomson Learning is pleased to provide you with an extensive selection of electronic and online supplements to help you lecture in economics. These resources have been specifically developed to supplement *Economics for Today.*

ExamView Testbank CD ROM

ExamView®

ExamView helps you create, customise and deliver tests in minutes for both print and online. The *Quick Test Wizard* and *Online Test Wizard* guide you step by step through the test-creation process. The program also allows you to see the test you are creating on the screen exactly as it will print or display online. With *ExamView's* complete word-processing capabilities, you can add an unlimited number of new questions to the bank, edit existing questions and build tests of up to 250 questions using up to 12 question types. You can now export the files into *Blackboard* or *WebCT*.

Instructor's Manual and PowerPoint Presentation on CD-ROM

The *Instructor's Manual* provides you with a wealth of content to help set up and administer an economics subject. It includes learning objectives, chapter outlines, key points, figures from the text, adjunct teaching and warm-up activities as well as solutions to problems in the text. Also included on the CD-ROMs are PowerPoint presentations to accompany *Economics for Today*. Use these slides to reinforce key economics principles.

Artwork CD-ROM

The *Artwork CD-Rom* includes digital files of graphs, tables, pictures and flow charts from the text that can be used in a variety of medias. Use them in WebCT or Blackboard, PowerPoint presentations or copy them onto overheads.

Acknowledgements

Many people have assisted us in very many ways to bring this project to fruition. They include Professor Ted Boss of University of Alabama, Birmingham, John Powell, Maria Robinson, Michael Robinson, Linda Taylor and Alan Williams. We also wish to thank the team at Thomson Learning, whose support and understanding have made the task so much easier for us. Thanks also to Veronica Horgan and Monica Layton for their help and continual support.

We would also like to thank the many reviewers who have provided numerous insightful suggestions for the current and previous editions, which we have attempted to take up wherever possible, particularly:

Chris Bajada – University of Technology, Sydney
Anis Chowdhury – University of Western Sydney
Jerry Courvisanos – University of Tasmania
Paul Flatau – Murdoch University
Anne Garnett – Murdoch University
Ross Guest – Griffith University
Anita Medhekar – Central Queensland University, Rockhampton
Tom Nguyen – Griffith University
Greg Parry – Edith Cowan University
Peter Slade – University of the Sunshine Coast
Ken Tester – Open Polytechnic Lower Hutt, New Zealand

Allan Layton
Tim Robinson
Irvin B. Tucker

Reviewers

The authors and publisher would like to gratefully credit or acknowledge the following:

Text

Allan Asher, former Deputy Chairperson of Australian Competition and Consumer Commission (ACCC), in a paper, 'International perspective: access to justice for consumers in the global electronic marketplace', to an 'Electronic Consumer' conference in NZ, p.198; Tables based on Australian Bureau of Statistics, 'International trade in goods and services', Dec 2004, Cat. No. 5368.0, Table 10, p.534, Cat. 5302, Table 1, p.552, Cat. No. 5206, Table 3, p.327 and p.329, Cat. No. 5302, Table 40, p.554 and p.559, Cat. No. 6202.0.55.001, Table 3, p.374, Cat. No. 6291.0.55.001, Table 1, p.383, Cat. No. 6401, Table 4A. p.357 and p.354, Cat No. 5206, Table 43, p.300, 317 and p.318, Cat. No. 5302, Table 1, p.316, various tables, p.313, Census, ABS 6310.0; ABS 6306.0, p.275 ABS data used with permission from the Australian Bureau of Statistics, www.abs.gov.au; David Bassanese, Comments section, *Australian Financial Review*, 12 August 2004, p.490; Central

Intelligence Agency, http://www.odci.gov, p.375, p.330, p.369; William S Comanor and Thomas A Wilson, 'Advertising market structure and performance', *The Review of Economics and Statistics*, 49:4 (Nov. 1967), pp. 423-40. © 1967 by the President and Fellows of Harvard College, p.239; Tim Costello, from 'Adam Smith problem offers ethical answers', *Weekend Australian Financial Review*, 25-26 Sept 2004, p. 62, reproduced on pp.16-18; Jennifer Dudley, 'Skivvy crew upset at scalpers' yummy profit', *The Courier Mail*, 1 October 2004, pp.101-2; 'Dollar dethroned by the might of frequent-flyer miles', edited article in *The Australian*, 10 January 2005, p. 27; reprinted originally from *The Economist*, pp.440-1; Federal Government Budget Paper No. 1, 2004-05, pp. 1-6, Chart 3, reproduced on p.522; Allan Fels, Chairman, ACCC 'Mergers and big business', speech presented at boardroom lunch, 'Mergers and Market Power', 15 March 2001, Sydney. Addressed to Australia-Israel Chamber of Commerce, p.226; Australian Competition and Consumer Commission (ACCC), December 2000 draft report, p.193; Charles Handy The Empty Raincoat, 1994, Hutchinson, London, p. 15; A Hawke and M Wooden, 'The changing face of Australian Industrial Relations', *Economic Record*, vol 74, no 224, 1998 and Australian Bureau of Statistics, 'Employee earnings, benefits and trade union membership', 6310 (Aug 2000), p.277; Kevin Helliker, 'Monster movies invade the cinema landscape', *Wall Street Journal*, 13 May 1997, p. B1, reproduced on p.163; David R Henderson, Preface, *The Fortune Encyclopedia of Economics*, 1993, p.12; Steven Jobs, cited in Deborah Wise & Catherine Harris, 'Apple's new crusade', *Business Week*, 26 November 1984, p 156, reproduced on p.164; Lini S. Kadaba, 'Futurists see more gizmos, fewer jobs', *Charlotte Observer*, 30 July 1995, p. 1A reproduced on pp.380-1; Wolfgang Kasper, 'Wolfgang Kasper says that good institutional rules make for prosperous nations', *Australian Financial Review*, Thursday 6 December 2001, p 55, pp.340-1; John Maynard Keynes, The General Theory of Employment, Interest and Money, Macmillan, London, 1936, p. 383. Reproduced by permission of Palgrave Publishers, p.403; Allan P Layton, 'A new approach to dating and predicting Australian business cycle phase changes', *Applied Economics*, v. 29, pp 861-8, and Reserve Bank of Australia, http://rba.gov.au; p.328; Slobodan Lekic, 'Belgrade puts rate of inflation in billions', *Charlotte Observer*, 2 December 1993, p. 24A, reproduced on pp.371-2; Stephen Long, 'A clever country wouldn't treat teachers like this', *Australian Financial Review Weekend*, 20-21 October 2001, pp. 274-5; Sophie Morris, 'Uni fees "deterrent": Macklin', *Australian Financial Review*, 8 December 1904, p. 7 reproduced on p.132; Paivi Munter, 'Russia's Gaidar: government to print money, trigger hyperinflation', Dow Jones Newswire, 2 October 1998, p.372; Courtesy of National Bureau of Economic Research, p.483; Sonia L. Nazario, 'When inflation rate is 116 000 %, prices change by the hour', *Wall Street Journal*, 7 February 1985, p. 1. Reprinted by permission of *Wall Street Journal*. © Dow Jones & Company, Inc. All Rights Reserved, Worldwide, (Copyright Clearance Center), p.371 ; James S. Newton, 'A death knell sounds for musical jobs', *New York Times*, 1 March 1983, sec. 3, p. 9. Reprinted with permission of *New York Times*, p.380; Mark Paterson, 'Australians all, let us get the numbers right', *Australian Financial Review*, 23 January 2001, p 48-49; Robert J Pember and Marie-Thérèse Dupré, 'Statistical aspects of minimum wage determination', International Labour Organization, Bulletin of Labour Statistics – Selection of

Articles, Originally pub in *Bulletin of Labour Statistics*, 1997-3, p.283; John Powell, Executive Officer of Caneharvesters, *Herbert River Express*, 3 October 2000, p. 2, reproduced on p.156; Reserve Bank of Australia Table 40.Annual data compiled by authors from monthly data, p.563, RBA derived from *RBA Bulletin*, September 2004, Table D3, p.446; James R. Rinehart, 'The marketing approach to organ shortages', Reprinted with permission from *Journal of Health Care Marketing*, pub by American Marketing Association, vol. 8, no. 1, March 1998, pp. 80-1; Richard Saltus, 'Telemedicing foresees robots as surgeons', *Boston Daily Globe*, 8 April 1996, sec. 3, p. 2. © 1996, Globe Newspaper Co. (MA) in the former Textbook via Copyright Clearance Center, p.380; Mark Skulley, 'Unions face last fight', *Australian Financial Review*, 9 November 2004, p.100; Treasury Department, *Budget Paper No. 1*, 2004-05, Statement 13, Table 1, pp. 13-14, reproduced on p.516; Irvin B. Tucker, *Survey of Economics*, p. 271, 3rd edn, 2001, South-Western Publishing (a division of Thomson Learning), p.382; US Dept of Labor, CPI Detailed Report, Oct 1998, Table 24; *Survey of Current Business*, www.bea.doc.gov/bea/dn1.htm, Table 2A; and *Economic Report of the President*, 1999, www.gpo.ucop.edu/catalog/erp99.html, Table B-31, p.383; Adapted from David N. Weil, Brown University, *Economic Growth*, Pearson/Addison Wesley, pp. 34-5, Figs 2.1 & 2.2, p.336; World Bank, worldbank.org/data/countrydata. Graph compiled from various tables on the website, (Copyright Clearance Center);p.306.

Photographs:

AAP/ © David Killick, p.49; APL / Corbis /© Bettmann, p.1 / © Steve Raymer, p.371 / © Bettmann, p.403 / © Premium Stock, p.419; Corbis John Feingersh, p. 12 / © Dewitt Jones, p.58 / © Franz-Marc Frei, p. 89 / © Kevin R. Morris, p.95 / © Franklin McMahon, P.238 / © Lake County Museum, p. 324 / © Jack Fields, p.346 / © John Springer Collection, p.384 / © Bossu Regis, p.525 /© Catherine Karnow, p.548; /© David Samuel Robbins, p.282 /© Bo Zaunders p. 435 / © Roger Ressmeyer, p.483; Copper Leife /Craig Forsythe, p.163; Digital Vision, p.567; Fairfax / Brendan Esposito p.470 / © Jason South, p.132 / Louie Douvis, p.193 /Craig Abraham, p.262 / Nick Moir, p.311; Getty Images / Christopher Furlong, p.208 / Mark Renders, p.217 / Gilles Mingasson, p. 340 / Cristina Quicler, p.380 / Roslan Rahman, p. 532 / Getty Images PhotoDisc, p.137 / © Justin Sullivan, p.75; Image Addict, p.156; National Pasta Association, p.233; Newspix, p. 99, p.101, p.144 / © Darren Edwards p.34, / Kelly Barnes, p.352, / Torsten Blackwood, p.499 / Greg Wood, p.457, / © John Hart, p.80, / © Norrish p.17; Photo Library/ © Peter Arnold Images Inc, p. 52, / p.440 / Dave Bartruff, p.252; Photos.com, p.173, p.390; Barry Smith Photography, p.226; National Bureau of Economic Research, p.483; © Bill Thomas, p.274; Zefa Images/ © D.Stewart, p. 115 / N.Schultze, p.293.

Every attempt has been made to trace and acknowledge copyright holders. Where the attempt has been unsuccessful, the publisher welcomes information that would redress the situation.

[illegible]

Photographs

[illegible]

Introducing the economic way of thinking

1

PART 1

Welcome to the exciting and useful way of looking at the world that we call 'the economic way of thinking'. As you learn this reasoning technique, it will become infectious. You will discover that the world is full of economic problems requiring more powerful tools than just common sense. As you master the methods explained in this book, you will appreciate that economics provides a valuable approach to solving many real-world puzzles and issues. The economic way of thinking is important because it provides a logical framework that can be used to help us understand a wide range of economic issues and events. Just to give you a sneak preview, in this text you will be studying the perils of government price-fixing. You will also find out why governments provide for coastal surveillance rather than leaving it to the private sector. You will investigate whether you should be concerned if the federal government does not balance its budget. You will learn why one famous economist once said that monetary policy

could be best handled by a smart horse. And the list of interesting and relevant topics explained continues through all the chapters. As you read these pages, your efforts will be rewarded with an understanding of just how economic theories and policies affect our daily lives – past, present and future.

Chapter 1 acquaints you with the foundation of the economic way of thinking. The first building blocks are the concepts of scarcity and choice. The next building blocks are the steps in the model-building process that economists use to study the choices people make. Then we look at some pitfalls of economic reasoning and explain why economists may disagree with one another.

In this chapter, you will examine these economics questions:

- Why are forecasts of future house prices sometimes wide of the mark?
- Why would you buy more Coca-Cola when the price increases?
- Why do economists disagree and why do the media emphasise these disagreements?
- How can self-interested behaviour possibly be beneficial to the community as a whole?

The problem of scarcity

Scarcity The condition in which human wants are forever greater than the available supply of time, goods, services and resources.

Our world is a finite place where people, both individually and collectively, face the problem of **scarcity**. Scarcity is the condition in which human wants are forever greater than the available supply of time, goods, services and resources. Because of scarcity, it is impossible to satisfy every desire. Pause for a moment to list some of your unsatisfied wants. Perhaps you would like a bigger home, more restaurant meals, cleaner air, better health care, shelter for the homeless, more leisure time and so on. Unfortunately, nature does not offer a utopia in which every desire is fulfilled. There are always limits on the economy's ability to satisfy unlimited wants. Alas, scarcity is pervasive: you really *can't* 'have it all'.

You may think your scarcity problem would disappear if you were rich, but wealth does not improve the situation. No matter how affluent an individual is, the wish list continues to grow. We are familiar with the 'rich and famous' who never seem to have enough. Although they live well, they still desire finer homes, faster planes and larger yachts. In short, the condition of scarcity means that all individuals, whether rich or poor, could be more satisfied with their lot. They would like more material goods and more leisure time in which to use them. What is true for individuals also applies to society. State governments search for innovative ways to raise taxes for the funding of schools. The federal government's desire to spend on the poor and on higher education, highways and defence exceeds the tax revenue it receives to pay for these programs. So not even the Australian government escapes the problem of scarcity.

Of course, scarcity is a fact of life throughout the world, regardless of whether a country has a command economy tightly controlled by government or a capitalist economy that relies primarily on free markets. In much of South America and Africa the problem of scarcity is often life-threatening. On the other hand, in North America, Europe, Australasia and much of Asia there has been substantial economic growth and development. Although life is much less gruelling in the more advanced countries, the problem of scarcity exists because individuals and countries never have as much of all the goods and services as they would like to have.

Scarce resources and production

Because of the economic problem of scarcity, no society has enough **resources** to produce all the goods and services necessary to satisfy all human wants. Resources are the basic categories of inputs used to produce goods and services. Resources are also called *factors of production*. Economists divide resources into three categories: *land*, *labour* and *capital* (see Exhibit 1.1).

Resources The basic categories of inputs used to produce goods and services. Resources are also called factors of production. Economists divide resources into three categories: land, labour and capital.

Exhibit 1.1 Three categories of resources

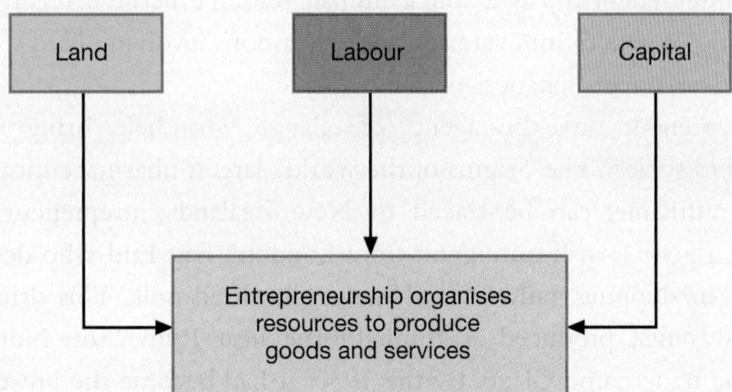

Resources are the basic categories of inputs organised by entrepreneurship (a special type of labour) to produce goods and services. Economists divide resources into the three categories of land, labour and capital.

Land

Land A shorthand expression for any resource provided by nature.

Land is a shorthand expression for any resource provided by nature. Land includes those resources that are gifts of nature available for use in the production process. Land includes anything natural above or below the ground, such as forests, minerals, oil, wildlife and fish. Other examples are rivers, lakes, oceans, the atmosphere, the sun and the moon. Pursuits such as farming, fishing, manufacturing and retailing all use land to a greater or lesser extent. Two broad categories of natural resources are *renewable resources* and *non-renewable resources*. Renewable resources are basic inputs that nature can automatically replace without interference from human beings. Examples include lakes, crops, animals and clean air. Non-renewable resources are basic inputs that nature will not automatically replace. There is only so much coal, oil, copper and iron ore in the world.

Labour

Labour The mental and physical capacity of workers to produce goods and services.

Labour is the mental and physical human capacity of workers to produce goods and services. The services of farmers, factory workers, lawyers, professional football players and economists are all *labour*. Both the number of people available for work and the skills or quality of workers measure the labour resource. One reason why nations differ in their ability to produce is that human characteristics, such as the education, experience, health and motivation of workers, differ among nations.

Entrepreneurship The creative ability of individuals to seek profits by combining resources to produce new or existing products.

Entrepreneurship is a special type of labour. Entrepreneurship is the creative ability of individuals to seek profits by combining resources to produce new or existing products. The *entrepreneur* is a motivated person who seeks profits by undertaking such risky activities as starting new businesses, creating new products or inventing new ways of accomplishing tasks. Entrepreneurship is a scarce human resource because relatively few are willing or able to innovate and make decisions involving hard work and greater-than-normal chances of failure.

Entrepreneurs are the agents of change who help bring material progress to society. The origins of the world's largest pharmaceutical group, GlaxoSmithKline, can be traced to New Zealand entrepreneur Joseph Nathan, a poor Jewish immigrant from London's East End who developed interests in shipping, railways and eventually dried milk. This dried milk, which was first produced at Bunnythorpe near Palmerston North, was given the trade name Glaxo. By the 1930s it had become the pre-eminent dried milk for babies, and Glaxo was a household word. At the end of the twentieth century the trade name that Nathan had registered in 1906 became GlaxoSmithKline after Glaxo had been involved in mergers with leading pharmaceutical companies. The Bunnythorpe dried milk factory was closed in 1974 but remains as a historic building – a lasting reminder of the entrepreneurial spirit of Joseph Nathan.

Read more about Joseph Nathan and the GlaxoSmithKline connection at **www.nzedge.com/heroes/nathan.html**.

PART 1

Capital

Capital is the physical plant, machinery and equipment used to produce other goods. Capital goods are human-made goods that do not directly satisfy human wants. *Capital* before the Industrial Revolution meant a tool, such as a hoe, an axe or a bow and arrow. In those days, these items served as capital to build a house or to provide food for the dinner table. Today, capital also consists of factories, office buildings, warehouses, robots, trucks and distribution facilities. University buildings, the printing presses used to produce this textbook, and software are also examples of capital.

Capital The physical plant, machinery and equipment used to produce other goods. Capital goods are human-made goods that do not directly satisfy human wants.

The term *capital* as it is used in the study of economics can be confusing. Economists know that capital in everyday conversation means money or the money value of assets, such as stocks, bonds or the deeds to real estate. This is actually financial capital. In the study of economics, capital does not refer to money assets. In economics, capital means human-made factors of production, such as factories or machinery. Money is not capital; it simply gives a measure of the value of assets, including capital goods.

Browse through some recent editions of *USA Today* (**www.usatoday.com**), the *Straits Times* (**www.straitstimes.asia1.com.sg**), the Sydney Morning Herald (**www.smh.com.au**) or the *New Zealand Herald* (**www.nzherald.co.nz**). Can you find some headline stories involving economics? What proportion are they of the headline stories?

Financial capital, which represents the monetary value of a wide range of assets, should not be confused with the economist's definition of capital, which encompasses only human-made goods used to produce other goods and services.

PART 1

Economics: the study of scarcity and choice

The perpetual problem of scarcity forcing people to make choices is the basis for the definition of **economics**. Economics is the study of how society chooses to allocate its scarce resources to the production of goods and services in order to satisfy unlimited wants. You may be surprised by this definition. People often think economics is the study of supply and demand, the stock market, or money and banking. In fact, there are many ways one could define *economics*, but economists accept the definition given here because it includes the link between *scarcity* and *choices*.

Economics The study of how society chooses to allocate its scarce resources to the production of goods and services in order to satisfy unlimited wants.

Society makes two kinds of choices: economy-wide or macro choices, and individual or micro choices. The prefixes *macro* and *micro* come from the Greek words meaning 'large' and 'small' respectively. Reflecting the macro and micro perspectives, economics consists of two main branches: *macroeconomics* and *microeconomics*.

Microeconomics

Microeconomics The branch of economics that studies decision-making by a single individual, household, firm or industry.

Microeconomics is the branch of economics that studies decision-making by a single individual, household, firm or industry. The focus is on the behaviour of small economic units, such as the economic decisions of particular groups of consumers or businesses. An example would be the use of microeconomic analysis to study economic units involved in the market for eggs. Will suppliers decide to supply more, fewer or the same amount of eggs to the market in response to price changes? Will individual consumers of these eggs decide to buy more, fewer or the same amount at a new price?

Macroeconomics

Macroeconomics The branch of economics that studies decision-making for the economy as a whole.

Macroeconomics is the branch of economics that studies the performance of, and decision-making in, the economy as a whole. Macroeconomics applies an overview perspective to an economy by examining economy-wide variables such as inflation, unemployment, the money supply and the flows of exports, imports and international financial capital. Macroeconomic decision-making considers such 'big picture' policies as the effect that balancing the federal budget may have on unemployment, the effect that changing the money supply may have on prices and the effect of strong economic growth on the value of the currency.

We have described macroeconomics and microeconomics as two separate branches, but they are related. Because the overall economy is the sum or aggregation of its parts, micro changes affect the macro economy, and macro changes produce micro changes.

Can the free market eliminate scarcity?

Vietnam is an economy in transition. As one of the few remaining communist economies, it is working towards reliance on the market rather than centralised controls to determine prices for goods and services. Nonetheless, there are sectors of the economy that continue to be subject to price controls and the shortages that these can cause. People explain that in Vietnam this scarcity is the result of low prices in relation to available supply. If a Vietnamese citizen were to say that the condition of scarcity in these regulated markets would be eliminated if the government were to allow free markets to operate as they do in other sectors of the economy, would you agree?

Visit the popular economics site (www.economy.com) for a survey of issues in the study of economics.

The methodology of economics

Economists use the same *scientific method* used in other disciplines such as criminology, biology, chemistry and physics. The scientific method

Exhibit 1.2 **The steps in the model-building process**

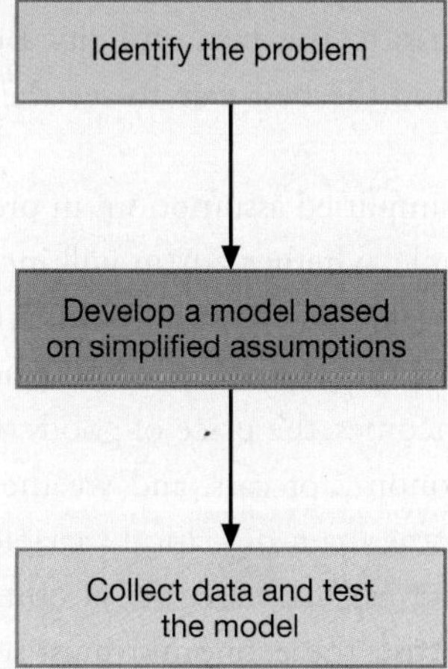

The first step in developing a model is to identify the problem. The second step is to select the critical variables necessary to formulate a model that explains the problem under study. Eliminating other variables that complicate the analysis requires simplifying assumptions. In the third step, the researcher collects data and tests the model. If the evidence supports the model, the model is accepted. If not, the model is rejected.

is a step-by-step procedure for solving problems by developing a theory, gathering data and testing whether the data are consistent with the theory. Exhibit 1.2 summarises the model-building process.

Economics is the only social science in which a Nobel Prize is awarded. Read about past winners and their contributions to economic thought at **www.almaz.com/nobel/economics/2004b.html.**

PART 1

Identifying the problem

The first step in applying the scientific method is to define the problem. Suppose an economist wishes to investigate the microeconomic question of why motorists have cut back on petrol consumption in a given year from, say, 5 billion litres per month in February to 4.5 billion litres per month in March.

Developing a model

The second step in our hypothetical example towards finding an explanation is for the economist to build a **model**. A model is a simplified description of reality used to understand and predict the relationship between variables. A model is built on the foundation of an underlying theory. It looks at the factors, often called *variables*, that explain an event. However, a model emphasises only those variables that are most important to explaining an event. In this respect, models are similar to their underlying theories which, according to Albert Einstein, 'should be as simple as possible, but not any simpler'. Paring a model down to its simplest possible form is sometimes

Model A simplified description of reality used to understand and predict the relationship between variables.

described as the pursuit of parsimony. The purpose of a model is to construct an abstraction from real-world complexities and make events understandable. A map of New Zealand's capital, Wellington, for example, is far from a precise duplication of a real trip to this beautiful city. But a map of the city does help a visitor understand the best way to see the sights by leaving out the clutter of details.

A model requires simplified assumptions in order to be useful. Someone must decide, for example, whether a map will include only symbols for the major highways or the details of every minor road. In our petrol consumption example, several variables may be related to the quantity of petrol consumed, including consumer incomes, the price of goods other than petrol, the price of petrol, the fuel economy of cars, and weather conditions. Because we wish to focus only on the main or critical variables, the economist must be a Sherlock Holmes and use a keen sense of observation to form a model. Using his or her expertise, the economist must select the relevant variables that are related to petrol consumption and reject variables that have only slight or no relationship to petrol consumption. In this simple case, the economist removes the cloud of complexity by formulating the hypothesis that increases in the price of petrol *cause* the quantity of petrol consumed to decrease during the time period.

Testing the model

economic model

An economic model can be formulated using verbal arguments, numerical tables, graphs or mathematical equations. You will soon discover that a major part of this book is devoted to building and using economic models. The purpose of an economic model is to enable us to *forecast* or *predict* the results of various changes in key variables. An economic model is useful only if it yields accurate predictions. When the evidence is consistent with the prediction that a change in *A* causes outcome *B*, all other factors remaining constant, there is confidence in the model's validity. This confidence in the model is maintained indefinitely unless there is some evidence that the model has lost its predictive power. So if repeated tests indicate that the evidence is inconsistent with the prediction that a change in *A* causes outcome *B*, the researcher rejects the model.

Returning to our petrol consumption problem, the economist gathers data to test the hypothesis that if the price of petrol rises, then petrol purchases fall – all other relevant factors held constant. Suppose the investigation reveals that there was a sharp rise in the price of petrol in March of the given year. The data are therefore consistent with the hypothesis that the quantity of petrol consumed per month falls when its price rises, assuming no other relevant factors change. Thus the model is valid if, for example, consumer incomes or population do not change at the same time as petrol prices rise.

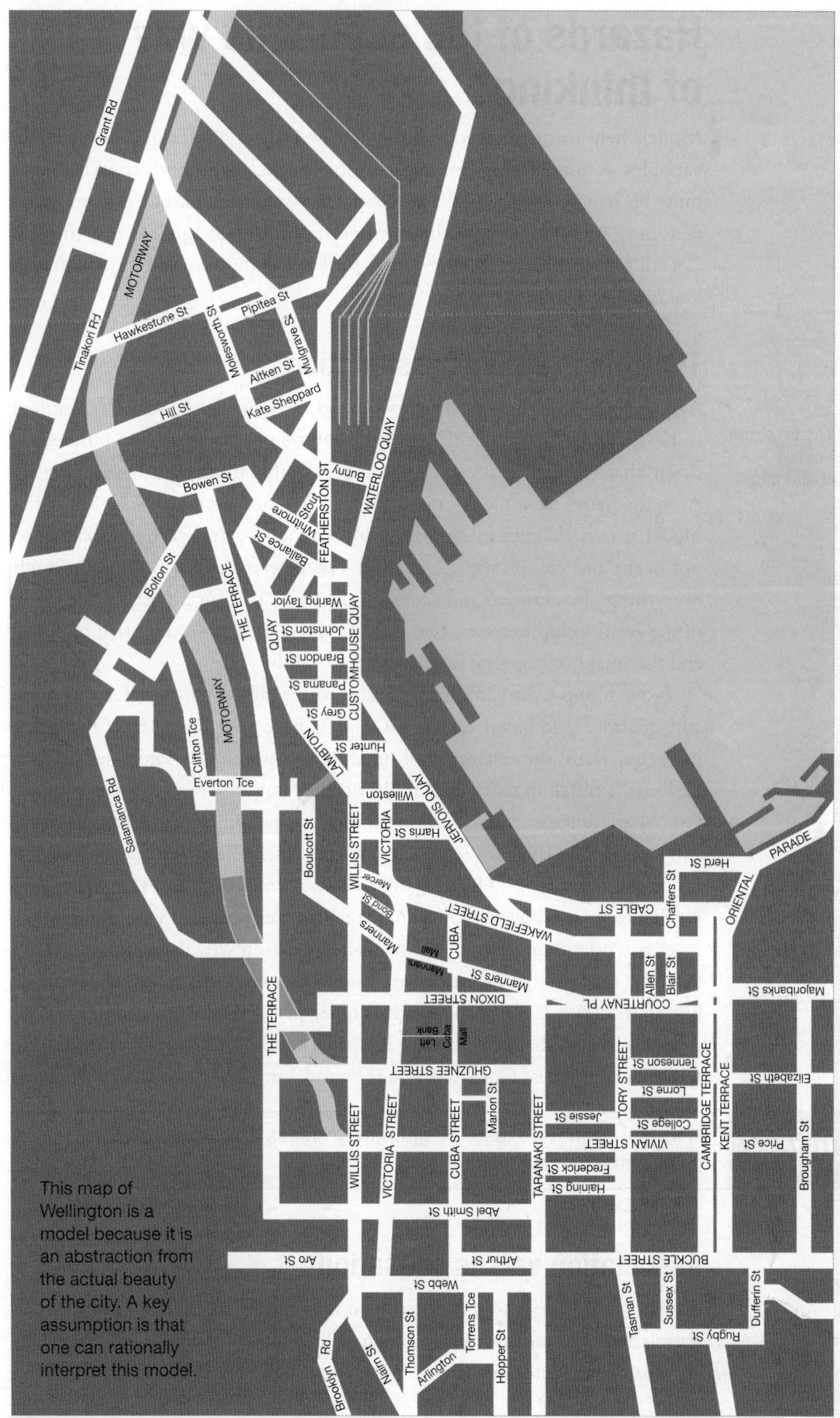

This map of Wellington is a model because it is an abstraction from the actual beauty of the city. A key assumption is that one can rationally interpret this model.

PART 1

Hazards of the economic way of thinking

Models help us understand and predict the impact of changes in economic variables. A model is an important tool in the economist's toolkit, but it must be handled with care. The economic way of thinking seeks to avoid reasoning mistakes. Two of the most common pitfalls to clear thinking are (1) failing to understand the *ceteris paribus* assumption and (2) confusing *association* and *causation*.

The ceteris paribus assumption

Ceteris paribus A Latin phrase meaning that, while certain variables change, all other things remain unchanged.

As you work through a model, try to think of a host of relevant variables assumed to be 'standing still', or 'held constant'. **Ceteris paribus** is a Latin phrase that means that, while certain variables change, 'all other things remain unchanged'. As in the petrol example discussed earlier, a key simplifying assumption of the model is that changes in consumer incomes and certain other variables do not occur and complicate the analysis. The ceteris paribus assumption holds everything else constant and therefore allows us to concentrate on the study of the relationship between two key variables: changes in the price of petrol and the quantity of petrol purchased per month.

Now suppose an economist wishes to explain the model for the price and quantity purchased of Coca-Cola. Assume the theory is 'If the price increases, then the quantity of Coca-Cola purchased decreases, ceteris paribus'. A pitfall in reasoning might occur if you observed that the price of Coca-Cola increased one summer and some people actually bought more and not less. On the basis of this real-world observation, you declare that the model does not work. Think again! The economist responds that the model is valid, based on the assumption of ceteris paribus, and that your observation gives you no reason to reject the model. The reason why the model appeared flawed is that another factor, a sharp rise in the temperature, *caused* people to buy more Coca-Cola in spite of its higher price. If the temperature and all other factors are held constant as the price of Coca-Cola rises, then people will indeed buy less Coca-Cola, as the model predicts.

CONCLUSION **A model cannot be tested legitimately unless its ceteris paribus assumption is satisfied.**

Association versus causation

Another of the most common errors in reasoning is to confuse *association* (or correlation) and *causation* between variables. Stated differently, you err when you read more into a relationship between variables than is actually there.

A model is valid only when there is a genuine cause-and-effect relationship. It is not valid when it relies on an association between variables; that is, where a change in the value of one variable does not cause any subsequent change that occurs in the other. Suppose that the hole in the ozone layer increases in size during three different months, and Indonesia's exports to Australia increase during each of these months. The change in the ozone layer is *associated* with the increase in exports, but this does not mean the ozone layer change *caused* the event. Even though there is a statistical relationship between two variables in a number of observations, economists would not be concerned if further increases in the size of the hole in the ozone layer were associated with a fall in Indonesian exports to Australia. The reason is that there is no true economic relationship between the ozone layer and Indonesian exports. A more likely explanation for the increase in Indonesian exports to Australia would be that currency movements have reduced the cost to Australians of buying these exports.

The fact that one event follows another does not necessarily mean that the first event caused the second event.

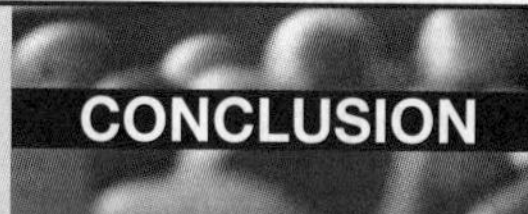

Can simple models explain house price movements?

Frequently in the press, in investment magazines and on Internet property sites there are explanations of the causes of the overall movement up or down in house prices, and forecasts of future changes. Property analysts, real estate agents and financial journalists variously attribute past or expected future ups and downs in the property market to migration patterns, changes in consumer confidence, changes in government policy, interest rate changes or seasonal differences. When the most recent property boom in Australia came to an end in 2004 it became apparent that there were flaws in some of these commentators' arguments. Reactions of the market to given events turned out to be different from what the pundits had been suggesting, leaving their forecasts wide of the mark. Why is it that explanations for house price movements are sometimes found to be incorrect?

Throughout this book, you will study economic theories and models that include variables linked by stable cause-and-effect relationships. These include the microeconomic theory that a change in the price of a good *causes* a change in the quantity purchased; and the macroeconomic model that estimates changes in the interest rate *caused* by changes in the money supply. The 'You make the call' above discusses an everyday example of the pitfalls of developing simple models to explain highly complex phenomena.

To find materials and data resources used by economists on the Internet, visit **www.helsinki.fi/WebEc.**

International focus

A prominent American economist explains why economists disagree

Writing in the preface to *The Fortune Encyclopedia of Economics* its editor, David R. Henderson. who is a research fellow at Harvard University's prestigious Hoover Institution, defends the charge against economists that their discipline is plagued by disagreements between its practitioners. The following excerpts from that preface summarise his case.

Applicable concepts: why economists disagree; positive economics; normative economics

> An old joke says that if you laid all the economists in the world end to end, they would not reach a conclusion. The popular perception behind the joke is that economists never agree. Implicit in that perception is the belief that economics is largely a matter of opinion and that economists (unlike biologists or the practitioners of any other science) do not share a common set of beliefs. Given all the conflicting pronouncements by economists that appear almost daily in the press, that perception is very understandable. It also is dead wrong. While economists disagree on many matters, they have reached virtually unanimous agreement on a multitude of others. ...
>
> Most of the disagreement among economists concerns 'macroeconomics', which deals with nationwide or worldwide phenomena such as inflation, unemployment, and economic growth. ... Some of their disagreements reflect different judgments about the relative importance of, say, inflation versus unemployment. Others stem from basic disagreement on the ability of government policy to affect the total economy in predictable ways. ...
>
> Macroeconomics, however, is only a small part of the total science of economics. The vast majority of economic questions (and public policy issues) fall in the realm of what is called microeconomics. And the vast majority of economists agree on the underlying economics of most micro issues, including rent controls, minimum wages, and the need to reduce pollution. Some may disagree on the policy implications of the analysis, but remarkably few disagree on the analysis itself.
>
> That economists agree on most micro issues became clear in the late seventies when the *American Economic Review*, the world's largest-circulation economics journal, published an opinion poll of 211 economists. The poll found that 98 percent agreed with the statement 'A ceiling on rents reduces the quantity and quality of housing available.' Similarly, 90 percent of economists agreed that 'a minimum wage increases unemployment among young and unskilled workers.' And 97 percent agreed with the statement 'Tariffs and import quotas reduce general economic welfare.' ...
>
> So why do people think economists disagree about everything? One reason is that the media present all

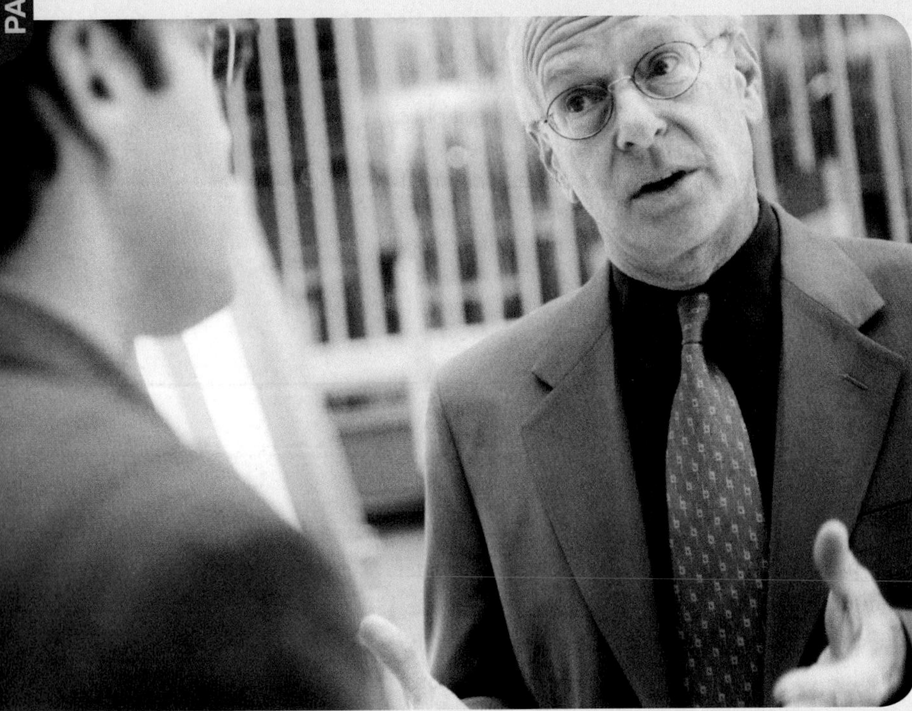

economic issues as if they are inherently controversial. The issues themselves are controversial, but the economics of the issues more often are not. …

Another equally important source of the misimpression about economics comes from the often overlooked distinction that economists make between 'positive' and 'normative' analysis. Positive analysis is the application of economic postulates and principles to a question – in other words, finding out the way things are and why the world behaves as it does. Normative analysis, in contrast, deals with the way things ought to be, and unavoidably involves the noneconomic value judgments of the analyst. For example, positive analysis says that licensing physicians will result in there being fewer doctors in society and higher prices for medical care. Whether states should license doctors to protect patients from quacks is a normative matter. In other words, there are no 'shoulds' in purely positive economic analysis, but [nonetheless] every economist has views on how things should be done.

In preparing this encyclopedia, we strived to separate positive and normative positions, to emphasize the areas where economists agree, while also specifying where and why they disagree. The goal is to communicate just how much economic analysis can teach us about the important issues we face as voters, consumers, employees, and as people who care about the world.[1]

1 David R. Henderson, *The Fortune Encyclopedia of Economics*, 1993, reprinted at www.econlib.org/library/Enc/bios/CEEPreface.html

Analyse the issue

Is it positive or normative issues that lead to most disagreements between economists? Explain and give some examples.

Why do economists disagree?

Why might one economist say a clean environment is the most important goal for society, and another economist say economic growth should be our goal? If economists share the economic way of thinking and carefully avoid reasoning pitfalls, then why do they disagree? Why are economists known for giving advice by saying, 'On the one hand, if you do this then *A* results and, on the other hand, doing this causes result *B*'? In fact, President Harry Truman once jokingly exclaimed, 'Find me an economist with one hand.' George Bernard Shaw offered another famous line in the same vein: 'If you took all the economists in the world and laid them end to end, they would never reach a conclusion.' These famous quotes imply that economists should agree, but ignore the fact that physicists, doctors, business executives, lawyers and other professionals often disagree.

It may appear that economists disagree more than other professions partly because it is more interesting to report disagreements than agreements. Actually, economists agree on a wide range of issues. Many economists, for example, agree on the benefits of free trade among nations, the elimination of farm subsidies and government-imposed rent ceilings, government deficit spending to recover from recession and many other issues. When disagreements do exist, the reason can often be explained by the difference between *positive economics* and *normative economics*.

Positive economics

Positive economics
An analysis limited to statements that are verifiable.

Positive economics deals with facts and therefore addresses 'what is' or 'verifiable' questions. Positive economics is an analysis limited to statements that are verifiable. Positive statements can be proved either true or false. Often a positive statement is expressed 'If A, then B.' For example, it might be stated that if the national unemployment rate is 7 per cent, then youth unemployment exceeds 80 per cent. This is a positive 'if-then' prediction, which may or may not be correct. The accuracy of the statement is not the criterion for being a positive statement. The key consideration for a positive statement is whether the statement is *testable* and not whether it is true or false. Suppose we read that if Australia's overall unemployment rate is 7 per cent, the youth unemployment rate would always be less than 7 per cent. A review of the official statistics relating to Australia's recent experience with unemployment would lead us to conclude that this positive statement is false. (In Australia in recent times, when the overall unemployment rate has been around 7 per cent, the rate for young people has been approximately 20 per cent.)

The Commonwealth Department of the Treasury (**www.treasury.gov.au**) and Zurich Financial Services (**www.zurich.com**) are just two examples of organisations that employ economists to, among other things, predict how the economy will behave and also interpret the latest data on economic performance.

Now we can explain one reason why economists' forecasts can diverge. The statement 'If event A occurs, then event B follows' can be thought of as a *conditional* positive statement. For example, two economists may agree that if the federal government cuts spending by 10 per cent this year, prices will fall about 2 per cent next year. However, their predictions about the fall in prices may differ because one economist assumes the government will not cut spending, while the other economist assumes it will cut spending by 10 per cent.

positive economics
normative economics

Forecasts of economists can differ because, using the same methodology, economists can agree that event A causes event B, but disagree over the assumption that event A will occur.

Normative economics

Normative economics
An analysis based on value judgements.

Instead of using objective statements, an argument can be phrased subjectively. **Normative economics** is concerned with 'what should be'. Normative economics is an analysis based on value judgements. Normative statements express an individual or collective opinion on a subject and cannot be proved by facts to be true or false. Certain words or phrases tell us clearly that we have entered the realm of normative economics. These include the words *good, bad, need, should* and *ought to*.

The point here is that people wearing different-coloured glasses see the same facts differently. Each of us has individual subjective preferences that we apply to a particular subject. An economist trained in the United States may argue that Asian nations *should* adopt Western values and institutions. Or one member of parliament argues, 'We *ought to* see that every teenager who wants a job has one.' Another counters by saying, 'Keeping inflation under control is *more important* than teenage unemployment.'

Normative statements involve opinions or points of view that are not scientifically testable.

When considering a debate, make sure you separate the arguments into their positive and normative components. This distinction allows you to determine if you are choosing a course of action related to factual evidence or to opinion. The material presented in this textbook, like most of economics, takes pains to stay within the boundaries of positive economic analysis. In our everyday lives, however, politicians, business executives, relatives and friends often use normative statements when discussing economic issues. Economists also may associate themselves with a political position and use normative arguments for or against some economic policy. When using value judgements, an economist's normative judgements may have no greater validity than those of others. As is the case with all human beings, an economist's own personal values or preconceptions can influence his or her thinking about many things ranging from deficit spending to whether petrol taxes should be reduced.

PART 1

Economics and ethics

As you study this book you will discover that the economic model is based on the assumption that economic agents pursue their own self-interest (or that of their family unit). This self-interest is said to be *enlightened* in that individuals pursue their own ends subject to the set of laws and social mores that prevails in society. Critics of economics sometimes argue, however, that the economic model promotes unenlightened self-interest – what is sometimes described as greed. Indeed, some individuals have used the notion of economic self-interest to justify their own greed – as did Gordon Gecko, played by actor Michael Douglas, when he famously declared that 'greed is good' in the film *Wall Street*.

Enlightened self-interest involves members of the community respecting the laws and social mores of society while they pursue their own individual goals.

In spite of some opportunistic interpretations of the relevance of the assumption of self-interested behaviour, the mainstream economic model does not set about promoting greed. It is concerned to promote the efficient working of free markets subject to conformity to an underlying set of ethical or moral principles – a set of principles that

INFOTRAC®
Adam Smith

are not to be traded for increased material welfare. The founder of modern economics, Adam Smith, whose image appears on the opening page of this chapter, pointed out over two centuries ago that the gaining of economic advantage by nonconformity to these principles does not promote the economic welfare of the community. Management guru Charles Handy, in *The Empty Raincoat*,[1] sums up the case by referring to Smith's eighteenth-century writings.

> Adam Smith, who was professor of moral philosophy not of economics, built his theories on the basis of a moral community. Before he wrote A Theory of the Wealth of Nations he had written his definitive work – A Theory of Moral Sentiments – arguing that a stable society was based on 'sympathy', a moral duty to have regard for your fellow human beings. The market is a mechanism for sorting the efficient from the inefficient, it is not a substitute for responsibility.

Determination of the set of ethical principles that underpin capitalist society is, of course, a normative exercise. The appropriateness of these principles cannot be tested objectively. Nonetheless, these principles constitute the foundation for economic behaviour that can be subjected to positive analysis.

1 Charles Handy, *The Empty Raincoat*, Hutchinson, London, 1994, p. 15.

Analyse the issue

Tim Costello on Adam Smith and business ethics

In the following extracts from an article in the *Weekend Australian Financial Review*, Tim Costello, a priest who is chief executive of World Vision Australia, points to the relevance of Adam Smith's understanding of the relationship between economics and ethics for Australian business.

Applicable concepts: economics and ethics; positive and normative analyses

I am frequently asked the question: Can it be profitable to be ethical? ...

Business has always been quick to sniff profit, and if it is profitable to be ethical then great, let's get on with it. But it's not that simple, as the past 20 years have borne out.

In the 1980s, Gordon Gecko and the mantra 'greed is good' represented a particular culture that virtually celebrated ruthlessness, without being troubled by conscience or ethics.

In the 1990s, a new doctrine permeated business – that business was morally neutral – value-free.

And if business was morally neutral, there was no embarrassment in maximising shareholder wealth – not in an exaggerated '80s style with machismo and shame, but as a proposition that moral neutrality can give us a clear focus to maximise shareholders' wealth.

Based on this doctrine, there's no need for business to give its wealth directly to the community. Maximise profit instead, so shareholders could bestow it wherever they wished in the community.

In the late 1990s it became clear there was no value-free place to stand, no neutrality for business. This is clearly illustrated by events at James Hardie, facing community censure over its approach to limiting liability for compensation to asbestos victims.

Like other companies found to have misled the community, James Hardie has found there is no neutral place to stand.

Over the past few years a new doctrine has emerged – the 'triple bottom line' – as the key to a company's sustainability. …

This doctrine emphasises that business is part of the community. It is in a relationship not just with shareholders, but with stakeholders. …

There are five reasons this doctrine has emerged: the increasing transparency of business affairs; improved communications in a global world; extensive social change in the last decade; the increased role played in the economy by the private sector; and the realisation that global business is not something apart from society.

So there have been significant shifts over the past 20 years – from greed is good, to neutrality, to today, where business is no longer neutral but in partnership with stakeholders.

We are in a different paradigm. But how committed is business to seeing through what this paradigm implies?

Adam Smith, the father of laissez-faire capitalism, provided a framework that I believe to be at the core of this paradigm: 'Human beings are simultaneously self-regarding and other-regarding.'

Most who have read Smith have understood instantly what he means by self-regarding. It covers the private profit motive, profit and self-interest that is mediated through the brilliant mechanism of the market, with billions of transactions every day. Indeed, no centralised or other system of planning, allocating preferences and distributing resources, can match it.

In picking up this part of Smith – the laissez-faire principle – we actually understood the truth of his first limb, that is, that humans are self-regarding.

Business understands this well and has led on this clearly.

But the second limb is where the great intellectual and personal challenge is for the corporate sector. 'Humans are simultaneously other-regarding.' The 'other' being environment, community, attention to spiritual non-visual materials, for instance. The other is the stakeholders referred to earlier.

But can we still find help from Smith? Interestingly, he was a moral philosopher before he was an economist.

In *The Theory of Moral Sentiments*, written before *The Wealth of Nations*, Smith says essentially that the foundation of a good society, a virtuous society, is moral sympathy. Today we would recognise this as empathy.

According to Smith, the foundation for a good society is a strong sense of connection to and responsibility for one another. Markets will create wealth, but they will not create a good society, or virtue. …

Smith essentially says markets don't have morals. They will create wealth, but they won't create it evenly, distribute it fairly, or create a virtuous society. …

Many societies, as in the West, have solved the problem of supply but found themselves faced with social dislocation: an epidemic of depression, high youth suicide rates, drug addiction and marital breakdown.

Why is this? Philosophers call this 'The Problem of Adam Smith' because the more we emphasise just one limb, the more we risk fragmenting the other. Individuals operating out of pure self-interest become atomised individuals lacking in sympathy, connection and social sustainability.

This is where we have to see corporations in the debate. They are not just the first limb of Adam Smith. They are beginning to understand that sustainable business happens in communities that are not fragmented. They need to be socially and environmentally aware of the context that surrounds them, the stakeholder, which is the other.

This is very important, ethically. If it is simply self – the financial bottom line, whatever the other rhetoric – there will be profound disillusionment and, ultimately, damage to the bottom line. …

But I understand why people get confused, and I understand why business – which asks if it is profitable to be ethical when the price tag is high – finds it difficult to find the answer.

There are no prescriptive answers to these dilemmas, but there is an answer to be found in holding together both limbs of Adam Smith's prose. …

People – whether they are corporate directors, finance managers or consumers – are simultaneously self-regarding and, to use Smith's words, other-regarding – self-seeking and other-seeking.

In that balance lie some of the answers to good corporate practice, good business and good ethics.[1]

Read more about Tim Costello, who was Victorian of the Year in 2004, at **www.lawfoundation.net.au/justice awards/bio tcostello.html.**

Using the information you have just read, answer the following questions:

1 Identify two positive and two normative statements relating to business ethics.
2 Give a positive and a normative argument as to why a business leader would take up Costello's challenge to have their business become more other-regarding as well as self-regarding.
3 Explain your own position on the issue of business being more ethically responsible. Identify positive and normative reasons for your decision. Are there alternative ways to ensure that businesses are good citizens?

1 Tim Costello, 'Adam Smith problem offers ethical answers', *Weekend Australian Financial Review*, 25–26 September 2004, p. 62.

Key concepts

Scarcity	Macroeconomics
Resources	Microeconomics
Land	Model
Labour	Ceteris paribus
Entrepreneurship	Positive economics
Capital	Normative economics
Economics	Enlightened self-interest

Summary

- **Scarcity** is the fundamental economic problem that human wants exceed the availability of time, goods, services and resources. Individuals and society therefore can never have everything they desire.
- **Resources** are factors of production classified as land, labour and capital. Entrepreneurship is a special type of labour. An entrepreneur combines resources to produce products.
- **Economics** is the study of how individuals and society choose to allocate scarce resources in order to satisfy unlimited wants. Faced with unlimited wants and scarce resources, we must make choices among alternatives.

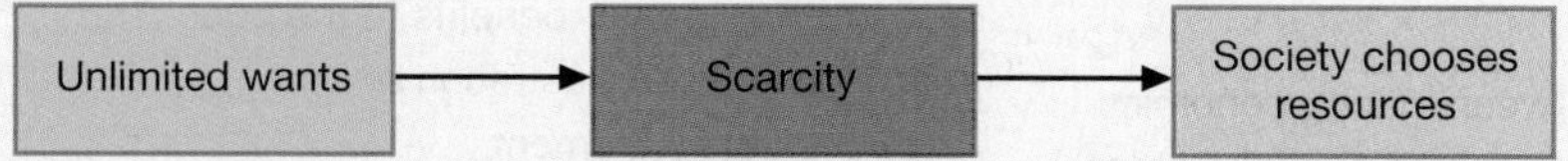

- **Macroeconomics** applies an economy-wide perspective that focuses on such issues as inflation, unemployment, the growth rate of the economy and international trade.
- **Microeconomics** examines individual decision-making units within an economy. Microeconomics studies such topics as a consumer's response to changes in the price of coffee and the reasons for changes in the market price of personal computers.
- **Models** are simplified descriptions of reality used to understand and predict economic events. An economic model can be stated verbally or in a table, graph or equation. If the evidence is not consistent with the model, the model is rejected.

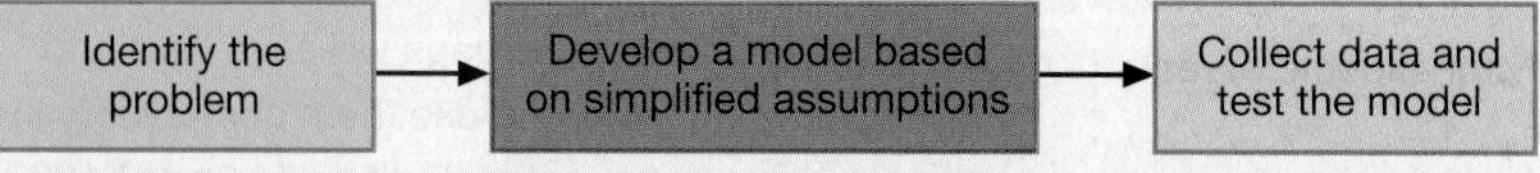

- **Ceteris paribus** means that all other factors that might affect a particular relationship remain unchanged. If this assumption is violated, a model cannot be tested. Another reasoning pitfall is to think that *association* means *causation*.
- Use of **positive** versus **normative** economic analysis is a major reason for disagreement among economists. **Positive economics** uses testable statements. Often a positive argument is expressed as an '*if-then*' statement. **Normative economics** is based on value judgements or opinions and uses words such as *good, bad, ought to* and *ought not to*.
- **Enlightened self-interest** involves members of the community respecting the laws and social mores of society while they pursue their own individual goals.

PART 1

Study questions and problems

1 Explain why nations with high living standards and nations with low living standards face the problem of scarcity. If you won $1 million in a lottery, would you escape the scarcity problem?

2 Why isn't money considered capital in economics?

3 Computer software programs are an example of
- a capital.
- b labour.
- c a natural resource.
- d none of the above.

4 Explain the difference between macroeconomics and microeconomics. Give examples of the areas of concern to each branch of economics.

5 Which of the following are microeconomic issues? Which are macroeconomic issues?
- a How will an increase in the price of Coca-Cola affect the quantity of Pepsi-Cola sold?
- b What will cause the rate of inflation in the nation to fall?
- c How does a quota on textile imports affect the textile industry?
- d Does a large federal budget deficit reduce the rate of unemployment in the economy?

6 A model is defined as a
- a value judgement of the relationship between variables.
- b presentation of all relevant aspects of real-world events.
- c simplified description of reality used to understand the way variables are related.
- d data set adjusted for irrational actions of people.

7 Explain the importance of an economic model being an abstraction from the real world.

8 Explain the importance of the ceteris paribus assumption for an economic model.

9 Not long after the completion of the Petronas Towers in Kuala Lumpur, the Malaysian economy experienced a recession. Is there causation in this situation, or are we observing an association between events?

10 Which of the following statements about Australian federal politics is an example of a proposition from normative economics?
- a If the Labor Party is in power, individual taxpayers will pay more tax than if the Coalition is in office.
- b The average rate of inflation has been higher during periods when the Labor Party has been in power.
- c The Coalition's economic policies are better for the economy.
- d Labor policies will result in a more equal distribution of income.

11 'The government should collect higher taxes from the rich and use the additional revenues to provide greater benefits to the poor.' This statement is an illustration of a
- a testable statement.
- b basic principle of economics.
- c statement of positive economics.
- d statement of normative economics.

12 Is there a contradiction in the behaviour of economists who profess to be adherents of a religious faith that emphasises regard for others but who also argue that people should pursue their own self-interest?

13 Analyse the positive versus normative arguments in the following case. Which are the positive statements used and which are normative?

Should airbags be compulsory in all new motor cars?

Airbag advocates say airbags will save lives and the government should make them compulsory in all cars. Airbags are estimated to add up to $1000 to the cost of a car, compared to about $160 for a set of seatbelts. Opponents argue that, because airbags are electronic devices, they are subject to failures and have caused injury or death. Opponents therefore believe the government should leave the decision about whether to spend an extra $1000 or so for an airbag to the consumer. They say the role of the government should be limited to providing information on the risks of having or not having an airbag.

Online exercises

Exercise 1

Does the Internet raise or lower the cost of purchasing goods such as antiques and collectables from other countries? As you ponder this question, visit an online auction site such as eBay (**www.ebay.com**). Which costs has the Internet reduced and which costs might it raise? Remember that we are considering all costs, not just monetary costs.

Exercise 2

Visit World Factbook (**www.odci.gov/cia/publications/factbook/index.html**) and follow these steps:

1. Select **Australia**.
2. Note the land area and population size of Australia.
3. Compute the land area per person by dividing the land area of Australia by its population size.
4. Select **Japan**. Repeat steps 2 and 3 for Japan.
5. How does the scarcity of land influence land-use choices? Would you find as many golf courses per capita in Japan as in Australia? Explain.

Exercise 3

Visit Job Openings for Economists (**www.aeaweb.org/joe/**) and select the most recent issue. Browse through the academic, foreign and non-academic job openings for economists. Study the job descriptions and earnings for economists. Can you explain why there are differences in salaries for different jobs where the qualifications and experience required are similar?

Exercise 4

Visit the official website of the Prime Minister of New Zealand (**www.primeminister.govt.nz**). Click on **Speeches & releases**. Choose a topic you think pertains to economics. Does the subject matter pertain to macroeconomics or microeconomics? Is the analysis primarily normative or positive?

Answers to 'You make the call'

Can the free market eliminate scarcity?

Scarcity is the condition in which human wants are forever greater than the resources available to satisfy those wants. Although the use of markets free from government interference will prevent shortages in these markets, it will not solve the scarcity problem. Scarcity exists at any price for a good or service. This means scarcity occurs at any price regardless of whether the price is determined in a capitalist, free market economy or in a government-controlled command economy. If you said you disagreed because free markets cannot eliminate scarcity, YOU ARE CORRECT.

Can simple models explain house price movements?

The commentators' explanations of the relationship between certain events and past or expected future house price movements are not necessarily based on true causal relationships because determination of the precise causes of house price movements would require surveys of the thousands of home buyers and sellers who operate in the market each year. Although there are some researchers whose analysis is based on sound models, what many commentators are doing is simply observing an *association* between certain events and movements in the market, and then attributing a *causal* role to the events they have observed. In some instances the link will be a causal one, but in others there will only be an association between the variables. Furthermore, even in cases where there is a causal link, other factors that would normally remain constant may change, with the result that the causal link no longer predominates. If you said that poor predictive power of the simple models linking house price movements to certain events can result from the confusion of association with causation or because the ceteris paribus assumption does not hold, YOU ARE CORRECT.

Multiple-choice questions

1 Scarcity exists
 a when people consume beyond their needs.
 b only in rich nations.
 c in all countries of the world.
 d only in poor nations.

2 Which of the following would eliminate scarcity as an economic problem?
 a moderation of people's competitive instincts.
 b discovery of sufficiently large new energy reserves.
 c resumption of steady productivity growth.
 d none of the above because scarcity cannot be eliminated.

3 Which of the following is *not* a factor of production?
 a land

PART 1

b labour
c a financial asset
d capital

4 Economics is the study of
a how to make money.
b how to operate a business.
c people making choices because of the problem of scarcity.
d the government decision-making process.

5 Microeconomics approaches the study of economics from the viewpoint of
a individual or specific markets.
b the operation of the Reserve Bank of Australia.
c economy-wide effects.
d the national economy.

6 A review of the performance of the Korean economy during the 1990s is primarily the concern of
a macroeconomics.
b microeconomics.
c both macroeconomics and microeconomics.
d neither macroeconomics nor microeconomics.

7 An economic model indicates that a rise in petrol prices will cause petrol purchases to fall, ceteris paribus. The phrase 'ceteris paribus' means that
a other relevant factors like consumer incomes must be held constant.
b the petrol prices must first be adjusted for inflation.
c the theory is widely accepted, but cannot be accurately tested.
d consumers' need for petrol remains the same regardless of price.

8 An economist notices that eclipses of the moon have preceded recessions, and concludes that these eclipses cause recessions. The economist has
a confused association and causation.
b misunderstood the ceteris paribus assumption.
c used normative economics to answer a positive question.
d built an untestable model.

9 Which of the following is a statement of positive economics?
a The income tax system collects a lower percentage of the incomes of the poor.
b Governments should attempt to reduce unemployment.
c Tax rates ought to be raised to finance health care.
d All of the above are primarily statements of positive economics.

10 Which of the following is a statement of positive economics?
a An unemployment rate greater than 8 per cent is good because prices will fall.
b An unemployment rate of 7 per cent is a serious problem.
c If the overall unemployment rate is 7 per cent, youth unemployment rates will average 20 per cent.
d Unemployment is a more severe problem than inflation.

11 Which of the following is a statement of normative economics?
a The minimum wage is good because it raises wages for low-income earners.
b The minimum wage is supported by unions.
c The minimum wage reduces jobs for less skilled workers.
d The minimum wage encourages firms to substitute capital for labour.

12 Which of the following statements best encapsulates the idea of enlightened self-interest?
a consumers making choices on the basis of complete information about the goods or services they are buying.
b businesses maximising their profits in a self-interested way.
c greed is good.
d individuals respecting socially derived constraints on their self-interested behaviour.

APPENDIX TO CHAPTER 1 Applying graphs to economics

Economists are well known for their use of graphs. The reason is that 'a picture is worth a thousand words.' Graphs are used throughout this text to present economic models. By drawing a line in a designated space, you can create a two-dimensional illustration to analyse the effects of a change in one variable on another. You could describe the same information using other devices, such as verbal statements, tables or equations. But the graph provides one of the simplest ways to present and understand relationships between economic variables.

Don't worry if graphs are unfamiliar to you. This appendix explains all the basic graphical language you will need for the economic analysis in this text.

A direct relationship

Basic economic analysis typically concerns the relationship between two variables, both of which have positive values. Thus we can confine our graphs to the upper right-hand (north-east) quadrant of the coordinate number system. In Exhibit A1.1, notice that the scales on the horizontal axis (x-axis) and the vertical axis (y-axis) do not necessarily measure the same variables.

The horizontal axis in Exhibit A1.1 measures annual income, and the vertical axis shows the amount spent per year on a personal computer (PC). The intersection of the horizontal and the vertical axes is the *origin* and the point where both income and expenditure are zero. In Exhibit A1.1, each point is a coordinate that matches the dollar value of income and the corresponding expenditure on a PC. For example, point *A* on the graph shows that people with an annual income of $10 000 spent $1000 per year on a PC. Other incomes are associated with different expenditure levels. For example, at $30 000 per year (point *C*), $3000 will be the annual amount spent on a PC.

The straight line in Exhibit A1.1 allows us to determine the direction of change in PC expenditure as annual income changes. This relationship is *positive* because PC expenditure, measured along the vertical axis, and annual income, measured along the horizontal axis, move in the same direction. PC expenditure increases as annual income increases. As income declines, so does the amount spent on a personal

Exhibit A1.1 **A direct relationship between variables**

Expenditure for a personal computer at different annual incomes

Point	Personal computer expenditure (thousands of dollars per year)	Annual income (thousands of dollars)
A	$1	$10
B	2	20
C	3	30
D	4	40

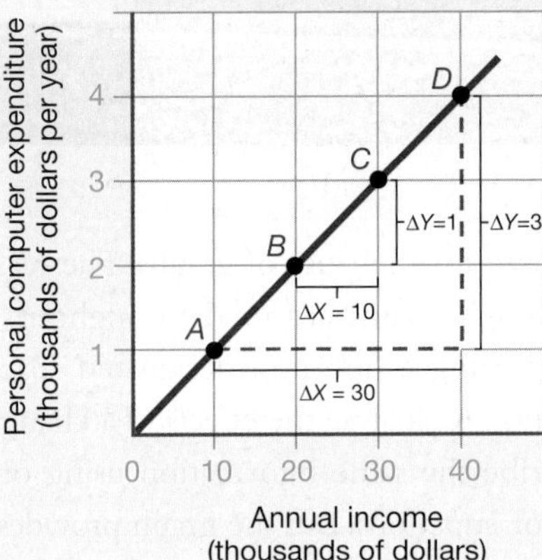

The line with a positive slope shows that the expenditure per year on a personal computer has a direct relationship to annual income, ceteris paribus. As annual income increases along the horizontal axis, the amount spent on a personal computer also increases, as measured by the vertical axis. Along the line, each 10-unit increase in annual income results in a 1-unit increase in expenditure on a personal computer. Because the slope is constant along a straight line, we can measure the same slope between any two points. Between points *B* and *C* or between points *A* and *D*, the slope is $\Delta Y/\Delta X = +3/+30 = 1/10$.

Direct relationship A positive association between two variables. When one variable increases, the other variable increases, and when one variable decreases, the other variable decreases.

computer. Thus, the straight line representing the relationship between income and PC expenditure is a **direct relationship.** A direct relationship is a positive association between two variables. When one variable increases, the other variable increases, and when one variable decreases, the other variable decreases. In short, both variables change in the *same* direction.

Finally, a two-variable graph, like any model, isolates the relationship between two variables and holds all other variables constant under the ceteris paribus assumption. In Exhibit A1.1, for example, other possible causal factors such as the prices of PCs and the education level of the individual are held constant by assumption. In Chapter 3, you will learn how to deal with changes in these variables as well.

An inverse relationship

Now consider the relationship between the price of compact discs and the quantity consumers will buy per year, shown in Exhibit A1.2. These data indicate a *negative* relationship between the price variable and the quantity variable. When the price is low, consumers purchase a greater quantity of compact discs than when the price is high.

In Exhibit A1.2 there is an **inverse relationship** between the price per compact disc and the quantity consumers buy. An inverse relationship is a negative association between two variables. When one variable increases, the other variable decreases, and when one variable decreases, the other variable increases. Stated simply, both variables move in *opposite* directions. Again we are dealing with only two variables, holding constant all other causal factors such as consumer income and sellers' expenditures on advertising compact discs.

Inverse relationship
A negative association between two variables. When one variable increases, the other variable decreases, and when one variable decreases, the other variable increases.

Exhibit A1.2 An inverse relationship between variables

Quantity of compact discs consumers purchase at different prices

Point	Price per compact disc	Quantity of compact discs purchased (millions per year)
A	$50	0
B	40	25
C	30	50
D	20	75
E	10	100

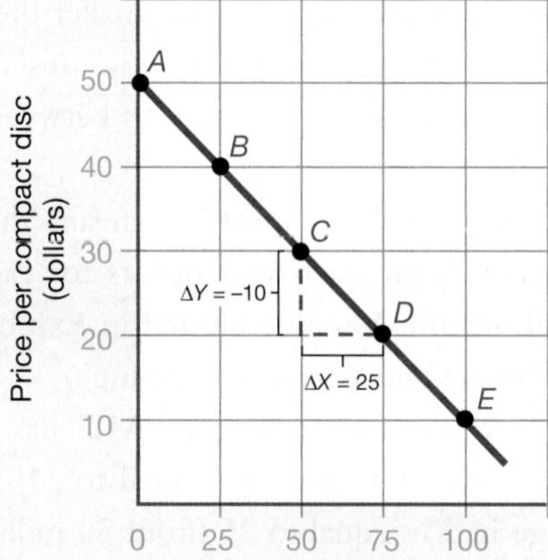

The line with a negative slope shows an inverse relationship between the price per compact disc and the quantity of compact discs consumers purchase, ceteris paribus. As the price of a compact disc rises, the quantity of compact discs purchased falls. A lower price for compact discs is associated with more compact discs purchased by consumers. Along the line, with each $10 decrease in the price of compact discs, consumers increase the quantity purchased by 25 units. The slope = $\Delta Y/\Delta X = -10/+25 = -1/2.5$.

The line drawn in Exhibit A1.2 is an inverse relationship. By long-established tradition, economists put price on the vertical axis and quantity on the horizontal axis. In Chapter 3, we will study in more detail the relationship between price and quantity demanded, which is called the *law of demand*.

In addition to the slope, you must interpret the *intercept* at point A in the exhibit. The intercept in this case means that at a price of \$50 no consumer is willing to buy a single compact disc.

The slope of a straight line

Slope The ratio of the changes in the variable on the vertical axis (the rise or fall) to the change in the variable on the horizontal axis (the run).

Plotting numbers gives a clear visual expression of the relationship between two variables, but it is also important to know how much one variable changes as another variable changes. To find out, we calculate the **slope**. The slope is the ratio of the change in the variable on the vertical axis (the rise or fall) to the change in the variable on the horizontal axis (the run). Algebraically, if Y is on the vertical axis and X on the horizontal axis, the slope is expressed as follows (the delta symbol, Δ, means 'change in'):

$$\text{Slope} = \frac{\text{rise}}{\text{run}} = \frac{\text{change in vertical axis}}{\text{change in horizontal axis}} = \frac{\Delta Y}{\Delta X}$$

Consider the slope between points B and C in Exhibit A1.1. The change in expenditure on a PC, Y, is equal to +1 (from \$2000 up to \$3000 per year) and the change in annual income, X, is equal to +10 (from \$20 000 up to \$30 000 per year). The slope is therefore +1/+10. The sign is positive because computer expenditure is directly or positively related to annual income. The steeper the line, the greater the slope because the ratio of ΔY to ΔX rises. Conversely, the flatter the line, the smaller the slope. Exhibit A1.1 also illustrates that the slope of a straight line is constant. That is, the slope between any two points along the line, such as between points A and D, is equal to $+3/+30 = 1/10$.

What does the slope of 1/10 mean? It means that a \$1000 increase (decrease) in PC expenditure each year occurs for each \$10 000 increase (decrease) in annual income. The line plotted in Exhibit A1.1 has a *positive slope*, and we describe the line as 'upward-sloping'.

On the other hand, the line in Exhibit A1.2 has a *negative slope*. The change in Y between points C and D is equal to –10 (from \$30 down to \$20), and the change in X is equal to 25 (from 50 million up to 75 million compact discs purchased per year). The slope is therefore $-10/+25 = -1/2.5$, and this line is described as 'downward-sloping'.

What does this slope of –1/2.5 mean? It means that raising (lowering) the price per compact disc by \$1 decreases (increases) the quantity of compact discs purchased by 2.5 million per year.

Suppose we calculate the slope between any two points – say, points B and C in Exhibit A1.3. In this case, there is no change in Y (expenditure for toothpaste) as X (annual income) increases. Consumers spend $20 per year on toothpaste regardless of annual income. It follows that $\Delta Y = 0$ for any ΔX, so the slope is equal to 0. When the relationship between two variables is indicated by a horizontal line (or a vertical line) there is an **independent relationship**. An independent relationship means there is no association between two variables. When one variable changes, the other variable remains unchanged.

Independent relationship No association between two variables. When one variable changes, the other variable remains unchanged.

The slope of a curve

So far we have looked at straight-line or linear relationships. Now we examine relationships between two variables that result in a curved-line or non-linear relationship. The slope of a curved line changes from one point to another. Suppose the relationship between the expenditure on a PC per year and annual income is not a straight line, but an upward-sloping curved line,

Exhibit A1.3 An independent relationship between variables

Expenditure for toothpaste at different annual incomes

Point	Toothpaste expenditure (dollars per year)	Annual income (thousands of dollars)
A	$20	$10
B	20	20
C	20	30
D	20	40

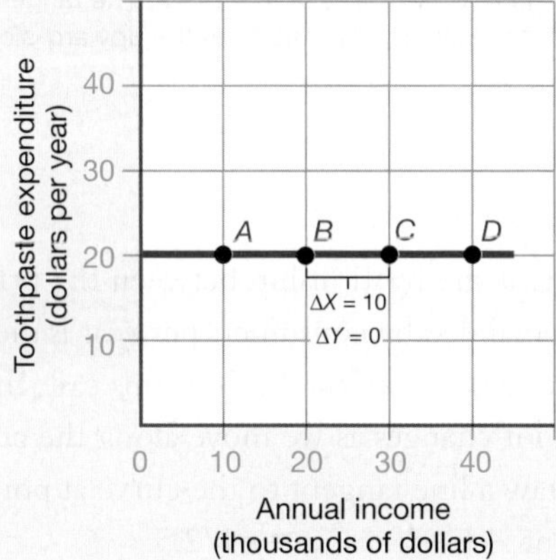

The horizontal line with a zero slope shows that the expenditure per year for toothpaste is unrelated to annual income. As annual income increases along the horizontal axis, the amount spent each year for toothpaste remains unchanged at 20 units. If annual income increases 10 units, the corresponding change in expenditure is zero. The slope = $\Delta Y/\Delta X = 0/+10 = 0$.

as drawn in Exhibit A1.4. The slope of the curve is *positive*, but it changes as we move along the curve. To calculate the slope of a given point on the curve requires two steps. For example, at point *A*, the first step is to draw a tangent line that just touches the curve at this point without crossing it. The second step is to determine the slope of the tangent line. In Exhibit A1.4, the slope of the tangent line, and therefore the slope of the curve at point *A*, is +2/+30 = 1/15. What does this slope of 1/15 mean? It means that at point *A* there will be a $1000 increase (decrease) in PC expenditure each year resulting from a $15 000 increase (decrease) in annual income.

Exhibit A1.4 The slope of an upward-sloping, non-linear curve

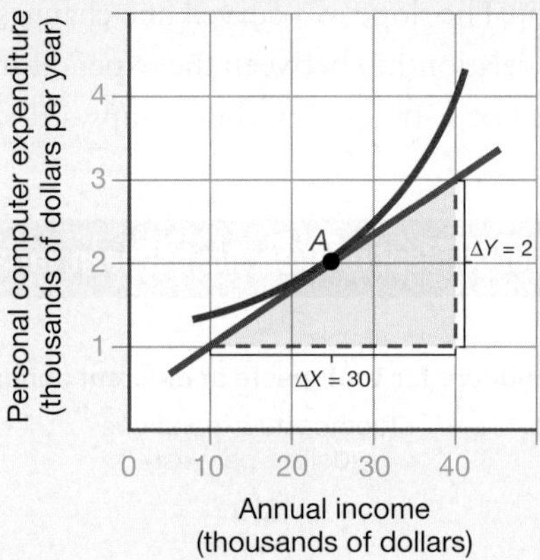

The slope of a curve at any given point, such as point A, is equal to the slope of the straight line drawn tangent to the curve at that point. The tangent line just touches the curve at point *A* without crossing it. The slope of the upward-sloping curve at point *A* is +2/+30 = +1/+15 = 1/15.

Now consider that the relationship between the price per compact disc and the quantity demanded by consumers per year is the downward-sloping, non-linear curve shown in Exhibit A1.5. In this case, the slope of the curve is *negative,* but again it changes as we move along the curve. To calculate the slope at point *A*, draw a line tangent to the curve at point *A*. Thus, the slope of the curve at point *A* is –20/+50 = –1/2.5.

Introducing a third variable to the graph

The two-variable relationships drawn so far conform to a two-dimensional flat piece of paper. For example, the vertical axis measures the price per compact disc variable, and the horizontal axis measures the quantity of

Exhibit A1.5 **The slope of a downward-sloping, non-linear curve**

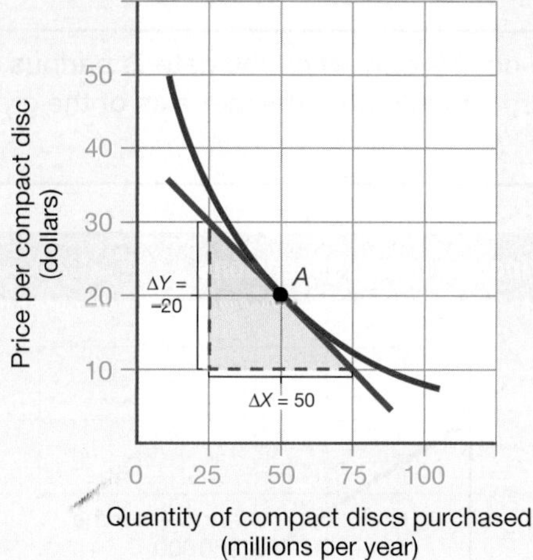

In this exhibit, the negative slope changes as one moves from point to point along the curve. The slope at any given point, such as point *A*, can be determined by the slope of the straight line tangent to that point. The slope of the downward-sloping curve at point *A* is −20/+50 = −1/+2.5 = −1/2.5.

compact discs purchased variable. All other factors, such as consumer income, that may affect the relationship between the price and quantity variables are held constant by the ceteris paribus assumption. But reality is frequently not so accommodating. Often a model drawn on a two-dimensional piece of graph paper must take into account the impact of changes in a third variable (say consumer income).

The method used to depict a three-variable relationship is shown in Exhibit A1.6. As explained earlier, the cause-and-effect relationship between price and quantity of compact discs determines the downward-sloping curve. A change in the price per compact disc causes a movement downward along either of the two separate curves in Exhibit A1.6. As the price falls, consumers increase the quantity of compact discs demanded. The location of each curve on the graph, however, depends on the annual income of consumers. As the annual income variable increases from $30 000 to $60 000 and as consumers choose to purchase more at each possible price, the price–quantity demanded curve shifts rightward. Conversely, as the annual income variable decreases and as consumers choose to buy less at each possible price, the price–quantity demanded curve shifts leftward.

This is an extremely important concept you must understand: throughout this book, you must distinguish between *movements along* and *shifts in* a curve. Here is how you tell the difference. A change in one of the variables shown on either of the coordinate axes of the graph causes *movement along* a curve. On the other hand, a change in a variable not shown on one of the coordinate axes of the graph causes a *shift in* a curve's position on the graph.

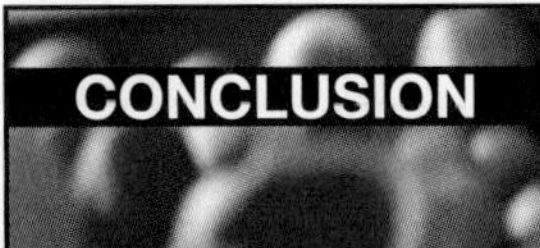

A shift in a curve occurs only when the ceteris paribus assumption is relaxed and a third variable not on either axis of the graph is allowed to change.

Exhibit A1.6 **Changes in price, quantity and income in two dimensions**

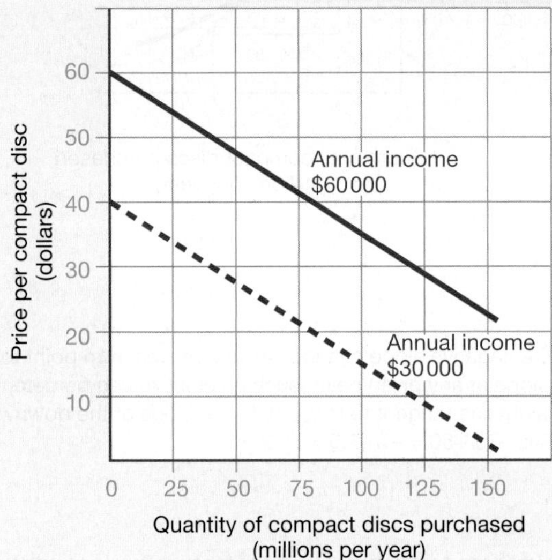

Economists use a multi-curve graph to represent a three-variable relationship in a two-dimensional graph. A decrease in the price per compact disc causes a movement downward along each curve. As the annual income of consumers rises, there is a shift rightward in the position of the demand curve.

A helpful study hint using graphs

Don't be the student who tries to memorise the graphs and then wonders why he or she failed economics. Instead of memorising graphs, you should use them as a valuable aid to learning the economic concepts they illustrate. After studying a chapter, go back to the graphs one by one. Hide the brief description accompanying each graph, and describe to yourself or other students what the graph means. Next, uncover the description and check your interpretation. If you still fail to understand the graph, read the text again and correct the problem before proceeding to the next chapter.

Key concepts

Direct relationship
Inverse relationship
Slope
Independent relationship

Summary

- **Graphs** provide a means of clearly showing economic relationships in two-dimensional space. Economic analysis is often concerned with two variables confined to the upper right-hand (north-east) quadrant of the coordinate number system.
- A **direct relationship** is one in which two variables change in the *same* direction.

Direct relationship

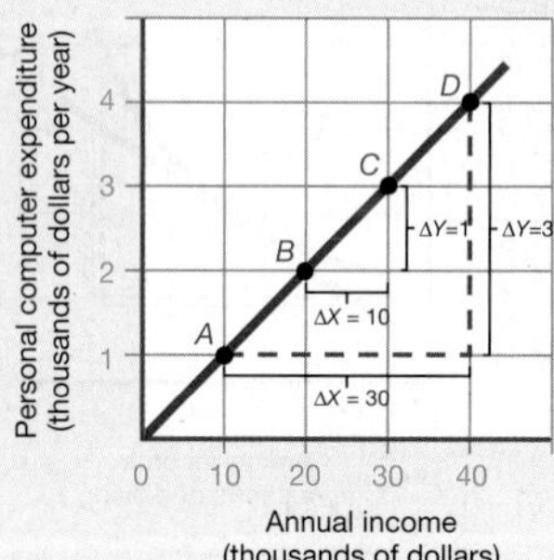

- An **inverse relationship** is one in which two variables change in *opposite* directions.

Inverse relationship

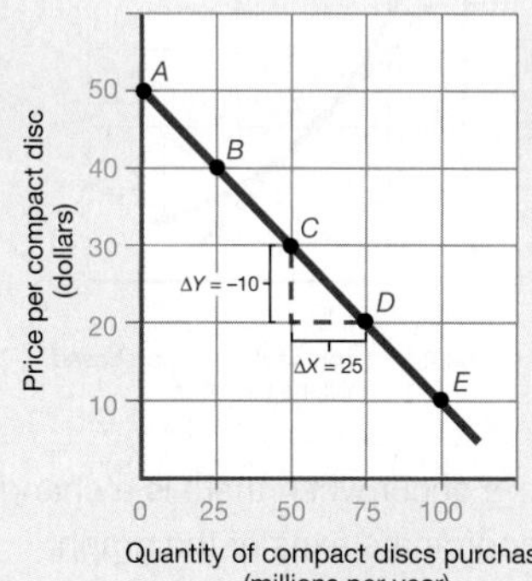

PART 1

- An **independent relationship** is one in which two variables are unrelated.

Independent relationship

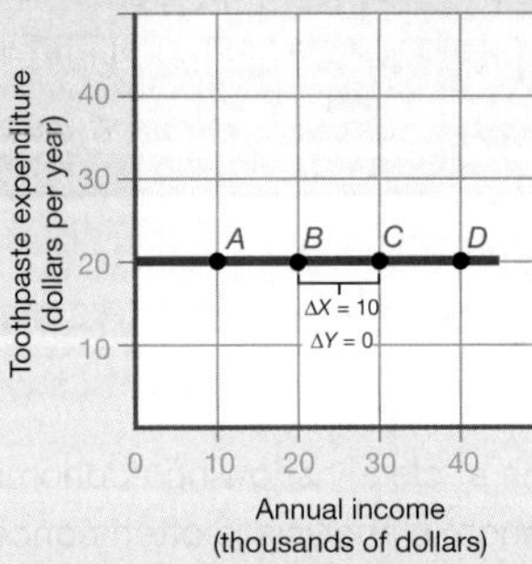

- **Slope** is the ratio of the vertical change (the rise or fall) to the horizontal change (the run). The slope of an *upward-sloping* line is *positive*, and the slope of a *downward-sloping* line is *negative*.

Positive slope of an upward-sloping curve

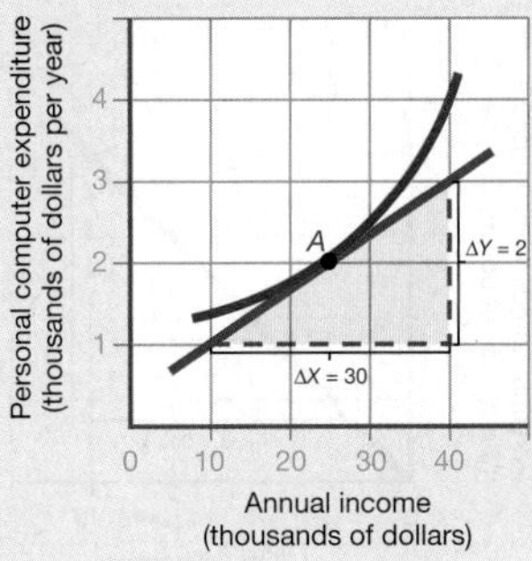

Negative slope of a downward-sloping curve

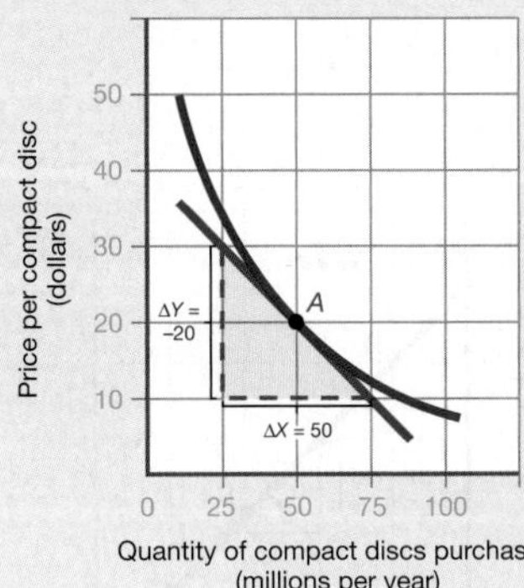

- **Movements along** a curve occur when there is a change in one of the variables shown on the coordinate axes of the graph.

- **Shifts in** a curve occur when there is a change in a variable that is not shown on the coordinate axes of the graph – that is, when the ceteris paribus assumption is relaxed.

Study questions and problems

1 Without using specific data, draw a graph for the expected relationship between the following variables:
   a life expectancy and age
   b annual income and years of education
   c rainfall and sales of umbrellas
   d distance from the equator and mean summer temperature

   In each case, state whether the expected relationship is *direct* or *inverse*. Explain an additional factor that would be included in the ceteris paribus assumption because it might change and influence your theory.

2 Assume a research firm collects survey sales data that reveal the relationship between the possible selling prices of hamburgers and the quantity of hamburgers consumers would purchase per year at alternative prices. The report states that if the price of a hamburger is $4.00, 20 000 will be bought. However, at a price of $3.00, 40 000 hamburgers will be bought. At $2.00, 60 000 hamburgers will be bought, and at $1.00, 80 000 hamburgers will be purchased.
   Based on these data, describe the relevant relationship between the price of a hamburger and the quantity consumers are willing to purchase, using
   a a verbal statement.
   b a numerical table.
   c a graph.

   Which device do you prefer and why?

Multiple-choice questions

1 Straight line *CD* in Exhibit A1.7 shows that
   a increasing the value of *X* will increase the value of *Y*.
   b decreasing the value of *X* will decrease the value of *Y*.
   c there is a direct relationship between *X* and *Y*.
   d all of the above are true.

2 In Exhibit A1.7, the slope of straight line *CD* is
   a 3. c −1.
   b 1. d 1/2.

3 In Exhibit A1.7, the slope of straight line *CD* is
   a positive. c negative.
   b zero. d variable.

Exhibit A1.7 Straight line

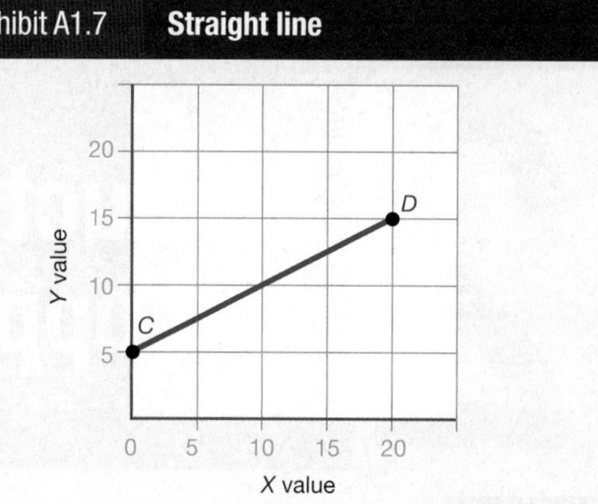

4 Straight line *AB* in Exhibit A1.8 shows that
   a increasing the value of *X* reduces the value of *Y*.
   b decreasing the value of *X* increases the value of *Y*.
   c there is an inverse relationship between *X* and *Y*.
   d all of the above are true.

5 As shown in Exhibit A1.8, the slope of straight line *AB*
   a decreases with increases in *X*.
   b increases with increases in *X*.
   c increases with decreases in *X*.
   d remains constant with changes in *X*.

6 In Exhibit A1.8, the slope for straight line *AB* is
   a 3. c −1.
   b 1. d −5.

7 A shift in a curve represents a change in
   a the variable on the horizontal axis.
   b the variable on the vertical axis.
   c a third variable that is not on either axis.
   d none of the above.

Exhibit A1.8 Straight line

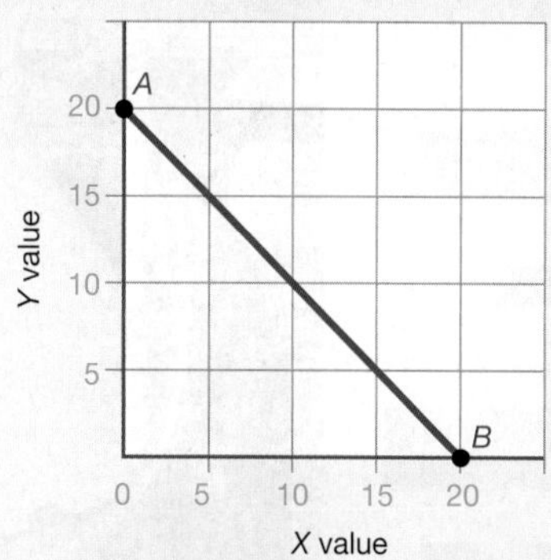

2 Production possibilities and opportunity cost

This chapter continues building on the foundation laid in the preceding chapter. Having learned that *scarcity* forces *choices*, here you will study the choices people make in more detail. This chapter begins by examining the three basic economic questions faced by society: *What*, *How* and *For whom*? Next, you will learn that the process of answering these basic questions introduces two other key building blocks in the economic way of thinking – *opportunity cost* and *marginal analysis*. Once you understand these important concepts, it will be easier to interpret our first formal economic model, the *production possibilities frontier*. This model illustrates how economists use graphs as a powerful tool to supplement words and develop an understanding of basic economic principles. You will discover that the production possibilities model explains many of the most important concepts in economics, including scarcity, the law of increasing opportunity costs, efficiency, investment

and economic growth. For example, the chapter concludes by using the production possibilities frontier to explain why many underdeveloped countries do not achieve economic growth, and thus fail to improve their standard of living.

In this chapter, you will examine these economics questions:

- Why did few established rock stars or movie stars go to university?
- Why would you spend an extra hour reading this text, rather than going to a movie or sleeping?
- Why are investment and economic growth so important?
- Why are some developing countries reluctant to enforce laws banning child labour?

The three fundamental economic questions

Whether rich or poor, every nation must answer these same three fundamental economic questions: (1) *What* goods and services will be produced? (2) *How* will they be produced? (3) *For whom* will they be produced?

What to produce?

Should society devote its limited resources to producing more military goods and fewer consumer goods and services? Should society produce more mobile phones and fewer cups of coffee? Should more small cars and fewer large cars be produced, or should more buses be produced instead of cars? The problem of scarcity imposes a restriction on the ability to produce everything we want during a given period, so the choice to produce 'more' of a good requires producing 'less' of another good. By and large, democratic societies determine what to produce on the basis of individual (or family) preferences expressed by consumers in the marketplace, and on the basis of collective preferences expressed through governments.

How to produce?

After deciding which goods and services to produce, the second question for society to decide is how to mix technology and scarce resources in order to produce them. For instance, a towel can be sewn primarily by hand (labour), partially by hand and partially by machine (labour and capital), or primarily by machine (capital). In short, the *How* question asks whether a production technique will be more or less capital-intensive.

Education plays an important role in answering the *How* question. Education improves the ability of workers to perform their work. The quality and quantity of education vary among nations; this is one reason why economies differ in their capacities to apply resources and technology to answer the *How* question. For example, many Asian and European countries are striving to catch up with the United States and Australia, which are among the world's biggest users of the Internet. Not only are appropriate hardware and software required for increased Internet use, but also there is a need for a vast array of trained staff.

For whom to produce?

Once the *What* and *How* questions are resolved, the third question is *For whom*. Of all the people who desire to consume the goods and services produced, who actually receives them? Who is fed well? Who drives a Lexus? Who receives organ transplants? This will depend largely on the way in which incomes are distributed among different members of the community. But the *For whom* question also means that society must ask whether governments should override market outcomes to ensure that the poorest members of society have a reasonable standard of living.

Opportunity cost

Because of scarcity, the three basic questions cannot be answered without considering sacrifice or cost. But what does the term *cost* really mean? The common response would be to say that the purchase price is the cost. A movie ticket *costs* $12, or a shirt *costs* $50. In the economic way of thinking, however, *cost* is a relative concept. A well-known phrase in economics is 'There is no such thing as a free lunch.' This expression captures the links among the concepts of scarcity, choice and cost. Because of scarcity, people must make choices, and each choice incurs a cost (sacrifice). Once one option is chosen, another option is given up. The money you spend on a night at the movies cannot also buy a DVD. A business may purchase a new textile machine to manufacture towels, but this same money cannot be used to buy a new recreation facility for employees.

Opportunity cost The best alternative sacrificed for a chosen alternative.

The DVD and the recreation facility examples illustrate that the relevant cost of these decisions is the **opportunity cost** of a choice. Opportunity cost is the best alternative sacrificed for a chosen alternative. If the best alternative to making a purchase is to keep the money, then the opportunity cost is the purchase price itself. This principle states that some most highly valued opportunity must be forgone in all economic decisions. The actual good or use of time given up for the chosen good or use of time measures the opportunity cost. We may leave off the word 'opportunity' before the word 'cost', but the concept remains just the same.

INFOTRAC®

opportunity cost

Examples are endless, but let's consider a few. Suppose your lecturer decides to become a rock star in the Rolling in Dough band. Now all his or her working hours are devoted to creating hit music, and the opportunity cost is the income and satisfaction that can no longer be derived from working as an academic. Opportunity cost also applies to national economic decisions. Suppose the federal government decides to spend tax revenues on homeland security. The opportunity cost depends on the next best program *not* funded. Assume roads and bridges are the highest-valued projects not undertaken as a result of the decision to increase expenditure on homeland security. Then roads and bridges are the opportunity cost of the decision to devote resources to security.

To illustrate the relationship between time and opportunity cost, ask yourself how much you could currently be earning if you were not spending many hours studying. If earning more income were the best alternative to studying, the opportunity cost of studying is the income you sacrifice. Established rock stars or movie stars would have to forgo a large amount of income to undertake further formal education. Now you know why so few of them make this choice.

What is the opportunity cost of attending university? Visit the official site of the Association of Tennis Professionals (ATP) at (**www.atptour.com**). Click on *PLAYER PROFILES* and look at the annual and career prize money for some of the top players. Although tennis professionals incur significant costs in the process of winning this prize money, you can see that taking time out to attend university would have a high opportunity cost.

Are we always conscious of opportunity cost?

You make the call

Public officials and elected representatives in cities and towns across Australia have rediscovered the humble rainwater tank. In spite of previously imposed bans on these devices – bans that were prompted by poor water quality and mosquitos breeding in inadequately maintained tanks – they are being promoted and subsidised by state governments and local authorities. It is argued that these tanks will result in lower demand for reticulated water, resulting in the need for less infrastructure such as dams and water mains and the adverse environmental effects this causes. As well as subsidising their installation by giving cash to householders, state and local governments also encourage home owners to install these tanks by emphasising the benefits of 'free' water for gardening, washing and, in some cases, drinking. But are home owners getting 'free' water when they install a tank? What a lot of people forget when they jump at the opportunity to have 'free' water from a rainwater tank is the opportunity cost of the money tied up in the system itself. Not only are there are funds tied up in the tank that could otherwise be earning interest or be used to help pay off a housing loan, but the tank is also slowly depreciating over time and will eventually need to be replaced. A 4500-litre tank costing $1500, including installation, will have an annual opportunity cost of $150 if interest forgone and depreciation total 10 per cent of the initial cost. An awful lot of water can be bought from the supplier of reticulated water for $150. In fact, at prices charged in Australia's capital cities, this would buy around 150 000 litres of water per year, or nearly 3000 litres per week. Furthermore, the funds used by local authorities to subsidise home owners'

purchases of tanks could be used for other worthwhile purposes; and the production and installation of tanks causes environmental damage that could well be much more per litre of water delivered than the environmental cost of infrastructure for reticulated water. If interest rates rise, are more or fewer people likely to choose to install a rainwater tank? What are some of the opportunity costs that environmentally conscious consumers should take into account when considering whether or not to install a tank?

To obtain an idea of the extent to which state and local governments are encouraging the installation of rainwater tanks by offering subsidies to consumers, enter the words *rainwater tank* and *rebate* into a web browser such as Google at **www.google.com**. Restrict your search to pages from Australia.

Marginal analysis

Marginal analysis An examination of the effects of additions to or subtractions from a current situation.

INFOTRAC®
marginal analysis

At the heart of many important decision-making techniques used throughout this text is **marginal analysis**. Marginal analysis examines the effects of additions to or subtractions from a current situation. This is a very valuable tool in the economic-way-of-thinking toolkit because it considers the effects of change. For example, you must decide how to use your scarce time. Should you devote an extra hour to reading this book, going to a movie, watching television, talking on the phone or sleeping? There are many ways to spend your time. Which option do you choose? The answer depends on marginal analysis. If you decide that the benefit of a higher grade in economics exceeds the opportunity cost of, say, sleep, then you allocate the extra hour to studying economics. Excellent choice!

Similarly, producers use marginal analysis. The farmer asks if he or she should add fertiliser to improve the wheat yield. Using marginal analysis, the farmer estimates that the wheat revenue yield will be about $75 per hectare without fertiliser and about $100 per hectare using fertiliser. If the cost of fertiliser is $20 per hectare, marginal analysis tells the farmer to fertilise. The additional fertiliser will increase profit by $5 per hectare because fertilising adds $25 to the value of each hectare at a cost of $20.

Marginal analysis is an important concept when considering changes in the overall composition of output produced within an economy. For example, as demonstrated in the next section, it is useful to know that an increase in the production of consumer goods will result in an opportunity cost of fewer consumer services produced.

The production possibilities frontier

Production possibilities frontier Shows the maximum combinations of two outputs that an economy can produce, given its available resources and technology.

The economic problem of scarcity means that society's capacity to produce combinations of goods is constrained by its limited resources. This condition can be represented in a model called the **production possibilities frontier**. The production possibilities frontier shows the maximum combinations of two outputs that an economy can produce, given its available resources and technology. Three basic assumptions underlie the production possibilities frontier model:

1 *Fixed resources.* The quantities and qualities of all resource inputs remain unchanged during the time period. But the 'rules of the game' do allow an economy to shift any resource from the production of one output to the production of another output. For example, an economy may shift workers from producing consumer goods to producing capital goods. Although the number of workers remains unchanged, this transfer of labour will produce fewer consumer goods and more capital goods.
2 *Fully employed resources.* The economy operates with all its factors of production fully employed and producing the greatest output possible without waste or mismanagement.
3 *Technology unchanged.* Holding existing technology fixed creates limits, or constraints, on the amounts and types of goods and services any economy can produce. **Technology** is the body of knowledge applied to the way goods and services are produced.

Technology The body of knowledge applied to the way goods and services are produced.

In modern economies an enormous range of goods and services is produced. Goods, which are tangible, include capital goods sold to the business sector and consumer goods such as food, clothing and furniture sold to consumers. Services, which are intangible, include accountants' and lawyers' services sold to businesses, and consumer services such as restaurant meals, electricity and education, which are sold to consumers. Exhibit 2.1 shows a hypothetical economy that has the capacity to manufacture any combination of consumer goods and consumer services per year along its production possibilities frontier (*PPF*), including points *A*, *B*, *C* and *D*. For example, if this economy uses all its resources to make consumer goods, it can produce a *maximum* of 160 billion units of consumer goods and zero units of consumer services (combination *A*). Another possibility is for the economy to use all its resources to produce a *maximum* of 100 billion units of consumer services and zero units of consumer goods (point *D*). Between the extremes of points *A* and *D* lie other production possibilities for combinations of goods and services. If combination *B* is chosen, the economy will produce 140 billion units of consumer goods and 40 billion units of consumer services. Another possibility (point *C*) is to produce 80 billion units of consumer goods and 80 billion units of consumer services.

At this stage it is important to point out that the production we are talking about is a *flow* of output that occurs over a particular time period – in this case one year. Whenever a variable is expressed as a quantity per time period, we are dealing with a flow concept. By contrast, a variable such as the amount of capital used to produce flows of output is described as a *stock*. It is simply expressed as a quantity without reference to a relevant time period. For example, we might say that a nation's stock of capital produces an annual flow of output of goods and services.

What happens if the economy does not use all its resources to their capacity? For example, some workers may not find work, or plant and equipment may be idle for any number of reasons. The result is that our hypothetical economy fails to reach any of the combinations along *PPF*. In

Exhibit 2.1, point *U* illustrates an *inefficient* output level for any economy operating without all its resources fully employed. At point *U*, our model economy is producing 80 billion units of consumer goods and 40 billion units of consumer services per year. Such an economy is under-producing because it could satisfy more of society's wants if it were producing at some point along the *PPF*.

Even if an economy fully employs all its resources, it is impossible to produce certain output quantities. Any point outside the production possibilities frontier is *unattainable* because it is beyond the economy's present production

Exhibit 2.1 The production possibilities frontier for consumer goods and consumer services

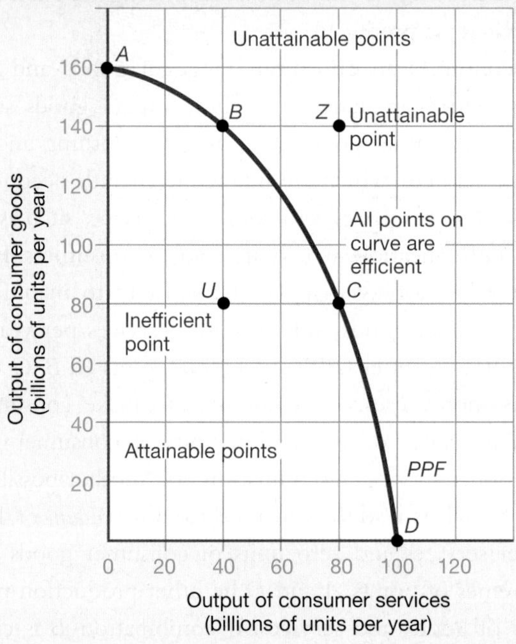

The production possibilities for consumer goods and consumer services per year

Output (billions of units per year)	Production possibilities			
	A	*B*	*C*	*D*
Consumer goods	160	140	80	0
Consumer services	0	40	80	100

All points along the production possibilities frontier (PPF) are maximum possible combinations of consumer goods and consumer services. One possibility, point A, would be to produce 160 billion units of consumer goods and zero units of consumer services each year. At the other extreme, point D, an economy uses all its resources to produce 100 billion units of consumer services and zero units of consumer goods each year. Points B and C are obtained by using some resources to produce each of the two outputs. If the economy fails to use its resources fully, the result is the inefficient point U. Point Z lies beyond the economy's present production capabilities and is unattainable.

capabilities. Point *Z*, for example, represents an unattainable output of 140 billion units of consumer goods and 80 billion units of consumer services. Society would prefer this combination to any combination along, or inside, *PPF*, but the economy cannot reach this point with its existing resources and technology.

Scarcity limits an economy to points on or below its production possibilities frontier.

Because all the points along the frontier are *maximum* output levels with the given resources and technology, they are all called *efficient* points. A movement between any two efficient points on the frontier means that *more* of one output is produced only by producing *less* of the other output. In Exhibit 2.1, moving from point *A* to point *B* produces 40 billion additional units of consumer services per year, but only at a cost of sacrificing 20 billion units of consumer goods. Thus, a movement between any two efficient points graphically illustrates that 'There is no such thing as a free lunch.'

The production possibilities frontier consists of all efficient output combinations where an economy can produce more of one output only by producing less of the other output.

The law of increasing opportunity costs

Why is the production possibilities frontier shaped the way it is? Exhibit 2.2 will help us answer this question. It presents a production possibilities frontier for a hypothetical economy that must choose between producing motor cars (goods) and producing university degrees (the services that comprise university education). Consider expanding the production of university degrees in 20 000-unit increments. Moving from point *A* to point *B*, the *opportunity cost* is 10 000 motor cars; between point *B* and point *C* the *opportunity cost* is 20 000 motor cars; and the *opportunity cost* of producing at point *D*, rather than point *C*, is 50 000 motor cars.

Exhibit 2.2 illustrates the **law of increasing opportunity costs**. The law of increasing opportunity costs states that the opportunity cost increases as production of one output expands. Holding the stock of resources and technology constant (ceteris paribus), the law of increasing opportunity costs causes the production possibilities frontier to display a *bowed-out* shape (concave to the origin).

Law of increasing opportunity costs The principle that the opportunity cost increases as the production of one output expands.

Why must our hypothetical economy sacrifice larger and larger amounts of motor car output in order to produce each additional batch of 20 000 university degrees? The reason is that the factors of production (primarily labour and capital) are not equally suited to producing one

Exhibit 2.2 **The law of increasing opportunity costs**

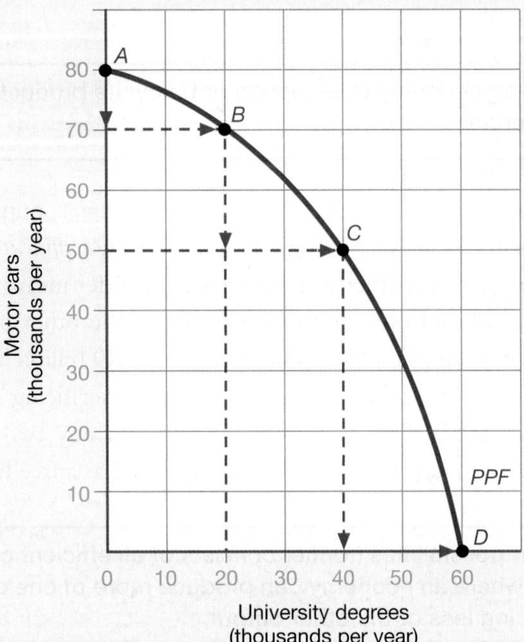

Production possibilities for motor cars and university degrees per year

Output (thousands per year)	Production possibilities			
	A	*B*	*C*	*D*
Motor cars	80	70	50	0
University degrees	0	20	40	60

A hypothetical economy produces equal increments of 20 000 university degrees per year as we move from point A to point D on the production possibilities frontier (PPF). If the hypothetical economy moves from point A to point B, the opportunity cost of 20 000 university degrees is a reduction in motor car output of 10 000 per year. This opportunity cost rises to 20 000 motor cars by selecting point C instead of point B. Finally, production at point D, rather than point C, results in an opportunity cost of 50 000 motor cars per year. The opportunity cost rises because factors of production are not equally suited to making motor cars and university degrees.

PART 1

good, compared to another good. To expand the output of labour-intensive university degrees requires a large amount of highly educated labour and some suitably equipped buildings and computers, whereas the expansion of output of capital-intensive motor cars requires a large amount of purpose-built machinery and computers and some workers with mostly moderate education levels.

Suppose our hypothetical economy has a range of capital goods and labour resources, some of which are best suited to production of motor cars and some of which are best suited to producing university degrees. Further, suppose that it currently produces no university degrees (point *A*). Now imagine that a decision is made to expand the economy's production of university degrees.

At first, a small amount of highly educated labour and a small amount of suitable capital such as buildings and desktop computers are transferred to produce 2000 university degrees. When this occurs, 10 000 motor cars are sacrificed. At this stage, few cars are sacrificed because the resources that are transferred are those best suited to production of university degrees. These resources make only a small contribution to the output of motor cars. As the economy moves from point *B* to point *C*, some less-educated car workers and some more buildings and computers are transferred to production of university degrees. But this time the opportunity cost rises to 20 000 cars. The opportunity cost has risen because the car makers are now losing labour and capital that are better suited to car making. Finally, the economy can decide to move from point *C* to point *D*, and the opportunity cost increases even more to 50 000 cars for the remaining 20 000 university degrees. In the process of moving from point *C* to point *D* the car makers have lost their most productive labour and capital. Now all workers, whether they are suited to it or not, are in the education sector, and all the capital – even the huge machines, robots and assembly lines – is in the education sector. Remember that our production possibilities frontier is constructed on the assumption that all of the economy's factors of production are fully employed. No matter how unsuited to the education sector some of them may be, *all* resources are now being used in this sector.

See if you can explain the law of increasing opportunity cost by considering what happens when society moves from producing only university degrees (point *D*) to producing only motor cars (point *A*).

If the factors of production employed in an economy were equally suited to the production of its two hypothetical outputs, then a situation of constant opportunity cost would prevail, and the production possibilities frontier would be a straight line. We will revisit this model in Chapter 18 when dealing with international trade and finance.

Shifting the production possibilities frontier

The economy's production capacity is not permanently fixed. If either the resource base increases or technology advances, the economy experiences **economic growth**, and the production possibilities frontier shifts outward. Economic growth is the ability of an economy to produce greater levels of output. In Chapter 12 theories of economic growth are discussed at length.

Economic growth The ability of an economy to produce greater levels of output, represented by an outward shift of its production possibilities frontier.

At this stage, however, we will undertake a simple explanation of the way in which economic growth can be represented by an outward shift of an economy's production possibilities frontier.

Exhibit 2.3 illustrates the importance of an outward shift. (Note the causation chain, which is often used in this text to focus on a model's cause-and-effect relationship.) At point *A* on production possibilities frontier PPF_1, a hypothetical full-employment economy produces 40 000 computers and 200 million pizzas per year. If the frontier shifts outward to new frontier PPF_2, the economy can expand its full-employment output options. One option is to produce at point *B* and increase computer output to 70 000 per year. Another possibility is to increase pizza output to 400 million per year. Yet another choice is to produce more of both at some point between points *B* and *C*.

Exhibit 2.3 An outward shift of the production possibilities frontier for computers and pizzas

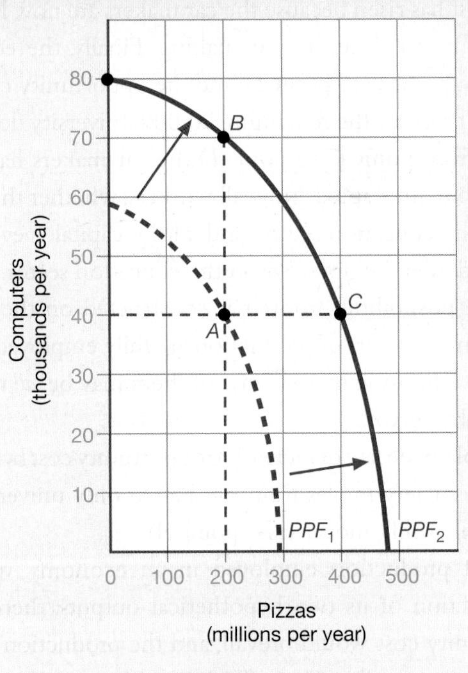

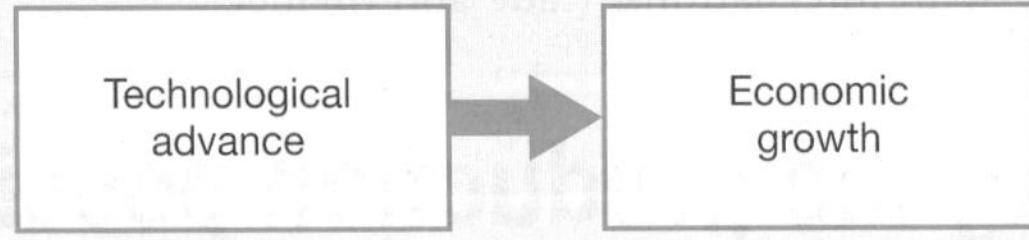

The economy begins with the capacity to produce combinations along production possibilities frontier PPF_1. Growth in the resource base or technological advance shifts the production possibilities frontier outward from PPF_1 to PPF_2. Points along PPF_2 represent new production possibilities previously impossible. This outward shift permits the economy to produce greater quantities of output. Instead of producing combination A, the economy can produce, for example, more computers at point B, or it can produce more pizzas at point C. If the economy produces at a point between B and C, more of both pizzas and computers can be produced compared to point A.

Changes in resources

One way to accelerate economic growth is to gain additional resources. Any increase in resources – for example more natural resources, increased immigration or more factories – will shift the production possibilities frontier outward. In Exhibit 2.3, assume frontier PPF_1 represents New Zealand's production possibilities for clothing and food in a given year. Suddenly, the terrorism threat to the rest of the world increases markedly, resulting in an unexpected influx of new resources including immigration of skilled labour. Such new resources will result in New Zealand having an expanded capacity to produce any combination along an expanded frontier, such as frontier PPF_2.

Reductions in resources will cause the production possibilities frontier to shift inward. Now assume frontier PPF_2 describes Japan's economy before World War II. After the destruction of its factors of production in the war, Japan's frontier shifted leftward to frontier PPF_1. Over the years Japan trained its workforce, built new factories and equipment, and used new technology to shift its frontier outward and surpass its original production capacity at frontier PPF_2.

Does the unpaid work of Australia's over 4 million volunteers shift the PPF?

You make the call

Roughly one-third of Australians over 18 years of age are volunteers. This group, comprising approximately 4.5 million people, contributes over 700 million hours of volunteer work to the Australian community each year. If the value of this unpaid work is estimated to average as little as $20 per hour, its total value amounts to more than $14 billion per annum. Whether these people are engaged in volunteering associated with youth groups, the arts, health services, sporting endeavours or any other of the myriad voluntary activities carried out in Australia today, their contribution makes an enormous difference to the well-being of Australians. If these volunteers were to suddenly decrease the level of their voluntary activity, would this have an effect on the position of the nation's *PPF*? What if the decrease in the level of hours of voluntary activity were to be exactly compensated by a rise in hours of paid employment?

Technological change

Another way to achieve economic growth is through research and development of new technologies. The knowledge of how to transform a block of stone into a wheel vastly improved the standard of living in prehistoric times. Technological change also makes it possible to shift the production possibilities frontier outwards by producing more from the same resources base. One source of technological change is *invention*. The light bulb, the

The CSIRO undertakes more research into Australian primary industries than any other organisation. Visit the CSIRO website (**www.csiro.au**). What types of research does the CSIRO conduct, and how might this research push out the production possibilities frontier for the areas of the economy affected by this research?

transistor, the computer chip and antibiotics are all examples of technological advances resulting from the use of science and engineering knowledge.

Technological change also includes the results of *innovation*. Innovation involves the creation and development of new products or productive processes. Seeking profits, entrepreneurs create new, better or less expensive products. This requires organising an improved mix of resources, which expands the production possibilities frontier.

For example one entrepreneur, Henry Ford, revolutionised manufacturing by pioneering the use of the assembly line for making cars. Chester Carlson, a law student, worked on his own to develop photocopying because the problem of copying documents frustrated him. After years of disappointment, a small firm named Xerox Corporation accepted Carlson's invention and transformed a good idea into a revolutionary product. An Australian, Dr David Warren, developed the black box flight recorder in Melbourne in the 1950s. In spite of early scepticism about its usefulness, it is now fitted to the aircraft of all commercial airlines. These and a myriad other business success stories illustrate the fact that entrepreneurs are important because they transform their new ideas into production and practical use. The link between technological change and growth will be analysed more fully in Chapter 12.

Present investment and future production possibilities frontier

When the decision for an economy involves choosing between capital and consumer goods, the output combination for the present period can determine future production capacity.

production possibilities frontier

Exhibit 2.4 compares two countries producing different combinations of capital and consumer goods. Part (a) shows the production possibilities frontier for the low-investment economy of Alpha. This economy was producing combination *A* in 2000, which is an output of C_a of consumer goods and an output of K_a of capital goods per year. Let's assume K_a is just enough capital output to replace the capital being worn out each year (that is, to cover depreciation). As a result, Alpha fails to increase its net amount of factories and equipment. This means that there can be no expansion of its production possibilities frontier outwards in future years. Why wouldn't Alpha simply move up along its production frontier by shifting more resources to capital goods production? The problem is that sacrificing consumer goods for capital formation causes the current standard of living to fall.

Comparing Alpha to Beta illustrates the importance of being able to do more than just replace worn-out capital. Beta operated in 2000 at point *A* in part (b), which is an output of C_b of consumer goods and K_b of capital goods. Assuming K_b is more than enough to replace worn-out capital, Beta is adding to its capital stock and creating extra production capacity. Newly

Exhibit 2.4 **Alpha's and Beta's present and future production possibilities frontiers**

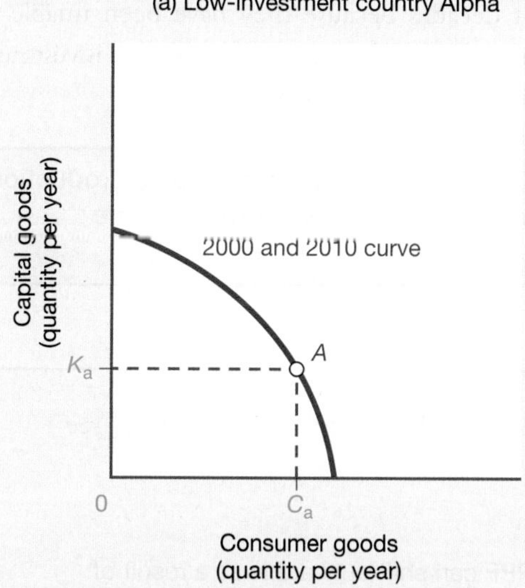

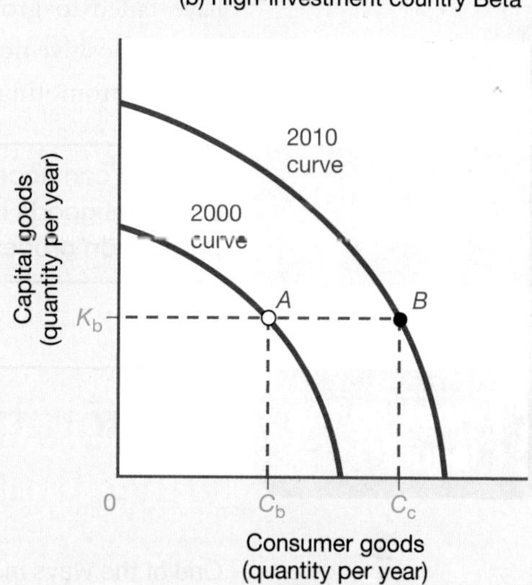

In part (a), each year Alpha produces only enough capital (K_a) to replace existing capital being worn out. Without greater capital and assuming other resources remain fixed, Alpha is unable to shift its production possibilities frontier outward. In part (b), each year Beta produces K_b capital, which is more than the amount required to replenish its depreciated capital. In the year 2010, this expanded capital provides Beta with the extra production capacity to shift its production possibilities frontier to the right. If Beta chooses point *B* on its frontier, it has the production capacity to increase the amount of consumer goods from C_b to C_c without producing fewer capital goods.

manufactured factories, machines and vehicles in excess of those required to replace the capital that wears out each year provide an economy with the capacity to expand its production options in the future. For example, the outward shift of its frontier allows Beta to produce C_c consumer goods at point *B* in the year 2010. This means Beta will be able to improve its standard of living by producing $C_c - C_b$ extra consumer goods, while Alpha's standard of living remains unchanged because the production of consumer goods remains unchanged.

Both Alpha and Beta produce capital goods, so they both undertake investment. **Investment** is the process of producing capital such as factories, machines and inventories. (Inventories are stocks of raw materials and finished goods.) In Alpha's case, where the investment just makes good the depreciation of the existing capital stock, we say that there is zero net investment. In Beta's case, where the investment is in excess of that required to cover depreciation, we say there is positive net investment.

Investment The process of producing capital, such as factories, machines and inventories.

Practical examples of the power of high levels of positive net investment to produce high growth rates can be found in many Asian countries including Singapore, China and Korea. By contrast, a number of Third World countries have failed to grow in recent decades because they have been unable to achieve positive net investment. Later, in Chapter 12, the role that investment plays in promoting growth will be discussed at length.

A nation can accelerate economic growth by increasing its production of capital goods in excess of the capital being worn out in the production process.

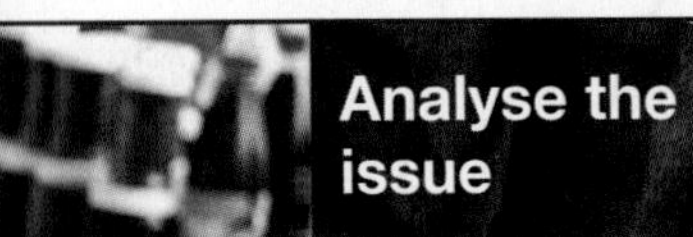

Immigration shifts the PPF in more ways than one

Applicable concepts: change in resources; technological change

One of the ways in which the PPF can shift outward is as a result of increased population, which provides for an increase in the labour force; one of the ways in which the population can be increased is through immigration. In many countries, including Australia, immigration is a contentious issue. On the one hand, conservationists concerned about additional pressure on natural resources, and conservative groups wishing to maintain homogeneity in the population, argue against immigration. On the other hand, the business community generally supports increased immigration. In the following article taken from the *Australian Financial Review*, Mark Paterson, chief executive of the Australian Chamber of Commerce and Industry, argues the business community's case for increased immigration.

> Australia's commercial and economic future is critically dependent upon our attitude to immigration.
>
> Without the massive post-war immigration intake, our population would now be about 13 million, instead of more than 19 million, and our society a much less interesting place in which to live.
>
> Recent reforms to some aspects of immigration policy have been beneficial, such as the rebalancing in favour of business and skilled labour migration.
>
> From a commercial standpoint, Australia has been well served by its economic migration programs. Research shows business migrants develop valuable international markets, transfer investment funds, expand the nation's capital base, create employment, introduce new technologies and boost exports.
>
> Like business migrants, skilled labour migrants bring with them financial as well as human capital. Research shows a positive relationship between the flows of skilled labour on the one hand and investment and trade on the other.
>
> Both groups also more than pay for themselves in terms of their impact on government fiscal programs. In short, greater business and skilled labour migration is a win-win-win situation – for the migrant, for business and for the nation as a whole.
>
> Official statistics indicate Australia is performing well in attracting business and skilled labour migrants.

However, this is not to say we can't do better. Regrettably, Australia is still seen by business migrants as a 'destination of second [or third] choice' behind the United States and Canada.

A more substantive and strategically targeted marketing campaign in priority markets is necessary to lift our share of the competitive business and skilled labour migration market-place.

An important yet little-noticed transformation in our migration intake has been the strong growth in longer-term temporary entrants, most notably business and skilled labour people coming to Australia for periods of between three months and four years.

According to official statistics, some 35 000 business and 42 000 skilled labour people entered Australia last year under these categories. Prominent sub-categories include experienced chief executives, financial and accounting experts and IT professionals.

These people fill gaps in the market-place for business and labour skills in short supply, and bring with them expertise and experience that may not otherwise be available in Australia.

Recent improvements to the operation of the skilled labour program, through enhanced occupation demand and supply matching, have helped businesses fill difficult gaps in their workforces.

The Skilled Occupation and the Migration Occupations in Demand lists have proved useful in drawing attention to business needs and in targeting those labour skills that are in the greatest demand.

Nevertheless, while adding commercial and economic value during their time in Australia, longer-term temporary entrants are not a substitute for permanent business and skilled labour migrants.

At the same time, we are also seeing strong growth in longer-term temporary exits – that is, younger and higher-skilled Australians leaving for extended periods to work overseas as part of their career-development strategies.

Such movements are wrongly regarded as a brain drain. In reality, many return to Australia after several years with their intellectual capital enhanced by their overseas experience. They bring home a greater understanding of international best practice as well as new management techniques and business and professional practices.

Similarly, the Working-Holiday Maker has made a substantial contribution to the Australian economy, allowing younger foreigners to visit Australia for up to a year at a time.

Key winners from this program are the tourism and agriculture industries, with such visitors adding around $500 million to the national economy annually. These people often return to their home countries with favourable views of Australia – to our long-term benefit.

Immigration policy is also an integral component of our (implicit) national population policy. On present trends, our population growth rate will slow in coming decades, peaking when the total hits about 23 million in the middle of the century. We will also experience an ageing of our population in the absence of any (unlikely) drastic changes in fertility.

The current aggregate levels of immigration of about 80 000 per year are little better than placing us, as a nation, in a holding pattern.

It would be good to see our immigration target move to about 0.67 per cent of the population – or 129 000 people in current terms – and remain there over time.[1]

PART 1

Although the analysis here suggests that immigration is a good thing, some opponents of immigration argue that it causes large-scale unemployment. Visit the Cato institute, a US free market think tank (**www.cato.org**). Use the search facility on this site to search for *immigration*. You should find a number of arguments directed against those who oppose immigration.

Using the above information, answer the following questions.

1. Draw a production possibilities frontier for an economy that has no immigration.
2. Explain how the introduction of a significant immigration program could shift this PPF.
3. Does the shift in the PPF result only from increased resources in the form of new labour, or do other resources and technological change also play a part?
4. In the above article the author, Mark Paterson, says that 'Australia's commercial and economic future is critically dependent on our attitude to immigration.' He is speaking on behalf of the business community. Are there other aspects of Australia's future that will be affected by immigration, and are there ethical issues that need to be considered when framing immigration policy?

1 Mark Paterson, 'Australians all, let us get the numbers right', *Australian Financial Review*, 23 January 2001, p. 32.

Gains from trade

Up to this point we have been considering the way in which an economy can choose between production of two different outputs given its endowment of resources and its production technology. This analysis can, of course, be extended to the full range of possible outputs that an economy might produce. The important point to recognise is that production of more of any given output must be accompanied, in the short run, by less production of one or a number of other outputs. A little reflection reveals that this analysis can also be applied to an individual. Thus, for example, if we assume that an individual has a certain number of hours per week to produce outputs, more output of child care services in the home must be accompanied by less output of other home-based outputs or work-based outputs.

So far in this chapter we have been making an important, but highly unrealistic, assumption. This is the assumption that nations (or individuals) do not engage in trade. The reality is that trade is a core activity for both individuals and nations. As individuals we tend to specialise in certain productive activities from which we earn income that can then be used to purchase goods and services produced by others. As you are aware from the continual references to our trading performance in the media, trade with other nations is a very important aspect of the national economy.

By engaging in trade, nations and individuals are able to benefit from levels of output that lie outside the confines of their own production possibilities frontiers. They do this by specialising in production of certain outputs for which they are well suited and then trading the output that is surplus to their own needs with other nations or other individuals. Thus the hairdresser specialises in cutting, shaping and colouring hair, using the income earned to buy cleaning services from a specialist cleaner, jewellery from jewellers, clothing from clothing stores, food from supermarkets and so on. Similarly, Australia specialises in activities such as primary production and tourism, using the proceeds of the export of these outputs to pay for imports such as manufactured goods, software and clothing.

The theory that enables us to analyse the nature and extent of specialisation undertaken by individuals and nations is called the *theory of comparative advantage*.

Comparative advantage

As you will see in Chapter 18, where comparative advantage is discussed at length, even if an individual or a nation could produce each of the goods and services it wants using fewer resources than another individual or nation, it will normally be better off if it chooses to specialise in certain outputs, trading its surplus production for those outputs it does not produce. The theory of comparative advantage tells us that it should specialise on the basis of a comparison of its ability to produce outputs at least cost in terms of output forgone with the ability of others to do likewise. The following example, which is used again later in Chapter 18, will help to clarify this idea.

comparative advantage

When Babe Ruth played baseball for the New York Yankees in the 1930s, he was both the best hitter and the best pitcher on the team. For example, Babe Ruth could produce the same number of home runs as any other team-mate with fewer times at bat, and he also had the best pitching figures of anyone in the team. The problem was that if he pitched, he would have to give up some batting because pitchers need rest after pitching. The coaches decided that even though he was the best player on the team at both hitting and pitching, the Babe had a comparative advantage in hitting. Other pitchers on the team could pitch almost as well as the Babe, but no one could come close to his hitting. The Yankees would get more runs and lose fewer games if the Babe specialised in hitting while other players specialised in pitching.

A similar argument explains why a hairdresser, who may perhaps be able to undertake more hairdressing and more cleaning in an hour than can his or her cleaner, is nonetheless better off using the income generated from specialising in hairdressing to pay for the services of the cleaner. In the same way in the global economy, nations that specialise in the outputs they can produce at least cost, in terms of other outputs forgone, can trade their surplus production with that of other nations that have also undertaken specialisation. The outcome of such international specialisation is that all nations are better off.

Comparative advantage is a powerful and important concept in economics, but it is not always easy to understand. At this stage we have done no more than try to get the basic idea across. A more comprehensive treatment is provided in Chapter 18, which deals with international trade and finance.

International focus

How would abolition of child labour affect the PPFs of developing countries?

Applicable concept: production possibilities frontier

Child labour in many developing countries is a problem that the governments of developed countries and organisations like the United Nations and Amnesty International would like to stamp out as quickly as possible. Yet it is not all that long ago that child labour was the rule rather than the exception in the world's richest countries. During the nineteenth century, at the height of the Industrial Revolution, child labour was common on both sides of the Atlantic; and it took decades of lobbying and subsequent legislative reform to stamp it out. Whether they are children at work in Asia producing brand name sporting goods for multinational companies, young girls knotting oriental carpets in the Indian Subcontinent, young girls working as prostitutes in parts of South America or boy soldiers in Africa, world-wide there are millions of children who should be playing or at school but are at work.

As part of the ongoing fight for the rights of children in 1989, the United Nations General Assembly adopted the Convention on the Rights of the Child which sets out civil, political, economic, social and cultural rights. It has been ratified by all but a few countries of the world.

Because of problems relating to the definition of child labour and the absence of relevant statistics in the generally poor countries where child labour is concentrated, no one knows precisely how many children are at work. Suffice it to say that leading international agencies in this area put the figure at hundreds of millions.

As was the case in Europe and North America in the nineteenth century, countries with high levels of child labour are in a bind. Facing severe resource limitations, they know that a reduction in child employment that reduces national income also reduces the capacity of the economy to fund the education that these children need.

Analyse the issue

Construct a production possibilities frontier that represents a developing country's goal of producing both consumer goods and education. On the assumption that child labour makes a significant contribution to total output in this economy, show the effect on the PPF of a discontinuation of this practice. Indicate a movement from point *A* to point *B* on the new PPF that would reflect a desire on the part of the community to increase educational outputs in order to educate the children released from child labour. What will be the eventual effect on the PPF of this increase in the overall educational standing of the community?

Key concepts

What, How and For whom questions
Opportunity cost
Marginal analysis
Production possibilities frontier
Technology
Law of increasing opportunity costs
Economic growth
Investment

Summary

- **Three fundamental economic** questions facing any economy are *What* to produce, *How* to produce it and *For whom* to produce it. The *What* question asks exactly which goods and services are to be produced and in what quantities. The *How* question requires society to decide the resource mix used to produce goods and services. The *For whom* problem concerns the division of output among society's citizens.

- A **production possibilities frontier** illustrates an economy's capacity to produce goods and services, subject to the constraint of scarcity. The production possibilities frontier is a graph showing the maximum possible combinations of two outputs that can be produced in a given period of time, subject to three conditions: (1) all resources are fully employed; (2) the resource base is not allowed to vary during the time period; and (3) *technology*, which is the body of knowledge applied to the production of goods, remains constant. **Inefficient** production occurs at any point inside the production possibilities frontier. All points along the frontier are **efficient** points because each point represents a maximum output possibility.

Production possibilities frontier

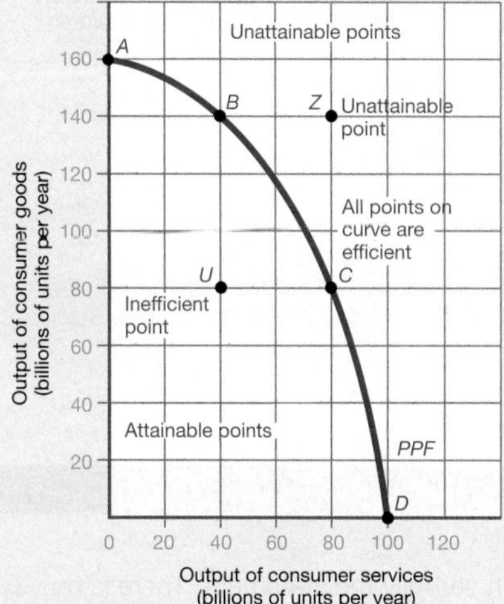

- **Marginal analysis** examines the impact of changes from a current situation and is a technique used extensively in economics. The basic approach is to compare the additional benefits of a change with the additional costs of the change.

PART 1

- **Opportunity cost** is the best alternative forgone for a chosen option. This implies that no decision can be made without cost.

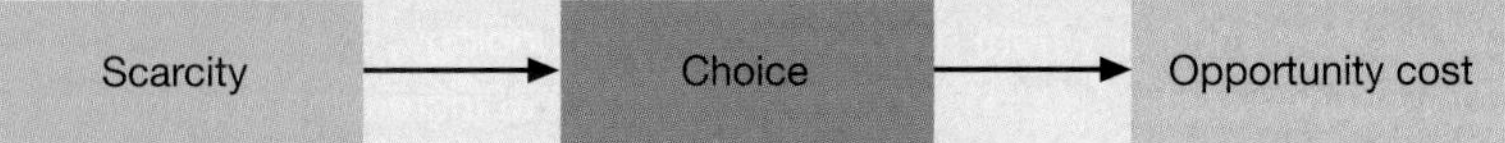

- The **law of increasing opportunity costs** states that the opportunity cost increases as the production of an output expands. The explanation for the law of increasing opportunity costs is that the suitability of resources declines sharply as greater amounts are transferred from producing one output to producing another output.

- **Investment** occurs when an economy produces new capital. Investment involves production of factories, machines and inventories. If the level of this production is great enough to more than compensate for wear and tear in the existing capital stock (depreciation), then the production possibilities frontier will shift outward in the future.

- **Economic growth** is represented by the production possibilities frontier shifting outward as the result of an increase in resources or an advance in technology.

Economic growth

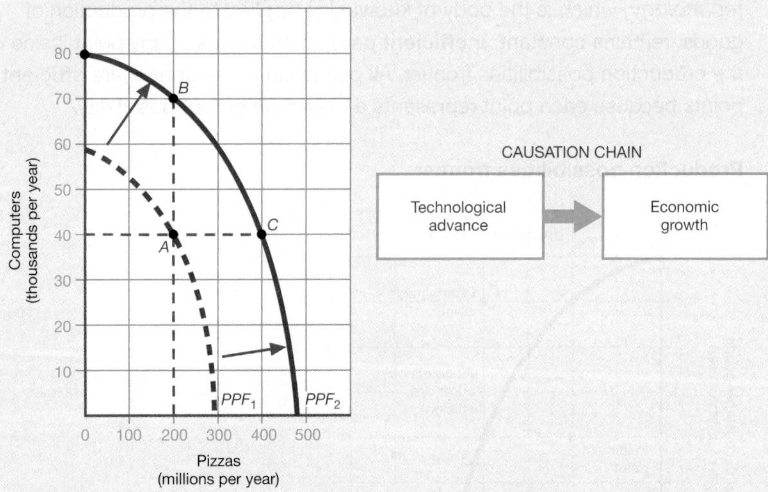

Study questions and problems

1 Explain why scarcity forces individuals and society to incur opportunity costs. Give specific examples.

2 Suppose a retailing company promotes its stores by advertising an opportunity to win a 'free car'. Is this car *free* because the winner pays *zero* for it?

3 Explain verbally the statement 'There is no such thing as a free lunch' in relation to scarce resources.

4 Which of the following decisions has the greater opportunity cost? Why?

a a decision to use an undeveloped lot in Tokyo for a park

b a decision to use a square kilometre in the Simpson Desert for a service station

5 Does your answer to Question 4 indicate that it is more economically sound to build a service station in the Simpson Desert than to provide a new park in Tokyo?

6 Attending university is expensive, is time-consuming and requires effort. Why do people decide to attend university?

7 The following is a set of hypothetical production possibilities for a nation.

Combination	Motor cars (thousands)	Lamb (thousands of tonnes)
A	0	10
B	2	9
C	4	7
D	6	4
E	8	0

a Plot these production possibilities data. What is the opportunity cost of the first 2000 cars produced? Between which points is the opportunity cost per thousand cars highest? Between which points is the opportunity cost per thousand tonnes of lamb highest?

b Label a point *F* inside the frontier. Why is this an inefficient point? Label a point *G* outside the frontier. Why is this point an unattainable point? Why are points *A* to *E* all efficient points?

c Does this production possibilities frontier reflect the law of increasing opportunity costs? Explain.

d What assumptions could be changed to shift the production possibilities frontier?

8 Why does a production possibilities frontier have a bowed-out shape?

9 Interpret the statements 'There is no such thing as a free lunch' and 'A free lunch is possible' in terms of the production possibilities frontier.

10 Suppose that, unfortunately, your accounting and your economics lecturers have both decided to give tests at different times two days from now and you realise that you can spend only a total of 12 hours studying for both exams. After some thought, you conclude that dividing your study time equally between each subject will give you an expected mark of 65% in each subject. For each increase of 3 hours' study time for one of the subjects, your mark will increase 10% for that subject and your mark will fall 10% for the other subject.

a Construct a table for the production possibilities and corresponding number of hours of study in this case.

b Plot these production possibilities data in a graph.

c Does this production possibilities frontier reflect the law of increasing opportunity costs? Explain.

11 Draw a production possibilities frontier for a hypothetical economy producing capital goods and consumer goods. Suppose a major technological breakthrough occurs in the capital goods industry and the new technology is widely adopted only in this industry. Draw the new production possibilities frontier. Now assume that a technological advance occurs in producing consumer goods, but not in producing capital goods. Draw the new production possibilities frontier.

12 The choice between investing in capital goods and producing consumer goods today affects the ability of an economy to produce in the future. Explain.

Online exercises

Exercise 1

Visit the Australian Bureau of Statistics (ABS) website (**www.abs.gov.au**). Using the search facility, search for **3101.0**. This is the number for the catalogue titled 'Australian Demographic Statistics'. Click on the links to the catalogue for the most recent quarter. You will find a discussion of recent population trends – including data for births, net overseas migration and interstate migration.

1 Note the relative contributions to Australia's population growth of births (natural increase) and net overseas migration (permanent arrivals minus permanent departures). Which of these has made the greater contribution to population growth? Which of these is more likely to shift the production possibility frontier over the next decade? In which direction will it shift?

2 Read the information about recent trends in interstate migration. Which Australian state or territory has gained the most migrants in the most recently reported period? Which has lost the most? Are these flows likely to have had any effect on the PPFs of these states?

Exercise 2

The number of Internet hosts in a country is sometimes used as an indicator of the extent to which that country has embraced the Internet and the productivity enhancement that it brings. Visit World Factbook, Field Listings at **www.odci.gov/cia/publications/factbook/index.html**.

1 In turn, select each of the following countries: **United States**, **Australia**, **Japan**, **Singapore** and **New Zealand**. For each country look up its population under the heading **People**, and look up the number of Internet hosts under the heading **Communications**. Compute the number of persons per Internet host for each country. Which country appears to have the greatest capacity for Internet connections? Which has the least?

2 Undertake the same exercise for the world as a whole. (**World** is listed at the top of the alphabetical list of countries.) How do the countries for which you have calculated individual person-to-Internet host ratios compare with the world as a whole?

Exercise 3

Visit the Department of Economics Resources website (**www.csuchico.edu/econ/resource.html**) and browse through **Economics Resources**. Do not select the index of Jokes about Economics or Economists.

Exercise 4

How might the officials of the People's Republic of China answer the three fundamental economic questions? For one perspective, visit the China Council for the Promotion of International Trade (CCPIT) (**www.ccpit.org**).

Answers to 'You make the call'

Are we always conscious of opportunity cost?

If you said a rise in interest rates means that installation of a rainwater tank involves an increase in interest income forgone, and fewer tank installations would occur as a result of this increased opportunity cost, YOU ARE CORRECT. In making a decision whether or not to install a tank, the environmentally conscious consumer would need to consider the opportunity cost of damage to the environment caused by using the tank as compared to the damage caused by using reticulated water. If you said the environmental damage caused by the manufacture and transport of the plastic or steel tank would need to be compared to the environmental damage that goes with flooding land and constructing infrastructure needed to supply reticulated water, YOU ARE CORRECT.

Does the unpaid work of Australia's over 4 million volunteers shift the PPF?

If the work of these volunteers were to suddenly decrease, the outcome would be an inward shift of the PPF. If the decrease in this voluntary work were to be exactly compensated by an increase in paid work, this would leave the PPF in approximately the same position; although, depending on whether workers were more or less productive in paid work as compared to volunteer work, the PPF could shift outwards or inwards slightly from its original position. Of course, substitution of paid work for volunteer work may well disadvantage the less well-off. Volunteering is thus likely to be a continuing feature of modern economies. If you identified the inward shift of the PPF as a result of reduced volunteering and little or no movement of the PPF as a result of substitution of paid work for volunteer work, YOU ARE CORRECT.

Multiple-choice questions

1 Which of the following sets of decisions must be made by all economies?

- **a** How much to produce? When to produce? How much does it cost?
- **b** What is the price? Who will produce it? Who will consume it?
- **c** What to produce? How to produce it? For whom to produce it?
- **d** None of the above.

2 If a diamond ring is priced at $5000, and the next best alternative to purchasing the ring is to keep the money and deposit it at interest in the bank, the opportunity cost of purchasing the ring, ceteris paribus, is

a more than $5000.
b less than $5000.
c $5000.
d the forgone opportunity to have an overseas holiday.

3 Opportunity cost is
a always the purchase price of a good or service.
b the value of leisure time plus out-of-pocket costs.
c the best alternative given up as a result of the choice that is made.
d the undesirable sacrifice required to purchase a good.

4 On a production possibilities frontier, the opportunity cost of good *X* in terms of good *Y* is represented by
a the distance to the frontier from the vertical axis.
b the distance to the frontier from the horizontal axis.
c the movement along the frontier.
d all of the above.

5 A band leader is deciding whether or not to take on a keyboard player. If the band adds one keyboard player, the price it can charge for a gig rises from $500 to $600. According to marginal analysis, the band leader should add a keyboard player if it costs less than
a $60.
b $100.
c $600.
d $1100.

6 On a production possibilities frontier, a change from economic inefficiency to economic efficiency is represented by
a movement along the frontier.
b movement from a point outside the frontier to a point on the frontier.
c movement from a point inside the frontier to a point on the frontier.
d a change in the slope of the frontier.

7 Any point inside the production possibilities frontier is
a an efficient point.
b a non-feasible point.
c an inefficient point.
d a maximum output combination.

8 Using a production possibilities frontier, unemployment is represented by a point located
a near the middle of the frontier.
b at the top of the frontier.
c at the bottom of the frontier.
d outside the frontier.
e inside the frontier.

9 Along a production possibilities frontier, an increase in the production of one good can be accomplished only by
a decreasing the production of another good.
b increasing the production of another good.
c holding constant the production of another good.
d a larger decrease in production of the other good.

10 Education and training that improve the skill of the labour force are represented on the production possibilities frontier by
a a movement along the frontier.
b an inward shift of the frontier.
c an outward shift of the frontier.
d a movement towards the frontier from an exterior point.

11 A nation can accelerate its economic growth by
a reducing the number of skilled migrants allowed into the country.
b adding to its stock of capital.
c reducing expenditure on research and development (R&D).
d imposing tariffs and quotas on all imported goods.

3 Market demand and supply

A cornerstone of modern economies is the use of markets to answer the basic economic questions discussed in the previous chapter. Consider movie tickets, compact discs, sushi, petrol, soft drinks, kiwi fruit and cocaine. In a *market economy*, each is bought and sold by individuals coming together as buyers and sellers in markets. Of course, cocaine is a product sold in an illegal market, but it is a market that determines the price and the quantity exchanged. This chapter is extremely important because it introduces basic supply and demand analysis. This technique will prove valuable because it is applicable to a multitude of real-world choices of buyers and sellers facing the problem of scarcity. For example, the International Focus section asks you to consider the highly controversial issue of international trade in human organs.

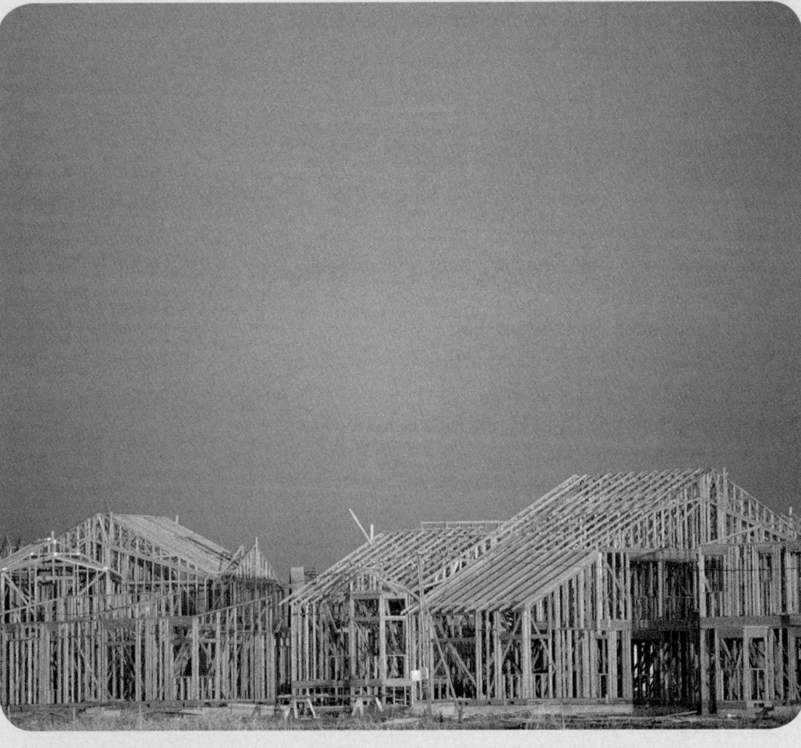

PART 1

Demand represents the choice-making behaviour of consumers, while supply represents the decisions of producers. This chapter begins by looking closely at demand and then at supply. Finally, it combines these concepts to see how prices and quantities are determined in the marketplace. Market supply and demand analysis is the basic tool of microeconomic analysis.

In this chapter, you will examine these economics questions:

- What is the difference between a 'change in quantity demanded' and a 'change in demand'?
- Can the law of supply help explain changes in the popularity of university courses?
- Can monetary incentives improve environmental outcomes?
- What are the economic and ethical issues involved in the transplantation of human organs?

The law of demand

Demand for goods and services in capitalist economies reflects a high degree of **consumer sovereignty**. Consumer sovereignty is the freedom of consumers to make their own choices about which goods and services to buy. If consumer sovereignty prevails, these choices are made without coercion on the part of business or government.

Consumer sovereignty The freedom of consumers to make their own choices about which goods and services to buy.

Exhibit 3.1 reveals an important 'law' in economics: the **law of demand**. The law of demand states that there is an inverse relationship between the price of a good or service and the quantity buyers are willing to purchase in a defined time period, ceteris paribus. The law of demand makes good sense. For example, consumers buy more when prices are reduced at a department store sale. More strawberries are purchased at the height of the season, when their price is lower than at other times.

Law of demand The principle that there is an inverse relationship between the price of a good or service and the quantity buyers are willing to purchase in a defined time period, ceteris paribus.

Economists are able to verify the law of demand from first principles by looking at human behaviour. When an individual consumes successive units of a good or service in a given time period, each unit provides less additional satisfaction than did the previous unit consumed. Just think about the additional satisfaction obtained from, say, the third slice of cake consumed compared with the second or the first. This characteristic of human behaviour is known as the law of diminishing marginal utility – 'utility' being the economist's preferred synonym for satisfaction. From this law, economists have derived the law of demand, which is consistent with the idea that consumers will purchase additional units of a good or service only if its price decreases.

INFOTRAC®
consumer sovereignty

In Exhibit 3.1, the *demand curve* is formed by the line connecting the possible price and quantity purchasing responses of an individual consumer. The demand curve therefore allows you to find the quantity demanded by a buyer at any possible selling price by moving along the curve. For example, Bob loves listening to music on his stereo while studying. Bob's demand curve shows that at a price of $30 per compact disc his quantity demanded is six compact discs purchased annually (point *B*). At the lower price of $20, Bob's quantity demanded increases to 10 compact discs per year (point *C*). Following this procedure, other price and quantity possibilities for Bob are read along the demand curve.

CONCLUSION

The law of diminishing marginal utility explains why consumers will buy more of a good only if its price decreases, ceteris paribus.

Note that, until we know the actual price, we do not know how many compact discs Bob will actually purchase annually. The demand curve is simply a summary of Bob's buying intentions. Once we know the market price, a quick look at the demand curve tells us how many compact discs Bob will buy.

Exhibit 3.1 An individual buyer's demand curve for compact discs

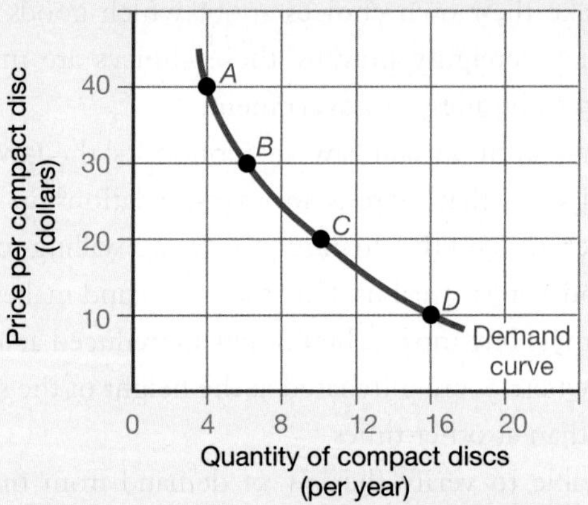

Individual buyer's demand schedule for compact discs

Point	Price per compact disc	Quantity demanded (per year)
A	$40	4
B	30	6
C	20	10
D	10	16

Bob's demand curve shows how many compact discs he is willing to purchase at different possible prices. As the price of compact discs declines, the quantity demanded increases and Bob purchases more compact discs. The inverse relationship between price and quantity demanded conforms to the law of demand.

Market demand

To make the transition from an *individual* demand curve to a *market* demand curve, we total, or sum, the individual demand schedules. Suppose the owner of Cool City, a small chain of retail music stores, employs a consumer research firm to help decide what to charge for compact discs in a new market. For simplicity, we assume Brett and Kim are the only two buyers in Cool City's new market, and they are each sent a questionnaire that asks how many compact discs each would be willing to purchase at several possible prices. Exhibit 3.2 reports their price–quantity demanded responses in tabular and graphical form.

The market demand curve D_{total} in Exhibit 3.2 is derived by summing *horizontally* the two individual demand curves D_1 and D_2 for each possible price. At a price of \$40, for example, we sum Brett's two compact discs demanded per year and Kim's one compact disc demanded per year to find that the total quantity demanded at \$40 is three compact discs per year. Repeating the same process for other prices generates the market demand curve D_{total}. For example, at a price of \$10, the total quantity demanded is 12 compact discs.

Exhibit 3.2 **The market demand curve for compact discs**

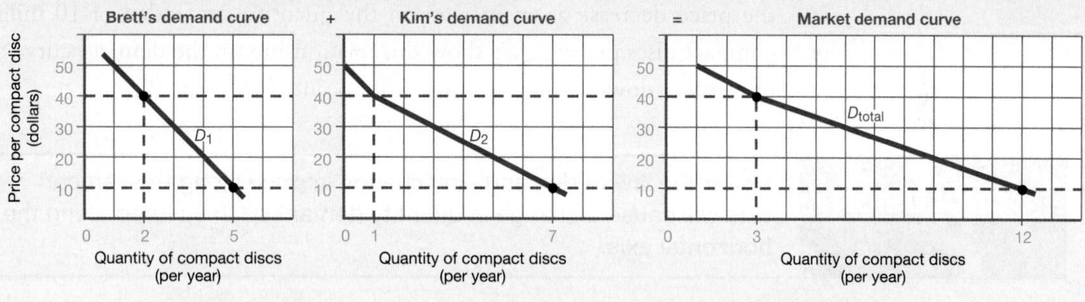

Price per compact disc	Quantity demanded (per year)		
	Brett	Kim	Total demand
\$50	1	0	1
40	2	1	3
30	3	3	6
20	4	5	9
10	5	7	12

Individual demand curves differ for consumers Brett and Kim. Assuming these are the only two buyers in the market, the market demand curve D_{total} is derived by summing horizontally the individual demand curves, D_1 and D_2.

PART 1

The distinction between changes in quantity demanded and changes in demand

Price is not the only variable that determines how much of a good or service consumers will buy. Recall from Chapter 1 that the price and quantity variables in our model are subject to the ceteris paribus assumption. If we relax this ceteris paribus assumption and allow other variables held constant to change, a variety of factors can influence the position of the demand curve. Because these factors are not the price of the good itself, these variables are called *non-price determinants*. The major non-price determinants include (1) the number of buyers, (2) tastes and preferences, (3) income, (4) expectations, and (5) prices of related goods.

Change in quantity demanded A movement between points along a stationary demand curve, ceteris paribus.

Before discussing these non-price determinants of demand, we must pause to explain an important and possibly confusing distinction in terminology. We have been referring to a **change in quantity demanded**, which results solely from a change in the price. A change in quantity demanded is a movement between points along a stationary demand curve, ceteris paribus. In Exhibit 3.3(a), at the price of $30, the quantity demanded is 20 million compact discs per year. This is shown as point *A* on the market demand curve. At the lower price of, say, $20, a larger quantity demanded of 30 million compact discs per year occurs, shown as point *B*. Verbally, we describe the impact of the price decrease as an increase in the quantity demanded of 10 million compact discs per year. We show this relationship on the demand curve as a movement down along the curve from point *A* to point *B*.

Under the law of demand, any change in price along the vertical axis will cause a change in quantity demanded, measured along the horizontal axis.

Change in demand An increase or decrease in the demand at each possible price. An increase in demand is a rightward shift in the entire demand curve. A decrease in demand is a leftward shift in the entire demand curve.

By contrast, a **change in demand** is an increase or a decrease in the demand at each possible price. If ceteris paribus no longer applies and if one of the five non-price factors changes, the demand curve shifts – to the right if demand increases, to the left if demand decreases.

Changes in non-price determinants can produce only a shift in the demand curve and not a movement along the demand curve, which is caused by a change in the price.

Exhibit 3.3 **Movement along a demand curve versus a shift in demand**

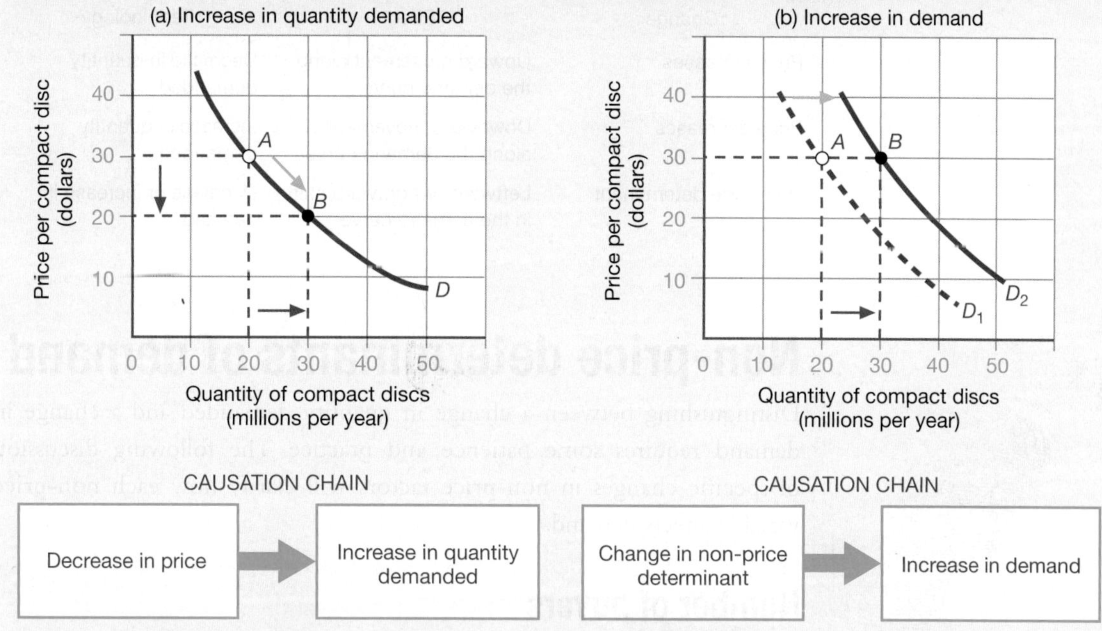

Part (a) shows the market demand curve *D* for compact discs per year. If the price is $30 at point *A*, the quantity demanded by consumers will be 20 million discs. If the price decreases to $20 at point *B*, the quantity demanded will increase from 20 million to 30 million compact discs.

Part (b) illustrates an increase in demand. A change in some non-price determinant can cause an increase in demand from D_1 to D_2. At a price of $30 on D_1 (point *A*), 20 million compact discs would be demanded per year. At this price on D_2 (point *B*), the demand increases to 30 million.

Comparing parts (a) and (b) of Exhibit 3.3 is helpful in making the distinction between a change in quantity demanded and a change in demand. In part (b), suppose the market demand curve for compact discs is initially at D_1 and there is a shift to the right (an increase in demand) from D_1 to D_2. This means that at *all* possible prices consumers wish to purchase a larger quantity than before the shift occurred. At $30 per compact disc, for example, 30 million CDs (point *B*) would be consumed each year, rather than 20 million CDs (point *A*).

Now suppose a change in some non-price factor (introduction of DVDs) causes demand curve D_1 to shift leftward (a decrease in demand). The interpretation in this case is that at *all* possible prices consumers will buy a smaller quantity than before the shift occurred.

Exhibit 3.4 summarises the terminology for the effect of changes in price and non-price determinants on the demand curve.

Exhibit 3.4 **Terminology for changes in price and non-price determinants of demand**

Change	Effect	Terminology
Price increases	Upward movement along the demand curve	Decrease in quantity demanded
Price decreases	Downward movement along the demand curve	Increase in quantity demanded
Non-price determinant	Leftward or rightward shift in the demand curve	Decrease or increase in demand

Non-price determinants of demand

Distinguishing between a change in quantity demanded and a change in demand requires some patience and practice. The following discussion of specific changes in non-price factors will clarify how each non-price variable affects demand.

Number of buyers

Look back at Exhibit 3.2 and imagine the impact of adding individual demand curves to the individual demand curves of Brett and Kim. At all possible prices, there is extra quantity demanded by the new customers, and the market demand curve for compact discs shifts rightward (an increase in demand). Population growth therefore tends to increase the number of buyers, which shifts the market demand curve for a good or service rightward. Conversely, a population decline shifts most market demand curves leftward (a decrease in demand).

The number of buyers can be specified to include both foreign and domestic buyers. Suppose the market demand curve D_1 in Exhibit 3.3(b) is for compact discs purchased in the United States by domestic and foreign customers. Also assume that China restricts the import of compact discs into China. What would be the effect of China removing this trade restriction? The answer is that the demand curve shifts rightward from D_1 to D_2 when Chinese consumers add their individual demand curves to the US market demand for compact discs.

Tastes and preferences

Notwithstanding the importance of consumer sovereignty, we know that fads, fashions, advertising and new products can influence consumer preferences to buy a particular good or service. Scooters became the rage in the early 2000s, and the demand curve for these products shifted to the right. When people tired of this product, the demand curve shifted back to the left. The physical fitness trend in the 1980s and 1990s increased the demand for health clubs and exercise equipment. On the other hand, have you noticed whether many shops still sell women's shoes with pointed toes and stiletto heels?

Why does Sunkist (**www.sunkist.com**), a major producer of oranges, provide free recipes on the web? To increase the demand for oranges, of course.

Income

Most students are all too familiar with how changes in income affect demand. There are two possible categories for the relationship between changes in income and changes in demand: (1) normal goods and (2) inferior goods.

A **normal good** is any good or service for which there is a direct relationship between changes in income and its demand. For most goods and services, an increase in income causes buyers to purchase more at any possible price. As buyers receive higher incomes, the demand shifts rightward for *normal goods* such as airline travel, new cars, bottled wine, expensive jewellery and DVDs. A decline in income has the opposite effect, and demand shifts leftward.

Normal good Any good or service for which there is a direct relationship between changes in income and its demand.

An **inferior good** is any good or service for which there is an inverse relationship between changes in income and its demand. A rise in income results in reduced purchases at any possible price. This is likely to happen with *inferior goods* such as interstate bus travel, second-hand cars, cask wine and cheap jewellery. Instead of buying these inferior goods, higher incomes allow consumers to buy airline tickets, new cars, bottled wine and expensive jewellery. Conversely, a fall in income causes the demand curve for inferior goods to shift rightward.

Inferior good Any good or service for which there is an inverse relationship between changes in income and its demand.

Some introductory economics texts state that normal goods with a high degree of responsiveness to income increases are *luxuries*, while those with low responsiveness are *necessities*. This distinction is often useful, but keep in mind that one person's luxury (for example, alcohol) can be another person's necessity.

Expectations of buyers

What is the effect on demand in the present when consumers anticipate future changes in prices, incomes or other factors? What happened in 2000 in the lead-up to the July introduction of the Australian government's goods and services tax (GST)? Because the GST was expected to raise home building costs there was a boom in housing construction. On the other hand, an expected fall in new motor car prices led to an unprecedented slump in motor vehicle sales. Suppose new graduates expect their incomes to grow rapidly in the first few years after graduation. On this basis, they are likely to commit to substantial levels of borrowing to finance the purchase of a home, a motor car or overseas travel. Another example is a change in the weather, which can directly or indirectly cause expectations to shift the demand curve for some products. Suppose a hailstorm destroys a substantial portion of the stone fruit crop. Consumers reason that the reduction in available supply will soon drive up prices, and they rush to buy before it is too late. This change in expectations causes the demand for stone fruit to increase.

Can housing become an exception to the law of demand?

The housing boom in Australia in the early years of this century saw house prices increasing by as much as 25 per cent per annum. At the height of the boom, both owner-occupiers and investors rushed to purchase houses and apartments because they feared they would have to pay higher prices in the future. In this case, as the price of houses and apartments increased, consumers bought more, not less. Is this an exception to the law of demand?

Visit the California Energy Commission page showing world gasoline prices in selected countries at **www.energy.ca.gov/gasoline/statistics/world_gasoline_prices.html**. Look at recent prices for gasoline (petrol) in the United States, Japan and Europe. Do these help explain why US citizens drive bigger, heavier and more powerful cars than their counterparts in Japan or Europe?

Prices of related goods

Possibly the most confusing non-price factor is the influence of other prices on the demand for a particular good or service. The term *non-price* seems to forbid any shift in demand resulting from a change in the price of *any* product. This confusion exists when one fails to distinguish between changes in quantity demanded and changes in demand. Remember that ceteris paribus holds all prices of other goods constant. Therefore, movement along a demand curve occurs solely in response to changes in the price of a product; that is, its 'own' price. When we draw the demand curve for Coca-Cola, for example, we assume that the prices of Pepsi-Cola and other colas remain unchanged. What happens if we relax the ceteris paribus assumption and the price of Pepsi rises? Many Pepsi buyers switch to Coca-Cola, and the demand curve for Coca-Cola shifts rightward (an increase in demand). Coca-Cola and Pepsi-Cola are one type of related goods, called **substitute goods**. A substitute good competes with another good for consumer purchases. As a result, there is a direct relationship between a price change for one good and the demand for its 'competitor' good. Other examples of substitutes include margarine and butter, new cars and second-hand cars, and DVD hire or a trip to the movies.

Substitute good A good that competes with another good for consumer purchases. As a result, there is a direct relationship between a price change for one good and the demand for its 'competitor' good.

DVDs and DVD players illustrate a second type of related goods, called **complementary goods**. A complementary good is jointly consumed with another good. As a result, there is an inverse relationship between a price change for one good and the demand for its complementary good. Although in many instances buying a DVD and buying a DVD player are seen as separate decisions, these two purchases are often related. The more DVD

Complementary good A good that is jointly consumed with another good. As a result, there is an inverse relationship between a price change for one good and the demand for its 'complementary' good.

players consumers buy, the greater is the demand for DVDs. What happens if the price of DVD players falls sharply from, say, $250 to $50? The market demand curve for DVDs shifts rightward (an increase in demand) because new owners of players add their individual demand curves to those of persons already owning players and buying DVDs. Similarly, if the price of DVDs were to fall, more people would consider purchasing a DVD player. The fall in the price of DVDs thus results in an increase in demand for DVD players and a shift to the right of the demand curve for DVD players.

Exhibit 3.5 summarises the relationship between changes in the non-price determinants of demand and the demand curve, accompanied by examples for each type of non-price factor change. Of course, what has been said about goods in this section applies equally to services.

Exhibit 3.5 Summary of the impact of changes in non-price determinants of demand on the demand curve

Non-price determinant of demand	Relationship with the demand curve	Examples
1 Number of buyers	Direct	• The Chinese remove import restrictions on American compact discs, and Chinese consumers increase the demand for American compact discs. • A decline in the birth rate reduces the demand for baby clothes.
2 Tastes and preferences	Direct	• For no apparent reason, consumers want scooters, and demand increases, but after a while the fad dies and demand declines.
3 Income		
a Normal goods	Direct	• There is an increase in consumers' income, and the demand for designer label clothes increases. • A decline in income decreases the demand for air travel.
b Inferior goods	Inverse	• There is an increase in consumers' income, and the demand for rice decreases. • A decline in income increases the demand for bus travel.
4 Expectations of buyers	Direct or inverse	• Consumers expect that introduction of a new tax next year will raise house prices. Consequently, consumers increase their demand for housing immediately to try to beat the introduction of the tax.
5 Prices of related goods		
a Substitute goods	Direct	• A reduction in the price of tea decreases the demand for coffee • An increase in the price of interstate bus fares causes higher demand for air travel.
b Complementary goods	Inverse	• A decline in the price of DVD players increases the demand for DVDs. • A higher price for rum decreases the demand for Coke.

Law of supply The principle that there is a direct relationship between the price of a good and the quantity sellers are willing to offer for sale in a defined time period, ceteris paribus.

The law of supply

In everyday conversations, the term *supply* refers to a specific quantity. A 'limited supply' of golf clubs at a sporting goods store means there are only so many for sale and that's all. This interpretation of supply is *not* the economist's definition. To economists, supply is the relationship between ranges of possible prices and quantities supplied, which is stated as the **law of supply**. The law of supply states that there is a direct relationship between the price of a good and the quantity sellers are willing to offer for sale in a defined time period, ceteris paribus. Interpreting the individual *supply curve* for Cool City, shown in Exhibit 3.6, is basically the same as interpreting Bob's demand curve shown in Exhibit 3.1. Each point on the curve represents a quantity supplied (measured along the horizontal axis) at a particular price (measured along the vertical axis). For example, at a price of $20 per disc (point *C*), the quantity supplied by the seller, Cool City, is 35 000 compact discs per year. At the higher price of $30, the quantity supplied increases to 45 000 compact discs per year (point *B*).

Exhibit 3.6 An individual seller's supply curve for compact discs

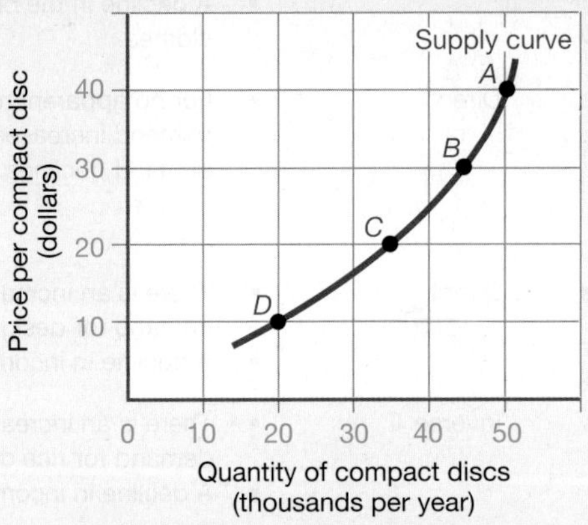

An individual seller's supply schedule for compact discs

Point	Price per compact disc	Quantity supplied (thousands per year)
A	$40	50
B	30	45
C	20	35
D	10	20

The supply curve for an individual seller, such as Cool City, shows the quantity of compact discs offered for sale at different possible prices. As the price of compact discs rises, a retail store has an incentive to increase the quantity of compact discs supplied per year. The direct relationship between price and quantity supplied conforms to the law of supply.

Why are sellers willing to sell more at a higher price? Suppose a grazier who produces both beef and lamb is trying to decide whether to redirect land, labour and capital to the production of more lamb. Recall from Chapter 2 the production possibilities frontier and the concept of increasing opportunity cost developed in Exhibit 2.2. If our grazier decides to produce more lamb, this will involve an increased opportunity cost, measured by the quantity of beef not produced. The logical question is: what would induce the grazier to produce more lamb for sale and overcome the higher opportunity cost of producing less beef? You guessed it! There must be the *incentive* of a higher price for lamb, ceteris paribus.

The Container Recycling Institute (**www.container-recycling.org**) promotes container and packaging recycling and re-use. Visit their site to see some of the reports on how increased incentives can increase the supply of materials for recycling or re-use.

Only at a higher price will it be profitable for sellers to incur the higher opportunity cost associated with producing and supplying a larger quantity.

Can the law of supply be applied to choice of university courses?

You make the call

At the turn of the century the rising importance of the Internet, e-commerce and computer technology in general led to an increased level of applications for computing and information technology courses in Australian universities. More recently, the lack of promise shown by the IT sector of the economy – in terms of career opportunities and salaries – has led to a sharp decline in enrolments in these courses from both international and Australian students. A similar phenomenon has been observed with enrolments in geology and earth science courses. When there is a minerals boom enrolments surge; when the boom is over they drop dramatically. Can these patterns of enrolments be explained by the law of supply?

Market supply

To construct a *market* supply curve, we follow the same procedure used to derive a market demand curve. That is, we *horizontally* sum all the quantities supplied at various prices that may prevail in the market.

Let's assume Super Sound Company and High Vibes Company are the only two firms selling compact discs in a given market. You can see in Exhibit 3.7 that the market supply curve S_{total} slopes upward to the right. At a price of \$50, Super Sound would supply 25 000 compact discs per year, and High Vibes would supply 35 000 compact discs per year. Thus, summing the two individual supply curves S_1 and S_2 *horizontally*, the total of 60 000 compact discs is plotted at this price on the market supply curve, S_{total}. Similar calculations at other prices along the price axis generate a market supply curve, telling us the total amount of compact discs these businesses offer for sale at different selling prices.

PART 1

Exhibit 3.7 **The market supply curve for compact discs**

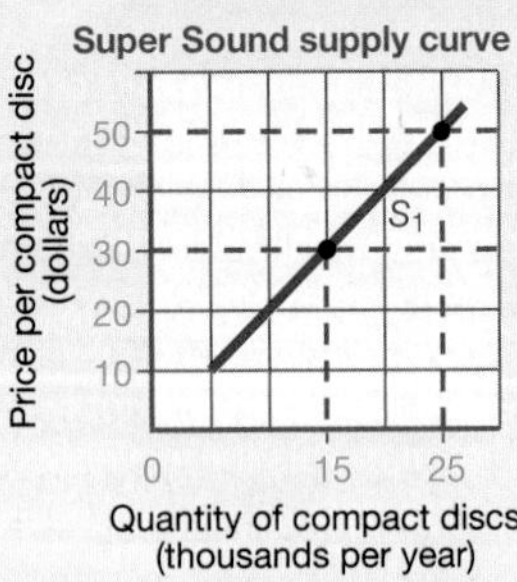

+

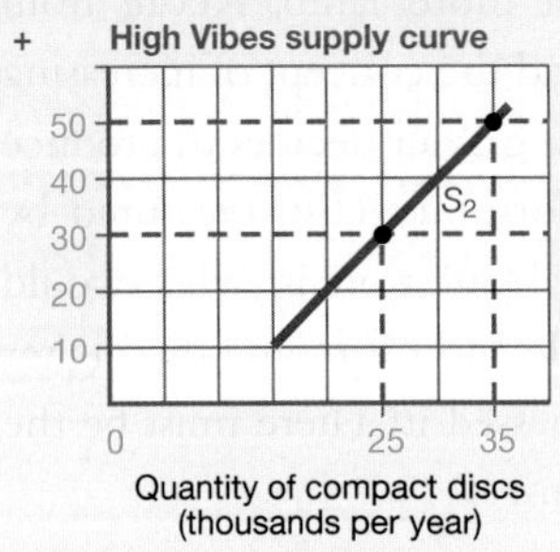

=

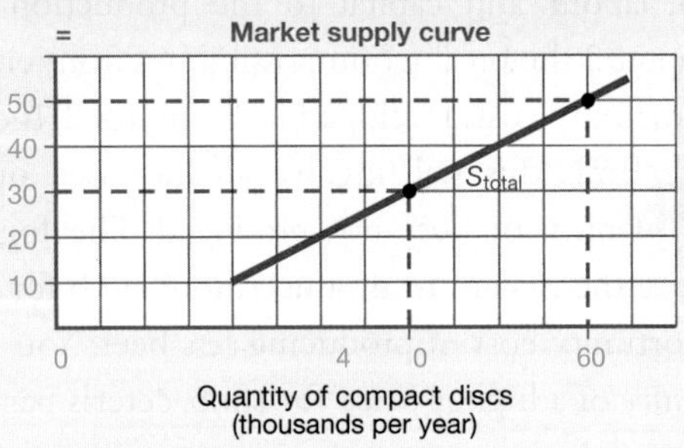

The market supply schedule for compact discs

Price per compact disc	Quantity supplied (thousands per year): Super Sound	+ High Vibes	= Total supply
$50	25	35	60
40	20	30	50
30	15	25	40
20	10	20	30
10	5	15	20

Super Sound and High Vibes are two individual businesses selling compact discs. If these are the only two firms in the compact disc market, the market supply curve S_{total} can be derived by summing horizontally the individual supply curves S_1 and S_2.

The distinction between changes in quantity supplied and changes in supply

The price of a product is not the only factor that influences how much sellers offer for sale. Once we relax the ceteris paribus assumption, there are six principal *non-price determinants* that can shift the supply curve's position: (1) the number of sellers, (2) technology, (3) input prices, (4) taxes and subsidies, (5) expectations and (6) prices of other goods. We will discuss these non-price determinants in more detail soon, but first we must distinguish between a change in quantity supplied and a change in supply.

Change in quantity supplied A movement between points along a stationary supply curve, ceteris paribus.

A **change in quantity supplied** is a movement between points along a stationary supply curve, ceteris paribus. In Exhibit 3.8(a), at the price of $20, the quantity supplied is 30 million compact discs per year (point *A*). At the higher price of $30, sellers offer a larger 'quantity supplied' of 40 million compact discs per year (point *B*). Economists describe the effect of the rise in price as an increase in the quantity supplied of 10 million compact discs per year.

Exhibit 3.8 **Movement along a supply curve versus a shift in supply**

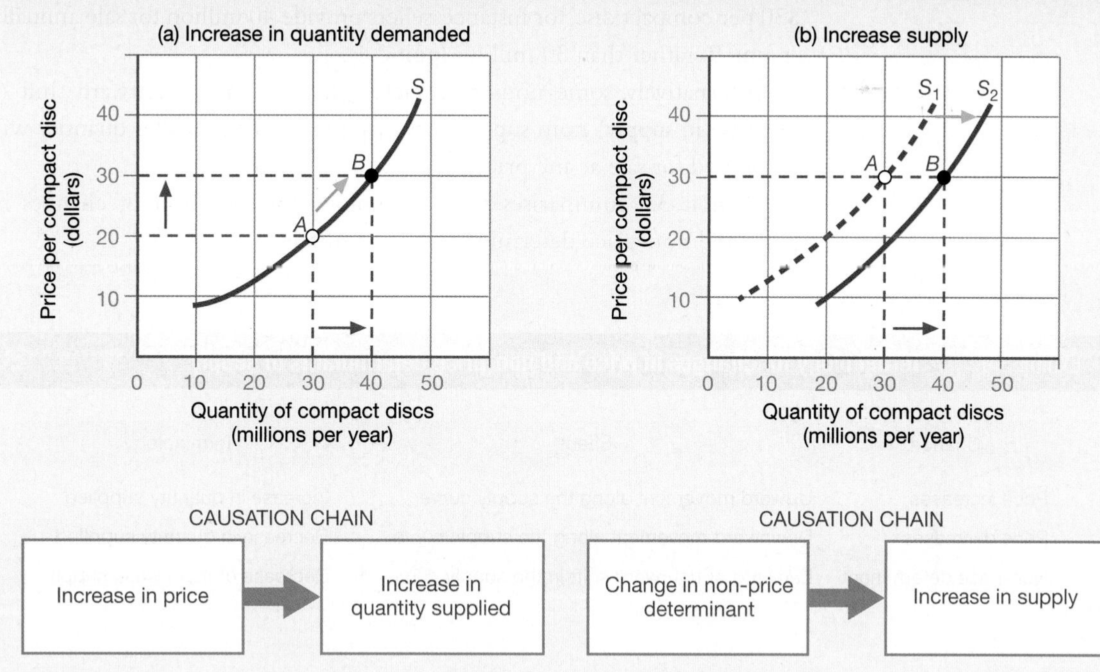

Part (a) presents the market supply curve, *S*, for compact discs per year. If the price is $20 at point *A*, the quantity supplied by firms will be 30 million discs. If the price increases to $30 at point *B*, the quantity supplied will increase from 30 million to 40 million compact discs.

Part (b) illustrates an increase in supply. A change in some non-price determinant can cause an increase in supply from S_1 to S_2. At a price of $30 on S_1 (point *A*), 30 million compact discs would be supplied per year. At this price on S_2 (point *B*), the supply increases to 40 million.

Under the law of supply, any increase in price along the vertical axis will cause an increase in the quantity supplied, measured along the horizontal axis.

A **change in supply** is an increase (rightward shift) or a decrease (leftward shift) in the supply at each possible price. If ceteris paribus no longer applies and if one of the six non-price factors changes, the effect is to alter the supply curve's location.

Change in supply An increase or decrease in the supply at each possible price. An increase in supply is a rightward shift in the entire supply curve. A decrease in supply is a leftward shift in the entire supply curve.

Changes in non-price determinants can produce only a shift in the supply curve and not a movement along the supply curve.

PART 1

In Exhibit 3.8(b), the rightward shift (an increase in supply) from S_1 to S_2 means that at all possible prices sellers offer a greater quantity for sale. At \$30 per compact disc, for instance, sellers provide 40 million for sale annually (point *B*) rather than 30 million (point *A*).

Alternatively, some non-price factor change causes a leftward shift (a decrease in supply) from supply curve S_1. As a result, a smaller quantity will be offered for sale at any price.

Exhibit 3.9 summarises the terminology for the effect of changes in price and non-price determinants on the supply curve.

Exhibit 3.9 **Terminology for changes in price and non-price determinants of supply**

Change	Effect	Terminology
Price increases	Upward movement along the supply curve	Increase in quantity supplied
Price decreases	Downward movement along the supply curve	Decrease in quantity supplied
Non-price determinant	Leftward or rightward shift in the supply curve	Decrease or increase in supply

Non-price determinants of supply

Now we turn to the way in which each of the six basic non-price factors affects supply.

Number of sellers

To see how business-to-business (B2B) applications of the Internet are revolutionising the way in which businesses operate, enter *B2B* into a search engine such as AltaVista (**www.altavista.com**). Look at just a few of the millions of pages devoted to ways in which Internet technology can enhance business productivity.

What happens when a severe drought destroys wheat, or an outbreak of disease ruins the orange crop? The damaging effect of the disease means that orange growers are able to supply fewer oranges at each possible price and supply decreases. Drought has a similar effect on the supply of wheat. When the government eases restrictions on hunting kangaroos, the number of kangaroo hunters increases and the supply curve for kangaroo meat and skins increases. Internationally, Australia may decide to lower trade barriers on textile imports, and this action will increase supply by allowing firms operating in countries such as China, Fiji and Indonesia to add their individual supply curves to the Australian market supply curve for textiles. Conversely, higher Australian trade barriers on textile imports shift the Australian market supply curve for textiles leftward.

Technology

Seldom have we experienced such an explosion of new production techniques as we see today. Throughout the world, new and more efficient technology is making it possible to manufacture more products at any possible selling price. For example, new, more powerful PCs reduce production costs and increase the supply of all sorts of goods and services. The Internet is greatly reducing the cost of business-to-business (B2B) transactions undertaken by firms.

Input prices

Natural resources, labour, capital and entrepreneurship are all required to produce products, and the prices of these resources affect supply. Supply is also affected by the prices of other inputs such as raw materials and semi-finished goods. Suppose many firms are competing for computer programmers to design their software and the salaries of these highly skilled workers increase. This increase in the price of labour adds to the cost of production. As a result, the supply of computer software decreases because sellers must charge more than before for any quantity supplied. Any reduction in production cost caused by a decline in the price of inputs will have an opposite effect and increase supply.

Taxes and subsidies

Certain taxes, such as company taxes, have the same effect on supply as an increase in the price of a resource. The impact of an increase in company tax would be similar to that of a rise in the salaries of computer programmers. An increase in company tax imposes an additional production cost on, for example, compact discs, and the supply curve shifts upward. On the other hand, payment of a subsidy by the government would have the same effect as lower prices for resources or a technological advance. That is, the supply curve shifts downward. In most developed countries governments subsidise the arts, leading to an increase in supply of services such as theatre productions, symphony concerts and operatic performances.

Visit the Irish Arts Council (**www.artscouncil.ie**), the Arts Council of New Zealand Toi Aotearoa (**www.creativenz.govt.nz**) or the Australia Council for the Arts (**www.ozco.gov.au**) to see how government funding provides incentives for people and organisations to increase the supply of artistic services.

Expectations of producers

Price expectations can affect current supply. For example, if wool growers expect the price of wool to rise with the onset of a harsh winter in the northern hemisphere, they may restrict current supply in order to have more wool to sell at higher prices during the coming winter months. The current supply curve shifts to the left. Looking at another example, suppose scooter manufacturers anticipate that the craze is over and the price of scooters will soon fall sharply. Their reaction is to sell down their inventories today before the downturn in price occurs tomorrow. Such a response shifts the supply curve for scooters to the right.

Prices of other goods the firm could produce

Business managers often consider shifting resources from producing one good or service to producing another good or service. A rise in the price of one product relative to the prices of other products signals to suppliers that switching production to the product with the higher relative price yields higher profit. If the price of tomatoes rises while the price of lettuces remains the same, many farmers will divert more of their land to tomatoes and less to lettuces. The result is an increase in the supply of tomatoes and a decrease in the supply of lettuces. This happens because the opportunity cost of growing lettuces, measured in forgone tomato profits, increases.

Exhibit 3.10 summarises the relationship between changes in the non-price determinants of supply and the supply curve, accompanied by examples for each type of non-price factor change.

Exhibit 3.10 **Summary of the impact of changes in non-price determinants of supply on the supply curve**

	Non-price determinant of supply	Relationship with the supply curve	Examples
1	Number of sellers	Direct	• Australia lowers trade restrictions on foreign textiles and the supply of textiles in Australia increases. • The popularity of law courses decreases and the supply of lawyers decreases.
2	Technology	Direct	• The development of new methods of producing motor cars reduces production costs, and there is an increase in the supply of cars. • The technological capability of a nation declines as a result of a decrease in government support for research and development. Production costs increase and there is a resultant decrease in supply.
3	Input prices	Inverse	• A decline in the price of computer chips increases the supply of computers. • An increase in the cost of farm equipment decreases the supply of tomatoes.
4	Taxes and subsidies	Inverse and direct	• An increase in the tax on tobacco companies reduces the supply of cigarettes. • A government payment to university researchers increases the supply of research output.
5	Price expectations	Inverse	• Oil companies anticipate a substantial rise in future oil prices, and this expectation causes these companies to decrease their current supply of oil. • Graziers expect the future price of wool to decline so they increase the present supply of wool.
6	Prices of other goods and services	Inverse	• A rise in the price of brand-name drugs causes drug companies to decrease the supply of generic drugs. • A decline in the price of tomatoes causes farmers to increase the supply of cucumbers.

Using the law of supply to help clean up the environment

Applicable concepts: law of supply; determinants of demand and supply

beverage container deposit

The discarding of containers that once held soft drink or alcohol results in wastage of raw materials and a significant litter problem. When environmentalists and government policy makers wish to reduce these problems, they exhort the public to stop littering and to make their waste beverage containers available for recycling. The various measures that sometimes accompany these exhortations – including recycling programs and fines for littering – have only a limited effect on recycling rates. In some jurisdictions these measures have been supplemented by the introduction of a beverage container deposit system. In Australia, the best known of these systems is the one introduced in South Australia in 1977.

A deposit system requires purchasers of beverages to pay a small deposit (5 or 10 cents) on the container when they purchase the beverage. When the container is returned – often by children rather than by the original purchasers – the deposit is refunded. Does this monetary incentive to return containers have a significant effect on recycle rates, or are existing measures the best we can do? Evidence from the Container Recycling Institute in the United States indicates that states with deposit schemes have recycle rates of 80 per cent – around twice the recycle rate of those without deposits. In Oregon, the deposit scheme has helped reduce beverage container litter to one-quarter of previous levels.

Large-scale 'litter' in the form of those shiny chrome supermarket shopping trolleys is the scourge of the modern city. They can be seen in waterways and on median strips and footpaths across the country. In recent years Aldi, the German supermarket chain, has opened a number of outlets in Australia. Use of a shopping trolley at these supermarkets requires payment of a deposit of $2 that is refunded when the trolley is returned. Not only does this reduce costs associated with attempts to recover lost trolleys – and Aldi competes primarily on price – but it also ensures a much higher rate of return of trolleys to the store. In fact, a number of local councils in Australia are considering the introduction of codes of practice that would require all supermarkets to introduce a scheme like Aldi's.

You can see that, although the deposit on a

container or a shopping trolley is small, it acts as a powerful incentive for someone to return it. This is an example of the law of supply at work – the increased incentive for people to return containers or shopping trolleys has increased the quantity of containers supplied for recycling and the number of trolleys returned to the store. The behaviour of these individuals is just the same as that of a firm responding to an increase in price by increasing the quantity of the product it produces.

Of course, there is no such thing as a free lunch. The container deposit schemes impose costs on both consumers and producers of soft drinks and alcohol. Consumers must pay a deposit that they may never recover, or that is recovered only after incurring the cost of returning the container. Producers, who generally oppose such schemes, must incur the cost of collection from locations at which refunds are paid. Supermarket operators are in favour of the savings that go with a higher return rate for their trolleys; however, the strong consumer resistance to payment of the deposit that led to the discontinuation of a Coles scheme similar to Aldi's suggests that trolley deposit systems come at a cost.

Using the above information, answer the following questions.

1 What is the likely effect of the introduction of a container deposit scheme on the quantity demanded of soft drinks and alcohol?
2 Can you identify any non-price demand determinants that would be affected?
3 Can you identify changes in supply that might result from the introduction of such a scheme?

A market supply and demand analysis

Market Any arrangement in which the interaction of buyers and sellers determines the price and quantity of goods and services exchanged.

Markets are one of the key institutions in capitalist economies. A **market** is any arrangement in which the interaction of buyers and sellers determines the price and quantity of goods and services exchanged. Let's consider the retail market for a particular type of tennis shoe. Exhibit 3.11 displays hypothetical market demand and supply data for this product. Notice that, in column 1 of the table, price serves as a common variable for both supply and demand relationships. Columns 2 and 3 list the quantity demanded and the quantity supplied for pairs of average quality tennis shoes per year.

The important question for market supply and demand analysis is: which selling price and quantity will prevail in the market? Let's start by asking what will happen if retail stores supply 75 000 pairs of tennis shoes and charge $105 a pair. At this relatively high price for tennis shoes, consumers are willing and able to purchase only 25 000 pairs. As a result, 50 000 pairs of tennis shoes remain as unsold inventory on the shelves of sellers (column 4) and the market condition is a **surplus** (column 5). A surplus is a market condition existing at any price where the quantity supplied is greater than the quantity demanded.

Surplus A market condition existing at any price where the quantity supplied is greater than the quantity demanded.

Exhibit 3.11 **Demand, supply and equilibrium for tennis shoes (pairs per year)**

(1) Price per pair	(2) Quantity demanded	(3) Quantity supplied	(4) Difference (3) – (2)	(5) Market condition	(6) Pressure on price
$105	25 000	75 000	+50 000	Surplus	Downward
90	30 000	70 000	+40 000	Surplus	Downward
75	40 000	60 000	+20 000	Surplus	Downward
60	50 000	50 000	0	Equilibrium	Stationary
45	60 000	35 000	–25 000	Shortage	Upward
30	80 000	20 000	–60 000	Shortage	Upward
15	100 000	5 000	–95 000	Shortage	Upward

How will retailers react to a surplus? Competition forces sellers to bring down their selling price in order to attract more sales (column 6). If they cut the selling price to $90, there will still be a surplus of 40 000 pairs of tennis shoes, and pressure on sellers to cut their selling price will continue. If the price falls to $75, there will still be an unwanted surplus of 20 000 pairs of tennis shoes remaining as inventory, and pressure will persist to charge a lower price.

Now imagine that, instead of being highly priced, tennis shoes are sold for just $15 per pair. This price is very attractive to consumers, and the quantity demanded is 100 000 pairs of tennis shoes each year. However, sellers are willing and able to provide only 5000 pairs at this price. The good news is that some consumers buy these 5000 pairs of tennis shoes at $15. The bad news is that potential buyers are willing to purchase 95 000 more pairs at that price, but cannot because the shoes are not on the shelves for sale. This out-of-stock condition signals the existence of a **shortage**. A shortage is a market condition existing at any price where the quantity supplied is less than the quantity demanded.

Shortage A market condition existing at any price where the quantity supplied is less than the quantity demanded.

In the case of a shortage, unsatisfied consumers compete to obtain the product by bidding to pay a higher price. Because sellers are seeking the higher profits that higher prices make possible, they gladly respond by setting a higher price of, say, $30 and increasing the quantity supplied to 20 000 pairs annually. A price of $30 will, however, also be temporary because the unfulfilled quantity demanded provides an incentive for sellers to further raise their selling price and offer more tennis shoes for sale. Even at a price of $45 a pair there is still a shortage of 25 000 pairs, and the market still gives the message to sellers to move upward along their market supply curve and sell for a higher price.

Equilibrium price and quantity

Equilibrium A market condition that occurs at any price for which the quantity demanded and the quantity supplied are equal.

Assuming that sellers are free to sell their product at any price, trial and error will make all possible price–quantity combinations unstable except at **equilibrium**. Equilibrium occurs at any price for which the quantity demanded and the quantity supplied are equal. Economists also refer to *equilibrium* as *market-clearing*.

In Exhibit 3.11, $60 is the *equilibrium* price and 50 000 pairs of tennis shoes is the *equilibrium* quantity per year. Equilibrium means that the forces of supply and demand are in balance and there is no reason for price or quantity to change, ceteris paribus. In short, all prices and quantities except a unique equilibrium price and quantity are temporary. Once the price of tennis shoes is $60, this price will not change unless a non-price factor changes demand or supply.

INFOTRAC®
Alfred Marshall

In his *Principles of Economics*, the famous English economist Alfred Marshall compared supply and demand to a pair of scissor blades. He wrote that we might as well argue whether it is the upper or the lower blade of a pair of scissors that cuts a piece of paper, as argue whether price is determined by demand or supply. Joining market supply and market demand as shown in Exhibit 3.12 allows us to see clearly the two 'blades'; that is, the demand curve *D* and the supply curve *S*. We can measure the amount of any surplus or shortage by the horizontal distance between the demand and the supply curves. At any price *above* equilibrium – say, $90 – there is an *excess quantity supplied* (surplus) of 40 000 pairs of tennis shoes. For any price *below* equilibrium – $30, for example – the horizontal distance between the curves tells us there is an *excess quantity demanded* (shortage) of 60 000 pairs. When the price per pair is $60, the market supply curve and the market demand curve intersect at point *E* and the quantity demanded equals the quantity supplied at 50 000 pairs per year.

Efficiency An efficient outcome is one in which society maximises the benefits it obtains from the use of its scarce resources.

When the forces of demand and supply are in balance at equilibrium, we say that the outcome is efficient or, alternatively, that the market is operating efficiently. An **efficient** outcome is one in which society maximises the benefits it gains from the use of its scarce resources. To see why the equilibrium outcome is efficient, consider a point to the left of the equilibrium point *E* in Exhibit 3.12. At this point the benefit to society measured by the demand curve is greater than the cost measured by the supply curve. (At this point consumers are willing to pay a price that is more than the seller's cost.) If output were to expand towards the equilibrium point, the benefit of additional output would be in excess of the additional cost of that output, and there would be a net gain to society from this expansion. Alternatively, consider a point to the right of the equilibrium point *E*. Here, the benefit as measured by the demand curve is less than the cost indicated by the supply curve. (At this point consumers are not willing to pay a price equal to the seller's cost.) If output were to contract towards the equilibrium point, the cost savings from reducing output would be greater than the value of the benefits forgone, and again there would be a net gain to society.

Exhibit 3.12 **The supply and demand for tennis shoes**

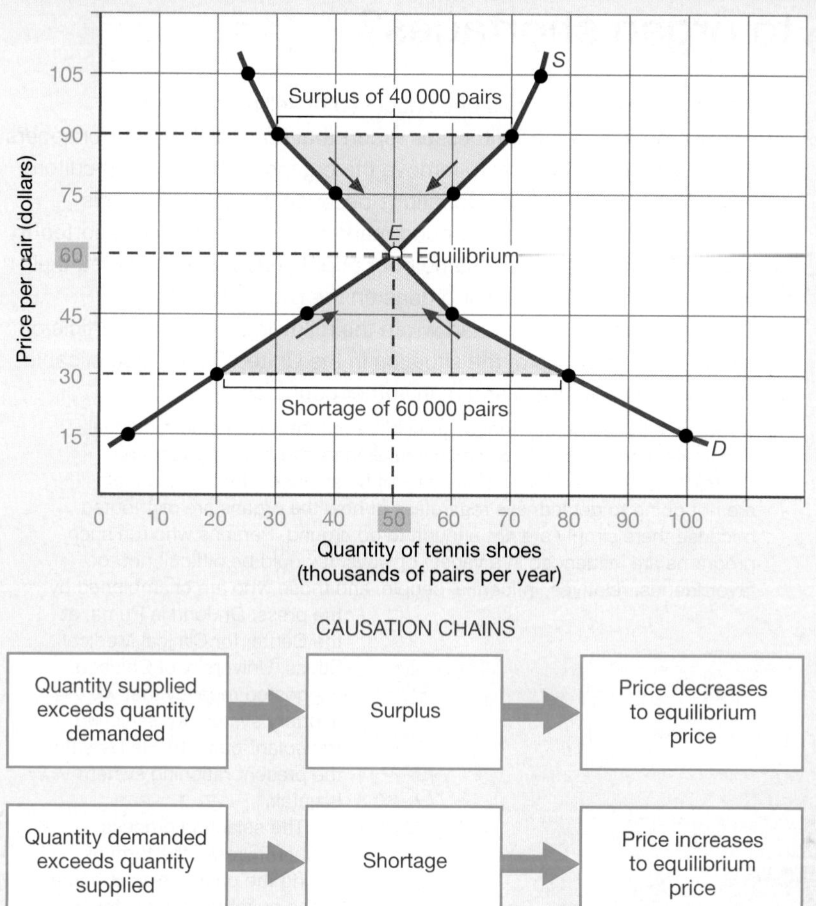

The supply and demand curves represent a market for tennis shoes. The intersection of the demand curve *D* and the supply curve *S* at point *E* indicates the equilibrium price of $60 and the equilibrium quantity of 50 000 pairs bought and sold per year. At any price above $60, a surplus prevails and pressure exists to push the price downward. At $90, for example, the excess quantity supplied of 40 000 pairs remains unsold. At any price below $60, a shortage condition provides pressure to push the price upward. At $30, for example, the excess quantity demanded of 60 000 pairs encourages consumers to bid up the price.

Graphically, the intersection of the supply curve and the demand curve is the market equilibrium price–quantity point. When all other non-price factors are held constant, this is the only stable point on the graph.

International focus

Should we adopt a market approach to organ shortages?

Applicable concepts: price system; markets and ethics

The Chinese government has been accused of selling organs from prisoners it puts to death. Witnesses report that immediately after prisoners are killed, surgeons stand by to remove the organs. In the Chinese culture, there are few voluntary organ donations because people believe this desecrates the body. An underground market for organs is also reported to be developing in India, where some poor people have supplemented their meagre incomes by selling their organs on the black market.

Economist James R. Rinehart wrote the following in a journal article on this subject. His analysis of the situation in the United States is applicable to the situation in Australia and many other countries.

> If you were in charge of a kidney transplant program with more potential recipients than donors, how would you allocate the organs under your control? Life and death decisions cannot be avoided. Some individuals are not going to get kidneys regardless of how the organs are distributed because there simply are not enough to go around. Persons who run such programs are influenced in a variety of ways. It would be difficult not to favor friends, relatives, influential people, and those who are championed by the press. Dr John la Puma, at the Center for Clinical Medical Ethics, University of Chicago, suggested recently that we use a lottery system for selecting transplant patients. He feels that the present rationing system is unfair.
>
> The selection process frequently takes the form of having the patient wait at home until a suitable donor is found. What this means is that, at any given point in time, many potential recipients are just waiting for an organ to be made available. In essence, the organs are rationed to those who are able to survive the wait.
>
> In many situations, patients are simply screened out because they are not considered to be suitable candidates for a transplant. For instance, patients with heart disease and overt psychosis often are excluded. Others with end-stage liver disorders are denied new organs on the grounds that the habits that produced the disease may remain to jeopardize recovery …

Under the present arrangements, owners receive no monetary compensation; therefore, suppliers are willing to supply fewer organs than potential recipients want. Compensating a supplier monetarily would encourage more people to offer their organs for sale. It also would be an excellent incentive for us to take better care of our organs. After all, who would want an enlarged liver or a weak heart …?[1]

The attention of Australians was drawn to the important role that organ donations can play when much-loved cricketer and broadcaster David Hookes died in tragic circumstances in early 2004. His untimely death, and his decision to donate his organs, led to the creation of the David Hookes Foundation, which has the objective of increasing the rate of organ donation in Australia. The most celebrated organ transplant in recent times occurred when media mogul Kerry Packer received a donor kidney from a personal friend employed as his helicopter pilot. When it comes to qualifying for a donated organ through official channels, wealth does not guarantee success.

Visit the David Hookes Foundation site to find more about organ donation in Australia. You'll find it at **www.davidhookesfoundation.com.**

1 James R. Rinehart, 'The marketing approach to organ shortages', *Journal of Health Care Marketing*, Vol. 8, No. 1, March 1988, pp. 72–5, published by the American Marketing Association. Reprinted with permission.

Analyse the issue

1 How would a decision to use the price system to allocate human organs affect the supply of organs and the demand for them?

2 What ethical issues are raised when considering whether to use the price system rather than a system such as the current one where organs are donated and then made available to those at the front of the queue?

PART 1

Our analysis leads to an important conclusion. The predictable or stable outcome in the tennis shoes example is that the price will eventually come to rest at $60 per pair. All other factors held constant, the price may be above or below $60, but the forces of surplus or shortage guarantee that any price other than the equilibrium price is temporary. This is in theory how the **price system** operates. The price system is a mechanism that uses the forces of supply and demand to create an equilibrium through rising and falling prices. Stated simply, price plays a rationing role. At the equilibrium price of $60, only those consumers willing to pay at least $60 per pair get tennis shoes, and there is no sale to buyers who will pay less.

price system

Price system A mechanism that uses the forces of supply and demand to create an equilibrium through rising and falling prices.

Key concepts

Consumer sovereignty
Law of demand
Change in quantity demanded
Change in demand
Normal good
Inferior good
Substitute good
Complementary good
Law of supply
Change in supply
Change in quantity supplied
Surplus
Market
Equilibrium
Shortage
Price system
Efficiency

Summary

- **Consumer sovereignty** is the freedom of consumers to make their own choices about which goods and services to buy. If consumer sovereignty prevails, these choices are made without coercion on the part of business or government.

- The **law of demand** states that there is an inverse relationship between the price and the quantity demanded, ceteris paribus. A market demand curve is the horizontal summation of individual demand curves.

- A **change in quantity demanded** is a movement along a stationary demand curve caused by a change in price. When any of the non-price determinants of demand changes, the demand curve responds by shifting. An increase in demand (rightward shift) or a decrease in demand (leftward shift) is caused by a change in one of the non-price determinants.

Change in quantity demanded and in demand

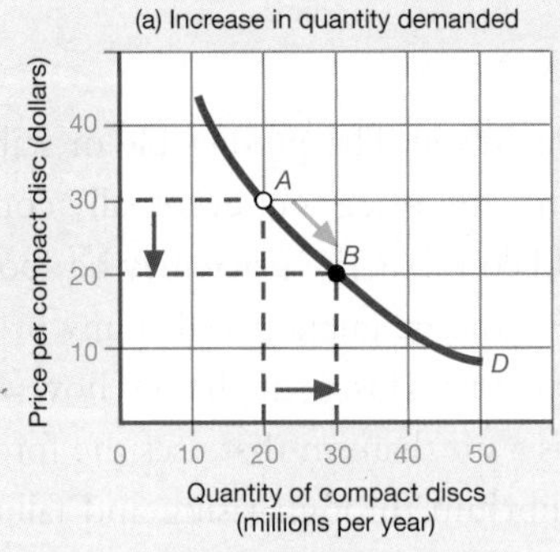

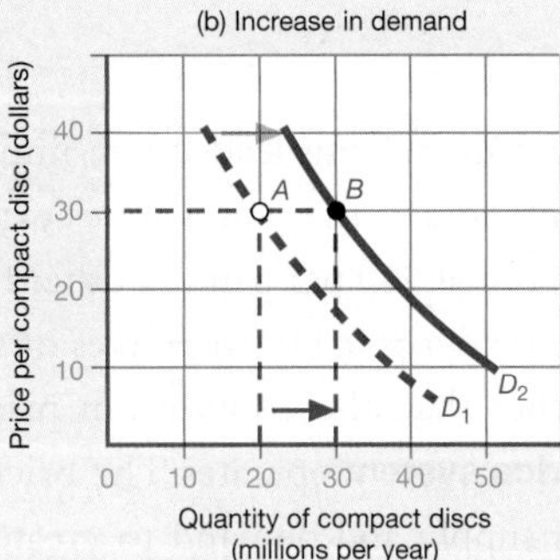

- **Non-price determinants of demand** are
  - **a** the number of buyers,
  - **b** tastes and preferences,
  - **c** income (normal and inferior goods),
  - **d** expectations, and
  - **e** prices of related goods (substitutes and complements).

- A **normal good** is any good or service for which there is a direct relationship between changes in income and its demand.

- An **inferior good** is any good or service for which there is an inverse relationship between changes in income and its demand.

- A **substitute good** is any good or service that competes with another good or service for consumer purchases. There is a direct relationship between a price change for one good or service and the demand for its 'competitor' good or service.

- A **complementary good** is any good or service that is jointly consumed with another good or service. There is an inverse relationship between a price change for one good or service and the demand for its 'complementary' good or service.

- The **law of supply** states that there is a direct relationship between the price and the quantity supplied, ceteris paribus. The market supply curve is the horizontal summation of individual supply curves.

- A **surplus** or **shortage** exists at any price where the quantity demanded and the quantity supplied are not equal. When the price of a good is greater than the equilibrium price there is an excess quantity supplied, which is called a *surplus*. When the price is less than the equilibrium price there is an excess quantity demanded, which is called a *shortage*.

- A **change in quantity supplied** is a movement along a stationary supply curve caused by a change in price. When any of the non-price determinants of supply changes, the supply curve responds by shifting. An increase in supply (rightward shift) or a decrease in supply (leftward shift) is caused by a change in one of the non-price determinants.

Change in quantity supplied and in supply

(a) Increase in quantity supplied

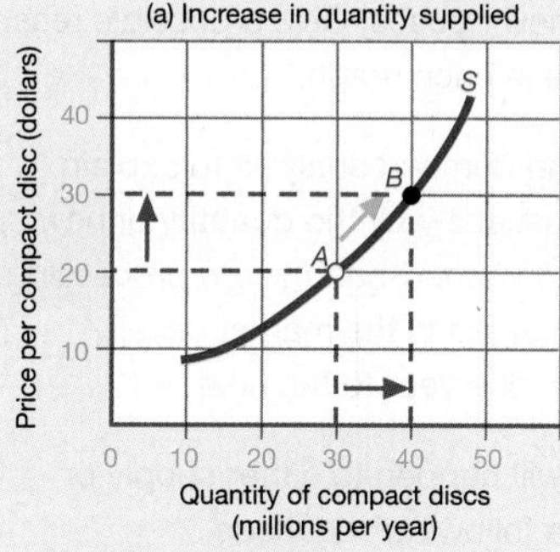

(b) Increase in supply

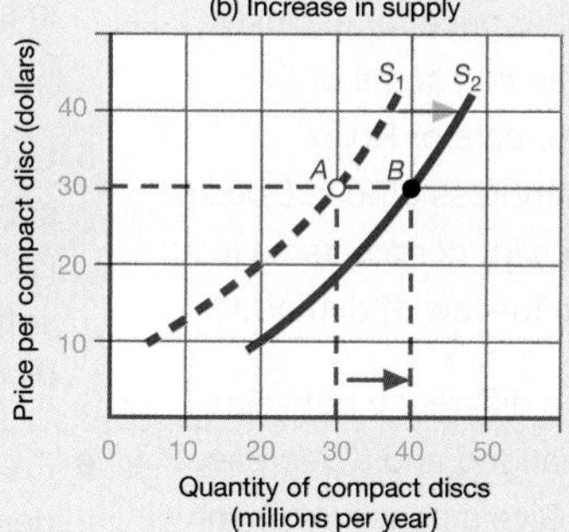

- **Non-price determinants of supply** are
  - **a** the number of sellers,
  - **b** technology,
  - **c** input prices,
  - **d** taxes and subsidies,
  - **e** expectations, and
  - **f** prices of other goods.

PART 1

- **Equilibrium** is the unique price and quantity established at the intersection of the supply and the demand curves. Only at equilibrium does quantity demanded equal quantity supplied.

Equilibrium

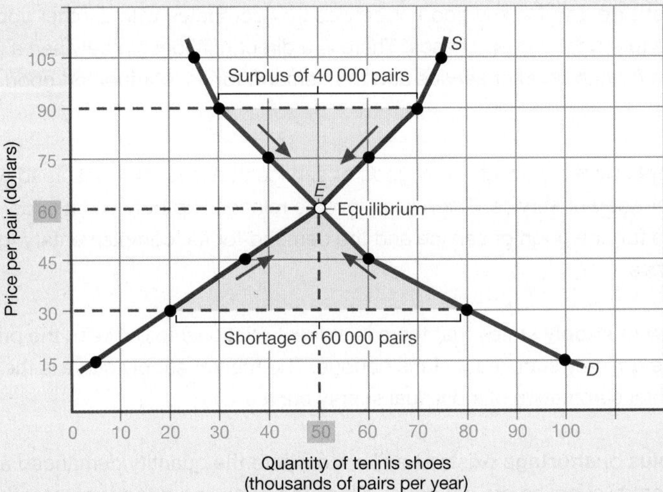

- An **efficient outcome** is one in which society maximises the benefits it gains from the use of its scarce resources.

- The **price system** is the supply and demand mechanism that establishes equilibrium through the ability of prices to rise and fall.

Study questions and problems

1 Some people will pay a higher price for exclusive brand-name goods. For example, some of the people who buy BMW motor cars or Rolex watches do so primarily to impress others. Does a decision to pay higher prices for certain items just for their 'snob value' violate the law of demand?

2 Draw graphs to illustrate the difference between a decrease in quantity demanded and a decrease in demand for cut flowers. Give a possible reason for the change you have shown in each graph.

3 Suppose oil prices rise sharply for years as a result of a war in the Middle East. What happens, and why, to the
   a demand for cars?
   b demand for home insulation?
   c demand for coal?
   d demand for tyres?

4 Draw graphs to illustrate the difference between a decrease in the quantity supplied and a decrease in supply for new houses. Give a possible reason for the change in each graph.

5 Use supply and demand analysis to explain some of the reasons why the quantity of new (as opposed to second-hand) word processing software exchanged in the market usually increases from one year to the next.

6 Predict what will happen to either supply or demand in the following situations.
   a Several large companies enter the accounting services industry.
   b Consumers suddenly decide that body piercing is unfashionable.
   c The health department issues a report that consumption of tomatoes prevents colds.
   d Frost threatens to damage the coffee crop, and consumers expect the price to rise sharply in the future.

e The price of tea falls. What is the effect on the coffee market?
f The price of sugar rises. What is the effect on the coffee market?
g Oil company and motoring association lobbyists persuade the government to remove the excise tax paid by sellers on each litre of petrol sold.
h A new type of robot is invented that will clean floors.

7 Using supply and demand analysis, explain and illustrate graphically the effect of the following situations.
a Population growth surges rapidly.
b The prices of resources used in the production of good *X* increase.
c The government is paying a $1 per unit subsidy for each unit of good *Y* produced.
d The income of consumers of normal good *X* increases.
e The income of consumers of inferior good *Y* decreases.
f Farmers are deciding what crop to plant and learn that, contrary to all expectations, the price of brussels sprouts has risen relative to the price of beans.

8 Explain why the market price is not necessarily the same as the equilibrium price.

9 If a new breakthrough in manufacturing technology reduces the cost of producing compact disc players by half, what would happen to the:
a supply of compact disc players?
b demand for compact disc players?
c equilibrium price and quantity of compact disc players?
d demand for compact discs?

10 Australia Post now faces increased competition from firms providing overnight delivery of packages and some letters. Additional competition has also emerged because messages can be sent by email and by fax machines. What will be the effect of this competition on the market demand for mail delivered by Australia Post?

11 In Melbourne, there is a shortage of Australian Rules football tickets for some games, and a surplus occurs for other games. Why do shortages and surpluses exist for different games?

12 Explain the statement 'People respond to incentives and disincentives' in relation to the demand curve and supply curve for good *X*.

Online exercises

Exercise 1

Visit the Economagic time series page for Australia (**www.economagic.com/aus.htm**).

1 Under the heading **Gross Domestic Product** select **Real GDP per Capita** and review the change over the past decade. Draw a graph to illustrate the effect of this change on the demand curve for domestic air conditioners. Show the effect on the demand curve for dish mops.

2 Under the heading **Indicators of Private Spending and Confidence**, select **Dwelling approvals**. Try to find evidence to support the idea that the introduction of the goods and services tax (GST) in July 2000 had an effect on home building approvals.

Exercise 2

As a result of his widely read work, *Principles of Economics*, the English economist Alfred Marshall was the person most responsible for dissemination of the simple ideas underlying the economist's concepts of demand and supply. Visit **www.econlib.org/library/Marshall/marP.html**, where you can search the text of the *Principles*. Search for **scissors** to find Marshall's famous paragraph in which he uses the blades of a pair of scissors as an analogy for demand and supply.

Exercise 3

If reticulated water is inexpensive and readily available, why does the demand for bottled water, which can cost more than $3 a bottle, remain strong? Why are consumers willing to pay such a steep price for bottled water? For some clues, visit the Evian water website at **www.evian.com**.

Exercise 4

To access a number of slide shows on supply and demand enter <**"slide show" + "supply and demand"**> into a web browser such as Google at **www.google.com**. Find a slide show that mirrors the material in this chapter.

Answers to 'You make the call'

Can housing become an exception to the law of demand?

As the price of houses and apartments began to rise rapidly, the expectation of still higher prices caused buyers to buy more now and, therefore, demand increased. As shown in Exhibit 3.13, suppose the price per dwelling unit was initially at P_1 and the quantity demanded was Q_1 on demand curve D_1 (point *A*). Then the frenzy of the boom caused the demand curve to shift rightward to D_2. Along the new demand curve D_2, consumers increased their quantity demanded to Q_2 at the higher price of P_2 per dwelling unit (point *B*).

The expectation of rising house and apartment prices in the future caused 'an increase in demand', rather than 'an increase in quantity demanded' in response to a higher price. If you said there are no exceptions to the law of demand, YOU ARE CORRECT.

Exhibit 3.13

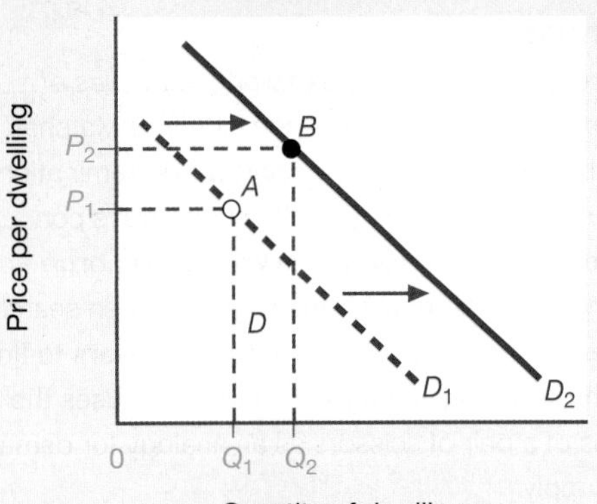

Can the law of supply be applied to choice of university courses?

When individuals make their choice of university course they are, in effect, making a decision to obtain qualifications that will enable them to supply their services to an industry that they hope will employ them when they graduate. Just as higher prices increase the quantity supplied of a good or service, so a rise in prospective salary or employment prospects will increase the quantity supplied of persons wishing to enter a particular profession. This explains the increase in enrolments in courses with improved salary and employment prospects and the subsequent decrease that occurs if these improved prospects evaporate. Labour economists tend to be critical of trends that involve increased enrolments based on short-term improvements in prospects for particular professions when there is little evidence that the situation will persist in the long run. They say that there is an unfortunate tendency for individuals to neglect the long run because they are short-sighted or myopic. If you said that the law of supply can be applied to choice of university courses, YOU ARE CORRECT.

Multiple-choice questions

1 The demand curve for good *X* is downward-sloping; this means that an increase in the price will result in

- **a** an increase in the demand for good *X*.
- **b** a decrease in the demand for good *X*.
- **c** no change in the quantity demanded for good *X*.
- **d** a larger quantity demanded for good *X*.
- **e** a smaller quantity demanded for good *X*.

2 The law of demand states that the quantity demanded of a good changes, other things being equal, when

- **a** the price of the good changes.
- **b** consumer income changes.
- **c** the prices of other goods change.
- **d** a change occurs in the quantities of other goods purchased.

3 Which of the following is the result of a decrease in the price of tea, other things being equal?

- **a** a leftward shift in the demand curve for tea.
- **b** a downward movement along the demand curve for tea.
- **c** a rightward shift in the demand curve for tea.
- **d** an upward movement along the demand curve for tea.

4 Which of the following will cause a movement along the demand curve for good *X*?

- **a** a change in the price of a close substitute.
- **b** a change in the price of good *X*.
- **c** a change in consumer tastes and preferences for good *X*.
- **d** a change in consumer income.

PART 1

5 Assuming beef and pork are substitutes, a decrease in the price of pork will cause the demand curve for beef to
  a shift to the left as consumers switch from beef to pork.
  b shift to the right as consumers switch from beef to pork.
  c remain unchanged, since beef and pork are sold in separate markets.
  d do none of the above.

6 Assuming coffee and tea are substitutes, a decrease in the price of coffee, other things being equal, results in
  a a downward movement along the demand curve for tea.
  b a leftward shift in the demand curve for tea.
  c an upward movement along the demand curve for tea.
  d a rightward shift in the demand curve for tea.

7 Assuming noodles and oyster sauce are complements, a decrease in the price of noodles will
  a decrease the demand for noodles.
  b increase the demand for noodles.
  c increase the demand for oyster sauce.
  d decrease the demand for oyster sauce.

8 Assuming prawns are a normal good, a decrease in consumer income, other things being equal, will
  a cause a downward movement along the demand curve for prawns.
  b shift the demand curve for prawns to the left.
  c cause an upward movement along the demand curve for prawns.
  d shift the demand curve for prawns to the right.

9 An increase in consumer income, other things being equal, will
  a shift the supply curve for a normal good to the right.
  b cause an upward movement along the demand curve for an inferior good.
  c shift the demand curve for an inferior good to the left.
  d cause a downward movement along the supply curve for a normal good.

10 Yesterday seller *A* supplied 400 units of a good *X* at $10 per unit. Today seller *A* supplies the same quantity of units at $5 per unit. Based on this evidence, seller *A* has experienced
  a a decrease in supply.
  b an increase in supply.
  c an increase in quantity supplied.
  d a decrease in quantity supplied.
  e an increase in demand.

11 An improvement in technology causes
  a a leftward shift of the supply curve.
  b an upward movement along the supply curve.
  c a firm to supply a larger quantity at any given price.
  d a downward movement along the supply curve.

12 Suppose bank employees receive a substantial wage increase. Other things being equal, the price of bank services will rise because of
  a an increase in the demand for bank services.
  b a rightward shift of the supply curve for bank services.
  c a leftward shift of the supply curve for bank services.
  d a reduction in the demand for bank services.

13 Assuming both grapes and tobacco can be grown on the same land, an increase in the price of tobacco, other things being equal, causes
  a an upward movement along the supply curve for grapes.
  b a downward movement along the supply curve for grapes.
  c a rightward shift in the supply curve for grapes.
  d a leftward shift in the supply curve for grapes.

14 If Q_d = quantity demanded and Q_s = quantity supplied at a given price, a shortage in the market results when
  a Q_s is greater than Q_d.
  b Q_s equals Q_d.
  c Q_d is less than or equal to Q_s.
  d Q_d is greater than Q_s.

15 Assume the equilibrium price for a good is $10. If the market price is $5,
  a a shortage will cause the price to remain at $5.
  b a surplus will cause the price to fall below $5.
  c a shortage will cause the price to rise towards $10.
  d a surplus will cause the price to rise towards $10.

16 In the market shown in Exhibit 3.14, the equilibrium price and quantity of good *X* are

- a $0.50, 200.
- b $1.50, 300.
- c $2.00, 100.
- d $1.00, 200.

Exhibit 3.14 Supply and demand curves

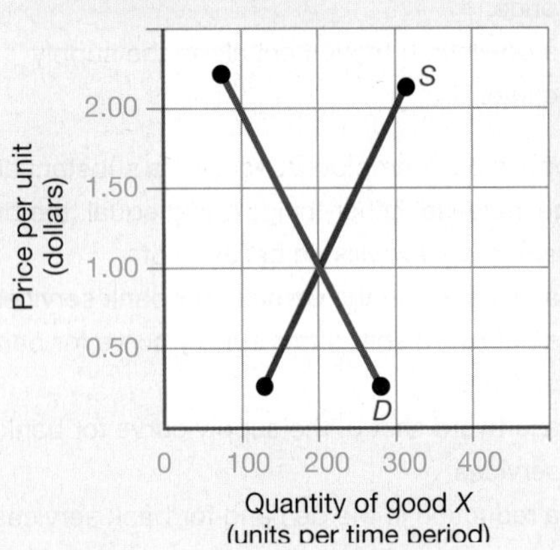

17 In Exhibit 3.14, at a price of $2.00, the market for good *X* will experience

- a a shortage of 150 units.
- b a surplus of 100 units.
- c a shortage of 100 units.
- d a surplus of 200 units.

18 In Exhibit 3.14, if the price of good *X* moves from $1.00 to $2.00, the new market condition will put

- a upward pressure on price.
- b no pressure on price to change.
- c downward pressure on price.
- d no pressure on quantity to change.

Markets in action

4

Once you understand how buyers and sellers respond to changes in equilibrium prices, you are progressing well in your quest to understand the economic way of thinking. This chapter begins by showing that changes in supply and demand influence the equilibrium price and quantity of goods and services exchanged around you every day. For example, you will study the impact of changes in supply and demand curves on the markets for New Zealand holiday packages, new homes and immunisation. Then you will see why the laws of supply and demand cannot be repealed. Using market supply and demand analysis, you will learn that government policies to control markets have predictable consequences. For example, you will understand what happens when the government limits the maximum rent landlords can charge and who benefits and who loses from minimum wage laws.

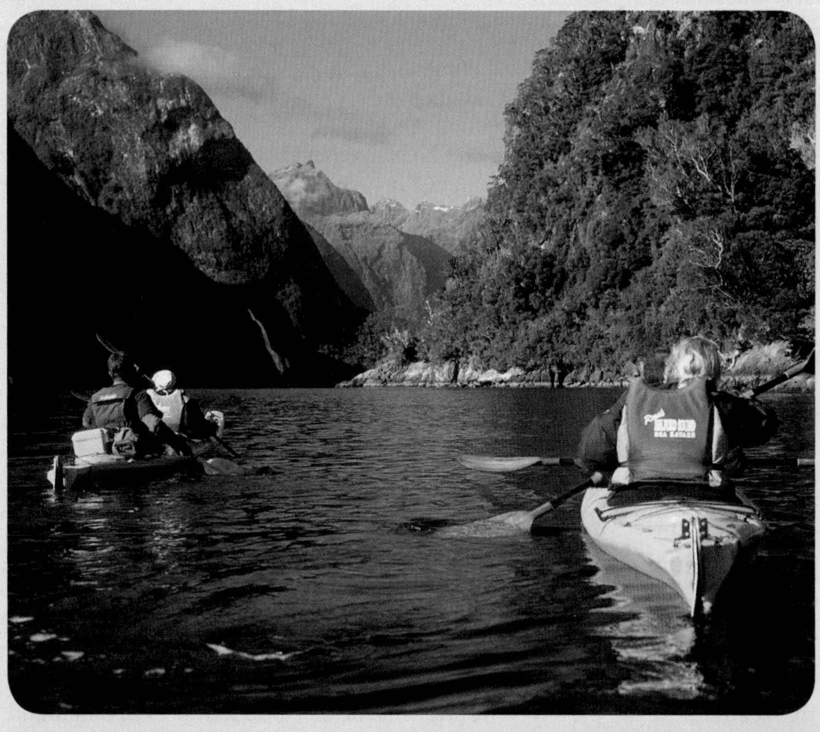

In this chapter, you will also study situations in which the market mechanism fails. Have you visited Taipei and lamented over the smog that sometimes blankets the beautiful surroundings? Or have you ever wanted to swim in a stream but could not because of pollution? These are obvious cases in which the market system has failed and the government must consider cures to reach socially desirable results.

In this chapter, you will examine these economics questions:

- How do endangered species affect the price of homes?
- What do ticket scalping and rent controls have in common?
- Why would governments offer to pay for immunisation against disease?
- When do markets work well and when do they fail?
- How can pricing policies reduce the need to add to public infrastructure?

Changes in market equilibrium

Using market supply and demand analysis is like turning on the windscreen wipers in your car. Suddenly the fuzzy world in front of you becomes clear. The following examples will open your eyes and help you to see that economic theory has something important to say about so many things in the real world.

Changes in demand

The market for a particular type of New Zealand packaged holiday is shown in Exhibit 4.1. In part (a) it is assumed that the position of the market supply curve, *S*, remains unchanged and that market demand increases from D_1 to D_2. Why has the demand curve shifted rightward in the figure? We will assume that the popularity of these holidays in New Zealand has suddenly risen sharply due to extensive advertising (changes in tastes and preferences). Given supply curve *S* and demand curve D_1, the initial equilibrium price is $1600 per holiday and the initial equilibrium quantity is 8000 holidays (holiday packages sold) per year, shown as point E_1. After the impact of advertising, the new equilibrium point, E_2, becomes 12 000 holiday packages per year at a price of $1900 each. Thus, the increase in demand causes both the equilibrium price and the equilibrium quantity to increase.

It is important to understand the force that caused the equilibrium to shift from E_1 to E_2. When demand initially increased from D_1 to D_2, there was a temporary shortage of 8000 holidays at $1600 per holiday. Firms in this segment of the packaged holiday business responded to excess demand

Exhibit 4.1 The effects of shifts in demand on market equilibrium

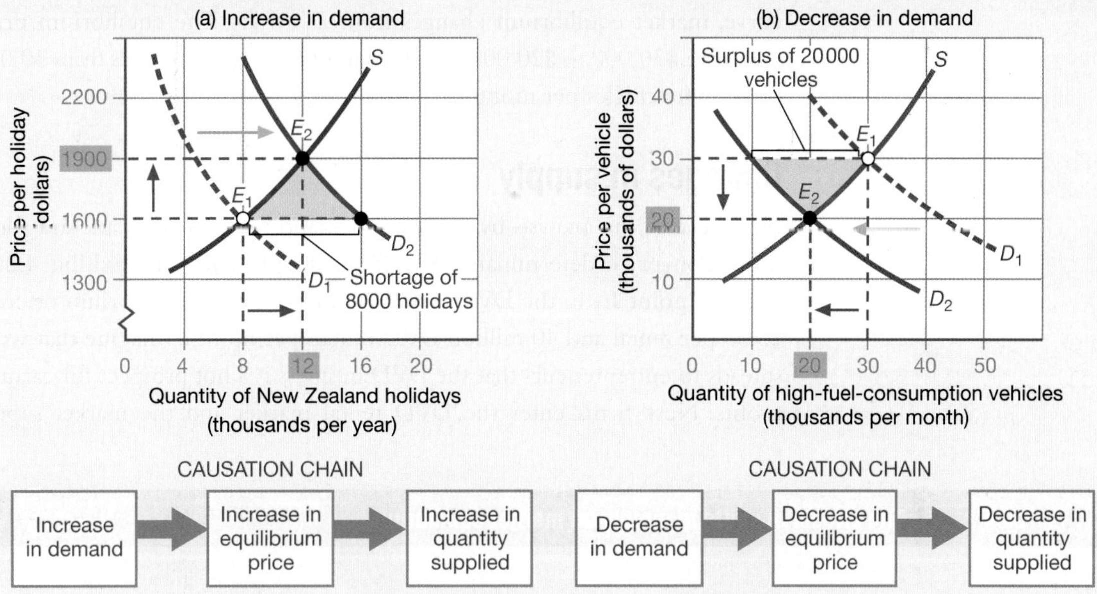

In part (a), there is an increase in the demand for New Zealand holiday packages because of extensive advertising and the demand curve shifts rightward from D_1 to D_2. This shift in demand causes a temporary shortage of 8000 holidays per year at the price associated with the initial equilibrium of E_1. This disequilibrium condition encourages firms in this segment of the holiday package industry to move upward along the supply curve to a new equilibrium at E_2.

Part (b) illustrates a decrease in the demand for high-fuel-consumption motor vehicles caused by a sharp rise in the price of petrol (a complement). This leftward shift in demand from D_1 to D_2 results in a temporary surplus of 20 000 vehicles per month at the price associated with the initial equilibrium of E_1. This disequilibrium condition forces car manufacturers to move downward along the supply curve to equilibrium E_2.

by hiring more people, offering more packaged holidays in New Zealand and raising the price. Tour companies will therefore move upward along the supply curve (increasing quantity supplied, but not changing supply). During some period of trial and error, sellers of packaged tours will increase their price and quantity supplied until a shortage no longer exists at point E_2. Therefore, the increase in demand causes both the equilibrium price and the equilibrium quantity to increase.

What will happen to the demand for high-fuel-consumption motor vehicles if the price of petrol triples and is expected to remain high? Because petrol and motor vehicles are complements, a rise in the price of petrol decreases the demand for such vehicles from D_1 to D_2 in Exhibit 4.1(b). At the initial equilibrium (E_1), with a price of $30 000 per vehicle the quantity supplied now exceeds the quantity demanded by 20 000 vehicles per month. This unwanted inventory forces car manufacturers to reduce the price and quantity supplied. As a result of this movement downward on the supply curve, market equilibrium changes from E_1 to E_2. The equilibrium price falls from \$30 000 to \$20 000 and the equilibrium quantity falls from 30 000 to 20 000 vehicles per month.

Changes in supply

Now reverse the analysis by assuming demand remains constant, and allow some non-price determinant to shift the supply curve. In Exhibit 4.2(a), begin at point E_1 in the DVD rental industry with an equilibrium price of \$3.00 per rental and 40 million DVD rentals per month. Imagine that word spreads to entrepreneurs that the DVD business is a hot prospect for earning profits. New firms enter the DVD rental market and the market supply

Exhibit 4.2 The effects of shifts in supply on market equilibrium

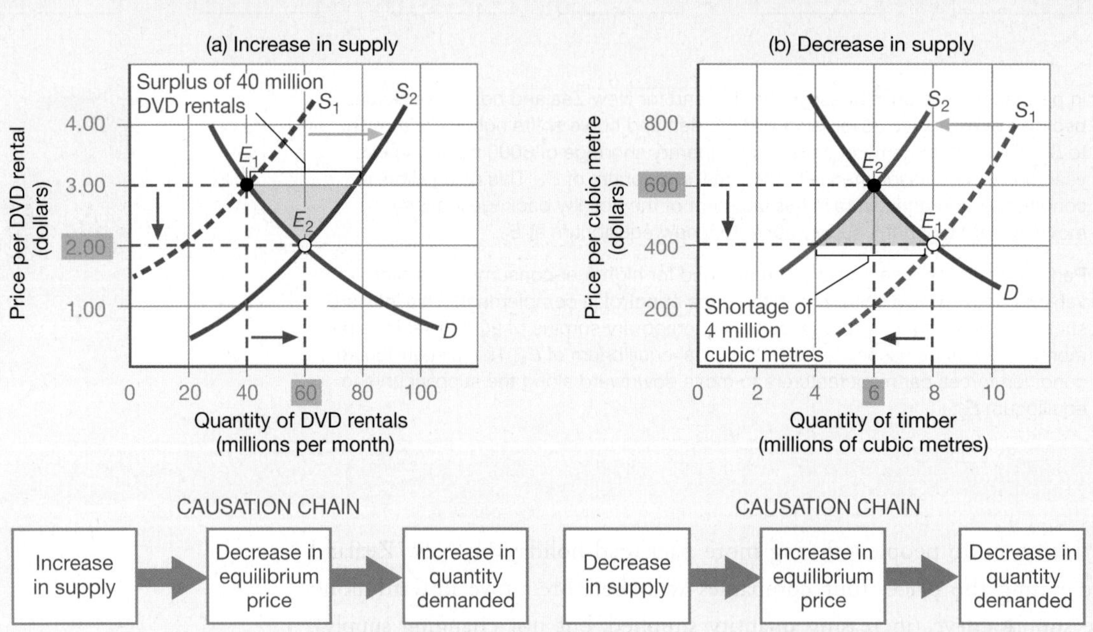

In part (a), begin at equilibrium E_1 in the DVD rental industry and assume that an increase in the number of DVD rental firms shifts the supply rightward from S_1 to S_2. This shift in supply causes a temporary surplus of 40 million DVD rentals per month. This disequilibrium condition causes a movement downward along the demand curve to a new equilibrium at E_2. At E_2, the equilibrium rental price declines and the equilibrium quantity rises.

In part (b), steps to protect the environment cause the supply curve for timber to shift leftward from S_1 to S_2. This shift in supply results in a temporary shortage of 4 million cubic metres per year. Customer bidding for the available timber raises the price. As a result, the market moves upward along the demand curve to a new equilibrium at E_2 and the quantity demanded falls.

curve shifts from S_1 to S_2. This creates a temporary surplus of 40 million DVD rentals at the initial equilibrium price of $3.00. DVD rental firms respond to having so many unrented DVDs on their shelves by reducing the rental price. As the price falls, buyers move down along their demand curve and rent more DVDs per month. When the rental price falls to $2.00, the market is in equilibrium again at point E_2 instead of E_1 and consumers rent 60 million DVDs per month.

Exhibit 4.2(b) illustrates the market for timber. Suppose this market is at equilibrium E_1, the going price is $400 per cubic metre, and 8 million cubic metres are bought and sold per year. Now suppose new legislation is introduced, and the federal government sets aside huge forest resources to protect endangered species and other wildlife. This means the market supply curve shifts leftward from S_1 to S_2 and a temporary shortage of 4 million cubic metres of timber exists at the initial equilibrium price of $400. Suppliers respond by raising their price from $400 to $600 per cubic metre and a new equilibrium is established at E_2, where the quantity is 6 million cubic metres. This higher cost of timber in turn raises the price of a new three-bedroom home by $4000 compared to the price of an identical home the previous year. One proposed solution to higher timber prices is to legislate to reduce sales of logs to foreign countries. Why or why not might this be a good idea?

Exhibit 4.3 gives a concise summary of the impact of changes in demand and supply on market equilibrium.

Exhibit 4.3 The effect of shifts in demand and supply on market equilibrium

Change	Effect on equilibrium price	Effect on equilibrium quantity
Demand increases	Increases	Increases
Demand decreases	Decreases	Decreases
Supply increases	Decreases	Increases
Supply decreases	Increases	Decreases

Can the laws of supply and demand be repealed?

In some markets, the objective of governments is to prevent prices from rising to the equilibrium price. In other markets, the government's goal is to maintain a price higher than the equilibrium price. Market supply and demand analysis is a valuable tool for understanding what might happen when the government considers fixing prices. There are two types of price controls: *price ceilings* and *price floors*.

Price ceilings

Price ceiling A legally established maximum price a seller can charge.

What happens if the government prevents the price system from setting a market price 'too high' by mandating a price ceiling? A **price ceiling** is a legally established maximum price a seller can charge. Rent controls are an example of the imposition of a price ceiling in the market for rental units. Many cities in the United States have rent controls, which set a maximum price that private landlords can ask for the rental accommodation they own. In Australia and in many Asian countries such controls over private landlords are rare. However, many of these countries do have rent control on government-provided housing, which is made available to tenants at subsidised rents well below the market equilibrium level. The rationale for rent control is to provide an 'essential service' that would be unaffordable to many people at the equilibrium rental price. Let's see why many economists believe that rent controls are counter-productive. In the following example we consider the private rental market. Many of the undesirable effects of rent control in this market can be shown to be equally applicable to rent controls applied in the government housing sector.

INFOTRAC®
rent control

Exhibit 4.4 is a supply and demand diagram for the quantity of rental units demanded and supplied per month in a hypothetical city. We begin the analysis by assuming that no rent controls exist and that the equilibrium is at point *E*, with a monthly rent of $600 per month and 6 million units occupied. Next, assume that the government imposes a rent control (ceiling price) designed to make housing more affordable. Assume the controlled rent is $400 per month. What does market supply and demand theory predict will happen? At the low rent ceiling of $400, the quantity demanded of rental units will be 8 million while the quantity supplied will be only 4 million. Consequently, the price ceiling creates a persistent market shortage of 4 million rental units because the rental price cannot rise.

What might be the impact of rent controls on consumers? First, consumers must spend more time on waiting lists and searching for housing, as a substitute for paying higher prices. This means consumers incur an *opportunity cost* added to the $400 rent set by government. Second, an illegal market, or *black market*, can arise because of the excess quantity demanded. Because the price of rental units is artificially low, a profit motive exists that encourages tenants to risk breaking the law in order to sub-let the unit to the highest bidder over $400 per month.

From the seller's perspective, rent control encourages two undesirable effects. First, a controlled low rent means landlords may skimp on maintenance, and housing deterioration will reduce the stock of decent rental units in the long run. Second, landlords may use discriminatory practices to replace the price system. Once owners realise that there is an excess demand for accommodation at the controlled price, they may resort to preferences based on family size, race and so on in order to determine how to allocate scarce rental space.

If governments accept economists' arguments against the use of rent controls, is there still some way to make housing available to targeted groups at a lower cost than the equilibrium rent? Many economists would argue for a system of welfare payments to low-income earners to enable them to pay market rents, leaving it up to the individual to choose how and when the welfare benefit might be spent. Other economists, who are concerned that welfare benefits may not be spent on housing, might propose a voucher system that would enable low-income earners to trade a permit issued by government for rental accommodation at market-determined rents. Such a scheme would ensure that recipients used their benefit for housing and also that the market for housing could achieve equilibrium.

Price controls on many goods and services, particularly those provided by government, were a common feature of many market economies throughout most of the twentieth century. In recent years, however, governments, acting on the advice of economists, have pursued policies such as deregulation and privatisation of government-owned enterprises. These policies have increased efficiency by reducing significantly the extent of market distortions associated with government controls on prices. In Australia, these policies have been part of a set of wide-ranging adjustments known as microeconomic reform. They are discussed in greater detail in Chapter 10.

Exhibit 4.4 Rent control results in a shortage of rental units

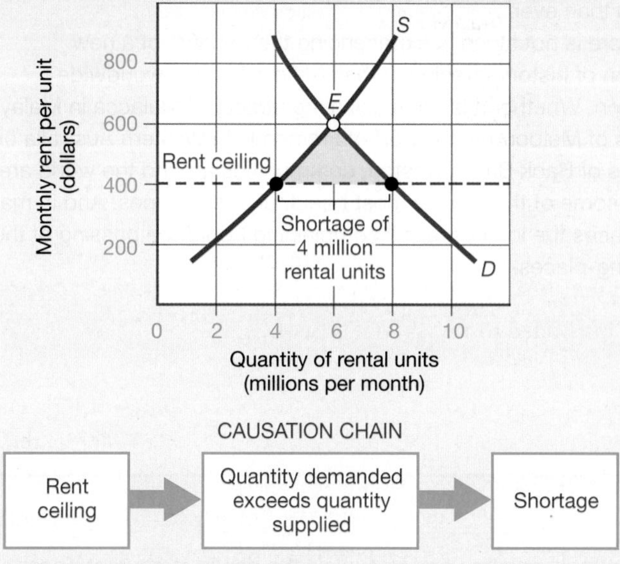

If no rent controls exist, the equilibrium rent for a hypothetical rental unit is $600 per month at point *E*. However, the government imposes a rent ceiling of $400 per month, and a shortage of 4 million rental units occurs. Because rent cannot rise by law, one outcome is that consumers must spend more time searching for an available unit. Other outcomes include a black market, bribes, discrimination and other illegal methods to deal with a shortage of 4 million rental units per month.

It should be noted that a rent ceiling at or above $600 per month would have no effect – a ceiling is only effective if it is below the market equilibrium price.

International focus

Can changes in demand and supply explain rising restaurant prices in Singapore's Chinatown?

Applicable concept: changes in market equilibrium

Visit Singapore's Urban Redevelopment Authority at **www.ura.gov.sg** to read about Chinatown and other conservation projects in Singapore.

For years, tourists have flocked to Singapore's fascinating Chinatown precinct. They have been attracted by good food at cheap prices, the charming streets with their small-scale nineteenth-century buildings and the specialty shops. Anyone who last visited Chinatown a decade or more ago would be amazed by the changes that have occurred. A return visit today would reveal that most of the shops, houses and restaurants have been beautifully restored. Although much of the character of the precinct has been retained, the overall impression is that it is experiencing a newfound prosperity.

Apart from the changes to the streetscape, there is another very significant change that a visitor returning after many years would notice: the prices of the meals in the restaurants seem higher than they used to be. Compared to restaurant prices in other parts of Singapore, the prices in Chinatown have increased noticeably. Although most tourists may be more than happy to pay the higher prices that accompany the changing face of Chinatown, some locals lament the passing of many of the cheap eating-places.

Of course, restoration of precincts like Chinatown does not come cheap, and many millions of Singapore dollars have been expended on refurbishment and new buildings. But this expenditure has had the desired effect. Singapore's Chinatown is a more popular tourist destination than ever.

Singapore is not alone in experiencing the benefits of a new appreciation of historic precincts; their restoration is a worldwide phenomenon. Whether it is the fascinating streets of Malacca in Malaysia, the villages of Melbourne, the port of Fremantle in Western Australia or the terraces of Back Bay in Boston, communities around the world are reclaiming some of the world's most beautiful streetscapes. And in many of these places the locals are still complaining about the passing of the cheap eating-places.

Analyse the issue

Show how changes in demand and supply can be used to explain the rise in restaurant prices in Singapore's Chinatown. Would these changes have resulted in an increase or a decrease in the number of restaurant meals purchased each year? Explain how the changes that have occurred in Singapore's Chinatown could have affected the markets for restaurant meals in other parts of Singapore.

How can better pricing policies help solve our infrastructure problems?

With strong growth in the Australian economy during the 1990s and early 2000s, the demands on infrastructure provided by governments have increased enormously. Power outages, water shortages and heavily congested roads are just some of the manifestations of this tendency. Many solutions have been suggested for these problems including calls for state governments, which are responsible for most of these services, to fund massive increases in public infrastructure. However, a policy of facilitating large increases in infrastructure is fraught with political dangers – not the least of which are the adverse environmental effects (negative externalities) that accompany construction of capital assets such as power plants, dams and highways. Rather than proposing increases in infrastructure as a solution to the problem, many economists suggest that an increase in the prices of these services is what is required. They say that in many cases the problems would be solved if prices were increased, but only during certain seasons, at certain times of the day or on certain days of the week. Thus water prices could be increased in summer, electricity prices could be higher when peak load occurs in the evening, and charges for toll roads and tunnels could be raised during weekday peak periods. In the examples cited, is the main reason why economists suggest different prices at different times related to demand factors or supply factors?

Price floors

price floor

Price floor A legally established minimum price a seller can be paid.

The other side of the price-control coin is that the government sets a price floor because it fears that the price system may establish a price viewed as 'too low'. A **price floor** is a legally established minimum price a seller can be paid. We now turn to the minimum wage as an example of a price floor.

We begin our analysis by noting that the demand for unskilled labour is the downward-sloping curve shown in Exhibit 4.5. The wage rate on the vertical axis is the price of unskilled labour, and the amount of unskilled labour that employers are willing to hire varies inversely with the wage rate. At a higher wage rate, businesses will hire fewer workers. At a lower wage rate, they will employ more workers.

On the supply side, the wage rate determines the number of unskilled workers willing and able to work per year. At higher wages, workers will give up leisure or schooling to work, and lower wages will result in fewer workers available for hire. The upward-sloping curve in Exhibit 4.5 represents the supply of labour.

To see how international airfares can differ significantly at different times of the year, visit STA Travel (**www.statravel.com.au**). Using the Search facility, search for the fare from any Australian capital city to London in January (when the northern winter discourages travellers). Now search for the fare for the same trip in July (at the height of the northern summer).

Assuming the freedom to bargain, the price system will establish an equilibrium wage rate of W_e and an equilibrium quantity of labour employed of Q_e. But suppose a central wage-fixing authority sets a minimum wage, W_m, which is a price floor above the equilibrium wage, W_e. The intent

Exhibit 4.5 **A minimum wage results in a surplus of labour**

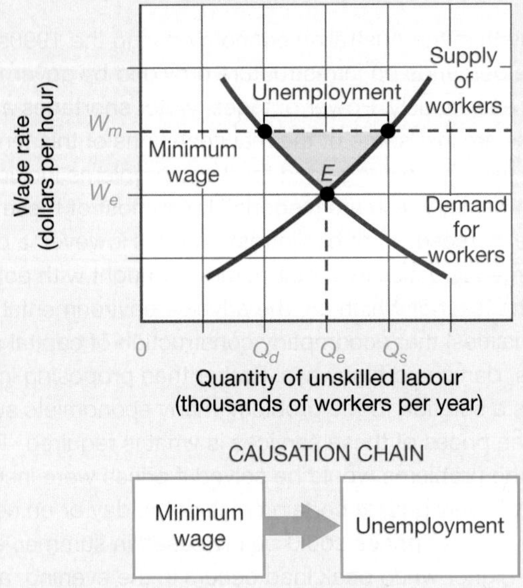

If the Australian Industrial Relations Commission sets a wage floor above the equilibrium wage, a surplus of unskilled labour develops. The supply curve shows the number of workers offering their services per year at each possible wage rate. The demand curve represents the number of workers employers are willing and able to hire at various wage rates. Equilibrium wage W_e will be the result if the price system is allowed to operate without government interference. At the minimum wage of W_m, there is a surplus of unemployed workers ($Q_s - Q_d$).

of this action which, in Australia, would be undertaken by the Australian Industrial Relations Commission, is to make lower-paid workers better off; but consider the undesirable consequences. One result of an artificially high minimum wage is that the number of workers willing to offer their labour increases upward along the supply curve to Q_s and the number of workers that firms are willing to hire decreases to Q_d on the demand curve. The predicted outcome is a labour surplus of unskilled workers, $Q_s - Q_d$, who are unemployed. Moreover, employers are encouraged to substitute machines and skilled labour for the unskilled labour previously employed at equilibrium wage W_e. The minimum wage is therefore considered counter-productive because employers lay off the lowest-skilled workers who are, ironically, the type of workers minimum wage legislation intends to help. It would be far better, according to many economists, to dispense with minimum wages and use the welfare system to top up the market-determined wages of low-income earners.

Analyse the issue

Would raising the minimum wage help low-income workers?

Applicable concepts: price floor; minimum wage laws

In Australia, regulation of the conditions of employment of workers is overseen by the Australian Industrial Relations Commission (AIRC). In 1907, in the famous Harvester case, its predecessor, the Conciliation and Arbitration Commission, determined that Australian workers should be protected by provision of a minimum wage. Today, in spite of this protection, a worker on the minimum wage who works full-time still earns a relatively low annual income. Nonetheless, like many economists, the Australian government takes the view that an increase in this relatively low income is likely to jeopardise the jobs of unskilled workers. The following extracts are from an article published in *The Australian Financial Review* newspaper in 2004, not long after the re-election of the Howard government with a majority in both houses of parliament. They show how the views of the government differ from those of the Australian Council of Trade Unions (ACTU), which represents workers in national wage cases.

> The ACTU's minimum wage claim for 2005 has renewed the struggle over the role of the Australian Industrial Relations Commission under the re-elected Howard government. ACTU secretary Greg Combet announced yesterday that the unions would be seeking a pay rise of $26.60 per week in next year's review of the award safety net.
>
> The claim would increase the minimum wage from about $12.30 an hour, or $467.40 a week, to $13 an hour, or $494 a week. Mr Combet argued that the pay rise for about 1.6 million low-paid Australians was 'completely affordable' ...
>
> The government's stated policy is to retain safety-net reviews, but it plans to push ahead with legislation that would require the AIRC to consider the effect of wage increases on the unemployed. ...

> Treasurer Peter Costello said the government would argue that the main priority should be to keep people in the labour market and increase workplace participation. 'As the economy grows, we ought to look for wage increases but we shouldn't leave behind people who might be locked out if those wage increases mean that their employment becomes threatened,' he said. ...[1]

As Treasurer Costello points out, the dilemma for policy-makers is that a higher minimum wage may be awarded at the expense of jobs for unskilled workers. Opponents of minimum wages forecast that the increased labour cost from an increase in the minimum wage would jeopardise tens of thousands of jobs of unskilled workers – many of whom are young. For example, employers may opt to purchase more capital and use less of the more expensive labour.

Another problem with raising the minimum wage is that studies show that the minimum wage is a blunt weapon for redistributing income. Only a small percentage of minimum-wage earners are full-time workers. For example, many minimum-wage workers are students living at home or workers whose spouses earn a much higher income. To help only poor families, some economists argue that the government should target only those who need it, rather than using the 'shotgun' approach of raising the minimum wage.

Supporters are not convinced by the case against raising the minimum wage. They say it is outrageous that a worker can work full-time and still earn a very low annual income. Moreover, these people believe that opponents exaggerate the dangers to the economy from a higher minimum wage. Economist Lester Thurow of Massachusetts Institute of Technology, for example, argues that a high minimum wage will force employers to upgrade the skills and productivity of workers. Increasing the minimum wage may therefore be a win-win proposition, rather than a win-lose proposition. Professor Thurow is supported by the research of David Card and Alan B. Krueger. These economists studied data on increases in the minimum wage in the United States. Their evidence shows that modest increases in the minimum wage have resulted in little or no loss of jobs.[2] Note that we will return to this issue in Chapter 10, where labour markets are discussed at length.

Using the information you have just read, answer the following questions:

1 Draw a diagram similar to Exhibit 4.5 above, which represents the labour market in Australia. On the vertical axis mark the equilibrium wage at $12.70 per hour.

2 Using this diagram, explain the outcome if the minimum wage were to be increased to $13 per hour in line with the ACTU's claim.

3 Explain the outcome if the claim were not allowed at all and the minimum wage remained at $12.30 per hour.

For a typical economic critique of minimum wage laws go to the Free Market Foundation's briefing paper on the subject at **www.freemarketfoundation.com/briefingpapers/minimumwages.htm.**

PART 1

1 Mark Skulley, 'Unions face last fight', *Australian Financial Review*, 9 November 2004.

2 David Card & Alan B. Krueger, *Myth and Measurement: The New Economics of the Minimum Wage*, Princeton University Press, Princeton, NJ, 1995.

Supporters of the minimum wage are quick to point out that those employed (Q_d) are better off. Even though the minimum wage causes a reduction in employment, some economists argue that a more equal or fairer income distribution is worth the loss of some jobs. Moreover, the slope of the labour demand curve may be much more vertical than is shown in Exhibit 4.5. If this is the case, the unemployment effect of a rise in the minimum wage would be small. In addition, they claim that opponents ignore the possibility that unskilled workers have much less bargaining power than their employers. It is also argued by advocates of minimum wage laws that the short-term incentive they give employers to substitute capital for labour may have the long-term effect of raising the productivity of workers, and with it the capacity of employers to pay higher wages.

Finally, a minimum wage set at or below the equilibrium wage rate is ineffective. If the minimum wage rate is set at the equilibrium wage rate of W_e, the quantities of labour demanded and labour supplied are equal regardless of the minimum wage. If the minimum wage rate is set below the equilibrium wage rate, the forces of supply of and demand for labour establish the equilibrium wage regardless of the minimum wage rate. We will look again at possible effects of minimum wages in Chapter 10 when we deal with microeconomic reform.

Skivvy crew upset at scalpers' yummy profit

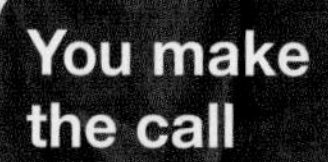

You make the call

PART 1

At sold-out concerts and sporting events, some of those with tickets try to resell them for more than they paid – a practice known as scalping. As the following excerpts from an article in *The Courier Mail* by Jennifer Dudley indicate, the practice of scalping is a contentious one – especially when it involves family entertainment.

> Children's entertainment supergroup The Wiggles may soon be pointing their famous fingers at ticket scalpers after the group instructed their lawyers to investigate recent eBay sales.
>
> Three tickets to one of the group's sold-out Brisbane concert were selling for $405 ... yesterday in a development the group's publicist said was 'ripping off families'.
>
> Publicist Dianna O'Neill said The Wiggles were in a difficult situation as they did not want their fans to pay excessive prices to see their concerts. ...
>
> But eBay Australia trust and safety director Alastair MacGibbon said sale prices were determined by demand and privately selling concert tickets was not illegal in Australia.
>
> He said ticket scalping was only illegal in Victoria for AFL grand finals and Commonwealth Games tickets and eBay had worked with police to ensure those tickets were not sold on the website.[1]

Read about the Wiggles and listen to them sing – if that's your thing – at **www.thewiggles.com**.

Scalping was also in evidence for certain events and ceremonies at the 2000 Sydney Olympics. For scalping to occur, must the original ticket price be akin to a price floor, the equilibrium price, or a price ceiling? Do you think that the Wiggles are pursuing enlightened self-interest when the low prices charged for tickets to their concerts result in a sell-out every time?

1 Jennifer Dudley, 'Skivvy crew upset at scalpers' yummy profit', *The Courier Mail*, 1 October 2004.

Market failure

market failure

Market failure A situation in which the price system fails to operate efficiently, creating a problem for society.

In this and the previous chapter, you have gained an understanding of how markets operate. Through the price system society coordinates economic activity, but markets do not always produce successful outcomes from society's point of view. It is now time to step back with a critical eye and consider markets that produce socially unacceptable results. **Market failure** means that the price system fails to operate efficiently, creating a problem for society. In this section, you will study four important examples of market failure: lack of competition, externalities, public goods and income inequality.

Lack of competition

There must be competition among both producers and consumers for markets to function effectively. In 1776 the Scotsman Adam Smith's famous work on economics, *The Wealth of Nations*, was published. Although Smith praised the virtues of the market system, he was acutely aware of the damage that anti-competitive practices could inflict. Smith observed that '… people of the same trade seldom meet together, even for merriment and diversion, but the conversation ends in a conspiracy against the public, or in some diversion to raise prices'. This famous quote clearly underscores the fact that in the real world, businesses will seek ways to replace consumer sovereignty with 'big business sovereignty'. What happens when a few firms rig the market and become the market's boss? By restricting supply through artificial limits on the output of goods or services, firms enjoy higher prices and profits. As a result, firms may reduce the well-being of the community by wasting resources and retarding technology and innovation.

Exhibit 4.6 illustrates how firms in the fire protection business could benefit from rigging the market for installation of fire alarms and fire sprinkler systems. Without collusive action, the competitive price for a typical installation is $1.5 million, the quantity sold is 20 per month, and efficient equilibrium prevails at point E_1. However, as long as their actions go undetected, it is in the financial interests of sellers to take steps that would make fire protection installations artificially scarce and raise the price. Graphically, the sellers wish to shift the competitive supply curve,

S_1, leftward to the restricted supply curve, S_2. This could happen as a result of an agreement among sellers to restrict supply (collusion) or as a result of government action. For example, the sellers could lobby the government to pass a law allowing an association of suppliers of fire protection equipment to set production quotas. The proponents might argue that this action raises prices and, in turn, profits. Higher profits would allow the industry to invest in new capital and become more competitive in world markets.

Opponents of artificially restricted supply argue that, whether the producers benefit or not, the lack of competition means that the economy loses. The result of restricting supply is that the efficient equilibrium point, E_1, changes to the inefficient equilibrium point, E_2. At point E_2 the higher price of $2 million is charged, and the lower equilibrium quantity means that firms devote too few resources to installing fire protection equipment.

In Australia, the Trade Practices Act, which is administered by the Australian Competition and Consumer Commission (ACCC), outlaws collusive behaviour of the type illustrated in Exhibit 4.6. Indeed, the example in Exhibit 4.6 resembles a recent case in Queensland, where a fire protection industry cartel was responsible for raising prices of alarm installations by 15 per cent and sprinkler installations by 10 per cent. The

To get a feel for the types of market failure that the Australian Competition and Consumer Commission (ACCC) deals with, visit their website at **www.accc.gov.au**.

Exhibit 4.6 Rigging the fire protection market

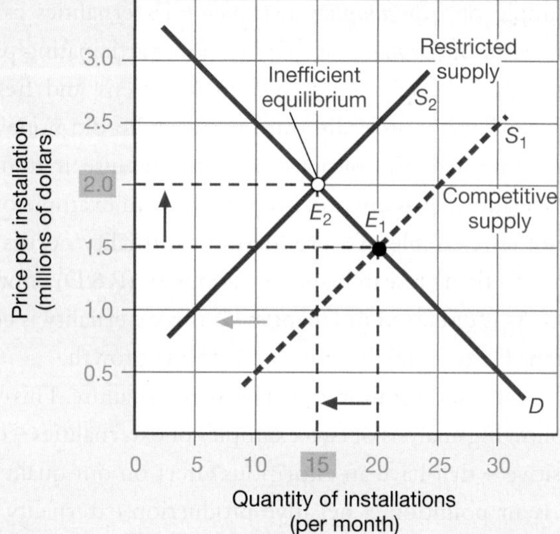

At efficient equilibrium point E_1, sellers compete. As a result, the price per installation charged is $1.5 million and the quantity of installations undertaken is 20. Suppose suppliers use collusion, government intervention or other means to restrict the supply of this product. The decrease in supply from S_1 to S_2 establishes inefficient equilibrium E_2. At E_2, firms charge the higher price of $2 million and the equilibrium quantity of installations falls to 15. Thus, the outcome of restricted supply is that the market fails because firms use too few resources to produce fire protection installations at an artificially higher price.

ACCC estimated that the effect of these higher prices was that members of the cartel could pocket an additional $5 million per annum at the expense of the building owners, their tenants and, ultimately, the consumer. Among the clients named as victims of the cartel were two large universities, an airport, an aged people's home, a soft drink manufacturer and two shopping centres. As a result of successful action by the ACCC against them, firms involved in the cartel, and some of their employees, have paid fines totalling millions of dollars as a penalty for their illegal (and unethical) behaviour.

Externalities

Externality A cost or benefit imposed on people other than the consumers and producers of a good or service.

INFOTRAC®
externalities

There must be competition among both producers and consumers for markets to function properly. However, even if markets are competitive, some markets may still fail because they suffer from the presence of side-effects economists call **externalities**. An externality is a cost or benefit imposed on people other than the consumers and producers of a good or service. Externalities are also called *spillover effects* or *neighbourhood effects*. People other than consumers and producers who are affected by these side-effects of market exchanges are called *third parties*. Externalities may be either negative or positive; that is, they may be detrimental or beneficial to the third party. Suppose you are trying to study and your neighbour is listening to Metallica at full blast on the stereo. The action of your neighbour is imposing an unwanted *external cost* or *negative externality* on you and other third parties who are trying to study or sleep. Because it results from your neighbour's consumption of music, this is an example of a *consumption externality*. Externalities can also result in an *external benefit* or *positive externality* to non-participating parties. When householders proudly display their beautiful gardens and freshly painted homes, neighbours and visitors are third parties who did none of the work but enjoy the benefit of the pleasant scenery. Because it results from the production of beautiful gardens and homes, this is an example of a *production externality*. Another example of a production externality occurs when some of the benefits of a firm's research and development (R&D) effort is captured by other firms. As is discussed in Chapter 12, this externality is considered to be an important factor contributing to economic growth.

Externalities are not a minor aspect of market failure. This will become clear in the following analysis of two examples of externalities – one negative, the other positive – that have an enormous effect on our quality of life. The first of these is air pollution, a negative production externality that has the potential to contribute to global warming and climate change. The second externality is the massive reduction in disease and death that accompanies widespread immunisation. This is a positive consumption externality.

A graphical analysis of pollution

Exhibit 4.7 provides a graphical analysis of two markets that fail to include externalities in their market prices unless the government takes corrective action. Exhibit 4.7(a) shows a market for steel in which steel firms burn coal and pollute the environment. Demand curve D and supply curve S_1 establish the inefficient equilibrium E_1 in the steel market. Not included in S_1 are the *external costs* to the public because the steel firms are not paying for the damage from smoke emissions. If steel firms discharge smoke and ash into the atmosphere, foul air reduces property values, raises health care costs, contributes to global warming and, in general, erodes the quality of life. Because supply curve S_1 does not include these external costs, they are also not included in the price of steel, P_1. In short, the absence of the cost of pollution in the price of steel means that the firms produce more steel and pollution than is socially desirable.

S_2 is the supply curve that would exist if the external costs of respiratory illness, dirty homes, climate change and other undesirable side-effects are included. Once S_2 includes the costs for environmental damage, the equilibrium price rises to P_2 and the equilibrium quantity becomes Q_2. At the efficient equilibrium point E_2, steel firms are paying the full cost and using fewer resources to produce the lower quantity of steel at Q_2.

When the supply curve fails to include negative external costs, the equilibrium price is artificially low and the equilibrium quantity artificially high.

CONCLUSION

Pollution taxes and regulation are just two of the ways in which society can correct the market failure of pollution.

1 *Pollution taxes.* This approach involves government levying a tax per tonne of output equal to the external cost imposed on society when the firm dumps pollution into the air. This action inhibits production by imposing an additional production cost per tonne from the pollution taxes, and shifts the supply curve leftward from S_1 to S_2. The objective is to change the equilibrium from E_1 to E_2 and eliminate the overuse of resources devoted to steel production and its pollution. Under this approach, the government is in effect charging the producer the amount that it would have to pay to affected third parties for them to willingly have the pollution costs imposed upon them. Thus, if the tax is set at the correct level, the revenue it raises could be used to fully compensate those damaged by the pollution. The market would be operating efficiently. Furthermore, the tax might encourage producers to install pollution-control equipment to minimise their pollution tax liability. Can you explain why this is sure to happen when pollution taxes are high but pollution control costs are low? (Tip: try using marginal analysis.)

2 *Regulation.* An alternative approach is to legislate standards that force firms to reduce their emissions as a condition of remaining in business. (Typically, emissions will be reduced but not eliminated because the costs of elimination are enormous compared with the costs of a substantial reduction.) Emissions reduction means a firm must buy, install and

Exhibit 4.7 **Externalities in the steel and immunisation markets**

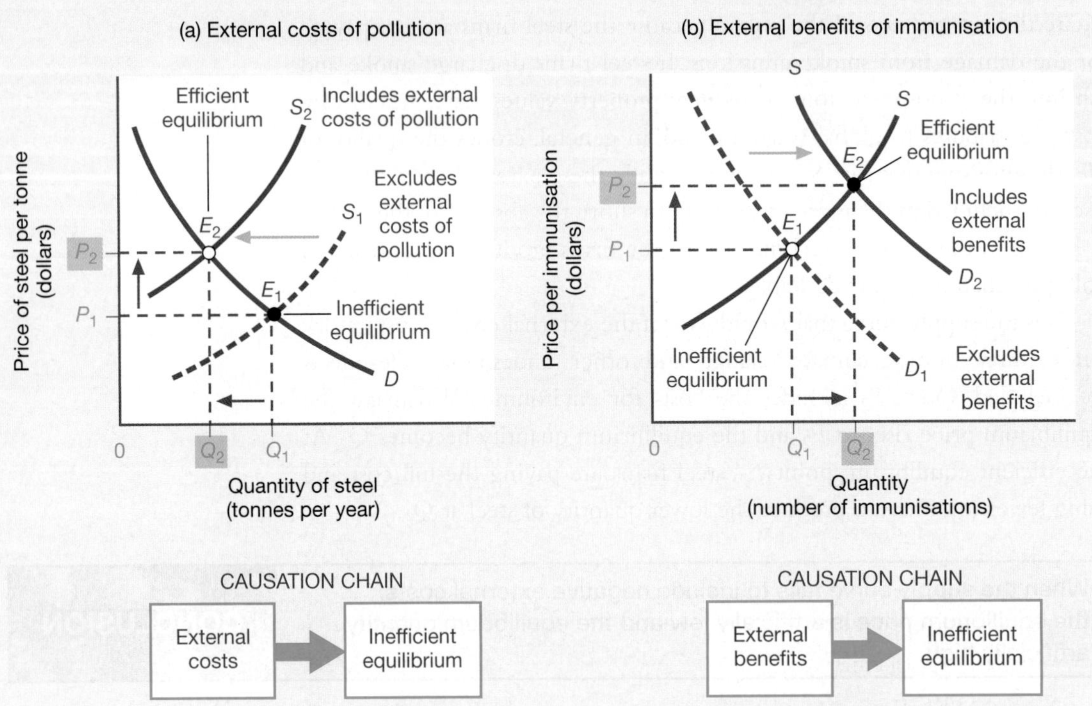

In part (a), resources are over-allocated at inefficient equilibrium E_1 because steel firms do not include the cost per tonne of pollution. Supply curve S_2 includes the external costs of pollution. If firms are required to purchase equipment to remove pollution or to pay a tax on pollution, the economy can move towards the efficient equilibrium of E_2.

Part (b) demonstrates that external benefits cause an under-allocation of resources. At equilibrium point E_2, the efficient output of immunisation services is obtained if the government pays a subsidy equal to the external benefit per shot.

maintain pollution-control equipment. When the extra cost of the pollution equipment is added to the production cost per tonne of steel, the initial supply curve S_1 shifts leftward. In order to simplify matters, let us assume it shifts to supply curve S_2. This means regulation has forced the market equilibrium to change from E_1 to E_2. At point E_2, the firm uses fewer resources to produce a smaller output of steel per year. Note that, because elimination of emissions is so costly, the community is still experiencing pollution and its attendant costs. That is, the negative externality continues. In this approach, because no tax revenue is raised, there is no basis for potential compensation for these remaining costs. The market will thus be operating more efficiently than previously, but it will not be operating as efficiently as it would with the tax-based approach, where tax revenues could fully compensate third parties.

Of the two approaches discussed here (there are more!) economists prefer the tax-based solution. Not only does it give greater efficiency, but it also allows greater flexibility to both the polluter and the government. Under the tax-based solution, polluters can choose between paying the tax and installing pollution control equipment, and the government can easily vary the tax rate.

A graphical analysis of immunisation

As explained above, the supply curve can understate the *external costs* of a good or service. Now you will see that the demand curve can understate the external benefits of a good or service. One of the marvels of modern medicine is that it is possible to vaccinate against many life-threatening diseases, including polio, measles and whooping cough. This is best done through immunisation of children – usually in the first two years of life. Should this immunisation be paid for by consumers, or should it be subsidised by government? Exhibit 4.7(b) illustrates the market for immunisation. Demand curve D_1 reflects the price consumers (the parents of children) would pay for shots to receive the benefit of a reduced probability of infection. Supply curve S shows the quantities of shots suppliers offer for sale at different prices. At equilibrium point E_1, the market fails to achieve an efficient allocation of resources. The reason is that, when children are vaccinated, other children whose parents did not purchase shots (called *free riders*) also benefit because these diseases are now less likely to spread. Once demand curve D_2 includes external benefits to non-consumers of child immunisation, the efficient equilibrium of E_2 is established. At Q_2, sellers devote greater resources to immunisation and the under-allocation of resources is eliminated.

How can society prevent market failure in the market for immunisation? Two approaches follow:

1 *Special subsidies*. One possible solution would be for the government to make a payment to parents for each child immunised. This would mean the government pays each citizen a dollar payment equal to the amount of external benefits per immunisation undertaken. Since the subsidy amount is payable at any price along the demand curve, the demand curve in Exhibit 4.7(b) shifts rightward from D_1 to D_2. In the process the efficient equilibrium price and quantity are achieved at E_2. In Australia, child immunisation is provided free of charge. Although this means that immunisation rates are far higher than they would be if parents were required to pay the full market price, declining immunisation rates in recent decades have led to the view that not enough children are being immunised. Rather than coax further immunisations from parents by paying a subsidy in addition to providing free immunisation, the Australian government has decided to regulate the market in another way. We now turn to the second approach.

Read about Australia's immunisation programs and policies on the Immunise Australia Program page at **www.immunise.health.gov.au**.

PART 1

2 *Regulation*. The government could boost consumption by passing laws requiring all parents to immunise their children. This would shift the demand curve rightward. This authoritarian approach to the problem is, however, difficult to pursue in a thriving democracy. This explains why the Australian government has tried to raise immunisation rates by restricting the benefits available to families whose children have not been immunised. Immunisation is not compulsory, but a decision not to immunise carries with it the high cost of loss of family benefits. This high cost results in the required rightward shift of the demand curve that might otherwise be brought about by a decision to make immunisation compulsory or by the payment of a subsidy.

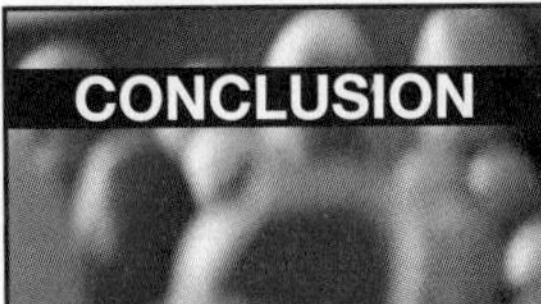

When externalities are present, market failure gives incorrect price and quantity signals and, as a result, resources are misallocated. External costs result in the market over-allocating resources, and external benefits result in under-allocating resources.

Public goods

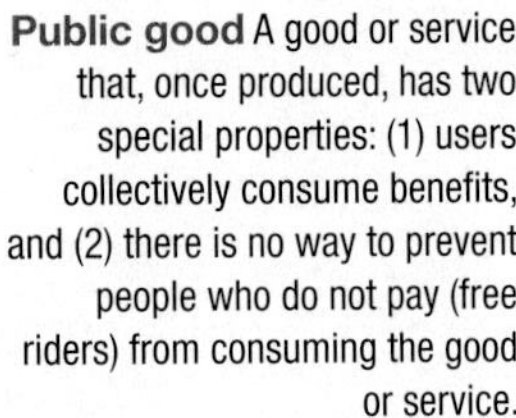

Public good A good or service that, once produced, has two special properties: (1) users collectively consume benefits, and (2) there is no way to prevent people who do not pay (free riders) from consuming the good or service.

National defence is an example of a **public good**, a good or service that the government, rather than the market, must provide if it is to be made available in sufficient quantity. A public good is a good or service that, once produced, has two special properties: (1) users collectively consume benefits, and (2) there is no way to prevent people who do not pay (free riders) from consuming the good or service.

public good

To see why the marketplace fails, imagine that a company called C-Surveillance commences patrols of the Australian coast, and offers to sell these coast watch services to people who want private protection against entry of illegal immigrants into Australia. First, once the system is operational, everyone in the country benefits from a reduced incidence of illegal immigration. Second, the *non-exclusive* nature of a public good means that it is impossible or very costly for any purchaser of coast watch services to prevent non-purchasers, the free riders, from reaping the benefits.

Given the two properties of a public good, why would any private individual purchase a C-Surveillance coast watch service? Why not take a free ride and wait until someone else buys coastal surveillance? Each person therefore wants a surveillance system, but each person does not want to bear the cost of the system when everyone shares in the benefits. As a result, C-Surveillance goes broke and the market fails to provide coast watch services. Everyone hopes that no illegal immigrants enter before someone finally decides to purchase a surveillance system. Government can solve this public goods problem by providing coastal surveillance services and taxing the public to pay. Note that, while government must provide public goods, there is no need for it to actually undertake their production. This task can be outsourced to the private sector. Unlike a private firm, the government can use force to collect payments and prevent the free-rider problem. Other examples of public goods include the judicial system, street lighting, maritime navigation marks and the quarantine service.

If public goods are made available only in the marketplace, people wait for someone else to pay and the result is an under-production or zero production of public goods.

Income inequality

In the cases of insufficient competition, externalities and public goods, the marketplace is inefficient because it allocates too few or too many resources to producing particular outputs. However, even when these market failures are absent and the market is operating efficiently, it may be instrumental in producing a very unequal distribution of income. Under the impersonal price system, top golfers, CEOs of large corporations and medical specialists can earn very high incomes, while unskilled workers and the disabled earn very low incomes – if they are able to earn an income at all. Not all economists agree that these differences in incomes constitute market failure. Those who believe they do not point to the strong incentive effects that income inequality provides. Nonetheless, there is widespread support for a policy of reducing income inequality below the level that would prevail if governments did not intervene in the market. This support is evidenced by the widespread adoption in all developed countries of income redistribution mechanisms such as progressive income taxes and payment of welfare benefits to those most in need. But how equal should the distribution of income be, and how much government intervention is required to achieve this goal? Some people wish to remove most inequality of income. Others argue for the government to provide a 'safety net' minimum income level for all citizens while higher incomes are lightly taxed so that they continue to act as an incentive to develop skills, work hard and accumulate wealth.

Should there be a war on drugs?

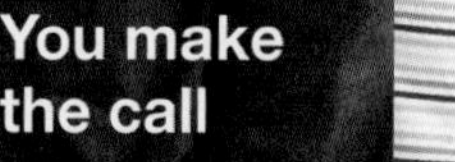

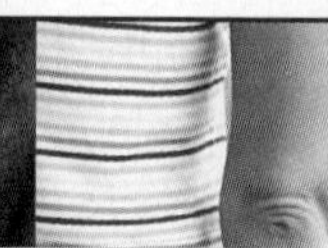

Australian governments fight the use of illegal drugs, such as marijuana, heroin and cocaine, in a variety of ways including close Customs scrutiny, confiscation of drugs and drug moneys and the imposition of jail sentences for dealers and users. Drug offences are taken so seriously in some Asian countries that drug trafficking carries a mandatory death sentence. What is the market failure that motivates governments to interfere with the market for drugs: lack of competition, externalities, public goods or income inequality?

Key concepts

Price ceiling
Price floor
Market failure
Public good
Externality

Summary

- **Price ceilings** and **price floors** are maximum and minimum prices enacted by law to prevent the forces of supply and demand determining prices in the market. A price ceiling is a maximum price mandated by government, and a price floor is a minimum legal price. If a price ceiling is set below the equilibrium price, a shortage will persist. If a price floor is set above the equilibrium price, a surplus will persist.

Price ceiling

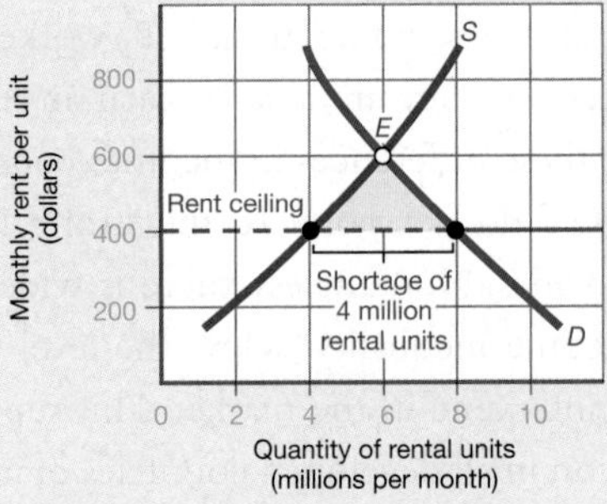

Price floor

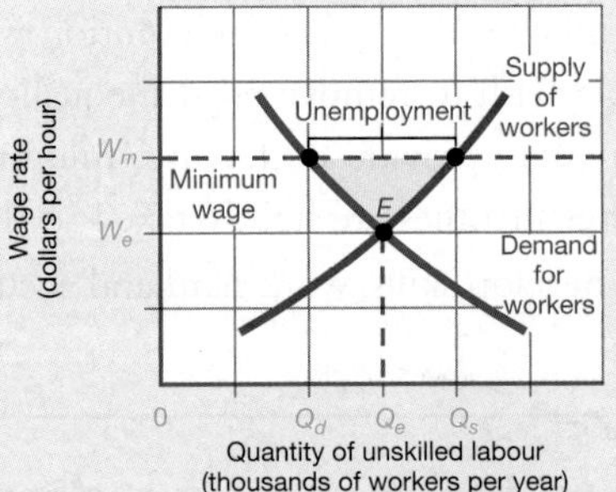

- **Market failure** is a situation in which the market mechanism operates inefficiently and, as a result, does not achieve the most desirable results. Sources of market failure include lack of competition, externalities, public goods and income inequality. Although sometimes controversial, government intervention is a possible way to correct market failure.

- An **externality** is a cost or benefit of a good or service imposed on people who are not buyers or sellers of that good or service. Pollution is an example of an external cost. Because this cost is not incurred by the polluting firm, it is using too many resources to produce too much of the product responsible for the pollution. Two basic approaches to solving this market failure are pollution taxes and regulation. Immunisation provides external benefits. Because buyers of immunisation services base their purchases on the benefit to themselves and ignore the benefits to those who are not immunised, the amount of immunisation services purchased is too low and too few resources are allocated to the production of these services. Two basic solutions to this type of market failure are special subsidies or laws making consumption compulsory.

Externalities

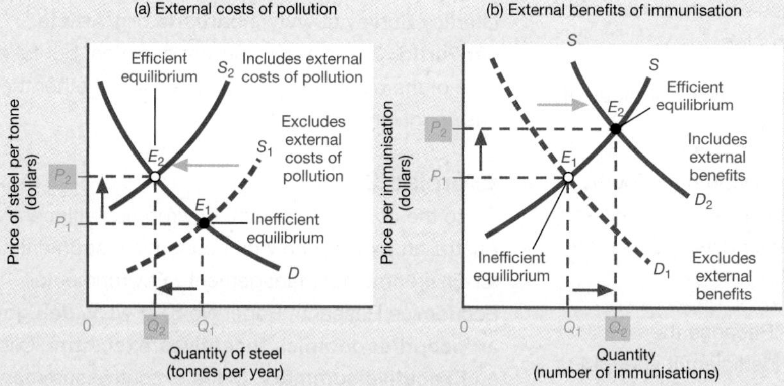

- A **public good** is a good or service that (1) is consumed collectively and (2) cannot be consumed by one person without others being able to consume it, regardless of whether they pay. If public goods such as national defence, coastal surveillance or street lighting are not provided by government they will be under-supplied or not provided at all.

Study questions and problems

1 Market researchers have studied the market for rice, and their estimates for the supply of, and the demand for, rice per month are as follows:

Price per kilo	Quantity demanded (millions of kilos)	Quantity supplied (millions of kilos)
$2.50	100	500
2.00	200	400
1.50	300	300
1.00	400	200
0.50	500	100

a Using the above data, graph the demand for rice and the supply of rice. Identify the equilibrium point as *E* and use dotted lines to connect *E* to the equilibrium price on the price axis and the equilibrium quantity on the quantity axis.

b Suppose the government enacts a rice support price of $2.00 per kilo. Indicate this action on your graph and explain the effect on the rice market. Why would the government establish such a support price?

c Now assume the government decides to set a price ceiling of $1.00 per kilo. Show and explain how this legally imposed price affects your graph of the rice market. What objective could the government be trying to achieve by establishing such a price ceiling?

2 Use a graph to show the impact on the price of Korean cars sold in Australia if Korean exporters restrict the number of cars destined for the Australian market. Now draw another graph to show the effect of the change in the Australian price of Korean cars on the price of Australian-made cars in Australia. Explain the market outcome in each graph and the link between the two graphs.

3 Using market supply and demand analysis, explain why it is sometimes said that one person's pay rise is another person's job.

4 What are the advantages and disadvantages of the price system?

5 Suppose a market is in equilibrium and both demand and supply increase. What happens to the equilibrium price if demand increases more than supply?

6 Consider this statement: 'Because the government is inherently inefficient it should not be responsible for providing any goods or services.' Do you agree or disagree? Explain.

7 Suppose firms that manufacture fertilisers are emitting large amounts of pollution into the air. Suggest two ways in which the government can deal with this situation.

8 Explain the impact of external costs and external benefits on resource allocation.

9 Why are public goods not produced in sufficient quantities by private markets?

10 Which of the following are public goods?
   a the judicial system
   b pencils
   c the quarantine service
   d the Great Wall of China
   e contact lenses

Online exercises

Exercise 1

For more than 100 years economists have used lighthouses as the example, par excellence, of a public good. They have argued that, if an attempt were made to charge users of lighthouses for the services of the light beam that enables them to determine their position, it would impossible to prevent vessels from using the services without paying (free riding). Nobel prize-winning economist, Ronald Coase, took issue with this view in a famous paper titled 'The Lighthouse in Economics'. Read more about Coase and the flavour of his argument about whether or not lighthouses are, in fact, public goods by reading a short biography of him in the *Concise Encyclopedia of Economics* at **www.econlib.org/library/Enc/bios/Coase.html**. Now go to the Heartland Institute's page containing the Minneapolis Federal Reserve Bank's National Economic Literacy Survey at **www.heartland.org/Article.cfm?artId=337**. Answer the last question, but take note of the editor's reservations about whether the answer given is correct.

Exercise 2

Go to the contents page of 'Environmental Incentives: Australian Experience with Economic Instruments for Environmental Management', Environmental Economics Research Paper No 5, at **www.deh.gov.au/pcepd/economics/incentives/exec.html**. Click on **Executive summary**. In the executive summary find and list the main advantages of using economic instruments as opposed to regulatory mechanisms for environmental control. What are some of the impediments to acceptance of environmental controls in the wider community?

Exercise 3

One solution often suggested for reducing pollution and lessening parking problems at the workplace is to promote alternative forms of transportation. For example, some people propose the increased use of bicycles to alleviate these problems. Review 'Bicycle Parking at the Workplace' at **www.ntl.bts.gov/DOCS/mapc.html**, a US study conducted by the Metropolitan Area Planning Council. What suggestions does this study offer? Does the study advance a realistic argument? Why or why not? Now consider the market for pushbikes. Using graphical analysis, explain how the development of small, lightweight, electric-powered scooters might affect this market.

Answers to 'You make the call'

How can better pricing policies help solve our infrastructure problems?

Exhibit 4.8 represents the market for reticulated water. You can see that an increase in demand for

PART 1

water in summer leads to a higher equilibrium price. If the water authority charges just one price no matter what the season, and if this price is lower than the equilibrium price for summer, then water shortages in summer can be expected to occur. Rather than solve this problem by building more infrastructure (and increasing the negative externalities it causes), a simple two-season pricing policy could bring about equilibrium in each season. Similar arguments can be applied to provision of roads and electricity. If you said that it is demand variations that prompt economists to call for different prices at different times of the day, week or year, YOU ARE CORRECT.

Exhibit 4.8

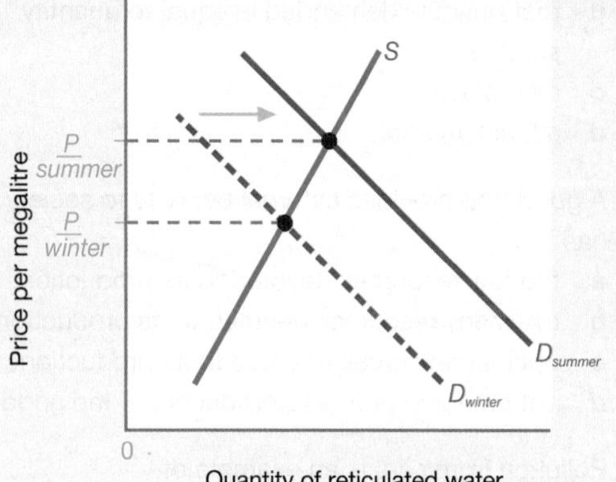

Skivvy crew upset at scalpers' yummy profit

Scalpers are evidence of a shortage, due to which not all buyers are able to find tickets at the official price. As shown in Exhibit 4.9, scalpers (sometimes illegally) sell tickets they have purchased at the official price for a higher price in order to profit from the shortage. Shortages result when prices are restricted below equilibrium, just as happens with a price ceiling. If you said scalping occurs when the set price is akin to a price ceiling, YOU ARE CORRECT.

The Wiggles may set concert prices below the market equilibrium because they believe that social mores dictate that prices should be within the reach of ordinary families. On the other hand, their concern may be that higher prices would alienate their customers, resulting in a sullying of their reputation and a subsequent drop in demand for their shows. If you identified the possibility of these two sources of motivation for the Wiggles' pricing policy but said that either could be regarded as the pursuit of enlightened self-interest, YOU ARE CORRECT. Nonetheless, you may think that the first motivation involves self-interest that is more enlightened than the second!

Exhibit 4.9

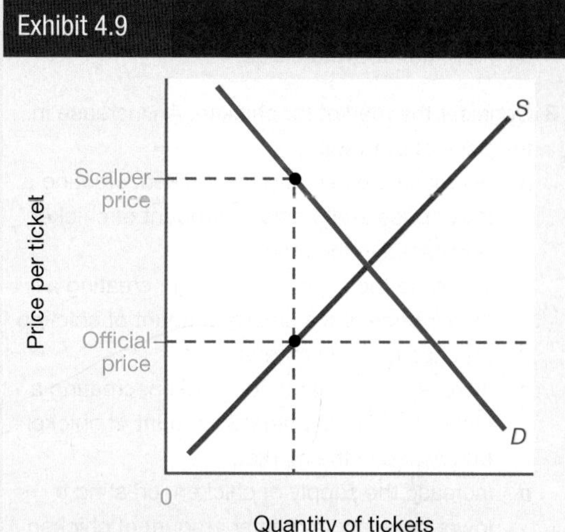

Should there be a war on drugs?

Drug use affects not only the person using the drugs, but other members of society as well. Drug use can be associated with diminished responsibility and low motivation. The spread of communicable diseases is also associated with intravenous drug use. When one person's actions affect others not involved in the decision to buy or sell, the market fails to operate efficiently. If you said the market failure motivating government intervention in the drug market is externalities because some drug users impose costs on non-users, YOU ARE CORRECT.

Multiple-choice questions

1 Suppose prices for new homes have risen, yet sales of new homes have also risen. We can conclude that
- **a** the demand for new homes has risen.
- **b** the law of demand has been violated.
- **c** new firms have entered the construction industry.
- **d** construction firms must be facing higher costs.

2 Which of the following statements is true of a market?
- **a** An increase in demand, with no change in supply, will increase the equilibrium price and quantity.

- **b** An increase in supply, with no change in demand, will decrease the equilibrium price and the equilibrium quantity.
- **c** A decrease in supply, with no change in demand, will decrease the equilibrium price and increase the equilibrium quantity.
- **d** All of the above are true.

3 Consider the market for chicken. An increase in the price of pork will

- **a** decrease the demand for chicken, creating a lower price and a smaller amount of chicken purchased in the market.
- **b** decrease the supply of chicken, creating a higher price and a smaller amount of chicken purchased in the market.
- **c** increase the demand for chicken, creating a higher price and a greater amount of chicken purchased in the market.
- **d** increase the supply of chicken, creating a lower price and a greater amount of chicken purchased in the market.

4 An increase in consumer income increases the demand for restaurant meals. As a result of the adjustment to a new equilibrium, there is

- **a** a leftward shift of the supply curve.
- **b** a downward movement along the supply curve.
- **c** a rightward shift of the supply curve.
- **d** an upward movement along the supply curve.

5 An increase in the wage paid to grape pickers will cause the

- **a** demand curve for grapes to shift to the right, resulting in higher prices for grapes.
- **b** demand curve for grapes to shift to the left, resulting in lower prices for grapes.
- **c** supply curve for grapes to shift to the left, resulting in lower prices for grapes.
- **d** supply curve for grapes to shift to the left, resulting in higher prices for grapes.

6 If the government wants to raise the price of cheese, it will

- **a** take cheese from government storage and sell it.
- **b** encourage farmers to research ways to produce more cheese.
- **c** subsidise purchases of farm equipment.
- **d** encourage farmers to produce less cheese.

7 Which of the following is the *least* likely result from rent controls set below the equilibrium price for rental housing?

- **a** Shortages and black markets will result.
- **b** The existing rental housing will deteriorate.
- **c** The supply of rental housing will increase rapidly.
- **d** People will demand more apartments than are available.

8 Suppose the equilibrium price set by supply and demand is lower than the price ceiling set by the government. The result will be

- **a** a shortage.
- **b** that quantity demanded is equal to quantity supplied.
- **c** a surplus.
- **d** a black market.

9 A good that provides external benefits to society has

- **a** too few resources devoted to its production.
- **b** too many resources devoted to its production.
- **c** optimal resources devoted to its production.
- **d** not provided profits to producers of the good.

10 Pollution from cars is an example of

- **a** a harmful opportunity cost.
- **b** a negative externality.
- **c** a production dislocation.
- **d** none of the above.

11 Which of the following is the *best* example of a public good?

- **a** medical services
- **b** education
- **c** defence
- **d** government buildings

12 A public good is any good or service that

- **a** cannot be made available to one consumer without other consumers benefiting from its availability.
- **b** must be distributed equally to all citizens in equal shares.
- **c** is never produced by government.
- **d** is described by answers **a** and **c** above.

Elasticity of demand and supply

5

Suppose you are the manager of the Feral Possums rock group. You are considering raising your ticket price for an upcoming concert, and you wonder how the fans will react. You have studied economics and know the law of demand. When the price of a ticket rises, the quantity demanded goes down, ceteris paribus. But you need to know more than this. You really need to know just how many fewer tickets fans will purchase if the band boosts the ticket price, because the proceeds from the concert will depend on both the ticket price and the number of tickets sold. Which ticket price should you choose? Is it better to charge a higher ticket price and sell fewer tickets or to charge a lower ticket price and sell more tickets?

The answer depends on changes in *total revenue* or sales as we move upward along points on Feral Possums' demand curve. Let us assume that, if the price for a Feral Possums concert is $25 per ticket, 20 000 tickets will be sold; and if the price is $30 per ticket, 10 000 tickets will be sold. Thus, a $5 increase price cuts in half the number of tickets sold. At $30 per ticket, sales revenue will be $300 000. But if you charge the lower price of $25, the group will take in $500 000 for a concert. Okay, you say, what happens at $20 per ticket?

This chapter teaches you to calculate price elasticity of demand, which is a measure of the responsiveness of quantity demanded of a good or service to changes in its price. Then you will see how this concept of elasticity relates to total revenue. This knowledge of the sensitivity of demand is vital for pricing and targeting markets for goods and services. Next, you will see how quantity demanded responds to changes in consumer income, and how it responds to changes in the prices of related goods. The chapter concludes by relating the concept of price elasticity to supply and to the impact of taxation on a market for a good or service.

In this chapter, you will examine these economics questions:

- Can total revenue from a Feral Possums concert remain unchanged regardless of changes in the ticket price?
- How sensitive is the quantity of university courses demanded to changes in their price?
- If the sellers of a product are required to pay a tax on the product they sell, does this mean that consumers are not affected by the tax?
- If the price of a good or service sold by a company rises, will the decrease in quantity demanded one year after the rise be larger or smaller than the decrease one month after the rise?
- Would a policy designed to increase the demand for scientific research bring about a large or a small increase in the quantity of scientific research supplied?

Price elasticity of demand

In Chapter 3, you studied the demand curve. The focus was on the law of demand, which states that there is an inverse relationship between the price and the quantity demanded of a good or service. This chapter stresses measuring the *relative size* of changes in the price and in the quantity demanded. Now we ask: by *what percentage* does the quantity demanded rise when the price falls by, say, 10 per cent?

The price elasticity of demand midpoint formula

Economists use a **price elasticity of demand** formula to measure the degree of consumer responsiveness, or sensitivity, to a change in price. Price elasticity of demand is the ratio of the percentage change in the quantity demanded of a product to a percentage change in its price. Suppose a private school's enrolment drops by 20 per cent because fees rise by 10 per cent. In this case, the price elasticity of demand is 2 (–20 per cent/+10 per cent). The number 2 means that the quantity demanded (enrolment) changes 2 per cent for each 1 per cent change in price (fees). Note that there should be a minus sign in front of the 2. This is because price and quantity under the law of demand are inversely related – they move in *opposite* directions. However, economists drop the minus sign because we know from the law of demand that quantity demanded and price are always inversely related.

Price elasticity of demand The ratio of the percentage change in the quantity demanded of a product to a percentage change in its price.

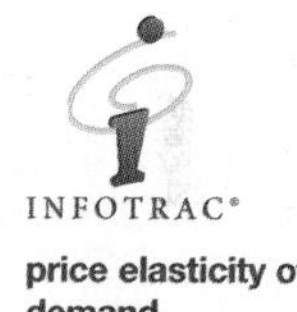

price elasticity of demand

The number 2 is an *elasticity coefficient*, which economists use to measure the degree of elasticity. The price elasticity of demand formula is

$$E_d = \frac{\text{percentage change in quantity demanded}}{\text{percentage change in price}}$$

where E_d is the elasticity of demand. Here you must take care – *there can be a problem using this formula*. Let's return to our rock group example from the Chapter Preview. Suppose Feral Possums *raises* its ticket price from \$25 to \$30 and the number of seats sold falls from 20 000 to 10 000. This would involve a move from point *B* to point *A* on the demand curve in Exhibit 5.1. We can compute the elasticity coefficient for this change as

$$E_d = \frac{\%\Delta Q}{\%\Delta P} = \frac{\dfrac{10\,000 - 20\,000}{20\,000}}{\dfrac{30 - 25}{25}} = \frac{50\%}{20\%} = 2.5$$

Now consider the elasticity coefficient computed between these same points on Feral Possums' demand curve when the price is lowered rather than raised. You can see in Exhibit 5.1 that starting at \$30 per ticket and lowering the ticket price to \$25 causes the number of seats sold to rise from 10 000 to 20 000. In the case of this move from point *A* to point *B*, the rock group computes a very different elasticity coefficient, as follows:

PART 2

Exhibit 5.1 **The midpoint formula**

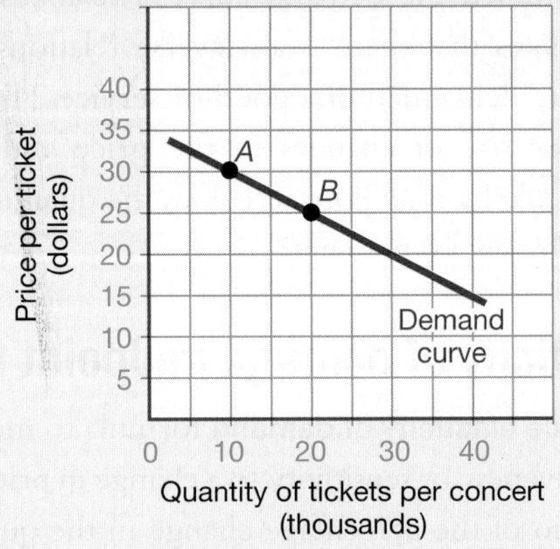

The price elasticity of demand coefficient calculated for a move from point *A* to point *B* is different from that calculated for a move from *B* to *A*. The midpoint formula enables an average coefficient to be calculated for the arc of the demand curve from *A* to *B*.

$$E_d = \frac{\%\Delta Q}{\%\Delta P} = \frac{\dfrac{20\,000 - 10\,000}{10\,000}}{\dfrac{25 - 30}{30}} = \frac{100\%}{17\%} = 5.9$$

There is a reason for the disparity in the elasticity coefficients between the same two points on a demand curve (2.5 if price is raised, 5.9 if price is cut). The natural approach is to select the initial point as the base and then compute a percentage change. However, price elasticity of demand involves changes between two possible initial base points (P_1, Q_1 or P_2, Q_2). Economists solve this problem of different base points by using the *midpoint* between the two possible initial base points. The *midpoint formula* for price elasticity of demand is

$$E_d = \frac{\text{change in quantity}}{\text{sum of quantities}/2} \div \frac{\text{change in price}}{\text{sum of prices}/2}$$

which can be expressed as

$$E_d = \frac{\%\Delta Q}{\%\Delta P} = \frac{\dfrac{Q_2 - Q_1}{(Q_1 + Q_2)/2}}{\dfrac{P_2 - P_1}{(P_1 + P_2)/2}}$$

where Q_1 represents the first quantity demanded, Q_2 represents the second quantity demanded and P_1 and P_2 are the first and second prices. Expressed this way, we divide the change in quantity demanded by the *average* quantity demanded. Then this value is divided by the change in the price divided by the *average* price. The midpoint formula is also commonly called the *arc elasticity formula* because it refers to elasticity over an arc of the demand curve. In our example, we are referring to the midpoint of the arc from point *A* to point *B* in Exhibit 5.1.

It does not matter if Q_1 or P_1 is the first number in each term. This is because we are finding averages. Also note that you can drop the 2 as a divisor of both the $(Q_1 + Q_2)$ and the $(P_1 + P_2)$ terms because the 2s in the numerator and the denominator cancel out. Now we can use the midpoint formula to show that the price elasticity of demand is 3.7 regardless of whether Feral Possums raises the ticket price from \$25 to \$30 or lowers it from \$30 to \$25.

$$E_d = \frac{\dfrac{Q_2 - Q_1}{Q_1 + Q_2}}{\dfrac{P_2 - P_1}{P_1 + P_2}} = \frac{\dfrac{10\,000 - 20\,000}{20\,000 + 10\,000}}{\dfrac{30 - 25}{25 + 30}} = \frac{33\%}{9\%} = 3.7$$

and

$$E_d = \frac{\dfrac{Q_2 - Q_1}{Q_1 + Q_2}}{\dfrac{P_2 - P_1}{P_1 + P_2}} = \frac{\dfrac{20\,000 - 10\,000}{10\,000 + 20\,000}}{\dfrac{25 - 30}{30 + 25}} = \frac{33\%}{9\%} = 3.7$$

The total revenue test of price elasticity of demand

As reflected in the midpoint formula, the *responsiveness* of the quantity demanded to a change in price determines the value of the elasticity coefficient. There are three possibilities, so far as the value of this coefficient is concerned: (1) the numerator is greater than the denominator (demand is elastic); (2) the numerator is less than the denominator (demand is inelastic); and (3) the numerator equals the denominator (demand is unitary elastic). Depending on the value of the elasticity coefficient, a decrease in price may lead to an increase in total revenue, a fall in total revenue or no change in **total revenue**. Total revenue is the total number of dollars a firm earns from sales of a good or service; it is equal to its price multiplied by the quantity demanded. Perhaps the simplest way to tell whether demand is elastic, unitary elastic or inelastic is to observe the response of total revenue as the price of a product changes. Exhibit 5.2 presents three cases that the Feral Possums rock band may confront.

Total revenue The total number of dollars a firm earns from sales of a good or service; it is equal to its price multiplied by the quantity demanded.

Elastic demand ($E_d > 1$)

Elastic demand is a condition in which the percentage change in quantity demanded is greater than the percentage change in price. Demand is elastic when the elasticity coefficient is greater than 1. Suppose Feral Possums' demand curve is as depicted in Exhibit 5.2(a). If the group decreases its ticket price from \$30 to \$20, the quantity demanded increases from 10 000 to 30 000. Using the midpoint formula, this means that a 40 per cent

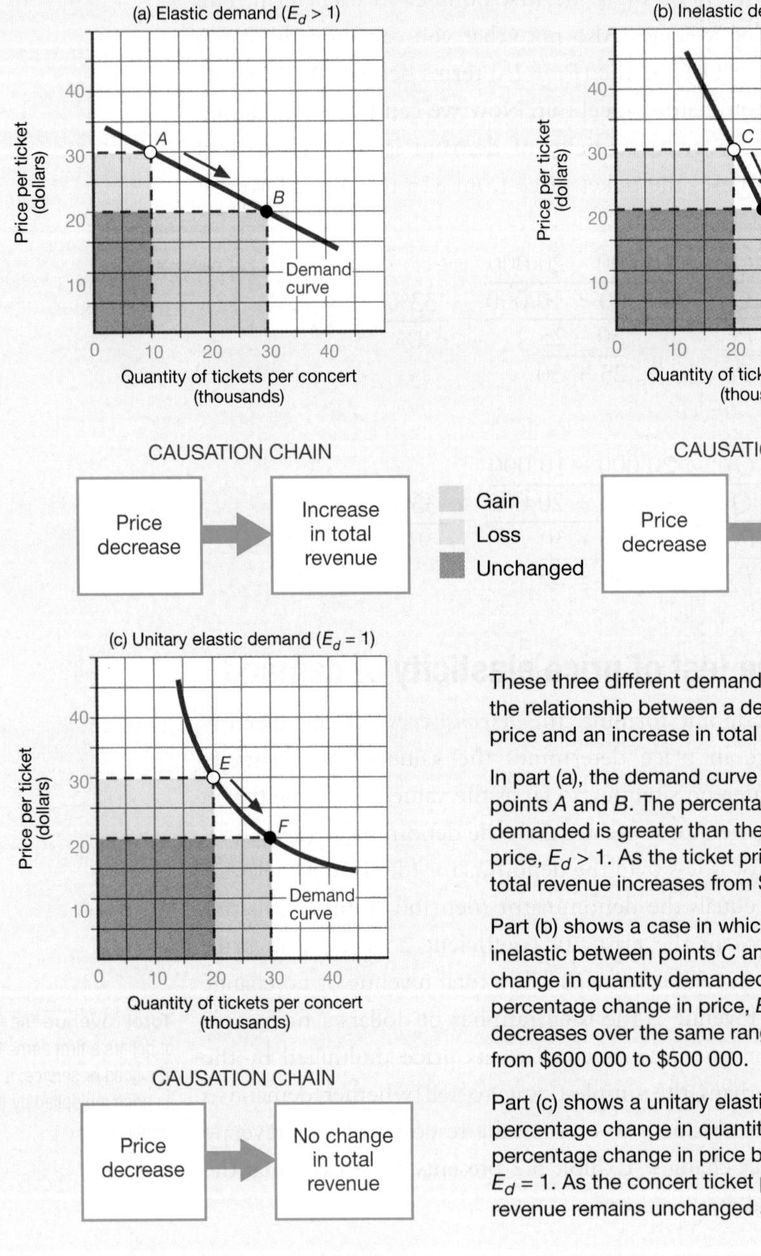

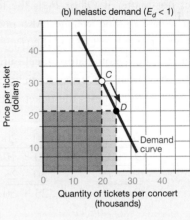

These three different demand curve graphs show the relationship between a decrease in concert ticket price and an increase in total revenue.

In part (a), the demand curve is elastic between points *A* and *B*. The percentage change in quantity demanded is greater than the percentage change in price, $E_d > 1$. As the ticket price falls from \$30 to \$20, total revenue increases from \$300 000 to \$600 000.

Part (b) shows a case in which the demand curve is inelastic between points *C* and *D*. The percentage change in quantity demanded is less than the percentage change in price, $E_d < 1$. As the ticket price decreases over the same range, total revenue falls from \$600 000 to \$500 000.

Part (c) shows a unitary elastic demand curve. The percentage change in quantity demanded equals the percentage change in price between points *E* and *F*, $E_d = 1$. As the concert ticket price decreases, total revenue remains unchanged at \$600 000.

reduction in the average ticket price brings about a 100 per cent increase in average quantity demanded. In other words, the ticket price has decreased by 40 per cent of its average (i.e. \$10/\$25) and demand has increased by 100 per cent of its average (i.e. 20 000/20 000) Thus, $E_d = 2.5$ and demand is **elastic**. Because the percentage change in quantity is greater than the percentage change in price, the drop in price is more than compensated by the rise in quantity and so *total revenue* rises. For example, in Exhibit 5.2(a) the total revenue at $30 is $300 000. The total revenue at $20 is $600 000. Compare the shaded rectangles under the demand curve, representing total revenue at each price. The orange area is an amount of total revenue unaffected by the price change. Note that the blue area gained at $20 per ticket ($400 000) is greater than the green area lost at $30 per ticket ($100 000). This net gain of $300 000 causes the total revenue to increase by this amount when Feral Possums lowers the ticket price from $30 to $20. The important point to note is that, when total revenue increases (decreases) as a result of a fall (rise) in price, demand is elastic.

Elastic demand A condition in which the percentage change in quantity demanded is greater than the percentage change in price.

Inelastic demand ($E_d < 1$)

Inelastic demand is a condition in which the percentage change in quantity demanded is smaller than the percentage change in price. The demand curve in Exhibit 5.2(b) is inelastic. Here a fall in Feral Possums' ticket price from $30 to $20 causes the quantity demanded to increase by just 5000 tickets (20 000 – 25 000 tickets). Using the midpoint formula, a 40 per cent fall in the average ticket price causes a 22 per cent rise in the average quantity demanded. This means that E_d = 0.55 and demand is **inelastic**. Inelastic demand is a condition in which the percentage change in quantity demanded is less than the percentage change in price. Demand is inelastic when the elasticity coefficient is less than 1. When demand is inelastic, the fall in price is not fully compensated by the rise in quantity, and this causes total revenue to fall from $600 000 to $500 000. Note the net change in the shaded rectangles. In general, when total revenue decreases (increases) as a result of a fall (rise) in price, demand is inelastic.

Inelastic demand A condition in which the percentage change in quantity demanded is smaller than the percentage change in price.

Unitary elastic demand ($E_d = 1$)

An interesting case exists when demand curves are neither elastic nor inelastic. Exhibit 5.2(c) is a demand curve in which the percentage change in quantity demanded is exactly the same as the percentage change in price everywhere along the demand curve. This situation occurs when the total amount of money spent on a good or service does not vary with changes in price. For example, if Feral Possums drops the ticket price from $30 to $20, the quantity demanded rises from 20 000 to 30 000. Therefore, using the midpoint formula, a 40 per cent decrease in average price brings about a 40 per cent increase in average quantity demanded. If this is the case, demand is **unitary elastic** (E_d = 1) and the total revenue remains unchanged at $600 000. With unitary elastic demand, because the percentage change in price equals the percentage change in quantity, total revenue does not change as price changes.

Unitary elastic demand A condition in which the percentage change in quantity demanded is equal to the percentage change in price.

Perfectly elastic demand ($E_d = 0$)

Perfectly elastic demand A condition in which a small percentage change in price brings about an infinite percentage change in quantity demanded.

Two extreme cases are shown in Exhibit 5.3. These represent the limits between which the three demand curves explained above fall. Suppose for the sake of argument that a demand curve is horizontal, as shown in Exhibit 5.3(a). At a price of $20, buyers are willing to buy as many tickets as Feral Possums are willing to offer for sale. At higher prices, buyers buy nothing. For example, this means that at $20.01 per ticket or higher, buyers will buy zero tickets. If so, $E_d = \infty$ and demand is *perfectly elastic*. **Perfectly elastic demand** is a condition in which a small percentage change in price brings about an infinite percentage change in quantity demanded.

Exhibit 5.3 Perfectly elastic and perfectly inelastic demand

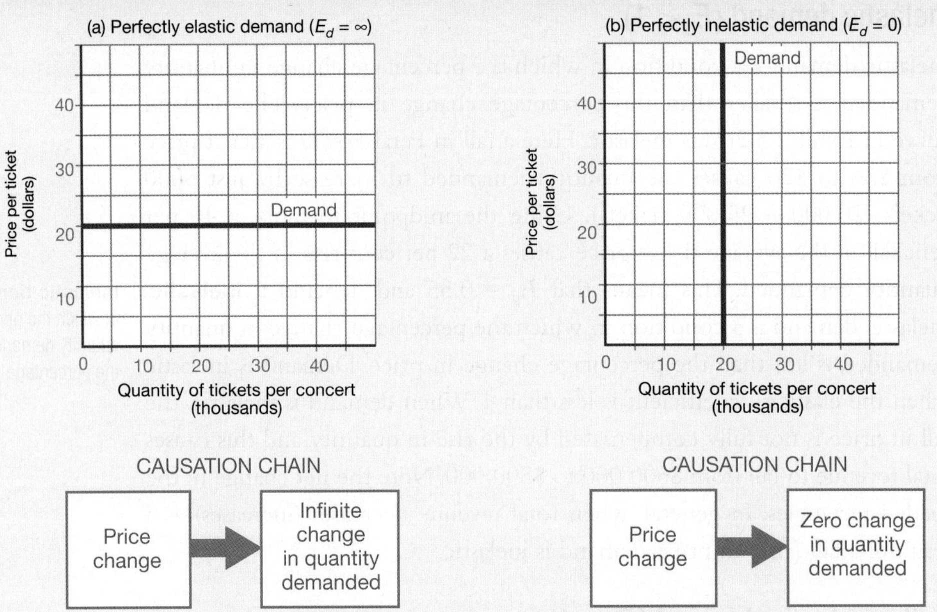

Here two extreme demand curves for Feral Possums concert tickets are represented. Part (a) shows a demand curve that is a horizontal line. Such a demand curve is perfectly elastic. At $20 per ticket, Feral Possums can sell as many concert tickets as they wish. At any price above $20, the quantity demanded falls from an infinite number to zero.

Part (b) shows a demand curve that is a vertical line. This demand curve is perfectly inelastic. No matter what the ticket price, the quantity demanded remains unchanged at 20 000 tickets.

Perfectly inelastic demand ($E_d = 0$)

Perfectly inelastic demand A condition in which the quantity demanded does not change as the price changes.

Exhibit 5.3(b) shows the other extreme case, in which a demand curve is vertical. No matter how high or low the Feral Possums' ticket price is, the quantity demanded is 20 000 tickets. Such a demand curve is **perfectly inelastic** and $E_d = 0$. Perfectly inelastic demand is a condition in which the quantity demanded does not change as the price changes.

Exhibit 5.4 summarises the ranges for price elasticity of demand.

Exhibit 5.4 **Price elasticity of demand terminology**

Elasticity coefficient	Definition	Demand	
$E_d > 1$	Percentage change in quantity demanded is greater than the percentage change in price	Elastic	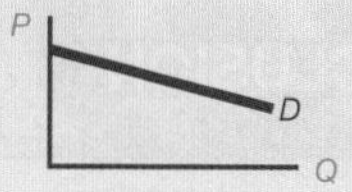
$E_d < 1$	Percentage change in quantity demanded is less than the percentage change in price	Inelastic	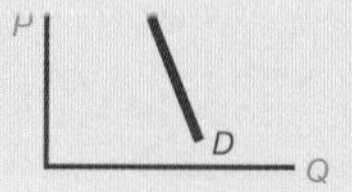
$E_d = 1$	Percentage change in quantity demanded is equal to the percentage change in price	Unitary elastic	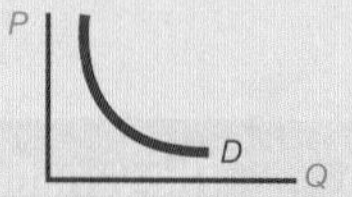
$E_d = \infty$	Percentage change in quantity demanded is infinite in relation to the percentage change in price	Perfectly elastic	
$E_d = 0$	Quantity demanded does not change as the price changes	Perfectly inelastic	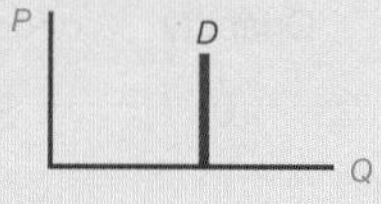

Price elasticity of demand variations along a straight-line demand curve

The price elasticity of demand for a downward-sloping straight-line demand curve varies as we move along the curve. Look at Exhibit 5.5, which shows a linear demand curve in part (a) and the corresponding total revenue curve in part (b). Begin at $40 on the demand curve and move down to $35, to $30, to $25 and so on. The table in Exhibit 5.5 lists variations in the total revenue and the elasticity coefficient (E_d) at different ticket prices. As we move down the upper segment of the demand curve, price elasticity of demand falls and total revenue rises. For example, measured over the price range of $35 to $30, the price elasticity of demand is 4.33 and therefore this segment of demand is elastic ($E_d > 1$). Between these two prices, total revenue increases from $175 to $300. At $20, price elasticity is unitary elastic ($E_d = 1$) and total revenue is maximised at $400. As we move down the lower segment of the demand curve, price elasticity of demand falls below a value of 1.0 and total revenue falls. Over the price range of $15 to $10, for example, the price elasticity of demand is 0.45 and therefore this segment of demand is inelastic ($E_d < 1$). Between these two prices, total revenue falls from $375 to $300.

CONCLUSION On a straight-line demand curve, the price elasticity of demand is different at every point along the curve.

It is no coincidence that the demand curve in Exhibit 5.5(a) displays elastic, unitary elastic, and inelastic demand at different points. In fact, *any downward-sloping straight-line demand curve displays all three of these types of price elasticity of demand*. As we move downward: first there is an elastic range; second, a unitary elastic point; and third, an inelastic range. Why?

Exhibit 5.5 The variation in elasticity and total revenue along a hypothetical demand curve

Calculation of total revenue and elasticity along a hypothetical demand curve

Price	Quantity	Total revenue (thousands of dollars)	Elasticity coefficient (E_d)	Demand
$40	0	$0		
			15.00	Elastic
35	5	175		
			4.33	Elastic
30	10	300		
			2.20	Elastic
25	15	375		
			1.29	Elastic
20	20	400	1.00	Unitary elastic
			0.78	Inelastic
15	25	375		
			0.45	Inelastic
10	30	300		
			0.23	Inelastic
5	35	175		

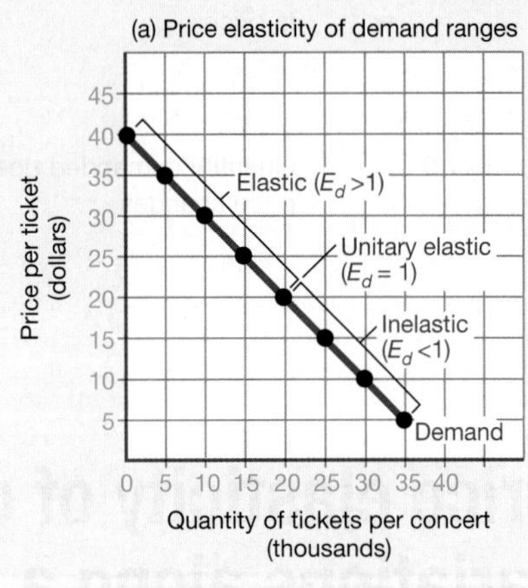

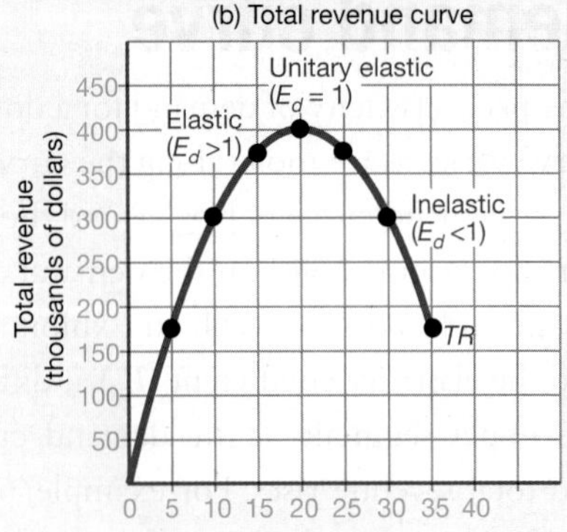

Part (a) shows a straight-line demand curve and the three elasticity possibilities. In the $40–$20 price range, demand is elastic. As price decreases in this range, total revenue increases. At $20, demand is unitary elastic and total revenue is at its maximum. In the $20–$5 price range, demand is inelastic. As price decreases in this range, total revenue decreases. The total revenue (*TR*) curve is plotted in part (b) in order to trace its relationship to price elasticity.

Recall that price elasticity of demand is a ratio of percentage changes. At the upper end of the demand curve, quantities demanded are lower and prices are higher. A change of one unit in quantity demanded is a large percentage change. On the other hand, a $1 price change is a relatively small percentage change. At the lower end of the curve, the situation reverses. A one-unit change in quantity demanded is a small percentage change. A $1 price change is a relatively larger percentage change. Now pause and refer back to parts (a) and (b) of Exhibit 5.2. If we examine changes in price along the entire length of these demand curves, they would have elastic, unitary elastic and inelastic segments.

Exhibit 5.6 summarises the relationships among elasticity, price change and total revenue.

Exhibit 5.6 **Relationships among elasticity, price change and total revenue**

Price elasticity of demand	Elasticity coefficient	Price	Total revenue
Elastic	$E_d > 1$	↑	↓
Elastic	$E_d > 1$	↓	↑
Unitary elastic	$E_d = 1$	↑↓	No change
Inelastic	$E_d < 1$	↑	↑
Inelastic	$E_d < 1$	↓	↓

What explains airline fare structures?

You make the call

The major competitors on Australian domestic airline routes – Qantas, Jetstar and Virgin Blue – have very complicated fare structures. However, if you look closely at their fares you will see that prices are higher for certain times of the day and for certain days of the week when air travel is most popular. Fares for early morning flights at 5 or 6 o'clock are particularly cheap compared to later times. Many fares for international trips are also higher for travellers who have an urgent need to travel – those who have not been able to book ahead. Do you think the creators of these pricing policies had some idea of the elasticity of demand for travel at the crack of dawn, and for travellers who find they have an urgent need to travel? (A cryptic clue may be found in Exhibit 5.7.) What about the ethics of charging higher prices to travellers who are unable to travel at unpopular times?

To see how domestic airfares vary according to the time of day and the day of the week go to the Qantas site (**www.Qantas.com.au**), the Virgin Blue site (**www.virginblue.com.au**) and the Jetstar site (**www.jetstar.com.au**).

Determinants of price elasticity of demand

Economists estimate price elasticity of demand for various goods and services. Exhibit 5.7 presents some of these estimates. You can see that the elasticity coefficients vary a great deal. For example, the demand for cars and for chinaware is elastic. On the other hand, the demand for jewellery and watches and for theatre and opera tickets is inelastic. The demand for tyres and tubes is approximately unitary elastic. What makes the price elasticities of demand for these products different? The following factors cause these differences.

Availability of substitutes

By far the most important determinant of price elasticity of demand is the availability of substitutes. Demand is more elastic for a good or service with close substitutes. If the price of cars rises, consumers can switch to buses, trains, bicycles and walking. The more public transportation is available, the more responsive is quantity demanded of cars to a change in their price.

Exhibit 5.7 **Estimated price elasticities of demand**

Item	Elasticity coefficient	
	Short run	Long run
Motor cars	1.87	2.24
Chinaware	1.54	2.55
Movies	0.87	3.67
Tyres and tubes	0.86	1.19
Commuter rail fares	0.62	1.59
Jewellery and watches	0.41	0.67
Medical care	0.31	0.92
Housing	0.30	1.88
Petrol	0.20	0.70
Theatre and opera tickets	0.18	0.31
Foreign travel	0.14	1.77
Air travel	0.10	2.40

Sources: Robert Archibald & Robert Gillingham, 'An Analysis of the Short-Run Consumer Demand for Gasoline Using Household Survey Data', *Review of Economics and Statistics*, Vol. 62, November 1980, pp. 622–8; Hendrik S. Houthakker & Lester D. Taylor, *Consumer Demand in the United States: Analyses and Projections*, Harvard University Press, Cambridge, 1970, pp. 56–149; Richard Voith, 'The Long-Run Elasticity of Demand for Commuter Rail Transportation,' *Journal or Urban Economics*, Vol. 30, November 1991, pp. 360–72.

When consumers have limited alternatives, the demand for a good or service is more price inelastic. Take the example of milk. Adult consumers find that milk has few substitutes, and it is an essential component in the diet of young children

The price elasticity of demand is closely related to the availability of good substitutes for a good or service.

Price elasticity also depends on how broadly or how narrowly we define the good or service for which we wish to calculate elasticity. For example, the price elasticity of demand for Ford motor cars is greater than that for cars in general. Fords compete with other cars sold by Holden, Toyota, Mitsubishi and other car makers. All of these other brands are substitutes for Ford. If we lump all brands together, however, we eliminate these specific brands of cars as competitors. In short, there are more close substitutes for Fords than there are for all cars.

Share of budget spent on the product

When the price of salt changes, consumers pay little attention. Why should they notice? The price of salt or matches could double and this purchase would still remain a small percentage of one's budget. If, however, international airfares, the prices of meals at restaurants or housing prices double, people will attempt to economise in their expenditure on these goods and services. These goods and services account for a large part of people's budgets.

The price elasticity coefficient of demand is directly related to the percentage of one's budget spent on a good or service.

Adjustment to a price change over time

Exhibit 5.7 separates the elasticity coefficients into short-run and long-run categories. As time passes, buyers can respond fully to a change in the price of a product by finding more substitutes. Consider the demand for petrol. In the short run, people find it hard to cut back the amount they buy when the price rises sharply. They are accustomed to driving back and forth to work alone in their cars. The typical short-run response is to cut unnecessary travel and reduce speed on trips. If high prices persist over time, car buyers will find additional ways to cut back. They can buy cars with better fuel economy, form car pools and use buses or trains. This explains why the short-run elasticity coefficient of petrol in the exhibit is more inelastic at 0.2 than the long-run elasticity coefficient of 0.7.

In general, the price elasticity coefficient of demand is higher the longer a price change persists.

Other elasticity measures

The elasticity concept has other applications beyond calculating the price elasticity of demand. Broadly defined, it is a technique for measuring the response of one variable to changes in some other variable.

Income elasticity of demand

Income elasticity of demand The ratio of the percentage change in the quantity demanded of a good or service to a given percentage change in income.

Recall from Chapter 3 that an increase in income can increase demand for a normal good or service and decrease demand for an inferior good or service, ceteris paribus. To measure exactly how consumption responds to changes in income, economists calculate the **income elasticity of demand**. Income elasticity of demand is the ratio of the percentage change in the quantity demanded of a good or service to the percentage change in income that brought about this change in quantity demanded. We use a midpoint formula similar to the one we used for calculating price elasticity of demand:

$$E_Y = \frac{\text{percentage change in quantity demanded}}{\text{percentage change in income}}$$

$$E_Y = \frac{\%\Delta Q}{\%\Delta Y} = \frac{\dfrac{Q_2 - Q_1}{Q_1 + Q_2}}{\dfrac{Y_2 - Y_1}{Y_1 + Y_2}}$$

where E_Y is income elasticity of demand, Q_1 and Q_2 represent quantities demanded before and after the income change, and Y_1 and Y_2 represent income before and after the income change.

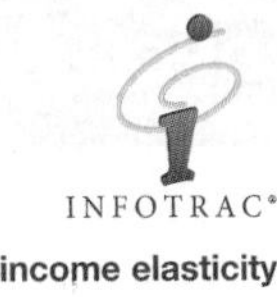

INFOTRAC®
income elasticity

For a *normal* good or service, the income elasticity of demand is *positive*, $E_Y > 0$. Recall that for this type of good demand and income move in the same direction. Thus, the variables change in the numerator and denominator in the same direction. For an *inferior* good or service the reverse is true, and the income elasticity of demand is *negative*, $E_Y < 0$.

Why is the income elasticity coefficient important? Returning to our rock group example, the Feral Possums need to know the impact of a recession on ticket sales. During a downturn when consumers' income falls, if a rock concert is a *normal good*, the quantity of ticket sales falls. Conversely, if a rock concert is an *inferior good*, the quantity of ticket sales rises. To illustrate, suppose consumers' income increases from \$1000 to \$1250 per month. As a result, the quantity of tickets demanded increases from 10 000 to 15 000. Based on these data, is a rock concert a normal or an inferior good? We compute as follows:

$$E_Y = \frac{\dfrac{Q_2 - Q_1}{Q_1 + Q_2}}{\dfrac{Y_2 - Y_1}{Y_1 + Y_2}} = \frac{\dfrac{15\,000 - 10\,000}{10\,000 + 15\,000}}{\dfrac{1250 - 1000}{1000 + 1250}} = \frac{0.20}{0.11} = 1.8$$

Exhibit 5.8 **Estimated income elasticities of demand**

Item	Elasticity coefficient	
	Short run	Long run
Potatoes	NA	−0.81
Furniture	+2.60	+0.53
Dental services	+0.38	+1.00
Motor cars	+5.50	+1.07
Physician services	+0.28	+1.15
Clothing	+0.95	+1.17
Shoes	+0.90	+1.50
Petrol and oil	+0.55	+1.36
Jewellery and watches	+1.00	+1.60
Toilet articles	+0.25	+3.74

Sources: Hendrik S. Houthakker and Lester D. Taylor, *Consumer Demand in the United States: Analyses and Projections*, Harvard University Press, Cambridge, 1970; Dale M. Helen, 'The structure of food demand: interrelatedness and duality', *American Journal of Agricultural Economics*, Vol. 64, No. 2, May 1982, pp. 213–21. Also see Rodney E. Falvey & Norman Gemmell, 'Are services income-elastic? Some new evidence', *Review of Income and Wealth*, Series 42, September 1996, pp. 257–69.

The computed income elasticity of demand coefficient of +1.8 summarises the relationship between changes in rock concert ticket purchases and changes in income. First, E_Y is a positive number, and therefore a rock concert is a normal good (or service) because people buy more when their income rises. Second, ticket purchases are very responsive to changes in income. When income rises by 11 per cent, ticket sales increase by more (20 per cent). Note that when we quote a figure for income elasticity we normally include the sign – either positive or negative – to ensure that there can be no doubt as to whether we are dealing with a normal or an inferior good (or service).

Are there some industries that do well in a recession?

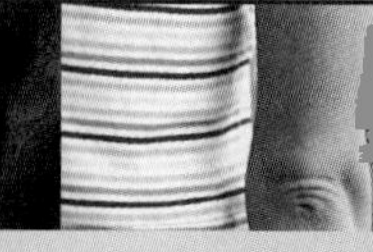

You make the call

When there is a downturn in the economy it is often said that the only businesses that escape its effects are those of the receivers and liquidators who help to wind up companies that have failed. Nothing could be further from the truth. Although sellers of luxury cars, expensive jewellery and overseas holidays may feel the pinch, many businesses tend to prosper during a recession. What are some of the goods and services that these businesses sell, and what characteristic of these goods and services enables their sellers to prosper?

For an alternative explanation of other demand elasticity measures go to The Digital Economist (**www.digitaleconomist.com/elas2.html**).

You make the call

Are children a normal good?

In 1798 Thomas Robert Malthus, a Church of England minister and economist, published his *Essay on the Principle of Population*. He argued that the population would continually outstrip the food supply, meaning that the future of humanity would be characterised by much misery unless checks to population growth occurred. In Malthus's day it was common for families to have ten or more children. Today the average family in developed countries has fewer than two children. Although many factors have contributed to this decline, including the improved effectiveness of contraception, some economists believe that one of the most important factors is the rise in family income that has occurred over the past 200 years. In making this point, are economists saying something about income elasticity of demand for children?

Exhibit 5.8 lists estimated income elasticity of demand for selected products. Here you can see that potatoes have a negative income elasticity. This means that they are an inferior good that people buy less (more) of when their income rises (falls). The long-run coefficient of –0.81 tells us that, ceteris paribus, a 1 per cent increase in income would lead to a fall in consumption of 0.81 per cent in the long run.

Cross-elasticity of demand

In Chapter 3 you learned that a change in the price of one good (say, *Y*) can cause the consumption of another good (say, *X*) to change (see prices of related goods in Exhibit 3.5 in Chapter 3). In Exhibit 4.1(b) in Chapter 4, for example, a sharp rise in the price of petrol (a complement) caused the number of high-fuel-consumption motor vehicles purchased to decline. This responsiveness of the quantity demanded to changes in the price of some other good is estimated by the **cross-elasticity of demand**. Cross-elasticity of demand is the ratio of the percentage change in the quantity demanded of a good or service to a given percentage change in the price of a related good or service. Again, we use the midpoint formula as follows to compute the cross-elasticity of demand:

Cross-elasticity of demand The ratio of the percentage change in the quantity demanded of a good or service to a given percentage change in the price of a related good or service.

$$E_c = \frac{\text{percentage change in quantity demanded of one good}}{\text{percentage change in price of another good}}$$

$$E_c = \frac{\%\Delta Q_X}{\%\Delta P_Y} = \frac{\dfrac{Q_{X2} - Q_{X1}}{Q_{X1} + Q_{X2}}}{\dfrac{P_{Y2} - P_{Y1}}{P_{Y1} + P_{Y2}}}$$

where E_c is cross-elasticity, Q_1 and Q_2 represent quantities demanded before and after the price of a related good or service changes and P_1 and P_2 represent the prices of the related good or service before and after the change.

The cross-elasticity coefficient reveals whether a good or service is a *substitute* or a *complement*. For example, Coke increases its price 10 per cent, which causes consumers to buy 5 per cent more Pepsi. The cross-elasticity of demand for Pepsi is +0.5 (+5 per cent/+10 per cent). Since $E_c > 0$, Coke and Pepsi are *substitutes* because the numerator and denominator variables change in the same direction. The larger the positive coefficient, the greater the substitutability between the two goods.

cross-elasticity

Now suppose that there is a 50 per cent increase in the price of motor oil and the quantity demanded of petrol decreases by 1 per cent. The cross-elasticity of demand for petrol with respect to the price of motor oil is –0.02 (–1 per cent/+50 per cent). Since $E_c < 0$, these two goods are complements. The larger the negative coefficient, the greater the complementary relationship between the two goods. With complementary goods or services, the variables in the numerator and denominator change in the opposite direction.

Note that when we quote a figure for cross-elasticity we normally include the sign – either positive or negative – to ensure that there can be no doubt as to whether we are dealing with substitutes or complements.

It is not only in relation to demand that we can make use of the elasticity concept. As you will see in the next section, this concept is equally applicable to supply.

Can elasticity of demand be calculated for university courses?

Analyse the issue

Applicable concepts: price elasticity of demand; cross-elasticity of demand

Prior to 2005, all Australian public universities charged a common tuition fee for individual courses that was determined by the Australian government. However, from 2005 on, these universities were given the opportunity to 'top up' the existing fee by up to 25 per cent. This resulted in most, but not all, of Australia's public universities increasing their tuition fees for commencing undergraduate students by the full 25 per cent from 2005.

The system by which Australian domestic students pay fees is known as the Higher Education Contribution Scheme, or HECS. Although students have the opportunity to pay their fees up front and receive a discount, by far the greatest majority choose to defer payment (in effect, take a loan from the Australian government) until graduation, when the fee is clawed back by the government over a number of years through an income tax surcharge.

In the run up to the 2005 academic year, a decline in commencing enrolments was observed. This caused Deputy Leader of the Federal Opposition and Education spokeswoman, Jenny Macklin, to argue that the 25 per cent increase in fees was responsible. In the following extracts from an article in the *Australian Financial Review*, the incidence and extent of the decline is briefly outlined. When you are reading this extract, think about whether the data provided could be used to gain rough estimates of elasticity of demand.

A decline in university applications shows that fee increases that start next year have deterred potential students, Labor Education spokeswoman Jenny Macklin said yesterday.

Data released yesterday by admission centres revealed a 3.1 per cent drop in first-preference applications for universities in NSW and the ACT …

Ms Macklin said the breakdown of applications to the 13 universities in NSW and the ACT showed 70 per cent of the overall decline had occurred at five universities which had chosen to increase fees next year …

The figures show the greatest increases in demand occurred at universities that have chosen not to increase fees next year, including the University of Wollongong (where applications were up 7.5 per cent on last year), Charles Sturt University (9.5 per cent) and Macquarie University (7.4 percent).

But the figures do not prove a watertight connection between fee rises and a drop in demand …

A spokesman for Education Minister Brendan Nelson rejected the suggestion that fee increases had affected demand for courses ...[1]

The following questions are based on an assumption that the universities that increased fees by 25 per cent experienced a combined decrease in applications of 2.5 per cent.

1 What is the own price elasticity of demand for courses at the universities that increased fees by 25 per cent?
2 Is demand for these courses elastic or inelastic?
3 What factors do you think are responsible for this degree of elasticity?
4 Is tuition fee revenue in 2005 likely to increase or decrease at these universities?

The next three questions are based on an assumption that the 25 per cent fee increase at the universities that increased fees caused a combined increase in applications of 8 per cent at those universities that did not increase their fees.

5 What is the price cross-elasticity of demand for courses at universities that did not increase their fees with respect to the price of courses at universities that did increase their fees? Don't forget to include the sign.

6 Are undergraduate courses at different universities substitutes or complements?
7 Is demand for courses at the universities that did not increase their fees elastic or inelastic with respect to the fees charged by universities that did increase their fees? What is the significance of this degree of elasticity?
8 Finally, what are some of the factors that might cause the author of the article and the spokesman for the Education Minister to argue that the changes in demand for courses are not necessarily related to the fee changes?

1 Sophie Morris, 'Uni fees "deterrent": Macklin', *Australian Financial Review*, 8 December 2004. p. 7.

Price elasticity of supply

Price elasticity of supply The ratio of the percentage change in the quantity supplied of a product to the percentage change in its price.

The **price elasticity of supply** is the ratio of the percentage change in the quantity supplied of a product to the percentage change in its price. This elasticity coefficient is calculated using the following formula:

$$E_s = \frac{\text{percentage change in quantity supplied}}{\text{percentage change in price}}$$

where E_s is the price elasticity of supply. Since price and quantity supplied change in the same direction, the elasticity coefficient is always positive. Economists use terminology corresponding to that for the elasticity of demand. Supply is *elastic* when $E_s > 1$, *unit elastic* when $E_s = 1$, *inelastic* when $E_s < 1$, *perfectly elastic* when $E_s = \infty$ and *perfectly inelastic* when $E_s = 0$. Exhibit 5.9 shows three of these cases.

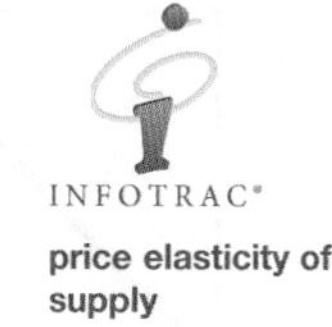

price elasticity of supply

Price elasticity of supply is a measure of the extent to which the quantity supplied of a good or service responds to a change in its price. In Chapter 7 we will explain why the time period of analysis is a primary determinant of the shape of the supply curve. It will be shown that, as is generally the case for demand, price elasticity of supply is greater in the long run than in the short run. Thus, the long-run supply curve will be flatter.

Exhibit 5.10 gives a summary of the three elasticity concepts presented in this section.

For an example of how price elasticity of supply is explained to farmers, go to the Alberta Agricultural Food and Rural Development site (**www1.agric.gov.ab.ca/$department/deptdocs.nsf/all/sis970?opendocument#elasticity**).

Price elasticity and the impact of taxation

Taxes imposed on sellers of goods with inelastic demand such as petrol, tobacco products and alcohol are an important source of revenue for governments in most countries. In Australia these taxes are known as excise taxes. They are typically levied at a much higher rate than applies in the case of broad-based consumption taxes such as Australia's goods and services tax (GST).

PART 2

Exhibit 5.9 **Price elasticity of supply**

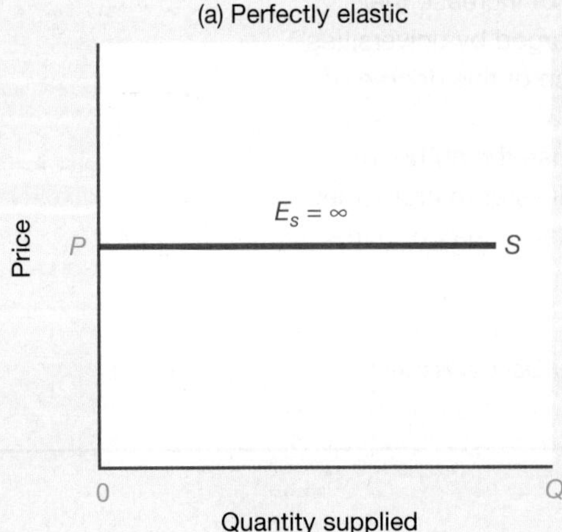

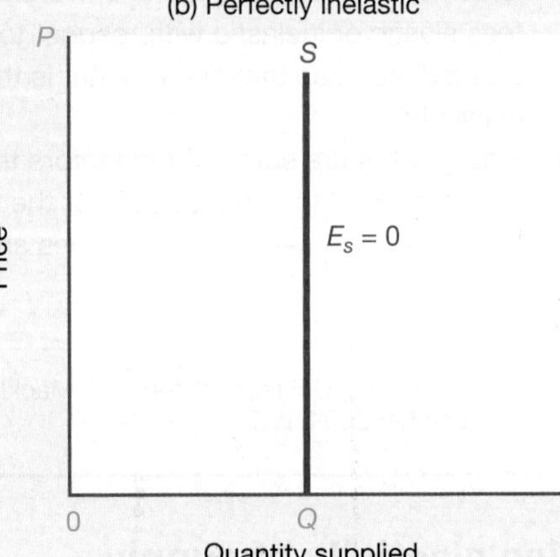

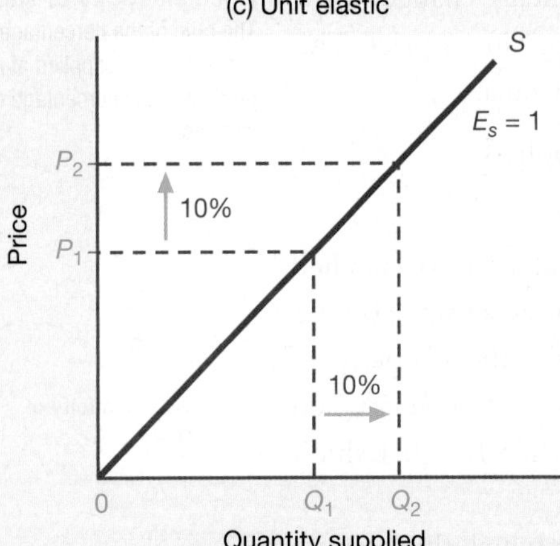

This figure shows three supply curves. As shown in part (a), a small change in price changes the quantity supplied by an infinite amount: $E_s = \infty$. Part (b) shows that the quantity supplied is unaffected by a change in price: $E_s = 0$, and supply is perfectly inelastic. In part (c), the percentage change in quantity supplied is equal to the percentage change in price: $E_s = 1$.

Exhibit 5.10 **Summary of elasticity concepts**

Type	Definition	Elasticity coefficient possibilities	Terminology
Income elasticity of demand	$\frac{\text{Percentage change in quantity demanded}}{\text{Percentage change in income}}$	$E_Y > 0$ $E_Y < 0$	Normal good Inferior good
Cross-elasticity of demand	$\frac{\text{Percentage change in quantity demanded of one good}}{\text{Percentage change in price of another good}}$	$E_c < 0$ $E_c > 0$	Complements Substitutes
Price elasticity of supply	$\frac{\text{Percentage change in quantity supplied}}{\text{Percentage change in price}}$	$E_s > 1$ $E_s = 1$ $E_s < 1$ $E_s = \infty$ $E_s = 0$	Elastic Unit elastic Inelastic Perfectly elastic Perfectly inelastic

But who pays the excise tax levied on sellers of goods such as petrol, cigarettes and alcoholic beverages? One way to answer this question is to say that if the government places an excise tax on, say, petrol, the petrol companies pay the tax. They collect the tax when they sell petrol and remit the proceeds to the government. But this is not the whole story. Instead of looking simply at who remits the proceeds, economists use the elasticity concept to analyse who 'really' pays a tax – the consumer or the seller. In this section, we show that even when taxes are collected from sellers, buyers do not escape a share of the tax burden. **Tax incidence** is the share of a tax ultimately paid by consumers or by sellers. The tax incidence depends on the price elasticities of demand and supply. Let's look at two examples.

tax incidence

Tax incidence The share of a tax ultimately paid by consumers or by sellers.

Exhibit 5.11 The incidence of a tax on petrol

(a) Partially shifted tax to buyers

Price per litre (dollars): 0.25, 0.50, 0.75, 1.00, 1.25, 1.50, 1.75, 2.00

Quantity of petrol (millions of litres per day): 0, 5, 10, 15, 20, 25, 30, 35, 40, 45, 50

S_2 After tax; S_1 Before tax; E_2; E_1; T; D

Paid by customers

Paid by sellers

(b) Fully shifted tax to buyers

Price per litre (dollars): 0.25, 0.50, 0.75, 1.00, 1.25, 1.50, 1.75, 2.00

Quantity of petrol (millions of litres per day): 0, 5, 10, 15, 20, 25, 30, 35, 40, 45, 50

D; S_2 After tax; S_1 Before tax; E_2; E_1; T

Paid by customers

CAUSATION CHAIN

Increase in petrol tax → Decrease in supply → Consumers and suppliers share burden of tax

CAUSATION CHAIN

Increase in petrol tax → Decrease in supply → Consumers bear full burden of tax

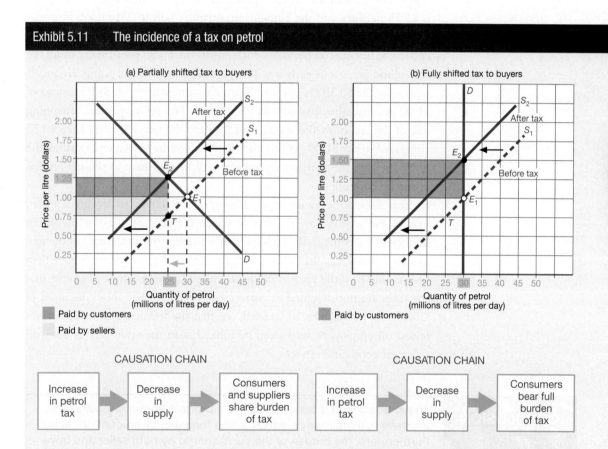

In parts (a) and (b), S_1 is the supply curve before the imposition of a tax of $0.50 per litre on petrol. The demand curve is not affected by this tax collected from the sellers. The initial equilibrium is E_1. Before the tax, the price is $1.00 per litre and 30 million litres are bought and sold.

In part (a), the equilibrium price rises to $1.25 per litre at E_2 as a result of the tax. After the tax is paid, sellers are paid only $0.75 per litre (point *T*) instead of $1.00, as they were before the tax. Thus, buyers pay $0.25 of the tax per litre and sellers bear the remaining $0.25. The shaded area is the total tax collected.

As shown in part (b), a tax collected from sellers can be fully shifted to buyers in the unlikely case that demand is perfectly inelastic. Since the quantity of petrol purchased is unresponsive to a change in price, sellers receive $1.00 per litre before and after they pay the tax.

PART 2

Suppose there is currently no tax on petrol. Now consider a decision by the federal government to impose a petrol excise of $0.50 per litre. Exhibit 5.11 shows the impact of the tax. At E_1 the equilibrium price before the tax is $1.00 per litre and the equilibrium quantity is 30 million litres per day. The effect of the tax is to shift the supply curve upward from S_1 to S_2. From the sellers' viewpoint, the production cost of each litre of petrol increases $0.50. The effect is exactly the same as if the price of crude oil or any resource used to produce petrol increased.

Sellers would like consumers to pay the entire amount of the tax. This would occur if consumers would pay $1.50 per litre for the same 30 million litres per day they purchased before the tax. But the shift upward of the supply curve establishes a new equilibrium at E_2. The new equilibrium price is $1.25 per litre and the equilibrium quantity falls to 25 million litres per day. At E_2 the entire shaded area represents the tax revenue. The government collects $12.5 million per day, which equals the $0.50 per litre tax times the 25 million litres sold each day. The vertical line between points E_2 and T represents the $0.50 tax per litre. Since consumers now pay $1.25 instead of $1.00 per litre, they pay one-half of the tax. The sellers pay the remaining half of the tax. Now the sellers send $0.50 to the tax office and keep $0.75 compared to the $1.00 per litre they kept before the tax. Ceteris paribus, the more inelastic the demand the greater will be the share of the tax burden borne by consumers.

You should be aware that, although taxes collected by government may be put to good use, the way in which they distort markets leads to an inefficient outcome in the sense that they prevent the attainment of the free market equilibrium. In general, output is lower and prices are higher than they would be if the tax had not been imposed. This assumes, of course, that the taxes are not designed to correct market failure like those discussed in Chapter 4. In Chapter 10 you will see that the incidence of income taxes levied on employees' wages can be looked at in the same way as taxes on sellers of goods and services.

CONCLUSION

The imposition of a tax on sellers of a product normally results in an increase in market price, which is less than the full amount of the tax. Furthermore, the burden of the tax is shared by both seller and buyer.

International focus

How will scientific research output respond to a policy-induced increase in its demand?

Applicable concept: price elasticity of supply

Today's knowledge-based globalised economies rely heavily on scientific research output to ensure continuing high productivity growth. Seeking to promote growth in their domestic economies, governments around the world subsidise scientific research in many different ways. One way to increase scientific research output would be to implement policies designed to increase demand for scientific research – for example, by paying a subsidy to purchasers. Such an increase in demand would be expected to lead to an increase in quantity supplied of scientific research and its market price. But how successful would such a policy be? Would the price rise caused by an increase in demand be associated with a relatively large or a relatively small increase in scientific research output? In other words, is the elasticity of supply of scientific research high or low?

Some clues to the answer to this question can be found in the estimate, contained in a US study, that a 100 per cent increase in the number of research scientists would give little more than a 50 per cent increase in research output. Further increases in the number of scientists would increase output by an even smaller proportion. The fundamental argument is that the best research scientists are already in the industry – any increase in the number of scientists would involve employment of researchers with lower skills than those already employed.[1]

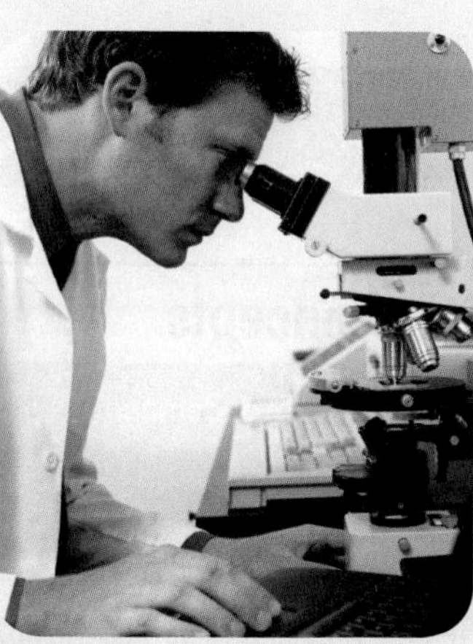

To get a feel for the way in which government subsidies can be used to increase demand for research, read about the history of the US research tax credit at **www.unclefed.com/GAOReports/ggd96-43_sum.html.**

1 See Stephen P. Dresch, 'The Economics of Fundamental Research', in J.W. Sommer, ed., *The Academy in Crisis: The Political Economy of Higher Education*, Transaction Publishers for the Independent Institute, San Francisco, New Brunswick, 1995.

Analyse the issue

Using the above clues and assuming that the wage rate paid to all research scientists is the same, answer the following questions.

1 If, as the demand for scientific research output increases, the companies and institutes undertaking this research respond to this increase in demand by employing more researchers, is the supply of research output likely to be elastic or inelastic?

2 As output increases further, does supply elasticity become smaller or larger?

3 Draw a diagram showing the effect of increased demand on the quantity of research output supplied.

4 Is the elasticity of supply of scientific research output likely to increase over a six-month period? Over a ten-year period?

Part (b) of Exhibit 5.11 is a special case in which the market price increases by the full amount of the tax per litre. Here the demand for petrol is perfectly inelastic. In this case, the decrease in supply caused by the tax does not result in buyers responding by decreasing the quantity demanded. The quantity demanded is 30 million litres per day before and after the tax. The price, however, increases by exactly the amount of tax per unit from \$1.00 to \$1.50 per litre. After paying the tax, sellers receive a net price of \$1.00 per litre. In this case, the burden of the tax is shifted entirely onto the buyers. The total tax revenue collected by the government is the shaded area. Each day \$15 million is collected, which equals the \$0.50 per litre tax multiplied by 30 million litres sold each day.

In the case where demand is perfectly inelastic, the price of a good or service will rise by the full amount of a tax and buyers will bear the full burden of the tax.

Key concepts

Price elasticity of demand
Total revenue
Elastic demand
Inelastic demand
Unitary elastic demand
Perfectly elastic demand
Perfectly inelastic demand
Income elasticity of demand
Cross-elasticity of demand
Price elasticity of supply
Tax incidence

Summary

- **Price elasticity of demand** is a measure of the responsiveness of the quantity demanded to a change in price. Specifically, price elasticity of demand is the ratio of the percentage change in quantity demanded to the percentage change in price. By definition it is always negative, but by convention it is always shown without the negative sign.

$$E_d = \frac{\%\Delta Q}{\%\Delta P} = \frac{\dfrac{Q_2 - Q_1}{(Q_1 + Q_2)/2}}{\dfrac{P_2 - P_1}{(P_1 + P_2)/2}}$$

- **Elastic demand** is a change of more than 1 per cent in quantity demanded in response to a 1 per cent change in price. Demand is elastic when the elasticity coefficient is greater than 1. When demand is elastic, total revenue (price times quantity) varies inversely with the direction of the price change (for example, if price goes up, total revenue goes down).

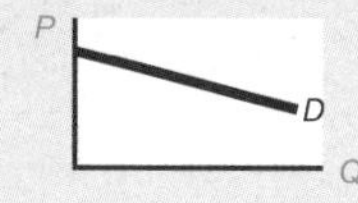

- **Inelastic demand** is a change of less than 1 per cent in quantity demanded in response to a 1 per cent change in price. Demand is inelastic when the elasticity coefficient is less than 1 and total revenue varies directly with the direction of the price change (for example, if price rises, total revenue also rises).

- **Unitary elastic demand** is a 1 per cent change in quantity demanded in response to a 1 per cent change in price. Demand is unitary elastic when the elasticity coefficient equals 1 and total revenue remains unchanged as the price changes.

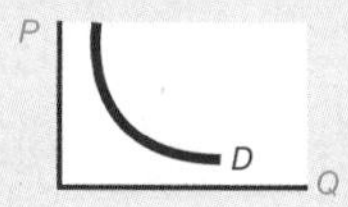

- **Perfectly elastic demand** is a decline in quantity demanded to zero for even the slightest rise in price. This is an extreme case, in which the demand curve is horizontal. In this case the elasticity coefficient equals infinity.

- **Perfectly inelastic demand** is no change in quantity demanded in response to price changes. This is an extreme case, in which the demand curve is vertical. In this case the elasticity coefficient equals zero.

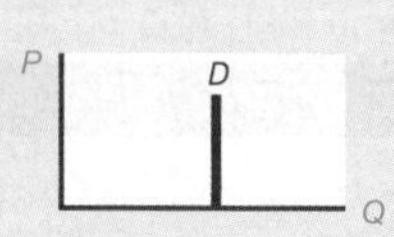

- **Determinants of price elasticity of demand** include (a) the availability of substitutes, (b) the proportion of the budget spent on the product and (c) the length of time allowed for adjustment. Each of these factors is directly related to the elasticity coefficient.
- **Income elasticity of demand** is a measure of the responsiveness of the quantity demanded to a change in income. Specifically, the income elasticity of demand is the percentage change in quantity demanded divided by the percentage change in income. For a normal good or service, income elasticity of demand is positive. For an inferior good or service, income elasticity of demand is negative.
- **Cross-elasticity of demand** is a measure of the responsiveness of the quantity demanded to a change in the price of a related good or service. Specifically, cross-elasticity of demand is the percentage change in the quantity demanded of one good or service caused by a 1 per cent change in the price of another good or service. When the cross-elasticity of demand is negative, the two products are complements; when it is positive they are substitutes.
- **Price elasticity of supply** is a measure of the responsiveness of the quantity supplied to a change in price. Price elasticity of supply is the ratio of the percentage change in quantity supplied to the percentage change in price.

- **Tax incidence** is the share of a tax paid by buyers and sellers. In most cases, the imposition of a tax on sellers of a good or service does not raise the price by the full amount of the tax and the burden of the tax is shared by both buyers and sellers. If, however, the demand curve was vertical, the price would rise by the full amount of the tax and the whole of the burden of the tax would be borne by buyers.

Tax incidence

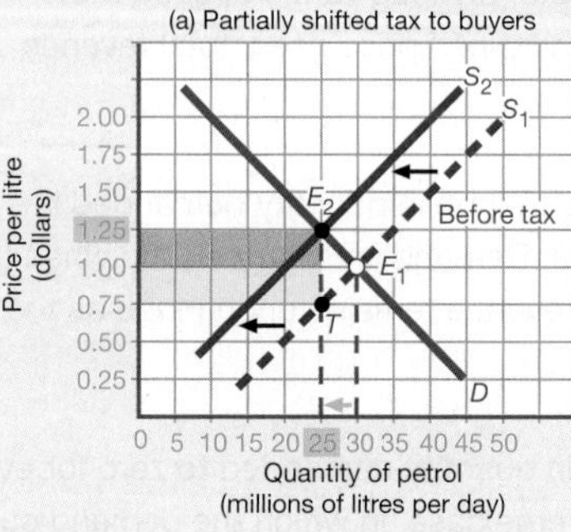

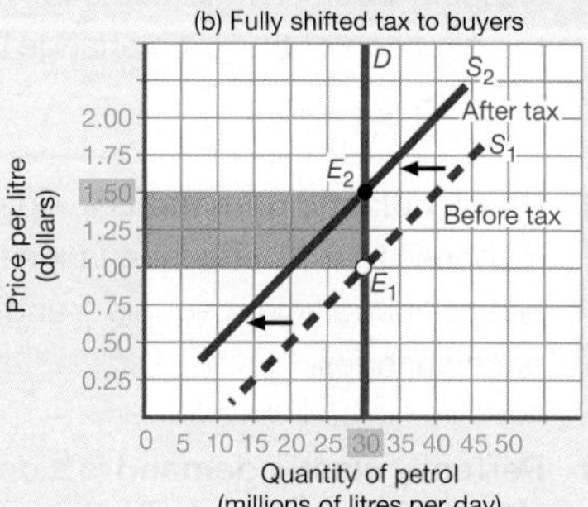

Study questions and problems

1 If the price of a good or service increases and the total revenue received by the seller declines, is the demand for this good over this segment of the demand curve elastic or inelastic? Explain.

2 Suppose the price elasticity of demand for rail travel is elastic. If the rail authority wants to raise revenue from fares, should it raise them or lower them?

3 Suppose the price elasticity of demand for used cars is estimated to be 3. What does this mean? What will be the effect on the quantity demanded for used cars if the price rises by 10 per cent?

4 Consider the following demand schedule.

Price	Quantity demanded	Elasticity coefficient
$25	20	
20	40	
15	60	
10	80	
5	100	

What is the price elasticity of demand between

a P = $25 and P = $20?
b P = $20 and P = $15?
c P = $15 and P = $10?
d P = $10 and P = $5?

5 Suppose a tour company raises the price of a particular packaged tour from $3000 to $3500. As a result, the number of persons taking the tours each year falls from 5000 to 4500. Calculate the price elasticity of demand. Is demand elastic, unitary elastic or inelastic?

6 Will each of the following changes in price cause total revenue to increase, decrease or remain unchanged?

a Price falls and demand is elastic.
b Price rises and demand is elastic.
c Price falls and demand is unitary elastic.
d Price rises and demand is unitary elastic.
e Price falls and demand is inelastic.
f Price rises and demand is inelastic.

7 Suppose a cinema complex raises the price of popcorn 10 per cent, but customers do not buy any less of it. What does this tell you about the price elasticity of demand, and what will happen to total revenue as a result of the price increase?

8 If the price of paper clips rose to $40 per box, would this have any effect on price elasticity of demand?

9 Which of the following goods and services has the higher price elasticity of demand?
  a oranges or Valencia oranges
  b cars or salt
  c holidays in New Zealand in the short run or in the long run

10 Is the price elasticity of supply of trips to the top of the Eiffel Tower (from the bottom) likely to be high or low?

11 Suppose the income elasticity of demand for furniture is +3 and the income elasticity of demand for doctors' services is +0.3. Compare the impact on furniture and doctors' services of a recession that reduces consumer income by 10 per cent.

12 How might you determine whether compact discs and restaurant meals are in competition with each other?

13 Assume that the cross-elasticity of demand for car tyres with respect to the price of cars is –2. What does this tell you about the relationship between car tyres and cars when the price of cars rises by 10 per cent?

14 Consider the following supply schedule.

Price	Quantity supplied	Elasticity coefficient
$10	50	
8	40	
6	30	
4	20	
2	10	
0	0	

What is the price elasticity of supply between
  a P = $10 and P = $8?
  b P = $8 and P = $6?
  c P = $6 and P = $4?
  d P = $4 and P = $2?
  e P = $2 and P = $0?

15 Why would consumers prefer that the government tax products with elastic, rather than inelastic, demand?

16 Opponents of increasing the tax on sellers of cigarettes argue that the big tobacco companies just pass the tax along to the consumers. Do you agree or disagree? Explain your answer.

Online exercises

Exercise 1

Visit the Non Smokers' Movement of Australia (**www.nsma.org.au**) and the tobacco overview page of the Australian Department of Health and Aged Care (**www.health.gov.au/internet/wcms/publishing.nsf/Content/health-pubhlth-strateg-drugs-tobacco-overview.htm**). You will find an array of strategies designed to reduce smoking in the community. Which of these strategies will have the effect of increasing the elasticity of demand for cigarettes?

Exercise 2

Do governments take economic concepts (such as elasticity) into consideration when they formulate energy and environmental policies? Visit the National Center for Environmental Economics at the US Environmental Protection Agency (EPA) and search for **elasticity**. The address is **yosemite.epa.gov/ee/epa/eed.nsf/pages/homepage?Opendocument**. Also visit the US Department of Energy, Energy Information Administration (**www.eia.doe.gov**).

Exercise 3

The Red Book is a major source of new and used car prices (**www.redbook.com.au**). Find the new car prices for base models of two popular Australian-made cars: Ford Falcon and Holden Commodore. Are the two cars closely priced? Do you think physically similar goods are closer substitutes when they are more closely priced than when they are less closely priced? Or do you think the issue of closeness in price is irrelevant to the degree of substitution? Explain your answer. Do you think the cross-price elasticity of demand between Falcon and Commodore is positive or negative? Explain your answer.

Exercise 4

Check out the rates of excise tax charged in Australia by visiting the Australian Taxation Office's site (**www.ato.gov.au**) and searching for **excise duty rates**. Why do you think the list is so long when excise is charged on a small number of categories of commodities such as petroleum and oil products, tobacco products and alcoholic beverages? You will see that home-brewed beer is not on the list, and neither are the materials used to make home brews. Can you explain why excise is not collected on home brew or its ingredients? Does your explanation tell you anything about the cross-elasticity of demand between home brew ingredients and beer purchased from the bottle shop?

Answers to 'You make the call'

What explains airline fare structures?

The determination of airline ticket prices is a complex process involving a knowledge of costs of supplying airline services as well as a knowledge of elasticities of demand. However, we can be pretty sure that the policy of charging higher fares at busy times of the day or busy days of the week, and charging higher fares for urgent travel is related to price elasticity of demand. For example, demand is likely to be more elastic for travel very early in the morning and for travel that is not urgent. If you said that the higher prices for travel at busy times and for urgent travel reflect less elastic demand, YOU ARE CORRECT. As far as the ethics of charging higher prices when demand is less elastic is concerned, economists would argue that this simply reflects reality in the market. They might also point out that, as long as there is competition in the market, the counterpart of higher prices paid by travellers who have less elastic demand is the lower prices paid by those who are willing to travel at less popular times or who can book ahead and thus have more elastic demand.

Are there some businesses that do well in a recession?

In a recession the incomes of many consumers fall. In the case of normal goods and services such as luxury cars, expensive jewellery and overseas holidays, this decline in income will reduce demand. Sellers of these goods and services will feel the full effects of recession. For inferior goods, however, the decline in income will lead to an increase in demand. Thus some businesses such as those producing generic brand groceries, those providing no-frills funerals and those selling low-cost domestic holidays may well prosper during a recession. If you said that businesses selling goods and services with high negative income elasticities of demand are likely to prosper in a recession, YOU ARE CORRECT.

Are children a normal good?

There is no doubt that the huge rise in family income that has occurred over the past 200 years has been *associated* with a dramatic decrease in the number of children per family. While some economists would argue that there are so many factors affecting family size that causation cannot be inferred from this relationship, others might argue that the relative increase in the prices of goods and services that are complements for children (clothes, entertainment, education etc.) has decreased the demand for children. Still others would argue that a causal relationship between income and demand for children almost certainly exists. If you said that economists who believe that rising incomes cause demand for children to decrease are asserting that children are not a normal good but an inferior good, YOU ARE CORRECT.

Multiple-choice questions

1 If an increase in ferry fares in Hong Kong reduces total revenue of the operators, this is evidence that demand is
- **a** price elastic.
- **b** price inelastic.
- **c** unitary elastic.
- **d** perfectly elastic.

2 Which of the following is the cause of an increase in total revenue?
- **a** Price increases when demand is elastic.
- **b** Price decreases when demand is elastic.
- **c** Price increases when demand is unitary elastic.
- **d** Price decreases when demand is inelastic.

3 You are on a committee that is considering ways to raise money to fund your city's symphony concerts. You would recommend increasing the price of concert tickets only if you thought the demand curve for these tickets was
- **a** inelastic.
- **b** elastic.
- **c** unitary elastic.
- **d** perfectly elastic.

4 The price elasticity of demand for a horizontal demand curve is
- **a** perfectly elastic.
- **b** perfectly inelastic.
- **c** unitary elastic.

- **d** inelastic.
- **e** elastic.

5 Suppose the quantity of steak purchased by the Nguyen family is 11 kilos per year when the price is $10.50 per kilo and 9 kilos per year when the price is $19.50 per kilo. The price elasticity of demand coefficient for this family is

- **a** 0.33.
- **b** 0.50.
- **c** 1.00.
- **d** 2.00.

6 If a 5 per cent reduction in the price of a good produces a 3 per cent increase in the quantity demanded, the price elasticity of demand over this range of the demand curve is

- **a** elastic.
- **b** perfectly elastic.
- **c** unitary elastic.
- **d** inelastic.
- **e** perfectly inelastic.

7 The manufacturer of Kool Kiwi Kakes hires an economist to study the price elasticity of demand for this product. The economist estimates that the price elasticity of demand coefficient for a range of prices close to the selling price is greater than 1. The relationship between changes in price and quantity demanded for this segment of the demand curve is

- **a** elastic.
- **b** inelastic.
- **c** perfectly elastic.
- **d** perfectly inelastic.
- **e** unitary elastic.

8 A downward-sloping demand curve will have a

- **a** higher price elasticity of demand coefficient along the upper half of the demand curve.
- **b** lower price elasticity coefficient along the upper half of the demand curve.
- **c** constant price elasticity of demand coefficient throughout the length of the demand curve.
- **d** positive slope.

9 The price elasticity of demand coefficient for a good will be less

- **a** if there are few or no substitutes available.
- **b** if a small portion of the budget will be spent on it.
- **c** in the short run than in the long run.
- **d** if all of the above are true.

10 The income elasticity of demand for shoes is estimated to be 1.50. We can conclude that shoes

- **a** have a relatively steep demand curve.
- **b** have a relatively flat demand curve.
- **c** are a normal good.
- **d** are an inferior good.

11 To determine whether two goods are substitutes or complements, an economist would estimate the

- **a** price elasticity of demand.
- **b** income elasticity of demand.
- **c** cross-elasticity of demand.
- **d** price elasticity of supply.

12 If the government wanted to raise tax revenue and shift most of the tax burden to the sellers, it would impose a tax on a good with an

- **a** inelastic demand curve and an inelastic supply curve.
- **b** inelastic demand curve and an elastic supply curve.
- **c** elastic demand curve and an inelastic supply curve.
- **d** elastic demand curve and an elastic supply curve.

6 Production costs

Suppose you dream of owning your own company. That's right, you want to experience the excitement of starting your own firm and making it successful. Instead of working for someone else, you want to be your own boss. You are under no illusions; it is going to take hard work and sacrifice.

You are an electrical engineer who is an expert at designing electronic components for automatic teller machines (ATMs) and similar applications. So you quit your job and invest your nest egg in starting Atmach (a mythical company). You lease factory space, hire employees and purchase raw materials, and soon your company's products begin rolling off the assembly line. In this new business venture, production cost considerations influence each decision you make. The purpose of this chapter is to study production and its relationship to various types of costs. Whether your company is new and small or an international giant, understanding costs is essential for success. In this chapter and the next chapter, you will follow Atmach and learn the basic principles of production and the way various types of costs vary with output.

In this chapter, you will examine these economics questions:

- Why would an accountant say a firm is making a profit and an economist say it is losing money?
- What is the difference between the short run and the long run?
- Why are multi-screen cinema complexes replacing single-screen theatres?
- Why do new Internet-based firms attempt to expand so rapidly?

Costs and profit

A basic assumption in economics is that the motivation for business decisions is profit maximisation. Economists realise that managers of firms may sometimes pursue other goals, such as seeking a satisfactory profit rather than maximum profit, or building an empire for the purpose of ego satisfaction. However, the profit maximisation goal has been shown to be a powerful way of explaining the behaviour of managers of firms who are responsible for making decisions about the appropriate level of output or price. To understand profit as a driving force for business firms, we must first distinguish between the way economists measure costs and the way accountants measure costs.

Explicit and implicit costs

Economists define the total opportunity cost of a business as the sum of explicit costs and implicit costs. **Explicit costs** are payments to non-owners of a firm for their resources. In our Atmach example, explicit costs include the wages paid to labour, the lease payments for vehicles, the cost of electricity, the cost of materials and the cost of workers compensation insurance. These resources are owned outside the firm and must be purchased with an actual payment to these 'outsiders'.

Explicit costs Payments to non-owners of a firm for their resources.

Implicit costs are the opportunity costs of using resources owned by the firm. These are opportunity costs of resources owned by the firm itself; therefore, the firm makes no actual payment to outsiders. When you started Atmach, you gave up the opportunity to earn a salary as an electrical engineer for someone else's firm. When you invested your nest egg in your own enterprise, you gave up earning interest. You also used a building that you own to warehouse finished Atmach products. Although you made no payment to anyone, you gave up the opportunity to earn rental payments on the building.

Implicit costs The opportunity costs of using resources owned by the firm.

Economic and accounting profit

In everyday use, the word *profit* is defined as follows:

$$\text{Profit} = \text{total revenue} - \text{total cost}$$

Economists call this concept *accounting profit*. This popular formula is expressed in economics as

$$\text{Accounting profit} = \text{total revenue} - \text{total explicit costs}$$

Economic profit Total revenue minus explicit and implicit costs.

economic profit

Because economic decisions include implicit as well as explicit costs, economists use the concept of **economic profit** instead of accounting profit. Economic profit is total revenue minus explicit and implicit costs. Economic profit can be positive, zero or negative (an economic loss). Expressed as an equation:

$$\text{Economic profit} = \text{total revenue} - \text{total opportunity costs}$$

or

$$\text{Economic profit} = \text{total revenue} - (\text{explicit costs} + \text{implicit costs})$$

Exhibit 6.1 illustrates the importance of the difference between accounting profit and economic profit. Atmach must know how well it is doing, so you hire an accounting firm to prepare a financial report. The figure shows that Atmach earned total revenue of $500 000 in its first year of operation. Explicit costs for wages, materials, interest and other payments totalled $470 000. Based on standard accounting procedures, this left an accounting profit of $30 000.

If the analysis ends with accounting profit, Atmach is profitable. But accounting practice overstates profit because it ignores implicit costs. A few

Exhibit 6.1 Atmach's accounting versus economic profit

Item	Accounting profit	Economic profit
Total revenue	$500 000	$500 000
Less explicit costs:		
Wages and salaries	400 000	400 000
Materials	50 000	50 000
Interest paid	10 000	10 000
Other payments	10 000	10 000
Less implicit costs:		
Forgone salary	0	70 000
Forgone rent	0	10 000
Forgone interest	0	5 000
Equals profit	$30 000	–$55 000

examples will illustrate the importance of implicit costs. Your $70 000-a-year salary as a manager was forgone in order to spend all your time as owner of Atmach. Also forgone were $10 000 in rental income and $5000 in interest that you would have earned during the year by renting your warehouse building to someone else and putting your savings in the bank. Subtracting both explicit and implicit costs from total revenue, Atmach had an economic loss of $55 000. The firm is failing to cover the opportunity costs of using its resources in the electronics industry. Thus, the firm's resources would earn a higher return if used for other alternatives.

How would you interpret a zero economic profit? It's not as bad as it sounds. Economists call this condition **normal profit**. Normal profit is the minimum profit necessary to keep a firm in operation. Zero economic profit signifies that there is just enough total revenue to pay the owners for all explicit and implicit costs. To state it differently, there is no benefit from reallocating resources to another use.

Normal profit The minimum profit necessary to keep a firm in operation. A firm that earns normal profit earns total revenue equal to its total opportunity cost (total explicit and implicit costs).

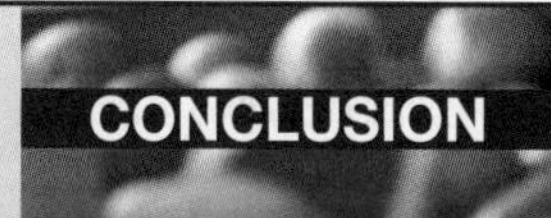

Since business decision-making is based on economic profit rather than accounting profit, the word *profit* in this text always means economic profit.

You make the call

Should the consultant go or stay?

Dr What is considering leaving her job with a large consulting firm to open her own consulting business as a sole practitioner. For her services as a consultant she would be paid $175 000 a year. To open this business, Dr What must use a house from which she collects rent of $16 000 per year as an office and hire a secretary at a salary of $40 000 per year. Also, she must withdraw $40 000 from savings for miscellaneous expenses and forgo earning 5 per cent interest per year on these savings. The consulting firm currently pays Dr What $120 000 a year. Based only on economic decision-making, do you predict that she will leave her current employer to start her own new business?

Short-run production costs

Having presented the basic definitions of cost, the next step is to study cost theory. In this section, we explore the relationship between output and cost in the short run. In the next section, the time horizon shifts to the long run.

Short run versus long run

Suppose we asked you, 'What is the difference between the short run and the long run?' Your answer might be that the short run is less than a year and the long run is over a year. Good guess, but wrong! Economists do not partition production decisions on the basis of any specific number of days, months or years. Instead, the distinction depends on the ability to vary the quantity of inputs of resources (factors of production) used in production. There are two types of resource inputs – **fixed inputs** and **variable inputs**.

Fixed input Any resource for which the quantity cannot change during the period of time under consideration.

Variable input Any resource for which the quantity can change during the period of time under consideration.

A *fixed input* is any resource for which the quantity cannot change during the period of time under consideration. For example, the physical size of a firm's plant and the production capacity of heavy machines cannot change easily within a short period of time. They must remain as fixed inputs while managers decide to vary output. In addition to fixed inputs, the firm uses *variable inputs* in the production process. A variable input is any resource for which the quantity can change during the period of time under consideration. For example, managers can hire fewer or more employees during a given year.

Short run A period of time during which there is at least one fixed input.

Long run A period of time of sufficient duration to allow all inputs to be varied.

Now we can link the concepts of fixed and variable inputs to the **short run** and the **long run**. The short run is a period of time during which there is at least one fixed input. For example, the short run is a period of time during which a firm can increase output by hiring more employees (variable input), while the size of the firm's plant (fixed input) remains unchanged. The firm's plant is the most difficult input to change quickly. The long run is a period of time of sufficient duration to allow all inputs to be varied. In the long run, the firm can build new factories or purchase new machinery. New firms can enter the industry and existing firms may leave the industry.

The production function

Production function The relationship between the maximum amounts of output a firm can produce and various quantities of inputs.

Having defined inputs, we can now describe the transformation of these inputs into outputs, using a concept called a **production function**. A production function is the relationship between the maximum amounts of output a firm can produce and various quantities of inputs. An assumption of the production function model we are about to develop is that the level of technology is fixed. Technological advances would mean that more output is possible from a given quantity of inputs.

production function

Exhibit 6.2 (a) presents a short-run production function for Eastern Slope Vineyard. The variable input is the number of employees employed per day, and each employee is presumed to have equal job skills. The amount of land, the number of vines, the number of machines and all other inputs are assumed to be fixed. Our production model is therefore operating in the short run. If no employees are employed, no grapes will be produced. A single employee can produce one tonne per day, but a lot of time is wasted when one employee picks, loads containers and transports the grapes to the storage shed. Adding the second employee raises output to 2.2 tonnes per day because the employees divide the tasks and specialise. Adding four more employees to these two raises total product to five tonnes per day.

Marginal product

The relationship between changes in total output and changes in labour is called the **marginal product**. Marginal product is the change in total output produced by adding one more unit of a variable input, with all other inputs used being held constant. When Eastern Slope increases labour from zero to one employee, output rises from zero to one tonne produced per day. This increase is the result of the addition of one more employee. Therefore, the marginal product is one tonne per employee. Similar marginal product calculations generate the marginal product curve shown in Exhibit 6.2(b). Note that marginal product is plotted at the midpoints shown in the table because the change in total output occurs between each additional unit of labour used.

Marginal product The change in total output produced by adding one unit of a variable input, with all other inputs used being held constant.

The law of diminishing returns

A long-established economic law – the **law of diminishing returns** – explains the shape of the marginal product curve. The law of diminishing returns states that, beyond some point, the marginal product decreases as additional units of a variable factor are added to a fixed factor. Because the law of diminishing returns assumes that there is at least one fixed input, this principle is a short-run, rather than a long-run, concept.

Law of diminishing returns The principle that beyond some point the marginal product decreases as additional units of a variable factor are added to a fixed factor.

diminishing return

Although we are using an agricultural example, this law can be expected to apply to production of all goods and services. Returning to Exhibit 6.2, we can identify and explain the law of diminishing returns in our Eastern Slope example. Initially, the total output curve rises quite rapidly as this firm hires the first two employees. The marginal product curve reflects the change in the total output curve because marginal product is the slope of the total output curve. As shown in Exhibit 6.2(b), the range from zero to two employees hired is called *increasing marginal returns*. In this range of output, the last employee adds more to total output than the previous employee.

Diminishing returns begin after the second employee is hired and the marginal product reaches its peak. Beyond two employees, diminishing returns occur and the marginal product declines. The short-run assumption guarantees this condition. Eventually, the amount of land, vines and machinery per employee falls as more employees are added to the fixed quantities of these and other inputs used to produce grapes.

Similar reasoning applies to the Atmach example introduced in the Chapter Preview. Assume that Atmach operates with a fixed plant size and a fixed number of machines, and that all other inputs except the number of employees are fixed. Those in the first group of employees hired divide the most important tasks among themselves, specialise, and achieve increasing returns. Then diminishing returns begin and continue as Atmach employs each additional employee. The reason is that, as more employees are added,

In the text we relate the production function to inputs of labour. To see that the familiar shape of the production function can be found in agriculture when the input is irrigated water, go to page 21 of the article on sugar cane irrigation by Tifley and Chapman at **www.canegrowers.com.au/irrigation/benchmarking.pdf**.

PART 2

Exhibit 6.2 A production function and the law of diminishing returns

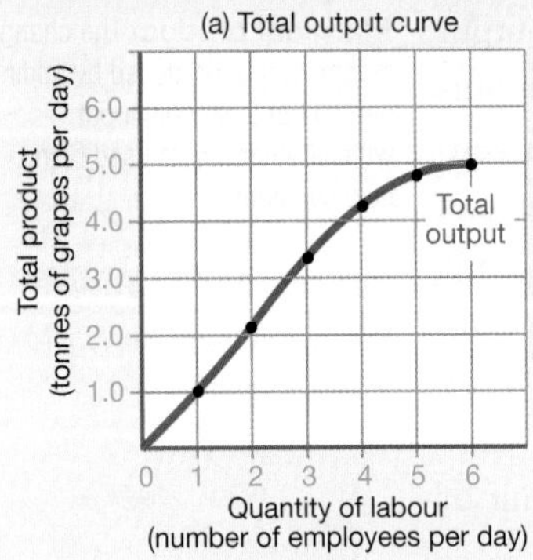

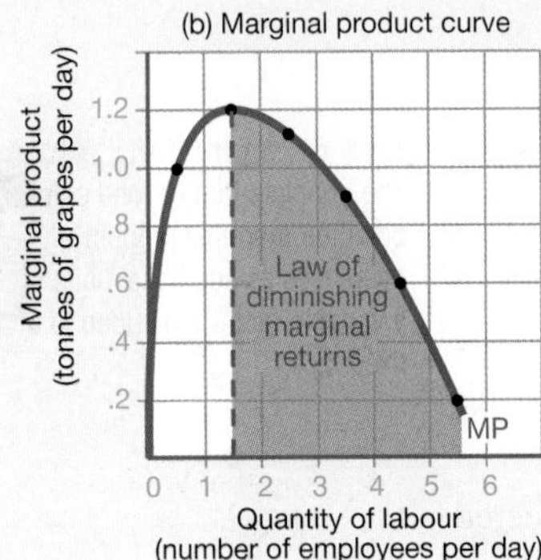

Short-run production function of Eastern Slope Vineyard

(1) Labour input (number of employees per day)	(2) Total output (tonnes of grapes per day)	(3) Marginal product (tonnes of grapes per day) [Δ(2)/Δ(1)]
0	0	
		1.0
1	1.0	
		1.2
2	2.2	
		1.1
3	3.3	
		.9
4	4.2	
		.6
5	4.8	
		.2
6	5.0	

Part (a) shows how the total output of tonnes of grapes per day increases as the number of employees increases while all other inputs remain constant. This curve is a short-run production function, which relates output to changes in a single variable input while all other inputs are fixed.

Part (b) illustrates the law of diminishing returns. The first employee adds one tonne of grapes per day and marginal product is one tonne per day. Adding a second employee adds another 1.2 tonnes of grapes per day to total output. This is the range of increasing marginal returns. After two employees, diminishing marginal returns set in and marginal product declines continuously.

they must share fixed inputs, such as machinery, with some employees standing around waiting for a machine to become available. As a result, marginal product declines. In the extreme case, marginal product could well be negative. At some point, as the number of employees increases, they start stepping on each other's toes and getting in each other's way when they have to work with a limited amount of floor space, machines and other fixed inputs. A profit-seeking firm would never intentionally hire employees with zero or negative marginal product. Chapter 10 explains the labour market in more detail and shows how Atmach decides exactly how many employees to hire.

Short-run cost formulas

In order to make production decisions in either the short run or the long run, a business must determine the costs associated with producing various levels of output. Using the Atmach example, we will study the relationship between short-run costs and output. We will look first at the total cost curves and then at the average cost curves.

For a breakdown of the fixed and variable costs of operating a multiplex cinema in the United Kingdom, look at the capital costs and operating costs respectively under the heading 'The profitability of multiplexes' on page 10 of Chapter 1.3 In Volume 2 of the *Whitebook of the European Exhibition Industry* at **www.mediasalles.it/whiteboo/wb2_1_3.htm**.

Total cost curves

Total fixed cost

As production expands in the short run, costs are divided into two basic categories: **total fixed cost** and **total variable cost**. Total fixed cost consists of costs that do not vary as output varies and that must be paid even if output is zero. These are payments for fixed inputs that the firm must make in the short run regardless of the level of output. Even if a firm such as Atmach produces nothing, it still must pay rent, interest on loans and general insurance. Fixed costs are therefore beyond management's control in the short run. The total fixed cost (*TFC*) for Atmach is $100, as shown in column 2 of Exhibit 6.3 (see p.152).

Total fixed cost Costs that do not vary as output varies and that must be paid even if output is zero. These are payments that the firm must make in the short run, regardless of the level of output.

Total variable cost Costs that are zero when output is zero and vary as output varies.

Total variable cost

As the firm expands from zero output, total variable cost is added to total fixed cost. Total variable cost consists of costs that are zero when output is zero and vary as output varies. These costs relate to the costs of variable inputs which, in our simple example, are confined to inputs of labour. Put simply, the variable cost is the cost of the wages of the employees employed. As a firm uses more input to produce output, its variable costs will increase. Management can control variable costs in the short run by changing the level of output. Exhibit 6.3 lists the total variable cost (*TVC*) for Atmach in column 3. Recall that, when explaining the production function, we assumed that all employees have the same level of job skills. We also assume that each of these employees receives the same wage.

Total cost

Given total fixed cost and total variable cost, the firm can calculate **total cost**. Total cost is the sum of total fixed cost and total variable cost at each level of output. As a formula:

Total cost The sum of total fixed cost and total variable cost at each level of output.

$$TC = TFC + TVC$$

Total cost (*TC*) for Atmach is shown in column 4 of Exhibit 6.3. Exhibit 6.4(a) (on p. 154) uses data in Exhibit 6.3 to construct graphically the relationships among total cost, total fixed cost and total variable cost. Note that the *TVC* curve varies with the level of output and the *TFC* curve does not. The *TC* curve is simply the *TVC* curve plus the *TFC* curve. That is, the vertical distance between the *TC* and *TVC* curves represents *TFC*.

Average cost curves

In addition to total cost, the *per-unit cost*, or *average cost*, is of great interest to firms. Average cost, like product price, is stated on a per-unit basis. The last three columns in Exhibit 6.3 are *average fixed cost* (*AFC*), *average variable cost* (*AVC*) and *average total cost* (*ATC*) calculated to the nearest whole dollar. These average, or per-unit, curves are also shown in Exhibit 6.4(b). These three concepts are defined as follows.

Average fixed cost

Average fixed cost Total fixed cost divided by the quantity of output produced.

As output increases, **average fixed cost** (*AFC*) falls continuously. Average fixed cost is total fixed cost divided by the quantity of output produced. Written as a formula:

$$AFC = \frac{TFC}{Q}$$

Exhibit 6.3 Short-run cost schedule for Atmach

(1) Total product (Q)	(2) Total fixed cost (TFC)	(3) Total variable cost (TVC)	(4) Total cost (TC)	(5) Marginal cost (MC)	(6) Average fixed cost (AFC)	(7) Average variable cost (AVC)	(8) Average total cost (ATC)
0	$100	$ 0	$100		--	--	--
				$ 50			
1	100	50	150		$100	$50	$150
				34			
2	100	84	184		50	42	92
				24			
3	100	108	208		33	36	69
				19			
4	100	127	227		25	32	57
				23			
5	100	150	250		20	30	50
				30			
6	100	180	280		17	30	47
				38			
7	100	218	318		14	31	45
				48			
8	100	266	366		13	33	46
				59			
9	100	325	425		11	36	47
				75			
10	100	400	500		10	40	50
				95			
11	100	495	595		9	45	54
				117			
12	100	612	712		8	51	59

As shown in Exhibit 6.4(b), the *AFC* curve approaches the horizontal axis as output expands. This is because larger output numbers divide into *TFC* and cause *AFC* to become smaller and smaller.

Average variable cost

The **average variable cost** (*AVC*) in our example forms a U-shaped curve. Average variable cost is total variable cost divided by the quantity of output produced. Written as a formula:

Average variable cost Total variable cost divided by the quantity of output produced.

$$AVC = \frac{TVC}{Q}$$

The *AVC* curve is also drawn in Exhibit 6.4(b). At first the *AVC* curve falls and then, after an output of 6 units per hour, the *AVC* curve rises. Thus, the *AVC* curve is U-shaped. The explanation for the shape of the *AVC* curve is given in the next section.

Average total cost

The **average total cost** (*ATC*) is total cost divided by the quantity of output produced. Written as a formula:

Average total cost Total cost divided by the quantity of output produced.

$$ATC = AFC + AVC = \frac{TVC}{Q}$$

Like the *AVC* curve, the *ATC* curve is U-shaped, as shown in Exhibit 6.4(b). At first the *ATC* curve falls because its component parts – *AVC* and *AFC* – are falling. As output continues to rise, the *AVC* curve begins to rise while the *AFC* curve falls continuously. Beyond the output of 7 units per hour, the rise in the *AVC* curve is greater than the fall in the *AFC* curve, which causes the *ATC* curve to rise in a U-shaped pattern.

PART 2

INFOTRAC®

marginal cost

Marginal cost

Marginal analysis asks how much it costs to produce an *additional* unit of output. Column 5 in Exhibit 6.3 shows **marginal cost**. Marginal cost is the change in total cost when one additional unit of output is produced. Stated differently, marginal cost is the ratio of the change in total cost to a one-unit change in output. Written as a formula:

Marginal cost The change in total cost when one additional unit of output is produced.

$$MC = \frac{\text{change in } TC}{\text{change in } Q} = \frac{\text{change in } TVC}{\text{change in } Q}$$

Note that marginal cost can also be calculated from changes in *TVC*. This is because the only difference between total cost and total variable cost is total fixed cost. Thus, the changes in *TC* and *TVC* with each unit change in output are the same amount. To check this relationship, look at the per-unit changes in *TC*, *TVC* and *MC* in Exhibit 6.3.

To be reassured that the concept of marginal cost is not just some irrelevant academic oddity, use a web browser such as Yahoo (**www.yahoo.com**) to search for *marginal cost*. How many pages did you find?

Changing output by one unit at a time simplifies the marginal cost calculations in our Atmach example. The marginal cost data are listed

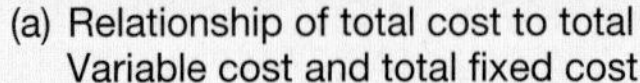
Exhibit 6.4 Short-run cost curves

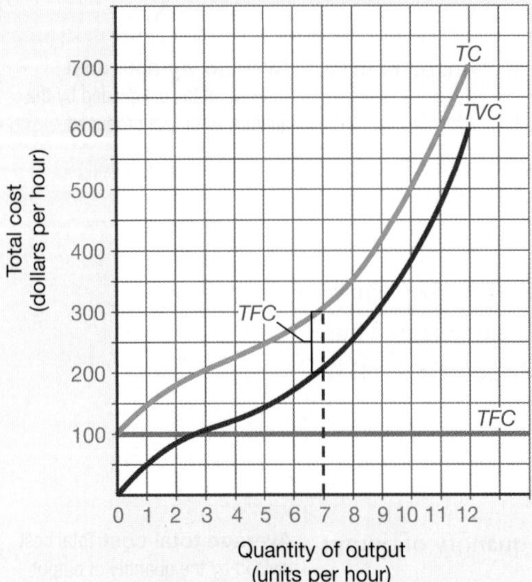

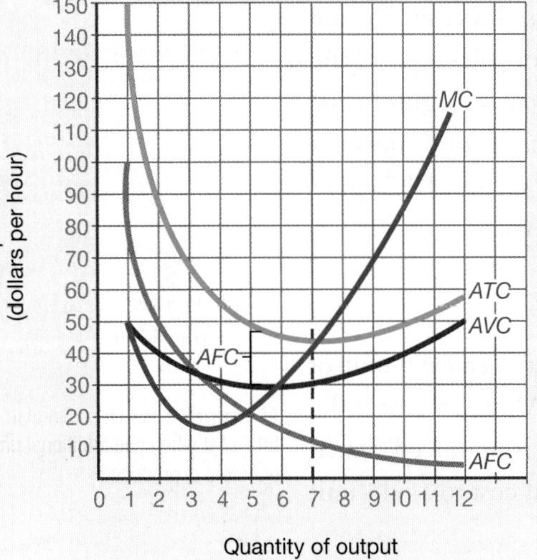

The curves in this figure are derived by plotting data from Exhibit 6.3. Part (a) shows that the total cost (*TC*) at each level of output is the sum of total variable cost (*TVC*) and total fixed cost (*TFC*). Because the *TFC* curve does not vary with output, the shape of the *TC* curve is determined by the shape of the *TVC* curve. The vertical distance between the *TC* and *TVC* curves is *TFC*.

In part (b), the marginal cost (*MC*) curve at first decreases, then reaches a minimum, and then increases as output increases. The *MC* curve intersects both the average variable cost (*AVC*) curve and the average total cost (*ATC*) curve at the minimum point on each of these cost curves. The average fixed cost (*AFC*) curve declines continuously as output expands. *AFC* is also the difference at any quantity of output between the *ATC* and the *AVC* curves.

between output levels to show that marginal cost is the change in total cost as the output level changes. Exhibit 6.4(b) shows this marginal cost schedule graphically. In the short run, a firm's marginal cost falls initially as output expands, eventually reaches a minimum and then rises, forming a U-shaped curve. Note that marginal cost is plotted at the midpoints because the change in cost occurs between each additional unit of output.

Exhibit 6.5 summarises a firm's short-run cost relationships.

Exhibit 6.5 **Short-run cost formulas**

Cost concept	Formula	
Total cost (*TC*)	$TC = TFC + TVC$	$ TC Q
Marginal cost (*MC*)	$\frac{\text{change in } TC}{\text{change in } Q} = \frac{\text{change in } TVC}{\text{change in } Q}$	$ MC Q
Average fixed cost (*AFC*)	$AFC = \frac{TFC}{Q}$	$ AFC Q
Average variable cost (*AVC*)	$AVC = \frac{TVC}{Q}$	$ AVC Q
Average total cost (*ATC*)	$ATC = \frac{TC}{Q}$	$ ATC Q

Marginal cost relationships

Part (b) of Exhibit 6.4 presents two important relationships that require explanation. First, we will explain the rule that links the marginal cost curve to the average cost curves. Second, we will return to the marginal product curve in Exhibit 6.2(b) and explain its connection to the marginal cost curve.

The marginal-average rule

Observe that the *MC* curve in Exhibit 6.4(b) intersects with both the *AVC* curve and the *ATC* curve at their minimum points. This is not accidental. It is the result of a relationship called the **marginal-average rule**. The marginal-average rule states that, when marginal cost is below average cost, average cost falls. When marginal cost is above average cost, average cost rises. When marginal cost equals average cost, average cost is at its minimum point. The marginal-average rule applies to grades, weights and any average figure.

Marginal-average rule When applied to cost relationships the rule states that, when marginal cost is below average cost, average cost falls. When marginal cost is above average cost, average cost rises. When marginal cost equals average cost, average cost is at its minimum point.

Perhaps the best way to understand this rule is to apply it to a non-economic example. Suppose there are 20 students in your classroom and each student has a grade point average (GPA) of 4.0. The average GPA of the class is therefore 4.0. Now let another student who has a GPA of 2.0 join the class. The new average GPA of 21 students in the class falls to 3.9. The average GPA was pulled down because the *marginal* GPA of the additional student was less than the *average* GPA of the other students. On the other hand, let's start with 20 students with a 2.0 GPA and add a student who has

Analyse the issue

Cane harvesting costs

At a meeting in Ingham in North Queensland in October 2000, John Powell, the executive officer of Caneharvesters, explained to managers of banks and other institutions that lend to the sugar cane harvesting industry that the industry was experiencing a crisis of profitability. This crisis had been brought about by lighter crops (less cane per hectare), higher fuel prices and increased capital requirements. Here is some of what he had to say when addressing these issues:

> In terms of fuel, the average operator uses roughly 1000 litres a day, and prices have increased by more than 40c a litre. That is an increase in cost of more than $400 a day over the past year.
>
> With light crops, harvesters are scratching to average 30 tonnes cut per hour but they are using the same amount of fuel as they would if they were cutting 60 tonnes. Effectively the cost of harvesting a tonne of cane has doubled.
>
> Capital repayments are being spread over half the tonnes, which effectively doubles capital costs.
>
> The low productivity also impacts on labour costs and the costs of maintaining the machinery doesn't change either.[1]

Which of the costs being discussed by Mr Powell are fixed costs and which are variable? Clue: In analysing this issue, Mr Powell is making the assumption that output of the cane harvesting industry is measured in tonnes of harvested cane rather than hectares of cane harvested. It will be easier to determine which costs are fixed and which are variable by treating hectares of harvested cane as the output. Do you think harvesting contractors are paid by the tonne or the hectare?

1 *Herbert River Express*, 3 October 2000, p. 2.

a 4.0 GPA. In this case, the new average GPA of 21 students rises from 2.0 to 2.1. Thus, the *marginal* GPA of the last student was greater than the *average* GPA of all students in the class before the addition of new students.

You make the call

Was Don Bradman's test average 100 before his last innings?

Australia's best-known cricketer, the late, great Don Bradman, needed just four runs in the last innings of his test career to have a test average of exactly 100. Unfortunately, he was out for a duck (out without scoring). Does the marginal-average rule enable us to work out whether Bradman's test average was more than 100 before his final innings?

To read a brief profile of Don Bradman, some highlights of his career and his batting statistics, go to **www.cricinfo.com/link_to_database/PLAYERS/AUS/B/BRADMAN_DG_02000492/**.

Now consider the *MC* curve in part (b) of Exhibit 6.4. In the range of output from 0 to 6 units per hour, the *MC* curve is below the *AVC* curve and *AVC* is falling. Beyond 6 units per hour, the *MC* curve is above *AVC* and *AVC* is rising. Hence, the relationship between *AVC* and *MC* conforms to the marginal-average rule. It follows that the *MC* curve intersects the *AVC* at its lowest point. This analysis also applies to the relationship between the *MC* and *ATC* curves. Initially, the *MC* curve lies below the *ATC* curve, which is falling. Beginning with 8 units of output, the *MC* curve exceeds the *ATC* curve, causing the *ATC* curve to rise.

Marginal cost and marginal product inversely related

Since the *MC* curve determines the U-shape of the *AVC* and *ATC* curves, we must explain the U-shape of the *MC* curve. Exhibit 6.6 shows how the shape of the *MC* curve is inversely related to the shape of the marginal product (*MP*) curve. Comparing parts (a) and (b) of Exhibit 6.6 gives us this conclusion: *The marginal cost declines as the marginal product of a variable input rises if the wage rate is constant. Beginning at the point of diminishing returns, the marginal cost rises as the marginal product of a variable input declines.* As explained earlier in this chapter, the law of diminishing returns explains the declining portion of the *MP* curve that corresponds to the rising portion of the *MC* curve.

To understand why this relationship exists, we return to the production relationships for Eastern Slope Vineyard, presented earlier in Exhibit 6.2. Now we again assume that labour is the only variable input and add the new important assumption that the wage rate is constant at $100 per day. When Eastern Slope moves from zero labour to hire one employee, its total output rises from zero to one tonne of grapes per day. As explained earlier, the marginal product is also one tonne and the marginal cost (per tonne) is $100/1 = $100. When Eastern Slope hires the second employee, this

Exhibit 6.6 The inverse relationship between marginal product and marginal cost

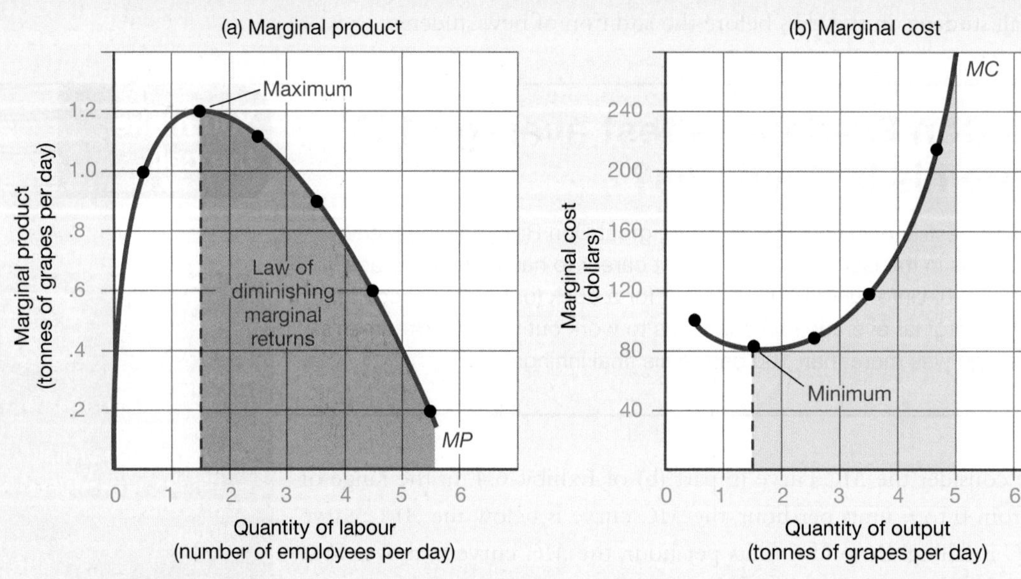

(1) Labour input (number of employees per day)	(2) Total output (tonnes of grapes per day)	(3) Marginal product (tonnes of grapes per day) [Δ(2)/Δ(1)]	(4) Total variable cost per day [$100 x (1)]	(5) Marginal cost per day [Δ(4)/(3)]
0	0		$0	
		1.0		$100.00
1	1.0		100	
		1.2		83.33
2	2.2		200	
		1.1		90.90
3	3.3		300	
		.9		111.11
4	4.2		400	
		.6		166.66
5	4.8		500	
		.2		500.00
6	5.0		600	

Part (a) represents the marginal product of labour (*MP*) curve. At first, each additional employee hired adds more to output than does the previously hired employee and the *MP* curve rises until a maximum is reached at two employees hired. At three employees, the law of diminishing returns has set in and each additional employee hired adds less output than previously hired employees.

Part (b) shows the marginal cost (*MC*) curve as a U-shaped curve that is inversely related to the *MP* curve. Assuming the wage rate remains constant, as the *MP* curve rises the *MC* curve falls. When the *MP* curve reaches a maximum between one and two employees, the *MC* curve is at a minimum. As diminishing returns set in and the *MP* curve falls, the *MC* curve rises.

increases the firm's total variable cost by $100, while the marginal product rises to 1.2 tonnes. The marginal cost associated with the second employee hired therefore falls to $100/1.2 = $83.33 per tonne. This is minimum marginal cost. At this point, it is noteworthy that the minimum point on the *MC* curve corresponds to the maximum point on the *MP* curve. Hiring of the third employee yields 1.1 additional tonnes of grapes per day, so marginal cost rises to $90.90. At this stage, diminishing returns are being experienced and the marginal cost continues to rise as more employees are hired.

Long-run production costs

As explained earlier in this chapter, the long run is a time period long enough to change the quantity of all fixed inputs. A firm can, for example, build a larger or smaller factory or vary the capacity of its machinery. In this section we will discuss how a decision to change the size of a firm's fixed inputs (for example, its factory and the machinery in it) affects the relationship between production and costs.

Long-run average cost curves

Suppose Atmach is making its production plans for the future. Taking a long-run view of production means that the firm is not locked into a small, medium or large-sized factory. However, once the factory is built in any of these sizes, the firm operates in the short run because the plant has become a fixed input.

PART 2

A firm operates in the short run when there is no need to alter fixed inputs or when there is insufficient time to do so. The firm plans in the long run when all inputs are variable.

Exhibit 6.7 illustrates a condition in which there are only three possible factory sizes Atmach might select. Short-run cost curves representing these three possible plant sizes are labelled $SRATC_s$, $SRATC_m$ and $SRATC_l$. *SR* is the abbreviation for short run, and *ATC* stands for average total cost. The subscripts *s*, *m* and *l* represent small, medium and large plant size respectively. In the previous sections, there was no need to use *SR* for short run because we were discussing only short-run cost curves and not long-run cost curves.

Suppose Atmach estimates that it will be producing an output level of 6 units per hour for the foreseeable future. Which plant size should the company choose? It will build the plant size represented by $SRATC_s$ because this affords a lower cost of $30 per unit (point *A*) than the factory size represented by $SRATC_m$, which is $40 per unit (point *B*).

What if production is expected to be 12 units per hour? In this case, the firm will choose the plant size represented by $SRATC_l$. This plant size gives a cost of $30 per unit (point *C*) rather than a cost of $40 per unit (point *D*).

CONCLUSION **The plant size selected by a firm in the long run will be the one that minimises cost for the expected level of production.**

Long-run average cost curve The curve that traces the lowest cost per unit at which a firm can produce any level of output when the firm can build any desired plant size.

Using the three short-run average cost curves shown in Exhibit 6.7, we can construct the firm's **long-run average cost curve** (*LRAC* curve). The long-run average cost curve traces the lowest cost per unit at which a firm can produce any level of output when the firm is in a position to build any desired plant size. The *LRAC* curve is sometimes called the firm's planning curve. In Exhibit 6.7, the green curve represents the *LRAC* curve.

Exhibit 6.8 shows the case where there are an infinite number of possible plant sizes from which managers can choose in the long run. As the number of short-run average total cost curves corresponding to these different-sized plants increases, the lumps in the *LRAC* curve shown in Exhibit 6.8 disappear. With an infinite number of plant sizes, the corresponding short-run *ATC* curves trace a smooth *LRAC* curve. When the *LRAC* curve falls, the points of tangency between the long-run and short-run curves are to the left of the minimum points on the short-run *ATC* curves. As the *LRAC* curve rises, the tangency points are to the right of the minimum points on the short-run *ATC* curves.

Exhibit 6.7 **The relationship between three factory sizes and the long-run average cost curve**

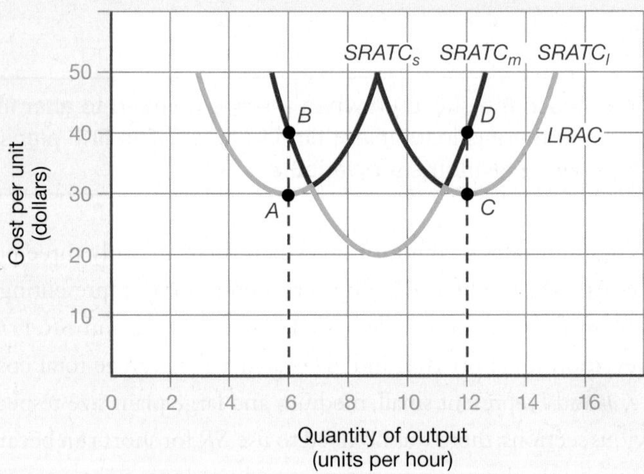

Each of the three short-run *ATC* curves in the figure corresponds to a different plant size. Assuming these are the only three plant-size choices, a firm can choose any one of these plant sizes in the long run. For example, a young firm may operate a small plant represented by the U-shaped short-run average total cost curve $SRATC_s$. As a firm matures and demand for its product expands, it can decide to build a larger factory, corresponding to either $SRATC_m$ or $SRATC_l$. The long-run average cost (*LRAC*) curve is the green, scalloped curve joining the short-run curves below their intersections.

Exhibit 6.8 **The long-run average cost curve when the number of factory sizes is unlimited**

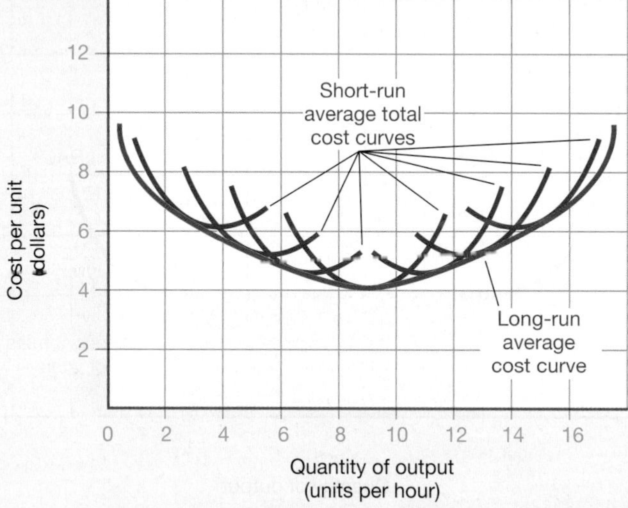

If there are an infinite number of possible short-run *ATC* curves that correspond to different plant sizes, the long-run average cost (*LRAC*) curve is the blue curve tangent to each of the possible red short-run *ATC* curves.

Different scales of production

Exhibit 6.8 depicts long-run average cost as a U-shaped curve. In this section, we will discuss the reasons why *LRAC* first falls and then rises when output expands in the long run. In addition, you will learn that the *LRAC* curve can have a variety of shapes. Note that the law of diminishing returns is not an explanation here, because in the long run there are no fixed inputs.

For simplicity, Exhibit 6.9 excludes the short-run *ATC* curves that touch points along the *LRAC* curve. Typically, a young firm starts small and builds larger plants as it matures. As the scale of operation expands, the *LRAC* curve can exhibit three different patterns. Over the lowest range of output from zero to Q_1, the firm experiences **economies of scale**. Economies of scale exist when the long-run average cost curve declines as the firm increases output.

Economies of scale
A situation in which the long-run average cost curve declines as the firm increases output.

economies of scale

There are several reasons for economies of scale. First, a larger firm can increase the *division of labour* and *use of specialisation*. Adam Smith noted in *The Wealth of Nations*, published in 1776, that the output of a pin factory is greater when, rather than having each employee make a complete pin, one employee draws the wire, a second straightens it, a third cuts it, a fourth grinds the point and a fifth makes the head. As a firm initially expands, having more employees allows managers to break a job into small tasks. Then each employee – including each manager – can specialise by mastering narrowly defined tasks rather than trying to be a jack-of-all-trades.[1] The classic example is Henry Ford's assembly line, which greatly reduced the cost of producing motor cars.

1 Adam Smith, *An Inquiry into the Nature and Causes of the Wealth of Nations*, 1776, reprint, Random House, New York, 1937, pp. 4–6.

Exhibit 6.9 **A long-run average cost curve including constant returns to scale**

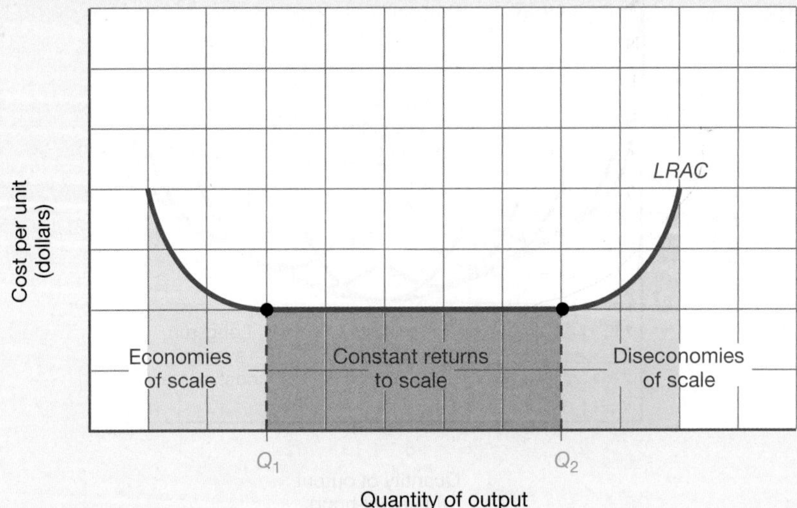

The long-run average cost (*LRAC*) curve illustrates a firm that experiences economies of scale until output level Q_1 is reached. Between output levels Q_1 and Q_2, the *LRAC* curve is flat and there are constant returns to scale. Beyond output level Q_2, the firm experiences diseconomies of scale and the *LRAC* curve rises.

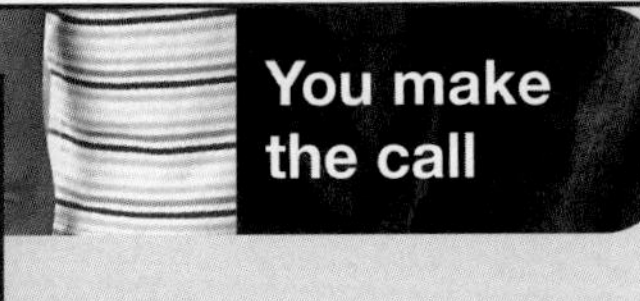

PART 2

Why were new Internet companies so keen to expand?

An important characteristic of the new Internet companies (dot-coms) that mushroomed in the second half of the 1990s was their incredible capacity to 'burn' shareholders' funds as they expanded rapidly. Many of these firms undertook expenditure on marketing and product development that was far in excess of their sales revenue. Some firms had no sales revenue at all! This led to many high-profile company crashes, culminating in the so-called tech stock crash of 2000. Why do you think these firms were so intent on rapid expansion?

Second, economies of scale result from greater *efficiency of capital*. Suppose machine *A* costs \$1000 and produces 1000 units per day. Machine *B* costs \$4000, but it is technologically more efficient and has a capacity of 8000 units per day. The low-output firm will find it too costly to purchase machine *B*, so it uses machine *A* and its average cost is \$1. The large-scale firm can afford to purchase machine *B* and produce more efficiently at a per-unit cost of only \$0.50. The scale of operation is important for competitive reasons. Consider a young firm producing less than output Q_1 and competing against a more established firm that has reaped all economies of scale and is now producing in the range of output between Q_1 and Q_2. The *LRAC* curve shows that the older firm has an average cost advantage.

International focus

Applicable concept: economies of scale

Invasion of the monster movie theatres

A few decades ago most movie theatres had a single screen and offered just one film, limited parking and a small range of products at the snack bar. Now theatres are bigger and better than ever, with one complex in South Australia having 27 screens. Multiplexes with fewer than 16 screens and megaplexes with 16 or more screens offer several movies at the same time, luxury seating, a bar and on-site parking. Patrons are increasingly choosing the premium offerings, involving food and drinks delivered to electric recliner lounge seats in intimate surroundings.

These large complexes have become the industry standard around the world and Australian companies are contributing, through industry partnerships, to their establishment in Asia, the Middle East and Germany. As the number of screens in these complexes increases, so does their output, measured in numbers of patrons per annum. A major reason for the development of these complexes is the economies of scale that they provide because their overheads can be shared by a larger number of screens. This leads to a situation where lower costs per screen, and greater flexibility of screen use, have the potential to increase owners' profits.

A US analyst who follows the movie theatre industry for First Union Capital Markets in Charlotte said the owners of second-run theatres – especially small ones – face several challenges. 'In the age of megaplexes, a four-screen theatre stands out on the negative side. In general we're moving to a lot more screens and a lot less theatres,' Bishop Cheen said. 'If you only have four screens, you only have four reasons for a patron to leave home and spend money.'[1]

Although these large complexes are providing economies of scale, it may be that diseconomies could occur if the complex becomes too large. For example, some industry analysts believe that the 14- and 18-screen complexes built in Germany are too big. In a similar vein, Kurt Hall, executive vice-president of United Artists Entertainment Co. in the United States, stated his concerns about complexes being too large:

> When building new theatres, United Artists is limiting its screens per site to about 15, half as many as AMC [American Multi-Cinema, Inc.]. United Artists fears that a larger megaplex won't pull in enough volume. 'Over 16 screens, the economics start to fall apart.'[2]

1 Audrey Y. Williams, 'Cut-rate movie theater has closed', *Charlotte Observer*, 9 October 1997, p. 1A.

2 Kevin Helliker, 'Monster movie theatres invade the cinema landscape', *Wall Street Journal*, 13 May 1997, p. B1.

Analyse the issue

1 Explain why the long-run average cost curve for movie theatres falls (economies of scale) as the number of screens they have increases.

2 Can you think of reasons why the long-run average cost curve for movie theatres might rise (diseconomies of scale) beyond some number of screens?

The *LRAC* curve may not turn upward and form the U-shaped cost curve in Exhibit 6.8. Between some levels of output, such as Q_1 and Q_2 in Exhibit 6.9, the *LRAC* curve no longer declines. In this range of output, the firm increases its plant size but the *LRAC* curve remains flat. Economists call this **constant returns to scale**. Constant returns to scale exist when long-run average cost does not change as the firm increases output.

Constant returns to scale
A situation in which the long-run average cost curve is horizontal as the firm increases output.

Diseconomies of scale
A situation in which the long-run average cost curve rises as the firm increases output.

As a firm becomes large and expands output beyond some level, such as Q_2 in Exhibit 6.9, it may encounter **diseconomies of scale**. Diseconomies of scale exist when the long-run average cost curve rises as the firm increases output. A large-scale firm becomes harder to manage. As the firm grows, the chain of command lengthens and communication becomes more complex. Everyone must use email to communicate instead of direct conversation. Firms become too bureaucratic and operations bog down in red tape. Layer upon layer of managers are paid to shuffle papers that may have little or nothing to do with producing output. Consequently, it is no surprise that a firm can become too big and these management problems can cause the average cost of production to rise. The managers of a firm in this situation may decide to break up the firm so that it consists of a number of smaller, more manageable units.

Steven Jobs, founder of Apple Computer Company, stated:

> When you are growing [too big], you start adding middle management like crazy … People in the middle have no understanding of the business, and because of that, they screw up communications. To them, it's just a job. The corporation ends up with mediocre people that form a layer of concrete.[2]

2 Deborah Wise and Catherine Harris, 'Apple's New Crusade', *Business Week*, 26 November 1984, p. 156.

Key concepts

- Explicit costs
- Implicit costs
- Economic profit
- Normal profit
- Fixed input
- Variable input
- Short run
- Long run
- Production function
- Marginal product
- Law of diminishing returns
- Total fixed cost
- Total variable cost
- Total cost
- Average fixed cost
- Average variable cost
- Average total cost
- Marginal cost
- Marginal-average rule
- Long-run average cost curve
- Economies of scale
- Constant returns to scale
- Diseconomies of scale

Summary

- **Marginal product** is the change in total output caused by a one-unit change in a variable input, such as labour. The **law of diminishing returns** states that, after some level of output in the short run, each additional unit of the variable input yields smaller and smaller marginal product. This range of declining marginal product is the region of diminishing returns.

- **Fixed cost** consists of costs that do not vary with the level of output, such as rent for office space and general insurance. **Total fixed cost** is the cost of inputs that do not change as the firm changes output in the short run. **Variable cost** consists of costs that vary with the level of output, such as wages. **Total variable cost** is the cost of variable inputs used in production at each level of output. **Total cost** is the sum of total fixed cost and total variable cost at each level of output.

Total cost

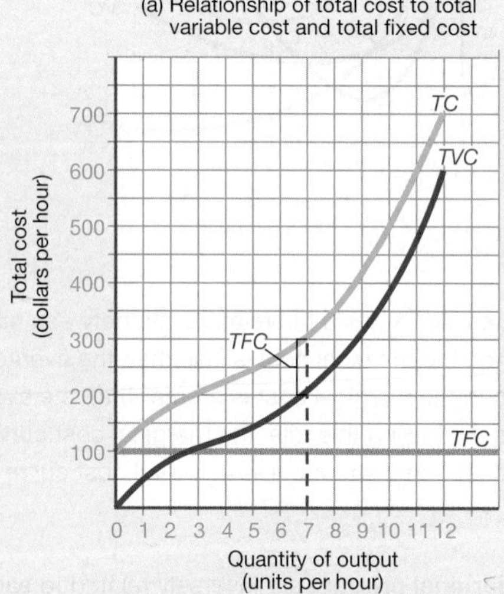

- **Economic profit** is equal to total revenue minus both **explicit** and **implicit costs**. Implicit costs are the opportunity costs of forgone returns to resources owned by the firm. Economic profit is important for decision-making purposes because it includes implicit costs, while accounting profit does not. Accounting profit equals total revenue minus explicit costs.

- The **short run** is a time period during which a firm has at least one fixed input, such as a factory of a given size. The **long run** for a firm is defined as a period during which all inputs are variable.

- A **production function** is the relationship between inputs and outputs. Holding all other factors of production constant, the production function shows the total output as the amount of one input, such as labour, varies.

- **Marginal cost** is the change in total cost associated with one additional unit of output. **Average fixed cost** is the total fixed cost divided by total output at each level of output. **Average variable cost** is the total variable cost divided by total output at each level of output. **Average total cost**, or the sum of average fixed cost and average variable cost, is the total cost divided by total output at each level of output.

Average total cost

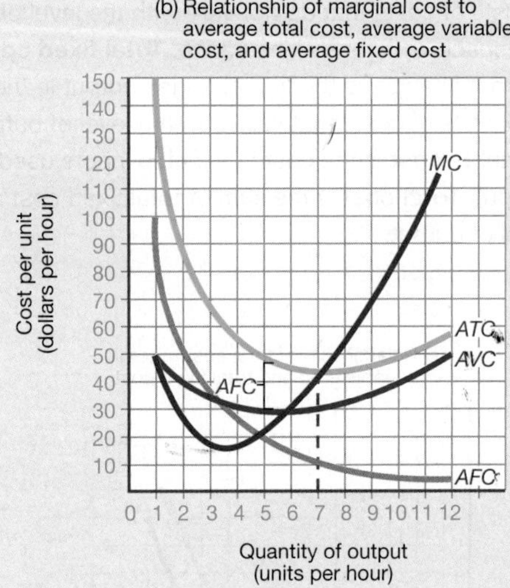

- The **marginal-average rule** explains the relationship between marginal cost and average cost. When the marginal cost is less than the average cost, the average cost falls. When the marginal cost is greater than the average cost, the average cost rises. Following this rule, the marginal cost curve intersects the average variable cost curve and the average total cost curve at their minimum points.

- **Marginal cost** and **marginal product** are inversely related to each other. Assuming a constant wage rate, marginal cost equals the wage rate divided by the marginal product. Increasing returns cause marginal cost to fall and diminishing returns cause marginal cost to rise. This explains the U-shaped marginal cost curve.

Marginal product

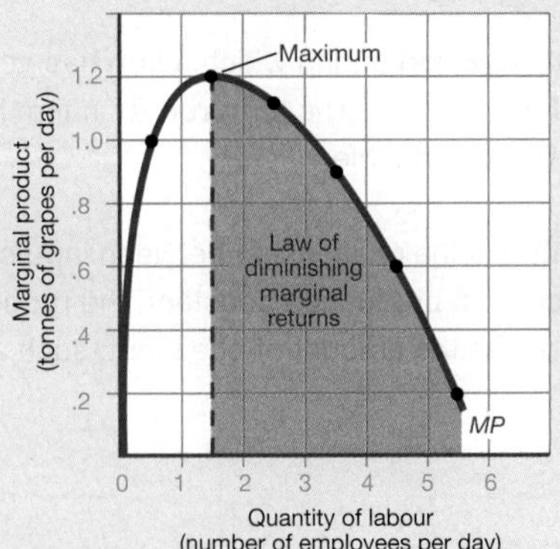

Marginal cost

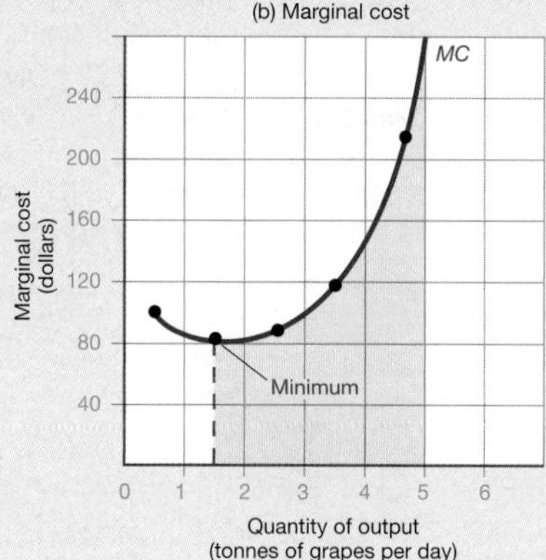

- The **long-run average cost curve** is a curve drawn at a tangent to all possible short-run average total cost curves. When the long-run average cost curve decreases as output increases, the firm experiences **economies of scale.** If the long-run average cost curve remains unchanged as output increases, the firm experiences **constant returns to scale.** If the long-run average cost curve increases as output increases, the firm experiences **diseconomies of scale.**

Long-run average cost curve

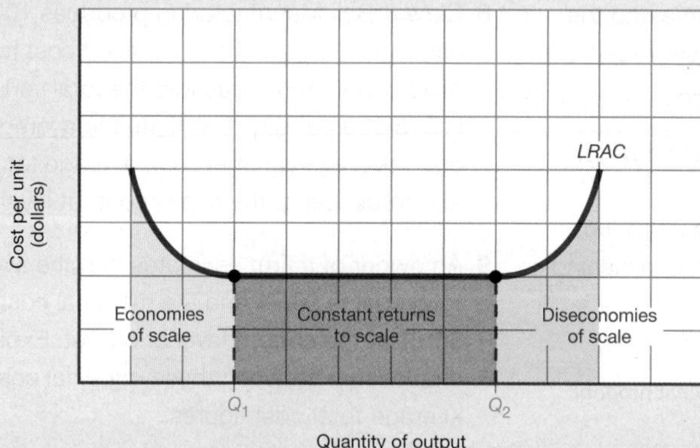

Study questions and problems

1 Indicate whether each of the following is an explicit cost or an implicit cost.

- **a** a manager's salary
- **b** payments to IBM for computers
- **c** a salary forgone by the owner of a firm by operating his or her own company
- **d** interest forgone on a loan an owner makes to his or her own company
- **e** workers compensation payments a company makes for its employees
- **f** income forgone while going to university.

2 Suppose you own a video rental store. List some of the fixed inputs and variable inputs you would use in operating the store.

3 Consider this statement: 'Total output starts falling when diminishing returns occur.' Do you agree or disagree? Explain.

4 What effect might an improvement in technology have on the short-run total product and marginal product curves?

5 a Construct the cost schedule below for a firm operating in the short run.

b Graph the average variable cost, average total cost and marginal cost curves.

Total product (*Q*)	Total fixed cost (*TFC*)	Total variable cost (*TVC*)	Total cost (*TC*)	Marginal cost (*MC*)	Average fixed cost (*AFC*)	Average variable cost (*AVC*)	Average total cost (*ATC*)
0	$50	$ ____	$50		$ ____	$ ____	____
				$ ____			
1	____	____	70		____	____	____
				____			
2	____	____	85		____	____	____
				____			
3	____	____	95		____	____	____
				____			
4	____	____	100		____	____	____
				____			
5	____	____	110		____	____	____
				____			
6	____	____	130		____	____	____
				____			
7	____	____	165		____	____	____
				____			
8	____	____	215		____	____	____
				____			
9	____	____	275		____	____	____

6 Explain why the average total cost curve and the average variable cost curve move closer together as output expands.

7 a Construct the marginal product schedule for the following production function.

b Graph the total output and marginal product curves and identify increasing and diminishing marginal returns.

Labour	Total output	Marginal product
0	0	
		____
1	8	
		____
2	18	
		____
3	30	
		____
4	43	
		____
5	55	
		____
6	65	
		____
7	73	
		____
8	79	
		____
9	82	
		____
10	80	

8 Claw & Ball Manufacturing produces 1000 hammers per day. The total fixed cost for the plant is $5000 per day and the total variable cost is $15 000 per day. Calculate the average fixed cost, average variable cost, average total cost and total cost at the current output level.

9 An owner of a firm estimates that the average total cost is $6.71 and the marginal cost is $6.71 at the current level of output. Explain the relationship between these marginal cost and average total cost figures.

10 In each commercial fishery in the world we observe a great similarity in the size of fishing vessels used to catch certain types of fish. Can cost theory help explain why this is so?

11 In the infancy of the development of the Internet for commercial purposes it was argued that firms could not afford to waste any time in developing their services and presenting them to the market. Why is it important to be an early entrant in a new industry having an L-shaped long-run average total cost curve?

Online exercises

Exercise 1

Visit the Alberta Agriculture, Food and Rural Development *crop cost and return calculator* at **www1.agric.gov.ab.ca** and select **Calculators**, then **Crop calculators** and **Crop enterprise**. Choose a soil type (say, black), choose a crop (say, CPS wheat) and then click to see the calculation. In the expenses (costs) list identify any costs that might be explicit rather than implicit on some farms. Are all the costs of growing the crop listed under the 'Expenses' heading?

Exercise 2

When Alfred Marshall, the great English economist, explained the concept of marginal product in his *Principles of Economics* he noted that the number of men required to look after a flock of sheep of a given size was much smaller in Australasia than in Britain. A table explaining the concept of marginal product can be found in Note 14 of Chapter 1 in Book VI of the *Principles* (**www.econlib.org/library/Marshall/marPNotes4.html#aa14**). Examine this table to see that the concept of marginal product (in the column headed 'product due to last man') is the same today as it was nearly a century ago when Marshall was writing about the wool industry. (Note, however, that Marshall is looking only at the falling section of the marginal product curve.) On the basis of the information provided in the note, do you think that the marginal product of employees in the Australasian wool industry would have been higher or lower than that of British employees? What is the relationship between the values in the column headed 'product due to last man' and that headed 'wages bill'?

Exercise 3

The *Whitebook of the European Exhibition Industry* includes a section (1.4 in Volume 2) about the economics of multiplexes. Go to this section at **www.mediasalles.it/whiteboo/ wb2_1_4.htm**. Under the heading 'costs of screens' read about the factors that are responsible for economies of scale at multi-screen sites. Now look at Figure 6 under the same heading. If we assume that the output of movie tickets is proportional to the number of screens in each cinema configuration, describe whether the following alternative company structures would have economies of scale, constant returns to scale or diseconomies of scale: a company having a number of single screen sites; a company having a multi-screen site; and a company having a multiplex.

Answers to 'You make the call'

Should the consultant go or stay?

In the new consulting business, the accounting profit is \$135 000. An accountant would calculate profit as the annual revenue of \$175 000 less the explicit cost of \$40 000 per year for the secretary's salary. However, the accountant would neglect implicit costs. Dr What's business venture would have implicit costs of \$16 000 in forgone rent, \$120 000 in forgone salary earnings and \$2000 in forgone annual interest on the \$40 000 she took out of savings. Her economic profit is –\$3000, calculated as the accounting profit of \$135 000 less the total implicit costs of \$138 000. If you said Dr What will pass up the potential accounting profit and stay with her current employer to avoid an economic loss, YOU ARE CORRECT.

Was Don Bradman's test average over 100 before his last innings?

If Bradman required four runs in his last test innings to end up with an average of exactly 100, his average before this final innings must have been over 100. The marginal-average rule tells us that, if the marginal score is lower than the average, it will pull the average down. Thus a marginal score of just four runs will have pulled down the average from something in excess of 100 runs to exactly 100 runs. For the record, Bradman went into his last innings with a run total of 6996 from 69 test innings. If he had been out for four runs in his last innings he would have had a run total of 7000 from 70 innings. If you said that the average was over 100, YOU ARE CORRECT.

Why were new Internet companies so keen to expand?

The development of the Internet with its very low costs of reaching potential customers almost anywhere in the world has seen many Internet-based firms attempting to increase the size of their market. It is widely believed that the larger an Internet-based firm becomes, the greater the extent to which it can

PART 2

spread many of its costs over an increasing number of customers. That is, the larger the scale of a firm's operation, the lower its per-unit cost will be. This means that the firm that can expand most rapidly and become the largest in the industry will be in a position to undercut its smaller rivals and drive them out of business. If you said that potential economies of scale prompted the mad rush by Internet companies to expand, YOU ARE CORRECT.

Multiple-choice questions

1 Explicit costs are payments to
- a employees.
- b insurance companies.
- c utility companies.
- d all of the above.

2 Implicit costs are the opportunity costs of using the resources of
- a outsiders.
- b owners.
- c banks.
- d accountants.

3 Which of the following equalities is true?
- a Economic profit = total revenue – accounting profit
- b Economic profit = total revenue – explicit costs – accounting profit
- c Economic profit = total revenue – implicit costs – explicit costs
- d Economic profit = opportunity cost + accounting cost

4 Fixed inputs are factors of production that
- a include all inputs except labour.
- b can be increased or decreased quickly to change output.
- c cannot be increased or decreased to change output.
- d are none of the above.

5 An example of a variable input is
- a raw materials.
- b energy.
- c hourly labour.
- d all of the above.

6 Suppose a car wash has two washing bays and five employees and is able to wash 100 cars per day. When it adds a third bay, but no more employees, it is able to wash 150 cars per day. The marginal product of the third washing bay is
- a 100 cars per day.
- b 150 cars per day.
- c 5 cars per day.
- d 50 cars per day.

7 If the units of variable input in a production process are 1, 2, 3, 4 and 5 and the corresponding total outputs are 10, 22, 33, 42 and 48 respectively, the marginal product of the fourth unit is
- a 2.
- b 6.
- c 9.
- d 42.

8 The total fixed cost curve is
- a upward-sloping.
- b downward-sloping.
- c upward-sloping and then downward-sloping.
- d unchanged with the level of output.

9 If the marginal cost curve is below the short-run average total cost curve, then as output increases the marginal cost curve must be
- a rising.
- b falling.
- c either rising or falling.
- d none of the above.

10 If both the marginal cost and the average variable cost curves are U-shaped, at the point of minimum average variable cost the marginal cost must be
- a greater than the average variable cost.
- b less than the average variable cost.
- c equal to the average variable cost.
- d at its minimum.

11 Which of the following is *true* at the point where diminishing returns set in?
- a Both marginal product and marginal cost are at a maximum.
- b Both marginal product and marginal cost are at a minimum.
- c Marginal product is at a maximum and marginal cost at a minimum.
- d Marginal product is at a minimum and marginal cost at a maximum.

12 As shown in Exhibit 6.10, total fixed cost for the firm is
- a zero.
- b $250.

PART 2

c $500.
d $750.
e $1000.

13 As shown in Exhibit 6.10, the total cost of producing 100 units of output per day is
a zero.
b $250.
c $500.
d $750.
e $1000.

Exhibit 6.10 **Total cost curve**

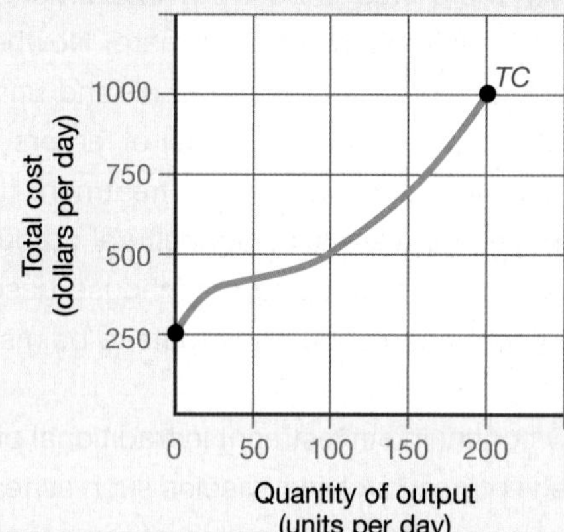

14 In Exhibit 6.10, if the total cost of producing 99 units of output per day is $475, the marginal cost of producing the 100th unit of output per day is approximately
a zero.
b $25.
c $475.
d $500.

15 Each potential short-run average total cost curve is tangent to the long-run average cost curve at
a the level of output that minimises short-run average total cost.
b the minimum point of the short-run average total cost curve.
c the minimum point of the long-run average cost curve.
d a single point on the short-run average total cost curve.

16 Suppose a firm is producing *X* units of output per day. Using any other of the infinite plant sizes, the long-run average cost would increase. The firm is operating at a point at which
a its long-run average cost curve is at a minimum.
b its short-run average total cost curve is at a minimum.
c both **a** and **b** are true.
d neither **a** nor **b** is true.

17 The downward-sloping segment of the long-run average cost curve corresponds to
a diseconomies of scale.
b both economies and diseconomies of scale.
c the decrease in average variable costs.
d economies of scale.

18 Long-run diseconomies of scale exist when the
a short-run average total cost curve falls.
b long-run total revenue curve rises.
c long-run average total cost curve falls.
d short-run average variable cost curve rises.
e long-run average cost curve rises.

19 Long-run constant returns to scale exist when the
a short-run average total cost curve is constant.
b long-run average cost curve rises.
c long-run average cost curve is flat.
d long-run average cost curve falls.

7 Perfect competition

Towards the end of last century there was a boom in investment in timber plantations in countries with suitable soil and climate. Nowhere was this more apparent than in Australia, where the area of land under plantation grew by 800 per cent during the 1990s. A number of factors led to this spectacular growth. They included favourable tax treatment that lowered growers' costs, falling prices for alternative agricultural outputs, recognition of the role that forests play in reducing greenhouse gases, and increasing dissemination of information about the profits to be made from plantation investments.

This boom in plantations saw continuing investment in traditional pine plantations as well as innovative ventures involving species such as teak, sandalwood, blue gum and blackwood. The combination of tax benefits and the expectation that demand would outstrip supply from existing sources led to expectations of handsome profits down the track when harvesting occurred.

Suddenly, however, at the turn of the century some commentators were warning that the high profits expected might never materialise. What factors were causing the alarm bells to ring? The problem appeared to be that too many growers were able to enter the market and supply timber of equal quality to that already being supplied. As the critics pointed out, tens of thousands of farmers and graziers in Australia alone had suitable land and could easily enter the industry. Furthermore, information on how to develop, maintain and harvest plantations was readily available and, so long as plantation management standards were maintained, each grower would be in a position to produce high-quality timber.

More recently, in the business pages of *The West Australian* in 2004 it was argued that the outlook for the plantation timber industry was again positive, with an expansion of sales and increased profitability encouraging further investment.[1]

Adam Smith concluded that competitive forces are like an 'invisible hand' that leads people who simply pursue their own interests to serve the

1 Cathy Bolt, 'Agribusiness agriboom', *The West Australian*, 20 November 2004, p. 86.

interests of society. In a competitive market such as the timber plantation industry, when the profit potential looks good, new and existing firms start developing more plantations. However, if too many participants branch out into this industry and the area under plantation explodes, prices and profits will eventually fall. This will cause growers to exit the industry. Thus the process of competition will eventually correct any tendency to move away from the appropriate level of output.

This chapter combines the demand, cost of production and marginal analysis concepts from previous chapters to explain how competitive markets determine prices, output and profits. The firms in these markets are small, like fruit and vegetable growers or providers of lawn mowing services, rather than huge, like Microsoft, Toyota or Singapore Airlines. Because they sell products or services that are very similar to those sold by their rivals, these competitive firms are also unlike small businesses such as restaurants or furniture manufacturers, which sell different kinds of services or products from those sold by their competitors. Other types of markets in which large and powerful firms operate, or in which small firms sell goods and services that are different from those sold by their rivals, will be discussed in subsequent chapters.

To read about opportunities for farmers in the timber plantation industry in Australia, go to the paper by Ross Garsden at **www.newcrops.uq.edu.au/acotanc/papers/garsden.htm**.

In this chapter, you will examine these economics questions:

- What is a market structure?
- Why would a firm stay in business while losing money?
- Why do governments around the world promote competition in markets?
- How is the Internet changing the structure of world markets?

Market structures

Market structure A classification system for the key characteristics of a market, including the number of firms, the similarity of the products they sell and the ease of entry into and exit from the market.

Firms sell goods and services under different sets of market conditions, which economists call **market structures**. There are a number of market structures, each of which has certain key characteristics that enable economists to understand the way in which firms behave in that market.

The characteristics of a market that define its structure include the number of firms in that market, the degree to which the products they sell are similar and the ease of entry into, and exit from, the market. These characteristics indicate the degree of competition faced by firms in their particular markets. Examination of the business sector of our economy reveals firms facing differing degrees of competition because they operate in very different market structures. As Exhibit 7.1 shows, these market structures range from a highly competitive market structure, characterised by a large number of firms, to one that is dominated by a single seller, which is called a monopoly. In this and subsequent chapters we will study each of the four market structures listed in Exhibit 7.1. In the process we will see how different market structures bring out differences in the behaviour of firms. The first market structure we examine is **perfect competition**, to which this entire chapter is devoted. Perfect competition is the most competitive market structure. It is characterised by (1) a large number of small firms, (2) a homogeneous product and (3) very easy entry into, or exit from, the market.

Perfect competition A market structure characterised by (1) a large number of small firms, (2) a homogeneous product and (3) very easy entry into or exit from the market.

Perfect competition

Large number of small firms

How many sellers is a large number? And how small is a small firm? Certainly one, two or three firms in a market would not be a large number. In fact, the

Exhibit 7.1 **Comparison of market structures**

Market structure	Number of sellers	Type of product	Entry conditions	Examples
Perfect competition	Large	Homogeneous	Very easy	Small crops, international commodity markets
Monopolistic competition	Large	Differentiated	Easy	Boutiques, restaurants, motels
Oligopoly	Few	Usually differentiated but sometimes homogeneous	Difficult	Car making, tobacco products, oil
Monopoly	One	Unique	Extremely difficult	Public utilities

exact number cannot be stated. This condition is fulfilled when each firm in a market has no significant share of total output and therefore no ability to affect the product's market price. Each firm acts independently, rather than coordinating decisions collectively. For example, there are thousands of independent egg farmers in Australia. If any single egg farmer raises or lowers his or her price, the going market price for eggs is unaffected.

The large-number-of-sellers condition is met when each firm is so small relative to the total market that no single firm can influence the market price.

Homogeneous product

In a perfectly competitive market, all firms produce a standardised or homogeneous product. This means that the goods or services of all the firms are identical. Fisherman Chek's prawns are identical to fisherman Joe's prawns. Similarly, buyers may believe that the transportation services of one independent trucking firm are about the same as another's services. This assumption rules out successful pursuit of competitive advantage through advertising, quality differences or locational advantage.

If a product is homogeneous, buyers are indifferent as to which seller's product they buy.

Very easy entry and exit

Very easy entry into a market means that a new firm faces no barriers to its entry into that market. Barriers can be financial, technical or government-imposed. These barriers include some classes of licences and permits, as well as patents. Anyone who wants to try his or her hand at commercial lawn mowing needs only a mower, a phone and a means of transport. Ease of exit from a market means that, if a firm decides against continuing to produce, it can easily close down. In other words, there are no contractual or legal reasons why it must continue. We shall see that this ability of firms to exit a declining industry is important, because it means that prices can be restored quickly to profitable levels.

Perfect competition requires that resources be completely mobile to freely enter or exit a market.

In addition to these assumptions, it is also presumed that economic agents – both businesses and consumers – are well informed about key aspects of the operation of the market, including knowledge of the product being sold, knowledge of the costs of production and knowledge of prices.

INFOTRAC®
perfect competition

No real-world market exactly fits the three assumptions of perfect competition. The perfectly competitive market structure is a theoretical

PART 3

or ideal model, but some actual markets do approximate the model fairly closely. Examples include farm product markets, the interstate road transport market and markets for home services such as lawn mowing or cleaning.

If no real-world market exactly fits the assumptions of perfect competition, you may be wondering why so much space is devoted to the model here. The answer is that the model provides a benchmark by which we may judge the structure and performance of markets that we observe in the real world. As you saw in Chapter 4, where we discussed market failure, a lack of competition in markets leads to a less efficient outcome than is potentially available if competition prevails. The notion that perfectly competitive markets deliver maximum efficiency is so important in contemporary market economies that every such economy in the world has a **competition policy** designed to promote efficiency through the encouragement of competition and the outlawing of anti-competitive practices.

Competition policy
Government policy that has the objective of increasing competition in the economy, or of encouraging firms that are not competitive to behave as if they were.

competition policy

In Australia, competition policy is overseen by the Australian Competition and Consumer Commission (ACCC), which is a Commonwealth government statutory authority responsible for ensuring compliance with relevant parts of the Trade Practices Act. This Act has the objective of enhancing the welfare of Australians through the promotion of competition and fair trading, and providing for consumer protection. The ACCC cooperates with, and complements, relevant state government bodies and also administers the Prices Surveillance Act.

The ACCC's objectives, which can be gleaned from its website, include the following:

- improve competition and efficiency in markets;
- foster adherence to fair trading practices in well-informed markets;
- promote competitive pricing wherever possible and restrain price rises in markets where competition is less than effective;
- inform the community at large about the Trade Practices Act and its specific implications for business and consumers; and
- use resources efficiently and effectively.

The New Zealand Commerce Commission (NZCC) has similar objectives, which are encapsulated in three strategic goals listed on their website. They are that:

- markets are dynamic and all goods and services are provided at competitive prices;
- consumers are confident of the accuracy of information they receive when making choices; and
- regulated industries are constrained from earning excess profits, face incentives to invest appropriately and share efficiency gains with consumers.

A brief resume of the Trade Practices Act and some discussion of the role of the ACCC can be found at **www.accc.gov.au**. Click on *About us*.

You can see that, even if perfect competition is evident only in some industries in modern economies, the aim of government competition policies is to encourage all industries to become more efficient by behaving *as if they were* competitive.

It is also worth noting that many of the regulatory activities of bodies like the ACCC or the NZCC are designed to curb unethical behaviour in the business sector – behaviour that Adam Smith might have described as displaying unenlightened self-interest. Some of the undesirable business activities that governments do their best to eliminate include colluding to raise prices and profitability, exercising monopoly power at the expense of consumers and engaging in misleading advertising.

Having established the importance of the presence of competition in contemporary market economies, we now turn to further development of the model of perfect competition.

The perfectly competitive firm as a price taker

Price taker A seller that has no control over the price of the product it sells.

As the first step in building our competitive model, suppose a firm operates in a market that conforms to all three of the above requirements for perfect competition. This would mean that the perfectly competitive firm is a **price taker**. A price taker is a seller that has no control over the price of the product it sells. From the individual firm's perspective, market supply and demand conditions over which the firm has no influence determine the price of its products. Look again at the characteristics of a perfectly competitive firm: a small firm that is one among many firms, sells a homogeneous product and is exposed to competition from new firms entering the market. These conditions make it impossible for the perfectly competitive firm to have the market power to affect the market price. Instead, the firm must adjust to, or 'take', the market price.

PART 3

Exhibit 7.2 The market price and demand for the perfectly competitive firm

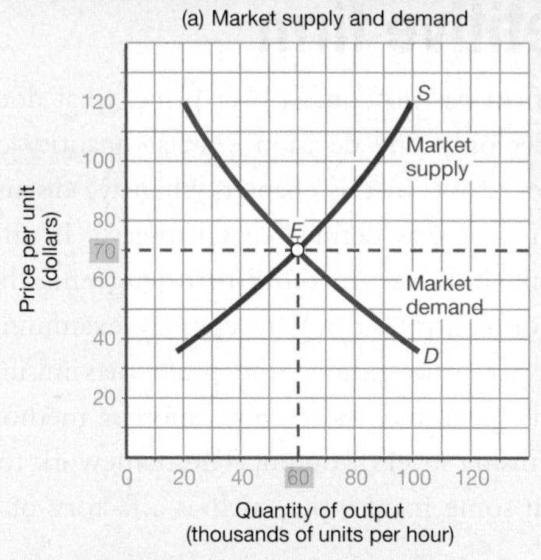

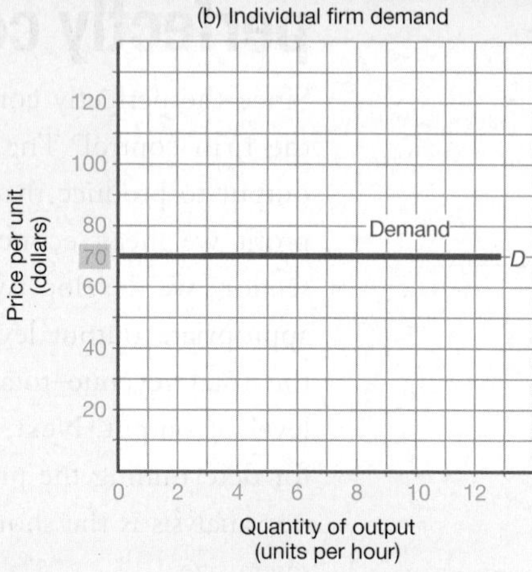

In part (a), the market equilibrium price is $70 per unit. The perfectly competitive firm in part (b) is a price taker because it is so small relative to the market. At $70, the individual firm faces a horizontal demand curve, *D*. This means that the firm's demand curve is perfectly elastic. If the firm raises its price even one cent, it will sell zero output.

Exhibit 7.2 is a graphical presentation of the relationship between the market supply and demand for electronic components and the demand curve facing a firm in a perfectly competitive market. Here we will assume that the electronic components industry is perfectly competitive, keeping in mind that the real-world market may not exactly fit the model. (Certainly, in the international market for electronic components there is likely to be a high level of competition, as there are a large number of suppliers worldwide.) Exhibit 7.2(a) shows market supply and demand curves for the quantity of output per hour. The theoretical framework for this model was explained in Chapter 4. The equilibrium price is $70 per unit and the equilibrium quantity is 60 000 units per hour.

Now we look at the demand curve faced by the individual firm. This demand curve shows the price–quantity combinations at which the firm can sell its output. Because the perfectly competitive firm 'takes' the equilibrium price, the individual firm's demand curve in Exhibit 7.2(b) is *perfectly elastic* (horizontal) at the $70 market equilibrium price. (Note the difference between the firm's units per hour and the industry's thousands of units per hour; this firm has but a small part of total industry output.) Recall from Chapter 5 that, when a firm facing a perfectly elastic demand curve tries to raise its price one cent higher than $70, no buyer will purchase its product (see Exhibit 5.3(a) in Chapter 5). The reason is that there are many other firms selling the same product at $70 per unit. Hence, the perfectly competitive firm will not set the price above the prevailing market price and risk selling zero output. Nor will the firm set the price below the market price because the firm can sell all it wants to at the going price and, therefore, a lower price would reduce the firm's revenue.

Short-run profit maximisation for a perfectly competitive firm

Since the perfectly competitive firm has no control over price, what does the firm control? The firm makes only one decision – what quantity of output to produce that maximises profit. In this chapter, when we discuss profit we mean economic profit as it was defined in Chapter 6. In this section, we develop two profit maximisation methods that determine the appropriate output level for a competitive firm. We begin by examining the total revenue–total cost approach for finding the profit-maximising level of output. Next, we use marginal analysis to show another method for determining the profit-maximising level of output. The framework for our analysis is the short run with some fixed input, such as a factory of a given size.

The total revenue–total cost method

Exhibit 7.3 provides hypothetical data on output, total revenue, total cost and profit for our typical electronic components producer, Atmach. Using Atmach as our example allows us to extend the data and analysis presented in previous chapters. The total cost figures in column 3 are taken from Exhibit 6.3 in Chapter 6. By looking at total cost at zero output you can see that total fixed cost is $100.

Total revenue is reported in column 2 of Exhibit 7.3 and is computed as the product price times the quantity. In this case, we assume that the market equilibrium price is $70 per unit, as determined in Exhibit 7.3. Because Atmach is a price taker, the total revenue from selling one unit is $70, from selling two units $140, and so on. Subtracting total cost in column 3 from total revenue in column 2 gives the total profit or loss (column 4) that the firm earns at each level of output. From zero to two units, the firm earns losses; then a *break-even point* (zero economic profit) occurs at about three units per hour. If the firm produces nine units per hour, it earns the maximum profit of $205 per hour. As output expands between nine and twelve units of output, the firm's profit diminishes. Exhibit 7.4 on p. 181 illustrates graphically that maximum profit occurs where the vertical distance between the total revenue and total cost curves is at a maximum.

Exhibit 7.3 Short-run profit maximisation schedule for Atmach as a perfectly competitive firm

(1) Output (units per hour)	(2) Total revenue	(3) Total cost	(4) Profit [(2) – (3)]	(5) Marginal cost [Δ(3)/Δ(1)]	(6) Marginal revenue [Δ(2)/Δ(1)]
0	$0	$100	–$100		
1	70	150	–80	$50	$70
2	140	184	–44	34	70
3	210	208	2	24	70
4	280	227	53	19	70
5	350	250	100	23	70
6	420	280	140	30	70
7	490	318	172	38	70
8	560	366	194	48	70
9	630	425	205	59	70
10	700	500	200	75	70
11	770	595	175	95	70
12	840	712	128	117	70

The marginal revenue equals marginal cost method

A second approach uses *marginal analysis* to determine the profit-maximising level of output by comparing marginal revenue (marginal benefit) and marginal cost. Column 5 of Exhibit 7.3 gives marginal cost data calculated in column 5 of Exhibit 6.3 in Chapter 6. Recall that marginal cost is the change in total cost as the output level changes one unit. As in Exhibit 6.3 in Chapter 6, these marginal cost data are listed between the quantity of output line entries.

Marginal revenue The change in total revenue from the sale of one additional unit of output.

Now we introduce **marginal revenue** (*MR*), a concept similar to marginal cost. Marginal revenue is the change in total revenue from the sale of one additional unit of output. Stated another way, marginal revenue is the ratio of the change in total revenue to a one-unit change in output. Mathematically,

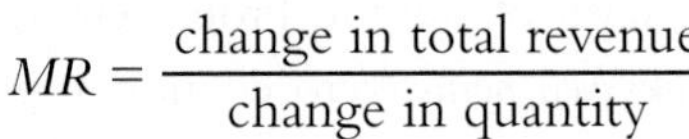

$$MR = \frac{\text{change in total revenue}}{\text{change in quantity}}$$

marginal revenue

As shown in Exhibit 7.2(b), the perfectly competitive firm faces a perfectly elastic demand curve. Because the competitive firm is a price taker, the sale of each additional unit adds to total revenue an amount equal to the price (price is the same as average revenue, *TR*/*Q*). In our example, Atmach adds $70 to its total revenue each time it sells one unit. Therefore, $70 is the marginal revenue for each additional unit of output in column 6 of Exhibit 7.3.

CONCLUSION **In perfect competition, the firm's marginal revenue equals the price that determines the position of the firm's horizontal demand curve.**

Columns 2 and 3 in Exhibit 7.3 show that both total revenue and total cost rise as the level of output increases. Now compare marginal cost and marginal revenue in columns 5 and 6. As explained, marginal revenue remains equal to the price, but marginal cost follows the U-shaped pattern introduced in Exhibit 6.4 in Chapter 6. At first marginal cost is below marginal revenue, and this means that producing each additional unit adds more to total revenue than to total cost. Economic profit therefore increases as output expands from zero until the output level reaches nine units per hour. Over this output range, Atmach moves from a $100 loss to a $205 profit per hour. Beyond an output level of nine units per hour, marginal cost exceeds marginal revenue and profit falls. This is because each additional unit of output raises total cost by more than it raises total revenue. In this case, profit falls from $205 to only $128 per hour if output increases from nine to twelve units per hour.

Our example leads to this question: how does the firm use its marginal revenue and marginal cost curves to determine the profit-maximising level of output? The answer is that the firm follows a guideline called the

Exhibit 7.4 **Short-run profit maximisation using the total revenue–total cost method**

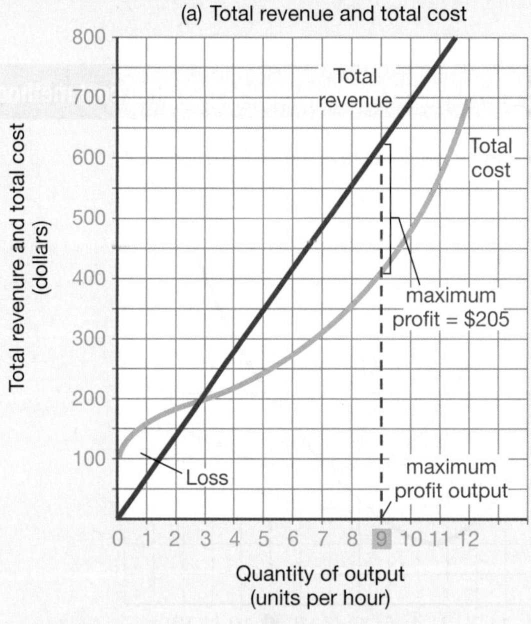

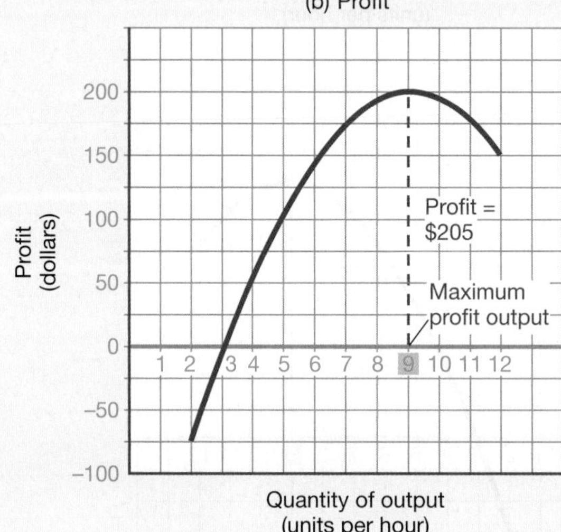

This exhibit shows the profit maximising level of output chosen by a perfectly competitive firm, Atmach. Part (a) shows the relationships between total revenue, total cost and output, given a market price of $70 per unit. The maximum profit is earned by producing nine units per hour. At this level of output, the vertical distance between the total revenue and total cost curves is the greatest.

Profit maximisation is also shown in part (b) of the figure. The maximum profit of $205 per hour corresponds to the profit-maximising output of nine units per hour, represented in part (a).

MR = *MC* rule: *The firm maximises profit or minimises losses by producing the output where marginal revenue equals marginal cost.* Exhibit 7.5 shows how use of the marginal revenue curve equals marginal cost rule leads to profit

Exhibit 7.5 **Short-run profit maximisation using the marginal revenue equals marginal cost method**

(a) Price, marginal revenue and cost per unit

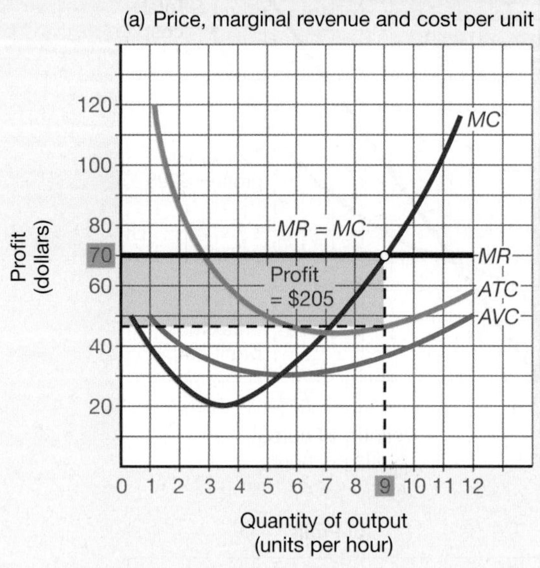

(b) Profit

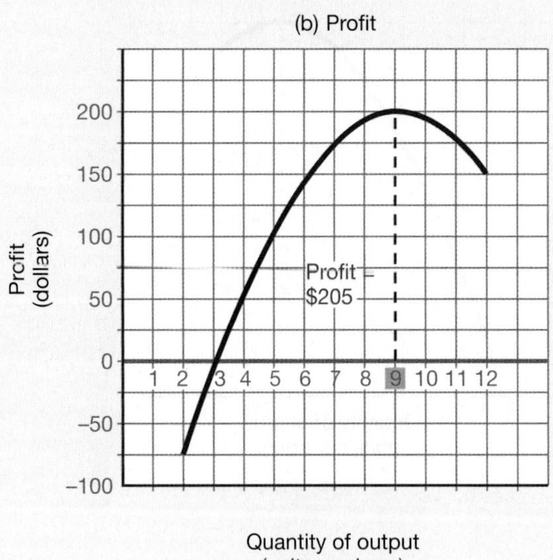

Quantity of output
(units per hour)

In addition to comparing total revenue and total cost, the profit-maximising level of output can be found by comparing marginal revenue and marginal cost. As shown in part (a), profit is at a maximum where marginal revenue equals marginal cost at $70 per unit. The intersection of the marginal revenue and the marginal cost curves establishes the profit-maximising output at nine units per hour.

A profit curve is depicted separately in part (b) in order to show that the maximum profit occurs when the firm produces at the level of output corresponding to the point at which marginal revenue equals marginal cost.

maximisation. In Exhibit 7.5(a) the perfectly elastic demand is drawn at the industry-determined price of \$70. The average total cost curve is traced from data given earlier in column 8 of Exhibit 6.3 in Chapter 6. Note that Exhibit 7.5(a) is a reproduction of Exhibit 6.4(b) in Chapter 6, except for the omission of the *AFC* curve.

Using marginal analysis, we can relate the *MR* = *MC* rule to the same profit curve given in Exhibit 7.4(b). Between eight and nine units of output, the *MC* curve is below the *MR* curve (\$59 < \$70) and the profit curve rises to its peak. Profit rises as we increase output because a rise in output adds more to revenue than it does to cost. (Marginal or additional revenue gained from increasing output is greater than the marginal or additional cost incurred in its production.) Beyond nine units of output, the *MC* curve is above the *MR* curve and the profit curve falls. For example, between nine and ten units of output, marginal cost is \$75 and marginal revenue is \$70. So an increase in output from nine to ten units increases cost by \$75 but gives only a \$70 increase in revenue. Profit must therefore fall. If the firm produces at nine units of output rather than, say, eight units or ten units of output, the *MR* curve equals the *MC* curve and profit is maximised.

You can also calculate profit directly from Exhibit 7.5(a). At the profit-maximising level of output of nine units, the vertical distance between the demand curve and the *ATC* curve is the *average profit per unit*. Multiplying the average profit per unit times the quantity of output gives the profit of \$205 [(\$70 – \$47.22) × 9 = \$205.02]. (Note that in Exhibit 6.3 in Chapter 6 the average total cost figure for nine units of output was rounded down from \$47.22 to \$47.) The shaded rectangle in Exhibit 7.5(a) also represents the maximum profit of \$205 per hour. We have arrived at the same profit maximisation amount (\$205) derived by comparing the total revenue and the total cost curves.

Short-run loss minimisation for a perfectly competitive firm

Because the perfectly competitive firm must take the price determined by market supply and demand forces, market conditions can change the prevailing price. When the market price drops, the firm can do nothing but adjust its output to make the best of the situation. This is why perfectly competitive firms are sometimes described as quantity adjusters. In the following analysis of loss minimisation principles, only the marginal revenue, marginal cost approach is used to predict output decisions of firms.

A perfectly competitive firm facing a short-run loss

Suppose a decrease in the market demand for electronic components causes the market price to fall to \$35. As a result, the firm's horizontal demand

Exhibit 7.6 **Short-run loss minimisation**

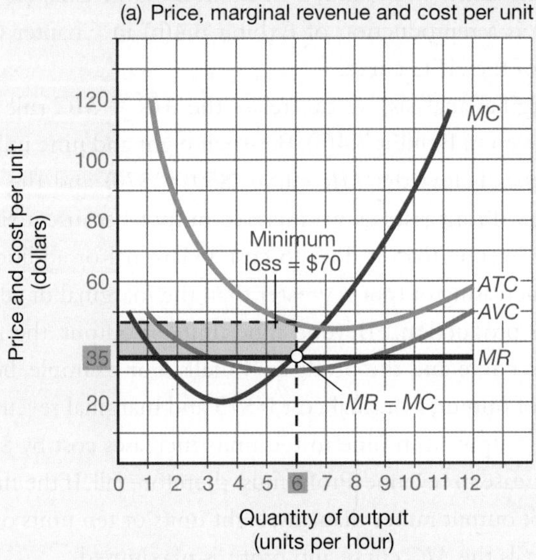

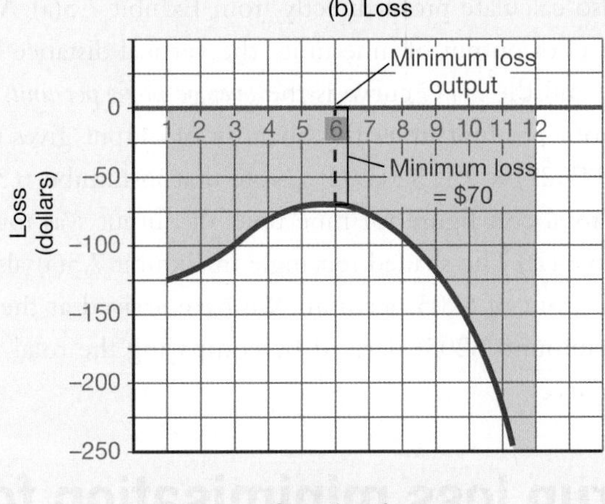

If the market price is less than the average total cost, the firm will produce a level of output that keeps its loss to a minimum. In part (a), the given price is $35 per unit and marginal revenue equals marginal cost at an output of six units per hour.

Part (b) shows that the firm's loss will be greater at any output other than where the marginal revenue and the marginal cost curves intersect. Because the price is above the average variable cost, each unit of output sold pays for the average variable cost and a portion of the average fixed cost.

curve shifts downward to the new position shown in Exhibit 7.6(a). In this case, there is no level of output at which the firm earns a profit because any price along the demand curve is below the *ATC* curve. The firm must now decide whether to continue to operate or to shut down. If it continues to operate it must also decide at what level of output to produce. (Keep in mind that we are continuing with our short-run analysis. This means that, although the firm must retain its fixed factors of production, it has the option of continuing to produce or shutting down. It cannot dispose of its fixed factors because a change in the quantity of the fixed factors can occur only in the long run.)

Since Atmach cannot make a profit at a price of $35, what output level should it choose? The logic of the *MR* = *MC* rule given in the profit-maximisation case applies here as well. At a price of $35, *MR* = *MC* at six units per hour. Comparing parts (a) and (b) of Exhibit 7.6 shows that the firm's loss will be at a minimum at this level of output. The minimum loss of $70 per hour is equal to the shaded area, which is the *average loss per unit* times the quantity of output [($35 – $46.66) × 6 = –$70]. (Again, note that in Exhibit 6.3 in Chapter 6 the average total cost figure for six units of output was rounded up from $46.66 to $47.)

Note that, although the price is not high enough to pay the average total cost, the price is high enough to pay the average variable cost. Each unit sold also contributes to paying a portion of the average fixed cost, which is the vertical distance between the *ATC* and *AVC* curves. Even though it is making a loss in this situation, the firm should continue to operate. If it were to shut down, the contribution that it is currently making to average fixed cost would discontinue. This analysis leads us to extend the *MR* = *MC* rule: *The firm maximises profit – or minimises loss – by producing the output where marginal revenue equals marginal cost.*

A perfectly competitive firm shutting down

What happens if the market price drops below the *AVC* curve, as shown in Exhibit 7.7? For example, if the price is $25 per unit, should Atmach produce some level of output? The answer is no. The best course of action is for the firm to shut down. *If the price is below the minimum point on the* AVC *curve, the revenue from each unit produced cannot cover the variable cost per unit, let alone make a contribution to fixed costs. To operate under these conditions would involve total losses in excess of those incurred if the firm were to shut down. If the firm shuts down, the maximum loss it can incur is equal to the total fixed cost.* Rather than losing more than the total fixed cost, the firm would be better off shutting down and producing zero output. While shut down, the firm would keep its factory, pay fixed costs and hope for higher prices soon. In the long run, if the firm does not believe market conditions will improve, it will avoid fixed costs by going out of business.

Exhibit 7.7 **The short-run shutdown point**

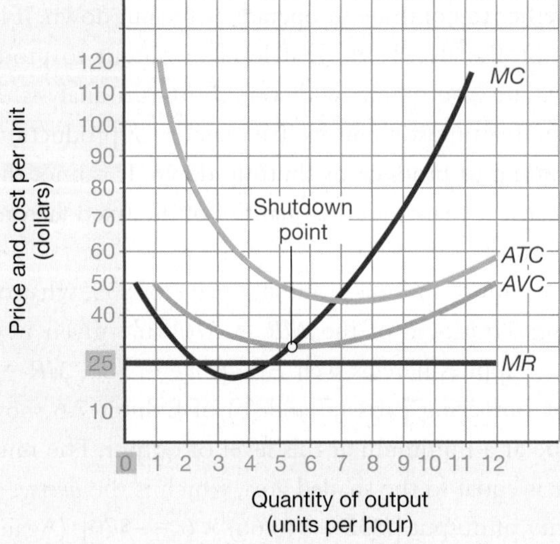

CAUSATION CHAIN

If the price falls below the minimum point on the average variable cost curve, the firm shuts down. The reason is that operating losses are now greater than the total fixed cost. In this exhibit, the price is $25 per unit and is below the average variable cost curve at any level of output.

You make the call

Should motels offer rooms at the beach for only $40 a night?

Using a search engine such as AltaVista (**www.altavista.com**), browse for *coffs harbour motel*. Check out the tariffs at some of the motels in this Northern New South Wales coastal town.

All along the Central and Northern coast of New South Wales there are motels offering basic accommodation – some of it within easy walking distance of the beach. During the school holidays and at other peak times the room rate is over $100 a night. But in the off-season, when the kids are back at school, one can find rooms for as little as $40 a night. Assume the average fixed cost of a room per night, including insurance, taxes and depreciation, is $50. The average guest-related cost for a room each night, including electricity, water, cleaning service and linen, is $25. Would these motels be better off renting rooms for $40 in the off-season or shutting down until the school holidays come round again?

Short-run supply curves under perfect competition

The preceding examples provide a framework for a more complete explanation of the supply curve than was given in Chapter 3. We now develop the short-run supply curve for an individual firm and then derive it for an industry.

The perfectly competitive firm's short-run supply curve

Exhibit 7.8 reproduces the cost curves from our Atmach example. Also represented in the exhibit are three different possible demand curves the firm might face: MR_1, MR_2 and MR_3. As the marginal revenue curve moves upward along the marginal cost curve, the $MR = MC$ point changes.

Suppose the initial market price for electronic components is \$30. Point *A* therefore corresponds to a price equal to MR_1, which equals *MC* at the lowest point on the *AVC* curve. At any lower price, the firm cuts its loss by

Exhibit 7.8 The firm's short-run supply curve

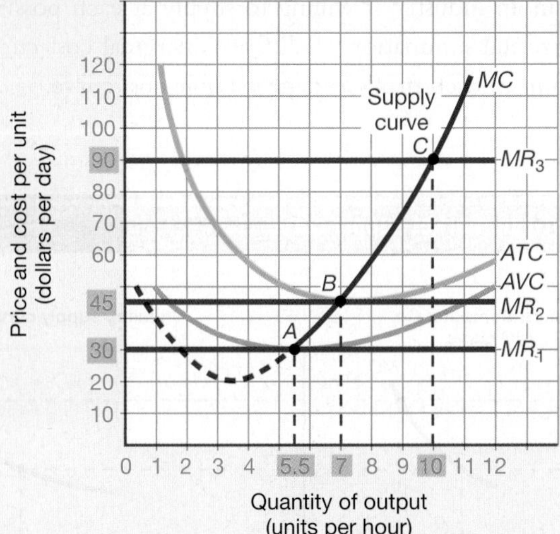

The exhibit shows how the short-run supply curve for Atmach is derived. When the price is \$30, the firm will produce 5.5 units per hour at point *A*. If the price rises to \$45, the firm will move upward along its marginal cost curve to point *B* and produce seven units per hour. At \$90, the firm continues to set price equal to marginal cost, and it produces 10 units per hour. Thus, the firm's short-run supply curve is the marginal cost curve above its average variable cost curve.

PART 3

shutting down. At a price of \$30, however, the firm produces 5.5 units per hour. Point *A* is therefore the lowest point on the individual firm's short-run supply curve.

If the price rises to \$45, represented in the exhibit by MR_2, the firm breaks even and earns a normal profit at point *B* with an output of seven units per hour. As the marginal revenue curve increases, the firm's supply curve is traced by moving upward along its *MC* curve. At a price of \$90, point *C* is reached. Now MR_3 intersects the *MC* curve at an output of ten units per hour and the firm earns an economic profit. If the price rises higher than \$90, the firm will continue to increase the quantity supplied and increase its maximum profit.

Perfectly competitive firm's short-run supply curve The firm's marginal cost curve above the minimum point on its average variable cost curve.

We can now define a **perfectly competitive firm's short-run supply curve**. The perfectly competitive firm's short-run supply curve is its marginal cost curve above the minimum point on its average variable cost curve.

The perfectly competitive industry's short-run market supply curve

Perfectly competitive industry's short-run market supply curve The supply curve derived from the horizontal summation of the short-run supply curves of all firms in the industry.

Understanding that the firm's short-run supply curve is the segment of its *MC* curve above its *AVC* curve enables us to derive the **perfectly competitive industry's short-run market supply curve**. The perfectly competitive industry's short-run market supply curve is simply the sum of the quantities that each of the firms in an industry is willing to supply at each possible price. It is thus the horizontal summation of all firms' marginal cost curves above the minimum point of each firm's average variable cost curve.

PART 3

Exhibit 7.9 **Deriving the industry short-run market supply curve**

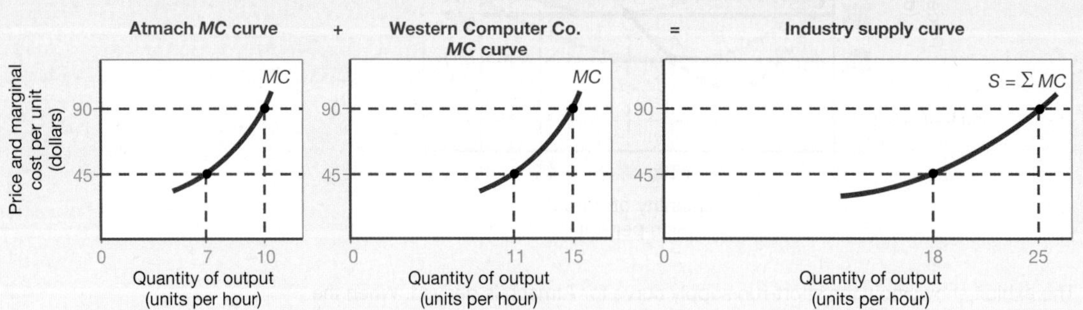

Assuming input prices remain constant as output expands, the short-run market supply curve for an industry is derived by the horizontal summation of quantities supplied at each price for all firms in the industry. In this exhibit, we assume there are only two firms in an industry. At \$45, Atmach supplies seven units of output, and Western Computer Co. supplies eleven units. The quantity supplied by the industry is therefore 18 units. Other points forming the industry short-run market supply curve are obtained similarly.

In Exhibit 3.7 in Chapter 3, we drew a market supply curve. Now we will reconstruct this market supply curve for a competitive industry using more precision. Although in perfect competition there are many firms, we will suppose for simplicity that the industry has only two firms, Atmach and Western Computer Co. Exhibit 7.9 illustrates the *MC* curves for these two firms. Note that the *MC* curve for Atmach is the same as the one shown in Exhibit 7.8. Each firm's *MC* curve is drawn for prices above the minimum point on the *AVC* curve. At a price of $45, the quantity supplied by Atmach would be seven units and the quantity supplied by Western Computer Co. would be eleven units. Now we horizontally add these two quantities and obtain one point on the industry supply curve corresponding to a price of $45 and 18 units. Following this procedure for all prices, we generate the competitive industry's short-run market supply curve.

Note that the market supply curve derived above is based on the assumption that input prices remain unchanged as output expands. Shortly you will learn how changes in input prices affect derivation of the supply curve. First, however, we need to examine short-run equilibrium for a perfectly competitive firm.

Exhibit 7.10 Short-run perfectly competitive equilibrium

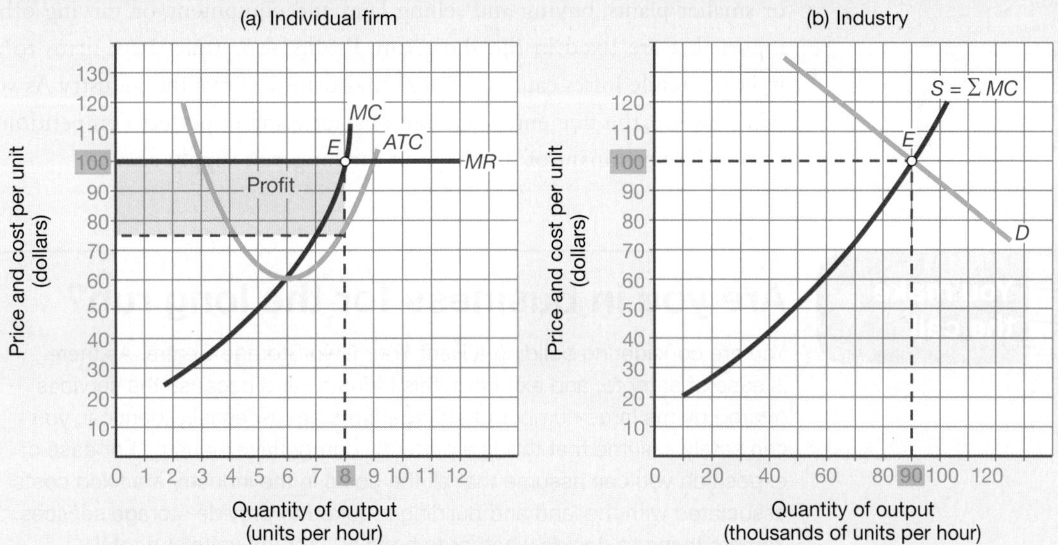

Short-run equilibrium occurs at point *E*. The intersection of the industry supply and demand curves shown in part (b) determines the price of $100 facing the firm shown in part (a). Given this equilibrium price, the firm represented in part (a) establishes its profit-maximising output at eight units per hour and earns an economic profit shown by the shaded area. Note in part (b) that the short-run industry supply curve is the horizontal summation of the marginal cost curves of all individual firms above their minimum average variable cost points.

Short-run equilibrium for a perfectly competitive firm

Exhibit 7.10 illustrates a condition of short-run equilibrium under perfect competition. Exhibit 7.10(a) represents the equilibrium price and cost situation for one of the many firms in an industry. As shown in the figure, the firm earns an economic profit in the short run by producing eight units. Exhibit 7.10(b) depicts short-run equilibrium for the industry. As explained earlier, the industry supply curve is the aggregate of each firm's *MC* curve above the minimum point on the *AVC* curve. Including industry demand establishes the equilibrium price of $100 that all firms in the industry must take. The industry's equilibrium quantity supplied is 90 000 units. This state of short-run equilibrium will remain until some factor changes and causes a new equilibrium condition in the industry. As you will see shortly, given that this short-run equilibrium is one in which firms are earning an economic profit, it cannot be sustained in the long run.

Long-run supply curves under perfect competition

Recall from Chapter 6 that *all* inputs are variable in the long run. Existing firms in an industry can react to profit opportunities by building larger or smaller plants, buying and selling land and equipment, or varying other inputs that are fixed in the short run. Profits also attract new firms to an industry, while losses cause some existing firms to leave the industry. As you will now see, the free entry and exit characteristic of perfect competition is a crucial determinant of the shape of the long-run supply curve.

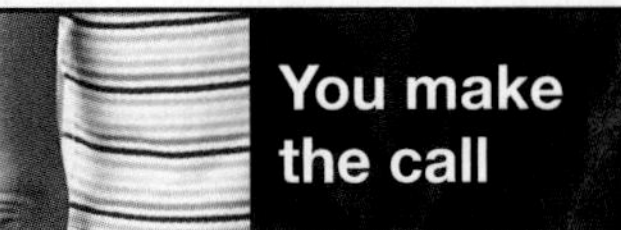

Are you in business for the long run?

You are considering building a Rent Your Own Storage Centre. As there is ease of entry to, and exit from, this industry, and because the services offered by the large number of storage firms are essentially identical, you can safely assume that this is a perfectly competitive industry. For ease of exposition you can assume that all the costs in the industry are fixed costs associated with the land and building required to provide storage services. You are trying to decide whether to build 50 storage units at a total economic cost of $200 000, 100 storage units at a total economic cost of $300 000, or 200 storage units at a total economic cost of $700 000. If you wish to survive in the long run, which size will you choose?

Long-run equilibrium for a perfectly competitive firm

The fact that firms can vary *all* inputs in the long run means that an established firm can decide to *leave* an industry if it earns below normal profits (negative economic profits) and that new firms may enter an industry in which earnings of established firms exceed normal profits (positive economic profits). This process of entry and exit of firms is the key to long-run equilibrium. If there are economic profits, new firms enter the industry and shift the short-run market supply curve to the right. This increase in short-run supply causes the price to fall until economic profits reach zero in the long run. On the other hand, if there are economic losses in an industry, existing firms leave, causing the short-run market supply curve to shift to the left and the price to rise. This adjustment continues until economic losses are eliminated and economic profits equal zero in the long run.

Exhibit 7.11 shows a typical firm in long-run equilibrium. Supply and demand for the market as a whole set the equilibrium price. In the long run, the firm faces an equilibrium price of $60. Following the $MR = MC$ rule, the firm produces an equilibrium output of six units per hour. At this output level, the firm earns a normal profit (zero economic profit) because marginal revenue (price) equals the minimum point on the short-run average total cost curve. Note that this outcome is different from the short-run equilibrium shown in Exhibit 7.10, where the firm was able to earn economic profit. It is different because ease of exit and entry in the long run means that firms attracted by the prospect of earning economic profits will enter the industry. When they do so, market supply will increase, price will fall and economic profits will disappear.

You can also see in Exhibit 7.11 that marginal revenue (price) equals the minimum point of the long-run average cost (*LRAC*) curve as well as the minimum point of the short-run average cost curve. Given the U-shaped *LRAC* curve, the firm is producing with the optimal (least cost) factory size. To see that this is optimal, consider firms with a larger or smaller factory size. In either case these firms would be at a point on the *LRAC* curve that involved higher costs than at the minimum point. This could not be a point of long-run equilibrium, because these firms would seek to change the size of their factories in order to decrease their costs and maximise their profits. Only when all firms in the industry are operating at the minimum point of the *LRAC* curve will long-run equilibrium be achieved.

These conditions for long-run perfectly competitive equilibrium can also be expressed as an equality:

$$P = MR = SRMC = SRATC = LRAC$$

Exhibit 7.11 Long-run perfectly competitive equilibrium

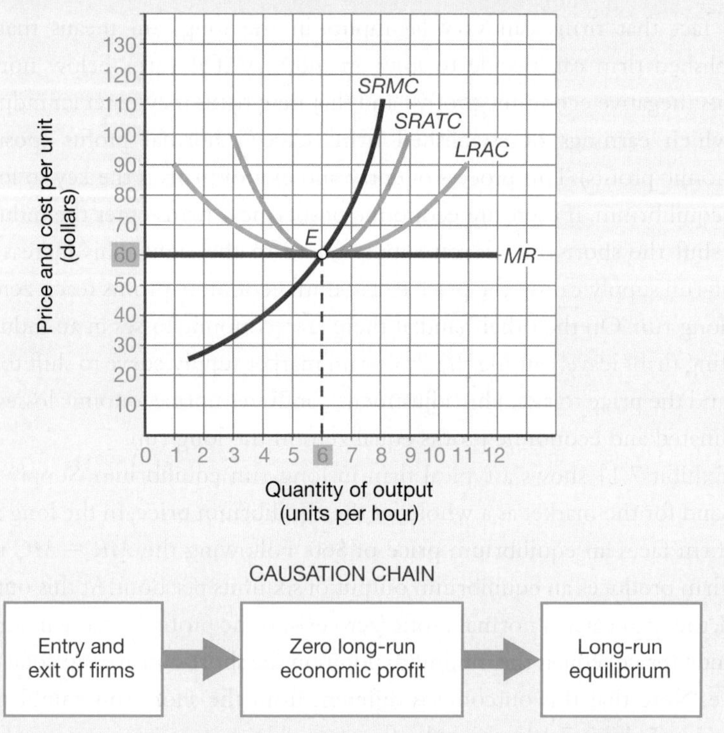

Long-run equilibrium occurs at point *E*. In the long run, the firm earns a normal profit. The firm operates where the price equals the minimum point on its long-run average cost curve. At this point, the short-run marginal cost curve intersects both the short-run average total cost curve and the long-run average cost curve at their minimum points.

As long as none of the variables in the above formula changes, there is no reason for a perfectly competitive firm to change its output level, factory size, or any aspect of its operation. Everything is just right! Because the typical firm is in a state of equilibrium, the industry is also at rest. Under long-run equilibrium conditions, there are neither positive economic profits to attract new firms to enter the industry nor negative economic profits to force existing firms to leave. In long-run equilibrium, the adjustment process of firms moving into or out of the industry is complete. The price that prevails in a perfectly competitive market in long-run equilibrium is the lowest possible price that can be achieved. The market is operating efficiently and consumer well-being is maximised. Note, however, that because market conditions change continually, long-run equilibrium may only be achieved from time to time. At other times the market will be moving towards equilibrium but not necessarily achieving it. Next, we will discuss how the firm and industry adjust when market demand changes.

Efficiency gains from holding prices at competitive levels

Analyse the issue

Applicable concept: long-run perfectly competitive equilibrium maximises efficiency

Because Australia's best-known telecommunications carrier, Telstra, has a monopoly in many areas of its operation, it is subject to government price controls implemented by the ACCC. These controls cover a broad range of telecommunications services including local calls, line rentals, mobile, STD and IDD services. In its December 2000 draft report, which reviewed these price control arrangements, the ACCC pointed to the gains to the community that flow from price controls, which prevent monopolists from raising their prices above the level that would prevail in a perfectly competitive market.

Note that, in the following extract from the draft report, the term *allocative efficiency* has the same meaning as the term *efficiency*, which we used in Chapter 3. In Chapter 3 you saw that the outcome that occurs when a market is in equilibrium is efficient. We described an efficient outcome as 'one in which society maximises the benefits it gains from its use of scarce resources'. The following extract comes from a section of the draft report on price control arrangements headed 'How price control arrangements can improve allocative efficiency'.

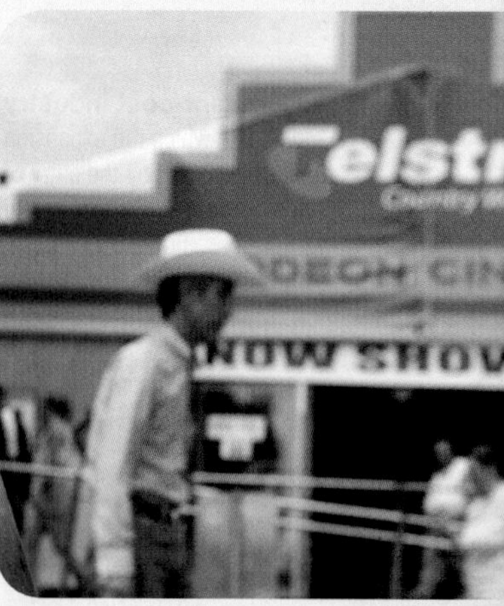

> In the absence of externalities, allocative efficiency is best achieved when the price of a given service equals the marginal cost of producing it. That way, consumers only pay for a service if they value it at least as much as the marginal cost of producing it. In contrast if the price of a service lies above its marginal cost, allocative inefficiency can arise as there will be some consumers who value the service at more than the marginal cost of producing it, but less than the price at which it is being sold and will therefore not purchase it.
>
> Similarly, if the price of a service lies below its marginal cost of production, allocative inefficiency can also arise. This is because there may be some consumers who value the service at less than the marginal cost of producing it, but at more than the price at which it is being sold. Hence, they will purchase the service despite not valuing it at least as much as its cost of production. Ideally, therefore, one would like the price of a service to reflect the marginal cost of producing it.
>
> In perfectly competitive markets, the forces of competition should ensure that the price of a service is driven towards the marginal cost of producing it. Hence, in perfectly competitive markets, allocative efficiency should be assured.
>
> In markets where a service provider has monopoly power, the incentive to drive prices towards marginal cost is removed.

Using the above information, answer the following questions.

1 In the absence of externalities, is it possible for an efficient outcome to occur if firms in an industry are earning economic profits in the long run?

2 If there were no externalities, would society benefit from a situation in which the price of a good or service was below its marginal cost of production?

3 In Chapter 4 you saw that government price controls in a market can lead to an inefficient outcome. What is the difference between the price controls discussed in Chapter 4 and the controls applied to Telstra?

To find a list of publications dealing with the ACCC's price control arrangements for Telstra, go to the ACCC website at **www.accc.gov.au** and use the search facility to search for *Telstra price control arrangements*.

PART 3

Three types of long-run supply curves

Perfectly competitive industry's long-run supply curve The curve that shows the quantities supplied by the industry at different equilibrium prices after firms complete their entry and exit.

There are three possibilities for a **perfectly competitive industry's long-run supply curve**. The perfectly competitive industry's long-run supply curve shows the quantities supplied by the industry at different equilibrium prices after firms complete their entry and exit. The shape of each of these long-run supply curves depends on the response of input prices as new firms enter the industry. The following sections discuss each of these three cases.

Constant-cost industry

Constant-cost industry An industry in which the expansion of industry output by the entry of new firms has no effect on the firm's cost curves.

In a **constant-cost industry**, input prices remain constant as new firms enter or exit the industry. A constant-cost industry is an industry in which the expansion of industry output by the entry of new firms has no effect on the firm's cost curves. Exhibit 7.12 reproduces the long-run equilibrium situation from Exhibit 7.11.

Begin in part (b) of Exhibit 7.12 at the initial industry equilibrium point E_1 with short-run industry supply curve S_1 and industry demand curve D_1. Now assume the industry demand curve increases from D_1 to D_2. As a result, the industry equilibrium moves temporarily to E_2. Correspondingly, the equilibrium price rises from \$60 to \$80 and industry output increases from 50 000 to 70 000 units.

The short-run result for the typical firm in the industry happens this way. As shown in part (a) of Exhibit 7.12, the firm takes the increase in price and adjusts its output from six to seven units per hour. At the higher price and output, the firm changes from earning a normal profit to making an economic profit because the new price is above the *SRATC* curve. All the other firms in the industry make the same adjustment by moving upward along their *SRMC* curves.

In perfect competition, new firms are free to enter the industry in response to a profit opportunity, and they will do so. The addition of new firms shifts the short-run supply curve rightward from S_1 to S_2. Firms will continue to enter the industry until profit is eliminated. This occurs at equilibrium point E_3, where short-run industry demand curve D_2 intersects short-run supply curve S_2. Thus the entry of new firms has restored the initial equilibrium price of \$60. The firm responds by moving back downward along its *SRMC* curve until it once again produces six units and earns a normal profit.

As shown in the exhibit, the path of these changes in industry short-run equilibrium points traces a horizontal line, which is the industry's long-run supply curve. What is the likely cause of this outcome? If an industry's use of particular inputs is small in relation to the overall availability of these inputs in the economy, it is unlikely that expansion of the industry will have a perceptible effect on the prices of these inputs. Thus a situation of constant costs is likely to prevail.

Exhibit 7.12 **Long-run supply in a constant-cost industry**

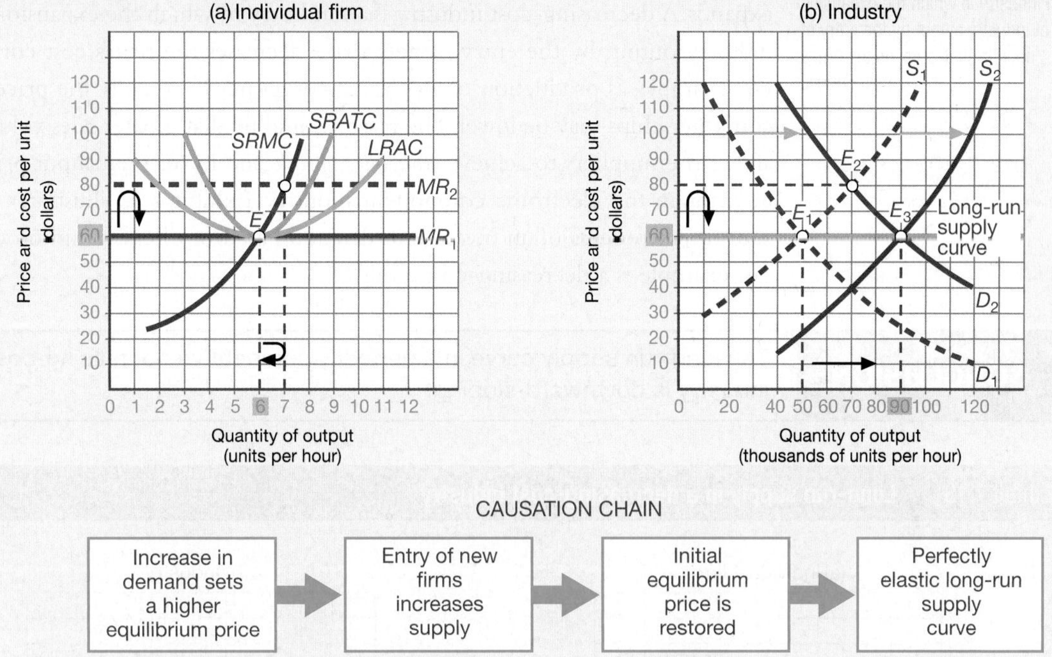

Part (b) shows an industry in equilibrium at point E_1, producing 50 000 units per hour and selling units at \$60 per unit. In part (a) the firm is in equilibrium, producing six units per hour and earning a normal profit. Then industry demand increases from D_1 to D_2 and the equilibrium price rises to \$80. Industry output rises temporarily to 70 000 units per hour and the individual firm increases output to seven units per hour. Firms are now earning an economic profit, which attracts new firms into the industry. In the long run, the entry of these firms causes the short-run supply curve to shift rightward from S_1 to S_2, the price is re-established at \$60 and a new industry equilibrium point, E_3, is established. At E_3, industry output rises to 90 000 units per hour and the firm's output returns to six units per hour. Now the typical firm earns a normal profit and new firms stop entering the industry. Connecting point E_1 to point E_3 generates the long-run supply curve.

The long-run supply curve in a perfectly competitive constant-cost industry is perfectly elastic.

Now we reconsider Exhibit 7.12 and ask what happens when the demand curve shifts leftward from D_2 to D_1. Beginning in part (b) at point E_3, the decrease in demand causes the price to fall temporarily below \$60. As a result, firms earn short-run losses and some firms leave the industry. The exodus of firms shifts the short-run supply curve leftward from S_2 to S_1, establishing a new equilibrium at point E_1. This decrease in supply restores the equilibrium price to the initial price of \$60 per unit. Once equilibrium is re-established at E_1, there are a smaller number of firms, each earning a normal profit.

Decreasing-cost industry

Decreasing-cost industry An industry in which the expansion of industry output by the entry of new firms decreases the firm's cost curves.

As new firms enter a **decreasing-cost industry**, input prices fall as output expands. A decreasing-cost industry is an industry in which the expansion of industry output by the entry of new firms decreases the firm's cost curves. For example, as production of electronic components expands, the price of computer chips may be lower. The reason could be that greater sales volume allows the suppliers to achieve *economies of scale* and lower their input prices to firms in the electronic component industry. Exhibit 7.13 illustrates the adjustment process of an increase in demand based on the assumption that our example is a decreasing-cost industry.

CONCLUSION **The long-run supply curve in a perfectly competitive decreasing-cost industry is downward-sloping.**

Exhibit 7.13 Long-run supply in a decreasing-cost industry

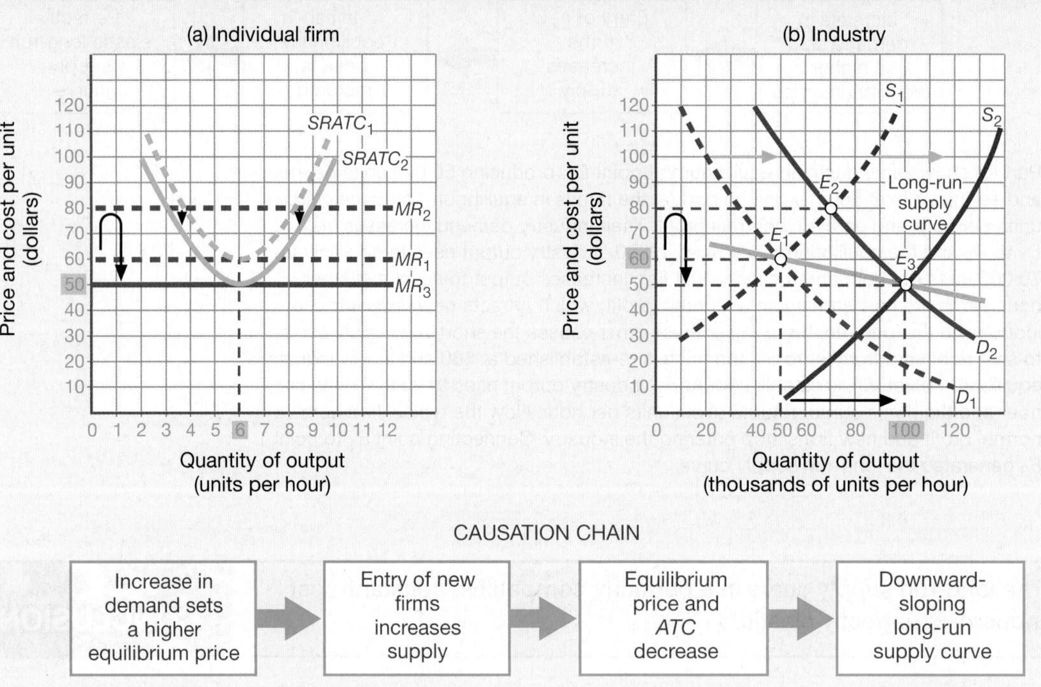

The long-run supply curve for a decreasing-cost industry is downward-sloping. The increase in industry demand shown in part (b) causes the price to rise to $80 in the short run. Temporarily, the typical firm illustrated in part (a) earns an economic profit. Higher profits attract new firms and supply increases. As the industry expands, the average total cost curve for the firm shifts lower and the firm re-establishes long-run equilibrium at the lower price of $50.

Increasing-cost industry

As new firms enter an **increasing-cost industry**, input prices rise as output expands. As this type of industry uses more labour, machines and raw materials, the demand for greater quantities of these inputs drives up some or all of their prices. An increasing-cost industry is an industry in which the expansion of industry output by the entry of new firms increases the firm's cost curves. Suppose the home appliance industry uses a significant proportion of all electrical engineers in the country. If this is the case, electrical engineering salaries will rise as firms hire more electrical engineers to expand industry output. In practice, it is believed that most industries are increasing-cost industries and, therefore, the long-run supply curve is upward-sloping.

Increasing-cost industry
An industry in which the expansion of industry output by the entry of new firms increases the firm's cost curves.

Exhibit 7.14 on page 200 shows what happens in an increasing-cost industry when an increase in demand causes output to expand. In part (b), the industry is initially in equilibrium at point E_1. As in the previous case, the demand curve shifts rightward from D_1 to D_2, establishing a new short-run equilibrium at E_2. This movement upward along short-run industry supply curve S_1 raises the price in the short run from \$60 to \$80, resulting in profit for the typical firm. Once again, new firms enter the industry and the short-run supply curve shifts rightward from S_1 to S_2. Part (a) of Exhibit 7.14 shows that the response of the firm's *ATC* to the industry's expansion differs from that in the constant-cost industry case. In an increasing-cost industry, the firm's *ATC* curve shifts upward from ATC_1 to ATC_2, corresponding to the new short-run equilibrium at point E_3. At this final equilibrium point, the price is higher at \$70 than the initial price of \$60. Normal profits are re-established because profits are squeezed from both the price fall and the rise in the *ATC* curve.

PART 3

The long-run supply curve in a perfectly competitive increasing-cost industry is upward-sloping.

Note that, in each of the three possible scenarios described above, the long-run industry supply curve is drawn by connecting the two long-run equilibrium points of E_1 and E_3. Equilibrium point E_2 is not a long-run equilibrium point because it is not established after the entry of new firms has restored normal profits.

Finally, it important to understand that each of the three models presented above can be observed in the real world. Some industries have constant costs when they expand, while others may have decreasing costs or increasing costs. Only direct observation and economic analysis of the industry can tell us which type of industry it is.

International focus

Applicable concept: the characteristics of perfect competition

Internet increases competition in global marketplace

The rise of the Internet as a global means of communication has led many commentators to argue that the ability of Internet users to connect with businesses and consumers anywhere in the world as easily as they might communicate with their next door neighbour means that the potential for international competition between firms has increased enormously. In other words, the Internet is increasing global competition and promoting the efficiency gains that are an acknowledged outcome of competitive markets. In a paper to an 'Electronic Consumer' conference in New Zealand, former Deputy Chairperson of the ACCC, Allan Asher, drew the following implications for global competition from the Internet revolution.

> [I]t seems almost certain that on-line markets and other forms of electronic commerce will expand rapidly to the point where a truly global retail marketplace will emerge. Already some industries are feeling the effects of these new technologies, especially those which are essentially information and booking services …
>
> [This] global electronic market will present both tremendous opportunities as well as some very real challenges for regulators, industry and consumers …
>
> Indeed, electronic commerce, and on-line commerce especially, has the potential to close the gap which so often exists between idealised economic models of perfect competition and the imperfect way that many markets actually work in practice … On-line commerce can do this by increasing competition amongst suppliers and by decreasing the opportunity and transaction costs faced by buyers in gathering and processing information …
>
> Electronic commerce has the potential to deliver significant gains to consumers in terms of price, quality and service through increased competition. This is likely to happen for two interrelated reasons – lower barriers to entry and increased numbers of suppliers competing in product markets.
>
> Traditionally, local or geographic monopolies have persisted because of high barriers to entry linked to large establishment (fixed) costs in such areas as physical infrastructure, distribution networks and advertising.
>
> The Internet, and to a lesser extent other electronic service delivery channels, lower barriers to entry significantly for providers of many products and services …
>
> Since the Internet allows newer and smaller players to promote and sell products in direct competition with larger players, it will increase the number of competitors in the market. Consumers can now tap into a global market and are not bound to a restricted number of physically nearby suppliers – improved choice, price and quality should result.

The excerpts in the text are from a paper by Allan Asher titled 'International perspective: access to justice for consumers in the global electronic marketplace'. You can find the complete paper by visiting the ACCC at **www.accc.gov** and searching for its title using the search facility.

Analyse the issue

1. How does the author of the above material see the Internet changing the extent to which markets conform to the three assumptions of the perfectly competitive market structure?
2. Why do you think the author welcomes the possibility that the Internet will close the gap between market structures observed in the real world and the idealised model of perfect competition?

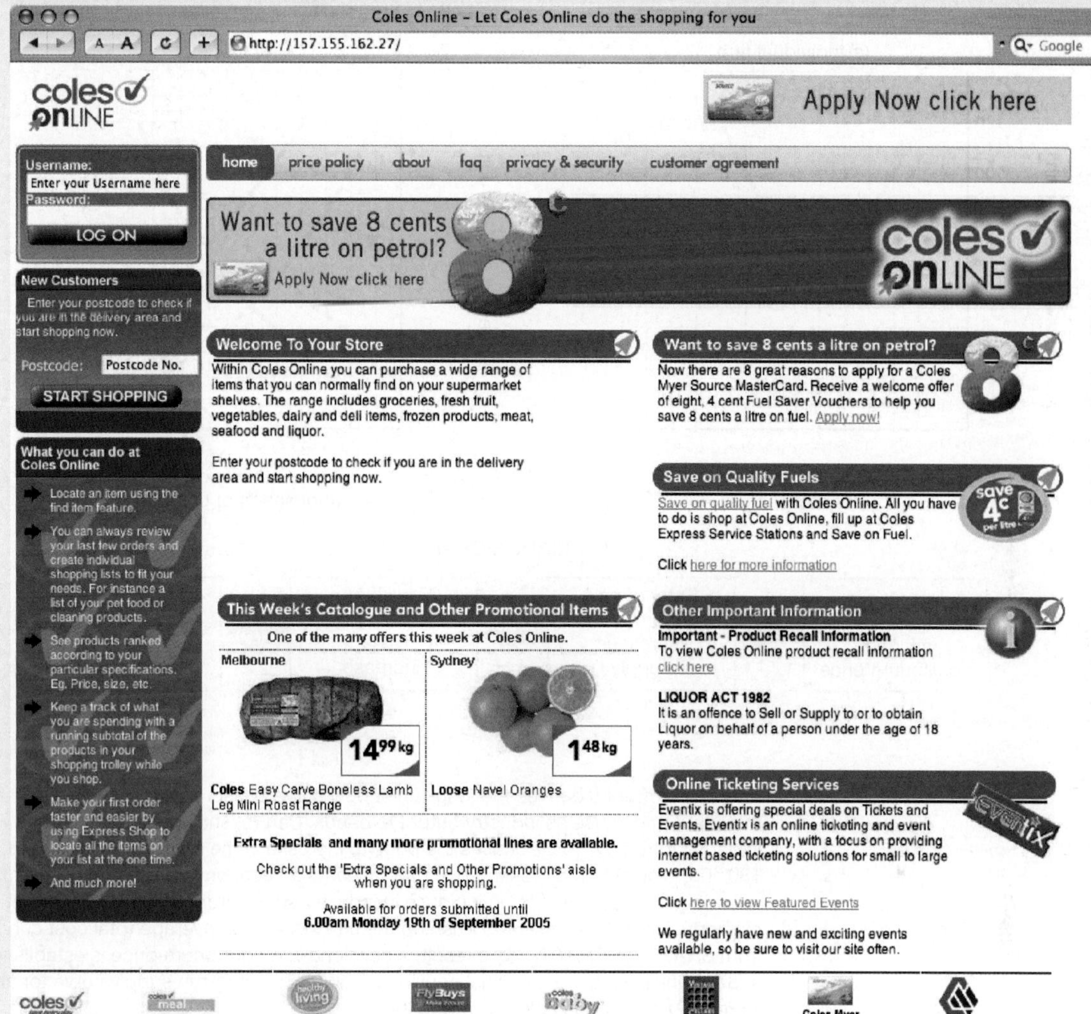
Coles Online – Let Coles Online do the shopping for you
http://157.155.162.27/
coles ONLINE
Apply Now click here
Username:
Password:
LOG ON
home
price policy
about
faq
privacy & security
customer agreement
Want to save 8 cents a litre on petrol?
Apply Now click here
New Customers
Enter your postcode to check if you are in the delivery area and start shopping now.
Postcode:
START SHOPPING
Welcome To Your Store
Within Coles Online you can purchase a wide range of items that you can normally find on your supermarket shelves. The range includes groceries, fresh fruit, vegetables, dairy and deli items, frozen products, meat, seafood and liquor.
Enter your postcode to check if you are in the delivery area and start shopping now.
Want to save 8 cents a litre on petrol?
Now there are 8 great reasons to apply for a Coles Myer Source MasterCard. Receive a welcome offer of eight, 4 cent Fuel Saver Vouchers to help you save 8 cents a litre on fuel. Apply now!
Save on Quality Fuels
Save on quality fuel with Coles Online. All you have to do is shop at Coles Online, fill up at Coles Express Service Stations and Save on Fuel.
Click here for more information
What you can do at Coles Online
Locate an item using the find item feature.
You can always review your last few orders and create individual shopping lists to fit your needs. For instance a list of your pet food or cleaning products.
See products ranked according to your particular specifications. Eg. Price, size, etc.
Keep a track of what you are spending with a running subtotal of the products in your shopping trolley while you shop.
Make your first order faster and easier by using Express Shop to locate all the items on your list at the one time.
And much more!
This Week's Catalogue and Other Promotional Items
One of the many offers this week at Coles Online.
Melbourne
Sydney
14.99 kg
1.48 kg
Coles Easy Carve Boneless Lamb Leg Mini Roast Range
Loose Navel Oranges
Extra Specials and many more promotional lines are available.
Check out the 'Extra Specials and Other Promotions' aisle when you are shopping.
Available for orders submitted until 6.00am Monday 19th of September 2005
Other Important Information
Important - Product Recall Information
To view Coles Online product recall information click here
LIQUOR ACT 1982
It is an offence to Sell or Supply to or to obtain Liquor on behalf of a person under the age of 18 years.
Online Ticketing Services
Eventix is offering special deals on Tickets and Events. Eventix is an online ticketing and event management company, with a focus on providing internet based ticketing solutions for small to large events.
Click here to view Featured Events
We regularly have new and exciting events available, so be sure to visit our site often.
Coles
Coles Meal Ideas
Healthy Living
FlyBuys Offers
Baby Club
Vintage Cellars
Coles Myer Source™ MasterCard
Colesmyer .com

Exhibit 7.14 **Long-run supply in an increasing-cost industry**

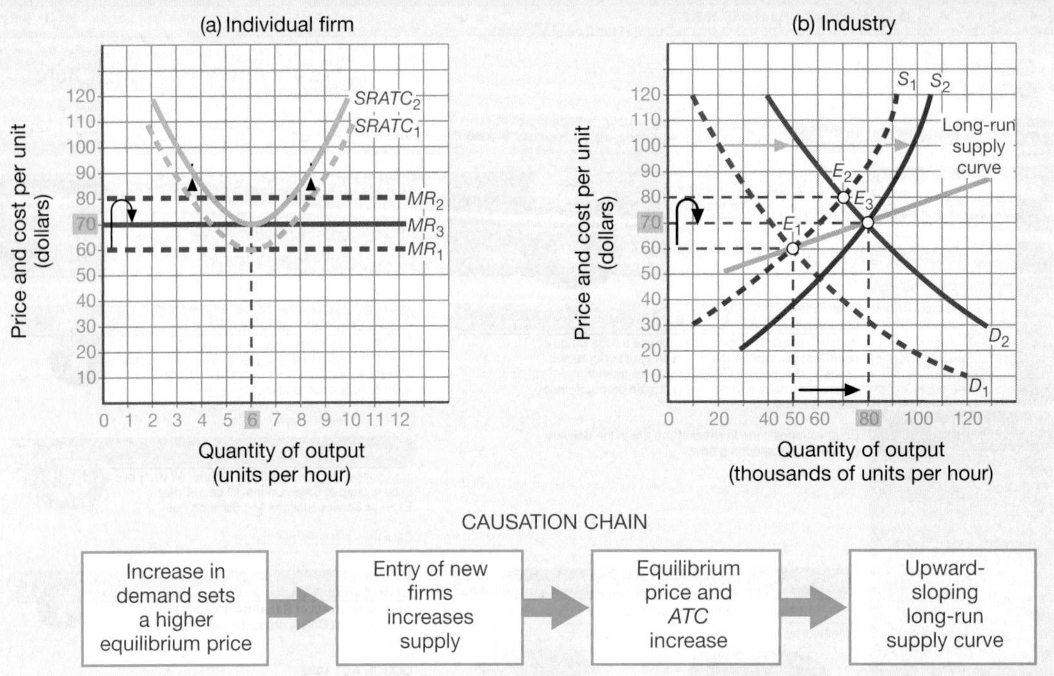

This pair of graphs derives the long-run supply curve based on the assumption that input prices rise as industry output expands. Part (b) shows that an increase in demand from D_1 to D_2 causes the price to increase in the short run from \$60 to \$80. The typical firm represented in part (a) earns an economic profit and new firms enter the industry, causing an increase in industry supply from S_1 to S_2. As output expands, input prices rise and push up the firm's short-run average total cost curve from $SRATC_1$ to $SRATC_2$. As a result, a new long-run equilibrium price is established at \$70, which is above the initial equilibrium price. The long-run supply curve for an increasing-cost industry is upward-sloping.

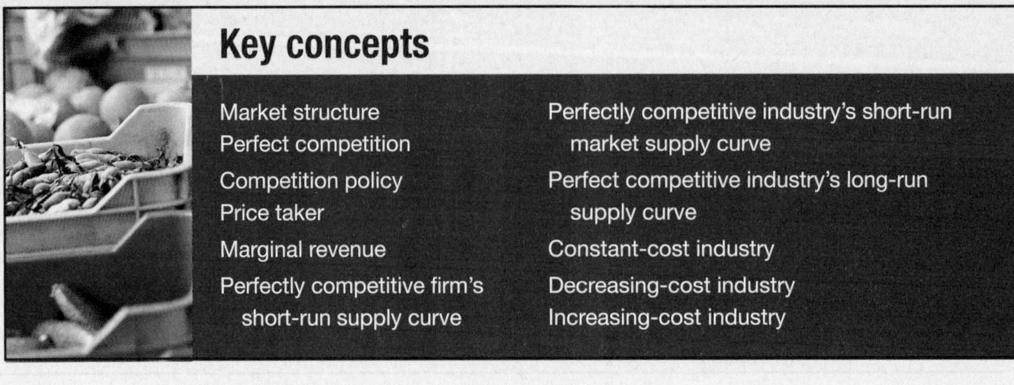

Key concepts

- Market structure
- Perfect competition
- Competition policy
- Price taker
- Marginal revenue
- Perfectly competitive firm's short-run supply curve
- Perfectly competitive industry's short-run market supply curve
- Perfect competitive industry's long-run supply curve
- Constant-cost industry
- Decreasing-cost industry
- Increasing-cost industry

Summary

- **Market structure** consists of three market characteristics: (1) the number of sellers, (2) the nature of the product and (3) the ease of entry into or exit from the market.

- **Perfect competition** is a market structure in which an individual firm cannot affect the price of the product it produces. Each firm in the industry is very small relative to the market as a whole, all the firms sell a homogeneous product and firms are free to enter and exit the industry.

- **Competition policy** has the objective of increasing competition in the economy, or of encouraging firms that are not competitive to behave as if they were. In its role as consumer advocate, the competition authority is often responsible for implementing policy directed at outlawing unethical behaviour by business.

- A **price-taker** firm in perfect competition faces a perfectly elastic demand curve. It can sell all it wishes at the market-determined price, but it will sell nothing above the given market price. This is because so many competitive firms are willing to sell at the going market price.

- The **total revenue–total cost method** is one way in which the firm determines the level of output that maximises profit. Profit reaches a maximum when the vertical difference between the total revenue and the total cost curves is at a maximum.

Total revenue–total cost method

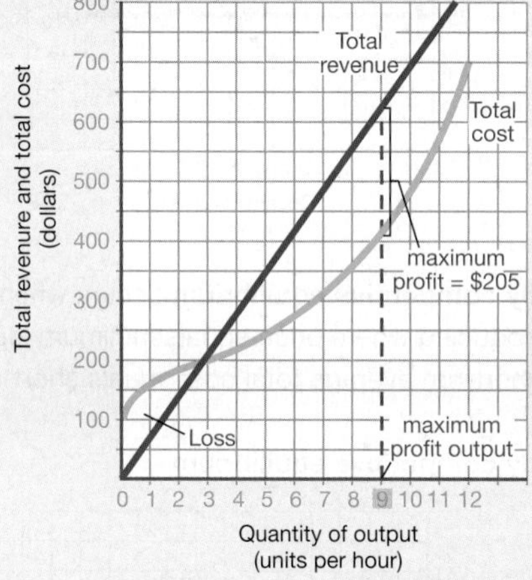

- The **marginal revenue equals marginal cost method** is a second approach to finding where a firm maximises profits. **Marginal revenue** is the change in total revenue from a one-unit change in output. Marginal revenue for a perfectly competitive firm equals the market price. The $MR = MC$ rule states that the firm maximises profit or minimises loss by producing the output where marginal revenue equals marginal cost. If the price (average revenue) is below the minimum point on the average variable cost curve, the $MR = MC$ rule does not apply and the firm shuts down to minimise its losses.

Marginal revenue–marginal cost method

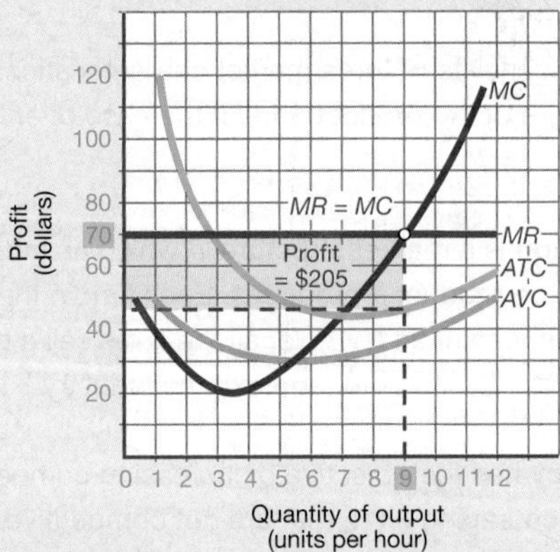

- The **perfectly competitive firm's short-run supply curve** is a curve showing the relationship between the price of a product and the quantity supplied in the short run. The individual firm always produces along its marginal cost curve above its intersection with the average variable cost curve. The **perfectly competitive industry's short-run market supply curve** is the horizontal summation of the short-run supply curves of all firms in the industry.

Short-run supply curve

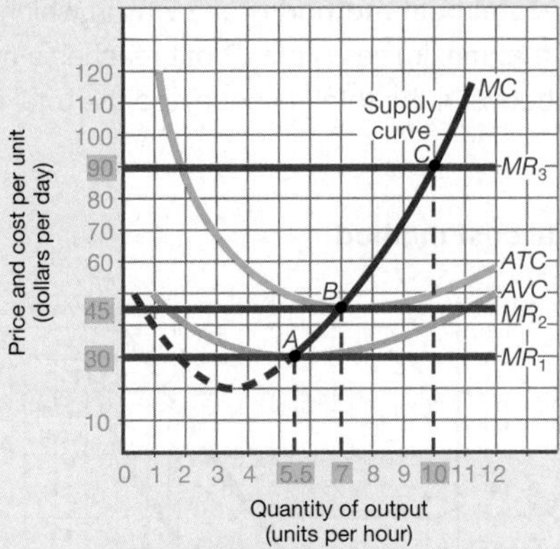

- **Long-run perfectly competitive equilibrium** occurs when the firm earns a normal profit by producing where price equals minimum long-run average cost equals minimum short-run average total cost equals short-run marginal cost.

Long-run perfectly competitive equilibrium

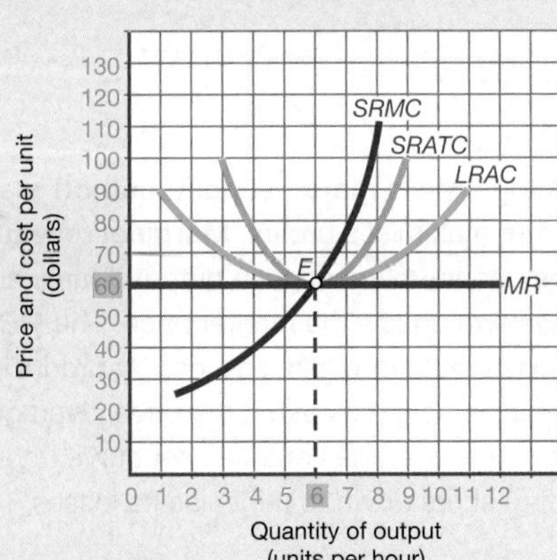

- A **constant-cost industry** is an industry in which expansion of total output involves neither an increase nor a decrease in each firm's average total cost. Because input prices remain constant, the long-run supply curve in a constant-cost industry is perfectly elastic.
- A **decreasing-cost industry is an industry** in which expansion of total output involves a decrease in each firm's average total cost. Lower input prices result in a downward-sloping long-run supply curve. As industry output expands, the long-run equilibrium market price falls.
- An **increasing-cost industry** is an industry in which expansion of total output involves an increase in each firm's average total cost. Higher input prices result in an upward-sloping long-run supply curve. As industry output expands, the long-run equilibrium market price rises.

Study questions and problems

1 Explain why a perfectly competitive firm would or would not advertise.

2 Does a New Zealand sheep farmer fit the perfectly competitive market structure? Explain.

3 If the ACCC or the NZCC is not able to promote increased competition in a particular industry, what action is it likely to take to increase the welfare of consumers?

4 Suppose the market equilibrium price of tomatoes is $2 per kilo in a perfectly competitive industry. Draw the industry supply and demand curves and the demand curve for a single tomato grower. Explain why the tomato grower is a price taker.

5 Assuming the market equilibrium price for tomatoes is $5 per kilo, draw the total revenue and the marginal revenue curves for the typical tomato grower in the same graph. Explain how marginal revenue and price are related to the total revenue curve.

6 Consider the following cost data for a perfectly competitive firm in the short run:

Output (Q)	Total fixed cost (TFC)	Total variable cost (TVC)	Total cost (TC)	Total revenue (TR)	Profit
1	$100	$120	$___	$___	$___
2	100	200	___	___	___
3	100	290	___	___	___
4	100	430	___	___	___
5	100	590	___	___	___

If the market price is $150, how many units of output will the firm produce in order to maximise profit in the short run? Specify the amount of economic profit or loss. At what level of output does the firm break even?

7 Consider this statement: 'A firm should increase output when it makes a profit.' Do you agree or disagree? Explain.

8 Consider this statement: 'When marginal revenue equals marginal cost, total cost equals total revenue and the firm makes zero profit.' Do you agree or disagree? Explain.

9 Consider Exhibit 7.15 which shows the graph of a perfectly competitive firm in the short run.

a If the firm's demand curve is MR_3, state whether the firm earns an economic profit or loss.

b Which demand curve(s) indicates the firm incurs a loss?

c Which demand curve(s) indicates the firm would shut down?

d Identify the firm's short-run supply curve.

Exhibit 7.15 **Perfectly competitive firm**

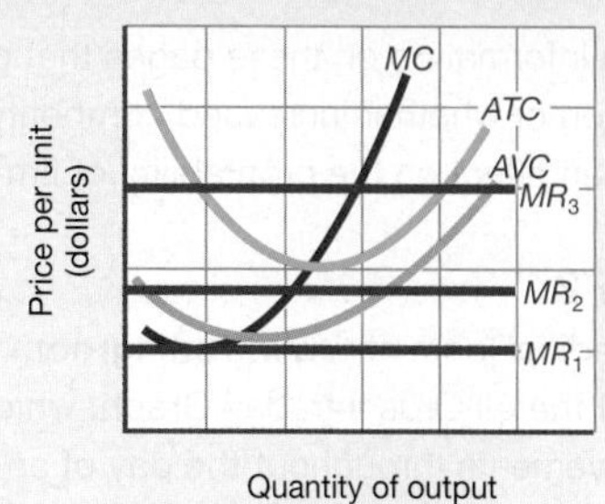

10 Consider this statement: 'The perfectly competitive firm will sell all the quantity of output that consumers will buy at the prevailing market price.' Do you agree or disagree? Explain your answer.

11 Suppose a perfectly competitive firm's demand curve is below its average total cost curve. Explain the conditions under which a firm continues to produce in the short run.

12 Suppose the industry equilibrium price of residential housing construction is $1000 per square metre and the minimum average variable cost for a residential construction contractor is $1100 per square metre. What would you advise the owner of this firm to do? Explain.

13 Suppose independent road transport operators are in a perfectly competitive industry. If these firms are earning positive economic profits, what happens in the long run to the following: the price of road transport services, the industry quantity of output, the profits of existing road transport operators? Given these outcomes, can you say whether the independent road transport industry is a constant-cost, increasing-cost or decreasing-cost industry?

Online exercises

Exercise 1

Read the New Economy Index pages dealing with the effects of the Internet and increased globalisation on business competition (**www.neweconomyindex.org/section1_page06.html**).

1 List the factors that are said to be driving increased competition between firms. Do these factors suggest that the structure of the markets in which firms operate are taking on more of the characteristics of the perfectly competitive market structure?

2 Is there information on these pages that gives an indication of whether increased competition is having an effect on the profitability of firms?

Exercise 2

Visit the TradingRoom at **www.tradingroom.com.au**. Look at the All Ords Intraday Graph, which graphs movements throughout the day of an index of Australian share prices. *Tip:* make your visit in the afternoon, when some hours of trading will have been recorded.

1 Study the extent to which prices have fluctuated during the day.

2 Apply the characteristics of a perfectly competitive market structure to the stock market. Why do stock prices fluctuate so much?

Answers to 'You make the call'

Should motels offer rooms at the beach for only $40 a night?

As long as price exceeds average variable cost, the motel is better off operating than shutting down. Since $40 is more than enough to cover the guest-related variable costs, the firm will operate. The $15 remaining after covering variable costs can be put towards the $50 of fixed costs. Were the firm to shut down, it could make no contribution to these overhead costs. If you said the motels should operate during the off-season because they can get a price that exceeds their average variable cost, YOU ARE CORRECT.

Are you in business for the long run?

In the long run, surviving firms will operate at the minimum of the long-run average cost curve. The average cost of 50 storage units is $4000 ($200 000/50), the average cost of 100 storage units is $3000 ($300 000/100) and the average cost of 200 storage units is $3500 ($700 000/200). Of the three sizes of storage-unit complex given, the one with the lowest average cost is closest to the minimum point on the *LRAC* curve. If you chose 100 storage units, YOU ARE CORRECT.

Multiple-choice questions

1 A perfectly competitive market is *not* characterised by
- **a** many small firms.
- **b** a great variety of different products.
- **c** free entry into and exit from the market.
- **d** any of the above.

2 Which of the following is a characteristic of perfect competition?

a entry barriers.
b homogeneous products.
c expenditures on advertising.
d differing quality of service.

3 Which of the following are the same at all levels of output under perfect competition?
a marginal cost and marginal revenue.
b price and marginal revenue.
c price and marginal cost.
d all of the above.

4 If a perfectly competitive firm sells 100 units of output at a market price of $100 per unit, its marginal revenue per unit is
a $1.
b $100.
c more than $1, but less than $100.
d less than $100.

5 Short-run profit maximisation for a perfectly competitive firm occurs where the firm's marginal cost equals
a average total cost.
b average variable cost.
c marginal revenue.
d all of the above.

6 A perfectly competitive firm sells its output for $100 per unit and the minimum average variable cost is $150 per unit. The firm should
a increase output.
b decrease output, but not shut down.
c maintain its current rate of output.
d shut down.

7 A perfectly competitive firm's supply curve follows the upward-sloping segment of its marginal cost curve above the
a average total cost curve.
b average variable cost curve.
c average fixed cost curve.
d average price curve.

8 Assume the price of the firm's product in Exhibit 7.16 is $15 per unit. The firm will produce
a 500 units per week.
b 1000 units per week.
c 1500 units per week.
d 2000 units per week.
e 2500 units per week.

9 The price in Exhibit 7.16 at which the firm earns zero economic profit in the short run is
a $5 per unit.
b $10 per unit.
c $20 per unit.
d $30 per unit.

Exhibit 7.16 A perfectly competitive firm's marginal revenue and cost per unit curves

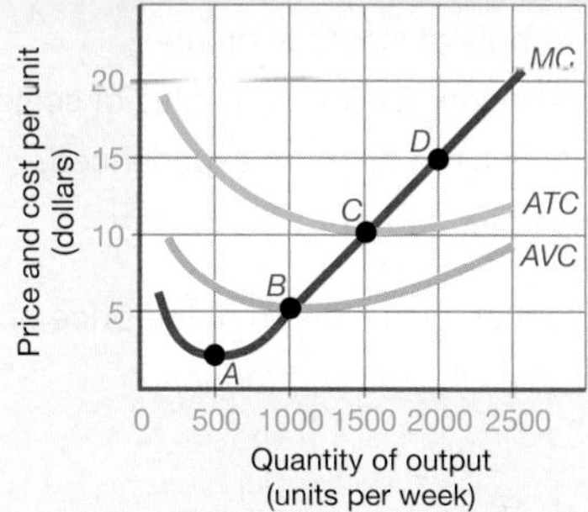

10 Assume the price of the firm's product in Exhibit 7.16 is $6 per unit. The firm should
a continue to operate because it is earning an economic profit.
b stay in operation for the time being even though it is earning an economic loss.
c shut down temporarily.
d shut down permanently.

11 Assume the price of the firm's product in Exhibit 7.16 is $15 per unit. The maximum profit the firm earns is
a zero.
b more than $10 000 per week.
c less than $10 000 per week.
d unable to be determined.

12 In Exhibit 7.16, the firm's total revenue at a price of $10 per unit pays for
a a portion of total variable costs.
b a portion of total fixed costs.
c none of the total fixed costs.
d all of the total fixed costs and total variable costs.

13 As shown in Exhibit 7.16, the short-run supply curve for this firm corresponds to which segment of its marginal cost curve?
a *A* to *D* and all points above.
b *B* to *D* and all points above.
c *C* to *D* and all points above.
d *B* to *C* only.

14 In long-run equilibrium, the perfectly competitive firm's price is equal to which of the following?

a short-run marginal cost.
b minimum short-run average total cost.
c marginal revenue.
d all of the above.

15 In a constant-cost industry, input prices remain constant as

a the supply of inputs fluctuates.
b firms encounter diseconomies of scale.
c workers become more experienced.
d firms enter and exit the industry.

16 Suppose that, in the long run, the price of feature films rises as the movie production industry expands. We can conclude that movie production is

a an increasing-cost industry.
b a constant-cost industry.
c a decreasing-cost industry.
d a marginal-cost industry.

17 Which of the following is *true* of a perfectly competitive market?

a If economic profits are earned, then the price will fall over time.
b In long-run equilibrium, *P* = *MR* = *SRMC* = *SRATC* = *LRAC*.
c A constant-cost industry exists when the entry of new firms has no effect on their cost curves.
d All of the above are true.

Monopoly

8

Playing the popular board game, Monopoly, teaches some of the characteristics of monopoly theory presented in this chapter. In the game version, players win by gaining as much economic power as possible. They strive to own sites with railway stations and utilities, or to acquire streets such as Regent Street or Bond Street. Then each player tries to gain maximum monopoly power by owning more than one railway station, more than one utility, or more than one street in a given location. Players who roll the dice and land on another player's property have no choice. They must pay rent on the capital improvements on the site – be it the railway station, the utility or the houses and hotels that have been erected on the street. The winning player is the one who is able, as a result of the high rents he or she charges, to bankrupt all other players.

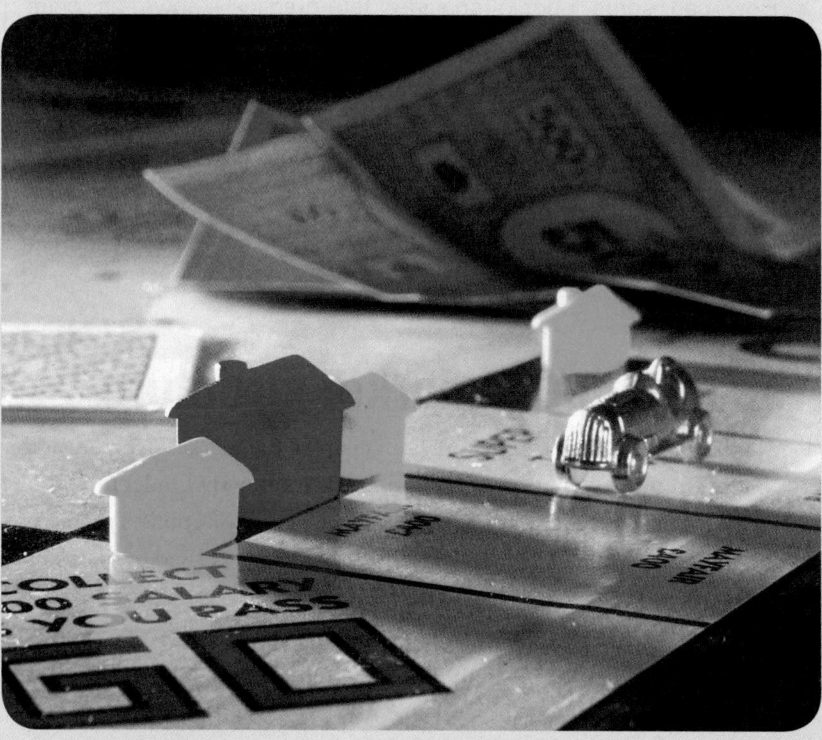

In the previous chapter we studied perfect competition, which may be viewed as the paragon of economic virtue. Why? Under perfect competition there are many sellers, each lacking any power to influence price. Perfect competition and monopoly are polar extremes. The word *monopoly* is derived from the Greek words *mono* and *poleo*, which translate as 'single seller'. A monopoly has the market power to set its price and not worry about competitors. Perhaps your campus has only one place where you can buy meals. If so, students may be paying higher prices for meals than would be the case if many sellers competed in the market for meals available on campus. Check out the campus vending machine prices. Are they higher than prices at shops in the local shopping centre?

This chapter explains why firms do not or cannot enter a particular market and compete with a monopolist. Then we explore some of the interesting actual monopolies around the world. We study how a monopolist determines what price to charge and how much to produce. The chapter ends with a discussion of the arguments for and against monopolies. Most of the analytical tools required here have been introduced in previous chapters.

In this chapter, you will examine these economics questions:

- Why doesn't a monopolist choose to charge consumers the highest possible price for its product?
- How can some people consider the practice known as price discrimination to be ethical?
- Should domestic monopolies be tolerated if they face international competition?
- With fish so abundant, how can there be a monopoly in certain fish products?

The monopoly market structure

Monopoly A market structure characterised by (1) a single seller, (2) a unique product and (3) extremely difficult or impossible entry into the market.

Recall that, in Exhibit 7.1 in the previous chapter, the market structure at the opposite extreme from perfect competition was monopoly. Under **monopoly**, the consumer has a simple choice – either to buy the monopolist's product or to do without it. Monopoly is a market structure characterised by (1) a single seller, (2) a unique product and (3) extremely difficult or impossible entry into the market. Unlike the product of a perfectly competitive firm, there are no close substitutes for the monopolist's product. Monopoly, like perfect competition, corresponds only approximately to real-world industries, but, as is the case with perfect competition, it serves as a useful benchmark model. Let's look at a brief description of each monopoly characteristic.

monopoly

Single seller

In perfect competition, many firms make up the industry. In contrast, a monopoly means that a single firm *is* the industry. One firm provides the total supply of a product in a given market. Local monopolies are more common real-world approximations of the model than national or world-market monopolies. For example, the campus bookshop, the local telephone service and the supplier of electric power to your home may be local monopolies. The only service station or hotel in a small, isolated country town and the only hot dog stand at a football game are also examples of monopolies. Nationally, Australia Post monopolises mail to households.

Unique product

barriers to entry

A unique product means there are *no close substitutes* for the monopolist's product. Thus the monopolist faces little or no competition. In reality, however, there are few products that do not have close or fairly close substitutes. For example, students can buy used textbooks from sources other than the campus bookshop. Gas is a good substitute for electricity for cooking and heating. Similarly, the fax machine and email are substitutes for the 'snail' mail service. On the other hand, there are no good substitutes for electricity for lighting, and it is likely that the firm that supplies electricity to your home is a monopoly.

PART 3

Barriers to entry

In perfect competition, there are no constraints to prevent new firms from entering an industry. In the case of monopoly, there are extremely high barriers that make it very difficult or impossible for new firms to enter an industry. We will now look at the three major barriers that prevent new sellers from entering a market and competing with a monopolist.

Ownership of a vital resource

Sole control of the entire supply of a strategic input is one way a monopolist can prevent a newcomer from entering an industry. A famous historical example is Alcoa's monopoly in the US aluminium market from the late nineteenth century until the end of World War II. The source of Alcoa's monopoly was its control of bauxite ore, which is necessary to produce aluminium.

Rather than the vital resource being a mineral, it could be human resources (labour) over which the monopolist has control. For example, it would be very difficult for a new professional tennis organisation to

The history of the ATP can be accessed at **www.atptennis.com/en/insidetheatp/theorganisation/history.asp**.

compete successfully with the ATP (Association of Tennis Professionals), which has contracts with the best players and links to the most prestigious tournaments.

Legal barriers

The oldest and most effective barriers protecting a firm from potential competitors are the result of government ownership or the issuing of franchises and licences. This means that government operates the monopoly itself or permits a single firm to provide a certain product or service and excludes competing firms by law. For example, in many countries the reticulation of electric power, water and gas is often undertaken by monopolies established by national, state or local government. Many of Australia's state governments issue licences for monopoly casinos and have a monopoly in off-course betting on horse races. These gambling monopolies are usually supported by laws that apply severe penalties to persons setting themselves up in competition to the state-sponsored monopoly. The purpose of these laws is to guarantee the stream of revenue that government collects from these monopolists in the form of licence fees and taxes.

Australia Post has exclusive rights to deliver certain classes of mail. Read about its monopoly at **www.aph.gov.au/library/pubs/bd/2000-01/01BD001.htm.**

Government-granted licences restrict entry into some industries and occupations. For example, radio and television stations must be licensed. In most cases doctors, lawyers, dentists, nurses, teachers, real estate agents, taxis, hotels and other professions and businesses are required to have a licence. In the case of the professions, the need for a licence does not preclude competition between licensed practitioners; however, it may serve to encourage them to form a professional association or union, which then behaves as a monopolistic supplier on behalf of its members.

Patents and copyrights are another form of government-initiated barrier to entry. The government grants patents to inventors, thereby legally prohibiting other firms from producing the patented product for the duration of the patent (twenty years in most countries). Copyrights give creators of literature, art, music and films exclusive rights to sell or license their works. The purpose behind granting patents and copyrights is to encourage innovation and new products by guaranteeing, for a limited period, exclusive rights to profit from new ideas.

Economies of scale

Why might competition among firms in a free market be unsustainable, so that eventually one firm becomes a monopolist? Recall the concept of economies of scale from the chapter on production costs (Chapter 6). As a result of large-scale production, the long-run average cost of production falls. This means that a monopoly can emerge in time naturally because of the relationship between average cost and the scale of an operation. As a firm becomes larger, its cost per unit of output is lower than it would be for a smaller competitor. In the long run, this 'survival of the fittest' cost advantage forces the smaller firms to leave the industry. Because new firms cannot hope to produce and sell quantities of output similar to that of the monopolist, thereby achieving the low costs of the monopolist, they will not enter the industry. Thus a monopoly can arise over time and remain dominant in an industry, even though the monopolist does not own an essential resource or have protection from legal barriers.

Economists call the situation in which one seller emerges in an industry because of economies of scale a **natural monopoly**. A natural monopoly is an industry in which the long-run average cost of production declines throughout the entire range of output. As a result, a single firm can supply the entire market demand at a lower cost than two or more smaller firms. Utilities such as electricity, gas, water and local telephone services are examples of natural monopolies. You can see why they are natural monopolies by considering whether a competitor would be likely to set up against, say, the monopoly supplier of water to householders. This competitor would have to risk spending millions of dollars to set up an additional distribution network in the knowledge that, because it would have to share the market with the existing supplier, it would have higher costs per unit of output than those currently experienced by the existing supplier. If a competitor were to enter, the outcome in this particular market would involve an approximate doubling of the fixed cost of the distribution network with no increase in sales volume.

Natural monopoly An industry in which the long-run average cost of production declines throughout the entire range of output. As a result, a single firm can supply the entire market demand at a lower cost than two or more smaller firms.

INFOTRAC®

natural monopoly

Exhibit 8.1 depicts the *LRAC* curve for a natural monopoly. A single firm can produce 100 units at an average cost of $15 and a total cost of

Exhibit 8.1 Minimising costs in a natural monopoly

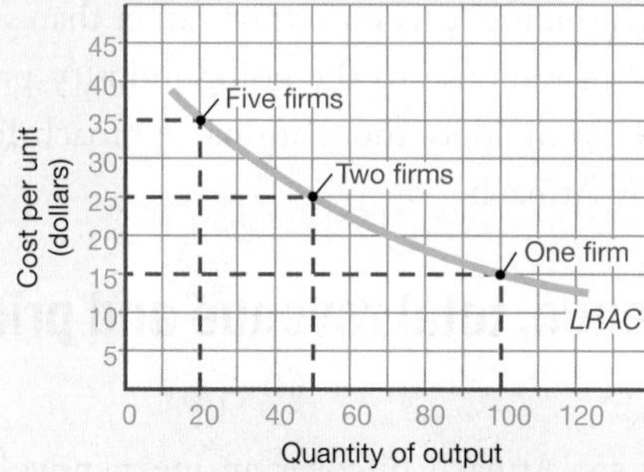

In a natural monopoly, a single firm can produce at a lower cost than two or more firms in an industry. This condition occurs because the *LRAC* curve for any firm decreases over the relevant range. For example, one firm can produce 100 units at an average cost of $15 and a total cost of $1500. Two firms in the industry can produce 100 units of output (50 units each) for a total cost of $2500, and five firms can produce the same total output for a total cost of $3500.

The Trade Practices Act provides for access by competitors to the infrastructure of certain natural monopolies. Read about aspects of this so-called *third party access* provision by bringing up the ACCC home page at **www.accc.gov.au** and using the search facility to search for *third party access*.

$1500. Another option is for two firms to produce 50 units each, with the total cost rising to $2500. With five firms producing 20 units each, the total cost rises to $3500.

In the past, in order to prevent exploitation of consumers by these powerful natural monopolies, it was usual for them to be government owned. Today, it is increasingly common to have these industries in private hands, with a regulatory authority such as the ACCC or the NZCC charged with preventing these private firms from exploiting their monopoly power. In some cases the regulatory authority limits exploitation by requiring these monopolists to give competitors access to their distribution network. For example, gas producers that own gas pipelines in Australia may be required to give access to other producers.

CONCLUSION

In a natural monopoly, a single firm will produce output at a lower per-unit cost than two or more firms in the industry.

Price and output decisions for a monopolist

A major difference between perfect competition and monopoly is the shape of the demand curve faced by the firm. Recall from the previous chapter that the demand curve faced by the firm shows the price–quantity combinations at which the firm can sell its output. As explained in the previous chapter, a perfectly competitive firm is a *price taker*. In contrast, the next sections explain that a monopolist is a **price maker**. A price maker is a firm that faces a downward-sloping demand curve. This means that a monopolist has the ability to select the product's price. In short, a monopolist can set the price with its corresponding level of output, rather than simply determining its production level in response to the going industry price. To understand the monopolist, we again apply the marginal approach to our hypothetical electronics company, Atmach.

Price maker A firm that faces a downward-sloping demand curve and can therefore choose among price and output combinations along the demand curve.

INFOTRAC®
price maker

Marginal revenue, total revenue and price elasticity of demand

Suppose engineers for Atmach discover an inexpensive miracle electronic device called 'SAV-U-GAS', which anyone can easily attach to their car's engine. Once installed, the device halves fuel consumption. The government grants Atmach a patent and the company becomes a monopolist selling these fuel-saving gadgets. Because of this barrier to entry, Atmach is the only seller in the industry. Although other firms try to compete with this invention, they create poor substitutes and fail. Because Atmach is the only supplier of an effective fuel-saver, it is the only firm in the industry. This means the downward-sloping demand curve for the industry and for the monopolist are identical.

Exhibit 8.2(a) on p. 214 illustrates the demand and the marginal revenue curves for a monopolist such as Atmach. As the monopolist lowers its price to increase the quantity demanded, changes in both price and quantity affect the firm's total revenue (price times quantity), as shown graphically in Exhibit 8.2(b). If Atmach charges $150, consumers purchase zero units and, therefore, total revenue is zero. To sell one unit, Atmach must lower the price to $138 and total revenue rises from zero to $138. Because the marginal revenue is the increase in total revenue that results from a one-unit change in output, the marginal revenue from selling the first unit of output is $138 ($138 – $0). Thus, the price and the marginal revenue from selling one unit are equal at $138. Like all marginal measurements, marginal revenue is plotted midway between the quantities. So in Exhibit 8.2(a) marginal revenue of $138 is plotted against 0.5 of a unit of output. To sell two units, the monopolist must lower the price to $125 and total revenue rises to $250. The marginal revenue of the second unit (plotted against 1.5 units of output) is $112 ($250 – $138). Now the marginal revenue from selling the second unit is $13 less than the price received. You can see that this outcome is different from the case of the perfectly competitive firm, for which marginal revenue and price are the same.

As shown in Exhibit 8.2(a), as a monopolist lowers its price the difference between price and marginal revenue becomes larger and larger. In Exhibit 8.2(a), observe that the *MR* curve cuts the quantity axis at six units, half of 12 units. Following an easy rule helps locate the point along the quantity axis where marginal revenue equals zero: *The marginal revenue curve for a straight-line demand curve intersects the quantity axis halfway between the origin and the quantity axis intercept of the demand curve.*

The demand and the marginal revenue curves of the monopolist are downward-sloping, in contrast to the horizontal demand and corresponding marginal revenue curves facing the perfectly competitive firm (compare Exhibit 8.2 with Exhibit 7.2 in the previous chapter).

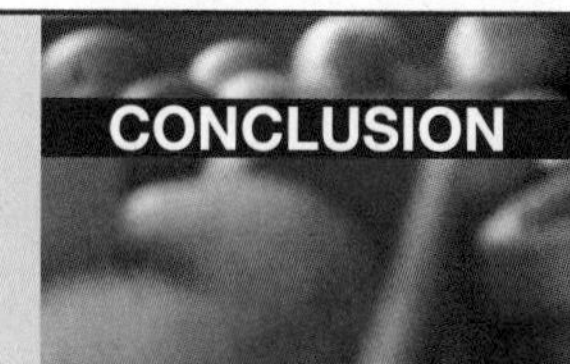

You can see that, starting from zero output, as the price falls, total revenue rises until it reaches a maximum at six units and then falls. Graphically, this is shown as the 'revenue hill' drawn in part (b) of Exhibit 8.2. The explanation was presented earlier in Chapter 5. Recall that a straight-line demand curve has an elastic ($E_d > 1$) upper half, a unit elastic ($E_d = 1$) midpoint and an inelastic ($E_d < 1$) lower half (see Exhibit 5.4 in Chapter 5). Recall from Chapter 5 that when $E_d > 1$, total revenue rises as the price drops and total revenue reaches a maximum where $E_d = 1$. When $E_d < 1$, total revenue falls as the price falls.

PART 3

Exhibit 8.2 Demand, marginal revenue and total revenue

Demand, marginal revenue and total revenue for Atmach as a monopolist

Output per hour	Price	Total revenue	Marginal revenue
0	$150	$0	
			$138
1	138	138	
			112
2	125	250	
			89
3	113	339	
			61
4	100	400	
			40
5	88	440	
			10
6	75	450	0
			−9
7	63	441	
			−41
8	50	400	
			−58
9	38	342	
			−92
10	25	250	
			−107
11	13	143	
			−143
12	0	0	

(a) Demand and marginal revenue curves

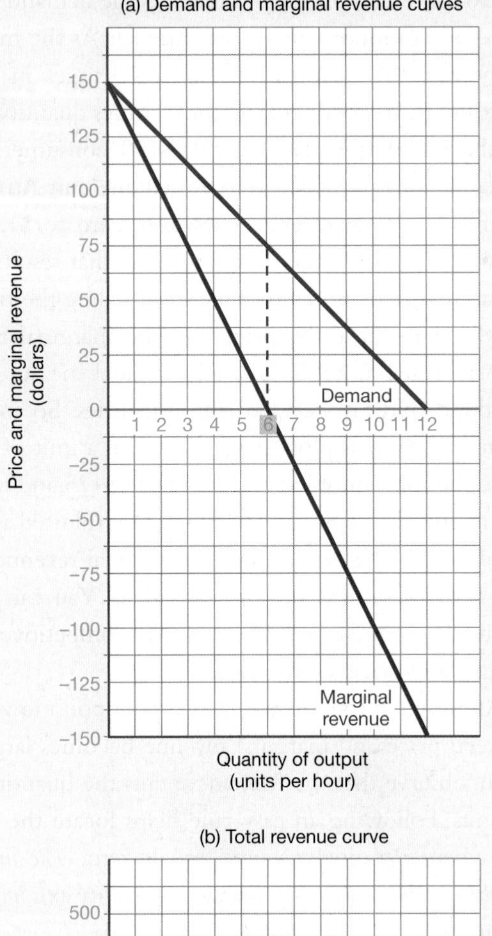

(b) Total revenue curve

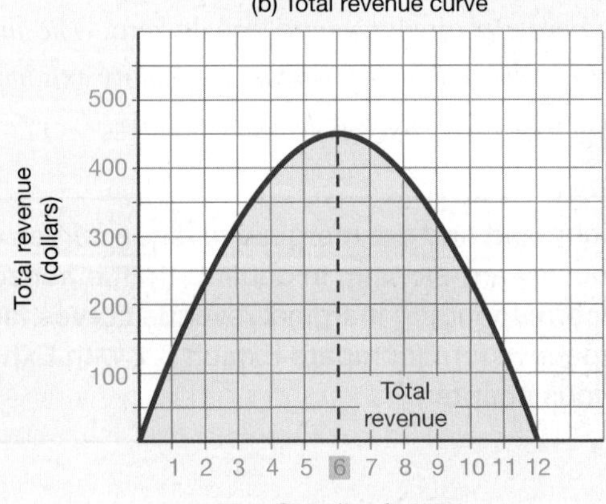

Part (a) shows the relationship between the demand and the marginal revenue curves. The *MR* curve is below the demand curve. Between zero and six units of output $MR > 0$; at six units of output $MR = 0$; beyond six units of output $MR < 0$.

The relationship between demand and total revenue is shown in part (b). When the price is $150, total revenue is zero. When the price is set at zero, total revenue is also zero. In between these two extreme prices, the price of $75 maximises total revenue. This price corresponds to six units of output, which is where the *MR* curve intersects the quantity axis, halfway between the origin and the intercept of the demand curve.

In Exhibit 8.2(b), you can see that total revenue for a monopolist is related to marginal revenue. When the *MR* curve is above the quantity axis (elastic demand), total revenue is increasing. At the intersection of the *MR* curve and the quantity axis (unit elastic demand), total revenue is at its maximum. When the *MR* curve is below the quantity axis, total revenue is decreasing (inelastic demand). The monopolist will never operate on the inelastic range of its demand curve that corresponds to a negative marginal revenue. The reason is that it would be silly for a firm to incur the extra cost of increasing output only to find that sales revenue (total revenue) from selling this level of output is lower than for a smaller output. If a firm was operating in this inelastic range, cutting output and raising price would reduce total cost and increase total revenue. In our example, Atmach would not charge a price lower than $75 or produce an output greater than six units per hour. But what price will the monopolist charge and how much output will it produce if it wishes to maximise profit? We will now look at the answer to this question.

Monopoly in the short run

Exhibit 8.3, which reproduces the demand and the marginal revenue curves from Exhibit 8.2, also shows the firm's cost curves. Note that these cost curves display the familiar shape developed in Chapter 6. Exhibit 8.3(a) illustrates a situation in which Atmach can earn monopoly economic profit in the short run. As with the perfectly competitive firm, a monopolist maximises profit by producing the quantity of output where *MR* = *MC* and charging the corresponding price on its demand curve. In this case, four units is the quantity at which *MR* = *MC*. As represented by point *A* on the demand curve, the price at four units is $100.

Point *B* represents the *ATC* of $75 at four units. Because price is greater than the *ATC* at the *MR* = *MC* output, the monopolist earns an economic profit of $25 per unit. At the hourly output of four units, total economic profit is $100 per hour, as shown by the shaded area. It is important to note here that, unlike the perfectly competitive firm, the monopolist charges a price that is greater than marginal cost. If you are wondering why the monopolist would not increase output even though price is greater than marginal cost, think for a moment about the implications of the *MR* = *MC* profit-maximising rule. As you can see from Exhibit 8.3(a), if the monopolist were to increase output beyond the level where *MR* = *MC*, marginal cost would be greater than marginal revenue. This means that an increase in output would add more to total cost than it would to total revenue, resulting in a fall in profit. As you will see shortly, the fact that the profit-maximising monopolist charges a price greater than marginal cost has important implications for the question of whether monopoly compromises economic efficiency.

Exhibit 8.3 **Profit maximisation and loss minimisation for a monopolist**

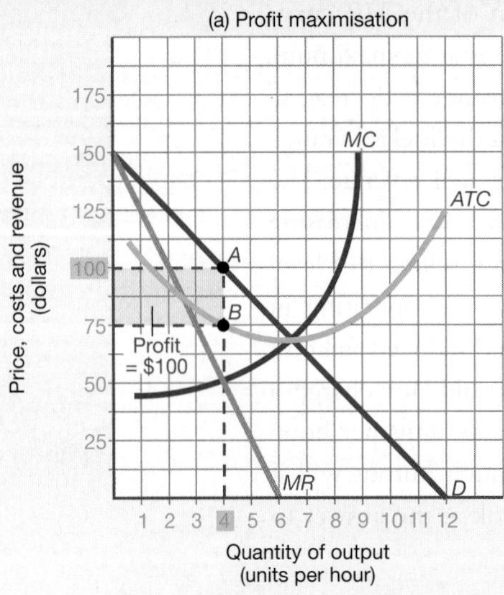

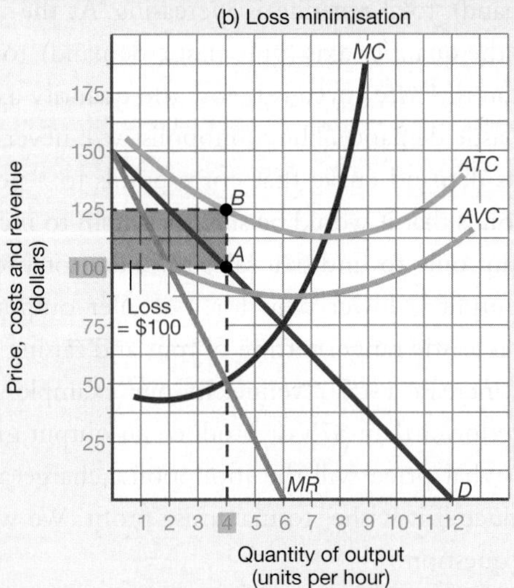

Part (a) illustrates a monopolist electronics firm – Atmach – maximising profit by producing four units of output, which corresponds to the intersection of the marginal revenue and the marginal cost curves. The price the monopolist charges is $100, which is point *A* on the demand curve. Because $100 is above the *ATC* of $75 at four units, the monopolist earns a short-run economic profit of $100 per hour, represented by the shaded area.

In part (b), Atmach is a monopolist minimising short-run losses by producing four units of output. Here the *ATC* curve is higher than it was in part (a), with the result that the demand curve lies below the *ATC* curve at all points. At a price of $100, the shaded area shows that total revenue is less than total cost and the loss is $100 per hour. If variable costs were to rise or if the demand curve shifts leftward, preventing the firm from charging a price that covers the *AVC*, the monopolist loses less money by shutting down.

Observe that a monopolist charges neither the highest possible price nor the revenue-maximising price. In Exhibit 8.3(a), $100 is not the highest possible price. Because Atmach is a *price maker*, it could have set a price above $100 and sold less output than four units. However, the monopolist does not maximise its profit by charging the highest possible price. Any price above $100 does not correspond to the intersection of the *MR* and *MC* curves. Now note that four units is below the output level of six units where *MR* = *0* and total revenue reaches its peak. If this monopolist did choose to maximise revenue by producing where *MR* = *0*, you can see that it would fail to maximise its profit because it would not be following the *MR* = *MC* profit-maximising rule. The only case in which a monopolist would maximise total revenue at the same time as it maximised profit would be where its marginal cost of production was zero. A monopolist producing with zero marginal cost is an unlikely case. Hence, the price charged to maximise profit is higher on the demand curve than the price that maximises total revenue.

International focus

Applicable concept: monopoly

Monopolies around the world

This section gives some interesting examples of monopolies in other countries. Let's begin with a historical example. In the period between the sixteenth and eighteenth centuries monarchs granted monopoly rights for a variety of businesses. For example, in Britain in 1600, Queen Elizabeth I gave a charter to the British East India Company, which established a monopoly over England's trade with India. This company was even given the right to coin money and to make peace or war with non-Christian powers. As a result of its monopoly, the company made substantial profits from the trade in Indian cotton goods, silks and spices. In the late 1700s, the growing power of the company and the huge personal fortunes of its officers provoked increasing government control. Finally, its trade monopoly, great power and patronage ended in 1858 when the company was abolished.

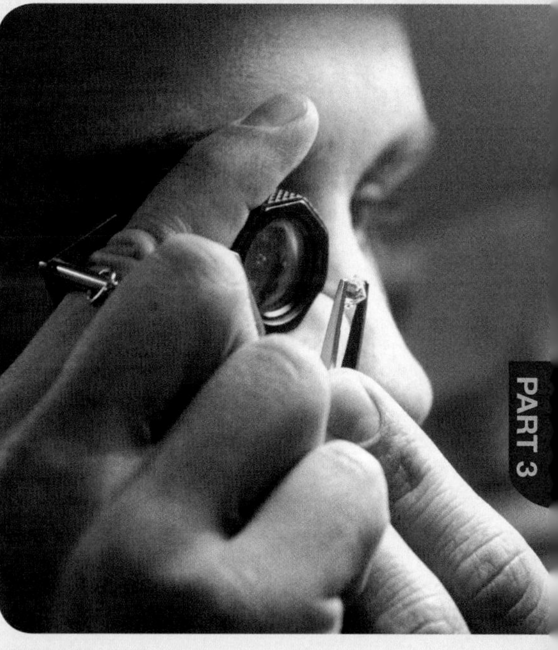

As the saying goes, 'diamonds are forever'. Whether or not the worldwide diamond monopoly that controlled the diamond market for most of the twentieth century can be revived is, however, another matter. Until recently De Beers, a South African corporation, was close to being a world monopoly. Through its Central Selling Organization (CSO), headquartered in London, De Beers controlled over 70 per cent of all the diamonds sold in the world. De Beers controlled the price of jewellery-quality diamonds by requiring suppliers in Russia, Zaire, Botswana, Namibia and other countries to sell their rough diamonds through De Beers' CSO. Why did the suppliers of rough diamonds allow De Beers to set the price and quantity of diamonds sold throughout the world? The answer is that, because the CSO controlled such a large proportion of the market, it could put any uncooperative seller out of business. All the CSO had to do was to reach into its huge stockpile of diamonds and flood the market with the type of diamonds being sold by an independent seller. Moreover, rather than the CSO actually doing this, it was its potential to do it that provided the ever-present threat to the non-compliant competitor. More recently, discovery of new diamond mines in countries such as Australia and Canada, along with a more independent stance on the part of some producers, has led to De Beers abandoning its monopoly control. Instead, it has chosen to use public relations and marketing strategies to differentiate its own diamonds from those of its smaller competitors.

Genuine caviar, the salty black delicacy, is naturally scarce because it comes from the eggs of sturgeon harvested at fisheries in the Caspian Sea near the mouth of the Volga River. After the Bolshevik revolution in 1917, a caviar monopoly was established under the control of the Soviet Ministry of Fisheries and the Paris-based Petrosian Company. The Petrosian brothers limited exports of caviar and pushed up prices to as much as $2200 a kilogram for some varieties. As a result of this worldwide monopoly, both the Soviet government and the Petrosian Company earned handsome profits. It is interesting to note that the vast majority of the tonnes of caviar harvested each year were consumed at government banquets or sold at bargain prices to top Communist Party officials.

With the fall of the Soviet Union it became impossible for the Ministry of Fisheries to control all exports of caviar. Various former Soviet republics claimed jurisdiction and negotiated independent export contracts. Caviar export prices dropped sharply. But caviar lovers should not be too overjoyed. Today the supply of caviar is dwindling because of overfishing and pollution of the Volga.

Read about the British East India Company and its monopoly in the online encyclopedia, *Wickipedia*, at **en.wikipedia.org/wiki/British_East_India_Company.**

CONCLUSION

The monopolist maximises profit by producing that level of output for which *MR* = *MC*. The corresponding price will be on the elastic segment of its demand curve.

The fact that a firm has a monopoly does not guarantee economic profits. A monopolist has no protection against changes in demand or cost conditions. Suppose that, following a spate of terrorist activity, Atmach incurs losses because higher insurance charges cause increases in its costs. If the *ATC* curve is everywhere higher than the demand curve, as shown in Exhibit 8.3(b), total cost exceeds total revenue at any price charged. Because the *MR* = *MC* price of \$100 (point *A*) is greater than the *AVC*, but not the *ATC*, the best Atmach can do is to minimise its loss. This means the monopolist, like the perfectly competitive firm, produces in the short run where *MR* = *MC* so long as the price exceeds *AVC*. At a price of \$100 (point *A*), the *ATC* is \$125 (point *B*) and Atmach takes a loss of \$100 per hour, as represented by the shaded area (\$2534 units). Note, in this example, that the marginal cost curve has not changed because the increase in insurance costs represents a change in fixed cost only.

What if *MR* = *MC* at a price below the *AVC* for a monopolist? As under perfect competition, the monopolist will shut down. To operate would only add further to losses. If this explanation is unclear, jog your memory by looking again at Chapter 7.

Monopoly in the long run

In perfect competition, economic profits are impossible in the long run. The entry of new firms into the industry drives the product's price down until economic profits reach zero. Extremely high barriers to entry, however, protect a monopolist.

If the factors determining the positions of a monopolist's demand and cost curves mean that it earns an economic profit, and if nothing disturbs these factors, the monopolist will earn economic profit in the long run.

In the long run, the monopolist has increased flexibility. The monopolist can alter its plant size in order to lower cost, just as a perfectly competitive firm can. But firms such as Atmach will not remain in business in the long run when losses persist – regardless of their monopoly status. Facing long-run losses, the monopolist will liquidate its resources or transfer them to a more profitable industry.

In reality, no monopolist can depend on barriers to protect it fully from competition in the long run. One threat is that entrepreneurs will find innovative ways to compete with a monopoly. For example, Atmach must fear that firms will use their ingenuity to develop a better and cheaper fuel-saving device. To dampen the enthusiasm of potential rivals, one alternative is to sacrifice short-run profits to earn greater profits in the long run. Returning to part (a) of Exhibit 8.2, the monopolist might wish to charge a price below $100 and produce an output greater than four units per hour. In this way it would send a signal to potential rivals that it is willing to sacrifice profits in the short run to discourage the entry of rival firms. A decision by a firm to discourage potential competition by temporarily reducing prices is known as *predatory pricing*.

predatory pricing

Price discrimination

Our discussion so far has assumed that the monopolist charges each customer the same price. What if Atmach decides to try to sell identical SAV-U-GAS units for, say, $100 to truck owners and $50 to car owners? Under certain conditions, a monopolist may practise **price discrimination** to maximise profit. Price discrimination occurs when, for the same product, a seller charges different customers different prices not justified by cost differences.

Price discrimination This occurs when, for the same product, a seller charges different customers different prices not justified by cost differences.

Conditions for price discrimination

Not all monopolists can engage in price discrimination. The following three conditions must exist before a seller can price discriminate.

1. The seller must be a price maker and therefore face a downward-sloping demand curve. As you will see in the next chapter, this means monopoly is not the only market structure in which this practice may appear.
2. The seller must be able to segment the market by distinguishing between consumers willing to pay different prices. This separation of buyers will be shown to be based on different price elasticities of demand.
3. It must be impossible or too costly for customers to engage in **arbitrage**. Arbitrage is the practice of earning a profit by buying a good or service at a low price and reselling it at a higher price. For example, suppose your campus bookshop tried to boost profits by selling textbooks at a 50 per cent discount to seniors. It would not take seniors long to cut the bookshop profits by buying textbooks at the low price, selling these texts

Arbitrage The practice of earning a profit by buying a good at a low price and reselling the good at a higher price.

for less than the list price to all the students who are not seniors, and pocketing the difference. In so doing, even without knowing the word *arbitrage*, the seniors would destroy the bookshop's price discrimination scheme. In our SAV-U-GAS gas example, Atmach might try to prevent arbitrage involving car owners buying units for $50 and reselling them to truck drivers for less than $100 by redesigning the unit so that the model sold to car owners cannot easily be fitted to trucks.

Although not typically monopolies, the providers of passenger train services meet the conditions for price discrimination. First, because a downward-sloping demand curve is faced, a lower (concession) fare will increase the quantity of tickets sold. Second, a passenger's age, or status as a student, can easily be determined and verified, allowing the rail authority to classify consumers with different price elasticities of demand. Children, pensioners and students usually have lower incomes and a lower willingness to pay than adults of working age. This means that their demand curve is more elastic than that of adults of working age. Third, the nature of the service and the conditions of travel prevent arbitrage. A child, pensioner or student cannot buy a rail ticket at a low price and sell it to an adult of working age for a higher price. Children are visibly younger than working-age adults, and pensioners and students are required to carry identification that indicates their eligibility for the lower (concession) fare.

Exhibit 8.4 **Price discrimination**

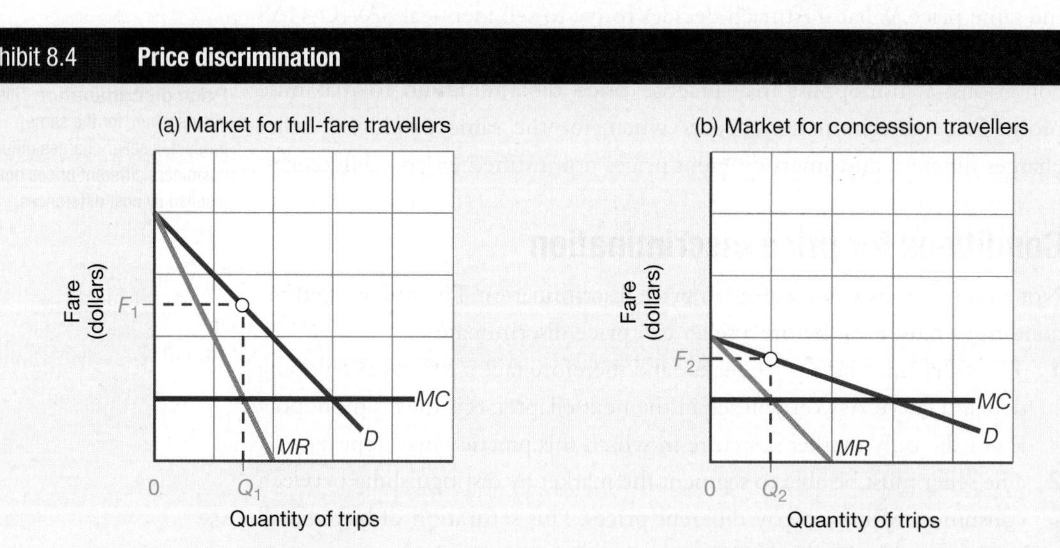

To maximise profit, the rail authority separates travellers into two markets. The demand curve for travel by working-age adults in part (a) is less elastic than the demand curve for travel by children, pensioners and students in part (b). Profit maximisation occurs when *MR* = *MC* in each market. Therefore, the rail authority sets a full fare for trips by working-age adults and a concession fare for trips by children, pensioners and students. By using price discrimination, the rail authority earns a greater profit than it would by charging a single price to all travellers.

Exhibit 8.4 illustrates how the rail authority practises price discrimination. For simplicity, assume the marginal cost of providing a seat on a train is constant and therefore represented by a horizontal *MC* curve. To maximise profit, the rail authority follows the *MR* = *MC* rule in each market. Given the different price elasticities of demand, the price at which *MR* = *MC* differs for the two markets. As a result, the rail authority sets a higher (full) fare for working-age adults and a lower (concession) fare for children, pensioners and students.

The ethics of price discrimination

Examples of price discrimination abound. Picture theatres offer lower prices for children than for adults, although the cost of providing a seat is the same for both. Hotels, restaurants and hairdressers often give discounts to senior citizens – and not because they eat less or have less hair! Local authorities such as city and shire councils offer lower rate charges to pensioners who own their homes.

A common reaction to price discrimination from those who do not benefit from it is that it is unfair. After all, if it costs the same to provide a meal to a pensioner as it does to anyone else, why should the hotel or restaurant give a discount to the pensioner? But look at the other side of price discrimination. First, the seller is pleased because price discrimination increases profits. Second, many buyers benefit from price discrimination by not being excluded from purchasing the product. In Exhibit 8.4, price discrimination makes it possible for concession fare travellers who could not afford to pay a higher fare to travel by train. Price discrimination allows retired people to enjoy hotels and restaurants they could not otherwise afford, it allows more children to go to the cinema, and it enables pensioners to more easily afford the costs of living in their own homes.

By and large, economists do not support price discrimination because it reflects the economic power of producers who are able to determine the prices they set rather than being constrained by the market, as occurs with perfect competition. Nonetheless, they understand that if price discrimination means that lower prices are available to the needy when they use public transport, visit the hairdresser, or use doctors' and lawyers' services then, from an ethical perspective, there is some merit in the practice.

Why don't adults pay more for popcorn at the movies?

At the movies, adults pay a higher ticket price than children and each group gets a different-coloured ticket. However, when adults and children go to the snack bar, both groups pay the same amount for popcorn and other snacks. Which of the following alternatives best explains why price discrimination stops at the ticket window? Is it: because the demand curve for popcorn is perfectly elastic; because the theatre has no way to divide the buyers of popcorn into separate groups based on different price elasticities of demand; or because the theatre cannot prevent resale?

Comparing monopoly and perfect competition

Now that the basics of the two extremes of perfect competition and monopoly have been presented, we can compare and evaluate these market structures. This is an important assessment, because the contrast between the disadvantages of monopoly and the advantages of perfect competition is the basis for many government policies, especially those enshrined in competition policy. To keep the analysis simple, we will assume that the monopolist charges a single price rather than engaging in price discrimination.

The monopolist as a resource misallocator

Recall the discussion of market efficiency from Chapter 3 and the explanation in Chapter 7 as to why perfect competition is efficient. Efficiency exists when a competitive market is in equilibrium. In a competitive market in equilibrium, each perfectly competitive firm produces that level of output for which price is equal to marginal cost. This means that production reaches the level of output where the price of the last unit produced matches the cost of producing it.

Exhibit 8.5(a) shows that, by following the $MR = MC$ profit-maximising rule, the perfectly competitive firm produces the quantity of output at which $P = MC$. The price, P_c (marginal benefit), of the last unit produced equals the marginal cost of the resources used to produce it. In contrast, when the monopolist shown in Exhibit 8.5(b) follows the $MR = MC$ rule, it charges a price, P_m, which is greater than marginal cost ($P > MC$). In this situation, there are some consumers who value the product at more than its marginal cost of production but at less than the price charged by the monopolist. In spite of valuing it at more than the cost of production, they are unable to purchase it. Consumers want the monopolist to use more resources and produce additional units that could only be sold at a lower price, but the monopolist restricts output to maximise profit.

Exhibit 8.5 Comparing a perfectly competitive firm and a monopolist

(a) Perfectly competitive firm

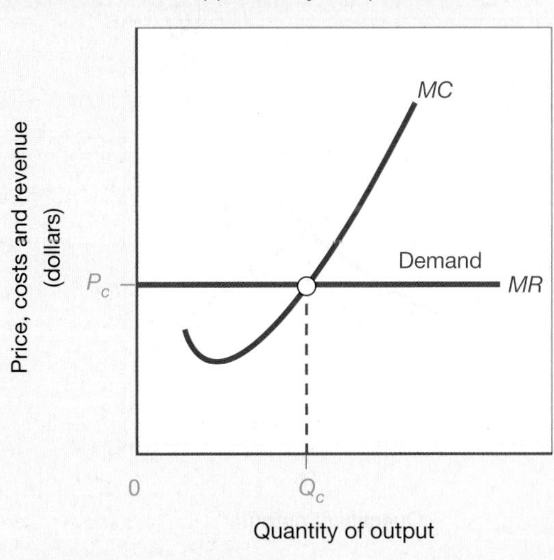

(b) Monopolist

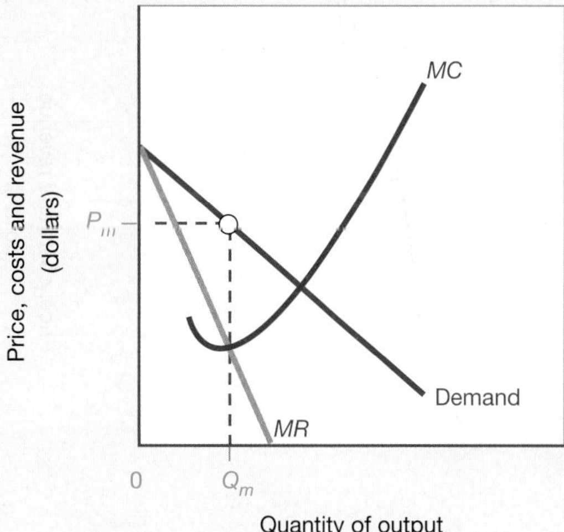

The perfectly competitive firm in part (a) sets $P = MC$ and produces Q_c output. Therefore, at the last unit of output, the marginal benefit is equal to the marginal cost of resources used to produce it. This condition means that perfect competition achieves efficiency.

Part (b) shows that the monopolist produces output Q_m, where $P > MC$. By so doing, consumers are short-changed because the marginal benefit of the last unit produced exceeds the marginal cost of producing it. Under monopoly, inefficiency occurs because the monopolist under-allocates resources to the production of its product.

A monopolist is characterised by inefficiency because resources are under-allocated to the production of its product.

Perfect competition means more output for less

Exhibit 8.6 presents a comparison of perfect competition and monopoly in the same graph. Suppose the industry begins as perfectly competitive. The market demand curve, *D*, and the market supply curve, *S*, establish a perfectly competitive price, P_c, and an output, Q_c. Recall from Exhibit 7.8 in the previous chapter that the competitive industry's supply curve, *S*, is the horizontal sum of the marginal cost curves of all the firms in the industry.

Now let's suppose the market structure changes when one firm buys out all the competing firms, and the industry becomes a monopoly. Assume further that the market demand curve remains unchanged and that the marginal cost curve for the monopolist is the same as the sum of the individual marginal cost curves of the previously competitive firms. In a monopoly, the market

Exhibit 8.6 **The impact of monopolising an industry**

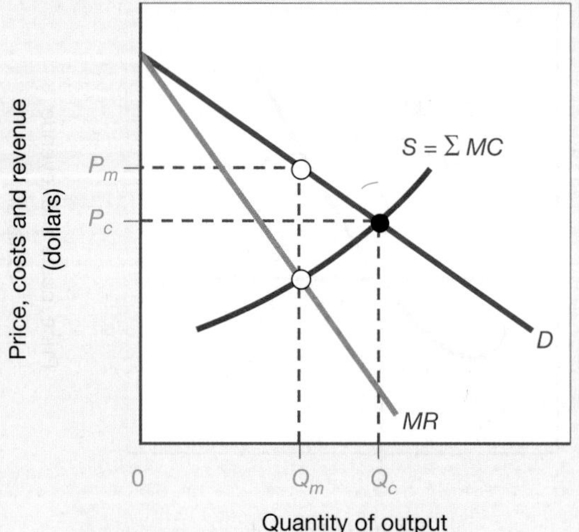

Assume an industry is perfectly competitive, with market demand curve *D* and market supply curve *S*. The market supply curve is the horizontal summation of all the individual firms' marginal cost curves above their minimum average variable costs. The intersection of market supply and market demand establishes the equilibrium price of P_c and the equilibrium quantity of Q_c. Now assume the industry suddenly changes to a monopoly. The monopolist produces the *MR* = *MC* output of Q_m, which is less than Q_c. By restricting output to Q_m, the monopolist is able to charge the higher price of P_m.

demand curve *is* the monopolist's demand curve. The monopolist's *MR* curve lies below the demand curve. To maximise profit, the monopolist sets *MR* = *MC* by restricting the output to Q_m and raising the price to P_m. The transformation of the industry to a monopoly disadvantages the consumer because prices rise, and advantages the new monopolist because, unlike perfect competitors, it is able to earn economic profits. Thus monopoly not only misallocates resources but also raises the income of the monopolist at the expense of the consumer.

Recall that one of the barriers to entry discussed earlier in this chapter was economies of scale. If monopoly exists because of economies of scale (natural monopoly) then it does not necessarily follow that perfect competition will produce more output for less. Any attempt by the competition policy agency to break up a natural monopoly into smaller firms will result in an increase in production costs, because economies of scale have been lost. In this case, the appropriate policy for the regulator is to allow the monopoly to continue but to cap the price. As you saw in Chapter 7, this is precisely what the ACCC did in relation to Telstra.

Monopoly harms consumers on two fronts. The monopolist charges a higher price and produces a lower output than would result under a perfectly competitive market structure.

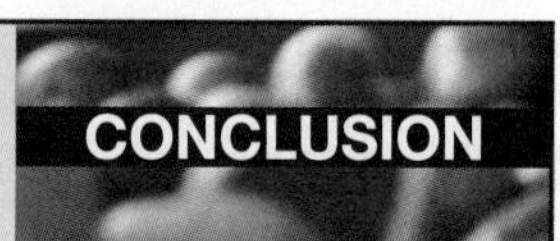

The case against and for monopoly

So far, a case has been made against monopoly and in favour of perfect competition. Now it is time to pause and summarise the economist's case against monopoly, as follows:

- A monopolist gouges (overcharges) consumers by charging a higher price than would be the case under perfect competition.
- Because a monopolist's profit-maximising output is less than that for a perfectly competitive industry, too few resources are allocated to production of the product. Stated differently, the monopolist is responsible for a misallocation of resources because it charges a price greater than marginal cost. In perfectly competitive industries, price is set equal to marginal cost and the result is an optimal allocation of resources.
- Monopolists earn long-run economic profit, which contrasts with the zero economic profit in the long run for a perfectly competitive firm.
- Monopoly alters the distribution of income in its favour.

Not all economists agree that monopoly is bad. Economists Joseph Schumpeter and John Kenneth Galbraith have praised monopoly power. They have argued that the rate of technological change is likely to be greater under monopoly than under perfect competition. Their view is that monopoly profits afford giant monopolies the financial strength to invest in the well-equipped laboratories and skilled labour necessary to create technological change.

The counter-argument is that monopolists are slow to innovate. Freedom from direct competition means the monopolist is not motivated and therefore tends to stick to the 'conventional wisdom'. As Nobel laureate Sir John Hicks put it, 'The best of all monopoly profit is a quiet life.' In short, monopoly offers the opportunity to relax a bit and not worry about the 'rat race' of technological change.

What does research on this issue suggest? Not surprisingly, many attempts have been made to verify or refute the effect of market structure on technological change. Unfortunately, the results to date have been inconclusive. It may well be that a mix of large and small firms in an industry is the optimal mix for creating technological change.

Nevertheless, the pervasiveness of competition policy in free market economies around the world does suggest that there is widespread support for the view that monopoly power should be curbed. Recall that in the previous chapter we noted that many of the regulatory activities of bodies like the ACCC or the NZCC, including the curbing of monopoly power, are designed to limit unethical behaviour in the business sector – behaviour that Adam Smith might have described as displaying unenlightened self-interest.

Analyse the issue

Does size matter?

Applicable concepts: competition versus monopoly; competition policy

Over the past two decades, the Australian government and many Australian firms have pursued the goal of globalisation. This has led to increasing integration of the Australian economy into the world economy. It has also resulted in a number of unforeseen developments, such as the desire of some Australian firms to shift their headquarters offshore to take advantage of more favourable tax regimes, and the emergence of arguments to the effect that Australia's competition policy should be less committed to the ideal of high levels of competition in the Australian economy. This latter development reflects the increasing competition faced by Australian firms in international markets.

The argument based on increasing international competition promotes the idea that Australian firms competing in world markets must get bigger or get out: if Australian firms are prevented by competition policy from merging with other Australian firms, there is no way that they can achieve sufficient size to be competitive in world markets. In pushing this argument, the business community points to examples like Qantas, which has more than half the Australian market but less than three per cent of the world market; or Australia's big four banks, which are nevertheless small by international standards.

The response from the ACCC to these arguments has been as vehement as the arguments themselves. Here is part of what the ACCC chairman at the time, Professor Allan Fels, had to say about the issue in a speech to the Australia–Israel Chamber of Commerce in March 2001:

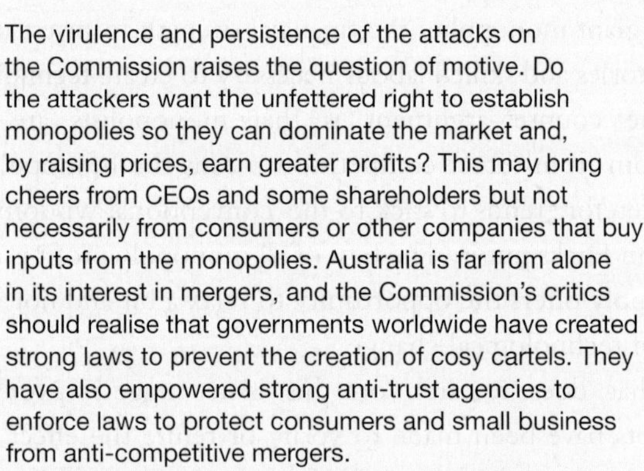

> The virulence and persistence of the attacks on the Commission raises the question of motive. Do the attackers want the unfettered right to establish monopolies so they can dominate the market and, by raising prices, earn greater profits? This may bring cheers from CEOs and some shareholders but not necessarily from consumers or other companies that buy inputs from the monopolies. Australia is far from alone in its interest in mergers, and the Commission's critics should realise that governments worldwide have created strong laws to prevent the creation of cosy cartels. They have also empowered strong anti-trust agencies to enforce laws to protect consumers and small business from anti-competitive mergers.
>
> If the big business critics were serious about promoting the development of large internationally competitive Australian companies it would acknowledge the benefits of competition. Would Australia's big companies be internationally competitive if they had to secure their raw materials, such as coal and petrol, from a monopoly supplier? How would they fare if they had to export their goods through a monopoly transport company and raise finance from a monopoly bank? Would they be better off if they purchased their products from a monopoly retailer, 'Colesworth'?[1]

Acknowledging that the foundations of competition policy are to be found in economic theory, Professor Fels concluded his speech by remarking that '[t]he anti-competitive conduct provisions of the Trade Practices Act, including the merger provisions, are an attempt to enact economics as law.'

With the 2003 appointment of a new chairman, Graeme Samuel, the ACCC appears to be taking a more relaxed position in relation to the effects of industry consolidation in Australia. In an article in the *Australian Financial Review* in late 2004, Samuel was quoted as backing the view of the Business Council of Australia that Australian companies are being pressured into consolidation within their industry sectors in order to be strong internationally.[2]

Using the above information, answer the following questions.

1 Using long-run cost concepts, explain why some Australian firms may need to get big if they are to compete internationally.

2 Elsewhere in his speech, Professor Fels pointed out that an overwhelming majority of merger applications were approved by the ACCC. Why do you think these mergers were approved?

1 Allan Fels, Chairman ACCC, 'Mergers and big business', speech presented at boardroom lunch, 'Mergers and market power', 15 March 2001, Sydney.

2 Toni O'Loughlin and Annabel Hepworth, 'Competition flourishing, argues BCA', *Australian Financial Review*, 6 December 2004, p. 5.

The views of the former chairman of the ACCC regarding the alleged need to promote the international competitiveness of Australian firms by watering down competition policy can be found in a speech to the Australia–Israel Chamber of Commerce. Go to (**www.accc.gov.au**) and use the search facility to search for *ACCC mergers and market power*.

PART 3

Key concepts

Monopoly
Natural monopoly
Price maker
Price discrimination
Arbitrage

Summary

- **Monopoly** is a single seller supplying the entire output of an industry. The demand curve that it faces is the entire industry demand curve for the good or service it sells. The monopolist sells a unique product, and extremely high barriers to entry protect it from competition.

- **Barriers to entry** that prevent new firms from entering an industry are (1) ownership of an essential resource, (2) legal barriers and (3) economies of scale. Government franchises, licences, patents and copyrights are the most obvious legal barriers to entry.

- A **natural monopoly** arises because of the existence of economies of scale in which the *LRAC* curve falls indefinitely as production increases. Without government restrictions, economies of scale allow a single firm to produce at a lower cost than any firm producing a smaller output. Thus, smaller firms leave the industry, new firms fear competing with the monopolist, and the result is that a monopoly emerges *naturally*.

Natural monopoly

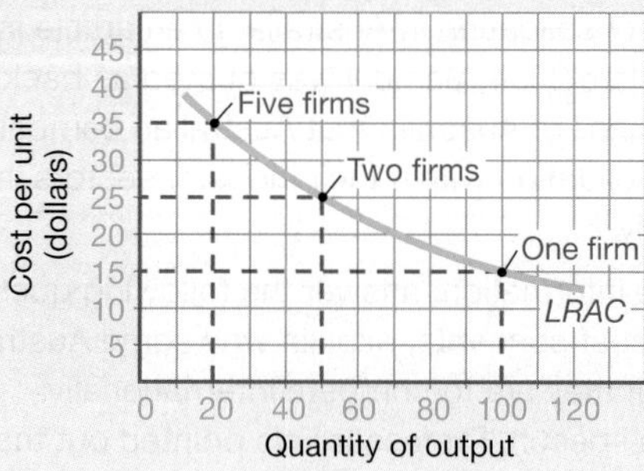

- A **price-maker** firm such as a monopolist faces a downward-sloping demand curve. It therefore searches for the price–output combination that maximises its profit or minimises its loss.

- The **marginal revenue** and the demand curves are downward-sloping for a monopolist. The marginal revenue curve for a monopolist is below the demand curve, and the total revenue curve reaches its maximum where marginal revenue equals zero.

- Because **price elasticity of demand** differs at different points along a straight-line demand curve, different points on the associated marginal revenue curve will correspond to different values of price elasticity. When *MR* is positive, price elasticity of demand is elastic, $Ed > 1$. When *MR* is equal to zero, price elasticity of demand is unit elastic, $Ed = 1$. When *MR* is negative, price elasticity of demand is inelastic, $Ed < 1$.

- The **short-run-profit-maximising monopolist**, like the perfectly competitive firm, locates the profit-maximising price on its demand curve by producing the quantity of output where the *MR* and the *MC* curves intersect. If this price is less than the *AVC* curve, the monopolist shuts down to minimise losses.

Short-run-profit-maximising monopolist

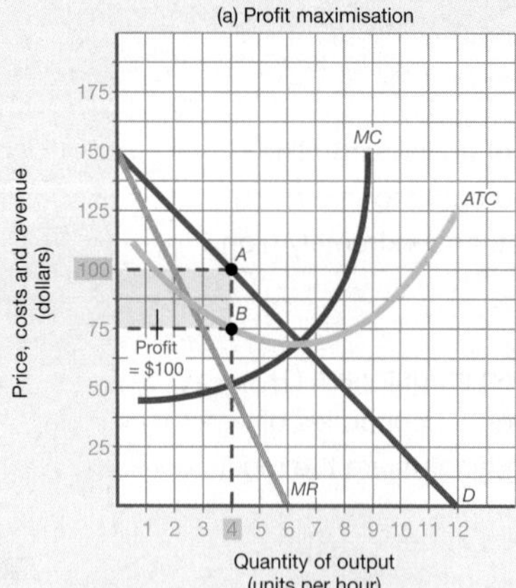

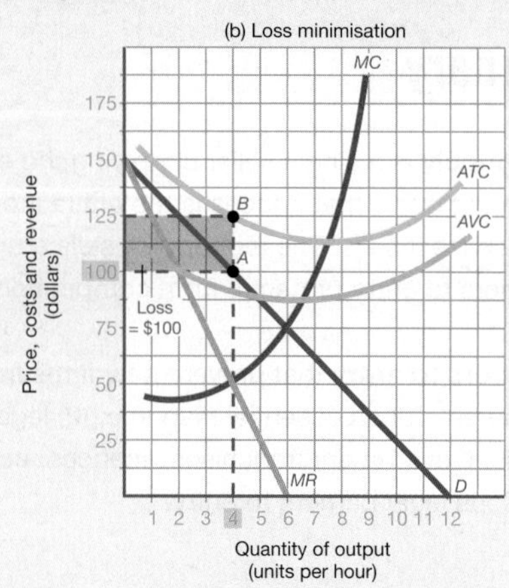

- The **long-run-profit-maximising monopolist** normally earns an economic profit because of barriers to entry. If, in the long run, demand and cost conditions prevent the monopolist from earning at least a normal profit, it will leave the industry.

- **Price discrimination** allows the monopolist to increase profits by charging different buyers different prices, rather than charging a single price to all buyers. Three conditions are necessary for price discrimination: (1) the demand curve faced by the firm must be downward-sloping, (2) buyers in different markets must have different price elasticities of demand and (3) buyers must be prevented from reselling the product at a higher price than their purchase price. Although economists do not generally support price discrimination, they nonetheless understand that if price discrimination means that lower prices are available to the needy when they use public transport, visit the hairdresser, or use doctors' and lawyers' services, then, from an ethical perspective, there is some merit in the practice.

Price discrimination

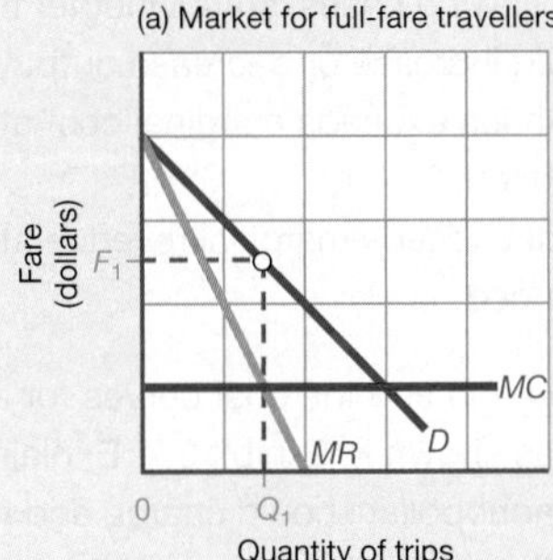

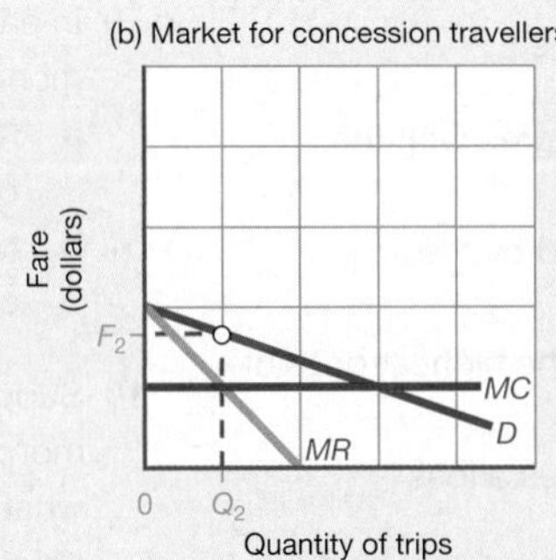

- Monopoly disadvantages are these: (1) a monopolist charges a higher price than a perfectly competitive firm; (2) resource allocation is inefficient because the monopolist produces less output than if competition existed; (3) monopoly produces higher long-run profits than if competition existed; and (4) monopoly transfers income from consumers to producers, compared with the outcome under perfect competition.

Monopoly disadvantages

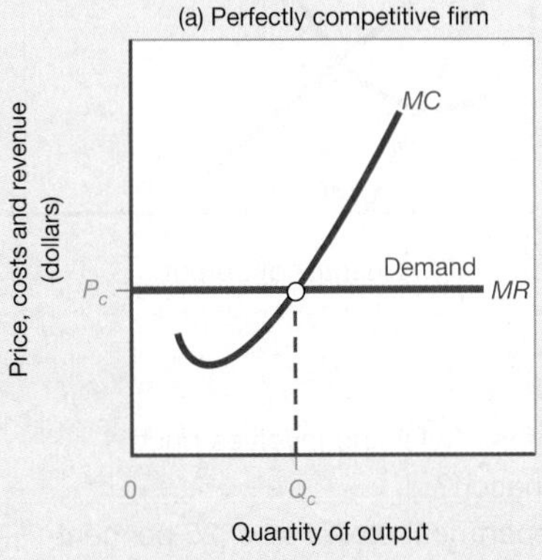

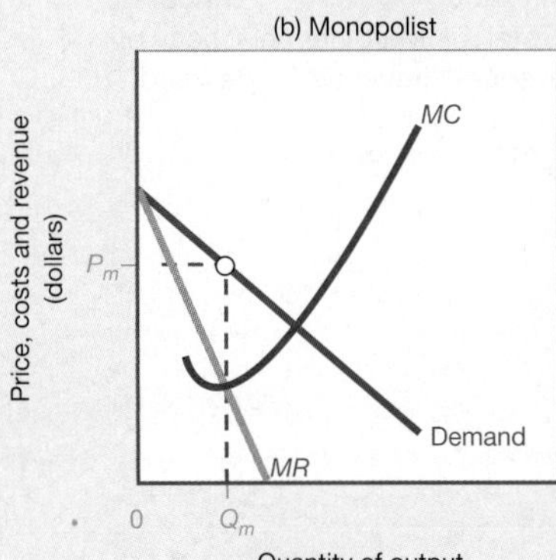

Study questions and problems

1 Using the three characteristics of monopoly, explain why each of the following is a monopolist in relation to at least some of the output it produces:
   a Telstra.
   b the only pharmacy in a country town.
   c the supplier of electricity to your home.

2 Why is the demand curve facing a monopolist downward-sloping and the demand curve facing a perfectly competitive firm horizontal?

3 Suppose an investigator reveals that the prices charged for pharmaceuticals at a hospital pharmacy are higher than the prices charged for the same products at pharmacies in the suburbs served by the hospital. What might the explanation for this situation be?

4 Explain why you agree or disagree with the following statements:
   a 'All monopolies are created by the government.'
   b 'The monopolist charges the highest possible price.'
   c 'The monopolist never takes a loss.'

5 Suppose the average cost of producing a kilowatt hour of electricity is lower for one firm than for another firm serving the same market. Without the government granting a franchise to one of these competing power companies, explain why a single seller is likely to emerge in the long run.

6 Use the following demand schedule for a monopolist to calculate total revenue and marginal revenue. For each price, indicate whether demand is elastic, unit elastic or inelastic. Using the data from the demand schedule, graph the demand curve, the marginal revenue curve and the total revenue curve. Identify the elastic, unit elastic and inelastic segments along the demand curve.

Price	Quantity demanded	Total revenue	Marginal revenue	Price elasticity of demand
$5.00	0	$	$	
4.50	1			
4.00	2			
3.50	3			
3.00	4			
2.50	5			
2.00	6			
1.50	7			
1.00	8			
0.50	9			
0.00	10			

7 Make the unrealistic assumption that production is costless for the monopolist in Question 6. Given the data from the demand schedule in Question 6, what price will the monopolist charge, and how much output should the firm produce? How much economic profit will the firm earn? What will be the effect on the price and output of the monopolist when marginal cost is above zero?

8 Explain why a monopolist would never produce in the inelastic range of the demand curve.

9 In each of the following cases, state whether the monopolist would increase or decrease output.
   a Marginal revenue exceeds marginal cost at the output produced.
   b Marginal cost exceeds marginal revenue at the output produced.

10 Suppose the demand and the cost curves for a monopolist are as shown in Exhibit 8.7. Explain what price the monopolist should charge and how much output it should produce.

Exhibit 8.7 A monopolist in the short run

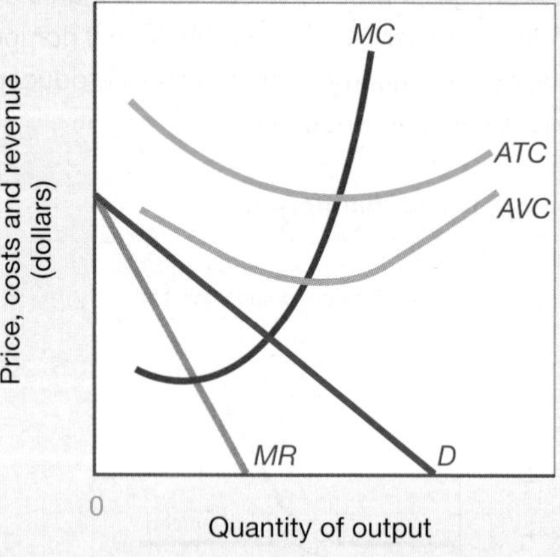

11 Which of the following involves price discrimination?
   a A department store has a '25 per cent off' sale.

b A publisher sells economics textbooks at a lower price in Bourke (in the far west of New South Wales) than in Sydney.
c Manufacturers of cars in Japan sell these cars at higher prices in the United States than in Japan.
d The phone company charges higher long-distance rates during the day (as compared to night rates).

12 Suppose the lawn mowing industry approximates a perfectly competitive industry. Suppose also that a single firm buys all the assets of the lawn mowing firms and establishes a monopoly. Contrast these two market structures with respect to price, output and allocation of resources. Draw a graph of the market demand and market supply for lawn mowing services before and after the takeover. Would you expect the monopoly to survive?

Online exercises

Exercise 1

Read the article 'Rethink the natural monopoly justification of electricity regulation' by Lynne Kiesling of the Reason Public Policy Institute at **www.rppi.org/naturalmonopoly.html**. What are some of the arguments used to suggest that electricity transmission and distribution are not natural monopolies? Do you think that there should be changes to the regulation of electricity transmission and distribution in your area?

Exercise 2

Visit the home pages of a number of Australian universities. (A list can be found at the Australian Government's 'going to uni' website at **www.goingtouni.gov.au/Main/CoursesAndProviders/ProvidersAndCourses/EligibleHigherEducationProviders.htm**. Do some of these universities offer scholarships to excellent students? If the effect of a scholarship is to reduce the price of tuition for the recipient, are the universities that offer them engaging in price discrimination?

Exercise 3

Read the rules of the Monopoly board game at **www.centralconnector.com/GAMES/ MONOPOL.html**. In what ways does the game realistically reflect the process of acquiring monopoly power in contemporary economies?

Answer to 'You make the call'

Why don't adults pay more for popcorn at the movies?

First, there are no other sellers in the foyer, so the theatre is a price maker for popcorn and the demand curve slopes downward. Second, the theatre could easily set up different lines for adults and children and charge different prices for popcorn. Third, is there a practical way to prevent resale? Could the theatre realistically try to stop children from reselling popcorn to their parents and other adults? If you said theatres do not practise price discrimination at the snack bar because resale cannot be prevented, YOU ARE CORRECT.

Multiple-choice questions

1 A monopolist always faces a demand curve that is
a perfectly inelastic.
b perfectly elastic.
c unit elastic.
d the same as the market demand curve.

2 A monopolist sets the
a price at which marginal revenue equals zero.
b price that maximises total revenue.
c highest possible price on its demand curve.
d price at which marginal revenue equals marginal cost.

3 A monopolist
a will never shut down because it always earns economic profits.
b will shut down if price is below average total cost.
c will shut down if its demand curve lies wholly below the average total cost curve.
d would do none of the above.

4 Which of the following is true for the monopolist?
a Economic profit is possible in the long run.
b Marginal revenue is less than the price charged.
c Profit maximising or loss minimising occurs when marginal revenue equals marginal cost.
d All of the above are true.

5 As shown in Exhibit 8.8, the profit-maximising or loss-minimising output for this monopolist is
a 100 units per day.
b 200 units per day.
c 300 units per day.
d 400 units per day.

Exhibit 8.8 Profit maximising for a monopolist

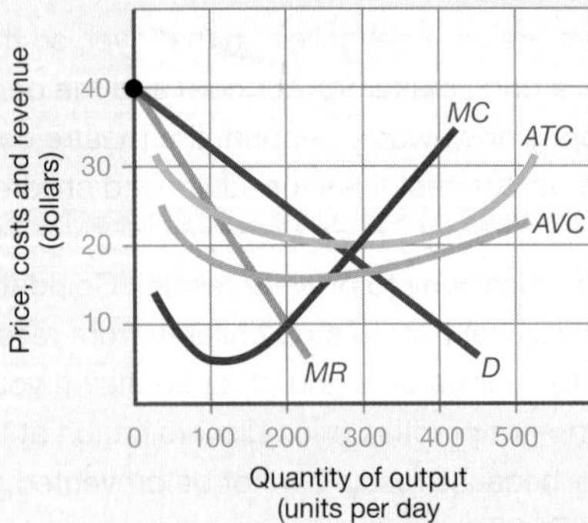

6 As shown in Exhibit 8.8, this monopolist
- **a** should shut down in the short run.
- **b** should shut down in the long run.
- **c** earns zero economic profit.
- **d** earns positive economic profit.

7 To maximise profit or minimise loss, the monopolist in Exhibit 8.8 should set its price at
- **a** $30 per unit.
- **b** $25 per unit.
- **c** $20 per unit.
- **d** $10 per unit.
- **e** $40 per unit.

8 If the monopolist in Exhibit 8.8 operates at the profit-maximising output, the ratio of its total revenue to its total fixed cost will be approximately
- **a** zero.
- **b** two.
- **c** five.
- **d** eight.

9 For a monopolist to practise effective price discrimination, one necessary condition is
- **a** different groups of buyers from different ethnic backgrounds.
- **b** differences in the price elasticity of demand among different groups of buyers.
- **c** a homogeneous product.
- **d** none of the above.

10 What is the act of buying a commodity in one market at a lower price and selling it in another market at a higher price?
- **a** buying short.
- **b** discounting.
- **c** tariffing.
- **d** arbitrage.

11 Under both perfect competition and monopoly, a firm
- **a** is a price taker.
- **b** is a price maker.
- **c** will shut down in the short run if price falls short of average total cost.
- **d** always earns a pure economic profit.
- **e** sets marginal cost equal to marginal revenue.

PART 3

Monopolistic competition and oligopoly

9

Suppose your favourite restaurant is Nat's Seafood Restaurant. Nat's does not fit either of the two extreme models studied in the previous two chapters. Instead, Nat's characteristics are a blend of monopoly and perfect competition. For starters, similar to a monopolist, Nat's demand curve is downward-sloping. This means Nat's is a *price maker* because it can consider charging a higher price, which means that, although it would lose some customers, many loyal customers would keep coming. The reason is that Nat's makes its product different from that of the competition by advertising, first-rate service, a convenient location and other factors. In short, like a monopolist, Nat's has a degree of *market power*. But like a perfectly competitive firm, Nat's is not the only place where you can buy a seafood meal in town. It must share the market with many other restaurants.

Even though Nat's small restaurant may not seem to have much in common with a gigantic firm such as Honda, you will see in this chapter that, in spite of the size difference, they are similar in many ways. These two firms compete in different market structures, both of which fall between perfect competition and monopoly. One of these market structures is *monopolistic competition* and the other is *oligopoly*. Nat's operates in the former, while Honda belongs to the latter.

Unlike monopolies, firms in these two market structures share the market with competing firms. But like monopolies, their profit-maximising behaviour results in a situation where industry output is restricted to below the level that would occur if the industry was perfectly competitive. The theories of perfect competition and monopoly presented in the previous two chapters will help you understand the impact of these new market structures on price and output decisions.

In this chapter, you will examine these economics questions:

- Why will Nat's Seafood Restaurant make zero economic profit in the long run?
- Does advertising increase or decrease prices and profits?
- Why do cartels, such as OPEC, tend to break down?
- Are Rice Bubbles, Vita Brits, Corn Flakes and other brands sold by firms in the breakfast cereal industry produced under monopolistic competition or oligopoly?

The monopolistic competition market structure

In the previous two chapters we have looked at the market structures at each end of the continuum presented in Exhibit 7.1. In this chapter we look at the two remaining structures. Later in the chapter we will look at the structure called oligopoly, which is closest to the monopoly end of the continuum. However, before we do that, we shall investigate the structure known as monopolistic competition, which is the structure closest to perfect competition.

Monopolistic competition
A market structure characterised by (1) many small sellers, (2) a differentiated product and (3) easy market entry and exit.

Economists define **monopolistic competition** as follows: monopolistic competition is a market structure characterised by (1) many small sellers, (2) a differentiated product and (3) easy market entry and exit. Monopolistic competition fits numerous real-world industries. In fact, most of the businesses you deal with on a day-to-day basis – the corner shop, your favourite coffee seller, the dry cleaner and the hot bread shop – are all monopolistic competitors. Monopolistic competition is the market structure in which we find more firms than in any other structure. Let's look at each of the characteristics of monopolistic competition in turn.

Many small sellers

Under monopolistic competition, as under perfect competition, the existence of a large number of firms means that no single firm can influence the market outcome. Nat's Seafood Restaurant, described in the Chapter Preview, is an example of a monopolistic competitor. Although Nat's cannot influence the market outcome, it can set prices slightly higher than those of rival restaurants without fear of losing all its customers, as would occur if it was a perfect competitor. As you will see, it is able to do this because it sells a differentiated product.

The many-sellers condition is met when each firm is so small relative to the total market that each firm's pricing decisions have no effect on the market outcome.

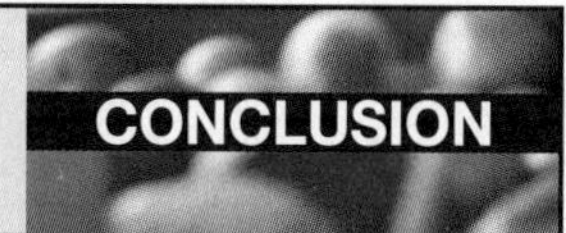

Differentiated product

The key feature of monopolistic competition is **product differentiation**. Product differentiation is the process of creating real or apparent differences between goods and services. A differentiated product means there are close, but not perfect, substitutes for the firm's product. While the products of each firm are very similar, the consumer views them as somewhat different or distinct. There may be 500 restaurants in a given city, but they are not all the same. They differ in location, atmosphere, style and quality of food, quality of service and so on.

Product differentiation The process of creating real or apparent differences between goods and services.

PART 3

How do Pepsi and Coke use their websites to differentiate their products? See **www.pepsi.com** and **www.cocacola.com**.

Product differentiation can be real or imagined, but it does not matter if it is only imagined so long as consumers believe such differences exist. For example, many customers think Nat's has the best seafood in town even though other restaurants actually offer a similar product. The importance of this consumer viewpoint is that Nat's can increase prices if it wishes because many of its customers will be willing to pay a slightly higher price to dine at Nat's. The greater the perceived difference between Nat's product and those of its rivals, the greater will be the capacity for Nat's to raise its prices without significant loss of customers. This gives Nat's the incentive to try to differentiate its product further by, for example, undertaking expenditure on appearances on local TV cooking shows and by developing a marketing campaign using ads showing Nat catching the fish her restaurant serves.

product differentiation

When a product is differentiated, buyers are not indifferent as to which seller's product they buy.

The example of Nat's restaurant makes it clear that, under monopolistic competition, rivalry centres not only on price competition but also on **non-price competition**. Non-price competition is the situation in which a firm competes using advertising, packaging, product development, quality and service, rather than lower prices. Non-price competition leads to important differences between monopolistic competition, perfect competition and monopoly. Under perfect competition, there is no non-price competition because the product is identical for all firms. Likewise, the monopolist may have little incentive to engage in non-price competition because it sells a unique product.

Non-price competition The situation in which a firm competes using differences in advertising, packaging, product development, quality and service, rather than lower prices.

INFOTRAC®

non-price competition

Easy entry and exit

Unlike a monopoly, firms in a monopolistically competitive market confront low barriers to entry. But entry into a monopolistically competitive market may not be quite as easy as entry into a perfectly competitive market. Because monopolistically competitive firms sell differentiated products, it is sometimes difficult for new firms to become established. Many persons who want to enter the seafood restaurant business can get a loan, lease a building and start serving seafood without too much trouble. However, new seafood restaurants may at first have difficulty attracting consumers because of Nat's established reputation as the best seafood restaurant in town. In spite of the possibility of slightly greater difficulty in entering monopolistically competitive markets, it should be emphasised that these are markets that remain very easy to enter. Just consider how anyone with a small amount of capital, the willingness to work hard and a modicum of common sense can start up a business such as a courier service, a shoe shop, a plant shop or a home maintenance service.

The monopolistically competitive firm as a price maker

Whereas the perfectly competitive firm is a price taker, the monopolistic competitor is a *price maker*. The primary reason is that its product is differentiated. This gives the monopolistically competitive firm, like the monopolist, limited control over its price. If it decides to raise its price it finds that, rather than losing all its customers as would be the case under perfect competition, a degree of loyalty to its product or service means that some customers will remain steadfast. On the other hand, a decision by a monopolistic competitor to lower its price will result in an increase in sales. This contrasts with the perfectly competitive case where the firm can sell as much as it likes at the market price, and thus has no incentive to reduce price. This control over price means that, as for a monopolist, the demand curve and the corresponding marginal revenue curve for a monopolistically competitive firm are downward-sloping. However, the existence of close substitutes causes the demand curve for the monopolistically competitive firm to be more elastic than the demand curve for a monopolist. When Nat's raises its price 10 per cent, the quantity of its seafood meals demanded declines, say, 30 per cent. Instead, if Nat's has a monopoly, no close substitutes exist and consumers are less sensitive to price changes. As a monopolist, Nat's might lose only 15 per cent of its quantity of seafood meals demanded from the same 10 per cent price hike.

The demand curve for a monopolistically competitive firm is less elastic (steeper) than for a perfectly competitive firm and more elastic (flatter) than for a monopolist.

Advertising pros and cons

Before presenting the complete graphical models for monopolistic competition, let's pause to examine further the topic of advertising. As explained at the beginning of this chapter, a distinguishing feature of a monopolistically competitive firm is that it engages in non-price competition, which may involve the use of advertising to differentiate its product. The desirability of this advertising is a subject that has exercised the minds of economists for more than half a century.

Critics of advertising argue that its main purpose is to persuade or mislead consumers into buying something they do not need. From society's viewpoint, the resources used in advertising could be used for schools, hospitals, food, clothing or other useful products and services. On the other hand, proponents of advertising cite its many benefits. Those on this side of the debate see ads as infusing the product with its characteristics (luxury cars for sophisticated people, off-road vehicles for adventurous types) and providing worthwhile information. Advertising informs consumers of the target market for the product and the availability of different products, as well as their advantages. So while advertising means that the product may cost a little more, this information saves consumers money and time. Ads may also increase price competition among sellers. Finally, protagonists of advertising argue that consumers are rational and cannot be fooled by advertising. If a product is undesirable, customers will not buy it.

Does non-price competition, which is a hallmark of monopolistic competition, lead to lower prices, greater output and better-informed consumers? Or does this market structure simply raise prices and annoy customers with useless and often misleading information? As long as there is advertising there will be continuing debate about its value to society. Nevertheless, a measure of the concern that society has about the ill effects of misleading advertising can be found in the regularity with which the ACCC imposes severe penalties on firms that contravene the Trade Practices

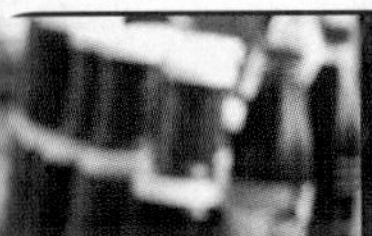

Analyse the issue

Applicable concepts: advertising; barriers to entry

The advertising game

In a departure from long-standing tradition, most Australian states partially deregulated advertising by doctors in the 1990s. In contrast to the traditional view that advertising by doctors would lead to unsavoury practices and a waste of scarce resources, it was decided that doctors should be allowed to undertake restricted types of advertising. In some states the restrictions were limited to prohibiting the use of patient testimonials and prohibiting implied criticism of other practitioners. In New South Wales, however, the restrictions also outlawed advertising that created unjustified expectations or promoted unnecessary or inappropriate use of medical services. Reactions to this deregulation have been mixed and, indeed, it may be too early to tell just what the overall effects may be. You can be sure, however, that one of the issues that critics will address is the effect of advertising costs on the price of medical services.

The Consumers' Health Forum (CHF) is an organisation devoted to maintenance of the rights of consumers of health services. Read about its activities at **www.chf.org.au**. To see how it tackles issues involving advertising of health services and products, use its search facility to search CHF publications for advertising.

In relation to effects of advertising on the price of professional services, some studies in the United States have provided results supportive of deregulation. In a 1983 study of lawyers, the Federal Trade Commission (FTC) surveyed 3200 lawyers in 17 states. The FTC concluded that fees for wills, bankruptcies, uncontested divorces and uncomplicated accident cases were 5 to 13 per cent lower in cities with the fewest restrictions on advertising.[1] Another study compared prices of eyeglasses in states that had restrictions on advertising to prices in states that did not. It found that in states without advertising the retail prices of eyeglasses were 25 to 40 per cent higher.[2]

Critics of advertising also claim that it serves as a barrier to entry against new firms. Brand loyalty allows firms to raise their prices without losing many customers. Researchers conducted an experiment in which

150 subjects from Detroit were given two plates of turkey meat. One plate displayed an advertised brand name and the other plate had an unknown brand. The advertised brand-name meat was preferred by 56 per cent of the subjects; 34 per cent preferred the unknown brand and only 10 per cent thought the two samples tasted alike. In fact, the slices of turkey meat in both samples came from the same turkey.[3]

In 1967, one study investigated the link between advertising expenditures and profits in 40 industries. The authors of the study reached the following conclusion:

> It is evident that advertising is a highly profitable activity. Industries with high advertising outlays earn, on the average, a profit rate which exceeds that of other industries by nearly four percentage points. This differential represents a 50 per cent increase in profit rates [from approximately 8 per cent to 12 per cent]. It is likely, moreover, that much of this profit rate differential is accounted for by the entry barriers created by advertising expenditures and by the resulting achievement of market power.[4]

Other economists claim that advertising is not a barrier to entry. In fact, a study by Yale Brozen found that advertising allows new entrants to penetrate markets dominated by long-established firms. Advertising gives new competitors a chance to introduce their products and win customers from their entrenched rivals.[5] A study by Woodrow Eckard is consistent with this theory. He found that market shares and profits of leading cigarette producers increased after the 1971 US government ban on cigarette advertising. Also, new cigarette brand entry virtually stopped for four years after the ban.[6]

Using the above information, answer the following questions.

1 Advertising is a waste of resources because it unnecessarily raises the cost of a good or service; therefore, all advertising should be banned. Give three arguments against this idea.

2 Some producers of essentially homogeneous products such as particular varieties of oranges, apples and tomatoes attempt to differentiate their products by attaching small stickers that give the name and logo of the producer. Why do you think these producers go to the added expense of attaching these stickers?

---

1 Ruth Marcus, 'Practicing law in the advertising age', *Washington Post*, 30 June 1987, p. A6.

2 Lee Benham, 'The effect of advertising on the price of eyeglasses', *Journal of Law and Economics*, Vol. 15, No. 2, 1972, pp. 337–52.

3 James C. Makens, 'Effect of brand preferences upon consumers' perceived taste of turkey meat', *Journal of Applied Psychology*, Vol. 49, 4 November 1965, pp. 261–3.

4 William Comanor & Thomas Wilson, 'Advertising, market structure, and performance', *Review of Economics and Statistics*, Vol. 49, November 1967, p. 437. Further evidence of this view is presented in William Comanor & Thomas Wilson, *Advertising and Market Power*, Harvard University Press, Cambridge, 1974.

5 Yale Brozen, 'Entry barriers: advertising and product differentiation', in *Industrial Concentration: The New Learning*, eds Harvey J. Goldschmid, H. Michael Mann & J. Fred Weston, Little, Brown, Boston, 1974, pp. 115–37.

6 Woodrow Eckard, 'Competition and the cigarette TV advertising ban', *Economic Inquiry*, Vol. 29, No. 1, January 1991, pp. 119–33.

Act by engaging in false or misleading advertising. In the next section, you will learn that advertising to differentiate a product is also a key characteristic of many firms in the oligopoly market structure.

Price and output decisions for a monopolistically competitive firm

Now we are prepared to develop the short-run and long-run graphical models for monopolistic competition. In the short run, you will see that monopolistic competition resembles monopoly. In the long run, however, entry by new firms leads to a more competitive market structure. This section presents a graphical analysis that shows why a monopolistically competitive firm has some of the characteristics of perfect competition and some of the characteristics of monopoly.

Monopolistic competition in the short run

Exhibit 9.1 shows the short-run equilibrium position for Nat's Seafood Restaurant, a typical firm under monopolistic competition. As explained

Exhibit 9.1 **A monopolistically competitive firm in the short run**

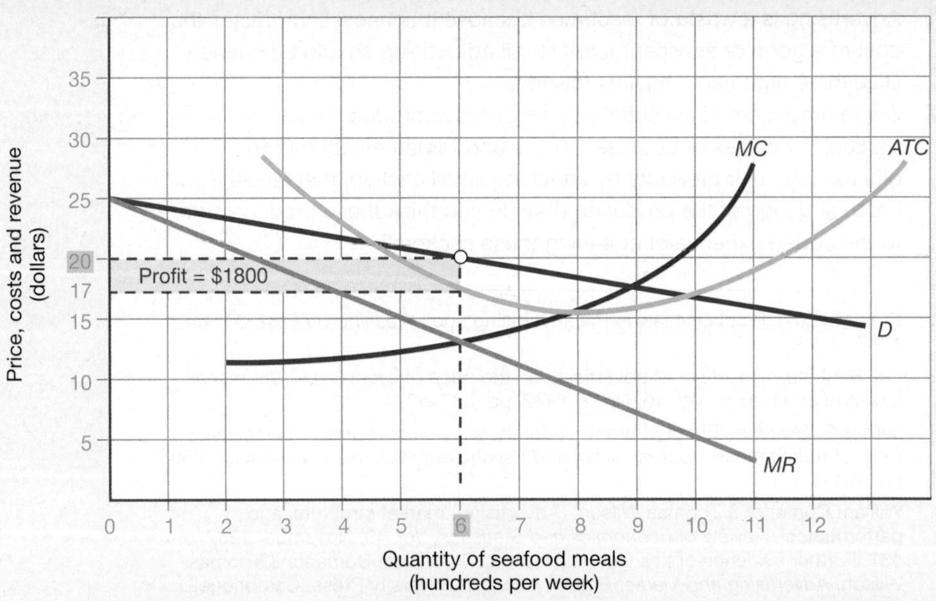

Nat's Seafood Restaurant is a monopolistically competitive firm that maximises short-run profit by producing the output where marginal revenue equals marginal cost. At a profit-maximising output of 600 seafood dinners per week, the price of $20 per dinner is determined by its demand curve. Given the firm's costs, output and prices, Nat's will earn a weekly short-run profit of $1800.

earlier, the demand curve faced by the firm slopes downward because customers perceive that Nat's product is different from its competitors' products. Nat's customers are attracted by its sophisticated atmosphere, its location and the quality of service provided. These non-price factors differentiate Nat's product and allow this restaurant to set its own price rather than 'take' the price that would be determined in the market if it were perfectly competitive. You can see in Exhibit 9.1 that Nat's marginal revenue curve lies below the demand curve, as is the case for a monopolist.

Like firms in any market structure, the monopolistically competitive firm maximises short-run profit by following the *MR* = *MC* rule. In this case, the marginal cost and the marginal revenue curves intersect at an output of 600 seafood meals per week. The profit-maximising price per meal of $20 is given by the point on the demand curve corresponding to this level of output. This price exceeds the *ATC* of $17 per meal, giving an economic profit of $3 per meal. Nat's thus earns a short-run weekly economic profit of $1800.

You can see that this short-run outcome, where price is in excess of marginal cost, looks just like that of the monopolist.

As is also the case under monopoly, if the price equals *ATC*, the firm earns a short-run normal profit; if the price is below the *ATC* curve, the firm suffers a short-run loss; and if the price is below the *AVC* curve, the firm shuts down. In the next section we will turn to the long run, which is just like perfect competition where ease of entry into the market ensures that short-run economic profits are competed away.

Monopolistic competition in the long run

Unlike a monopolist, the monopolistically competitive firm will not earn an economic profit in the long run. Rather, like a perfectly competitive firm, the monopolistically competitive firm earns only a normal profit (that is, zero economic profit) in the long run. The reason is that short-run profits and easy entry attract new firms into the industry. When Nat's Seafood Restaurant earns a short-run profit, the entry of new firms will affect Nat's demand curve, which will shift downward as some of each seafood restaurant's market share is taken away by new firms seeking profit. Nat's, as well as other seafood restaurants, may try to recapture market share by advertising, improving the atmosphere of the restaurant and using other forms of non-price competition. If this does happen, these firms may succeed in moderating the decrease in demand for their product; but the flip side is that they will see their average costs increase. In the analysis that follows, we ignore the possibility of firms engaging in increased non-price competition in these circumstances so that we can concentrate on the effects of increased competition on the demand curve alone. These effects are explained in Exhibit 9.2.

Exhibit 9.2 shows the result of the leftward shift in the firm's demand curve, which continues in the long run until the firm earns zero economic, or normal, profit. The result shown in Exhibit 9.2 is the long-run equilibrium condition. At a price of $17 per meal, the demand curve is tangent to the *LRAC* curve at the *MR* = *MC* output of 500 meals per week. Once long-run equilibrium is achieved in a monopolistically competitive industry, there is no incentive for new firms to enter or leave. You can see that this outcome (zero economic profit) is similar to the long-run outcome for a firm in a perfectly competitive market. Note that, because we are in the long run, existing firms may change the size of their plant to ensure that they are producing at the lowest average cost possible. Given that demand for the firm's output has decreased as a result of entry of new firms, this could mean that existing firms would use smaller-sized plant than they had previously. In Nat's case, the restaurant's floor area, number of tables and kitchen size may be reduced.

You should now be able to analyse the long-run outcome for monopolistic competitors incurring short-run losses rather than profits. See if you can describe the shift in the demand curve that will occur when firms exit the industry, the consequent direction of change in price, and whether

Exhibit 9.2 A monopolistically competitive firm in the long run

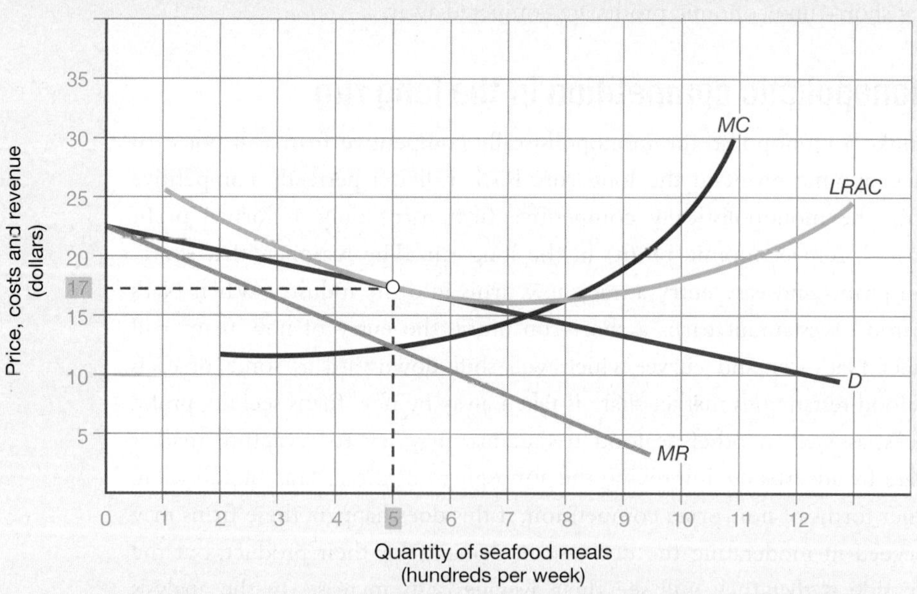

In the long run, profitability of existing firms encourages the entry of new seafood restaurants, which decreases the demand for Nat's seafood. In addition, Nat's may choose a smaller scale of plant, which minimises average costs at the lower level of output being produced. In the long run, the firm earns zero economic profit at a price of $17 per seafood meal and produces an *MR* = *MC* output of 500 meals per week.

remaining firms are likely to increase or decrease the scale of plant they employ. One thing you can be sure of is that, in long-run equilibrium, the firms remaining in the industry will be earning normal profits.

Comparing monopolistic competition and perfect competition

Some economists argue that the long-run equilibrium state for a monopolistically competitive firm, as shown in Exhibit 9.2, results in poor economic performance. Other economists contend that the benefits of a monopolistically competitive industry outweigh the costs. In this section, we again use the standard of perfect competition to help us understand both sides of the debate.

Is the monopolistic competitor a resource misallocator?

As in the case of monopoly, the monopolistically competitive firm fails the standard efficiency test. Exhibit 9.3(a) reproduces the long-run condition from Exhibit 9.2. In Exhibit 9.3(b) it is assumed that the seafood restaurant market is perfectly competitive. For ease of exposition, it is also assumed that Nat's costs remain unchanged when the market structure changes to become perfectly competitive. Recall from Chapter 7 that the characteristics of perfect competition include the condition that customers perceive seafood meals as *homogeneous* and that no firms engage in advertising or other forms of non-price competition. Because we now assume, for the sake of argument, that Nat's product is identical to all other seafood restaurants, Nat's becomes a *price taker*. In this case, the industry's long-run supply and demand curves set an equilibrium price of $16 per meal. Consequently, Nat's faces a horizontal demand curve with the price equal to marginal revenue. Also recall from Chapter 7 that long-run equilibrium for a perfectly competitive firm is established by the entry of new firms until the minimum point of $16 per meal on the firm's *LRAC* curve equals the price (*MR*).

A comparison of parts (a) and (b) of Exhibit 9.3 reveals two important points. First, both the monopolistic competitor and the perfect competitor earn zero economic profit in the long run. Second, the long-run equilibrium output of the monopolistically competitive firm is to the left of the minimum point on the *LRAC* curve. Like a monopolist, the monopolistically competitive firm therefore charges a higher price and produces less output than a perfectly competitive firm.

In our example, Nat's would charge $1 less per meal and produce 300 more seafood meals per week in a perfectly competitive market. The criticism

Exhibit 9.3 **A comparison of monopolistic competition and perfect competition in the long run**

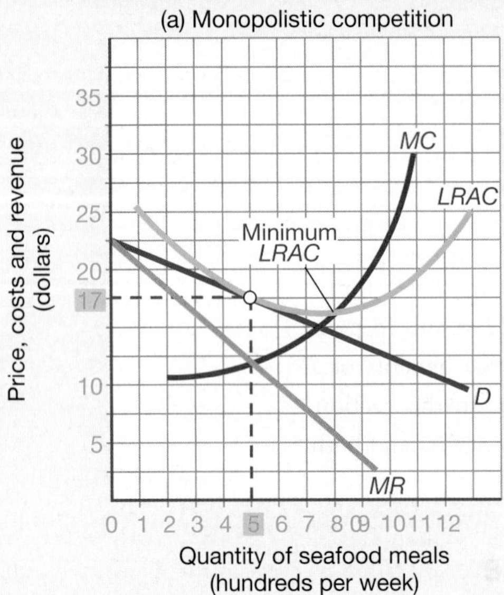

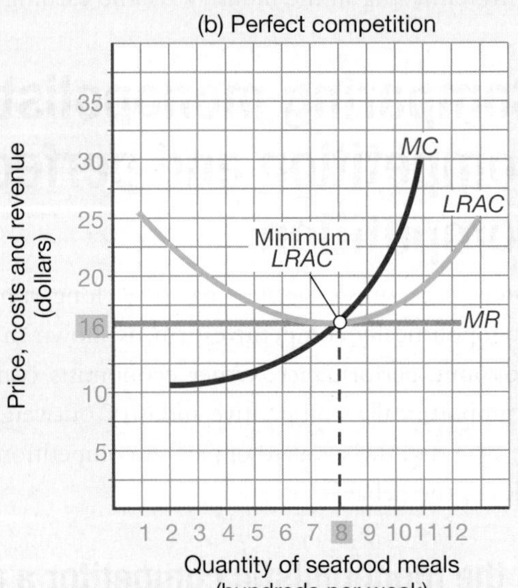

In part (a), Nat's Seafood Restaurant is a monopolistically competitive firm that sets its price at $17 per seafood meal and produces 500 meals per week. As a monopolistic competitor, Nat's earns zero economic profit in the long run and does not produce at the lowest point on its *LRAC* curve.

Under conditions of perfect competition in part (b), Nat's becomes a price taker rather than a price maker. Here the firm faces a horizontal demand curve at a price of $16 per seafood meal. The output is 800 meals per week, which corresponds to the lowest point on the *LRAC* curve. Therefore, the price is lower and the output is 300 meals per week higher when Nat's operates as a perfectly competitive firm rather than as a monopolistically competitive firm.

of monopolistic competition, then, is that firms produce too little output at inflated prices and waste society's resources in the process. With perfect competition, each firm would produce a greater output at a lower price and with a lower average cost.

Although monopolistic competition fails the standard efficiency test, opinions differ as to whether some of the benefits of monopolistic competition might not outweigh these efficiency losses. These benefits arise from the greater consumer choice available under monopolistic competition compared with perfect competition. If there are many seafood restaurants offering differentiated products, this gives consumers much more choice than if the restaurants were all the same. Each seafood restaurant may cook different kinds of seafood in a variety of ways in premises that have a different atmosphere and a different location. If you do not like Nat's seafood basket, you may be able to find a version you like on the menu of another restaurant. Then again, you may like Nat's cooking but simply want a change from Nat's style of food next time you eat out. Most of us appreciate having this range of choices.

All things considered, we can be pretty sure that, in the case of most goods and services, consumers would prefer the variety that comes with product differentiation in monopolistically competitive markets rather than be faced with no choice in a perfectly competitive market in which all firms sell identical products. Although product differentiation means lower output and higher prices, it would seem that the benefits of variety usually far outweigh the benefit from lower prices that would result from production of identical goods and services in a perfectly competitive market. It seems that governments see it this way too. Can you imagine a competition policy that proposed penalties for small firms that attempted to use product differentiation and advertising to make their products or services more attractive to consumers?

As with monopoly, the monopolistically competitive firm can, because it faces a downward-sloping demand curve, try to practise price discrimination. In order to do this it must, like the monopolist, fulfil the three conditions for price discrimination that were discussed in Chapter 8. Examples of price discrimination by monopolistic competitors include restaurants that charge lower prices for seniors and travel agencies that give discounts to students.

The oligopoly market structure

Now we turn to oligopoly, a market structure in which a few large firms dominate the market. Many industries, such as steel, aluminium, motor vehicle manufacturing, airlines, banking, insurance, pharmaceuticals and tobacco, are best described as oligopolistic. This is the 'big business' market structure, in which firms often aggressively compete by using forms of non-price competition such as costly marketing campaigns and image-building exercises.

Economists define an **oligopoly** as follows: oligopoly is a market structure characterised by (1) few sellers, (2) either a homogeneous or a differentiated product and (3) barriers to market entry. Although the number of oligopolistic firms in the economy is relatively small, between them they have a large share of total output produced in the economy. Let's examine each of the characteristics of oligopoly in turn.

Oligopoly A market structure characterised by (1) few sellers, (2) either a homogeneous or a differentiated product and (3) barriers to market entry.

Few sellers

Oligopoly is competition 'among the few'. Here we cover industries that have too few firms to be classed as monopolistically competitive. We use the terms 'Big Three' or 'Big Four' to mean that three or four firms dominate an industry. But what does 'a few' firms really mean? Does this mean at least two, but fewer than ten? As with other market structures, the answer is not that a specific number of firms must dominate an industry if it is to be described as oligopolistic. Economists measure the extent to which the largest firms in an industry dominate the market by using a measure called a **concentration ratio**. This measure indicates the percentage of total sales in the industry that are generated by its largest firms. For example, it might be determined that the four largest firms in industry A have 90 per cent of the market, while in industry B they have only 50 per cent of the market. The important point to understand is that in oligopoly a small number of firms *dominate* the market regardless of the total number of firms that operate in that market. Because a small number of firms dominate the market, this means that a decision by a single large firm to alter the amount of output it sells in the market will affect overall market supply and thus the market price. It follows from this that, like the monopolist and the monopolistic competitor, the oligopolist is a *price maker* facing a downward-sloping demand curve. If it wishes to sell more it must lower its price; if it sells less it can raise its price.

Concentration ratio
A measure indicating the percentage of total sales in the industry that are generated by its largest firms.

concentration ratio

CONCLUSION **The few-sellers condition is met when these few firms are so large relative to the total market that they can affect the market price.**

Because they face a downward-sloping demand curve, oligopolists can, like monopolists and monopolistically competitive firms, endeavour to engage in price discrimination. Some examples of price discrimination practised by oligopolists would include banks having lower fee structures for students and pensioners, and supermarket chains charging different prices for the same product in different stores where there is no difference in costs between stores.

An important feature of firms in an oligopoly market structure is that they tend to be mutually interdependent. **Mutual interdependence** is a condition in which an action by one firm may cause a reaction on the part of other firms. When the ANZ Bank considers raising its fees or offering new financial products, it must predict how the Commonwealth Bank, the National Australia Bank and Westpac will change their fees or products in response. Therefore, the decisions under oligopoly are more complex than under perfect competition, monopoly or monopolistic competition.

Mutual interdependence
A condition in which an action by one firm may cause a reaction on the part of other firms.

An extreme case of mutual interdependence occurs when oligopolistic firms collude – usually with the intention of raising profits. For example, they may carve up the market to give each player exclusive (monopoly) rights to a defined territory, or they may agree to restrict output and raise prices across the market as a whole. Collusion is, of course, facilitated by the fact that only a small number of players must 'join the party'. The large number of firms under perfect competition or monopolistic competition rule out mutual interdependence and collusion in these market structures.

Homogeneous or differentiated product

Under oligopoly, firms can produce either a homogeneous or a differentiated product or service. The aluminium ingots produced by Alcan are virtually identical to the ingots manufactured by Alcoa. The oil sold by Saudi Arabia is very similar to the oil from Iran. Similarly, raw zinc, copper and steel are standardised products. But cars produced by the four Australian manufacturers are differentiated products. Domestic air travel, soft drinks, tobacco products and insurance are also differentiated services or products sold by firms in oligopoly market structures.

To read about the world aluminium oligopoly, go to **www.unu.edu/unupress**, locate the search facility and key in *aluminium* in the search box, then select *4. Control of the world mineral industry* and *The aluminium oligopoly*.

Buyers in an oligopolistic market may or may not be indifferent as to which seller's product they buy.

Barriers to entry

Similar to monopoly, formidable barriers to entry in an oligopoly market protect firms from new entrants. These barriers include very large financial requirements to enter the market, control of an essential resource by existing firms, patent rights held by existing firms, and other legal barriers such as licences required by operators of banks and hotels. But the most significant barrier to entry in an oligopoly market structure is *economies of scale*. For example, larger car manufacturers achieve lower average total costs than those incurred by smaller firms. Consequently, the world motor car manufacturing industry has moved from having hundreds of firms prior to World War II to having no more than twenty significant players today.

Price and output decisions for an oligopolist

Mutual interdependence among firms in an oligopoly makes this market structure more difficult to analyse than perfect competition, monopoly or monopolistic competition. Nevertheless, we can be sure that the market power that oligopolists derive from significant barriers to entry means that, like the monopolist, they can earn economic profits in the long run. However, the price–output decision of an oligopolist is not simply a matter of charging the price where $MR = MC$. Making price and output decisions in an oligopoly is like playing a game of chess, or like a sporting game in which one player's move depends on the anticipated reactions of the opposing player. Indeed, the behaviour of oligopolists is so like that of players of a game that this market structure is often analysed by a specialised discipline called *game theory*. As you will see shortly, this theory has evolved to help analyse and explain situations where mutual dependency of players determines the strategy they employ. Just as in a game, there are many different possible reactions that one firm in an oligopoly can make to the price, non-price and output changes of another firm. Consequently, there are different oligopoly models because no single model can cover all cases. The following is a discussion of four well-known oligopoly models: (1) non-price competition, (2) the kinked demand curve, (3) price leadership and (4) the cartel.

Non-price competition

When we observe major oligopolies, they often compete using advertising and product differentiation. Instead of 'slugging it out' with price cuts, oligopolies can try to capture business away from their rivals with better advertising campaigns and improved products. This model of behaviour explains why advertising expenditures are often large in the cigarette, soft drink, athletic shoe and motor vehicle industries. It also explains why the research and development (R&D) function is so important to oligopolies. For example, much effort is put into developing new products and improving existing products.

Why might oligopolies compete through non-price competition rather than price competition? The answer is that each oligopolist perceives that its rival will easily and quickly match any firm's price reduction. On the other hand, it is much more difficult to combat a clever or important product improvement.

The kinked demand curve

Kinked demand curve
A demand curve faced by an oligopolist who assumes that rivals will match a price decrease but ignore a price increase.

Unlike other market structures, different assumptions define different models for any given oligopolistic industry. In relation to some oligopolistic industries it is argued, for example, that the behaviour of firms can be explained by the **kinked demand curve**. (No, this is not the *kinky* demand curve one hard-of-hearing student reported it to be after the lecture!) The strange shape of this curve explains why prices in an oligopolistic market for motor cars, for example, would change far less often than prices in a perfectly competitive market selling tomatoes.

The kinked demand curve is a demand curve faced by an oligopolist who assumes that rivals will match a price decrease but ignore a price increase. Assuming there is no collusion, the kinked demand curve exists because management tacitly believes that the competition will match its price cuts to ensure that it will not be 'undersold'. On the other hand, a price hike by one firm allows its competitors to increase their share of the market by leaving their prices unchanged. As you have seen, oligopolistic firms must make pricing decisions and, therefore, they are *price makers* rather than price takers. But as we will demonstrate in the kinked demand curve model, the high degree of interdependence among oligopolists restricts their pricing discretion.

Exhibit 9.4 **The kinked demand curve**

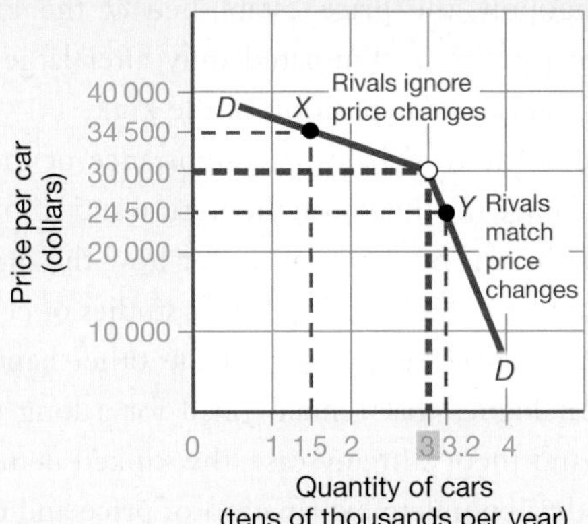

An oligopolist's demand curve may be kinked. In this graph, a car manufacturer believes it faces two demand curves. A price increase from $30 000 to $34 500 per car causes a sizeable reduction in the quantity demanded from 30 000 to 15 000 cars (point *X*). Demand above the kink is relatively elastic, because rivals ignore the firm when it raises the price. Below the kink, the demand curve is less elastic. A price reduction from $30 000 to $24 500 attracts very few new customers, and the quantity demanded increases only from 30 000 to 32 000 cars per year (point *Y*). Under the kinked demand curve theory, prices will be sticky.

In Exhibit 9.4, a kinked demand curve is drawn for Aussica, which we assume competes with Holden, Ford, Toyota and Mitsubishi in the market for six-cylinder family cars in Australia. The current price per car is $30 000 and the quantity demanded at this price is 30 000 Aussica cars per year. Aussica's management assumes that, if it raises its price even slightly above $30 000, the other car makers *will not follow* with higher prices. This price gap between the Aussica and other cars would drive many of Aussica's customers over to its rivals. The segment of the demand curve above $30 000 is therefore relatively flat. Stated differently, above the 'kink' in the demand curve, demand is relatively elastic.

If Aussica raises the price to, say, $34 500 at point *X*, this price hike cuts Aussica's quantity demanded to 15 000 cars per year. Since raising its price is ill advised, management can consider a price reduction strategy. Suppose Aussica cuts the price of its cars to $24 500 at point *Y*. The model shows that Aussica gains few customers and the quantity demanded rises slightly to only 32 000 cars per year. The reason for such a small sales boost is that Holden, Ford, Toyota and Mitsubishi also cut their prices so that each firm might keep its initial market share. However, the lower price does attract some new buyers who would not buy a car at the higher price. The segment of the demand curve below the kink is therefore relatively steep. Here demand is less elastic, meaning the quantity demanded is less responsive to a price drop.

Given the kinked demand curve facing the oligopolist, management fears the worst and is afraid to raise or lower the price of its product. Under this model of oligopoly, the price established at the kink changes very infrequently. Price rigidity is eliminated only after large cost increases or decreases force a change in the position of the kink.

Economists continue to debate the importance of the kinked demand model. Critics challenge the theory on theoretical and empirical grounds. On a theoretical level, there is no explanation for how the original price at the kink was determined. On empirical grounds, studies of certain oligopolistic industries fail to find price stickiness. On the other hand, widespread use of price lists in catalogues that remain fixed for a long time is consistent with kinked demand theory. In any case, the kinked demand theory is not intended to provide a complete explanation of price and output decisions.

Price leadership

Price leadership A pricing strategy in which a dominant firm sets the price for an industry and the other firms follow.

price leadership

Without formal agreement, firms can play a game of follow-the-leader that economists call **price leadership**. Price leadership is a pricing strategy in which a dominant firm sets the price for an industry and the other firms follow. Following this tactic, firms in an industry simply match the price of perhaps, but not necessarily, the biggest firm. For example, suppose GMH initiates a price increase for its popular six-cylinder family car. Reacting to this price hike, other Australian car manufacturers quickly follow the leader's example and boost the price of their cars by a similar amount. Price leadership is not uncommon.

The cartel

The price leadership model assumes that firms do not explicitly collude to avoid price competition. Instead, firms avoid price wars by informally playing by the established follow-the-leader pricing rules. Another way to avoid price wars is for oligopolists to formally, but often covertly, agree to act in concert. Instead of approaching mutual interdependence from a competitive angle, firms openly, or in secret, agree with one another to

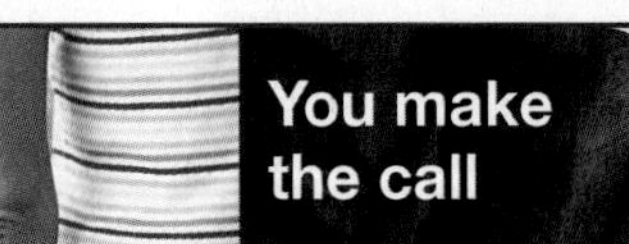

Is price leadership illegal?

The Trade Practices Act, which is administered by the ACCC, prohibits contracts, arrangements or understandings that have the purpose or effect of fixing, controlling or maintaining prices. Do you think that this provision of the Trade Practices Act means that the ACCC would consider taking action against a firm like a bank if it were to make a public announcement foreshadowing the revised interest rate it will charge on home loans in the future?

cooperate to form a monopoly called a **cartel.** A cartel is a group of firms formally agreeing to control the price and the output of a product. The goal of a cartel is to reap monopoly profits by raising prices and restricting output. Cartels are illegal in Australia and in most other developed countries. However, they are common in some developing countries and also across international boundaries where there is no legal authority to regulate them. The best-known cartel is the Organization of Petroleum Exporting Countries (OPEC). The members of OPEC divide crude oil output among themselves according to quotas openly agreed upon at meetings of the OPEC oil ministries. Saudi Arabia is the largest producer and has the largest quota. Let's see how these cartels work.

Cartel A group of firms formally agreeing to control the price and the output of a product.

OPEC is one of the most successful cartels in history. Visit its site at **www.opec.org.**

Using Exhibit 9.5 (see p. 253), we can demonstrate how a cartel works and why keeping members from cheating is a problem. Our analysis begins before oil-producing firms have formed a cartel. For simplicity, we will assume that the oil industry is initially perfectly competitive rather than oligopolistic. Keep in mind, however, that because there are so many firms in a competitive market, it is usually not possible to achieve consensus on forming a cartel. It is easier, but still difficult, to form a cartel in an oligopolistic industry where only a small number of firms must come to the party. Assume each firm has the same cost curve as shown in Exhibit 9.5. Competition has driven each firm to charge \$30 a barrel, which is equal to the minimum point on its *LRAC* curve. Because oil is a fairly homogeneous product, each firm fears that raising its price will result in the loss of many, if not all, of its customers. Thus, the typical firm can be described as being in long-run competitive equilibrium at a price of \$30 per barrel (MR_1), producing six million barrels per day. In this condition, economic profits are zero. There is thus a strong incentive for the firms to attempt to increase profitability by organising a meeting of all oil producers to establish a cartel.

INFOTRAC®
cartel

Now assume the cartel is formed. After examining the price/output combinations dictated by the market demand curve for oil, it is decided that each firm should charge \$45 per barrel and reduce its output to four million barrels per day. At the cartel price, each firm earns an economic profit of \$40 million, rather than a normal profit. The cartel is behaving in the same way as would a monopolist that owned all the world's oil reserves. But what if one firm decides to cheat on the cartel agreement by stepping up its output and other firms stick to their quotas? The marginal revenue curve for the cheater is represented by the horizontal curve MR_2. Output corresponding to the point at which $MR_2 = MC$ is eight million barrels per day. If a cheating firm expands output to this level, it can increase its profit by earning an extra \$40 million. There is thus a strong incentive for cartel members to cheat. However, if all firms cheat and the cartel breaks up, the price and output of each firm return to the initial levels and economic profit again falls to zero. Of course, if we had assumed that the firms were oligopolists earning economic profits before the cartel was formed, the increase in profitability

PART 3

International focus

Applicable concept: cartel

Major cartels in global markets

Cartels, which try to exploit consumers by raising prices and reducing output, have been outlawed in most English-speaking countries for a century or more. However, they flourished in Germany and other European countries in the first half of the twentieth century. Many were international in membership. Although European countries passed laws against such restrictive trade practices after World War II, it is difficult for truly international cartels to be outlawed. Here are brief details of some of these international cartels.

- *Organization of Petroleum Exporting Countries (OPEC)*. OPEC was created by Iran, Iraq, Kuwait, Saudi Arabia and Venezuela in Baghdad in 1960. Today, OPEC's membership consists of eleven countries that control around 70 per cent of the world's oil reserves. OPEC's objective is to set oil production quotas for members and, in turn, raise global prices of oil and petroleum products. Since the oil crises of the 1970s, when threefold increases in the world oil price demonstrated just how powerful this cartel could be, the developed countries have greatly reduced their reliance on oil with the result that the cartel is less powerful than previously.
- *International Airline Cartel (IATA)*. Most of the world's international airlines belong to the IATA. This cartel controls access to airports, fixes airline rates and promotes mutual objectives for its members. The market power of the IATA may decline as more nations follow the example of the United States and reduce protection and regulation of airlines.
- *International Telecommunications Union (ITU)*. Formerly known by its French acronym CCIT, this is perhaps the world's least-known but most effective cartel. This cartel is based in Switzerland and sets the minimum price you pay for an international telephone call. As a result, rates for international calls are usually higher than competitive long-distance telephone calls within a country. In recent years, action by the Federal Communications Commission in the United States has resulted in a weakening of the power of the cartel.

Another little-known group of cartels that are of particular importance to countries like Australia and New Zealand, which rely heavily on ships for transport of exports and imports, are the international container lines cartels. Although immunity from national competition laws has allowed these cartels to flourish in the past, the European Commission and the Australian government have recently been considering ways to end these arrangements.

PART 3

Exhibit 9.5 **Why a cartel member has an incentive to cheat**

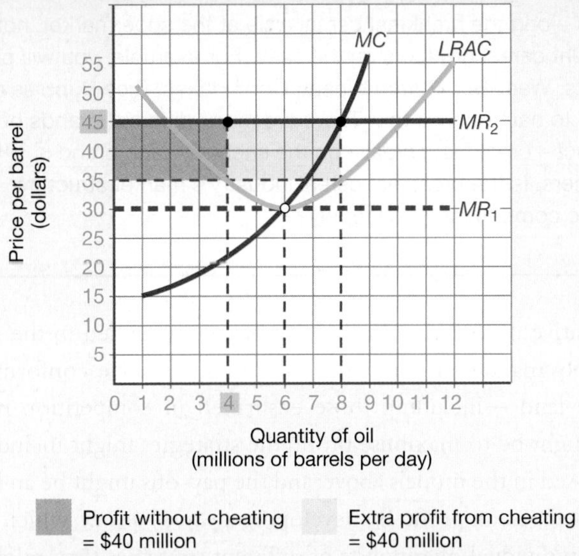

A representative oil producer operating in a perfectly competitive industry would be in long-run equilibrium at a price of $30 per barrel, producing six million barrels per day and making zero economic profit. A cartel can agree to raise the price of oil from $30 to $45 per barrel by restricting the firm to four million barrels per day. As a result of this quota, the cartel price is above $35 on the *LRAC* curve and the firm earns a daily profit of $40 million. However, if the firm cheats on the cartel agreement, it will set the cartel price equal to the *MC* curve and earn a total profit of $80 million by adding an additional $40 million. If all firms cheated, the original long-run equilibrium would be re-established.

would not have been as great as was shown here. Nevertheless, oligopolists would generally find it worthwhile to form a cartel if cheating could be eliminated and if a country's competition policy did not prohibit it.

Game theory

Game theory Analyses the strategic decisions of players when the outcome for each is dependent on the behaviour of others.

Each of the oligopoly models above involves strategic analysis of the responses that firms make, or are likely to make, to the actions of their rivals. Thus *non-price competition* may be preferred to price competition because it is more difficult for rivals to match non-price strategies; the *kinked demand curve* is the outcome of asymmetrical responses of rivals to price increases as compared to price decreases; *price leadership* assumes that rivals will follow the leader; and the *cartel* will work only if rivals cooperate unreservedly. As foreshadowed earlier, much of this interdependent behaviour can be analysed by a discipline called game theory. **Game theory** analyses the strategic decisions of players when the outcome for each is dependent on the behaviour of others. These strategic decisions can be competitive or cooperative.

Every game – even one as simple as noughts and crosses – must be played by a set of rules, and must have a clear-cut goal or objective for those trying to win the game. Every game will also be characterised by a number of possible strategies and their corresponding outcomes or pay-offs, which

Mathematician John Nash, who won the Nobel Prize in Economics in 1994, developed a game-theory-based concept of equilibrium that can be applied to oligopolists. Nash was the subject of a Hollywood movie called *A Beautiful Life*, starring Russell Crowe. Read about Nash by entering the movie title into a web browser such as Google at **www.google.com**.

Which model fits the cereal aisle?

As you walk along the breakfast cereal aisle at the supermarket, notice the many different cereal products on the shelf. For example, you will probably see Vita Brits, Weet-Bix, Puffed Wheat, Corn Flakes, Rice Bubbles and Coco Pops, to name only a few. There are many different brands of the same product – breakfast cereal – on the shelves. Each brand is different from the others. Is the breakfast cereal industry's market structure monopolistic competition or oligopoly?

may be positive or negative. In the case of games applied in the context of the oligopoly market structure, the rules might involve conformity to the laws of the land – including those enshrined in competition policy. The objective might be to maximise profit; the strategies might include some of those discussed in the models above; and the pay-offs might be an increase in profit or a decrease in profit. By developing a *pay-off matrix*, which shows the pay-offs to individual oligopolists of different strategies they might employ, game theory is able to show that market outcomes can be very different depending on whether rivals follow the same or different strategies. For example, the kinked demand curve model above shows that, when all players employ the same strategy of cutting prices, the outcome is very different from the outcome that occurs when rivals do not follow when one player pursues a strategy of increasing price.

In the case of many games, it can be shown that the outcome will be a stable equilibrium in which players have no incentive to change their behaviour. Thus, for example, a game based on rivals' reactions to price changes could result in the sticky price outcome in the kinked demand curve model discussed above. Another example might be a game based on the pay-offs from conforming to a collusive agreement as opposed to cheating. Such a game might result in a stable equilibrium in which firms continue to cheat and a cartel is impossible.

An evaluation of oligopoly

Oligopoly is much more difficult to evaluate than other market structures. None of the models presented above gives a definite answer to the question of efficiency under oligopoly. Depending on the assumptions made, an oligopolist can behave much like a perfectly competitive firm or more like a monopoly. Nevertheless, let's look at a comparison of outcomes under perfect competition compared with an oligopoly selling a differentiated product.

First, the price charged for the product will be higher than under perfect competition. The smaller the number of firms there are in the oligopoly and the more difficult it is to enter the industry, the greater the oligopoly price will be in comparison to the perfectly competitive price.

Second, an oligopoly is likely to spend money on advertising, product differentiation and other forms of non-price competition. These expenditures can shift the demand curve to the right. As a result, both price *and* output may be higher under oligopoly than under perfect competition.

Third, in the long run, a perfectly competitive firm earns zero economic profit. The oligopolist, however, can charge higher prices and earn economic profits because it is more difficult for competitors to enter the industry.

Overall, we can conclude that, as is the case with monopoly, the market power wielded by oligopolists results in a misallocation of resources.

Review of the four market structures

Now that we have completed the discussion of perfect competition, monopoly, monopolistic competition and oligopoly, you are in a better position to appreciate the differences that were summarised in Exhibit 7.1, where we first introduced the concept of market structure. These differences can be seen in Exhibit 9.6, which is the same as Exhibit 7.1. You should now be familiar with the idea that market structures cover a continuum from the most competitive (perfect competition) to the least competitive (monopoly). You should also be aware that there is a strong case for preferring structures that are towards the competitive end of the continuum.

Exhibit 9.6 Comparison of market structures

Market structure	Number of sellers	Type of product	Entry conditions	Examples
Perfect competition	Large	Homogeneous	Very easy	Small crops, international commodity markets
Monopolistic competition	Large	Differentiated	Easy	Boutiques, restaurants, motels
Oligopoly	Few	Usually differentiated but sometimes homogeneous	Difficult	Car making, tobacco products, oil
Monopoly	One	Unique	Extremely difficult	Public utilities

Key concepts

Monopolistic competition
Product differentiation
Non-price competition
Oligopoly
Concentration ratio
Mutual interdependence
Kinked demand curve
Price leadership
Cartel
Game theory

Summary

- **Monopolistic competition** is a market structure characterised by (1) many small sellers, (2) a differentiated product and (3) easy market entry and exit. Given these characteristics, firms in monopolistic competition are price makers but cannot affect the *market* outcome.

- **Product differentiation** is a key characteristic of monopolistic competition. It is the process of creating real or apparent differences between products.

- **Non-price competition** includes advertising, packaging, product development and quality differences. Monopolistically competitive firms and oligopolistic firms may compete using non-price competition rather than price competition.

- **Short-run equilibrium** for a monopolistic competitor can yield economic losses, zero economic profits or economic profits. In the long run, monopolistic competitors make zero economic profits.

Short-run equilibrium for a monopolistic competitor

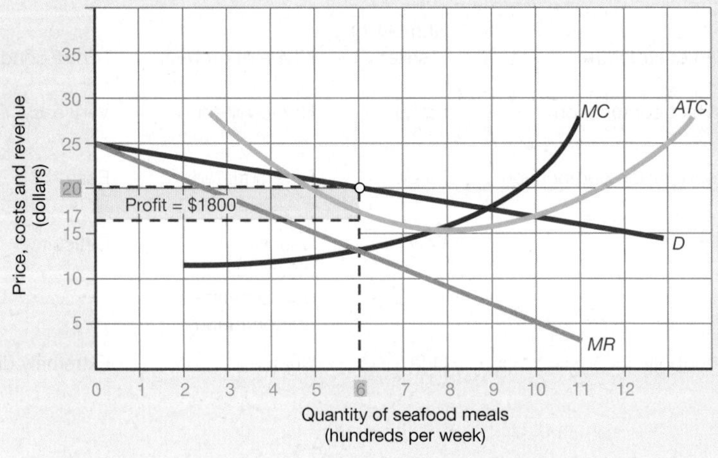

PART 3

- **Comparing monopolistic competition with perfect competition**, we find that the monopolistically competitive firm does not achieve allocative efficiency. It charges a higher price, restricts output and does not produce where average costs are at a minimum.

Comparison of monopolistic and perfect competition

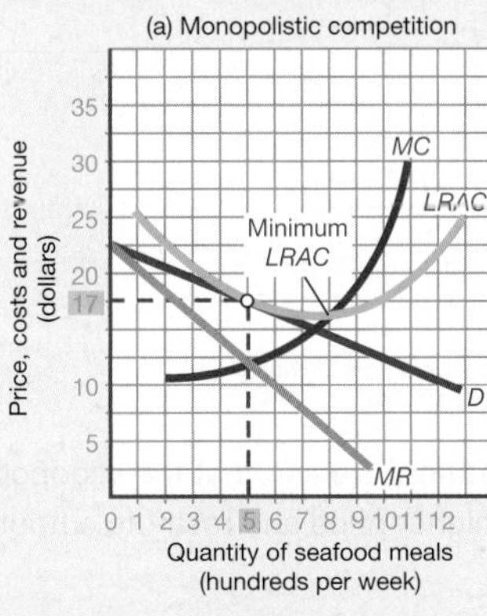

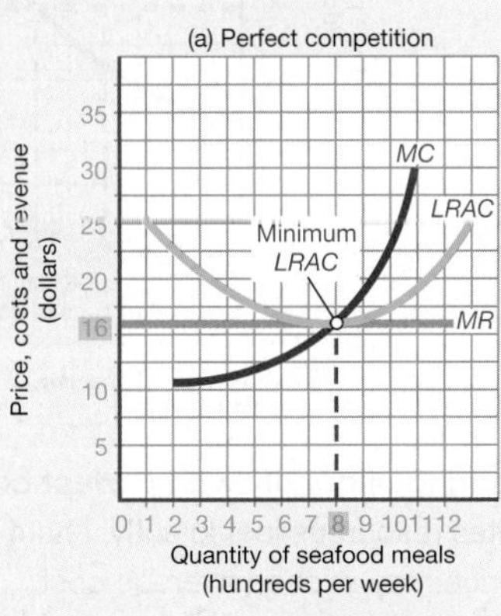

- **Oligopoly** is a market structure characterised by (1) few sellers, (2) a homogeneous or a differentiated product and (3) significant barriers to entry. Oligopolies are **mutually interdependent** because an action by one firm may cause a reaction on the part of other firms.

- A **concentration ratio** for an industry measures the percentage of total sales that are generated by its largest firms.

- **Price leadership** is a theory of pricing behaviour under oligopoly. When a dominant firm in an industry raises or lowers price, other firms follow suit.

- The **kinked demand curve** is a model that explains why prices may be sticky in an oligopoly. The kink is established because an oligopolist assumes that rivals will match a price decrease but ignore a price increase.

Kinked demand curve

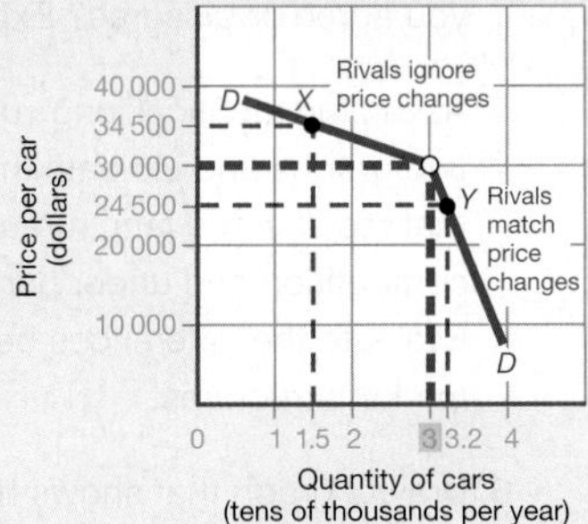

- A **cartel** is a formal agreement among firms to raise prices and set output quotas. The goal is to maximise profits, but firms have an incentive to cheat, which is a constant threat to a cartel.

Cartel

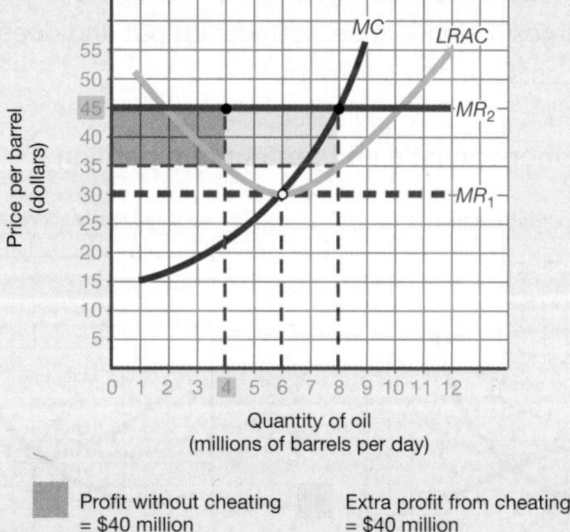

- **Comparing oligopoly with perfect competition**, we find that the oligopolist allocates resources inefficiently, charges a higher price and restricts output so that price may exceed average cost.

Study questions and problems

1 Compare the monopolistically competitive firm's demand curve to those of a perfect competitor and a monopolist.

2 Suppose the minimum point on the *LRAC* curve of a soft drink firm's cola is $1 per litre. Under conditions of monopolistic competition, will the price of a litre bottle of cola in the long run be above $1, equal to $1, less than $1 or impossible to determine?

Exhibit 9.7

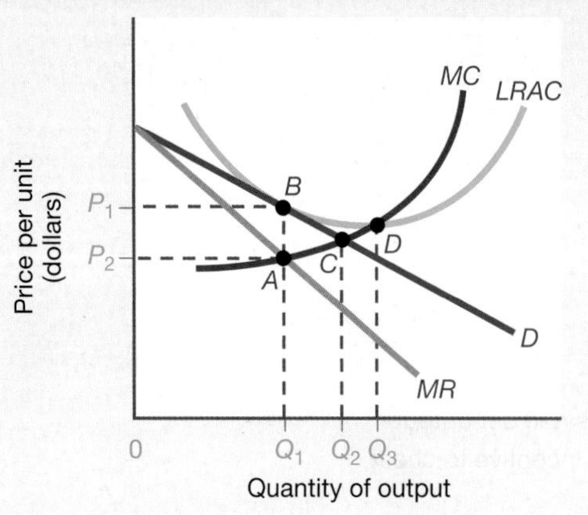

3 Exhibit 9.7 represents a monopolistically competitive firm in long-run equilibrium.

a Which price represents the long-run equilibrium price?

b Which quantity represents the long-run equilibrium output?

c At which quantity is the *LRAC* curve at its minimum?

d Is the long-run equilibrium price greater than, less than or equal to the marginal cost of producing the equilibrium output?

4 Consider this statement: 'Because price equals long-run average cost and profits are zero, a monopolistically competitive firm is efficient.' Do you agree or disagree? Explain.

5 Assuming identical long-run cost curves, draw two graphs and indicate the price and output that result in the long run under monopolistic competition and under perfect competition. Evaluate the differences between these two market structures.

6 Draw a graph that shows how advertising affects a firm's demand curve. Could advertising lead to a situation in which monopolistically competitive firms earn economic profits in the long run?

7 List four goods or services that you have purchased which were produced by an oligopoly.

Why are these industries oligopolistic, rather than monopolistically competitive?

8 Why is mutual interdependence important under oligopoly, but not so important under perfect competition, monopoly or monopolistic competition?

9 Suppose the jeans industry is an oligopoly in which each firm sells its own distinctive brand of jeans. Each firm believes its rivals will not follow its price increases but will follow its price cuts. Explain the demand curve facing each firm. Given this demand curve, does this mean that firms in the jeans industry do or do not compete against one another?

10 Why do you think the ACCC is more likely to be interested in the activities of oligopolists than monopolistic competitors or perfect competitors?

11 Suppose IBM raised the price of its printers but Hewlett-Packard (the largest seller) refused to follow. Two years later IBM cut its price and Hewlett-Packard retaliated with an even deeper price cut, which IBM was forced to match. For the next five years, Hewlett-Packard raised its prices five times, and each time IBM followed suit within 24 hours. Does the pricing behaviour of these computer industry firms follow the cartel model or the price leadership model? Why?

12 Evaluate the following statement: 'A cartel will put an end to price wars, which is a barbaric form of competition that benefits no one.'

Online exercises

Exercise 1

The Trade Practices Act outlaws misleading conduct by businesses. Visit the ACCC web page at **www.accc.gov.au** and enter the words **misleading conduct** into the search box. This will give you the opportunity to read about numerous cases of misleading conduct by Australian firms. Can you think of everyday examples of misleading conduct that you have witnessed yourself? Would there be instances where it would be ethical for firms to mislead the public?

Exercise 2

How do Australia's major motor vehicle manufacturers use the Internet to advertise their products? Look at the websites for Holden (**www.holden.com.au**), Ford Australia **www.ford.com.au**), Toyota (**www.toyota.com.au**) and Mitsubishi (**www.mitsubishi-motors.com.au**). These companies' products compete with numerous imported brands including Nissan, Honda, Mazda, Kia, Daewoo, Audi, VW and Chrysler. Are these companies operating within a monopolistically competitive or oligopolistic market environment? Explain your answer.

Exercise 3

To see how the New Zealand Commerce Commission (NZCC) uses concentration ratios to determine whether mergers of firms would substantially lessen competition, go to **www.comcom.govt.nz/BusinessCompetition/MergersAcquisitions/MergersAcquisitionsGuidelines/Overview.aspx**. Click on **Mergers & Acquisitions Guidelines** to go to a page where you can open the Mergers and Acquisitions Guidelines document. Open the document and search in it (Ctrl+F) for **concentration ratio**. After you have read about the NZCC's use of concentration ratios, go to Section 13 on page 40 of the same document, where there is a list of web addresses for guidelines for other jurisdictions including Australia, Canada, Europe and the U.S. In which jurisdictions are the guidelines most strict; in which are they most liberal?

Exercise 4

In his *Wealth of Nations*, published in 1776, the father of modern economics, Adam Smith, made clear his objection to collusion. In a famous passage, he warned that when business people meet, even for merriment and diversion, they tend to conspire against the public, and contrive to raise prices. Read the relevant passage from *Wealth of Nations* at the Library of Economics and Liberty site at **www.econlib.org** by keying in **merriment** in the Search Site box and selecting **Smith, Wealth of Nations** in the Search Book box. What do you think of Smith's suggestion that, although business people should not be prevented by law from meeting together, the law should not facilitate or render necessary such meetings?

Answers to 'You make the call'

Is price leadership illegal?

The answer to this question can be found in media release 254/99 issued by the ACCC on 23 December

PART 3

1999. In that release, the Chairman of the ACCC, Professor Allan Fels, said that '[b]anks, like other businesses, run the risk of breaching the *Trade Practices Act 1974* if they 'telegraph' possible rises in interest rates to their competitors – and especially when they refer publicly to specific numbers such as "up to 0.5 percentage points".' He concluded by saying that '[t]he ACCC will maintain a close watch on bank behaviour in the coming period to ensure that there is no collusion.' If you said the ACCC would consider taking action against banks that overtly engage in price leadership, YOU ARE CORRECT.

Which model fits the cereal aisle?

The fact that there are many differentiated products does not necessarily mean that there are many firms competing along the cereal aisle. The different cereals listed in this example are produced by only three companies: Uncle Toby's, Sanitarium and Kellogg. In fact, there are relatively few firms in the cereal industry, so even though they sell a large number of differentiated products, the market structure cannot be monopolistic competition. If you said the cereal industry is an oligopoly, YOU ARE CORRECT.

Multiple-choice questions

1 An industry with many small sellers, a differentiated product and easy entry would *best* be described as which of the following?
- **a** an oligopoly
- **b** monopolistic competition
- **c** perfect competition
- **d** a monopoly

2 Which of the following industries is the best example of monopolistic competition?
- **a** wheat growing
- **b** retail jewellery
- **c** car manufacturing
- **d** household water supply

3 Which of the following is *not* a characteristic of monopolistic competition?
- **a** a large number of small firms
- **b** a differentiated product
- **c** easy market entry
- **d** a homogeneous product

4 A monopolistically competitive firm will
- **a** maximise profits by producing where $MR = MC$.
- **b** probably not earn an economic profit in the long run.
- **c** shut down if price is less than average variable cost.
- **d** do all of the above.

5 The theory of monopolistic competition predicts that in long-run equilibrium a monopolistically competitive firm will
- **a** produce the output level at which price equals marginal revenue.
- **b** operate at minimum long-run average cost.
- **c** produce more output than if it were perfectly competitive.
- **d** produce the output level at which price equals long-run average cost.

6 A monopolistically competitive firm is inefficient because the firm
- **a** earns positive economic profit in the long run.
- **b** is producing at an output where marginal cost equals price.
- **c** is not maximising its profit.
- **d** produces an output where average total cost is not minimum.

7 A monopolistically competitive firm in the long run earns the same level of economic profit as
- **a** a perfectly competitive firm.
- **b** a monopolist.
- **c** a cartel member.
- **d** none of the above.

8 One possible effect of advertising on a firm's long-run average cost curve is to
- **a** raise the curve.
- **b** lower the curve.
- **c** shift the curve rightward.
- **d** shift the curve leftward.

9 Monopolistic competition is an inefficient market structure because
- **a** firms earn zero profit in the long run.
- **b** marginal cost is less than price in the long run.
- **c** there is a wider variety of products available compared to perfect competition.
- **d** all of the above.

10 The 'big four' Australian banks operate alongside dozens of smaller banks in an industry described as
- **a** a monopoly.
- **b** perfect competition.
- **c** monopolistic competition.
- **d** an oligopoly.

11 The clothing manufacturing industry in Australia is described as
- **a** a monopoly.
- **b** perfect competition.
- **c** monopolistic competition.
- **d** an oligopoly.

12 A characteristic of an oligopoly is
- **a** mutual interdependence in pricing decisions.
- **b** easy market entry.
- **c** both **a** and **b**.
- **d** neither **a** nor **b**.

13 The kinked demand theory attempts to explain why an oligopolistic firm
- **a** has relatively large advertising expenditures.
- **b** fails to invest in research and development.
- **c** infrequently changes its price.
- **d** engages in excessive brand proliferation.

14 According to the kinked demand theory, when one firm raises its price other firms will
- **a** also raise their prices.
- **b** refuse to follow.
- **c** increase their advertising expenditures.
- **d** exit the industry.

15 Which of the following is evidence that OPEC is a cartel?
- **a** agreement on price and output quotas by oil ministries.
- **b** ability to raise prices regardless of demand
- **c** mutual interdependence in pricing and output decisions.
- **d** ability to completely control entry.

10 Labour markets and microeconomic reform

There has been a constant theme running through the previous chapters of this book. This theme, which is central to the study of economics, involves the idea that economic efficiency and the well-being of the community are promoted by competition. In Chapters 3 and 4 you saw how competitive markets promote efficiency and how market failure, which reduces efficiency, can be corrected. In Chapters 7, 8 and 9 we established that, although a perfectly competitive industry structure maximises well-being, departures from this ideal – involving the exercise of market power by oligopolists and monopolists – are common. We also looked at ways in which government might lessen market power and promote competition through *competition policy*.

In this chapter we will look at some of the ways in which governments in Australia have promoted economic efficiency on a national scale by implementing a broad range of policies that have come to be known as *microeconomic reform*. A number of aspects of microeconomic reform will be discussed in the second half of this book, which deals with the macro economy. In this chapter we concentrate on two aspects of microeconomic reform that can be analysed by examining the way in which they affect the labour market. These two aspects are taxation reform and labour market reform.

Have you ever asked why some governments claim that we would actually be better off if wages were reduced? How can governments argue that wages should be reduced, while at the same time claiming that there should be personal income tax cuts to increase workers' take-home pay? The analysis undertaken in this chapter will help answer these questions by developing a model of the competitive labour market that explains how equilibrium wages are determined. This model also enables us to explain how union wage demands can cause unemployment.

In this chapter, you will examine these economics questions:

- What determines the wage rate an employer pays?
- How can labour unions cause unemployment?
- Do lower personal income taxes raise national output?
- Could a partially deregulated labour market increase the supply of skilled labour?

Microeconomic reform

Microeconomic reform encompasses government policies that deregulate or re-regulate markets for goods, services or factors of production so as to increase competition and raise efficiency. These policies, which apply to both the private and the public sectors, have included: tariff reform designed to make domestic producers more efficient by reducing tariffs (taxes) on imported goods with which they compete (discussed in Chapter 18); financial deregulation aimed at increasing the efficiency of markets in which banks and other financial institutions operate (discussed in Chapter 15); the removal of long-standing impediments to competition and efficiency in key sectors of the economy such as electricity, telecommunications and the waterfront; improvement in the efficiency of government by privatising or corporatising government-owned enterprises; reform of the tax system aimed at reducing distortions and increasing incentives; and labour market reform. In this chapter we will look more closely at tax reform and labour market reform, using a simple model of the labour market to illustrate aspects of the reform process.

Microeconomic reform
Government policies that deregulate or re-regulate markets for goods, services or factors of production so as to increase competition and raise economic efficiency.

Both the Commonwealth government and the state governments have been involved in microeconomic reform. It is, however, the Commonwealth government that has the greater capacity to instigate reform and which has initiated most programs of reform. These reforms have been carried out at the commonwealth and state levels by successive governments of both political persuasions since the mid-1970s. Although many of the key microeconomic reforms have been implemented, the program is an ongoing one, which is best thought of as involving a process of continual improvement.

In late 2004 the Productivity Commission produced a draft report on reform of national competition policy that was seen as setting the agenda for continuing microeconomic reform over the duration of the Howard government's fourth term. The report identified many areas for further reform including health, energy, water, telecommunications and transport. As you might expect, although the overall effect of microeconomic reform is to raise economic efficiency, there have been many losers as a result of the reforms. This has led to a sometimes vociferous defence of the status quo at the political level.

The implementation of reform policies occurs in a great variety of ways. At the national and state levels there are organisations charged with coordinated implementation of many of the reforms aimed at increasing competition in key markets – particularly those involving natural monopolies such as electricity reticulation, water supply and gas. Other policies have involved privatisation of government-owned businesses by selling them to private-sector firms or selling them to the public by issuing shares. Examples of the former include the sales of capital-city airports to firms or consortiums; examples of the latter include the sale of shares in Qantas and in the Commonwealth Bank.

In many cases, microeconomic reform policies are the responsibility of existing government agencies, which are ideally placed to put into effect the legislative changes made. As you have seen in previous chapters, many aspects of competition policy, which has been strengthened as part of the microeconomic reform agenda, are implemented by the ACCC. As you will see shortly, the Australian Industrial Relations Commission has played a key role in implementing labour market reform.

The tax system in Australia has undergone significant reform over the past quarter-century. An understanding of the fundamentals of the tax system is an important prerequisite for understanding some aspects of macroeconomic theory and policy discussed in the second half of this book. A good way to understand the fundamentals of the tax system is to look at the way in which taxation policy has changed over recent years as part of the microeconomic reform process.

Taxation reform

In order to fund their expenditures, all levels of government – national, state and local – must raise revenue. Rates and charges for services rendered are the major sources of revenue for local government, which has no power to raise revenue through taxation. State governments have very limited taxation powers, with taxes on employers' payrolls (payroll tax) being the major source of taxation revenue. The states do, however, receive a large proportion of their total revenue from the Commonwealth government, which has the greatest capacity of all levels of government to levy taxes. This means that the Commonwealth government not only funds most of its own expenditure from taxes it collects, but also uses these taxes to provide substantial revenues to the states.

As the primary tax collector in the nation, it is the Commonwealth government that has the greatest capacity to increase economic efficiency by pursuing tax reform. Before looking at some of the details of taxation reform at the national level, we should first explain the different types of taxes that can be levied.

Types of taxation

Economists divide taxes into two broad categories. The first category is **direct taxes**. Direct taxes are taxes levied on income. In Australia these taxes provide the greater part of tax revenue raised by the Commonwealth government. Income taxes in Australia are levied on individuals and on companies. As you will see, the nature of the tax scales that apply to individuals (personal income tax) are quite different from those that apply to companies (company tax).

Direct taxes Taxes levied on income.

The second category of taxes is **indirect taxes**. These are taxes levied on the sale of goods and services. They are sometimes called *sales taxes*. In Chapter 5 we looked briefly at the different types of indirect taxes levied in Australia when we discussed the incidence of a tax. We noted in that chapter that the two major types of indirect tax levied in Australia are *excise taxes* (levied at a high rate on sellers of a small number of categories of inelastic goods including petrol, alcohol and tobacco products), and the *goods and services tax* (GST), which is a broad-based consumption tax levied at a relatively low rate on buyers of all goods and services, excepting some special exempt categories such as education, health care and some types of food.

Indirect taxes Taxes levied on the sale of goods and services.

indirect taxes

Now that you understand the basic categories of taxation, we can examine the process of taxation reform. When reading about recent tax reform in the sections that follow, you should keep in mind that the re-election of the Howard government in 2004 with a majority in both houses of parliament is likely to mean further refinement of the reforms already undertaken.

Direct tax reform

Economists generally support direct taxation reform because they believe there are strong disincentive effects associated with this type of tax. In the case of firms, income taxes provide a disincentive to invest and take risks in the pursuit of profit. In the case of individuals, income taxes provide a disincentive to work. Put simply, the more of your income that you can take home, the more you are likely to work. Microeconomic reform of the taxation system will therefore look for ways to make the economy more efficient by reducing these disincentives.

Personal income tax scales in Australia – as in most countries – are *progressive*. This means that high-income earners pay a higher proportion of their income in tax than do low-income earners. Generally speaking, progressive income taxes thus act as a greater disincentive to work for high-income earners than for low-income earners. The thrust of reform of personal income taxes has involved attempts to lessen their disincentive effects by reducing the progressivity of the personal income tax scales. The re-jigging of the personal income tax scales that has occurred from the mid-1980s through to the present has resulted in a decrease in the income tax burden of middle- and high-income earners. Although these changes have the potential to increase efficiency, many critics have noted that they also have the effect of reducing the extent to which income is redistributed from the well-off to the less well-off. Later in this chapter we will use a model of the labour market to show how a reduction in personal income taxes can increase output.

Company taxes in Australia are *proportional*. This means that they are levied at the same rate on company profits regardless of the level of profit. The rate has been reduced on a number of occasions since the late 1980s to bring it down from nearly 50 per cent to 30 per cent today. Critics have noted, however, that the efficiency gains flowing from an increased willingness of firms to invest and take risks as a result of the lower tax regime have been accompanied by an increase in the relative burden of taxation borne by individuals.

As you will see in the next section, personal income taxes were reduced significantly from mid-2000, when additional revenues resulted from the introduction of the GST.

Indirect tax reform

Like direct taxes, indirect taxes can also have significant adverse effects on economic efficiency. Sales taxes can result in the distortion of consumer choice in the market if they are levied at higher rates on some goods and services than on others. The effect of a tax on a good or service is for consumers to buy less of that good than they would buy if it were untaxed. Likewise, if some goods or services are taxed at higher rates than others, those goods and services attracting the higher tax will be purchased in relatively smaller quantities than would be the case if all goods and services were taxed at the same rate. This distortion of consumers' choices means that they differ from those that would occur if they were exercising their preferences in a free market with no government intervention.

The Australian government's proposals for tax reform that were implemented in 2000 can be found in Chapter 1 of the Senate Committee's GST Inquiry Main Report at **www.aph.gov.au/senate/committee/gst/main/contents.htm**. Read sections 1.3 to 1.17 dealing with income tax and indirect tax reform.

It was noted above that there are currently two types of indirect tax levied by the Commonwealth government – excise taxes and the GST. The GST was introduced in July 2000 as part of the Commonwealth government's taxation reform agenda. At the time of the introduction of the GST, Australia was one of the few OECD countries without a broad-based consumption tax. Until then indirect taxes in Australia had consisted of excise taxes levied on petrol, alcohol and tobacco products, and wholesale sales taxes that were levied in a somewhat arbitrary way at different rates on different goods, with many goods and *all* services being exempt.

The distortions created by this regime were very marked, with large variations in the proportion of the retail price of a good attributable to indirect tax. Expenditure patterns were tilted towards consumption of goods that attracted low or zero sales taxes, and towards the consumption of services that attracted no indirect taxes. Not only did the introduction of the GST increase efficiency by removing distortions in consumption patterns but, because it brought a significant increase in indirect tax revenues, it allowed reductions in personal income taxes, which also raised efficiency by reducing their disincentive effects.

A major objection to a broad-based consumption tax such as the GST is that it is *regressive*. This means that lower-income earners pay a higher proportion of their income in consumption taxes than do higher-income earners. How can this be, you might ask, when the rate is a flat 10 per cent? The answer is because, on average, low-income earners spend a higher proportion of their income on consumption than do high-income earners. Assume, for the moment, that income taxes are not levied and that the only form of taxation is a 10 per cent GST. If low-income earners spend 100 per cent of their income on consumption, a GST rate of 10 per cent means they will pay 10 per cent of their income in GST. By contrast, high-income earners who spend 90 per cent of their income on consumption will pay only 9 per cent of their income in GST.

We now turn to the issue of labour market reform.

Labour market reform

For most of the twentieth century Australia had a highly centralised wage-fixing process. On the basis of public hearings involving unions, employer groups, government and other interested parties, the Australian Industrial Relations Commission (AIRC) and its predecessors were charged with determining pay and conditions for virtually all classes of employees. These included unskilled workers, tradespeople such as plumbers and toolmakers, and some classes of professionals such as engineers and academics. It was illegal for an employer to provide less pay and lower-grade conditions than those prescribed by the AIRC. In effect, this centralised process provided for a minimum wage for every class of employee.

Read about the AIRC, its history and its functions at **www.airc.gov.au/research/ about/about.html**.

PART 3

Since the early 1990s, however, the process of labour market reform has wrought unimagined change to the industrial relations scene. Today, around one-third of employees have their terms and conditions of employment (including wage rates) determined by a decentralised process known as **enterprise bargaining**. This typically involves unions in each workplace undertaking direct bargaining as a group with their employer to determine terms and conditions of employment for a period of up to five years. These agreements are registered with the AIRC and are monitored by the peak union body, the Australian Council of Trade Unions (ACTU). The major advantage of enterprise bargaining is the increased flexibility it brings.

enterprise bargaining

Enterprise bargaining This typically involves unions in each workplace undertaking direct bargaining as a group with their employer to determine terms and conditions of employment for a period of up to five years.

A simple explanation of how enterprise bargaining works can be found on the ACTU website at **www.worksite.actu.asn.au**. Select *FACT SHEETS*, then *Awards, Enterprise Agreements, AWAs and Contracts – all you need to know*.

A brief resume of the history and activities of the ACTU can be found at **www.worksite.actu.asn.au**. Select *FACT SHEETS*.

It enables employees to be paid wages that reflect their productivity in a particular workplace rather than being paid wages that are judged by a central wage-fixing authority to be reflective of productivity across the entire nation. Thus, workers' remuneration in different enterprises may differ according to factors such as the market in which the enterprise operates, its location, the natural resources it controls, the nature of its capital equipment and, more generally, its overall potential to earn profits.

Although the labour market for skilled workers has been largely deregulated, the AIRC continues to determine a minimum wage for unskilled workers. This is the so-called *safety net* wage, which sets a floor to wages for all workers. The effect on unemployment of setting this wage above the equilibrium wage for unskilled workers was discussed in Chapter 4 and analysed graphically in Exhibit 4.5. We will look again at this effect later in this chapter.

Now that you know more about taxation reform and labour market reform, we are in a position to develop a model of the labour market that will help to explain the effects of some aspects of these reforms in reasonable detail. We will also use this model to examine how union power can, under certain circumstances, cause unemployment.

Labour markets

How are earnings determined? What accounts for the wide differences in earnings we observe in the economy? What is the effect on wages and employment of a reduction in personal income taxes or the substitution of indirect taxes for income taxes? How does union power affect wages and employment? The model we are about to develop provides answers to these questions by explaining aspects of labour markets that determine workers' remuneration and the number of workers firms hire. As you will see, understanding employers' hiring decisions and workers' willingness to work is a key to understanding how labour markets operate. We will begin by developing a model of a competitive labour market in which no single buyer or seller can influence the price (wage rate) of labour.

The labour market under perfect competition

Recall from Chapter 7 that we assumed that the hypothetical firm called Atmach produces and sells electronic components in a perfectly competitive market. Here we will also assume that Atmach hires workers in a perfectly competitive labour market. In a perfectly competitive labour market there are many sellers and buyers of labour services. Consequently, wages and salaries are determined by the intersection of the demand for labour and the supply of labour.

The demand for labour

How many workers should Atmach hire? To answer this question, Atmach must understand the way in which workers contribute to its output. Following our earlier discussion of production costs in Chapter 6, column (1) of Exhibit 10.1 lists possible numbers of workers Atmach might hire per day and column (2) shows the total output per day. One worker would produce five units per day, two workers together would produce an output of nine units per day and so on. Note that columns (1) and (2) constitute a short-run *production function* as represented in Exhibit 6.2(a) in Chapter 6. Column (3) lists the additional output from hiring each worker. The first worker hired would add five units of output per day, the second would produce an additional four units (9–5) and so on. Recall from Chapter 6 that the additional output from hiring another unit of homogeneous labour is defined as the *marginal product of labour;* see Exhibit 6.2(b) in Chapter 6. Consistent with the *law of diminishing returns*, the marginal product falls as the firm hires more workers. (Note that, in order to simplify our analysis, we are assuming there is no initial phase of increasing return, and thus that diminishing returns are experienced from the first unit of homegeneous labour employed.)

The next step in Atmach's hiring decision is to convert marginal product into dollars by calculating the **marginal revenue product** (*MRP*). The *MRP* is the increase in total revenue to a firm resulting from hiring an additional unit of labour or other variable resource. Stated simply, *MRP* is the dollar value of worker productivity. It is the extra revenue a firm earns from selling the output produced by an extra worker. Let us assume, as we did in Exhibit 7.2 in Chapter 7 on perfect competition, that the market equilibrium price is $70 per unit. Because Atmach operates in a perfectly competitive market, the firm can sell any quantity of its product at the market-determined price of $70. Given this situation, the first unit of labour contributes a marginal revenue product of $350 per day to revenue ($70 per unit times the five units of output). Column (5) of Exhibit 10.1 lists the marginal revenue product of each additional worker hired.

Marginal revenue product (*MRP*) The increase in total revenue to a firm resulting from hiring an additional unit of labour or other variable resource.

PART 3

Exhibit 10.1 Atmach's demand for labour

Reference points	(1) Labour input (workers per day)	(2) Total output (units per day)	(3) Marginal product (units per day)	(4) Product price	(5) Marginal revenue product [(3) × (4)]
	0	0	–	$70	–
A	1	5	5	70	$350
B	2	9	4	70	280
C	3	12	3	70	210
D	4	14	2	70	140
E	5	15	1	70	70

CONCLUSION **A perfectly competitive firm's marginal revenue product is equal to the marginal product of its labour times the price of its product.**

Demand curve for labour A curve showing the different quantities of labour employers are willing to hire at different wage rates in a given time period, ceteris paribus. It is equal to the marginal revenue product of labour.

Now assuming all other inputs are fixed, Atmach can derive its **demand curve for labour**, which conforms to the law of demand explained in Chapter 3. The demand curve for labour is a curve showing the different quantities of labour employers are willing to hire at different wage rates. It is equal to the *MRP* of labour. The *MRP* numbers from Column (5) of Exhibit 10.1 are duplicated in Exhibit 10.2. As shown in the exhibit, the price of labour in terms of daily wages is measured on the vertical axis. The quantity of workers Atmach will hire per day at each wage rate is measured on the horizontal axis. The demand curve for labour is downward-sloping: as the wage rate falls, Atmach will hire more workers per day. If the wage rate is above $350 (point *A*), Atmach will hire no workers because the cost of a worker is more than the dollar value of any worker's contribution to its

Exhibit 10.2 **Atmach's demand curve for labour**

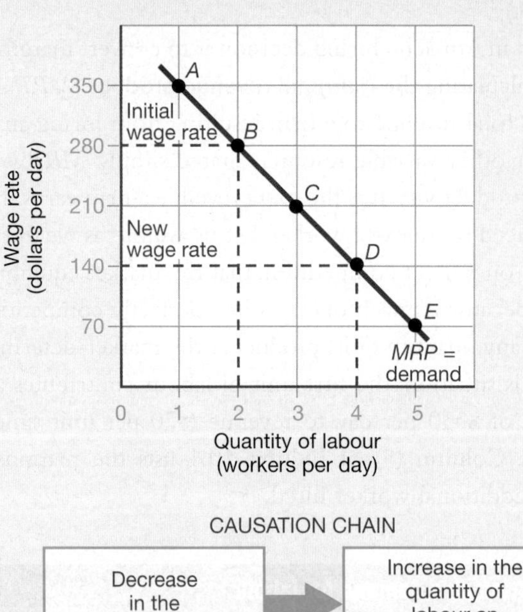

Atmach's downward-sloping demand curve for labour is derived from the marginal revenue product (*MRP*) of labour, which declines as additional workers are hired. The *MRP* is the change in total revenue that results from hiring one more worker. At point *B*, the wage rate is $280 per day and Atmach finds it profitable to pay this wage to two workers because each worker's *MRP* equals or exceeds the wage rate. If the wage rate falls to $140 per day at point *D*, it is not profitable for Atmach to hire the fifth worker because this worker's *MRP* of $70 is below the wage rate of $140 per day.

total revenue (*MRP*). But what happens if the wage rate is \$280 per day? At point *B*, Atmach finds it profitable to hire two workers because the *MRP* of the first worker is greater than the wage rate (extra cost) and the second worker's *MRP* equals the wage rate. If the wage rate is \$140 per day at point *D*, Atmach will find it profitable to hire four workers. In this case, Atmach will not hire the fifth worker. Why? The fifth worker contributes an *MRP* of \$70 to total revenue (point *E*), but this amount is below the wage rate paid of \$140. Consequently, Atmach cannot maximise profits by hiring the fifth worker because it would be adding more to costs than to revenue.

A firm hires additional workers up to the point where the *MRP* equals the wage rate.

Each firm in the market has a demand for labour based on its *MRP* data. Summing these individual demand curves for labour provides the market demand curve for labour in the electronic components industry. Although we do not derive the market demand curve for labour at this stage, it appears shortly when we look at the market demand and supply curves for labour in Exhibit 10.4(a). Another important point must be made here. The demand for labour is called **derived demand**. The derived demand for labour – and other factors of production – depends on the demand for the goods and services the factor produces. If, for example, demand for electronic components were to increase, the price of these components would rise and the *MRP* of firms in the electronic components industry would also rise. The result is a rightward shift in the market demand curve for labour. This means that Atmach would be willing to hire more labour at any given wage rate.

derived demand

Derived demand The derived demand for labour – and other factors of production – depends on the demand for the goods and services the factor produces.

PART 3

The supply of labour

The **supply curve of labour** is consistent with the law of supply discussed in Chapter 3. The supply curve of labour is a curve showing the different quantities of labour that workers are willing to offer employers at different wage rates. Summing the individual supply curves of labour for workers having the requisite skills and experience to work in the electronic components industry provides the *market* supply curve of labour. As shown in Exhibit 10.3, as the wage rate rises, more workers are willing to supply their labour. At point *A*, 20 000 workers offer their services to the industry for \$140 per day. At the higher wage rate of \$280 per day (point *B*), the quantity of labour supplied is 40 000 workers. (To simplify matters we are assuming here that the only effect of higher wages is to call forth extra workers. In reality, higher wages may also encourage existing workers to work longer hours.)

Supply curve of labour A curve showing the different quantities of labour workers are willing to offer employers at different wage rates in a given time period, ceteris paribus.

Why do you think that, ceteris paribus, workers are likely to supply more labour at higher wages? Consider for a moment the alternatives to paid work. For most people these are either leisure time or unpaid work (including

Exhibit 10.3 The market supply curve of labour

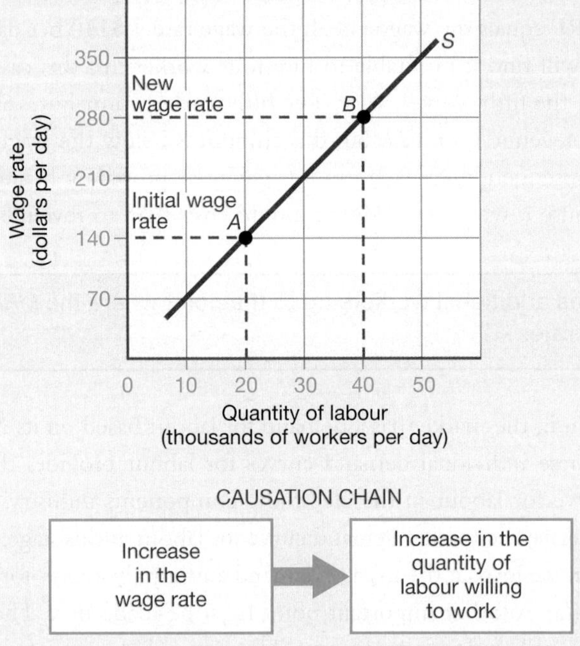

The upward-sloping supply curve of labour for the electronic components industry indicates that a direct relationship exists between the wage rate and the quantity of labour supplied. At point *A*, 20 000 workers are willing to work for $140 per day in this market. If the wage rate rises to $280 per day, 40 000 workers supply their services to the electronic parts labour market.

study), which is often carried out at home. Higher wages attract workers away from these activities. In relation to enjoyable leisure, an increase in the wage tilts the trade-off between paid work and leisure more in favour of paid work. In other words, the opportunity cost of leisure increases as wages increase, leading people to choose extra work rather than leisure. (Because we are dealing with the short run here, we can safely ignore the long-run tendency for workers to demand more leisure as their wages grow over time. This occurs because leisure is seen as a *normal good* for which demand increases as income increases.)

In relation to the alternative of unpaid work, an increase in the wage means that the incentive for workers to engage in paid work increases. Workers who choose more paid work can use their income from this source to pay others to do the unpaid work that they are now unable to undertake. Parents who use the proceeds of paid employment to pay for childcare services provide a good example of this phenomenon. The increased income from wages could also be used to purchase labour-saving capital equipment, such as a dishwasher, which would decrease the burden of home-based unpaid work.

The equilibrium wage rate

Wage rates are determined in perfectly competitive markets by the interaction of labour supply and demand. Exhibit 10.4(a) on p. 276 shows the market supply curve of labour from Exhibit 10.3 intersecting the market demand curve for labour, which has been derived by summing the individual labour demand curves of each of the firms in the electronic components industry. You can see that the equilibrium wage rate for the entire electronic components market is $210 per day. This wage rate clears the market, because the quantity of 30 000 workers demanded equals the quantity of 30 000 workers who are willing to supply their labour services at that wage rate. In a competitive labour market, no single worker can set his or her wage above the equilibrium wage. Such a worker knows he or she will not be hired because there are so many workers who will work for $210 per day. Similarly, there are so many firms hiring labour that a single firm cannot influence the wage by paying workers more or less than the prevailing wage. Hence, a wage rate above $210 per day would create a surplus of workers seeking employment (unemployment) in the electronic components market, and a wage rate below $210 per day would cause a shortage.

Although the supply curve of labour is upward-sloping for the electronic components market, this is not the case shown in Exhibit 10.4(b) for an individual firm such as Atmach. Because a competitive labour market assumes that each firm is too small to influence the wage rate, Atmach is a 'wage taker' and therefore pays the market-determined wage rate of $210 per day regardless of the quantity of labour it employs. For this reason, the labour supply to Atmach is represented by a horizontal line at the equilibrium wage rate. Given this wage of $210 per day Atmach then hires labour up to the equilibrium point *E*, where the wage rate equals the third worker's marginal revenue product.

In the Atmach example we have been using, we have assumed that all workers employed have the same level of skill and suitability for this employment. As you are aware, in reality an enormous range of skills and capabilities are displayed by workers in the economy. Atmach itself may employ electronics engineers alongside tradespeople and unskilled workers. Furthermore, the wages of these different categories of workers are likely to be very different. On the supply side, the supply of engineers is likely to be less than that of tradespeople and much less than that of unskilled workers. On the demand side, the productivity of engineers is likely to be higher than that of tradespeople and even higher than that of unskilled workers.

INFOTRAC®
human capital

An important explanation of these differences is the **human capital** required to perform various occupations. Human capital is the accumulation of education, training, experience and health status that helps a worker to be productive in an occupation. Less human capital is required to be an unskilled worker than to be a tradesperson or an engineer. The interaction of the separate demand and supply curves in each of the different markets

Human capital The accumulation of education, training, experience and health status that help a worker to be productive in an occupation.

Analyse the issue

Why does the clever country have a shortage of teachers?

Applicable concepts: equilibrium wage; supply of labour

The following is an edited version of a story, 'A clever country wouldn't treat teachers like this' by Stephen Long, which appeared in the *Australian Financial Review Weekend* for 20–21 October 2001.

Three weeks ago teachers from schools in the London Borough of Greenwich boarded Qantas flight 32 at Heathrow Airport, bound for Sydney. Their mission: to poach some of Australia's best and brightest classroom teachers.

The poachers find no shortage of locals willing to relocate to Britain. About 15 000 teachers from Australia and New Zealand are employed in the Greater London area – and it's not hard to see why. Even taking into account England's higher cost of living, its real salaries dwarf what a dedicated classroom teacher can command here.

Under reforms introduced by the Blair Government last year, a classroom teacher with advanced skills can earn almost £45 000 a year in England … On current exchange rates that equates to about $140 000 a year. But even if the Australian dollar wasn't in the doldrums, Britain's new pay deal would compare favourably. A top classroom teacher's salary in England is well over double [England's] average weekly full-time earnings.

Contrast the aforementioned salary with the top money a classroom teacher can earn in a government school here: about $55 000, which is less than 25 per cent more than our average weekly full-time adult rate of pay.

The average age of an Australian teacher has risen to 42, and the biggest cohort of teachers is aged between 40 and 50. With large numbers set to retire during this decade, Australia faces a looming, dire shortage of teachers.

Why has this once-revered vocation become so unattractive? Pay is just one issue in the complex and myriad explanations for the decline in teaching. Yet a staggering decline in the relative earnings of teachers must have played a part.

AFR Weekend commissioned an exclusive analysis of how teachers' salaries have fared over the past 15 years against a series of other professions [see table].

Consider earnings of GPs aged 30-plus: on average, they have risen by more than triple the rate of salaries for experienced teachers, according to research by labour-market analyst Rodney Stinson, author of *What Jobs Pay*.

Estimates of increases in weekly full-time earnings

Profession	Percentage change (1986–2000) 20–24 years	30+ years
Civil engineers	73.5	98.1
General medical practitioners	109.5	220.8
Primary school teachers	65.9	74.2
Secondary school teachers	65.0	71.8
University lecturers	104.6	80.2
Lawyers:		
barrister	91.7	94.4
solicitor	165.6	123.7
Accountants	54.5	90.8
Economists	72.2	116.3
All occupations	67.1	93.0

Source: Census; ABS 6310.0; ABS 6306.0

The average earnings for solicitors have increased at almost double the rate of those of teachers and the relative gain is even more pronounced for barristers.

[Research also shows that] fifteen years ago, an experienced teacher earned more than three-quarters of the average economist's salary; now she or he earns less than 60 per cent.

Money has never been the main motive for choosing to become a teacher. Teaching has always been seen as a vocation, a calling. It used to attract the brightest young women who, had they been men, might have become doctors and lawyers. Women like Helen Jackson, Head Language Teacher at the Sydney private girls' school SCEGGS, Darlinghurst, who has been teaching for 30 years. She finished second in her final year at a selective school at Newcastle where all of the girls in the top class had an IQ of 130 or above. 'We were a bright bunch,' she concedes. 'Seven of the top ten became teachers.'

Now [that] the new generation of Helen Jacksons *are* becoming doctors and lawyers, it's harder to attract highly capable people to education. Partly as a consequence, teaching's status has declined, exacerbating the problem.

Using the above information, answer the following questions.

1 Without using specific data, draw a diagram showing the current demand and supply curves for teachers in Australia.

2 On the basis of information contained in the article, do you think teachers' wages today are above, below or at the equilibrium level? Show the current level of wages on your diagram.

3 In the article it is suggested that the attitude to teaching as a profession has changed. Once it was seen as a vocation or calling; now it is seen as no different from other professions. On your diagram show what the effect would be if teaching were to regain its former status as a vocation or calling.

4 If teaching were to regain its former status as a vocation or calling, would the current shortage of teachers be increased or reduced?

for engineers, tradespeople and unskilled workers will lead to a different equilibrium wage in each market. The equilibrium wage is likely to be highest for engineers and lowest for unskilled workers.

In the next section, our model of the labour market is used to explain why union power can, under certain circumstances, result in unemployment.

Exhibit 10.4 A competitive labour market determines the firm's equilibrium wage

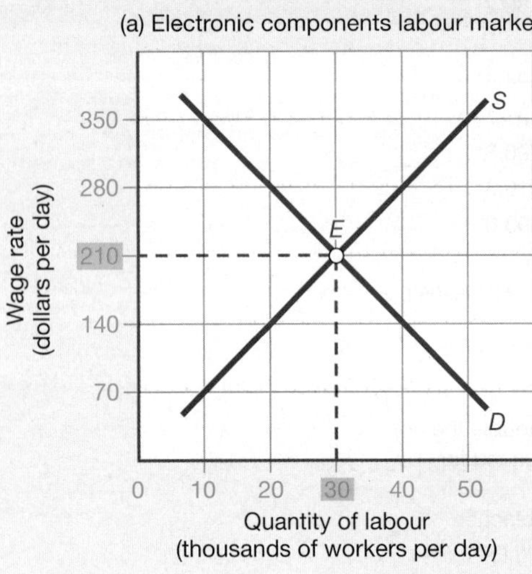

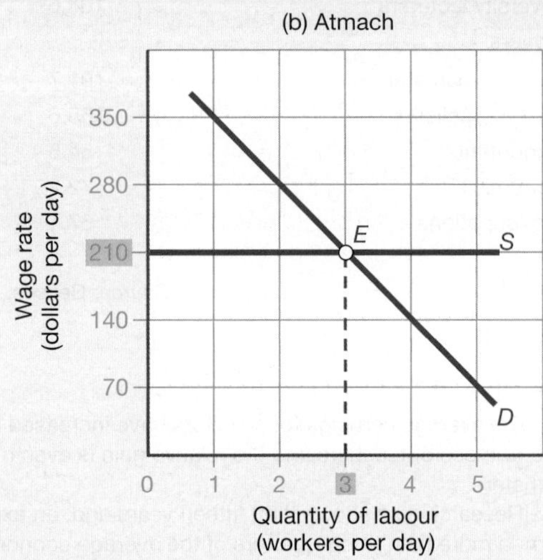

In part (a), the intersection of the supply of and the demand for labour curves determines the equilibrium wage rate of $210 per day in the electronic components industry. Part (b) illustrates that a single firm, such as Atmach, is a 'wage taker'. The firm can hire all the workers it wants at this equilibrium wage, so its supply curve, *S*, is a horizontal line. Atmach chooses to hire three workers, where the firm's demand curve for labour (from Exhibit 10.2) intersects its supply curve of labour.

You make the call

Why do the best-paid rock stars beat the best-paid surgeons in the earnings stakes?

The best-paid surgeons in the world earn many hundreds of thousands of dollars a year; some even earn millions. By contrast, the best-paid rock stars earn millions of dollars a year; some even earn tens of millions. Good surgeons must be dexterous and highly intelligent. They go through many years of post-secondary-school training to learn their craft. On the other hand, many highly successful rock stars left school when they were young and have often undertaken little formal training. Furthermore, many people would argue that the services provided by rock stars are of less intrinsic value to society than those provided by surgeons. Can you explain why the earnings of some rock stars exceed those of surgeons?

Labour unions

An idea of the breadth of occupations and industries that are unionised can be gleaned from the ACTU's list of member unions. Go to **www.directory.actu.asn.au** and select *Unions*.

The perfectly competitive model does not apply to workers who belong to unions. Unions arose because workers recognised that acting together gave them more bargaining power than acting individually in their negotiations with employers. In Australia prior to the 1980s there were hundreds of unions. In order to simplify the labour market and prevent disputes between unions, a process of union amalgamations was then implemented. Some of the biggest unions today are: the Construction, Forestry, Mining and Energy Union; the Textile, Clothing and Footwear Union and the Australian Manufacturing Workers' Union. A primary objective of unions is to improve working conditions and raise the wages of union members. Unions first evolved at the height of the Industrial Revolution. Although employers fought long and hard to prevent the formation of unions, their ultimate success reflected the view, held by many economists, that the bargaining power of a single employee was much less than that of a large employer. These economists included the father of modern liberalism, John Stuart Mill, who argued in the mid-nineteenth century that the imbalance of power would be redressed only if associations of workers (unions) could be legally formed. Traditionally, Australia has had a high level of unionisation of its workforce. However, as Exhibit 10.5 shows, in the past two decades the proportion of full-time employees who are union members has more than halved.

To raise wages, unions employ a wide variety of strategies. Here we look at the most important of these – exertion of power to force employers to pay higher wages. Although the exercise of power by unions (through strike action, for example) may do no more than redress the imbalance of power

Exhibit 10.5 Australian trade union membership, 1982–2003

Year	Union members (% of full-time employees)
1982	54
1986	50
1990	46
1994	39
1998	31
2003	26

As a percentage of workers, trade union membership in Australia has fallen continuously since 1982.

Source: A. Hawke & M. Wooden, 'The changing face of Australian Industrial relations', *Economic Record*, Vol. 74, No. 224, 1998, pp. 74–8, Table 1; Australian Bureau of Statistics, 'Employee earnings, benefits and trade union membership', 6310, August 2000; and Australian Bureau of Statistics, 'Australian labour market statistics', 6105, April 2004

Exhibit 10.6 **The effects of a successful union demand for higher wages**

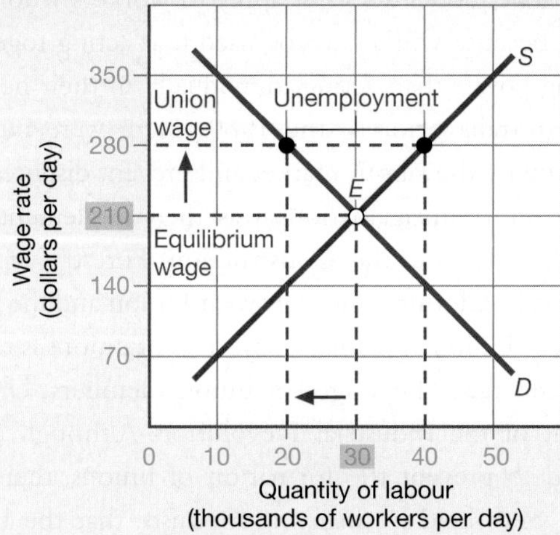

A union exerts its power through enterprise bargaining. Instead of the competitive wage rate of $210 at point *E*, firms in the industry reluctantly agree to a wage of $280 per day. The effect is to artificially create a labour surplus (unemployment) of 20 000 workers at the negotiated wage.

between employer and employee, there are also cases where unionisation gives employees the upper hand. If the wage that employers are forced to pay as a result of the exercise of union power is higher than the competitive equilibrium wage in this market, then unemployment will be created.

This outcome is shown in Exhibit 10.6. Again, we return to the situation depicted for the electronic components market in Exhibit 10.4(a). Recall that this is a perfectly competitive labour market where neither employers nor employees have market power and where labour is not unionised. At the equilibrium wage rate of $210 per day (point *E*) there is no surplus or shortage of workers. Then the industry is unionised and an enterprise bargaining agreement takes effect in which firms, perhaps fearful of strike action, reluctantly agree to pay the union wage rate of $280 per day. (For simplicity we are assuming that enterprise bargains in each firm in the industry have the same outcome.) At the higher wage rate, employment offered falls from 30 000 to 20 000 workers. However, the number of workers who wish to work for $280 per day is 40 000 workers. Consequently, there is a surplus of 20 000 unemployed workers in this industry. Because firms now hire fewer workers and pay higher wages, how might firms react? Employers might react by substituting capital for labour or by transferring operations overseas where labour costs are lower than in Australia. Some firms will be forced to close down.

CONCLUSION **If union bargaining power results in wages that are above the equilibrium level, unemployment will result.**

The case of unions having more bargaining power than their employees is the most commonly cited example of the effect of market power in the labour market. In some labour markets, however, employers have the upper hand. In this case the outcome is one in which labour is paid wages below the competitive equilibrium level.

The next section looks at why reduction of personal income taxes is an important element in taxation reform.

Income tax reform

In our discussion of the role of taxation reform as part of microeconomic reform it was pointed out that personal income taxes are seen as a disincentive to work. A reduction in income taxes can thus be expected to increase employment and, with it, the output of the nation.

To understand how this happens, we first imagine an economy in which all markets are perfectly competitive and in which there are initially no taxes of any kind. Exhibit 10.7 shows the labour market for the electronic components industry in such an economy. Equilibrium in this market is the same as is represented in Exhibit 10.4(a). At point E_1 there is no surplus or shortage of labour at the equilibrium wage of $210 per day. Now imagine that the government introduces a personal income tax of $70 per day. Personal income taxes are, as we have seen, normally expressed as a percentage of income. In the example being used here, it is assumed that income taxes are a

Exhibit 10.7 Personal income taxes reduce employment and output

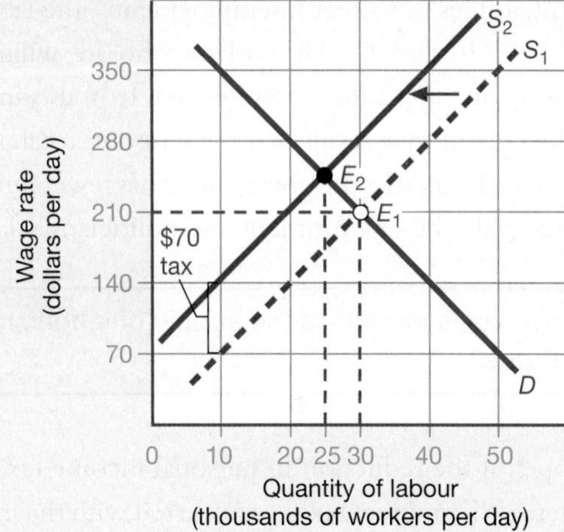

Introduction of a personal income tax of $70 per day shifts the supply curve of labour leftward from S_1 to S_2. As a result, the equilibrium pre-tax wage rises and the equilibrium level of employment falls from 30 000 to 25 000. Taxation reform in the form of personal income tax cuts would shift the supply curve from S_2 towards S_1, bringing about a rise in employment and output.

flat dollar amount per day regardless of income. This simplifying assumption allows us to undertake an analysis of the imposition of an income tax that is easier to explain but which still shows the overall effect that will occur.

Imposition of an income tax of $70 per day has the effect of reducing the supply of labour. Now that workers have a smaller take-home pay, the trade-off between work and leisure (or unpaid work) is tilted more in favour of leisure (or unpaid work). In Exhibit 10.7 the supply curve has shifted from S_1 to S_2. This represents an upward shift of $70, which has occurred because workers will be willing to supply any given amount of labour only if the pre-tax wage they receive is $70 higher. For example, after the imposition of the tax the 30 000 workers who would have supplied their labour at a wage of $210 will now supply their labour only if the wage rises to $280.

The intersection of the new supply curve with the existing demand curve for labour gives a new equilibrium at point E_2. The equilibrium pre-tax wage has increased and the quantity of labour employed has decreased from 30 000 workers to 25 000 workers. If such an income tax is imposed on all workers in the economy, the outcome will be a fall in employment and total output in the economy.

To complete our explanation of the effects of income tax reform, we now consider what would happen if the government, in its microeconomic reform agenda, were to implement a policy of reducing the $70 per day tax. The effect in the electronic components industry would be to shift the labour supply curve S_2 to the right towards S_1, bringing about a rise in employment and output. For the economy as a whole, the effect of a reduction in personal income taxes would be to raise national output and employment. It is important to understand that, although this tax reduction increases employment, it does not affect unemployment – the labour market is in equilibrium at both E_1 and E_2. All workers who are willing to work at the equilibrium wage in each case are employed. It is also important to keep in mind that the tax cut may result in a reduction in total government taxation revenue, with the result that the government has fewer funds available to spend on roads, hospitals, the environment and politicians' salaries.

CONCLUSION **A reduction in income taxes increases the supply of labour, raising employment and output.**

What would happen if the reduction in personal income tax were more or less offset by an increase in indirect taxes, as occurred with the introduction of the GST? The effect of the reduction in income taxes would be exactly as described in the above paragraph. However, the raising of indirect taxes through the imposition of a broad-based consumption tax would reduce demand for the typical firm's product, leading to a fall in the price it receives. This would have the effect of reducing each firm's demand for labour curve, because it would adversely affect its marginal revenue product curve. The net effect of the increase in employment brought about by the decrease in personal income taxes, combined with the decrease in employment brought about by the rise in indirect taxes, cannot be known with certainty. However, most commentators argued that the introduction of the GST with offsetting income tax cuts would raise employment and output.

Labour market reform and the minimum wage

When minimum wage laws were discussed in Chapter 4, it was shown that a minimum wage that is set at a level above the equilibrium wage leads to a surplus of labour because the quantity of labour supplied exceeds the quantity demanded. The demand and supply curves drawn in Exhibit 4.5 in Chapter 4 are based on precisely the same principles as have been used to derive the curves that are drawn above in the labour market model described by Exhibit 10.4(a).

As you saw in the section above dealing with labour market reform, the reform process has effectively resulted in the irrelevance of minimum wages for skilled workers. Despite vigorous attempts by conservative governments to reduce minimum wages for unskilled workers to well below their current 'safety net' level, the goal of deregulation of wages for unskilled workers has, at the time of writing, yet to be achieved. Nonetheless, the re-election of the Howard government in 2004 with a majority in both houses means that it is likely that significant reform of minimum wage legislation will occur.

The AIRC has special pages for students that can be accessed at www.airc.gov.au.

The philosophy behind the safety net minimum wage is that this wage should provide an adequate standard of living for its recipients. Although the issue of worker productivity is taken into account by the AIRC when it determines the minimum wage, the overriding consideration is maintenance of the standard of living rather than matching wages with labour productivity. This has resulted in a situation where the minimum wage for unskilled workers is a floor price in excess of the equilibrium wage. Evidence of this can be found in the much higher rate of unemployment experienced by unskilled as opposed to skilled workers.

minimum wage

Not only does the minimum wage affect the market for unskilled workers but, because of the interdependency between different labour markets, it may also affect the deregulated market for skilled workers.

Exhibit 10.8(a) on page 284 shows the effect of minimum wages using the labour supply and demand curves that are relevant for the market for unskilled workers. The wage rate Wm represents the minimum, or safety net, wage, which is in excess of the equilibrium wage We_{us} and which is responsible for unemployment, represented by the distance $Qs_1 - Qd$.

Exhibit 10.8(b) shows the labour market for skilled workers. On the assumption that labour market reform in the form of enterprise bargaining has resulted in the achievement of an equilibrium outcome in this market, the

International focus

Why do governments around the world legislate for minimum wages?

Applicable concept: minimum wage

An idea of the broad range of employment issues that the ILO deals with can be easily seen by going to its home page at **www.ilo.org**. Click on an issue that you think might be better understood by a person with a grounding in economics.

The International Labour Organization (ILO) is the United Nations (UN) specialised agency responsible for promotion of social justice and internationally recognised human and labour rights. It was created in 1919 following World War I. The ILO formulates international labour standards for basic labour rights: freedom of association, the right to organise, collective [enterprise] bargaining, abolition of forced labour, equality of opportunity and treatment, and other standards relating to issues surrounding work. In 1969 the ILO was awarded the Nobel Peace Prize.

In spite of the opposition of many economists, a major aim of the ILO has been to promote the adoption of minimum wages in countries around the world. Its current policy is embodied in the Minimum Wage Fixing Recommendation, 1970. The Recommendation states that the purpose of minimum wages is to give wage earners necessary social protection as regards minimum permissible levels of wages, and to ensure the satisfaction of the needs of all workers and their families.

According to the ILO's Recommendation, some of the criteria that should be used to determine the level of minimum wages are: the needs of workers and their families, the general level of wages in the country, the cost of living, social security benefits, the relative living standards of other social groups, and economic factors including levels of productivity and the desirability of maintaining a high level of employment.

As you can see, labour productivity which, with a given level of labour supply, has been explained in this chapter as the sole determinant of the equilibrium wage in competitive markets, is only one of a number of criteria that the ILO says should be used to determine the minimum wage. A number of the other criteria are clearly aimed at maintenance of an adequate standard of living.

In their article 'Statistical aspects of minimum wage determination' published by the ILO, Robert Pember and Marie-Thérèse Dupré point out that:

> [m]inimum wages along with other measures of economic and social policy aim at reducing poverty and meeting basic needs. The concept of minimum wage is related to work, as distinct from that of 'minimum income' which is intended to guarantee minimum living conditions regardless of whether a person has an employment from which he/she gets a wage.[1]

Minimum wages are applied in most countries in spite of the objections of economists, employers and many politicians. A small sample of countries in which a minimum wage applies includes Australia, the United States, Canada, France, the Netherlands, Denmark, Germany and Japan.

---

1 Robert J. Pember & Marie-Thérèse Dupré, 'Statistical aspects of minimum wage determination', International Labour Organization, *Bulletin of Labour Statistics – Selection of Articles*, www.ilo.org/public/english/bureau/stat/publ/bulletin/artminw.htm, last updated 9 April 1999. Originally published in the *Bulletin of Labour Statistics* 1997–93.

Analyse the issue

If economists (and others) are so sure that minimum wages have the potential to cause unemployment, why is it that they are promoted by the ILO and adopted by most countries? Explain why you agree or disagree with the economists' position. Are there ethical considerations that have led to your conclusion?

equilibrium wage We_{sk} will prevail and there will be no unemployment. (In Chapter 13 you will learn that, for various reasons, a national unemployment rate of zero cannot be achieved. In order to make the analysis undertaken here simpler, we assume that it can. This assumption does not alter the thrust of the argument.)

You can see from the two parts of Exhibit 10.8 that the equilibrium wage for skilled workers, We_{sk}, is higher than the minimum wage for unskilled workers, Wm, and that it is even higher than the equilibrium wage for unskilled workers, We_{us}. Labour market reform has increased efficiency in the market for skilled labour, but it has not affected the market for unskilled labour. What is the likely effect of this difference between the two markets?

A comprehensive answer to this question requires a knowledge of many relevant factors. For example, can the unemployed unskilled workers find employment as self-employed contractors at lower rates of remuneration than the minimum wage? There are many unskilled persons undertaking cleaning, gardening and letterbox deliveries under these conditions. Are some of the unemployed unskilled workers happy to receive unemployment benefits rather than endeavour to hold down a job at the minimum wage? Here we ignore these possibilities to look at what might happen if unskilled workers who are unemployed as a result of the minimum wage attempt to

Exhibit 10.8 **Partial labour market deregulation**

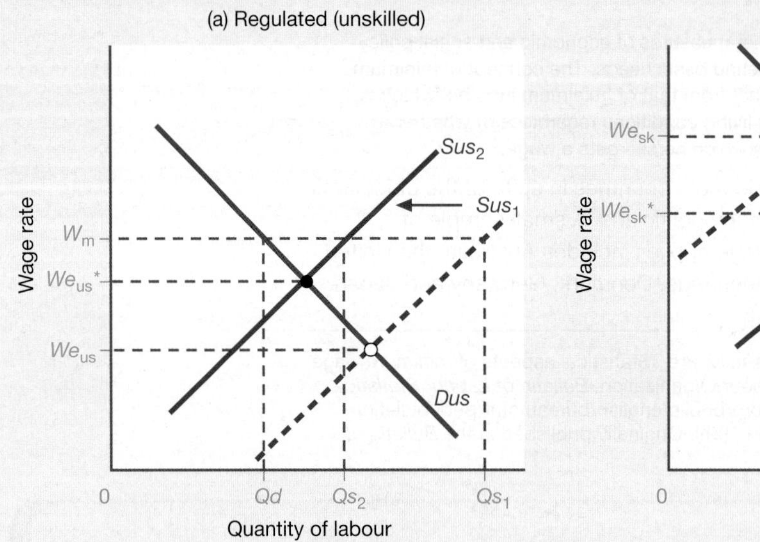

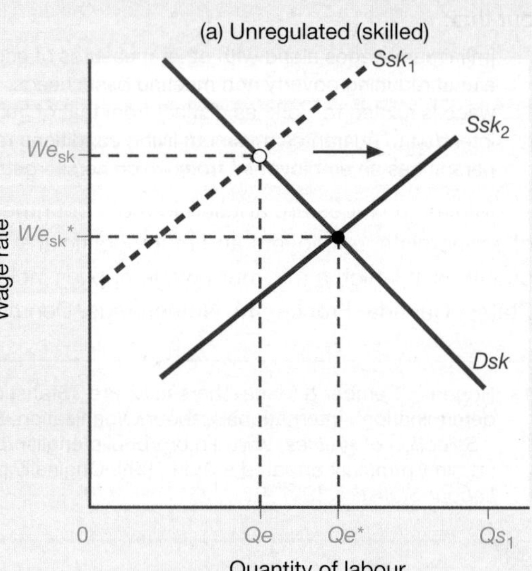

Workers who suffer, or fear, unemployment in the regulated market for unskilled labour may exit this market to undertake training in order to raise their level of skill. They may then enter the unregulated market for skilled labour. The exit from the regulated market shown in part (a) results in a shift to the left of the supply curve from Sus_1 to Sus_2. Unemployment caused by the minimum wage is reduced. The entry of newly skilled workers into the unregulated market shown in part (b) causes a rightward shift in the supply curve from Ssk_1 to Ssk_2. Employment in this market increases.

raise their level of skill so that they can find employment in the market for skilled labour.

The effect on the market for unskilled labour is for some of the unemployed workers to no longer offer their services in this market. This is represented by a leftward shift in the supply curve from Sus_1 to Sus_2 in Exhibit 10.8(a). In this market the equilibrium wage rises to We_{us}^*, a wage that is now closer to, but still below, the minimum wage Wm. Unemployment caused by the minimum wage is now reduced to $Qs_2 - Qd$.

In the market for skilled labour there will be an increase in supply resulting from the entry of newly skilled workers who have exited the unskilled labour market and undertaken education and training. This change is shown in Exhibit 10.8(b) by a shift to the right in the supply curve from Ssk_1 to Ssk_2. The effect of this increase in supply of skilled workers is to

Do workers pocket all of a cut in income tax?

When a government foreshadows a decrease in income taxes, most employees accept the government argument that the proposed dollar value of the income tax cut will increase their take-home pay by the same amount. Examine the validity of this argument, using the model of a competitive labour market developed in this chapter. Are there conditions under which the argument is valid, and conditions under which it is not?

reduce the equilibrium wage in this unregulated market from We_{sk} to We_{sk}^*. Total employment in this market increases from Qe to Qe^*.

You can see that the effect of the partial deregulation of the labour market may be to unwittingly bring about a desirable increase in the level of skill of Australian workers. Although this outcome may not appear obvious to the casual observer, there is no doubt that the Australian government is conscious of the possibility of reducing unemployment among the unskilled by implementing policies designed to raise their skill levels. Thus the government has policies designed to retrain and skill workers who are unemployed, and it encourages acquisition of skills by providing allowances to students from low-income families to enable them to continue their education beyond year ten.

The ethics of minimum wages

The question of whether ethical considerations lead us to the appropriate wage regulation regime is a difficult one. As we have seen, imposition of minimum wages based on ethical motives may have the perverse result of raising unemployment. Fulfilment of the objective of paying higher wages to unskilled workers may mean that their ability to find jobs and keep them is compromised. On the other hand, if provision of minimum wages encourages unskilled workers to seek to raise their level of skill and, subsequently, their pay, the ethical considerations that prompted the implementation of minimum wages may indeed lead to a desirable outcome. There is more to the issue of minimum wages than meets the eye.

Key concepts

Microeconomic reform
Direct taxes
Indirect taxes
Enterprise bargaining
Marginal revenue product (*MRP*)
Demand curve for labour
Derived demand
Supply curve of labour
Human capital

Summary

- **Microeconomic reform** encompasses government policies that deregulate or re-regulate markets for goods, services or factors of production so as to increase competition and raise efficiency.

- **Direct taxes** are taxes levied on income. The primary sources of income tax are individuals and companies. In Australia, direct taxes are collected only by the Commonwealth government.

- **Indirect taxes** are levied on the sale of goods and services. The two major types of indirect tax levied in Australia are excise taxes and the goods and services tax (GST).

- The **demand curve for labour** is the curve showing the quantities of labour a firm is willing to hire at different prices of labour. The marginal revenue product (*MRP*) of labour curve is the firm's demand curve for labour. Summing individual demand for labour curves gives the market demand curve for labour.

Demand for labour

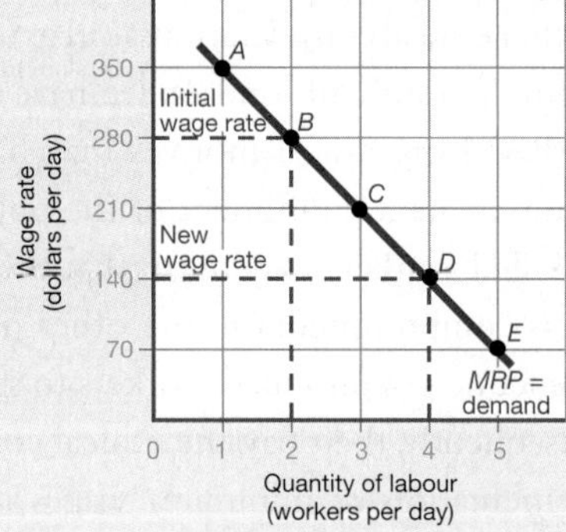

- **Enterprise bargaining** typically involves workers in each workplace undertaking direct bargaining as a group with their employer to determine terms and conditions of employment for a period of up to five years.

- **Marginal revenue product** (*MRP*) is determined by a worker's contribution to a firm's total revenue. Algebraically, the *MRP* equals the price of the product times the worker's marginal product (*MP*).

- **Derived demand** describes the situation in which changes in demand for a good or service cause changes in demand for labour and for other resources used to produce the good or service.
- The **supply curve of labour** is the curve showing the quantities of workers willing to work at different prices of labour. The market supply curve of labour is derived by adding the individual supply curves of labour.

Supply curve of labour

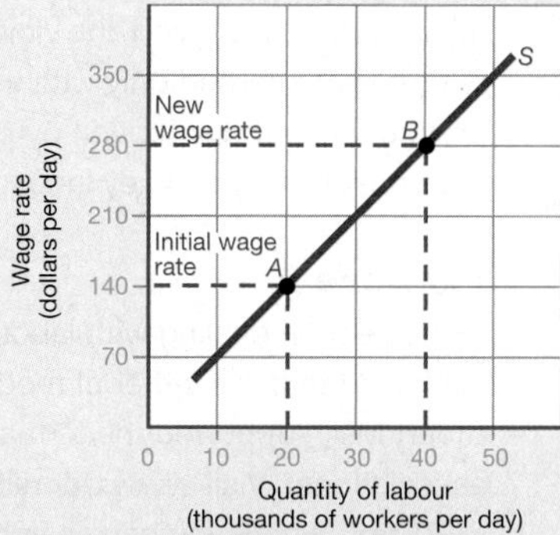

- **Human capital** is the accumulation of education, training, experience and health status that help a worker to be more productive in an occupation. One explanation for earnings differences is differences in human capital.

Study questions and problems

1 Consider this statement: 'Workers demand jobs, and employers supply jobs'. Do you agree or disagree? Explain.

2 The Zippy Paper Company has no control over either the price of paper it sells or the wage it pays its workers. The following table shows the relationship between the number of workers Zippy hires and total output.

Labour input (workers per day)	Total output (boxes of paper per day)
0	0
1	15
2	27
3	36
4	43
5	48
6	51

Answer the following questions, assuming that the selling price is $10 per box.

a What is the marginal revenue product (*MRP*) of each worker?

b How many workers will Zippy hire if the wage rate is $100 per day?

c How many workers will Zippy hire if the wage rate is $75 per day?

d Assume the wage rate is $75 per day and the price of a box of paper is $20. How many workers will Zippy hire?

3 Assume the Grand Slurp Ice Cream Stall sells $500 worth of ice creams each day, with one employee operating the store. The owner decides to hire a second worker, and the two workers together sell $750 worth of ice creams. What is the second worker's marginal revenue product (*MRP*)? If the price per ice cream sold is $5, what is the second worker's marginal product (MP)?

4 What is the relationship between the marginal revenue product (*MRP*) and the demand curve for labour?

5 The market supply curve of labour is upward-sloping, but the supply curve of labour for a single firm is horizontal. Explain why.

6 Assume the labour market for timber workers is perfectly competitive. How would each of the following events influence the wage rate paid to those workers?
   a Consumers boycott products made with wood.
   b Timber workers reassess the risks of injury in the industry, finding that it is less risky than they had imagined.
   c Timber workers form a union that requires longer apprenticeships, charges high fees and uses other devices designed to reduce union membership.

7 How does a human capital investment in education increase your lifetime earnings?

8 Suppose state governments pass laws requiring nurses to have a master's degree in order to retain their registration as nurses. What effect would this legislation have on the labour market for nurses?

9 Use the data in Question 2 and assume that there is a perfectly competitive labour market in equilibrium, with an equilibrium wage rate of $90 per day. Now explain the impact of a union-negotiated enterprise bargaining agreement that changes the wage rate to $100 per day.

10 Some economists argue that the Australian Medical Association (AMA) creates an effect on the labour market for doctors similar to that of a labour union. Do you agree?

11 If the Commonwealth government were to successfully deregulate the market for unskilled workers, would this have an effect on the supply of skilled workers?

12 Why is it that taxation reform usually involves greater personal income tax relief for high-income earners than low-income earners? Is the same policy followed with reform of company taxes?

Online exercises

Exercise 1

The Productivity Commission is the Australian government's principal review and advisory body on microeconomic policy and regulation. Go to the November 1999 Commission Research Paper, 'Microeconomic Reforms and Australian Productivity: Exploring the Links', at **www.pc.gov.au/research/commres/meraap/index.html**. Click on Volume 1: Report, then **Chapter 2 'Microeconomic reform, productivity and living standards'**. Read the contents of Box 2.4 on page 15. Describe the ultimate aim of microeconomic reform. Explain why microeconomic reform may not mean that government intervention in the economy must be minimised. Explain why the view that microeconomic reform is concerned only with the processes of production and distribution by private and public enterprises in certain key industries is incorrect.

Exercise 2

In the section dealing with labour unions it was explained that the father of modern liberalism, John Stuart Mill, supported the formation of unions (or associations). Visit **www.econlib.org/library/Mill/mlP.html**, where you can search the text of his *Principles of Political Economy*, published in 1848. Search for 'higgle' to find the paragraph in which Mill makes his point. Take particular note of Mill's discussion of the unequal bargaining power between individual workers and their employers. Note also that Mill describes strikes as a 'valuable part of the machinery of society'. Do you think Mill's arguments are relevant today?

Exercise 3

The full text of the ILO article 'Statistical aspects of minimum wage determination' by Robert Pember and Marie-Therésè Dupré can be found on the ILO website at **www.ilo.org/public/english/bureau/stat/publ/bulletin/artminw.htm**. Go to the heading 'Statistics needed for Criterion 2: General level of wages in the country'. Note the authors' observation that periodic adjustment of the minimum wage is often undertaken to maintain a particular ratio of the minimum wage to the average wage. Using the model of the labour market developed in this chapter, can you explain how this practice might result in increasing unemployment of workers on the minimum wage?

Exercise 4

Find the glossary of terms on the ACTU website by going to **www.worksite.actu.asn.au/** and selecting **GLOSSARY**. Look up Collective Bargaining, Enterprise Bargaining and Enterprise Agreement. What is the relationship between these concepts?

Look up the Harvester Case. Was labour productivity or the standard of living of workers' families the main consideration in determining Australia's first national minimum wage?

Answers to 'You make the call'

Why do the best-paid rock stars beat the best-paid surgeons in the earnings stakes?

Like the world's best-paid rock stars, most of the world's best-paid surgeons are self-employed. However, this does not prevent us from using our understanding of labour markets to explain why their earnings differ. In the market for rock stars and in the market for surgeons there will be a supply curve showing the quantity of labour offered in each market at each possible level of earnings. Ceteris paribus, its position will be determined by the trade-off between work and leisure. (At the level of earnings of these people we can safely assume that they do not see unpaid work as an alternative to paid work.) In each market there will also be a demand for labour curve based on marginal revenue product. It shows the additional revenue accruing to the rock star or the surgeon when they, in effect, employ themselves for an additional period of time in the recording studio or the operating theatre. As is shown in Exhibit 10.9, all that is required for the earnings of rock stars (E_r) to exceed those of surgeons (E_S) is for the equilibrium point in the market for rock stars to be at a higher level of earnings than for surgeons. Perhaps you can think of some reasons why the demand and supply curves in each market give this outcome? As Adam Smith noted over 200 years ago, diamonds, which have far less intrinsic value to society than water or food, are, as a result of the interaction of demand and supply, far more valuable in the marketplace. If you said that the forces of supply and demand in the labour markets for the best-paid rock stars and the best-paid surgeons determine the differences in their earnings, YOU ARE CORRECT.

Exhibit 10.9

(a) Surgeons

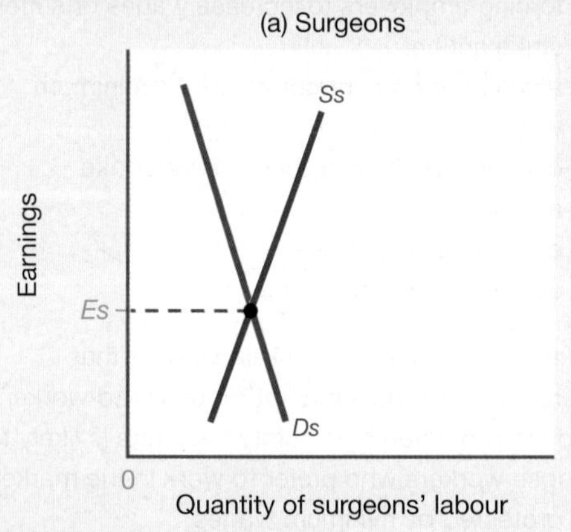

(b) Rock stars

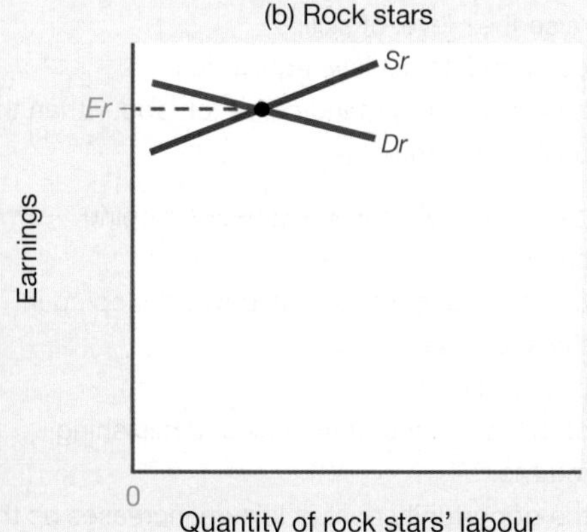

Do workers pocket all of a cut in income tax?

Exhibit 10.10 (on p. 290), which uses the same demand and supply curves as Exhibit 10.7, shows the effect of the imposition of a \$70 income tax on workers. The effect is to shift the market equilibrium from E_1 to E_2, increasing the equilibrium wage rate for workers from \$210 to \$245. This wage of \$245 is now a pre-tax wage from which the government's \$70 income tax must be deducted. When it is deducted, workers receive an after-tax wage of \$175 (\$245 – \$70). The imposition of a \$70 tax has thus resulted in a decrease in the wage that workers pocket from the original \$210 to \$175 – a fall of only \$35. Similarly, if the government were to abolish the \$70 tax, the supply curve would shift from S_2 to S_1 and the wage pocketed by workers would increase from \$175 to the original equilibrium wage of \$210, a rise of only \$35. The case in which a reduction in income tax would result in an equal increase in after-tax wages of workers occurs in the unlikely event of the demand for labour curve being perfectly inelastic (vertical). These outcomes parallel those that we discussed when we looked at the incidence of a tax on sellers of goods and services in Chapter 5. If you said that, contrary to the assertions of governments, workers pocket only part of a cut in income taxes unless labour demand is perfectly inelastic, YOU ARE CORRECT.

Exhibit 10.10

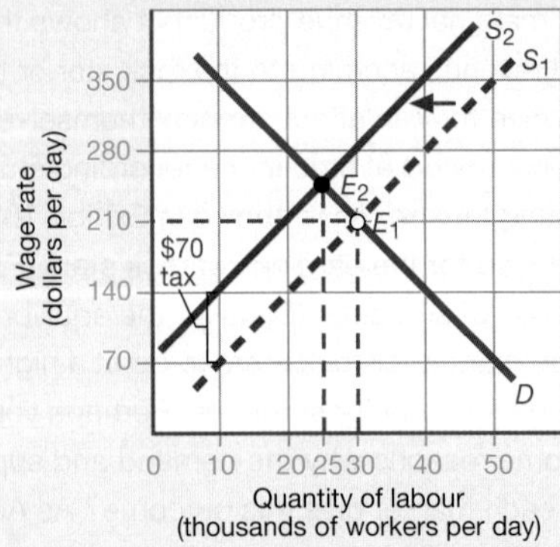

Multiple-choice questions

1 Marginal revenue product measures the increase in
- a output resulting from one more unit of labour.
- b total revenue resulting from one more unit of output.
- c revenue per unit from one more unit of output.
- d total revenue resulting from one more unit of labour.

2 Droll Corporation sells dolls for $10 each in a market that is perfectly competitive. Increasing the number of workers from 100 to 101 would cause output to rise from 500 to 510 dolls per day. Droll should hire the 101st worker only when the wage is
- a $100 or less per day.
- b more than $100 per day.
- c $5.10 or less per day.
- d none of the above.

3 Derived demand for labour depends on the
- a cost of factors of production used in the product.
- b market supply curve of labour.
- c consumer demand for the final goods produced by labour.
- d firm's total revenue less economic profit.

4 If market demand for a product falls, the demand curve for labour used to produce the product will
- a shift leftward.
- b shift rightward.
- c remain unchanged.
- d do none of the above.

5 The owner of a restaurant will hire additional waiters if
- a supply equals demand.
- b marginal product is at the maximum.
- c the additional output of these employees adds more to total revenue than to costs.
- d waiters do not belong to a union.

6 Suppose a firm hires 100 workers at $8 per hour in a perfectly competitive labour market. If the marginal revenue product of the 101st worker is also $8, the firm should
- a hire the additional worker.
- b not hire the additional worker.
- c hire more than one additional worker.
- d do none of the above.

7 In a perfectly competitive market, the demand curve for labour
- a slopes upward.
- b slopes downward because of diminishing marginal productivity.
- c is perfectly elastic at the equilibrium wage rate.
- d is described by all of the above.

8 A union can influence the equilibrium wage rate by
- a forcing employers to increase wages or suffer strike action.
- b agitating for the introduction of a minimum wage.
- c encouraging its members to undertake additional training.
- d doing all of the above.
- e doing none of the above.

9 A deregulated market for skilled labour that operates alongside a market for unskilled workers who are protected by a safety net wage is likely to
- a lose workers who prefer to work in the market protected by minimum wages.
- b attract unskilled workers who are willing to raise their level of skill.
- c be unable to achieve equilibrium.
- d have a lower demand curve for labour than the unskilled market.

10 The labour supply curve is upward-sloping because
- a the firm's supply curve is upward-sloping in the short run.
- b it is elastic.
- c of the relevance of the law of diminishing returns.
- d the opportunity cost of leisure increases as the wage increases.

11 A minimum wage causes unemployment only if
- **a** it is below the equilibrium wage.
- **b** it is equal to the equilibrium wage.
- **c** it applies to the demand for labour and not the supply.
- **d** it is above the equilibrium wage.

12 An important reason for the substitution of income tax revenue with revenue from a broad-based consumption tax is that it
- **a** gives a more equitable outcome.
- **b** costs less to collect consumption taxes than the cost of collecting income taxes.
- **c** reduces the disincentive to work.
- **d** does all of the above.

13 Which of the following is not an element of microeconomic reform in Australia?
- **a** taxation reform.
- **b** financial market reform.
- **c** strengthening of competition policy.
- **d** electoral reform.

14 Since 1990, employee membership of unions in Australia has
- **a** been replaced by enterprise bargaining.
- **b** stayed about the same.
- **c** increased.
- **d** declined.

11 Measuring the size of the economy

Measuring the performance of the economy is an important part of life. In December 2000, the Australian Treasurer proclaimed that the economy's performance in the 1990s had been the best since 1959 and yet the Leader of the Opposition argued that the economy could perform better, particularly in respect of the level of unemployment. These days governments are – rightly or wrongly – considered by the people to have an important influence on macroeconomic outcomes such as the level of unemployment, inflation, interest rates, the value of the exchange rate and so on. The outcomes of elections are often very significantly determined by the electorate's judgement of the current and likely future state of the economy and the relative macroeconomic management abilities of those running for office. Indeed, in the run-up to the 2004 federal election a significant electoral issue was the relative macroeconomic management credentials of the two major parties.

How then should we assess the macroeconomic performance of the economy? In addressing this kind of issue, which statistics would you seek to provide relevant information on how well the economy is doing? The answer requires an understanding of some of the nuts and bolts of *national income accounting*. National income accounting is the system used to measure the aggregate income and expenditures for a nation. Despite certain limitations, the national income accounting system provides a valuable indicator of an economy's performance. For example, as an exercise you can visit the Internet and check the website for the Australian Bureau of Statistics to compare the size or growth of the Australian economy between 2003 and 2004, or some other years.

Prior to the Great Depression in 1929–33, there were no national accounting procedures for estimating the data required to assess an economy's performance. In order to provide accounting methodologies for macroeconomic data, the late economist Simon Kuznets published a small report in 1934 titled *National Income, 1929–32*. For his pioneering work Kuznets, 'the father of GDP', earned the Nobel Prize in Economics

in 1971. Also deserving of mention in terms of developing the system of national accounts is the late Colin Clark.

Today, most countries use common national accounting methods, thanks in large part to Kuznets and Clark. National income accounting serves the nation in a way similar to the manner in which accounting serves a business or household. In each case, the use of proper accounting methodology is vital in order to identify economic problems and formulate plans for achieving goals.

In this chapter, you will examine these economics questions:

- Why doesn't economic growth include increases in spending for social welfare payments and unemployment programs?
- If one news report maintains that the economy grew, while another suggests that for the very same year the economy declined, can both reports be correct?
- How is the calculation of national output affected by environmental damage and, more generally, what are the limitations in using it as a measure of economic welfare?

Gross domestic product

Gross domestic product (GDP) The market value of all final goods and services produced within a nation's geographic borders during a period of time, usually a quarter or a year.

Gross national product (GNP) The income accruing to a country's residents from the production of all final goods and services during a period of time, no matter where in the world the goods and services were produced.

The most widely reported measure throughout the world of a nation's economic performance is **gross domestic product**. Gross domestic product (GDP) is the market value of all final goods and services produced within a nation's geographic borders during a period of time, usually a quarter or a year. GDP therefore excludes production abroad by the nation's businesses. An alternative but less commonly used measure is that of **gross national product**. Gross national product (GNP) is the income accruing to a country's residents from the production of all final goods and services during a period of time, no matter where the goods and services are produced in the world. For example, Australian GNP includes Billabong's profits on its foreign operations, but GDP does not. On the other hand, GNP excludes Toyota's profits from its Australian car manufacturing operations, while GDP includes it.

gross domestic product

The main reason for the emphasis on GDP is that it is the measure more relevant to the level of domestic economic activity and therefore to the generation of domestic jobs. A country's GDP and GNP may differ only slightly or very significantly, depending on the importance of international trade to the country. In the case of countries such as many countries in East Asia, which are very open to trade, GNP can be quite different from GDP. For instance, in 2003 Hong Kong's GDP was US$158.6 billion and its GNP was US$173.3 billion, a difference of over 9 per cent.

Why is GDP important? One advantage of GDP is that it avoids the 'apples and oranges' measurement problem. If an economy produces nothing but ten apples one year and nothing but ten oranges the next, can we say that the quantity and value of output has changed in any way? To answer this question, we must attach price tags so that we can evaluate the relative value of apples and oranges to society. This is the reason GDP uses dollars to measure value, rather than a list of the number of cars, computers, aluminium, heart transplants, legal cases, haircuts, toothbrushes, tanks and so on produced. Instead, the market-determined dollar value establishes the monetary importance of production. In GDP calculations, 'money talks'. That is, GDP relies on prices (and therefore markets) to establish the relative value of goods and services to the community.

The Australian Bureau of Statistics (ABS) **www.abs.gov.au**, an agency of the federal government, is the nation's economic accountant, preparing data on all components of GDP. The ABS also provides a rich source of international and regional data, among other information.

GDP also requires that we give the following two points special attention.

Point 1: GDP counts only new domestic production

National income accountants calculating GDP carefully exclude transactions in two major areas: second-hand transactions and non-productive financial transactions.

Second-hand transactions

GDP does not include the sale of a used car or the sale of a house constructed some years ago. Such transactions are merely exchanges of ownership of previously produced goods and are not *current* production of new goods that add to the existing stock of cars and homes. However, the sales commission paid to the salesperson on account of the sale of a used car or a home produced in an earlier period counts in current GDP, because the salesperson performed a service during the current period of time.

Non-productive financial transactions

GDP does not include purely financial transactions (either private or public), such as giving private gifts, trading in financial securities (such as stocks and bonds) – although, again, any brokerage charged would be included, as this represents a current period service provision – and making **transfer payments.** A transfer payment is a government payment to individuals not in exchange for goods or services currently produced. Social welfare payments, veterans' benefits, other types of pensions and unemployment benefits are transfer payments. These transactions are not included in GDP because they do not represent production of any new or *current* output. Similarly, stock market transactions represent only the exchange of certificates of ownership (stocks) or indebtedness (bonds) and not actual new production.

Transfer payment
A government payment to individuals not in exchange for goods or services currently produced.

Point 2: GDP counts only final goods

The popular press usually defines GDP as simply 'the value of all goods and services produced'. This is technically incorrect, because GDP counts only final goods and services. Including all goods and services produced would inflate GDP by *double counting* (that is, many items would be counted more than once). **Final products** are finished goods and services produced for the ultimate user. In order to count only final goods and services and avoid overstating GDP, national income accountants must take care not to include **intermediate products**. Intermediate products are goods and services used as inputs into the production of final goods and services. Stated differently, intermediate products are not produced for consumption by the ultimate user.

Final products Finished goods and services produced for the ultimate user.

Intermediate products
Goods and services used as inputs for the production of final products.

Suppose a wholesale distributor sells glass to a house builder. This transaction is not included in GDP. The glass is an intermediate good used in the production of the house. When a customer buys the house from the builder, the value of the glass is included as part of the selling price of the house, which is the value of a final good counted in GDP. Let's consider another example. A wholesale distributor sells glass to a hardware store. GDP does not include this transaction because the hardware store is not the final user. When a customer buys the glass from the hardware store to repair a broken window, the final purchase price of the glass is added to GDP as a consumer expenditure.

DismalScientist **(www.dismal.com)** is an economic news and analysis service, part of which is devoted to the GDP.

The concept of value added

An important concept in macroeconomics to which readers should be introduced at this point is that of economic value added. It is particularly important from a national accounting perspective. For example, suppose a retail store sells a woollen suit for $420 ($20 of which is paid to the government in sales tax), which it buys from the manufacturer for $300. At earlier stages of the production chain, the manufacturer purchased the raw material from its fabric supplier for $150 and the supplier, in turn, purchased the raw wool for $40. The sum of expenditures at the various stages of production is $910 ($420 + $300 + $150 + $40), but the value of final output (that is, its price to the final consumer), which embodies the value added of each stage of production plus the sales tax, is only $420. So far, this is simply another example of the principle of only counting final goods and services when measuring GDP.

GDP at factor cost A measure of GDP arrived at by adding all the incomes of all factors of production (including labour, land and capital).

GDP at market prices A measure of GDP arrived at by valuing GDP produced at the prices at which the goods and services sell. The difference between this and GDP at factor cost is the existence of indirect taxes less subsidies.

Indirect taxes less subsidies Government taxes levied on the production and/or sale of goods and services sold, less any subsidies paid to business from government. Examples include general sales taxes (like the GST in Australia), excise taxes and customs duties.

However, to further illustrate the idea of value added, consider another perspective on the above example. The retailer paid the manufacturer $300 for the suit and received $400 for it (after the sales tax had been deducted). This $100 represents the value added by the retailer and is made up of wages, salaries and supplements of employees (such as delivery and sales people) plus the retailer's gross operating surplus, which covers an allowance for interest payments on borrowings plus profit. The profit is the income of the owners of the retail store, while the interest is the income of any lenders of funds to the store. Thus all the value added at this stage in the production process accrues to somebody as income. This is also true of all other stages and, by adding the value added for all the production stages (here 100 + 150 + 110 + 40), we get what is called **GDP at factor cost**. In this example it is equal to $400. However, looking at it from the expenditure side, **GDP at market prices** is $420 since this is how much the end buyer paid for the suit. The difference between the two measurements is accounted for in the national accounts by **indirect taxes less subsidies**, here $20.

PART 4

Further on measuring GDP

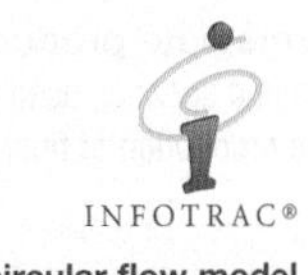

circular flow model

Circular flow model A diagram showing the flow of products from businesses to households and the flow of resources from households to businesses. In exchange for these resources, money payments flow between businesses and households.

GDP consists of many puzzle pieces to fit together, including markets for products, markets for resources, consumers spending and earning money and businesses spending and earning money. How can one fit the puzzle pieces together? One way to understand how all these concepts fit together is to use a simple macroeconomic model called the **circular flow model**. The circular flow model shows the flow of products from businesses to households and the flow of resources from households to businesses. In exchange for these resources, money payments flow between businesses and households. Exhibit 11.1 shows the circular flow in a hypothetical economy with no government, no financial markets and no foreign trade. In this ultra-simple pure market economy, only the households and the businesses make decisions.

The circular flow model

The upper half of the diagram in Exhibit 11.1 represents *product markets*, in which households exchange money for goods and services produced by firms. The *supply* arrow in the top loop represents all finished products and the value of services produced, sold and delivered to consumers. The *demand* arrow in the top loop shows why the businesses make this effort to satisfy the consuming households. When consumers decide to buy products, they are actually voting with their dollars. This flow of consumption expenditures from households is sales revenues to businesses and expenses from the viewpoint of households. Notice that the box labelled *product markets* contains a supply and demand graph. This represents the idea that the forces of supply and demand in individual markets determine the price and quantity of each product exchanged.

Exhibit 11.1 The basic circular flow model

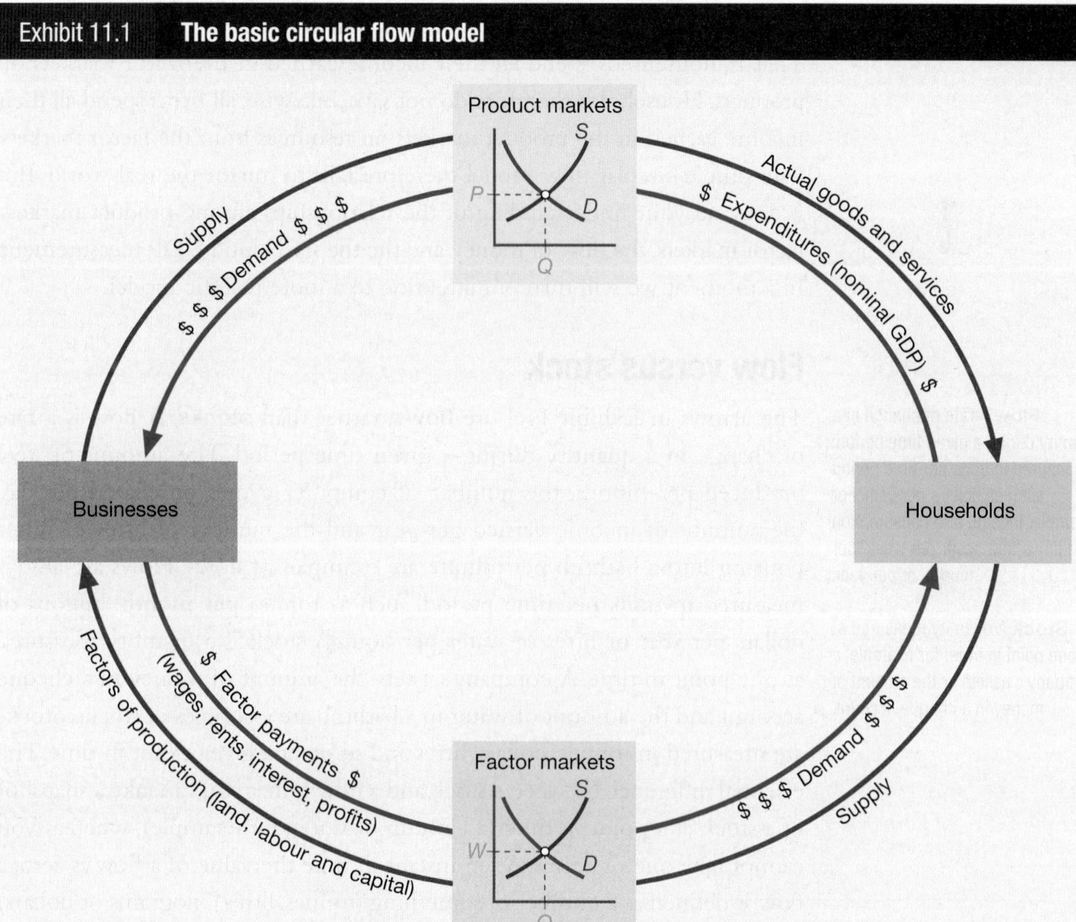

In this simple economy, households spend all their income in the upper loop and demand consumer goods and services from businesses. Businesses seek profits by supplying goods and services to households through the product markets. Prices and quantities in individual markets are determined by the market supply and demand model. In the factor markets in the lower loop, resources (land, labour and capital) are owned by households and supplied to businesses that demand these factors in return for money payments. The forces of supply and demand determine the returns to the factors – for example, wages and the quantity of labour supplied. Overall, goods and services flow clockwise and the corresponding payments flow counter-clockwise.

The bottom half of the circular flow diagram consists of the *factor markets*, in which firms *demand* the natural resources, land, labour, capital and entrepreneurship needed to produce the goods and services sold in the product markets. In our hypothetical economy it is assumed for simplicity that households own all the factors of production. Businesses therefore must purchase all their resources from the households. The *supply* arrow in the bottom loop represents this flow of resources from households to firms and the *demand* arrow is the flow of money payments for these resources. These payments are also income earned by households in the form of wages, rents, interest and profits. As in the product markets, market supply and demand determine the prices of factors and the factor quantities supplied.

Our simple model also assumes that all households live from hand to mouth. That is, households spend all their income earned in the factor markets on products. Households therefore do not save. Likewise, all firms spend all their income earned in the product markets on resources from the factor markets. The simple circular flow model therefore fails to mirror the real world. But it does aid your understanding of the relationships among product markets, factor markets, the flow of money and the theory behind GDP measurement. In a moment we will turn our attention to a more realistic model.

Flow versus stock

Flow A rate of change in a quantity during a given time period, measured in units per time period such as dollars per year. For example, income and consumption are flows that occur per week, per month, or per year.

Stock A quantity measured at one point in time; for example, a company's assets or the amount of money in a cheque account.

The arrows in Exhibit 11.1 are **flows**, rather than **stocks**. A flow is a rate of change in a quantity during a given time period. The amount of steel produced per month, the number of computer games purchased per day, the amount of income earned per year and the number of litres of water pouring into a bathtub per minute are examples of flows. Flows are always measured in units per time period, such as tonnes per month, billions of dollars per year or litres of water per hour. A stock is a quantity measured at one point in time. A company's assets, the amount of money in a cheque account and the amount of water in a bathtub are examples of stocks. Stocks are measured in tonnes, dollars, litres and so on at a given point in time. The essential difference between a stock and a flow is that you can take a snapshot of a stock at a point in time (a bathtub of water, for example), whereas you cannot take one of a flow. At an instant in time the value of a flow is zero; a flow is defined as a number of something (tonnes, litres, kilograms or dollars) per unit of time (per day, hour, month and so on).

An important point here is this: *All measurements in the circular flow model are flows. As such, they tell us what has been added during a period to the total stocks of goods, services, money or whatever is available in the economy, but they do not represent the total stocks themselves.* Consumption expenditures, business production, wages, rents, interest payments and profits are flows of money arising from newly produced products in the period in question that affect the total level of stocks in the economy, but which themselves – that is, the underlying stocks – are not shown in the model.

A four-sector circular flow model

Exhibit 11.2 puts all the puzzle pieces together. It presents a more complex circular flow model by adding three sectors: financial markets, government and foreign markets. Other than household spending on the output of firms, these additions add three *leakages* from the amount of income paid to households that reduce their spending. First, part of households' income is saved. Second, part of it is taxed. Third, part of the income is spent on

Exhibit 11.2 The circular flow model of an open economy

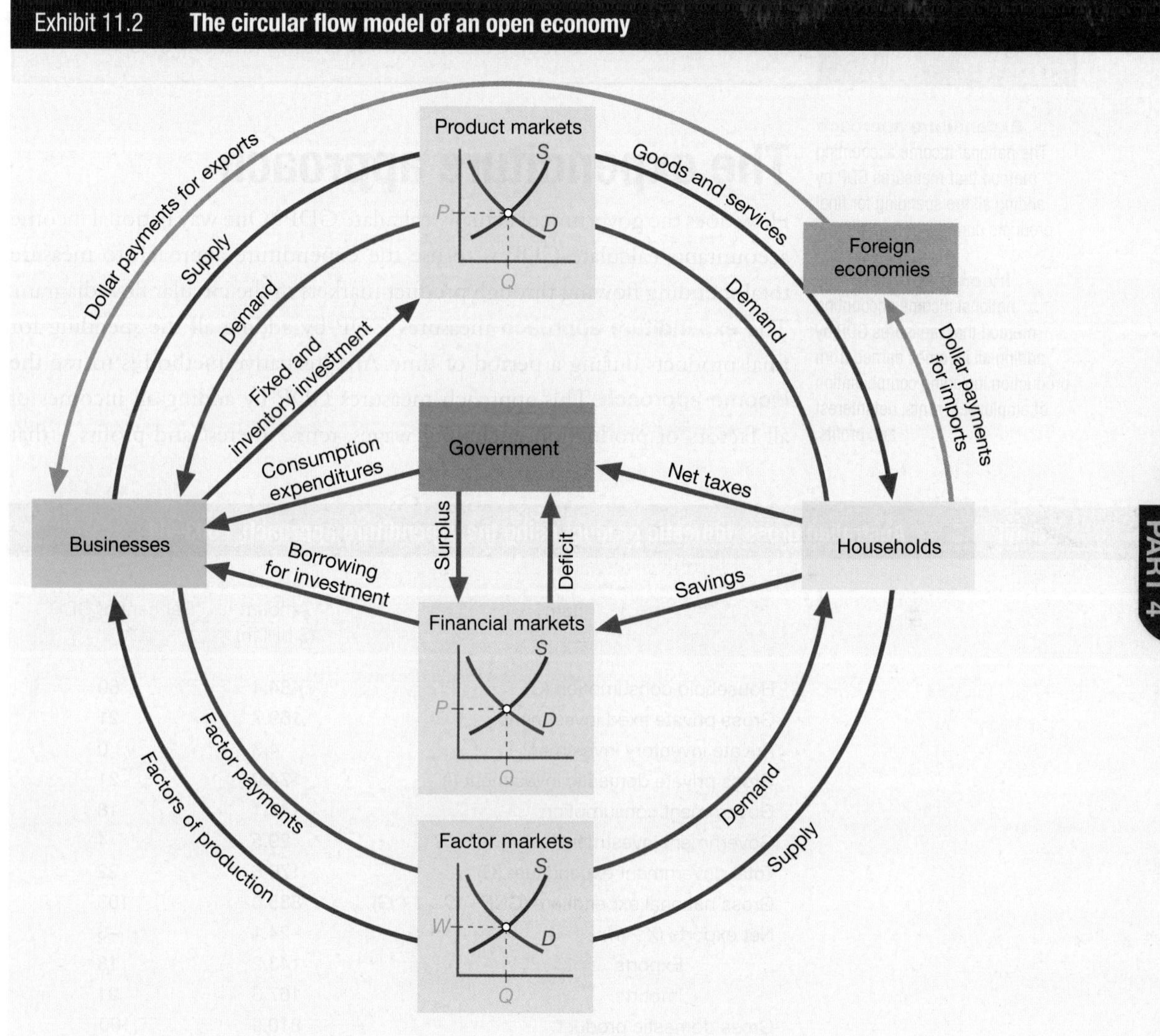

This exhibit presents a circular flow model for a real-world economy (such as Australia's) that has a financial section and a government sector, and engages in international trade. The model includes links between the product and factor markets in the domestic economy and the financial markets, government and foreign economies. To simplify the model, only dollar payments are shown for the foreign sector.

imports. On the other hand, there are three sources of spending *injections* for firms' output other than from households. First, firms invest in new plant, equipment and inventories (investment) purchased from other firms. Second, government uses taxes raised for expenditures on goods and services from firms. Third, foreigners purchase exports from the firms.

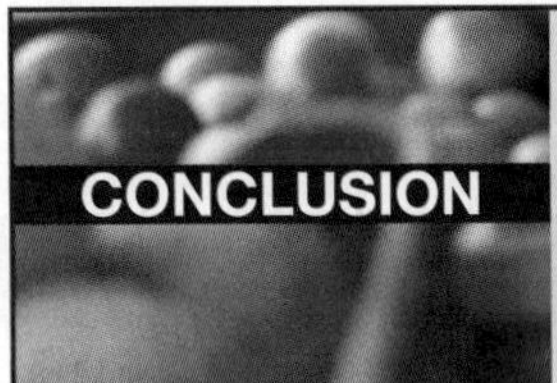

The dollar value of all output produced is accounted for by virtue of the fact that the dollar value of all leakages from the income flow (savings, taxes, imports) equals the dollar value of all injections of spending (investment [including firms' voluntary or involuntary spending on inventories], government spending and exports).

Expenditure approach The national income accounting method that measures GDP by adding all the spending for final products during a period of time.

Income approach The national income accounting method that measures GDP by adding all incomes earned from production including compensation of employees, rents, net interest and profits.

The expenditure approach

How does the government actually calculate GDP? One way national income accountants calculate GDP is to use the expenditure approach to measure total spending flowing through product markets in the circular flow diagram. The **expenditure approach** measures GDP by adding all the spending for final products during a period of time. An alternative method is to use the **income approach**. This approach measures GDP by adding all incomes of all factors of production, including wages, rents, interest and profits – that

Exhibit 11.3 Australian gross domestic product using the expenditure approach, 2003–04

Item	Amount ($ billion)	Per cent of GDP
Household consumption (*C*)	484.4	60
Gross private fixed investment	169.7	21
Private inventory investment	4.3	0
Gross private domestic investment (*I*)	174.0	21
Government consumption	147.1	18
Government investment	29.5	4
Total government expenditure (*G*)	176.6	22
Gross national expenditure (GNE = $C + I + G$)	835.0	103
Net exports ($X - M$)	–24.1	-3
Exports	143.2	18
Imports	167.3	21
Gross domestic product (GDP = $C + I + G + X - M$)[1]	810.9	100 (difference due to rounding)

Source: Australian Bureau of Statistics, www.abs.gov.au, Cat. No. 5206, Table 43.

1 In practice, there is always a statistical discrepancy involved in estimating GDP. For our purposes the statistical discrepancy calculated by the ABS for 2003–04 ($1.6 billion) was distributed proportionally across the expenditure categories to ensure consistency of GNE with GDP.

is, all the income generated in the production process. Conceptually, both approaches should yield the same result. However, in practice, measurement issues result in small differences between the two estimates.

Two months after the end of each quarter the Australian Bureau of Statistics (ABS) publishes calculations of GDP on both the expenditure and income bases. In practice, GDP estimates based on a third approach, which involves valuing the quantities of products produced – the output approach – come about a month later in another publication. Although conceptually each should give exactly the same figure, all three (expenditure, income and output estimates) are calculated independently and in practice yield somewhat different estimates due to the different measurement approaches.

The ABS website (**www.abs.gov.au**) was used to obtain data discussed in this chapter. On the main page of the site select *AusStats*, then *Publications & Data*, then *Time Series Spreadsheets*, then *By Catalogue/Subject*, then *52. National accounts*, then *5204.0* and *5206.0* for a range of data sets.

Exhibit 11.3 shows 2003–04 GDP using the expenditure approach, which breaks down expenditures into four components. The data in this table show that all production in the Australian economy is ultimately purchased by spending from households, businesses, government or foreigners. Let's discuss each of these expenditure categories.

Household consumption expenditures (*C*)

The largest component of GDP in 2003–04 was \$484.4 billion for *household consumption expenditures*, represented by the letter *C*. Household consumption expenditures comprise total spending by households for durable goods, non-durable goods and services. Durable goods include such items as cars, appliances and furniture, because they last longer than one year. Food, clothing, soap and petrol are examples of non-durables, because they are considered used up or consumed in less than a year. There is obviously an element of arbitrariness involved here. For instance, the authors would each admit to having shirts that are older than some cars on the road. Nevertheless, by convention, shirts are non-durable and cars are durable goods.

household consumption expenditures

The services category, which these days is the largest category, includes recreation expenditures (such as movies, football games, the theatre), legal advice, medical treatment, education and any transaction not in the form of a tangible object (that is, one that you pay for but cannot drop on your foot!).

The total consumption of goods and services by households (*C*) in a modern developed economy is by far the largest component of GDP and comprises around 60 per cent or more of the total production of all goods and services.

gross private domestic investment

Gross private domestic investment (*I*)

In 2003–04, \$174 billion was spent for what is officially called *gross private domestic investment* (*I*). This figure includes 'gross' (that is, all spending, regardless of whether the spending was to replace equipment or buildings that were wearing out), 'private' (not government), 'domestic' (not foreign) spending by businesses for investment. At this point it is worth emphasising the distinction between **gross investment** and **net investment**.

Gross investment Any spending that maintains or increases the capital stock in the country.

Net investment Only that spending that actually increases the nation's capital stock.

PART 4

Gross investment is any spending that maintains or increases the capital stock in the country. Net investment is only that spending that actually increases the nation's capital stock. As an example, suppose the owner of a trucking company spends $1 million on the company's fleet of trucks, but $800 000 of that is for repairs and other maintenance in order to keep the current stock of trucks in good shape. The other $200 000 is for actual additions to the fleet. In this case, gross investment was $1 million, while net investment was $200 000. It is gross investment that is counted in GDP.

Gross private domestic investment is the sum of two components: (1) *fixed investment* expenditures for newly produced capital goods, such as commercial and residential structures, machinery, equipment and tools; and (2) changes in *private-sector inventories*, which is the net change in spending for unsold finished goods and raw materials. Note that gross private domestic investment is simply the national income accounting category for 'investment' defined in Chapter 2. The only difference is that investment in Exhibit 2.4 in Chapter 2 was in physical capital rather than the dollar value of capital.

At this point we caution you with respect to the use of the terms 'investment' and 'capital'. In everyday usage, any time a person or a company uses some of their accumulated savings – or borrows money – to buy shares, fixed interest securities, a piece of existing real estate or the like, they will usually say that they are 'investing'. Similarly, you will often hear of people 'needing capital' for some venture or other. Here they mean they need some financing to fund their venture.

However, in economics we use the term 'investment' to refer to spending on physical products that are intended to be used as inputs in production processes. The reason for this is that, in everyday parlance, much of what is commonly referred to as investment is merely the transfer of existing assets from one person to another (as occurs, for instance, when someone buys some shares from someone else on the share market). To avoid confusion, from now on whenever we use the word 'investment' it will be meant in the sense used in this discussion of the national accounts. Alternatively, we will use the term 'financial investment' when we are referring to the acquisition of financial assets.

Similarly, the term 'capital' – or 'capital stock' – is used in economics and in this book to refer to the existing stock of buildings, factories and machinery available to be used in production processes. In terms of the above discussion on flows and stocks, investment is a flow while capital is a stock.

Now we will take a closer look at gross private domestic investment. Note that national accountants include the value of newly constructed residential housing in the $174 billion spent for fixed investment. A new factory, warehouse or manufacturing robot is surely a form of investment, but why include residential housing as business investment, rather than consumption by households? The debatable answer is that a new home is considered investment because it provides services over time into the future, which the owner can choose to rent out for financial return. For this reason, all newly produced housing is investment whether the owner rents out or occupies the property. In addition, a motor car purchased by a firm to use in its business is regarded as investment and is part of fixed investment ('fixed' not in the sense that it is stationary, but in the sense that it continues to exist from one period to another, whereas inventory investment may be sold in the next period).

Also note that, again, the important issue is the use to which the purchase is being put. A motor car purchased by a company to assist it in producing further output (even if it is just to carry the CEO around) is investment. On the other hand, the same motor car purchased by a household to take the children to netball and to school is considered consumption expenditure because it is not being used to assist in the further production of output.

Finally, the $4.3 billion change in private-sector inventories in Exhibit 11.3 means that this amount of net dollar value of unsold finished goods and raw materials was added to the stock of inventories by firms during 2003–04. Note that this run up in inventories is considered to have been purchased by the firms concerned, and it is in this way that the total value of production must always equal the total value of spending in any period. The production is either purchased by somebody (either a domestic resident or a foreign buyer) or assumed to have been implicitly purchased by the firm in question (at least until it is sold in some future period). When businesses have more on their shelves at the end of this year than last, more new production has taken place than is consumed during this year, but this is still part of production for that year and is therefore included in GDP. Conversely, a decline in inventories from one period to the next means that measured GDP would be less than total dollar sales in the period in question because households would have spent more on production than firms actually produced during that period.

Government consumption and gross public investment expenditures (*G*)

This category includes the value of all goods and services that the government (including federal, state and local levels) purchases in a particular period. For example, spending on the salaries of police, the defence forces and other government employees, as well as spending on such things as paper, stationery, garbage disposal and New Year fireworks displays, enters the GDP accounts as government consumption at the prices the government pays for them.

An interesting aspect of national income accounting convention is that government spending on the salaries of teachers, university lecturers, health workers and so on is also treated as government consumption, even though a reasonable case can be made that such expenditures represent valuable expenditure on so-called **human capital** and as such could be regarded as an investment type of expenditure. 'Human capital' is a term used to distinguish

Human capital A term used to distinguish spending on physical capital – that is, spending on physical goods and services to improve the productive process – from spending that has the purpose of enhancing the productivity of the human input into production.

spending on physical capital – spending on physical goods and services to improve the productive process – from spending intended to enhance the productivity of the human input into production. For example, when people spend money on their education you could say they are enhancing their human capital stock. Similarly, when a government spends money on teachers so as to enhance the educational and skill level of the members of the community, you could argue that this is just as integral a part of investment expenditure (rather than expenditure of a consumption kind) as spending money on the construction of a new bridge.

In addition, the government spends money on investment-type goods, such as highways, bridges and government buildings. In 2003–04, federal, state and local government consumption expenditures and gross investment (*G*) were $176.6 billion (147.1 + 29.5). You should also note that consumption expenditures and gross investment of state and local governments far exceed those of the federal government. This is because much of the federal government's 'spending' is really transfer payments either to individuals or to other tiers of government. It is very important to understand that consumption and gross investment expenditures by government (what we mean by *G*) exclude *transfer payments* because, as defined at the beginning of the chapter, they do not represent newly produced goods and services. Instead, transfer payments such as social welfare benefits, pensions, unemployment benefits, benefits from other social programs and federal government grants to state and local government are simply a transfer of purchasing power from one section of the community to another via government.

Net exports (*X* – *M*)

INFOTRAC®
net exports

The last GDP expenditure item is *net exports*, expressed in the formula (*X* – *M*). *Exports* (*X*) are expenditures by foreigners for domestically produced goods and services. *Imports* (*M*) are the dollar amount of a nation's purchases from producers in other countries. Because we are using expenditures for domestically produced output to measure GDP, one might ask why imports are subtracted from exports. The answer concerns how the government actually collects data from which GDP is computed. Spending for imports is not subtracted when spending data for consumption (*C*), investment (*I*) and government spending (*G*) are reported.

Gross national expenditure (GNE) The sum of consumption, investment and government spending in the economy in a quarter or a year (= *C* + *I* + *G*), irrespective of whether the spending was on domestic production or on imports.

When these three components of GDP are added, the result is what is referred to as **gross national expenditure (GNE).** This is the total spending by Australian residents on goods and services, irrespective of whether that spending was on domestic production or on imported production. Thus GNE will overstate the value of expenditures on domestically produced products by the extent of imports (*M*). On the other hand, GNE will not include the expenditure by foreigners on Australian production. Thus, GNE will understate expenditure on Australian production by the extent of exports (X). To get GDP we therefore need to add net exports ($X - M$) to GNE.

To elaborate further, consider the data collected to compute consumption (C). In reality, personal consumption expenditures reported to the ABS include expenditures for both domestically produced and imported goods and services. For example, car dealers report to the government that Australian consumers purchased a given dollar amount of new cars during 2004, but they are not required to separate their figures between sales of Australian-produced cars and sales of foreign cars. Because GDP measures only domestic economic activity, foreign sales must be removed. Subtracting imports in the net exports category removes all foreign sales, including new foreign cars, from consumption (C) and likewise from investment (I) and government expenditures (G). Similarly, the ABS needs to add to domestic sales any export sales to foreigners of domestically produced goods and services such as iron ore, sugar, computing software, intellectual property (movie rights, for example) and educational services. Adding exports in the net exports category adjusts for this type of expenditure to obtain a picture of total Australian production in a particular period.

The 2003–04 GDP outcome is obtained by subtracting \$167.3 billion in imports from GNE ($C + I + G$) and adding in the \$143.2 billion in exports to yield GDP of \$810.9 billion. The negative value for net exports of –\$24.1 billion (around 3 per cent of GDP) indicates that in 2003–04 Australia spent more dollars to purchase foreign products than it received from the rest of the world for its exports of goods and services. Issues relating to international trade are discussed in more detail later in the chapter and again in the last chapter of the book.

A formula for GDP

Given the above discussion, using the expenditure approach, GDP is expressed mathematically in billions of dollars as

$$\text{GDP} = C + I + G + (X - M) \qquad \textbf{(1)}$$

For 2003–04 (see Exhibit 11.3),

$$810.9 = 484.4 + 174.0 + 176.6 + (143.2 - 167.3)$$

This simple equation plays a central role in macroeconomics. It is the basis for analysing many macroeconomic problems and formulating macroeconomic policy. When economists study the macro economy, they can apply this equation to predict the behaviour of the major sectors of the economy: consumption (C) is spending by households; investment (I) is gross investment spending by firms; government consumption and government gross investment expenditures (G) is spending by the government and net exports ($X - M$) is net spending by foreigners.

Exhibit 11.4 **An international comparison of GDP, 2003**

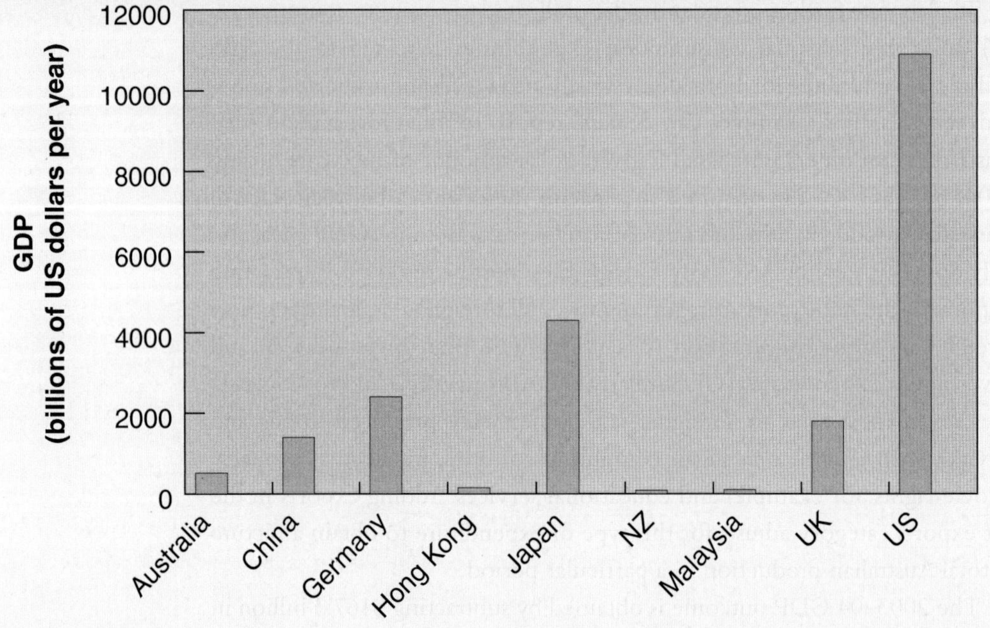

Source: World Bank, worldbank.org/data/countrydata, various tables

GDP in other countries

Exhibit 11.4 provides GDP comparisons among selected countries. For example, the United States has the world's highest GDP, which is more than twice Japan's and about 120 times that of New Zealand. Australia's GDP is about 5 per cent of the size of that of the United States.

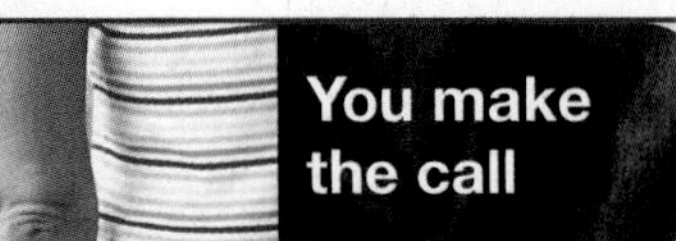

How much does Mark add to GDP?

Mark works part-time at Pizza Hut and earns an annual wage of $15 000. He sold 4000 pizzas at $5 per pizza during the year. He was unemployed part of the year, so he received unemployment benefits of $3000. During the past year, Mark bought a used car for $1000. Using the expenditure approach, how much has Mark contributed to GDP?

GDP shortcomings as a measure of economic welfare

For various reasons, GDP omits certain measures of overall economic welfare (or well-being). Because GDP is the basis of government economic policies, the concern is that a false impression of the nation's material well-being may result from an imperfectly measured GDP. GDP is a less-than-perfect measure of the nation's economic pulse because it excludes the following factors.

The Organisation for Economic Co-operation and Development (OECD) is a forum for monitoring economic trends in its 25 member countries, which include Australia, the United States, the United Kingdom and Japan. Visit the OECD at www.oecd.org.

Non-market transactions

Because GDP counts only market transactions, it excludes certain unpaid activities such as household production, child-rearing and do-it-yourself home repairs and services. For example, if you take your dirty clothes to the cleaners, GDP increases by the amount of the cleaning bill paid. But GDP ignores the value of cleaning these same clothes if you clean them yourself at home. Finally, non-market activities such as house-and-yard and charity work are not included in the estimates, nor are the not insubstantial activities of students in adding to their (and the community's) stock of human capital.

There are two reasons for excluding non-market activities from GDP. First, it would be extremely imprecise to attempt to collect data and assign a dollar value to services people provide for themselves or others without compensation. Second, it is difficult to decide which non-market activities to exclude and which ones to include. Perhaps mending your own roof, painting your own house and repairing your own car should be included. But what about washing your car, mowing your lawn and pruning your shrubs?

Distribution, kind and quality of products

GDP data provide no information as to whether a small fraction of the population consumes most of a country's GDP or whether consumption is evenly divided. Furthermore, GDP data alone provide no information in respect of the quality and kinds of goods and services that comprise a nation's GDP. Consider the fictional economies of Zuba and Econa. Zuba has a GDP of $2000 billion and Econa has a GDP of $1000 billion. At first glance, Zuba appears to possess superior economic well-being. However, suppose a very large proportion of Zuba's GDP consists of military goods, while Econa's products include some military goods but comprise mostly computers, entertainment goods and services, clothing, tractors, wheat, milk, houses and other consumer items.

Moreover, imagine that the majority of the people of Zuba couldn't care less about the output of military goods and would be more pleased with the production of consumer goods. It would be reasonable to conclude therefore that, as far as the people of Zuba are concerned, not many of them would feel as though they were better off than the people of Econa. Furthermore, suppose that the population of Zuba is twice that of Econa. Therefore, *GDP per capita* in the two countries is actually the same. Moreover, in Zuba, 20 per cent of its people are actually the beneficiaries of 80 per cent of its GDP production, while in Econa 60 per cent of its people are the beneficiaries of 80 per cent of its output. In other words, the GDP is shared more widely in Econa than in Zuba. All these additional issues will contribute to the overall economic well-being felt by the two communities in question.

CONCLUSION GDP is a quantitative, rather than a qualitative, measure of the output of goods and services.

Another very important practical issue involved in measuring GDP is how to allow appropriately for changes in output quality over time. For example, if from one year to the next the number of bananas produced increases from 100 to 105 we would be fairly safe in saying that banana output has increased by 5 per cent. This is because it is reasonable to assume that the basic quality of the bananas has remained similar. However, now suppose the good we are considering is a personal computer and there is the same percentage increase in number produced from one year to the next. This is a much more complex good with many different quality characteristics. If there are enhancements to any of these characteristics, how are they to be measured and compared? For example, suppose the 105 PCs in year two have 20 per cent more memory and extra colour monitor features, require less CPU time for tasks and have slightly better monitor resolution than the 100 from the year before. Is it appropriate to still say GDP increased by only 5 per cent? After all, in the banana case, if each of the 105 bananas in year two was also 20 per cent bigger should we still simply count them? The vexed question of quality change is one that is a continual challenge for the Australian Bureau of Statistics.

Neglect of leisure time

The wealthier a nation becomes, in general, the more leisure time its citizens can afford. Rather than continuing to work long hours, people often choose to increase their time for recreation and travel. During this century, the length of the typical work week in most developed countries has declined steadily from about 50 hours in 1900 to about 35 hours in 2004. As another example, suppose a community voluntarily chooses at some point to spend less time working to produce output and more time meditating about the mysteries of life. Its GDP will certainly reduce, but has its welfare reduced, increased or stayed the same?

CONCLUSION It can be argued that GDP understates national well-being because no allowance is made for people not working as many hours as they once did.

The underground economy

Illegal gambling, prostitution, loan-sharking and illegal drugs are goods and services that meet all the requirements for GDP. They are final products with a value determined in markets (although the markets are illegally conducted!) but GDP does not include unreported criminal activities. Some argue that even if some way could be found to estimate accurately the quantum of these outputs, they should be excluded from GDP anyway because they are 'bads' rather than 'goods'. In the language we developed in Chapter 1 when discussing economics and ethics, these activities clearly do not represent the pursuit of 'enlightened self-interest'. Others, however, argue – although fairly controversially – that if people derive satisfaction from such activities and are willing to pay for them, they should be included in the same way that the purchase of alcohol and certain magazines and videos of questionable social value are currently included.

The 'underground' economy also includes activities not reported because of tax evasion. One way to evade paying taxes on a legal activity is to trade or barter, rather than selling goods and services. One person fixes a neighbour's car in return for baby-sitting services and the value of the exchange is unreported. Other legal sales are made by some individuals and businesses for cash, with no report of the income earned to the Australian Taxation Office. Estimates of the size of this subterranean economy vary from time to time and from country to country. Some studies by economists estimate the size of the underground sector in Australia at between 5 and 10 per cent of GDP. This range of estimates is comparable to the estimated size of the underground economy in most European countries.

If the underground economy is sizeable, GDP will understate an economy's performance.

Economic 'bads'

More production means a larger GDP, regardless of the level of pollution created in the process. Recall from Chapter 4 the discussion of negative externalities, such as pollution caused by steel mills, chemical plants and cigarettes. Air, water and noise pollution are other examples of economic 'bads' (which are not illegal) that impose costs on society that are often not reflected in private market prices and quantities bought and sold. When a polluting company sells its product, this transaction increases GDP. However, critics of GDP argue that it fails to account for the diminished quality of life from the 'bads' not reported in the GDP. Another 'bad' that many people are very concerned about is ecological degradation. For this reason a number of economists prefer to use a measure known as the 'genuine progress indicator' (GPI). This measures attempts to adjust measured GDP for the creation of such 'bads' as mentioned above, as well as to allow for any reduction or degradation of the nation's ecological systems and resources.

Finally, in some perverse ways reductions in community well-being may actually manifest as increases in measured GDP. For instance, suppose that due to a reduction in public safety resulting from, say, increased street violence, more police are employed. Their salaries will show up as an increase in GDP and yet it is difficult to see how the use of more scarce human resources to try to counteract increased community violence is an increase in welfare.

Other national accounts

In addition to GDP, several other national accounts are often reported in the media because they are necessary for studying the macro economy. We will now have a brief look at each. The relationships among them are illustrated in Exhibit 11.5.

Net domestic product (NDP)

Net domestic product (NDP) Gross domestic product minus depreciation of the capital worn out in producing output.

It can be argued that depreciation should be subtracted from GDP. Recall that GDP is not entirely a measure of newly produced output, because it includes the estimated value of the capital goods required to replace those worn out in the production process. The measurement designed to correct this deficiency is **net domestic product (NDP)**. Net domestic product is gross domestic product minus depreciation of the capital worn out in producing output. Stated as a formula:

NDP = GDP – depreciation (also known as consumption of fixed capital)

Exhibit 11.5 Six measures of the macro economy

C + I + G + X = GNE + X	Imports of goods and services	Imports of goods and services	Imports of goods and services	Imports of goods and services	Imports of goods and services	Imports of goods and services
					Net income paid overseas	Net income paid overseas
						Net transfers overseas
	Gross domestic product = C + I + G + (X – M)	Gross domestic product at factor cost	Domestic factor incomes	Net domestic product	Net national product	National disposable income
			Indirect taxes less subsidies			
		Indirect taxes less subsidies	Depreciation allowances	Depreciation	Depreciation allowances	Depreciation allowances

The seven bars show the relationships among six major measurements of the Australian macro economy.

Is GDP a false beacon steering us into the rocks?

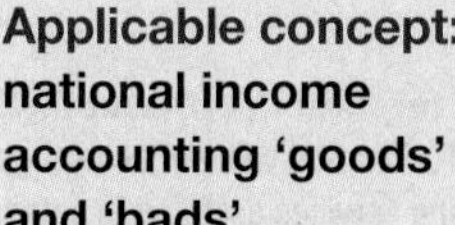
Analyse the issue

Applicable concept: national income accounting 'goods' and 'bads'

Suppose a factory in your community has been dumping hazardous wastes in the local water supply and people have contracted cancer and other illnesses from drinking polluted water. The Department of the Environment discovers this pollution and, under state law, orders a clean-up and a fine for the damages. Initially the company defends itself against the charge by hiring lawyers and experts and takes the case to court. After years of trial, the company loses the case and has to pay for the clean-up and damages.

In terms of the GDP, an amazing 'good' result occurs: the primary measure of national economic output, GDP, increases. GDP counts the millions of dollars spent to clean up the water supply. GDP even includes the health-care expenses of anyone who develops cancer or other illnesses caused by drinking polluted water. GDP also includes the money spent by the company on lawyers and experts to defend itself in court. And GDP includes the money spent by the government to regulate the polluting company.

Now consider what happens when raw materials like oil and minerals are used to produce houses, cars and other goods. The value of the oil and minerals is an intermediate good implicitly computed in GDP because the value of the final goods is explicitly computed in GDP. Using scarce resources to produce goods and services therefore raises GDP and is considered a 'good' result. On the other hand, don't we lose the value of the oil and minerals in the production process and isn't this a 'bad' result?

The Australian Bureau of Statistics is the Australian government department vested with the responsibility for compiling estimates of GDP. Critics of current methods used to estimate GDP have called for a new measure designed to estimate such damage as described above. These new accounts would adjust for changes in air and water quality and depletion of non-renewable raw materials like oil and minerals. These accounts would also adjust for changes in the stock of renewable natural resources, such as forests and fish stocks. Also, it is argued by some that accounts should be created to measure global warming and destruction of the ozone layer.

As explained in this chapter, a dollar estimate of physical capital depreciation is subtracted from GDP to compute net domestic product (NDP). The argument here is that a dollar estimate of the damage to the environment should also be subtracted. To ignore measuring such environmental problems, critics argue, threatens future generations.

Critics of so-called 'green national accounts', however, argue that assigning a dollar value to environment damage and resource depletion requires a methodology that is extremely subjective and complex. Notwithstanding these difficulties, the ABS has not ignored the criticisms and continues to make efforts to refine – but in prudent, considered and appropriate ways – its methods.

Suppose there is a nuclear power plant disaster. How could GDP be a 'false beacon' in this case?

Consumption of fixed capital is the official government term for an estimate of the depreciation of capital. This somewhat imposing term is simply an allowance for the portion of capital worn out producing GDP. Over time, capital goods such as buildings, machines and equipment wear out and become less valuable. Because it is impossible to measure depreciation accurately, an estimate is entered. In 2003–04, $129 billion was the estimated amount of GDP attributable to depreciation during the year, leaving NDP of $682 billion.

Net national product (NNP) The market value of all final goods and services accruing to a nation's residents, no matter where in the world the goods and services were produced, after an allowance for depreciation is subtracted.

National disposable income (NDI) Obtained after subtracting net transfers overseas (mainly foreign aid and pensions paid to recipients living abroad) from net national product.

Net national product (NNP)

As noted above, from gross domestic product, depreciation is subtracted to obtain net domestic product. Removing net income (interest and dividends) paid overseas yields **net national product**. This represents the volume of production net of depreciation accruing to Australian residents. From this, net transfers overseas (mainly foreign aid and pensions paid to recipients living abroad) can be subtracted to obtain **national disposable income (NDI).**

Domestic factor income (DFI)

Domestic factor income (DFI) The total income earned by domestic resource owners, including wages, rents, interest and profits (after depreciation), conceptually also equal to net domestic product less indirect taxes.

Suppose we are interested in how much income is *earned* by domestic households that are the suppliers of resources. The figure that measures the total flow of payments to the owners of the factors of production is **domestic factor income (DFI).** Domestic factor income is the total income earned by resource owners domiciled in Australia, including wages, rents, interest and profits (after depreciation). One way to compute domestic factor incomes is to add compensation of employees, rents, profits and net interest using the income approach to estimating GDP. Another way is to use the expenditure approach; given the conceptual equivalence of the two approaches, it is the simpler estimation method. To obtain DFI we use the following formula:

$$\text{DFI} = \text{NDP} - \text{indirect business taxes}$$

Domestic factor income equals NDP minus *indirect business taxes*. As defined earlier in this chapter, indirect business taxes include sales taxes, federal excise taxes, licence fees, business property taxes and customs duties. Indirect taxes are not income payments to suppliers of resources. Instead, firms collect indirect business taxes and send these funds to the government. Because indirect business taxes are included in the price, but are not income for individuals, they must be subtracted from NDP to determine DFI. Exhibit 11.6 derives the values for these various aggregates for 2003–04.

Exhibit 11.6 **Calculations of various national macroeconomic aggregates for 2003–04**

		Amount (billions of dollars)
(1)	GDP	= 811
(2)	Depreciation	= 129
(3)	NDP	= 682 [(1) – (2)]
(4)	Net income payable to foreigners	= 24
(5)	GNP	= 787 [(1) – (4)]
(6)	NNP	= 658 [(5) – (2)]
(7)	Net transfers to foreigners	= 0.1
(8)	NDI	= 657.9 [(6) – (7)]

Source: Australian Bureau of Statistics, www.abs.gov.au, various tables.

Relationship between community saving and investment

One relationship not represented in Exhibit 11.5 is that linking a community's saving and its (economic) investment.

In very simple economies a community's saving is by definition its investment (S = I). For example, imagine a desert island economy where the sole resident, Robyn Crusoe, is both the household sector and firm sector. Each period she survives quite happily by catching fish and gathering coconuts just sufficient for her needs (GDP = C). One day she realises that, by giving up some of her usual fish catching/coconut gathering time to make a fishing net, she will be able to catch even more fish in the future (or, alternatively, have more leisure time). The island's national accounts for that period would be as follows. Total output (GDP) would now equal a smaller-than-usual number of fish and coconuts, which Robyn readily consumes (C), plus an inedible fishing net, which is her investment for that period (I). The difference between the island's total production and consumption (GDP – C) is the economy's saving (S) by its (rather hungry) inhabitant. This saving is identical to the island's investment during the period (S = I = the net). In the following periods Robyn enjoys the fruits of her earlier thrift by being able to have greater consumption than was possible before.

Of course, in a more complex real-world economy the saving and investment decisions are not made by the same person (Robyn) but are being undertaken by different groups of individuals. Households decide how much to save, while firms decide how much to invest in capital. How can it be the case that these two sets of decisions will always be consistent with each other so that S = I?

The answer is that *desired* saving by households will not in fact always be equal to *desired* investment by firms, but actual *measured* saving and *measured* investment will always be equal. Whenever desired saving by households is different from desired investment by firms, there will be an unintended inventory accumulation or decumulation. For example, if planned household saving is greater than expected by firms when they made their production and investment plans, they will experience an unexpected (and unwanted) increase in their levels of inventories. As noted earlier, however, these inventories are nonetheless considered part of investment spending.

Now let's have a quick look at how it all works for an open economy with a government sector, like modern real-world economies. Here, the private sector (households and firms) saves whenever its income is greater than its consumption. Similarly, the government saves whenever its tax revenue is greater than what it spends on consumption. The total of both these sources of saving is a country's **national saving**. This national saving – which is just total production not consumed – must, by definition, be part of the country's aggregate investment (like Robyn's net). But this is not the only source of saving for aggregate national investment.

National saving A country's total income accruing to its residents less its consumption.

In an open economy, the rest of the world can also contribute some of its saving to further increase a country's aggregate **national investment**. This foreign saving that flows into a country is known as 'foreign investment', and it occurs if foreigners believe they can get a good financial return on their saving by investing in other countries. Thus, for an open economy, a country's aggregate investment can be greater (or less) than its national saving. For example, Australia's is usually greater while Japan's is typically less. The difference is accounted for by the country's external trade with the rest of the world and is referred to as its current account balance. If a country's aggregate investment in some period is greater than its national saving, it will have a negative current account balance. This is called a current account deficit (or CAD).

National investment A country's total spending on capital goods by the private sector and government. If national investment is greater than national saving, then the country will have a current account deficit.

More precisely, a country's **current account balance** is the total of its exports of goods and services less its imports of goods and services and less its net income (dividends and interest payments) paid overseas. (Recall the earlier discussion of GDP versus GNP and refer again to Exhibits 11.5 and 11.6.) Whenever a country's aggregate investment is greater than its own national saving, its current account balance will be negative and so it will have a current account deficit. The size of its CAD therefore records the extent to which its total investment was facilitated by foreign sources.

Current account balance The total value of a country's exports of goods and services less its imports of goods and services and less the net income (interest and dividends) paid overseas.

INFOTRAC®

current account balance

To finance its CAD (investment not funded by its own saving) a country must in return either incur debts to foreigners or else provide them with a share of the ownership of domestic factors of production. The sum of these financing flows is, as was mentioned earlier, called net foreign investment. The breakdown of these flows is provided in the capital account of the balance of payments.

The capital and current accounts of the balance of payments must conceptually exactly offset each other, since the capital account simply reflects the money flow equivalent of the physical goods and services flow on the current account. To understand this, consider a simple analogy. A family-run grocery earns $100 000 in a year and spends $80 000 on its own consumption. Its saving is therefore $20 000. During the year it also invests in three new refrigerators for its business, for $10 000 each. To do this it uses its own $20 000 saving and it borrows $10 000 from a bank. Here we could say the family (analogous to a domestic economy) had aggregate investment of $30 000 but its saving (analogous to the domestic economy's national saving) was only $20 000. Because its aggregate investment exceeded its saving, it has a CAD of $10 000 in the form of one of the three refrigerators. At the same time, it borrowed $10 000 from the bank (analogous to foreign investment) to finance its CAD and so had a capital account surplus of $10 000.

The obverse of a current account deficit is therefore an exactly equal capital account surplus (KAS). In practice, however, measurement errors result in these two accounts failing to balance exactly. Therefore a balancing item is included to achieve the conceptual balance. Exhibit 11.7 presents a breakdown of Australia's balance of payments accounts for the year 2003–04. A more detailed discussion of these matters is presented in Chapter 18.

Changing nominal GDP to real GDP

So far, GDP has been expressed as **nominal GDP**. Nominal GDP is the value of all final goods based on the prices existing during the period of production. Nominal GDP is also referred to as *current dollar or money GDP*. Nominal GDP grows over time not only as a result of increases in output but also as a result of general price rises. In order to get a clearer picture of how much an economy is growing over time, it is necessary to adjust nominal GDP so that it reflects only changes in output and not changes in prices. This adjusted GDP allows meaningful comparisons of aggregate economic activity over time when prices are changing.

Nominal GDP The value of all final goods based on the prices existing during the time period of production.

Measuring the difference between changes in output and changes in the price level involves making an important distinction between nominal GDP and **real GDP**. Real GDP is the value of all final goods and services produced during a given period based on the prices existing in a selected reference year. The Australian Bureau of Statistics currently uses 2002–03 as the reference year. Real GDP is also referred to as *constant-dollar GDP*.

Real GDP The value of all final goods and services produced during a given time period based on the prices existing in a selected reference year.

Exhibit 11.7 **Australia's balance of payments 2003–04**

Current account transactions	Amount (billions of dollars)
Goods	
1 Exports (credits)	109.2
2 Imports (debits)	–132.9
3 Balance on merchandise trade (1 + 2)	–23.7
Services	
4 Exports (credits)	34.0
5 Imports (debits)	–34.4
6 Net services (4 + 5)	–0.4
7 **Balance on goods and services (3 + 6)**	**–24.1**
Foreign income	
8 Credits	15.8
9 Debits	–39.1
10 Net income paid overseas (8 + 9)	–23.3
Transfers	
11 Credits	4.3
12 Debits	–4.3
13 Net transfers (11+12)	0.0
Balance on current account (7 + 10 + 13)	**–47.4**
Capital and financial account transactions	
14 Capital account	1.2
Financial account	
Direct investment	
15 Abroad	–24.4
16 In Australia	9.6
17 Portfolio investment	77.4
18 Financial derivatives	0.9
19 Other investment	–11.3
20 Change in official reserve assets	–5.1
21 **Balance on capital account (14 + … + 20)**	**48.3**
Balancing item	–0.9

Source: Australian Bureau of Statistics, www.abs.gov.au, Cat. No. 5302, Table 1.

The GDP chain price index

GDP chain price index
A measure that compares changes in the prices of all final goods and services during a given period to the prices of those goods and services in a reference year.

The most broadly based measure used to take the changes-in-the-price-level 'air' out of the nominal GDP 'balloon' and compute real GDP is officially called the **GDP chain price index**. The GDP chain price index is a measure that compares changes in the prices of all final goods and services produced during a given period relative to the prices of those goods and services in a reference year. The GDP chain price index is a broad 'deflator' index calculated by a complex chain-weighted geometric series. It is highly inclusive, because it measures not only price changes of consumer goods but also price changes of business investment, government consumption expenditures, exports and imports. Do not confuse the GDP chain price index with the *consumer price index* (CPI), which is widely reported in the news media. The CPI is a different index, measuring only consumer prices, which we will discuss in the chapter on inflation and unemployment.

Now it's time to see how it works. We begin with the following conversion equation:

$$\text{Real GDP} = \frac{\text{nominal GDP} \times 100}{\text{GDP chain price index}}$$

Using 2003–03 as the reference year, suppose you are given the 2003–04 nominal GDP of $810.9 billion and the 2003–04 GDP chain price deflator of 103.48. To calculate 2003–04 real GDP, use the above formula as follows:

$$\text{2003–04 real GDP} = \frac{810.9 \text{ billion}}{103.48} \times 100$$

$$= 783.6 \text{ billion}$$

Exhibit 11.8 shows actual Australian nominal GDP, real GDP and GDP chain price index computations for selected years. Column (1) reports nominal GDP, column (2) gives real GDP figures for these years and column (3) lists corresponding GDP chain price indexes. Notice that the GDP chain price index exceeds 100 in the year after 2002–03. This means that prices, on average, rose from 2002–03, causing the real purchasing power of the

PART 4

Exhibit 11.8 Australian nominal and real GDP

Year	(1) Nominal GDP (billions of dollars)	(2) Real GDP (billions of 2002–03 dollars)	(3) GDP chain price index 2002–03 reference year
1990–91	397.8	498.1	79.9
1991–92	406.6	499.3	81.4
1992–93	426.2	517.6	82.3
1993–94	447.0	537.8	83.1
1994–95	471.3	560.4	84.1
1995–96	502.8	583.9	86.1
1996–97	529.9	606.1	87.4
1997–98	561.2	633.4	88.6
1998–99	592.0	667.0	88.8
1999–00	626.0	692.3	90.4
2000–01	671.1	706.1	95.0
2001–02	714.3	733.6	97.4
2002–03	756.2	756.2	100
2003–04	810.9	783.6	103.5

Source: Australian Bureau of Statistics, www.abs.gov.au, Cat. No. 5206, Table 3.

dollar to fall. In years before 2002–03 the GDP price index is less than 100, which means the real purchasing power of the dollar was higher relative to the 2002–03 reference year. At the reference year of 2002–03, nominal and real GDP are identical and the GDP price index equals 100.

Exhibit 11.9 traces real GDP and nominal GDP for the economy since 1984–85. Note that nominal GDP usually grows faster than real GDP. For example, if we calculate the economy's growth rate in nominal GDP between 1996–97 and 1997–98, the economy's annual growth rate was 5.9 per cent. If instead the calculation is made for real GDP growth between the same years, the growth rate was 4.5 per cent. You must therefore pay attention to which measure of GDP is being used in an analysis.

Exhibit 11.9 Changes in real GDP and nominal GDP, 1984–85 to 2003–04

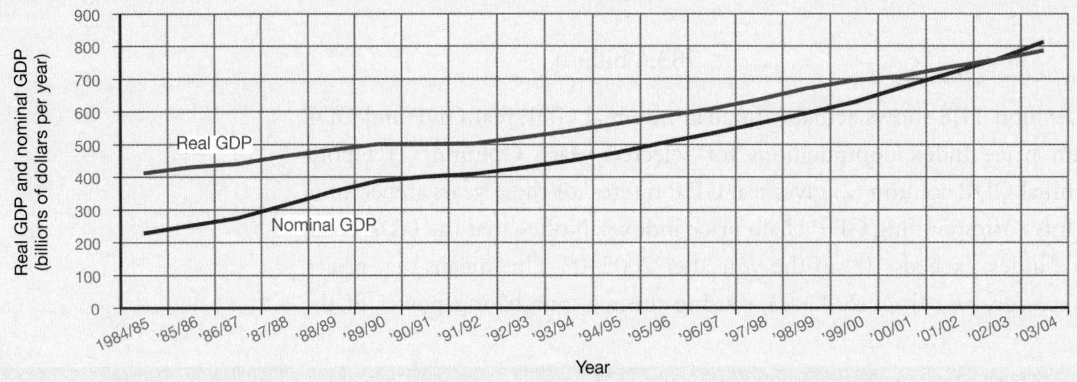

Source: Australian Bureau of Statistics, www.abs.gov.au, Cat. No. 5206, Table 3.

Each year's real GDP reflects output valued at 2002–03 base-year prices, but nominal GDP is annual output valued at prices prevailing during the current year. The intersection of real and nominal GDP occurs in 2002–03 because in the reference year both nominal GDP and real GDP measure the same output at 2002–03 prices. Note that the nominal GDP curve has risen more sharply than the real GDP curve since 1985 as a result of inflation included in the nominal figures.

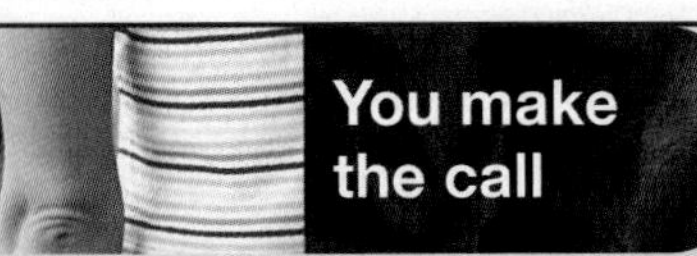

Is the economy up or down?

One person reports, 'GDP rose this year by 9 per cent.' Another says, 'GDP fell by 0.3 per cent.' Can both reports be right?

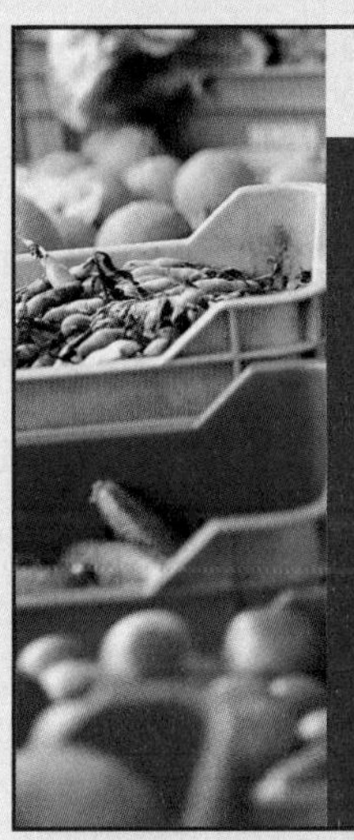

Key concepts

Gross domestic product (GDP)
Gross national product (GNP)
Transfer payment
Final products
Intermediate products
Circular flow model
Flow
Stock
Expenditure approach
Income approach
Indirect business taxes
Net domestic product (NDP)
Domestic factor incomes (DFI)
Net national product (NNP)
Nominal GDP
Real GDP
GDP chain price index
Balance of payments, balance of goods and services
Current account balance
Capital account balance
Saving
Investment – gross and net
Consumption

Summary

- **Gross domestic product** (GDP) is the most widely used measure of a nation's economic performance. GDP is the market value of all **final goods and services** produced within a nation's geographical borders during a period of time regardless of who owns the factors of production. Second-hand and financial transactions are not counted in GDP. To avoid double counting, GDP also does not include **intermediate products**. GDP is calculated by either the expenditure approach or the income approach.

- **Gross national product** (GNP) is the income accruing to a country's residents from the production of all final goods and services during a period of time, no matter where in the world the goods and services are produced.

- The **circular flow model** is a diagram representing the flow of products and resources between businesses and households in exchange for money payments. **Flows** must be distinguished from **stocks**. Flows are measured in units per time period – for example, dollars per year. Stocks are quantities that exist at a given point in time measured in dollars.

Circular flow model

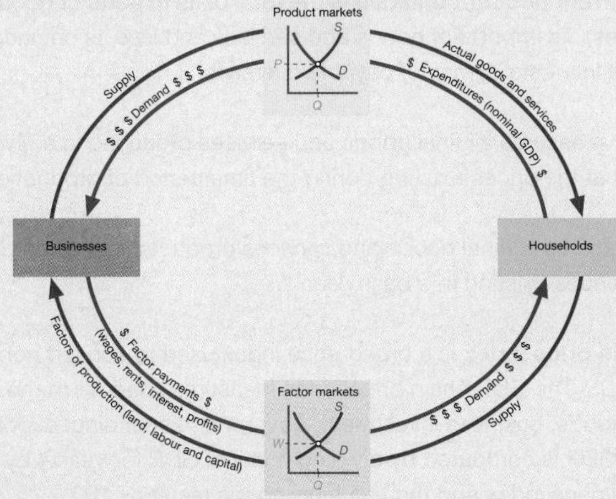

- The **expenditure approach** sums the four major spending components of GDP: consumption, investment, government and net exports. Algebraically, $GDP = C + I + G + (X - M)$, where X equals foreign spending for domestic exports and M equals domestic spending for foreign products.
- **Net domestic product** (NDP) is GDP minus depreciation.
- **Domestic factor incomes** (DFI) is total income *earned* by households domiciled in a country. It is calculated as NDP minus indirect business taxes.
- **Net national product** (NNP) is the total net production accruing to a country's residents. It is calculated as NDP minus net income paid overseas.

Measures of the macro economy

C + I + G + X = GNE + X	Imports of goods and services	Imports of goods and services	Imports of goods and services	Imports of goods and services	Imports of goods and services	Imports of goods and services
	Gross domestic product = C + I + G + (X − M)	Gross domestic product at factor cost	Domestic factor incomes	Net domestic product	Net income paid overseas	Net income paid overseas
					Net national product	Net transfers overseas
						National disposable income
			Indirect taxes less subsidies			
		Indirect taxes less subsidies	Depreciation allowances	Depreciation	Depreciation allowances	Depreciation allowances

- A country's **national saving** is the total of the income accruing to its residents less its consumption. It is equal to its total national investment plus its current account balance.
- A country's **national investment** is the total of its spending on its stock of physical capital by both the private sector and the government.
- A country's **current account balance** is the total of its exports of goods and services less its imports of goods and services and less its net income (dividends and interest payments) payable overseas.
- **Nominal GDP** measures all final goods and services produced in a given period, valued at the prices existing during the time period of production.
- **Real GDP** measures all final goods and services produced in a given period, valued at the prices existing in a base year.
- The **GDP chain price index** is a broad price index used to convert nominal GDP to real GDP. The GDP chain price index measures changes in the prices of consumer goods, business investment, government spending, exports and imports. Real GDP is computed by dividing nominal GDP for year X by year X's GDP chain price index and then multiplying the result by 100.

Study questions and problems

1 Which of the following are final goods or services and which are intermediate goods or services?
  a a haircut purchased from a barber.
  b a new car.
  c car seats purchased by a motor vehicle manufacturer.
  d crude oil.

2 Using the basic circular flow model, explain why the value of businesses' output of goods and services equals the income of households.

3 A small economy produced the following final goods and services during a given month: 3 million kilograms of food, 50 000 shirts, 20 houses, 50 000 hours of medical services, one motor car plant and two tanks. Calculate the value of this output at the following market prices:
  a $1 per kilogram of food.
  b $20 per shirt.
  c $50 000 per house.
  d $20 per hour of medical services.
  e $1 million per motor car plant.
  f $500 000 per tank.

4 An economy produces final goods and services with a market value of $5000 billion in a given year, but only $4500 billion worth of goods and services is sold to domestic or foreign buyers. Is this nation's GDP $5000 billion or $4500 billion? Explain your answer.

5 Explain why a new forklift sold for use in a warehouse is a final good, even though it is fixed investment (capital) used to produce other goods. Is there a double-counting problem if this sale is added to GDP?

6 Explain why the government consumption expenditures component of GDP falls short of actual government expenditures.

7 Explain how net exports affect the Australian economy. Describe both positive and negative impacts on GDP. Why do national income accountants use net exports to compute GDP, rather than simply adding exports to the other expenditure components of GDP?

8 Suppose the following are national accounting data for a given year for some particular country. Calculate GDP, using the expenditure approach.

	Amount (billions of dollars)
Consumption of fixed capital	279
Gross private domestic investment	716
Government consumption expenditures	724
Government investment expenditures	124
Imports	547
Exports	727
Household consumption expenditures	2 966
Indirect taxes less subsidies	370
Net property income paid overseas	328

9 Using the data given in Question 8, compute net domestic product (NDP). Explain why NDP might be a better measure of economic performance than GDP. What is the country's gross national expenditure?

10 Again using the data from Question 8, determine domestic factor income (DFI) by making the required subtractions from GDP. Next, derive the country's gross national product (GNP) and its net national product (NNP). Also, calculate GDP at factor cost. What is the country's current account balance? What is the country's gross national saving?

11 Suppose a country's nominal GDP increases from $5000 billion in 1997 to $5500 billion in 1998. Can you conclude that these figures present a misleading measure of economic growth? What alternative method would provide a more accurate measure of the rate of growth?

12 Which of the following are counted in this year's expenditure-based estimates of GDP? Explain your answer in each case.
  a Flashy Car Company sold a used car.
  b Nancy Wong cooked meals for her family.
  c IBM paid interest on its bonds.
  d Jose Suarez purchased 100 shares of IBM stock.
  e Bob Smith received a welfare payment.
  f Carriage Realty earned a brokerage commission for selling a previously owned house.
  g Air and water pollution increases.
  h Some previously illegal forms of gambling are legalised in all states.

i A retired worker receives a government pension payment.

13 Explain why comparing the GDPs of various nations might not tell you which nation is better off.

Online exercises

Exercise 1

Visit *World Factbook* (**www.odci.gov/cia/publications/factbook**). Select **Australia**. Scroll down to **Economy** and note the GDP composition by sector for Australia. What is your conclusion?

Exercise 2

Review the most recent Parliamentary Statement by the Governor of the Reserve Bank of Australia for a summary of national economic conditions available through the Reserve Bank of Australia at **www.rba.gov.au**. Select **Speeches** on the Home Page and then **Parliamentary Committee Appearances**. Is the economy healthy? Why or why not?

Exercise 3

Go to the Australian Bureau of Statistics at **www.abs.gov.au**. Select **AusStats**, **Publications & Data**, **Time Series Spreadsheets**, **By Catalogue/Subject**, **52. National accounts**, then **5206.0 – Australian National Accounts: National Income, Expenditure and Product**. How much has real GDP changed in the last couple of years listed?

Exercise 4

Go to the Australian Bureau of Statistics (**www.abs.gov.au**), follow the sequence in Exercise 3 and go to Table 43. Note the components of GDP and compare with the text.

Answers to 'You make the call'

How much does Mark add to GDP?

Measuring GDP by the expenditure approach, Mark's output production is worth $20 000 because consumers purchased 4000 pizzas at $5 each. Transfer payments and purchases of goods produced in other years are excluded from GDP. The $3000 in unemployment benefits received and the $1000 spent for a used car are therefore not counted in GDP. Mark's income of $15 000 is also not counted using the expenditure approach. If you said that using the expenditure approach to measure GDP Mark contributes $20 000 to GDP, YOU ARE CORRECT.

Is the economy up or down?

This can happen when nominal GDP rises but real GDP falls, as happens during a recession. It is rare for this to occur in annual data but happens more frequently with quarterly data. An annual example occurred in the Australian economy in 1982–83. Between 1982 and 1983, nominal GDP rose by 7.8 per cent. During the same period, real GDP fell by 2.4 per cent. If you said both reports can be correct because of the difference between nominal and real GDP, YOU ARE CORRECT.

Multiple-choice questions

1 The dollar value of all final goods and services produced within the borders of a nation is the
  a GNP deflator.
  b gross national product.
  c net domestic product.
  d gross domestic product.

2 Based on the circular flow model, money flows from businesses to households in
  a factor markets.
  b product markets.
  c neither factor nor product markets.
  d both factor and product markets.

3 Which of the following is not included in the circular flow model?
  a the quantity of shoes in inventory on 1 January.
  b the total wages paid per month.
  c the percentage of profits paid out as dividends each year.
  d the total profits earned per year in the Norwegian economy.

4 The expenditure approach measures GDP by adding all the expenditures for final goods made by
  a households.
  b businesses.
  c government.
  d foreigners.
  e all of the above.

5 GDP is a less-than-perfect measure of the nation's economic pulse because it
  a excludes non-market transactions.

PART 4

b does not measure the quality of goods and services.

c does not report illegal transactions.

d does all of the above.

6 Subtracting an allowance for depreciation of fixed capital from gross domestic product yields

a real GDP.

b nominal GDP.

c national income.

d net domestic product.

7 Adding all incomes earned by Australian resident households from the sale of resources and after allowing for depreciation on capital gives

a intermediate goods.

b indirect business taxes.

c domestic factor income.

d personal income.

8 Net national product equals net domestic product minus

a personal savings.

b transfer payments.

c dividend payments.

d net property income paid overseas.

9 Gross national expenditure

a includes spending on exports.

b includes transfer payments.

c excludes transfer payments.

d includes imports.

10 Gross domestic product data that reflect actual prices as they exist in a given year are expressed in terms of

a fixed dollars.

b current dollars.

c constant dollars.

d real dollars.

11 The GDP chain price index is

a a measure designed to represent percentage changes in real output.

b a broadly based measure of price changes in the goods and services in GDP.

c adjusted for government spending.

d a measure of changes in consumer prices.

12 Which of the following statements is true?

a The inclusion of intermediate goods and services in GDP calculations would underestimate our nation's production level.

b The expenditure approach sums the compensation of employees, rents, profits, net interest and non-income expenses for depreciation and indirect business taxes.

c Real GDP has been adjusted for changes in the general level of prices due to inflation or deflation.

d Real GDP equals nominal GDP multiplied by the GDP deflator.

12 Business cycles and economic growth

The headline in the morning newspaper reads 'Economy Slumps.' Later in the day, a radio announcer begins the news by saying 'The unemployment rate increased for the fourth consecutive month.' On television, the evening news broadcasts an interview with several economists who predict that the downturn in the business cycle will last for another three months. Next, the Leader of the Opposition appears on the screen and says, 'It's time for change.' These events show that the growth rate of the economy and the state of the business cycle are headline-catching news. Indeed, these measures of macroeconomic instability are important because they affect your future. When real GDP rises and the economy 'booms', jobs are more plentiful. A fall in real GDP means a 'slump' in that the state of the economy is such as to force some firms into bankruptcy and cause workers to lose their jobs. Not being able to find a job when you want one is a painful experience not easily forgotten.

This chapter looks behind the macro economy at a story that touches each of us. It begins by discussing the business cycle. How are the expansions and contractions of business cycles measured? And what creates the business cycle roller coaster? The business cycle – although sometimes very painful – may be considered short-term in nature. The other crucial thing to understand about modern economies is what factors cause them to grow over the longer term and, in particular, why some countries grow more rapidly than others.

In this chapter, you will examine these economics questions:

- What is a recession and what is the difference between a recession and a depression?
- What are the phases of the business cycle?
- What macroeconomic indicators are used to determine the phase of the business cycle and to forecast where it may be headed in the near future?
- Can an economy produce more output than its potential?
- What are the long-term determinants of economic growth and what can governments do to influence a country's long-term rate of economic growth?

The business cycle roller coaster

One central concern of macroeconomics is the upswings and downswings in the level of real output that make up the **business cycle**. The business cycle is alternating periods of economic growth and contraction. Business cycles are inherent in market economies. A key indication of cycles is the rise and fall in real GDP. These rises and falls are mirrored in other key measures of the macro economy such as employment growth, the rate of unemployment, retail sales and industrial production growth. For instance, in a downturn we would see a drop in real GDP, industrial production, sales and employment, with unemployment rising. For the sake of simplicity of exposition, here we will use real GDP as a proxy for the business cycle. However, remember that this is only for expositional purposes; in reality, downturns and upturns in the business cycle are more than just fluctuations in real GDP. Also recall from the previous chapter that changes in real GDP measure changes in the value of national output while ignoring changes in the price level.

Business cycle Alternating periods of economic growth and contraction, which can be dated by changes in output, income, sales and employment measures.

business cycle

PART 4

The four phases of the business cycle

Although it is an over-simplification, it is useful to represent the long-term growth in a modern economy as following a fairly smooth (let's say, for argument's sake, a straight line) growth path. What we call the business cycle is the succession of short-run fluctuations around this long-term trend. Exhibit 12.1(a) illustrates a highly stylised theoretical business cycle. Although real-world business cycles vary in duration and intensity, each cycle can be divided into four phases: **peak**, **recession**, **trough** and **expansion**. The business cycle looks like a roller coaster. It begins at a peak, drops to a bottom, climbs steeply, begins to level out and then reaches another peak. Once the trough is reached, the upswing starts again. Although forecasters cannot precisely predict the timing of the phases of a cycle, the economy is always operating in one of these phases. Over time, there has also been a fairly smooth long-term upward trend, despite shorter-term cyclical fluctuations around the long-run trend.

Peak The phase of the business cycle during which the economy reaches its maximum after rising during an expansion.

Recession A downturn in the business cycle during which output, sales and employment decline.

Trough The phase of the business cycle in which the economy reaches its cyclical minimum after falling during a recession.

Expansion An upturn in the business cycle during which real GDP, employment and other measures of aggregate economic activity rise.

Two *peaks* are illustrated in Exhibit 12.1(a). At each of these peaks, the economy would be close to or at full employment. (The concept of full employment is discussed in more detail in the next chapter.) That is, as explained in Chapter 2, the economy is operating near its production possibilities frontier and real GDP is at its highest level relative to recent years. A macro setback, called a *recession* or *contraction*, follows each peak. A recession is a downturn in the business cycle during which real GDP (and other measures of aggregate economic activity) declines. During a recession, the economy is functioning inside its production possibilities frontier. The ABS and the Reserve Bank of Australia usually consider a recession to be at least two consecutive quarters (six months) in which there is a decline in real GDP. In general, during a prolonged recession consumer demand drops significantly, business profits fall, the percentage of the workforce without jobs rises and production capacity is under-utilised.

PART 4

Visit the Melbourne Institute (**www.ecom.unimelb.edu.au**) and the National Bureau of Economic Research (**www.nber.org/cycles.html**) for a history of Australian and US business cycle expansions and contractions respectively.

The *trough* is the point where the level of real GDP 'bottoms out'. At the trough, unemployment and idle productive capacity are at their highest levels relative to recent years. The length of time between the peak and the trough is the duration of the recession. Since the end of World War II, recessions in Australia have averaged about 15 months. However, as shown in Exhibit 12.2, the last recession lasted over two years – from April 1990 to June 1992. The percentage decline in real GDP was 1.9 per cent and the national unemployment rate hit a peak rate of 11.2 per cent in 1992.

What is the difference between *recession* and *depression*? There is an old saying: 'A recession is when your neighbour loses his or her job and a depression is when you lose your job!' This one-liner is close to the true distinction between these two concepts. As explained earlier, economists use 'recession' to refer to any decline in the business cycle lasting at least six months, so why not use the term 'Great Recession' for the contraction of 1929–33? Because no subsequent recession has approached the prolonged severity of the Great Depression, the term 'depression' is primarily a historical reference to the extremely deep and long recession of the early 1930s. Nevertheless, the recession in Australia in the early 1990s was certainly the most severe experienced in this country since World War II. The Great Depression is discussed again in the next chapter and in the chapter on monetary policy.

Exhibit 12.1 **Hypothetical and actual business cycles**

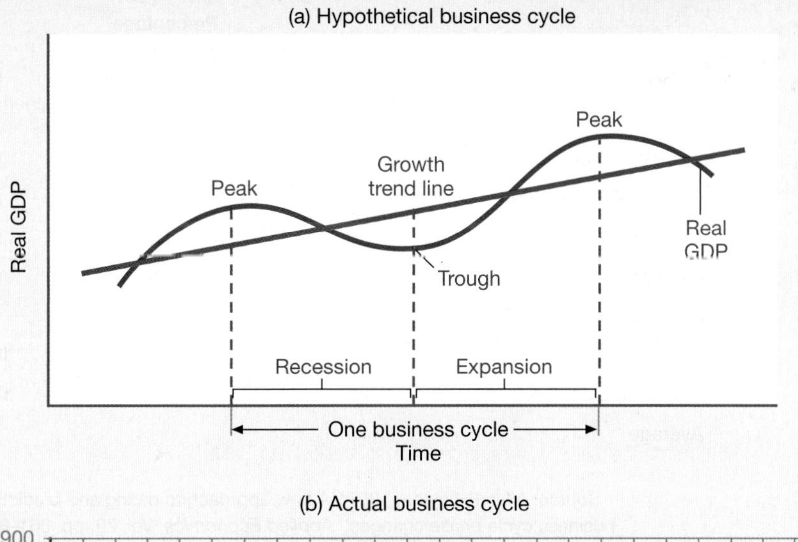

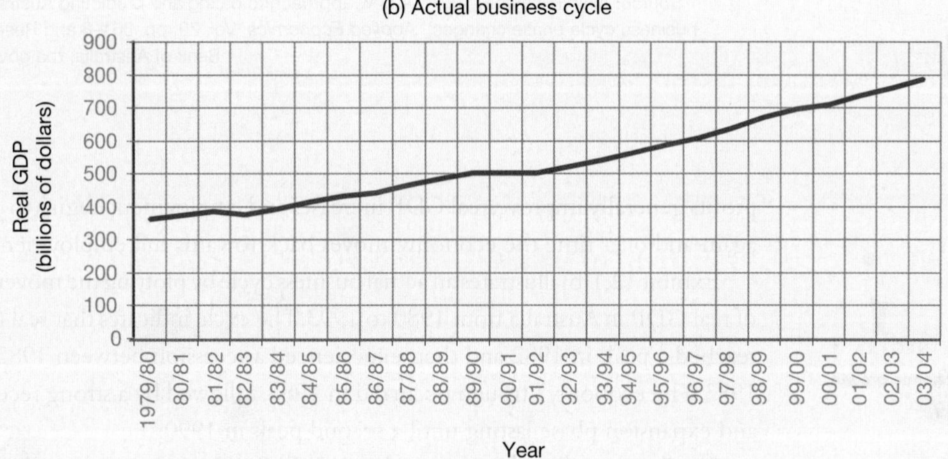

Part (a) illustrates a hypothetical business cycle consisting of four phases: peak, recession, trough and expansion. These fluctuations of real GDP can be measured by a growth trend line, which shows that over time real GDP has trended upward. In reality, the fluctuations are not so clearly defined as those in this graph.

Part (b) illustrates actual ups and downs of the business cycle. The Australian economy was experiencing an upswing in 1981. After a recession during 1982–83, a strong upswing continued until another recession during 1990–92.

Source for (b): Australian Bureau of Statistics, Cat. No. 5206, Table 3.

The trough is bad news and good news. It is simultaneously the bottom of the 'valley' of the downturn and the foot of the 'hill' of improving economic conditions called an *expansion*. Expansion is an upturn in the business cycle during which real GDP rises, sometimes quite rapidly, in the early quarters immediately following a trough. During the expansion phase of the cycle,

Exhibit 12.2 **Severity of post-war recessions in Australia**

Recession dates (peak–trough)	Duration (months)	Percentage change in GDP (from peak to trough)	Peak unemployment
Apr. 1951–Sep. 1952	17	n/a	n/a
Dec. 1955–Aug. 1956	8	n/a	n/a
Dec. 1960–Sep. 1961	9	−3.3	n/a
Jul. 1974–Mar. 1975	8	−3.5	n/a
Aug. 1976–Nov. 1977	15	−0.8	6.7
Sep. 1981–May 1983	20	−3.8	10.4
Apr. 1990–Jun. 1992	26	−1.9	11.2
Average	15		

Source: Allan P. Layton, 1997, 'A new approach to dating and predicting Australian business cycle phase changes', *Applied Economics*, Vol. 29, pp. 861–8 and Reserve Bank of Australia, rba.gov.au.

profits generally improve, real GDP increases and employment begins to grow again and over time the economy moves back towards full employment.

economic growth

Exhibit 12.1(b) illustrates an actual business cycle by plotting the movement of real GDP in Australia from 1980 to 1993. The cycle indicates that real GDP reached a peak in 1982 and then experienced a recession between 1982 and 1983. The economy's trough occurred in 1983, followed by a strong recovery and expansion phase lasting until a second peak in 1990.

Economic growth
An expansion in national output measured by the annual percentage increase in a nation's real GDP.

Finally, we will expand upon the definition of **economic growth** given in Chapter 2. Economic growth is an expansion in national output measured by the annual percentage increase in a nation's real GDP. The growth trend line in the hypothetical model in Exhibit 12.1(a) represents the fact that over time our real GDP tends to rise. This general, long-term upward trend in real GDP persists in spite of the peaks, recessions, troughs and expansions. As shown by the dashed line in Exhibit 12.3, since 1960 real GDP in Australia has grown at an average annual rate of about 4 per cent. This may seem to be a small annual change, but about 4 per cent annual growth will lead to a doubling of real GDP in only 18 years. One of our challenging ongoing economic policy goals is to maintain that long-term growth rate at around 4 per cent per annum.

Information on Australia's economic growth can be obtained from the Australian Bureau of Statistics (**www.abs.gov.au**) or the Reserve Bank of Australia (**www.rba.gov.au**).

We value economic growth as one of our nation's economic goals because it increases our standard of living – it creates a bigger 'economic pie'.

PART 4

Exhibit 12.3 **A historical record of business cycles in Australia since 1959–60**

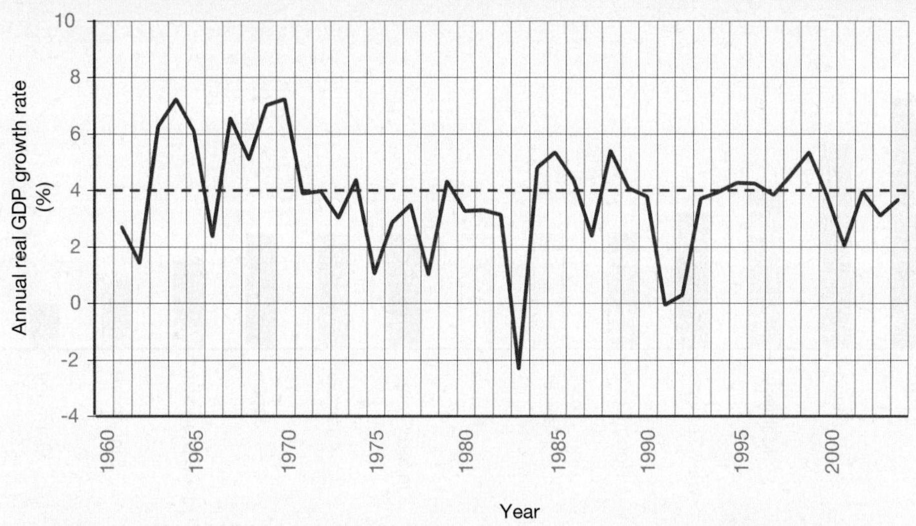

Real GDP has increased at an average annual growth rate of 4 per cent since 1959–60. Above-average annual growth rates alternated with below-average annual growth rates. During a recession year, such as 1990–91, the annual growth rate is negative and therefore below the zero growth line. The economy entered the recovery phase in 1991–92 and the growth rate reached 4.5 per cent in 1994–95 before falling to 3.6 per cent in 1996–97. In 2003–04, the growth rate was above 3.5 per cent and the economy completed its 13th year of expansion, the longest in the post World War II era.

Source: data calculated from Australian Bureau of Statistics, Cat. No. 5206, Table 3.

An examination of Exhibit 12.3 reveals that the growth path of the Australian economy over time is not smooth, but consists instead of a series of year-to-year variations in real GDP growth. In some years, such as 1998 and 1999, the economy experienced above-average growth. In other years, such as 1983, the economy slipped below the zero growth line. Note that the annual growth for the 1991–92 recession year was also negative and therefore dipped below the zero growth line. However, the economy entered the recovery phase in late 1992 and the annual growth rate had reached 4.5 per cent in 1995 before dropping back to 3.6 per cent in 1997. In 2003–04, the growth rate was again around 4 per cent (3.63%) and had been around 4 per cent or higher for the majority of the years since 1992–93.

Real GDP growth rates in a selection of countries

Exhibit 12.4 presents real GDP growth rates for selected countries in 2003: Australia, the United States, the United Kingdom, Germany, Japan, New Zealand, Malaysia, the Philippines, Taiwan, Korea, Singapore, Hong Kong and Thailand. As the exhibit shows, by 2003 (in fact by 1999) most East Asian economies had recovered from the 1997–98 economic and financial crises.

Exhibit 12.4 **Real GDP growth rates in 2003, selected countries**

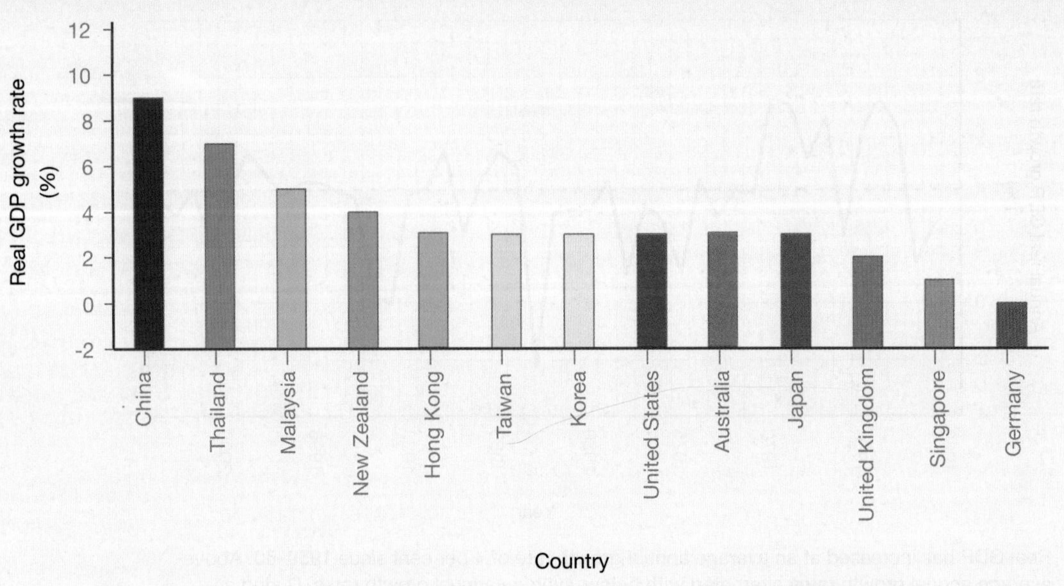

Source: Central Intelligence Agency, www.odci.gov.

Where are we on the business cycle roller coaster?

Suppose the economy has been in a recession and everyone is asking when it will recover. To find an answer to the state of the economy's health, a television reporter interviews Terence Asaud, a local car dealer. Asaud says, 'I do not see any recovery. This year our second quarter sales were down on the first quarter. In the third and fourth quarters we then sold a lot more cars than in the second quarter, but sales in both these two quarters are still down on what they were in the same quarters last year.' Is Mr Asaud correct? Are his observations consistent with the peak, recession, trough or expansion phase of the business cycle?

A wealth of economic information can be obtained from the website of the Central Intelligence Agency (**www.odci.gov**).

Business cycle indicators

In addition to changes in real GDP, the media often report several other macroeconomic variables published by the ABS and other agencies that measure business activity. These economic *indicator* variables are usually classified into three categories: leading indicators, coincident indicators and lagging indicators. While the third set is mentioned in the discussion below, they are not often referred to these days and so a detailed list is not provided here. Exhibit 12.5 lists the variables corresponding to each of the other sets of indicators.

Exhibit 12.5 Business cycle indicators for Australia

Leading indicators
Average work week
New businesses formed as proxied by net demand for new telephone installations
New building approvals
Material prices
Stock prices
Money supply, M3
Gross operating surplus of companies
A macroeconomic measure of price mark-up: the ratio of the GDP deflator to unit labour costs
Coincident indicators
Unemployment rate (inverted)
Total civilian employment
Household income
Industrial production
Retail sales
Gross domestic non-farm product

One highly monitored forecasting gauge for business cycles is the *index of leading indicators,* published monthly by the Melbourne Institute of Applied Economic and Social Research. **Leading indicators** are variables that change direction before the economy shifts from one phase into another (say, from an expansion into a recession). This index captures the headlines when there is concern over swings in the economy. The first set of variables in Exhibit 12.5 is used to forecast the business cycle about six months in advance. For example, a downturn ahead is signalled when declines exceed advances in the components of the leading indicators data series. But beware! The leading indicators may rise for a couple of consecutive months and then fall for several. Economists are therefore cautious and wait for the leading indicators to move in a new direction for several months before forecasting a change in the cycle.

INFOTRAC®
leading indicators

Leading indicators Variables that change direction before the economy shifts from one business cycle phase into another.

INFOTRAC®
goals of macroeconomic policy

Goals of macroeconomic policy These are to reduce the severity of the ups and downs of the business cycle and to assist with the achievement of the highest possible sustainable economic growth trajectory consistent with the economic, social and cultural aspirations of the community.

Goals of macroeconomic policy are used to reduce the severity of the ups and downs of the business cycle and to assist with the achievement of the highest possible sustainable economic growth trajectory consistent with the economic, social and cultural aspirations of the community.

The second group of variables listed in Exhibit 12.5 are referred to as **coincident indicators**. Coincident indicators are variables that change at the same time as the economy shifts from one phase into another. For example, as real GDP rises economists expect employment, personal income, industrial production and sales to rise, while the unemployment rate usually falls.

Coincident indicators Variables that change at about the same time as the economy shifts from one business cycle phase into another.

Lagging indicators Variables that change after a phase change in the economy has occurred.

Information on Australia's indexes of coincident and leading indicators can be obtained from the Melbourne Institute (**www.ecom.unimelb.edu.au**).

The third group of variables sometimes used in analyses of the business cycle are the so-called **lagging indicators**. Lagging indicators are variables that change direction after real GDP changes. For example, the duration of unemployment is a lagging indicator. As real GDP increases, the average time that workers remain unemployed does not fall until some months after the beginning of the recovery. The prime interest rate (the rate charged by banks on business loans to their best corporate customers) is another example. As noted above, in practice lagging indicators are not used extensively these days and so a comprehensive list is not supplied in Exhibit 12.5.

Total spending and the business cycle

The uneven historical pattern of economic growth for the Australian economy gives rise to the question: what causes business cycles? The theory generally accepted by economists today is that changes in total or aggregate expenditures (also referred to as aggregate demand) are the principal cause of variations in real GDP. However, as will be explained later, business cycles can also be caused by shocks to so-called aggregate supply. For now, think of aggregate supply as a kind of amalgam of all the nation's microeconomic production and cost functions. A major shock to these – for example, as occurred in 1973–74 when the world price of oil quadrupled in less than a year – can throw the economy into disequilibrium and cause a recession.

Recall from the previous chapter that aggregate expenditures refer to total spending for *final products* by households, businesses, government and foreign buyers. Expressed as a formula:

$$\text{GDP} = C + I + G + (X - M)$$

Why do changes in total spending cause the level of GDP to change? Stated simply, if total spending increases, businesses may find it profitable to increase output. When firms increase production they use more land, labour and capital. Hence, increased spending leads to economic growth in output, employment and incomes. When total spending falls, businesses will find it profitable to produce a lower volume of goods and avoid unsold inventory accumulation. In this case, output, employment and incomes fall. These cutbacks can in turn lead to recession.

The situation described above assumes that the economy is operating below full employment so that any changes in total spending bring forth changes in the supply of goods and services to the market. Once the economy reaches full employment, increases in total spending have no impact on real GDP. Further spending in this case will simply pull up the price level and 'inflate' nominal GDP, resulting in higher inflation.

In subsequent chapters, much more will be explained about the causes of business cycles. Using the aggregate demand and supply analytical framework described in Chapter 14, you will learn to ascertain why changes occur in national output, unemployment and the price level. Understanding the nature and determinants of the business cycle and the extent to which government policies can reduce its severity is the first major concern of macroeconomics.

The GDP gap

When people in an economy would like to have a job but are unemployed, society forfeits the production of goods and services that such people could have helped produce. To determine the dollar value of how much society loses if the economy fails to reach full employment (see the next chapter for a more detailed discussion of unemployment), economists estimate the **GDP gap**. The GDP gap is the difference between full-employment real GDP and actual real GDP in a particular period. Full employment does not literally mean an unemployment rate of zero. In a dynamic economy, with changing tastes and technology, there will always be some level of measured unemployment while people, having left their current employment, find suitable alternative employment. More will be said on this in the next chapter.

GDP gap The difference between full-employment real GDP and actual real GDP.

The level of GDP that could be produced at full employment is also called *potential real GDP*. Because the GDP gap is estimated on the basis of the difference between GDP at full employment and GDP at the actual unemployment rate, the GDP gap measures the cost of what is known as *cyclical unemployment*. Expressed as a formula:

$$\text{GDP gap} = \text{potential real GDP} - \text{actual real GDP}$$

PART 4

The gap between actual and potential real GDP measures the opportunity cost to the nation of reduced production of real goods and services from operating at less than full employment.

Economic growth in the longer term

In the preceding discussion we indicated that, over short time horizons, real GDP may deviate from its long-term growth path as a result of shocks to aggregate demand. Such shocks may result in real GDP being above or below its long-term growth path for sometimes quite long periods of time (sometimes even several years). In the longer term, though, it is generally believed that an economy will revert to some underlying long-term growth path. This long-term growth path can vary considerably in different countries and, over time, these different trajectories can have a very significant impact on living standards in those countries. For instance, an annual per capita growth in real GDP of 3 per cent results in a doubling of living standards every 25 years (or, say, each generation), while a 5 per cent growth rate will result in more than a trebling over such a time frame.

A second central concern in macroeconomics, therefore, is to understand the underlying determinants of economic growth and whether government policies may be able to influence an economy's growth trajectory.

In Exhibit 12.6, changes in real GDP per capita over long periods of time are provided for a range of countries. Real GDP per capita (per person) is a commonly used international measure of changing income levels per person and, despite the limitations of GDP mentioned in the last chapter, it is nevertheless a useful way of comparing changes in living standards around the world. Looking at these data, a number of questions will immediately come to mind. Why did Japan's real GDP per person increase almost twenty-fold over the 100 years from 1890 to 1990 while other countries – like India and Bangladesh – experienced almost no growth in real income per person over similarly long periods of time? Of the countries listed, why did Australia have the highest real income per person in the late nineteenth century – higher even than in the United States – but then subsequently slip down the rankings? And why does the United States now have the highest real income per person of all the countries listed?

Furthermore, over the last 15–20 years the world has witnessed the strong and sustained economic growth of the Asian Tigers (South Korea, Taiwan, Hong Kong and Singapore), which continued largely uninterrupted from the 1960s through until the Asian financial crisis of 1997–98. And again, since 1999 these countries' economic performance has continued at a fast albeit less spectacular pace than it did prior to 1997–98. Finally, possibly the most

Exhibit 12.6 A variety of growth experiences

Country	Period	Real GDP per person at beginning of period* $	Real GDP per person at end of period* $	Growth rate (per year) %
Japan	1890–1990	842	16 144	3.00
Brazil	1900–1987	436	3 417	2.39
West Germany	1870–1990	1 223	14 288	2.07
United States	1870–1990	2 244	18 258	1.76
China	1900–1987	401	1 748	1.71
United Kingdom	1870–1990	2 693	13 589	1.36
Australia	1870–1990	3 143	13 514	1.22
Thailand	1900–1987	626	2 294	1.09
Indonesia	1900–1987	499	1 200	1.01
India	1900–1987	378	662	0.65
Bangladesh	1900–1987	349	375	0.08

*Real GDP is measured in 1985 dollars.

Source: amended from *Principles of Macroeconomics* by Robin Stonecash, Joshua Gans, Stephen King & Gregory Mankiw, Harcourt, 1997, p. 171.

notable and most impressive economic growth performance of all since the 1970s has been that of China. Incredibly, China's production of real GDP per capita per year has grown more than 500 per cent since 1980, implying that, in just one generation, economic living standards in China have improved more than five-fold. What might be the explanation for these growth performances? All these questions lead us to try to understand what the important factors are that drive a country's long-term economic growth.

The most significant early contribution to an understanding of economic growth was made by **Robert Solow**. In 1987 Solow won the Nobel Prize in Economics for his contributions to growth theory. His first significant article was 'A contribution to the theory of economic growth'.[1] A very recent book by David Weil,[2] *Economic Growth*, provides excellent foundation reading on the topic, while a more mathematical treatment of growth theory is provided in *Macroeconomics* by N. Gregory Mankiw.[3] The growth discussion that follows below borrows somewhat from both Weil's and Mankiw's presentations.

Solow growth model
An early growth model that sought to explain how consumption, saving, capital, labour and technological change combine in the longer term to determine a nation's economic growth. In the Solow model, technological change is assumed to be exogenous.

At the most basic level, a country's economy grows over time as a result of growth in both demand and supply. In what follows, we will consider demand and supply separately, but you should remember that at each point in time it is the interaction of these forces that determines the quantity of output produced, consumed, saved and invested. Over the longer term a community's demand for goods and services cannot outstrip its productive capacity and equally, without sufficient increase in demand, there will be no incentive for an increase to occur in the productive capacity of the country.

The determinants of growth

Let's consider the supply side first. Fundamentally, output growth is the result of increases over time in the factor inputs of land (productive land), labour and capital – combined with improvements in technology – into the production process. For the purposes of simplifying our discussion below, we will refer to the non-labour production factor inputs collectively as simply 'production factors'. Now recall the concept of the production function introduced in Chapter 6 and imagine, for argument's sake, that all of a country's many separate existing production processes were represented by just one stylised aggregate production function, as illustrated by Exhibit 12.7.

The aggregate production function of Exhibit 12.7(a) indicates that, as the quantity of production factors per worker increases, the output per worker of the country increases, but at a decreasing rate. This is just the law of diminishing marginal productivity in action again, which you first read about in Chapter 6. (If necessary, refer back to that discussion for a refresher.) Now consider the impact of a wide-ranging improvement in production

1 *Quarterly Journal of Economics*, 1956, pp. 65–94.
2 Published by Addison-Wesley, 2005.
3 Published by Worth, 2000

Exhibit 12.7 Stylised aggregate production functions for a country

(a) A stylised aggregate production function for a country with a given production technology

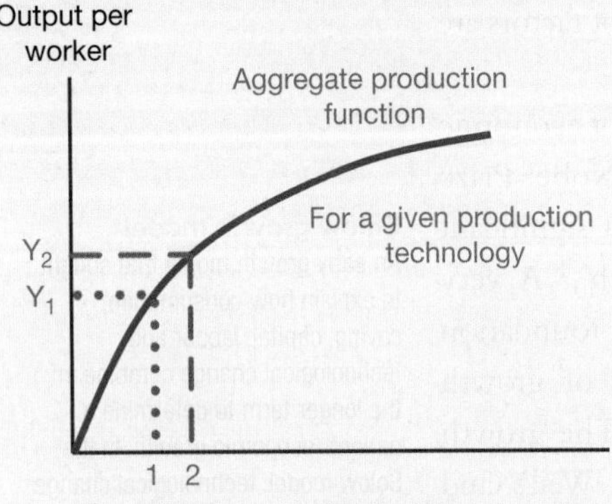

(b) Two stylised aggregate production functions for a country – technological progress

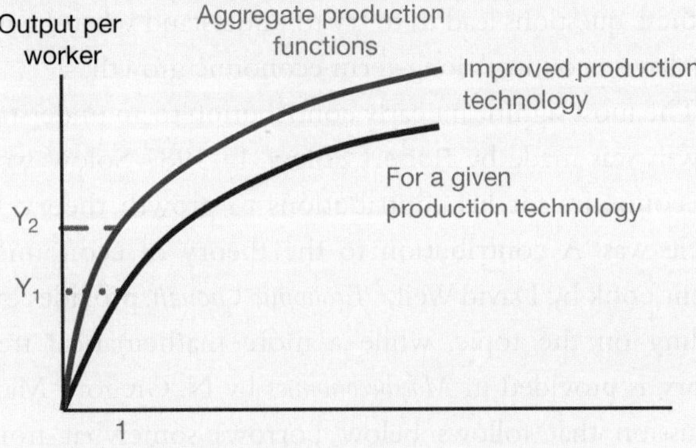

(c) Possible sources of differences in output per worker across countries

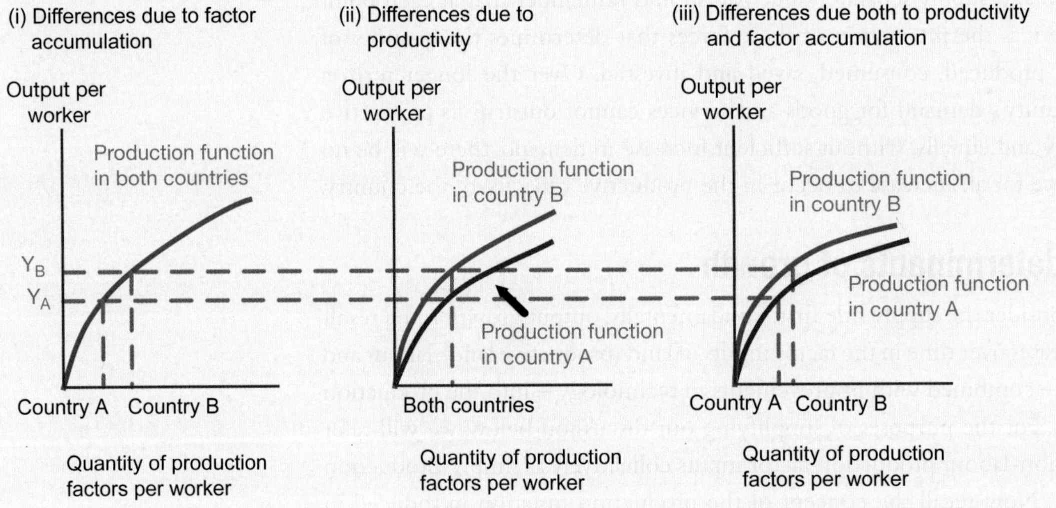

Source: adapted from David N. Weil, *Economic Growth* (Addison-Wesley, USA, 2005) pp. 34–5.

technologies available in the country, which allowed any given quantity of production factors to be used more productively by the workforce to produce higher levels of output per worker. This is illustrated in Exhibit 12.7(b) by an upward shift in the aggregate production function.

Exhibits 12.7(a) and (b) illustrate a simple yet very powerful point. A country may enjoy a higher level of output per worker – or, in the language of the earlier discussion, a higher level of real GDP per person – by either somehow increasing the quantity of production factors available to the workforce or by improving its available production technologies. This logic also applies when we think about different countries. One country may be experiencing a higher level of real GDP per capita than another, either because its workforce has a greater quantity of production factors available to it per worker, or because its production technologies allow it to be more productive in the use of its production factors, or because of a combination of both these determinants.

This is illustrated in Exhibit 12.7(c). In each case, country B is experiencing higher output per worker (real GDP per person). In the first panel, both countries are using the same production technologies. However, country B has the higher output per worker because each of its workers has a higher quantity of production factors available to use. In the second panel, both countries' workers have the same quantity of production factors available to them, but country B has superior production technologies. In the third panel, a combination of these two determinants contributes to country B enjoying a higher level of output per worker than country A. In fact, it is this third case of superior production technologies plus a greater quantity of production factors per worker that would be the most common explanation for one country's higher per capita GDP in comparison to that of another.

So far we have been talking in this section about the factors that influence the level of output per person in a country. However, our introductory discussion was all in terms of growth rates over time in output per person in different countries! Of course, it is just the same two determinants as described above that influence the growth in a country's output per person. A country will experience such growth if it *either*: increases its quantity of production factors per worker; *or* improves its production technologies so that its workforce becomes more productive; *or* if it experiences a combination of these two influences. Following on from this, therefore, countries that have recorded relatively higher growth over time in output per person than others have either been able to more rapidly accumulate the quantity of production factors per worker than other countries, or been able to increase the productivity of their production technologies more rapidly than others, or some combination of the two.

This being the case, one is naturally led to ask how a country might increase the quantity of production factors available to each worker and/or improve its production technologies. Let's take the first issue first. We will discuss technology in the following subsection.

Production factor accumulation and the 'Golden Rule'

The quantum of production factors available to workers boils down to the amount of (economic) investment per person a country is making and this leads inevitably to a consideration of the other side of the economic growth equation, viz. demand. Fundamentally, a nation's output is ultimately either consumed or used for investment. The output not consumed is the saving of the inhabitants, which in turn allows for the investment undertaken by firms. As explained briefly in the previous chapter, a nation can augment its investment by also utilising the saving of foreigners. However, for our purposes at the moment, we can abstract from this consideration since the essential ideas discussed here are applicable to the more complex (but more realistic) situation also.

Thus, it is saving by the country's inhabitants that is one very crucial determinant of the quantity of investment possible in the economy and it is this investment that maintains and adds to the available quantity of non-labour production factors per capita. Higher levels of saving per person imply higher levels of investment per person, a larger quantity of production factors per person, and therefore higher levels of output per person.

A natural question then to ask is whether there is one unique level of saving per capita that is optimal, 'optimality' here being defined as the saving rate that would allow the community to maximise its consumption over time. Since saving is just forgone present consumption, the only motivation for saving is, after all, to be able to enjoy a higher standard of living in the future. (Remember Robyn Crusoe from the last chapter.)

Intuitively, as mentioned above, we could say that a higher saving rate in the community will allow a higher quantity of production factors, which will allow for a higher level of output. What saving rate is optimal? Obviously it is not zero (otherwise, for example, the nation's capital stock would eventually wear down to zero through depreciation), nor could it possibly be 100 per cent (that is, no consumption at all!) but what criterion could we use to decide on the optimal rate? This is actually quite important, because policy makers have a range of policy measures at their disposal, which they can use to influence the community's rate of saving.

The 'Golden Rule' steady-state quantity of production factors per capita The quantity of production factors per capita – and associated saving rate – that results in the maximum level of consumption per capita in the long-run steady state.

The so-called **'Golden Rule' quantity of production factors per capita**, which in turn will imply an optimal saving rate, will be determined by the following consideration: the larger the economy's total quantity of non-labour production factors – say capital, for example – the larger will be the amount wearing out each period through depreciation. Therefore, in order to maintain a higher stock of non-labour production factors in the economy, a higher level of output will be needed each period just to cover for the higher depreciation. This implies higher gross investment per period, which will in turn require a higher level of saving per capita each period. Of course, with a higher capital stock, the community will also be able to produce more output and so the community's consumption per capita could well be higher as well, thereby leaving the community better off.

However, there is a limit to how much to increase the quantity of production factors per capita. This is because, with fixed production technologies, diminishing marginal productivity means that the increase in output made possible by a larger stock of production factors reduces as the stock is increased (recall the shape of the production functions in Exhibit 12.7). A point will therefore be reached where the extra saving per capita needed out of the higher output simply to cover the depreciation in production factors will be such as to leave the community with less consumption per capita. At that point, no further increases in the saving rate would be rational.

The point at which consumption per capita cannot be made any larger is called the 'Golden Rule' level of saving. Beyond this point, the extra output produced by even more saving and investment by the community is simply being used to maintain the higher stock of production factors with no extra output available for extra consumption. If consumption is what the inhabitants of the community are interested in, then the extra saving is of no value to them. They would be better off with a lower saving rate!

It is important to understand that an economy left to its own devices may not necessarily gravitate towards the 'Golden Rule' saving rate. This is an example where there may be a role for a policy maker to put in place suitable incentives to bring about the necessary transition. However, the task may not be an easy one for the policy maker, particularly if what is required is a lifting in the saving rate.

In this case, while in the longer term the community may well be better off in terms of higher ongoing consumption per capita, in the short term the community will have to give up current consumption. The situation is complicated even further when it is recognised that the future beneficiaries of the short-term sacrifices may be quite different from the group making the consumption sacrifice. If the policy maker depends for his or her survival – say through the ballot box – on the support of the current community group, then bringing about the required lifting of the saving rate may be very difficult politically. Some of the less developed countries in Asia and the Indian subcontinent could be thought of as examples of this type of situation.

It should be noted that no such problem should exist if what is required is a movement to a lower saving rate. Given Japan's very high saving rate over many decades last century, it may well be an example of a country in this type of situation. In the long term the level of consumption per capita in such a country would be higher with a lower saving rate, since the country was above its 'Golden Rule' saving rate, which implies that the community was initially saving 'too much'. However, not only will future consumption per capita be higher as a result of this transition, but it would also involve an immediate short-term increase in consumption as well. Theoretically, few political skills would be required in this type of situation.

International focus

Applicable concept: economic growth and government policies

Tried and true way to economic growth

The following is an edited version of an article that appeared in the *Australian Financial Review*.

Wolfgang Kasper says that good institutional rules make for prosperous nations.

The Heritage Foundation in Washington recently published its economic freedom ratings for 2002, with Australia ranking 14th – that is, behind the economic high-flyers who set world-best institutional standards, but well ahead of the interventionist and sclerotic welfare states of western Europe.

But the Heritage report also adds convincing evidence to a new theory of economic growth, namely that 'it's the traffic rules and the institutions, stupid, that make for poverty or prosperity!'

The same conclusion emerges from weighty new empirical research by two American researchers, John Talbot and Richard Roll of the University of California. All this has forceful implications for economic policy.

Their research has shown that 85 per cent of all differences between the poorest and richest societies – from $US440 (A$853.98) per capita annual income in Sierra Leone to more than $US41,000 (A$79,500) in Luxembourg – can be explained by differences in the protection of private property, civil liberties, political and press freedom, as well as the absence of black markets, discriminatory regulations, inflation and barriers to free trade. Liberal economic reforms and the assertion of basic economic freedom have invariably boosted economic growth, as well as high employment, a reduction in poverty and improvements on many other social fronts.

Postwar economic reforms in Germany and Japan, subsequent improvements in economic freedom in East Asia, even the People's Republic of China and more recent reforms in countries such as Australia have been rewarded by economic prosperity.

Only economists who disregard institutions could call these episodes 'economic miracles' – that is, outcomes that cannot be rationally explained. Interest groups that seek and extract political favours, parliaments and judges that grant them and politicians that distribute opportunistic handouts have to be seen as the main enemies of broad-based prosperity.

The research confirms what common sense and some economic theories have asserted all along. Prosperity and all its benefits depend on

PART 4

the division of labour and the effectiveness of co-ordinating millions of specialised producers. If these are made to compete, time and again and can do so with trust in simple, reliably enforced 'traffic rules', they will result in a genuine knowledge nation and offer bountiful economic opportunity: growth and high employment for most.

[One] implication for national policy makers … is to make foreign aid conditional on institutional reform. With economic reforms that implement high standards of economic freedom, a good investment climate will be ensured and 'the investment dollars will magically appear', as Roll and Talbot put it, so that aid becomes superfluous.

Another policy implication of the new growth theory has to do with the fact that prosperity is not driven by what many economists have asserted; that is, a high investment rate, high spending on research and development or a big share of foreign trade. These are proximate causes of growth.

In fact, government policies that promote investment or R & D by artificial means target superficial symptoms and induce a waste of resources on lousy projects. Even worse, they introduce favouritism and detract from the equality of all before the law. Over time, governments thus erode genuine economic freedom and weaken the spontaneous growth potential. The Australian Government should not favour research and development spending by big firms over other costs that producers incur. The mercantilistic promotion of exports and the maintenance of the costly Austrade bureaucracy [the government agency created to facilitate Australian exports], which the Productivity Commission has rightly lambasted for its ineffectiveness, aim tax dollars at tokenism and detract from basic freedom and equality.

The research by the Heritage Foundation, the (Canadian) Fraser Institute and a rapidly growing network of researchers that look at the fundamental institutions of economic freedom and genuine economic reforms is rapidly changing the policy scene overseas. It will eventually trickle down to Canberra and State capitals. The question is: with what time lag? And will the electorate accept the lessons?

Wolfgang Kasper is a senior fellow at the Sydney-based Centre for Independent Studies.

Source: *Australian Financial Review*, Thursday, 6 December 2001, p. 55.

Analyse the issue

Kasper is a prominent Australian economist. Here he expresses quite strong views about the role of government in assisting the economic development of nations. Analyse the ideas in this article in the context of the text's discussion of growth theory. If you disagree with him, outline the basis of your disagreement. If you agree, do you see any role for government in facilitating growth beyond that proposed by Kasper? What broad role would you see as appropriate for government and policy to play? Is the role that they might play also important for determination of the underlying laws and social mores that were said in Chapter 1 to underpin the pursuit of 'enlightened self-interest' in capitalist society?

The impact of technological change

The above discussion of the 'Golden Rule' leads invariably to the interesting – and, at first, surprising – conclusion that, for a given state of unchanging production technologies, consumption (and output) per capita for any particular country will eventually become constant. In other words, as saving and investment per person increase, output per person could be expected to increase. However, eventually a level of saving and investment per person would be attained beyond which there would be no further growth in the country's consumption per capita.

What then is the explanation for the clearly evident persistent growth in living standards in most countries over the past couple of centuries? The ultimate answer to this must be the other fundamental determinant of growth, viz. technological change, and an important question to ask is: How does technological progress occur? Also, perhaps even more importantly, can the rate of technological progress be influenced by government policy?

In the earliest economic models of growth – like, for example, the Solow model mentioned earlier – technological progress was accounted for by recognising that new additions to the capital stock might be more than simply additional units of the same type of capital as had previously existed. On the contrary, the new capital might be highly likely to embody some type of technological progress (for example, not simply more computers, but more powerful computers with a greater range of capabilities and functions). This new capital allows the productivity of labour to increase and it is this increased productivity of labour that allows living standards – that is, real output per capita – to increase over time rather than remain static. In the language of Chapter 2, society's production possibilities frontier per person continues to shift out and, using Exhibit 12.7 as a reference and as mentioned earlier, technological progress would be represented by an upward shifting aggregate production function.

Furthermore, there are other ways to enhance the productivity of labour than through 'pure' technological progress. Better organisation of the workforce, improved management practices and a more skilled, better educated and more highly trained workforce can all add to the productivity of labour. All of these things can therefore shift out the aggregate production function of Exhibit 12.7. For our purposes, all these factors that can operate to improve the efficiency of labour will be grouped under the rubric of technological progress.

In the Solow model all technological change is assumed to be exogenous, meaning that these labour productivity-enhancing technological advances are determined outside the economic system. They simply occur randomly and are not influenced in any way by the economic activities of consumers and producers or the policy actions of government. While most economists regard the Solow model of economic growth as a very important introduction to the issue of growth, the assumed exogeneity of technological progress means that it is far from being a comprehensive explanation of the growth phenomenon. We will now briefly introduce a more modern model of economic growth, known as **endogenous growth** theory.

Endogenous growth Modern explanations of the economic growth process argue that the process of technological change is endogenous to economic growth rather than being treated as exogenous, as in the earlier Solow growth model.

Extending the Solow model – endogenous growth theory

endogenous growth

The Solow growth model is silent regarding the source of the technological progress that has been so crucial to the explanation of persistent increases in living standards in most countries of the world during the past century. However, in the past twenty years or so, a view that has become increasingly popular among economists and policy makers is that, far from being entirely exogenous, technological progress may be largely endogenous to the economic growth process itself. What do we mean by this?

Suppose a new production technology is developed that drastically reduces production costs. Not only will this be of direct benefit across society as new capital is put in place using the new production technology, but it also embodies increased knowledge held by society at large and this increased knowledge base may act as a platform to produce even more advanced technologies, and so the process could go on indefinitely. The development of the microprocessor in the 1960s as a result of the space race leading to more powerful mainframe computers in the 1970s, and then the widespread use of PCs and other smart devices in the 1980s and early 1990s 'culminating' in the incredibly rapid development of superfast communication technologies of the late 1990s and 2000s is clearly an example of this.

Recognition of the powerful role played by knowledge in the growth process has led to suggestions that governments can potentially play a very significant positive role. For example, once knowledge exists and is used in the economic process it is difficult for any one group to maintain a monopoly of that knowledge. However, the research and development (R&D) required to develop the knowledge can involve very large investments of resources and much R&D – particularly R&D that is very applied in nature and focused on the development of specific new products – is carried out by private firms. Such firms are not altruistic and need to earn profits for their shareholders. They will only invest in R&D if they feel they can get a temporary advantage over their rivals, either through an innate 'first mover' market advantage or through the existence of a legal patent over the product or process. The patent system is a good example of the government's recognition that it is in society's longer-term interest if a temporary monopoly right over a resource (the knowledge of the production process or product) is granted to someone. This monopoly right provides some incentive for firms to engage in significant R&D.

Notwithstanding the patent system, it is fairly clear that an individual firm will not necessarily be able to capture all the resulting benefits from its own R&D expenditure. There will inevitably be some 'spillover' or positive externalities that benefit other firms in the economy. From the standpoint of society at large these spillovers are of very real benefit, but from the viewpoint of the individual firm incurring the original R&D cost they represent a disincentive to invest. The existence of these knowledge externalities is the basis of arguments about the government providing tax breaks for R&D investment. The fact that the potential societal benefit of firms' R&D expenditures may be greater than their own private benefits is a justification for the government considering some sort of tax incentive to encourage more private R&D expenditure. Some studies in fact have estimated that, for every $1 private benefit from private R&D expenditure, there is almost another $2 of wider public benefit. This strongly suggests that, from a societal perspective, if left to itself the private sector could very well under-invest in R&D. These positive externalities are similar in their effects to those arising from immunisation against disease, which were discussed in Chapter 4.

There is another interesting aspect worth pointing out about 'knowledge' as an additional production factor. In the basic Solow model, additional capital was assumed to add to output at a decreasing rate. This is reasonable for physical capital. After all, using the construction industry as an example, just how many bulldozers per work gang on a one-kilometre length of road construction is optimal? Probably one or two. To add further bulldozers could easily be sub-optimal and would involve diminishing returns to the capital input. However, the same intuition does not necessarily apply to knowledge when viewed as a factor of production. As the above example about the development of the microprocessor illustrated, the acquisition of new knowledge might not have diminishing returns. It may indeed have increasing returns.

Thus, again we are led to the conclusion that government policies designed to encourage further knowledge development – even if such policies involve considerable subsidisation from the community's taxpayers – may pay handsome dividends to the community in the longer term. This argument is often used in support of publicly funded basic research (as opposed to very applied commercial research) undertaken by universities. Such research may have huge long-term benefits to the community even if, in the short run, there may be no obvious commercial application. Let's not forget that the Internet was created because a group of university researchers simply wanted to develop a quick way of communicating with one another using their computers and telephone wire links! It's almost certain that they would not have anticipated the resulting information technology revolution that developed out of their early tinkering.

You make the call

Should the taxpayer subsidise private-sector R&D expenditure?

For normal expenses incurred in the generation of income, a company can claim 100 per cent of these expenses as a deduction against its income for tax purposes. Shortly after winning government in Australia in 1996, the Coalition reduced the depreciation allowance on a firm's R&D expenditure from 150 per cent of the expenditure (i.e., for $100 expenditure the firm could claim as a tax deduction $150 of expenses) – what it had been for some time – to 125 per cent. Their argument for doing this was that the 150 per cent deduction had resulted in a lot of spurious claims by firms for deductions for expenditures that were not at all proper R&D expenditure, but merely attempts to rort the tax system. In the lead-up to the 2001 election many organisations representing employers pressured the government to increase the deduction back up to 150 per cent, arguing that, as a matter of national priority, Australia needed to lift its game as far as R&D expenditure was concerned. They agreed that a good way to do this would be to increase the deduction, thereby decreasing the after-tax cost of such expenditure.

What is your assessment of this policy issue?

The goals of macroeconomic policy

In Chapter 11 we introduced important issues dealing with the measurement of the macro economy. In this chapter we have extended that to consider how an economy grows over time. In particular, we have highlighted the determinants of its long-term growth path as well as the fact that, over the shorter term, an economy experiences fluctuations around this long-term growth path known as business cycles. In the following chapters we will extend this by elaborating on the goals of macroeconomic policy in some detail, but first we will briefly outline them here.

First, it is desirable wherever possible to follow policies that will reduce the severity of the ups and downs of the business cycle. There are two aspects to this. For reasons that will be explained in the next chapter, it is desirable to reduce the severity of recession, thereby limiting the rise in unemployment that is inevitably associated with such downturns. It is, however, also important to try to avoid situations where the economy is growing 'too fast'. Such periods often ultimately result in excessively increasing inflation (see next chapter) leading to poor business and investment decisions, which in their turn can precipitate a subsequent recession.

Second, where possible, macroeconomic policies should be followed that enable the economy to achieve the highest possible sustainable long-term economic growth trajectory that is consistent with – and indeed will

Analyse the issue

Applicable concept: productivity growth always increases economic well-being

Does productivity growth increase unemployment and therefore reduce economic well-being?

You sometimes hear that, even though GDP grew in a period, unemployment actually increased because labour productivity grew so strongly during the period that fewer new workers were needed than the additional entrants into the workforce during the period. As a result, unemployment went up. Some see this as an argument against technological advance and attempts to achieve the highest possible rate of productivity growth.

It is certainly true that a lot of technological change may in the short run throw some workers out of a job in a particular firm or industry. However, technological change will also create jobs in other firms and industries. It is easier to identify the short-term losers and, unfortunately, such identification seems to make for more sensational media stories. They are usually concentrated and more vocal than the diverse groups who gain jobs, especially when these gains may come gradually over time. The fact that there are some losers from technological change is no reason to resist it. However, there is an important role for government to play here in that appropriate transitional arrangements need to be available to enable the displaced workers to retrain or relocate to find gainful employment again elsewhere in the economy.

As a simple thought experiment, imagine an island economy where the inhabitants live on fish, coconut milk, fruit and nuts – no McDonald's burgers for these folk! Some of the inhabitants gain their livelihood from fishing, others from growing and gathering coconuts and so on, and then they exchange their products at going rates of barter exchange. Let's also suppose the technology used for fishing is by spear from the beach or off rocks. As a result there is also a group of spear makers who make a nice living from the fishing industry by supplying their capital (the spears).

Now suppose one morning the inhabitants wake up to find a few boats (they've never seen these before) and fishing nets in good repair washed up on the beach. A couple of enterprising fishing types experiment with this new technology and find that, by using a boat to go out into deeper water and using a net, they can catch a whole heap more fish in half the time. A few others catch on quickly, and before you know it the small number of boats and nets are appropriated. After a few days the others in the fishing industry catch on to the fact that they are using outmoded technology and find they are being undercut by those using the new methods. As a result, they find they are not getting as many coconuts and so on for their efforts as they used to. The spear makers are also concerned at developments. What do these groups do? They immediately band together to decry the unfair practices of the few with the new technology and try to get the community's elders to ban it. They succeed and the boats and nets are immediately burned and things quickly return to the way they were before.

Given this outcome, the community is no worse off than before but it is no better off either. Think about what alternative actions could have been taken when the little island community found itself with the potentially very beneficial, but socially disruptive, new technology. What could have happened to the community's economic well-being? How could short-term transitional costs have been handled? What lessons does this parable teach us?

facilitate the achievement of – the economic, social and cultural aspirations of the community. Of course, lifting or reducing a nation's long-term growth trajectory will entail a range of government policies, many of which will be more microeconomic in nature. However, good macroeconomic policy will certainly have a role to play. For example, many economists believe that business cycle downturns have not only a short-term negative economic impact on the community but, to the extent that such downturns may adversely affect the capital stock and the skills of the workforce, they may also actually permanently affect the long-term growth path of the economy. Also, raising a nation's saving rate may well involve a raft of government expenditure and taxation policies (see Chapter 17 on fiscal policy) that may be regarded as macroeconomic in nature.

More will be said on these issues in later chapters.

Key concepts

- Business cycle
- Peak
- Recession
- Trough
- Recovery
- Economic growth
- Leading indicators
- Coincident indicators
- Lagging indicators
- GDP gap
- Solow model of economic growth
- The 'Golden Rule' level of saving per capita
- Technological change
- Endogenous growth model

Summary

- **Business cycles** are recurrent rises and falls in real GDP over a period of years. Business cycles vary greatly in duration and intensity. A cycle may be considered to comprise four phases: **peak**, **recession**, **trough** and **expansion**. The generally accepted theory today is that changes in the forces of demand and supply cause business cycles. A **recession** is officially defined as at least two consecutive quarters of real GDP decline. However, a more comprehensive definition is that it is defined as at least six months of contraction in a range of macroeconomic measures of output, income, sales and employment. A **trough** is the turning point in national output between recession and recovery. During an **expansion** there is an upturn in the business cycle during which real GDP begins to rise again, quite often very rapidly, in the early periods after the trough and eventually becomes more representative of normal economic growth.

Business cycle

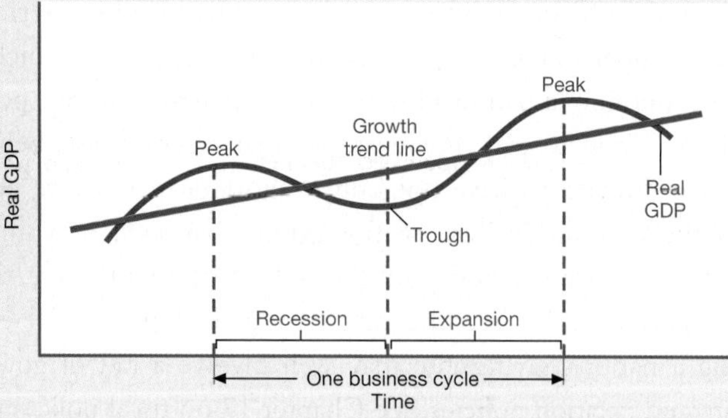

- **Economic growth** is measured by the annual percentage change in real GDP in a nation. The long-term annual average growth rate in Australia is around 3.5 to 4 per cent.

- **Leading**, **coincident** and **lagging indicators** are groups of economic variables that change before, at the same time as, and after changes in real GDP respectively.

- The **GDP gap** is the difference between full employment (or potential) real GDP and actual real GDP. Therefore, the GDP gap measures the loss of output due to **cyclical unemployment**.
- The **Solow growth model** explains how consumption, saving, the capital stock, the labour force and technological change combine in the longer term to determine a nation's economic growth. In the Solow model, technological change is assumed to be exogenous.
- **Endogenous growth models** incorporate technological change that is endogenous to the economic system and represent a richer understanding of the way technological progress happens and its role in the economic system.

Study questions and problems

1 What is the basic cause of the business cycle?

2 Shown here are real GDP figures for each of ten quarters.

Quarterly real GDP (billions of dollars)

Quarter	Real GDP (billions of dollars)	Quarter	Real GDP (billions of dollars)
1	400	6	500
2	500	7	800
3	300	8	900
4	200	9	1000
5	300	10	900

Plot these data points and identify the four phases of the business cycle. Give a theory that may explain the cause of the observed business cycle. What are some of the consequences of a prolonged decline in real GDP? Is the decline in real GDP from $1000 billion to $900 billion a recession?

3 Explain the GDP gap.

4 In the Solow model, without technological change, how does the saving rate affect the steady-state level of income per capita and the steady-state rate of growth in income per capita?

5 Why might a policy maker choose a steady state with a lower quantity of non-labour production factors per person than in the 'Golden Rule' steady state?

6 In recent years a number of prominent economists have argued that, if a larger share of national output were devoted to investment, the result would be rapid productivity growth and rising living standards. Do you agree with this? Explain your position with respect to both the Solow and the endogenous growth models.

7 It has been predicted that Australia will have much reduced annual rates of population growth in the first three decades of the twenty-first century compared with those of the twentieth century. What would you forecast to be the effect of this slow-down in population growth on the growth of total output and the growth of output per person?

8 In any model of economic growth a community's saving rate is an important determinant. How can policy makers influence a nation's saving rate?

9 What is the ultimate explanation for the steady increase in living standards (output per capita) since World War II?

10 How does endogenous growth theory explain persistent growth without needing to make the assumption of exogenous technological progress? How does this differ from the Solow model?

Online exercises

Exercise 1

Visit the ABS website (**www.abs.gov.au**). Select **AusStats, Publications & Data, Time Series Spreadsheets, By Catalogue/Subject, National**

Accounts, then **5206: Australian National Accounts**, then **Table 3**. Locate **real gross domestic product** (**Chain volume GDP**). Graph real GDP from 1980 to the present and observe the business cycle.

Exercise 2

By further studying the real GDP graph from Exercise 1 and by taking account of other current developments of which you are aware, make an economic forecast for the next year.

Exercise 3

As in Exercise 1, locate Real GDP per capita and graph it from 1980 to the present. How much did Australia's annual Real GDP per person grow from 1980 to 2004?

Exercise 4

Visit the Melbourne Institute website (**www.melbourneinstitute.com**). Select Research **Programs**, Applied **Macroeconomics** then **Business cycle dates**. Analyse the table and compare it with dates in the text.

Answers to 'You make the call'

Where are we on the business cycle roller coaster?

The car dealer's sales in the first quarter may be viewed as conforming to the recession phase of the business cycle, while those in the second quarter may suggest the trough, given the subsequent increased sales in both the third and fourth quarters. This suggests that the economy may have entered a recovery phase in the third quarter. The fact that sales in these quarters were below the corresponding quarters in the previous year may simply be a reflection of the severity of the recession from which the economy was just beginning to recover. If you can see that real GDP during the first few quarters of a recovery phase can be lower than real GDP during some quarters of a recession, YOU ARE CORRECT.

Should the taxpayer subsidise private-sector R&D expenditure?

The issue here is that the 150 per cent deduction recognises – quite properly – the existence of significant spillovers to the rest of the community when a private firm produces new knowledge as a result of its R&D. In theory then, such a policy has considerable justification. However, there does exist the incentive for some unscrupulous people to finesse the system in order to improperly claim expenses as R&D expenditures when they are really just ordinary business expenses. To the extent that this occurs, taxpayers are unnecessarily and unfairly increasing the profits of such firms with no wider benefit to society. If the government were to reintroduce such a substantial tax incentive, there would need to be strong measures included in the policy to guard against such attempted rorts. If you thought about the issue in these terms YOU ARE CORRECT.

Multiple-choice questions

1 The phases of a business cycle are
   a upswing and downswing.
   b full employment and unemployment.
   c peak, recession, trough and expansion.
   d full employment, depression, expansion and plateau.

2 The phase of a business cycle during which real GDP reaches its minimum level is the
   a recession.
   b depression.
   c recovery.
   d trough.

3 Which of the following is *not* a variable in the index of leading indicators?
   a new building approvals.
   b stock prices.
   c new businesses formed.
   d prime rate.

4 Which of the following is *not* a coincident indicator?
   a personal income.
   b industrial production.
   c manufacturing and trade sales.
   d none of the above.

5 In the Solow growth model – with no technological progress – at the 'Golden Rule' saving rate per capita
   a output per capita is constant.
   b output per capita grows over time.
   c the capital stock increases at the community's savings rate.
   d none of the above occurs.

6 In the Solow model incorporating technological change, at the 'Golden Rule' stock of capital per capita, output per capita
   a is constant.
   b grows at the rate of population growth.
   c grows at the rate of technological growth.
   d has none of the above characteristics.

7 In the Solow model, technological change
   a is assumed to be exogenous.
   b is assumed to enhance labour productivity.
   c cannot be incorporated into the model.
   d has all of the above characteristics.

8 Endogenous growth models differ from the Solow model of growth in that
   a technological progress is incorporated into the model.
   b the process of technological changes is assumed to be endogenous.
   c a role exists for government policies to affect the rate of technological progress.
   d all of the above characteristics apply.

9 The steady increase in living standards in many countries over the twentieth century can be explained
   a only by endogenous growth models.
   b only by the Solow model.
   c by both **a** and **b**.
   d by neither **a** nor **b**.

10 Other things being equal, a country with a higher saving rate per person than another will necessarily
   a have a higher steady-state growth in output per capita.
   b have a higher steady state growth in consumption per capita.
   c have neither **a** nor **b**.
   d have both **a** and **b**.

PART 4

13 Inflation and unemployment

Maintaining an economy at or near full employment with strong, sustainable economic growth and keeping prices reasonably stable are the most important economic goals facing a nation. In Australia, the Great Depression of the 1930s produced profound changes in our lives. Similarly, the 'Great Inflation' of the 1970s and early 1980s left memories of the miseries of inflation. Concern that inflation would again become a major problem continued into the 1990s, even though the underlying rate of inflation since 1992 had dropped significantly and has remained at under 3 per cent from 1997 until the time of writing. As with high unemployment, voters are very quick to blame any administration that fails to keep inflation under control.

This chapter explains what is meant by unemployment and inflation. You will study how the government measures unemployment and how it computes the rate of inflation. The chapter includes a discussion of the consequences of both unemployment and inflation and explains who the winners and losers are in each case. For example, you will learn about the types of unemployment, what 'full employment' is, and what the monetary, non-monetary and demographic costs of unemployment are. Similarly, you will learn about demand-pull and cost-push inflation, who wins from inflation and who loses. As an example, you will see what happened in Bolivia when the inflation rate was, for a time, running at 116 000 per cent per year. After studying this chapter, you will have a much clearer understanding of why unemployment is such a burden on society and why inflation is so feared.

In this chapter, you will examine these economics questions:

- What is the inflation rate of your university education?
- Can a person's income fall, even though he or she received a rise in salary?
- Can an interest rate be negative?
- Does inflation harm everyone equally?
- Is a worker who has given up searching for work counted as unemployed?
- What is structural versus cyclical unemployment?
- What does the term 'full employment' mean?

Meaning and measurement of inflation

Fifty years ago a 350 ml bottle of Coke sold for about 10 cents in Australia. Nowadays, a similar bottle sells for more than twenty times that price. Clearly, however, the bottle of Coke has not become twenty times more valuable. Much of the price rise is simply accounted for by a general increase in the prices of the vast array of goods and services produced in the economy. **Inflation** is an increase in the *general* (average) price level of goods and services in the economy. Inflation's opposite is **deflation**. Deflation is a decrease in the *general* (average) price level of goods and services in the economy (negative inflation).

inflation

Inflation An increase in the general (average) price level of goods and services in the economy.

Deflation A decrease in the general (average) price level of goods and services in the economy.

Note that inflation does not mean that *all* prices of *all* products in the economy rise during a given period. For example, the annual percentage change in the average overall price level during the 1970s reached double digits, but the prices of pocket calculators and digital watches actually declined. The reason that the average price level rose in the 1970s was that the rising prices of many other goods and services produced in the economy outweighed the falling prices of pocket calculators, digital watches and other such electronic goods and services.

Inflation is an increase in the overall average level of prices and not an increase in the price of any specific product.

Disinflation A reduction in the rate of inflation.

You will sometimes also hear the word **disinflation**. This is a situation in which the rate of inflation is dropping (from, say, 10 per cent per annum to 5 per cent per annum).

The consumer price index

Consumer price index (CPI) An index that measures changes in the average prices of consumer goods and services.

consumer price index

The most widely reported measure of inflation is the **consumer price index (CPI)**. The CPI is an index that measures changes in the average price of consumer goods and services. It is sometimes called the *cost-of-living index*. The CPI includes only consumer goods and services, in order to determine how rising prices affect the income of consumers. Unlike the *GDP chain price index* explained in the earlier chapter on the measurement of GDP, the CPI does not cover items purchased by businesses and government, nor does it include items that are exported. Also unlike the GDP chain price index, it does seek to measure changes in the prices of imported consumer goods and services.

The ABS prepares the CPI. Each quarter the ABS 'price collectors' contact a sample of retail stores, other businesses supplying consumer products or services, home owners and tenants in Australia's capital cities. Based on these quarterly sample surveys, the ABS estimates average prices for a 'market

Exhibit 13.1 **Composition of the consumer price index**

Category (All items 100.0%)	Percentage Weight in Index	% Price change June qtr 2004→ Sept qtr 2004	% Price change Sept qtr 2003→ Sept qtr 2004
Food	17.7	–0.6	2.1
Alcohol and tobacco	7.4	0.9	3.4
Housing	19.7	1.4	3.6
Housing furnishings, supplies and services	8.1	–0.1	–0.7
Clothing and footwear	5.2	–0.2	–0.7
Transportation	15.3	0.8	2.8
Health	4.7	–0.7	5.8
Recreation	12.3	0.5	–0.1
Education	2.7	0.0	7.6
Communication	2.9	0.5	1.1
Other goods and services	4.0	1.2	2.5
All groups	**100**	**0.4**	**2.3**

Note: In 2004, the ABS was using its 14th CPI Series, which employed the estimated spending patterns for 1998–99 (i.e. 1998–99 was the 'weighting base period' for the 14th Series).

Source: Australian Bureau of Statistics, www.abs.gov.au/ausstats, Cat. No. 6401.

basket' of different items purchased by the typical *urban* family in each of Australia's capital cities. These items are included under the following categories: food and beverages, clothing, housing expenses, transportation, medical care, entertainment and a range of other goods and services.

Exhibit 13.1 presents a breakdown of these categories and the relative importance of each as a percentage of total expenditures. The survey reveals, for example, that about 20 cents out of each consumer dollar is spent on housing and about 15 cents on transportation. The composition of the market basket generally remains unchanged from one period to the next, so the CPI is called a *fixed-weight price index*. If 20 per cent of consumer spending was on housing in 1998–99 (the 'weighting base period' for the 14th (current) Series of the CPI), the assumption is that 20 per cent of spending is still spent on housing in, say, 2004. The weighting base period is changed roughly every five years. Over time, the composition of items in the CPI has changed considerably. For example, recent revisions have added personal computers, mobile phones, VCRs, compact disc players and DVD rentals.

Read more about some interesting episodes of hyperinflation around the world at **www.sjsu.edu/faculty/watkins/hyper.htm.**

How the CPI is computed

Exhibit 13.2 illustrates the basic idea behind the CPI and how this price index measures inflation. Suppose that in 1994 a typical family in Australia lived a very meagre existence and purchased a market basket of only hamburgers, petrol and jeans. Column (1) shows the quantity purchased for each of these items and column (2) lists the corresponding average selling price. Multiplying the price by the quantity gives the market basket cost in column (3) of each consumer product purchased in 1994. The total cost paid by our typical family for the market basket, based on 1994 prices and quantities purchased, is $245.

Ten years later it is 2004 and we wish to know the impact of rising prices on consumer purchases. To calculate the CPI, we determine the cost of the

PART 4

Exhibit 13.2 Consumer price index for a simple economy

Products in consumers' market basket	(1) 1994 quantity purchased	(2) 1994 price	(3) Market basket cost in 1994 (1) x (2)	(4) 2004 price	(5) Market basket cost in 2004 (1) x (4)
Hamburgers	50	$0.80	$40.00	$1.00	$50.00
Litres of petrol	250	$0.70	$175.00	$0.90	$225.00
Jeans	2	$15.00	$30.00	$30.00	$60.00
		Total 1994 cost = $245.00		Total 2004 cost = $335.00	

$$2004 \text{ CPI} = \frac{\$335}{\$245} \times 100 = 136.7$$

Note: All figures are fictitious.

Base year A year chosen as a reference point for comparing price levels with some earlier or later year.

same market basket, valued at 2004 *current-year prices* and compare this to the cost at 1994 **base-year** prices. Expressed as a general formula:

$$\text{CPI} = \frac{\text{cost of the market basket of products at current year (2004) prices}}{\text{cost of the same market basket of products at base-year (1994) prices}} \times 100$$

As shown in Exhibit 13.2, the 2004 cost for our market basket example is calculated by multiplying the 2004 price for each item in column (4) by the 1994 quantity purchased in column (1). Column (5) lists the result for each item in the market basket and the total market basket cost in 2004 is $335. The CPI value of 136.7 is computed as the ratio of the current 2004 cost of the 1994 market basket of quantities ($335) to the cost of the exact same market basket in the 1994 base year ($245) multiplied by 100.

The value of the CPI is always 100 in the base year because the numerator and the denominator of the CPI formula are the same in the base year. At the time of writing, the base year for Australia's CPI was 1989–90. However, as indicated above, the ABS was using 1998–99 as its 'weighting base period'. This means the spending patterns in that year were used to weight price changes in the component groups of the CPI (see Exhibit 13.1) to get the value of the overall index for each period. Once the ABS selects the base year and uses the market basket technique to generate the CPI numbers, the annual *inflation rate* is computed as the percentage change in the official CPI index from one year to the next. In 2003–04, for example, the CPI was 143.5, while in 2002–03 it was 140.2. The rate of inflation for 2003–04 was therefore 2.4 per cent (obtained as (143.5/140.2 – 1) × 100). Mathematically,

$$\text{Annual rate of inflation} = \frac{\text{CPI in given year} - \text{CPI in previous year}}{\text{CPI in previous year}} \times 100$$

History of Australia's inflation rates

Exhibit 13.3 records how rapidly prices have changed in Australia since 1949, as measured by annual changes in the CPI. During the early years after the war, the CPI reached a double-digit inflation rate. From the mid-1950s until the inflationary pressures in the early 1970s, the inflation rate was generally around 3 per cent. Then the inflation rate climbed to more than 10 per cent in the mid-1970s, reaching a high of 16 per cent in 1975. Following the 1981–82 recession, the annual inflation rate moderated and averaged about 8 per cent between 1983 and 1990. After the end of the recession of the early 1990s, Australia's inflation rate was quite low and has kept historically very low until the time of writing. In fact, underlying inflation (abstracting from the temporary impact of the introduction of the GST in July 2000) since 1994 has been lower than at any time since the 1960s.

Exhibit 13.3 **Australia's inflation rate, 1950–2004**

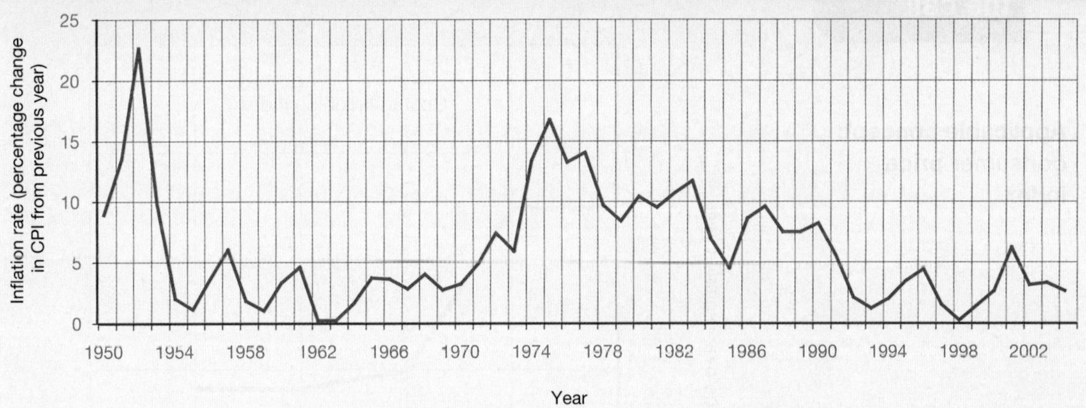

Source: Australian Bureau of Statistics, www.abs.gov.au, Cat. No. 6401, Table 4A.

Criticism of the consumer price index

Just as there is criticism of the unemployment rate (discussed shortly), the CPI is not a perfect measure of inflation and it has been the subject of much public debate. Here are the key reasons.

First, changes in the CPI are based on a 'typical' basket of products purchased, but it is often argued that it does not match the actual market basket purchased by many consumers. Suppose you spend your nominal annual income entirely on lemonade, meat pies and jeans. During the year, the inflation rate is 5 per cent, but assume that the prices of lemonade, meat pies and jeans actually fall. In this case, your own personal real income (that is, the quantities of lemonade, meat pies and jeans that you can buy with your income) will rise and the official inflation rate based on the CPI will *overstate* the negative impact of inflation on your cost of living.

Retired people, for example, buy a bundle of products that differs quite markedly from that of the 'typical' family. Because retired people purchase proportionally more medical services than the typical family – and fewer children-related items – the inflation rate may understate the impact of inflation on older people if the cost of medical services is rising faster than other items in the CPI. While this is a valid criticism, it is a very difficult issue to remedy, short of the ABS trying to construct a separate CPI for all the special-interest groups in the community. The cost of doing so would be prohibitive and, in the absence of the community being willing to significantly increase funding to the ABS, it is unlikely to occur.

Second, the ABS has difficulty adjusting the CPI for changes in *quality*. As noted in the chapter on measuring GDP, how do you compare a personal computer made in the past with a new personal computer? The new computer may cost more, but it is much better than the old computer.

You make the call

Applicable concept: consumer price index

Does it cost more to laugh?

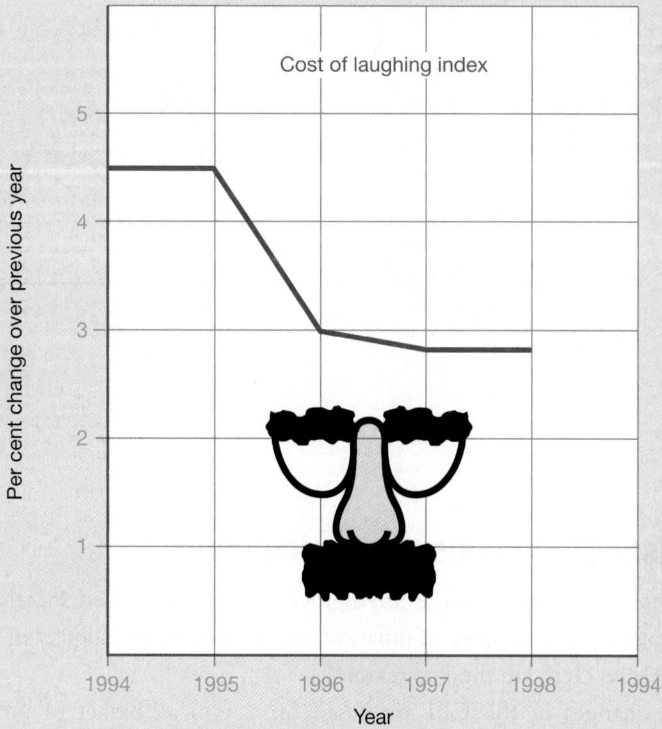

Are we paying bigger bucks for smaller yuks? Is there a bone to pick with the price of rubber chickens? Is the price of Groucho glasses raising eyebrows, the cost of *Mad* magazine driving you mad? … well, you get the idea.

Malcolm Kushner, an attorney-turned-humour consultant based in Santa Cruz, California, developed an index based on a compilation of leading humour indicators to measure price changes in things that make us laugh. Mr Kushner created the Cost of Laughing index to track how trends in laughter affect the bottom line. He is a humour consultant who advises corporate leaders on making humour work for business professionals. For example, humour can make executives better public speakers and laughter also reduces stress and can even cure illnesses. Mr Kushner believes humour is America's greatest asset and his consulting business gets a lot of publicity from publication of the index. His latest book is *Successful Presentations for Dummies*, which provides the reader with ten sites on the World Wide Web where speakers can find everything from quotations of famous people, to an appropriate Murphy's Law, to general information material for a speech. To combat rising humour costs, Kushner has established a website at **www.kushnergroup.com**. It organises links to databases of funny quotes, anecdotes, one-liners and other material for business speakers and writers.

The exhibit with the Groucho face traces the annual percentage change in the cost of laughing that Mr Kushner reported to the media. On an annual basis, the Cost of Laughing index remained flat as a pancake at 4.4

per cent between 1994 and 1995 and then did a belly flop to 3 per cent in 1996, where it remained through 1998.

Closer examination of the laughing index over the years gives both happy and sad faces. The good news is that the prices of an arrow through the head, singing telegrams and ticket prices for several comedy clubs have remained unchanged since 1995. The bad news is that all the other items increased. The major source of more expensive humour is the price of writing a half-hour television situation comedy.

Just like the CPI, Kushner's index has been criticised. Note that the fee for writing a TV sitcom dominates the index. Kushner responds to this issue by saying, 'Well, I wanted the index to be truly national. The fact that this price dominates the index reflects that TV comedy shows dominate our national culture. If you can laugh for free at a sitcom, you don't need to buy a rubber chicken or go to a comedy club.'

No question here. This one is just for fun.

Cost of Laughing index

Item	1995	1996	1997	1998
Rubber chicken[1]	$60.00	$66.00	$66.00	$66.00
Groucho glasses[1]	15.00	15.00	15.00	15.00
Arrow through head[1]	6.00	6.00	6.00	6.00
Mad magazine[2]	3.95	2.50	2.50	2.50
Singing telegrams[3]				
Pink gorilla	75.00	75.00	75.00	75.00
Dancing chicken	65.00	65.00	65.00	65.00
Fee for writing a TV sitcom[4]	10 883.00	11 209.00	11 545.00	11 891.00
Comedy clubs[5]				
Atlanta: The Punch Line	14.00	14.00	14.00	15.00
Chicago: Second City	16.00	15.50	16.00	16.00
Houston: Laff Stop	10.00	10.83	10.00	10.00
Denver: Comedy Club	8.00	8.00	8.00	8.00
Indianapolis: Crackers Comedy Club	10.00	10.00	10.00	10.00
Los Angeles: Laugh Factory	10.00	10.00	10.00	10.00
New York: Comic Strip	12.00	12.00	12.00	12.00
Pittsburgh: The Funny Bone	10.00	11.00	11.00	11.00
San Francisco: Punch Line Comedy Club	10.00	10.00	10.00	12.00
Seattle: Comedy Underground	10.00	10.00	10.00	10.00
Total cost of humour basket	**$11 217.45**	**$11 549.83**	**$11 885.50**	**$12 234.50**
Annual inflation rate	**4.4%**	**3.0%**	**2.9%**	**2.9%**

1 One dozen wholesale from Franco-American Novelty Co., Long Island City, New York.
2 April issue.
3 Available from Bellygrass, New York Metropolitan Area.
4 Minimum fee under Writers Guild of America Basic Agreement.
5 Admission on Saturday night.

Source: data provided by Malcolm Kushner.

PART 4

A portion of the price increase therefore reflects better quality rather than simply a higher price for the same item. If the quality of items improves, increases in the CPI will *overstate* inflation. Similarly, deteriorating quality means that increases in the CPI *understate* inflation. The ABS attempts to make adjustments for quality changes in automobiles, electronic equipment and other products in the market basket, but these adjustments are difficult to determine accurately.

Third, the use of a single unchanging 'weighting base period' market basket ignores the law of demand. As you learned in earlier chapters, if the relative price of a product rises, consumers will tend to purchase substitutes, and so a smaller quantity is demanded. Suppose orange growers suffer from severe frosts and the supply of oranges decreases. Consequently, the relative price of oranges increases sharply. According to the *law of demand*, consumers will tend to decrease the quantity demanded of oranges and substitute consumption of, say, apples for oranges. Because the market basket does not automatically change by reducing the percentage or weight of oranges and increasing the percentage of apples, the CPI will *overstate* the impact of higher prices for oranges on the measured change in price level. To deal with this *substitution* bias problem, the ABS regularly (about every five to seven years) updates the year it uses as its 'weighting base period' and uses household expenditure survey data for that year to try to keep up with changing consumption patterns and correct for the fixed market-basket limitations of the CPI.

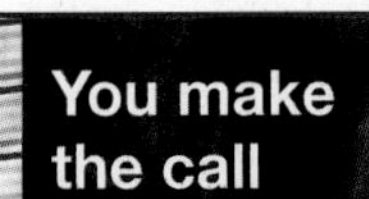

You make the call

The university education price index

Suppose your market basket for a university education consisted of only the four items (fictitious costs) listed in the following table, with quantities of each item fixed in both periods and indicated in the notes below the table.

Item	2003	2004
Tuition and fees[1]	$2 500	$3 000
Room and board[2]	6 000	6 200
Books[3]	1 000	1 0
Soft drinks[4]	150	200

1 Tuition for two semesters
2 Payment for nine months
3 Twenty books of 800 pages with full colour
4 One hundred 350 ml Coca-Colas

Using 2003 as your base year, what is the percentage change in the university education price index in 2004?

In 1996, in the United States, a Senate-appointed commission of five economists headed by Barry Boskin of Stanford University studied the methods used to compile the CPI in that country and reported that, primarily because of quality improvements, they believed the CPI overstated inflation by about one whole percentage point each year. This is a significant overstatement and it is likely that the CPIs of other countries that use very similar compilation methodologies – including Australia – may have similar degrees of overstatement. We will refer to this issue again in Chapter 16 when we discuss the appropriate target for monetary policy.

Consequences of inflation

We now turn from the issue of measuring inflation to its effects on people's income, wealth and purchasing power. Why should inflation cause concern? You will learn that inflation is feared because it can significantly alter one's standard of living. In this section, you will see that inflation can quite arbitrarily create winners who enjoy a larger slice of the national income pie, and losers who receive a smaller slice. You will also learn that inflation can potentially impede proper business decision-making and the efficiency with which resources are allocated in the economy.

Inflation shrinks income

Economist Arthur Okun once stated, 'This society is built on implicit and explicit contracts … They are linked to the idea that the dollar means something. If you cannot depend on the value of the dollar, this system is undermined. People will constantly feel they've been fooled and cheated'.[1] When prices rise, people worry whether the rise in their income will keep pace with inflation. And the more quickly prices rise, the more people suffer from the stresses of inflation and its uncertainties.

Inflation tends to reduce our standard of living through declines in the purchasing power of money. The greater the rate of inflation, the greater the decline in the quantity of goods we can purchase with a given **nominal income**, or *money income*. Nominal income is the actual number of dollars received over a period of time. The source of such income can be wages, salary, rent, dividends, interest or pensions.

Nominal income The actual number of dollars received over a period of time.

Nominal income does not measure your real purchasing power. Finding out if you are better or worse off over time requires converting nominal income to **real income**. Real income is the actual number of dollars received (nominal income) adjusted for changes in the general level of prices as measured by, for example, the CPI. Real income measures the amount of goods and services that can be purchased with one's nominal income. If the CPI increases and your nominal income remains the same, your real income (purchasing power) falls. In short, if your nominal income fails to keep pace with inflation, your standard of living falls. Suppose your nominal income

Real income The actual number of dollars received (nominal income) adjusted for changes in the CPI.

real income

1 'How inflation threatens the fabric of US society', *Business Week*, 22 May 1978, p. 118.

in 2003 is \$40 000 and the 2003 CPI value is 136. Your real income relative to the CPI base year is

$$\text{Real income} = \frac{\text{nominal income}}{\text{CPI (as decimal, i.e. CPI/100)}}$$

$$\text{2003 real income} = \frac{\$40\ 000}{1.36} = \$29\ 411$$

Now assume your nominal income rises in 2004 by 10 per cent, from \$40 000 to \$44 000, and the CPI increases by 5 per cent, from 136 to 143. Thus you earn more money, but how much better off are you? To answer this question, you must compute your 2004 real income as follows:

$$\text{2004 real income} = \frac{\$44\ 000}{1.43} = \$30\ 769$$

Using the preceding two computed real-income figures, the percentage change in real income between 2003 and 2004 was 4.6 per cent (\$1358/\$29 411 × 100). This means that your standard of living has risen because you effectively have an extra \$1358 of purchasing power in 2004 to spend on movies, clothes, travel and so on. Even though the general price level has risen, your purchasing power has increased – but by less than the 10 per cent increase in your nominal income – because the percentage rise in nominal income more than offset the rate of inflation. Instead of precisely calculating this relationship, a good approximation can be obtained through the following simple formula:

Percentage change in real income = Percentage change in nominal income − Percentage change in CPI

Based on the examples given above, you can see why inflation can be an income redistribution mechanism. Other examples of this follow below.

People whose nominal incomes rise faster than the rate of inflation gain purchasing power, while people whose nominal incomes do not keep pace with inflation lose purchasing power.

Economics and ethics

In this section we have concentrated on using CPI movements to inflation-adjust nominal income changes in order to gauge changes in real income. Movements in the CPI are also very useful when one is interested in comparing particular prices or expenditure over time. For instance, in the 'Analyse the issue' box on page 364 we look at the inflation-adjusted A\$ price of oil over time. Also, when we look at announced increases in levels of annual government spending in areas like, for example, health and education, it is very important to look at the inflation-adjusted increases to properly judge the extra real spending increases involved.

If nominal spending on a government program increased by 5 per cent when inflation was running at 8 per cent, then the government actually committed less in real resources to that program. In relation to the economics and ethics considerations mentioned in Chapter 1, it unfortunately occurs too often that government ministers will announce program expenditure increases in nominal terms rather than real, inflation-adjusted terms. Without adjustment, such announcements can give quite a misleading impression of the implied funding level commitments.

Inflation and wealth

Wealth The value of the stock of assets owned at some point in time.

Income is one measure of economic well-being and **wealth** is another. Income is a flow of money earned by selling factors of production. Wealth is the value of the stock of assets owned at some point in time. Wealth includes real estate, shares, bonds, bank accounts, life insurance policies, cash, collectibles (such as art), cars, boats and other things. A person can have high income and little wealth, or great wealth and little income.

Inflation can benefit holders of wealth because the value of assets often tends to increase faster than consumer prices rise. Consider a yacht purchased in 1980 for $100 000. By 2004, this yacht may have sold for $320 000 – a 220 per cent increase in wealth. If the CPI happened to be 100 in 1980 (the base year in this case) and rose to 250 in 2004 – indicating consumer prices had risen by 150 per cent – then the yacht owner has clearly profited from ownership of this asset. Thus, people who own forms of wealth that can increase in value faster than the inflation rate, such as real estate, are often winners. Of course, physical (or financial) assets sometimes do not increase in price faster than the general level of prices. If that happens, the assets lose their real value (the real purchasing power they would yield if sold) over time.

On the other hand, the impact of inflation on wealth penalises people without it. Again, consider younger couples wishing to purchase a home. If house prices rise faster than the inflation rate and wages growth, it becomes more difficult for them to buy their first home.

Inflation and the real interest rate

real interest rate

Nominal interest rate The actual rate of interest earned over a period of time.

Real interest rate The nominal rate of interest minus the inflation rate.

Borrowers and savers may be winners or losers, depending on the rate of inflation. Understanding how this may happen requires making a distinction between the **nominal interest rate** and the **real interest rate**. The nominal interest rate is the actual rate of interest earned over a period of time. The nominal interest rate, for example, is the interest rate specified on a loan or savings account. If you borrow $10 000 from a bank at a 10 per cent annual interest rate for five years, this is more accurately called a 10 per cent annual nominal interest rate. Similarly, a $10 000 certificate of deposit that yields

Analyse the issue

Just how high really was the price of oil in 2004?

Applicable concept: inflation-adjusting nominal data

Most readers will recall that the price of crude oil accelerated quite sharply during 2004 and that this was the cause of considerable concern in the community generally, and also to economic policy makers in Australia and elsewhere. The causes were both of a demand-side and a supply-side nature. On the demand side, for example, the rapidly growing Chinese economy was needing increasing supplies of oil and other energy products. On the supply side, for example, uncertainties associated with Iraqi oil supplies (in the aftermath of the Iraq war of 2003) were putting upward pressure on prices.

The result of these pressures saw the US$ price of crude oil shoot up from around $30 a barrel in late 2003 to an average price of around US$44 a barrel in the September quarter of 2004 (and up above US$55 a barrel for a brief time in the month of October). This increase in crude oil prices resulted in quite significant increases in petrol prices at the pump. Such higher prices for petrol pose potential problems for economic growth, as higher spending on petrol leaves less money in the hands of consumers for spending in other areas. This can lead to reduced consumer spending and, thereby, lower production, slower economic growth and possibly higher unemployment. In addition, higher fuel prices feed directly through into higher transport costs, putting upward pressure on product prices. Finally, oil is a very important component in the production of many different products (for example, plastics), so higher oil prices again feed through into higher production costs for a wide range of goods and services.

For these reasons some feared that, should oil prices not stabilise or fall back to more 'normal' levels of around US$25–30 a barrel, then the world might well see a repeat of the 'stagflation' episode of 1973–74, where an international recession occurred along with high inflation. Indeed, it was this 1970s episode that actually gave rise to the word 'stagflation'. At that time the price of oil quadrupled and is referred to now as the first 1970s 'oil price shock'. Another international recession also coincided with the second 1970s oil price shock of 1979–80, when the oil price per barrel doubled.

At the time of writing in late 2004, an international recession did not seem very likely and there were late signs, especially after the US election

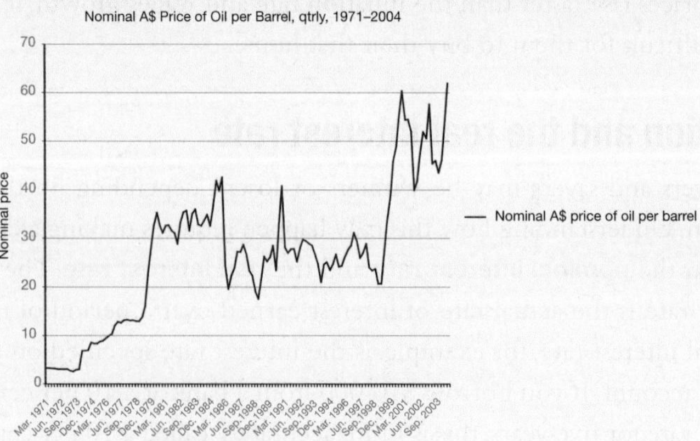

Source: data supplied by Economagic (www.economagic.com)

was concluded, that the oil price might have been on its way down, thus considerably alleviating such concerns.

As far as Australia is concerned, to gauge the impact on prices and economic activity in Australia we also need to adjust the US$ price of oil for the A$ exchange rate against the US$. In the first graph, the quarterly A$ price of oil per barrel is graphed for the years 1971–2004 (September quarter). As can be seen, the nominal A$ price of oil averaged around A$62 per barrel in the September quarter of 2004 and was considerably higher than the average price of oil in both the 1973–74 and 1979–80 episodes. In fact, the previous peak in the A$ price of oil was only around A$40 a barrel back in the mid-1980s. From this graph it would seem that the price of oil in the 2000s was considerably higher than in the 1970s, 1980s and even throughout most of the 1990s.

However, it's important to remember that the general level of prices in the Australian economy rose steadily throughout the 1970s, 1980s and 1990s. In fact, as measured by the CPI, the average price level in late 2004 was actually about three times as high as it was around the time of the second oil price shock in 1979–80. Therefore, to gauge the relative 'real price' of oil over this long period of time we have to adjust the nominal price for inflation. This is done in the next graph.

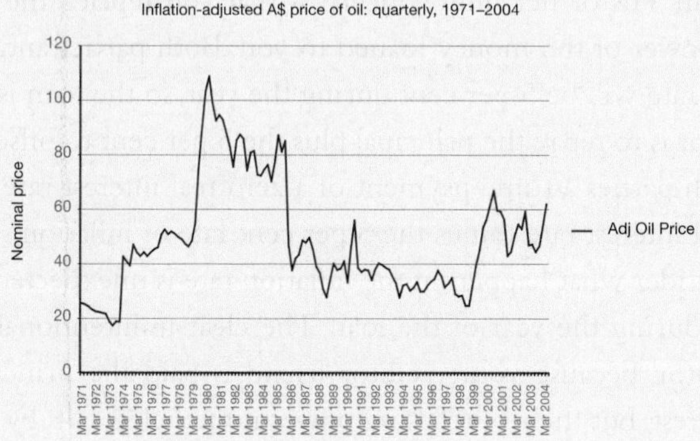

Source: data supplied by Economagic (www.economagic.com)

As can be seen from this second graph, a very different picture emerges once the oil price data are inflation-adjusted. In the figure all prices are adjusted into 2004 terms; that is, 2004 was used as the base period. Thus, the 2004 price remains unchanged from the nominal price. However, oil prices in all earlier periods are adjusted upwards to account for the generally lower average price levels in these earlier periods. Now the real price of oil in 1979–80 can be seen in terms of 2004 prices.

1 What was the price of oil in 1979–80 equivalent to in 2004 terms?
2 Alternatively, from a different perspective, to what level would the price of oil in late 2004 need to have risen to be as high in real terms as it was back in 1979–80?

This should demonstrate just how important it is to adjust for general price level changes when you want to compare the real price of something over different time periods.

10 per cent annual interest is said to have a 10 per cent annual nominal interest rate.

The real interest rate is approximately the nominal interest rate minus the inflation rate. The occurrence of inflation means that the real interest rate will be less than the nominal rate. Suppose the inflation rate during the year is 5 per cent. This means that a certificate of deposit for $5000 you may have at a bank that yields 10 per cent annual nominal interest only earns approximately 5 per cent *real interest*. Even though you receive $5500 at the end of the year, the general level of prices of goods and services has gone up by 5 per cent, which has reduced the real purchasing power of your $5500. Thus the effective real purchasing power of your $5500 at the end of the year in terms of the prices prevailing will be 5500/1.05, or $5238, representing a growth in real purchasing power of 4.8 per cent (approximately 5 per cent).

$$\text{Real interest rate} = \text{nominal interest rate} - \text{inflation rate}$$

To understand how inflation can make those who borrow winners, suppose you receive a one-year loan from a close friend in order to start a business. Your friend has no desire to earn a profit and knows you will repay the loan. His or her only concern is that you replace the decline in purchasing power of the money loaned to you. Both parties anticipate that the inflation rate will be 5 per cent during the year, so the loan is made and the agreement is to repay the principal plus the 5 per cent to offset inflation. In short, both parties assume payment of a zero real interest rate (the 5 per cent nominal interest rate minus the 5 per cent rate of inflation).

The Australian Bureau of Statistics (ABS) is the principal fact-finding agency for the federal government in the field of labour economics and statistics. Visit the ABS website (**www.abs.gov.au**). The Reserve Bank of Australia (**www.rba.gov.au**) also maintains a reasonable database of macroeconomic data, including data on unemployment and inflation.

Now consider what happens if the inflation rate is unexpectedly actually 10 per cent during the year of the loan. The clear unintentional winner is you, the debtor, because your creditor friend is paid the principal plus 5 per cent interest, but their purchasing power nonetheless falls by 5 per cent because the actual inflation rate is 10 per cent. Stated differently, instead of zero, the real interest rate you paid on the loan was –5 per cent (the 5 per cent nominal interest rate minus the 10 per cent rate of inflation). In real terms, your friend has actually paid you for the privilege of lending their money to you!

Finally, it is important to note that the nominal interest rate is never negative, but the real interest rate can be either positive or negative depending on the rate of inflation relative to the nominal interest rate. During the 1970s in Australia (and elsewhere around the world) real rates of interest were sometimes negative. This was because lenders had not fully adjusted their inflationary expectations to the higher rates of inflation prevalent in the 1970s compared with the low inflation rates of the 1960s.

CONCLUSION

When the real rate of interest is negative, lenders and savers lose at the expense of borrowers because interest earned does not keep up with the inflation rate.

Inflation and investment and business decisions

It is generally considered that a low and stable level of inflation is reasonably conducive to efficient investment and business decision-making. Such decisions should be based on the relative expected real (inflation-adjusted) rates of return from investing economic resources in alternative activities. When inflation has been and continues to be stable, most economic agents will be able to correctly forecast general price changes in coming periods. This means they will probably be able to abstract from this general change in prices and form a view about likely relative real rates of return from alternative investments. However, when inflation is higher it is also usually more unstable. This makes it more difficult to abstract correctly from future expected general price level changes so as to focus on relative real rates of return from alternative investments. In aggregate, this can lead to greater numbers of inappropriate decisions being made by firms and individuals, resulting in reduced efficiency with which the community's scarce resources are allocated.

The situation is made worse when tax considerations are factored into the decision process. The interaction of high inflation and the tax system can result in some forms of investment being favoured, not because of their inherent high relative rate of economic return but simply because, with high inflation, they are more tax effective. From the individual's or company's perspective such an investment may be rational but, from the viewpoint of the community as a whole, it can lead to sub-optimal outcomes. Over-investment may occur in some areas and under-investment in others, to the long-run detriment of the wider community. For example, in the 1970s, house prices in Australia increased dramatically. Since the nominal interest on borrowings to finance investment in rental properties was (and is) tax deductible, but the nominal capital gains resulting from the sale of such investments were not taxed (at that time), the acquisition of such assets as investments proved very popular for many. In the opinion of many analysts, the result was that the community was left with an over-supply of housing and an under-supply of other forms of investment – such as investment in plant and equipment.

Demand-pull and cost-push inflation

Economists often distinguish between two basic types of inflation, depending on whether it originates from the buyers' or the sellers' side of the market. The analysis presented in this section returns to the cause-and-effect relationship between total spending and the business cycle discussed in the previous chapter.

Demand-pull inflation

Demand-pull inflation A rise in the general price level resulting from an excess of total spending (demand) over supply.

Perhaps the most familiar type of inflation is called **demand-pull inflation**. This is a rise in the general price level resulting from an excess of total spending (demand). Demand-pull inflation is often expressed as 'too much money chasing too few goods'. When sellers are unable to supply all the goods and services buyers demand, sellers typically respond by raising prices. If such an excess in nominal demand is widespread across many markets, the general price level in the economy will be 'pulled up' by the pressure from buyers' total expenditures.

Demand-pull inflation occurs where the economy is operating at or near full capacity. Here, not only is total or aggregate demand for goods and services high, but the capacity of the economy to meet this demand is also being stretched. In these circumstances, and if such very strong nominal demand is expected by firms to continue into the future, they would find it profitable to expand their plant and production to meet the buyers' demand. However, they cannot do this in the short run. As a result, national output remains largely unchanged, but prices will tend to rise as buyers try to outbid one another for the available supply of goods and services. If total spending subsides, so will the pressure on the available supply of products, and prices will not rise as rapidly or may even fall.

A word of caution: consumers may not be the only actors in the demand-pull story. Recall that total aggregate spending includes consumer spending (C), business investment (I), government spending (G) and net exports ($X - M$). Even foreigners may contribute to inflation by bidding up the price of Australia's exports. The increase in export income will, through the circular flow described in Chapter 11, feed through into additional demand in other parts of the economy, thereby possibly resulting in increases in domestic prices.

PART 4

Cost-push inflation

An excess of total spending is not the only possible explanation for rising prices. In 1973, for example, the Organization of Petroleum Exporting Countries (OPEC) sharply increased the price of oil. This action meant a significant increase in the cost of producing many goods and services (not just in the price of petrol). The result was **cost-push inflation**. Cost-push inflation is a rise in the general price level resulting from a general increase in the costs of production.

Cost-push inflation A rise in the general price level resulting from an increase in the cost of production, irrespective of demand conditions.

The source of many cost-push inflations is not such a dramatic event as the one described above. Any increased costs to businesses are a potential source of cost-push inflation. This means that upward pressure on prices may be caused by cost increases for labour, raw materials, construction, equipment, borrowing and so on.

The influence of *expectations* on both demand-pull and cost-push inflation is an important consideration. Suppose buyers see prices rise and believe they should purchase that new television set or car today before these items cost much more tomorrow. At or near full employment, this demand-pull pressure results in a rise in prices. On the suppliers' side, firms may expect their production costs to rise in the future and this causes them to raise prices in anticipation of the higher costs. The result is cost-push inflation. So you can see that, in reality, the two types of inflation can be closely interlinked and, in any given inflationary episode, it may be impossible to ascribe the cause to one or the other type of mechanism. The important point of distinguishing between the two in theory is to give you an understanding of the different types of factors that may result in increasing prices.

Here you should take note of a coming attraction. The next chapter on aggregate demand and supply develops a modern macroeconomic model that you can use to analyse with more precision the factors that determine national output, employment and the price level. In particular, the last section of that chapter applies the aggregate demand and supply model to the concepts of demand-pull and cost-push inflation.

Inflation in other countries

Of course, inflation is not a distinctly Australian phenomenon. Exhibit 13.4 reveals that inflation rates vary widely among nations. In 2003, for example, Brazil and Indonesia had, relatively speaking, quite high inflation rates while New Zealand, Malaysia, France and the UK all had quite low rates. Taiwan actually experienced slight deflation in 2003.

Exhibit 13.4 **Average annual inflation rates in selected countries, 2003**

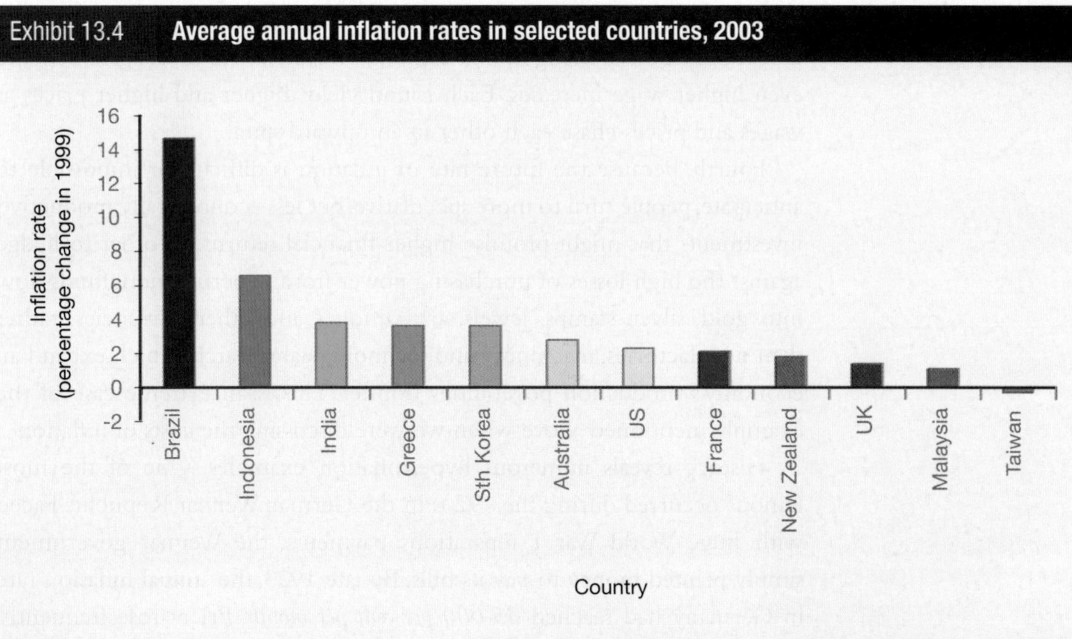

Source: Central Intelligence Agency, www.odci.gov, *World Factbook*.

Inflation on a rampage

Hyperinflation An extremely rapid rise in the general price level.

INFOTRAC®
hyperinflation

At different times during the twentieth century in a few different countries, some people had to carry a large stack of money to pay for something as simple as a chocolate bar because of the disastrous consequences of **hyperinflation**. Hyperinflation is an extremely rapid rise in the general price level. There is no consensus on when a particular rate of inflation becomes 'hyper'. However, most economists would agree that an inflation rate of about 1000 per cent per year (that is, prices going up ten-fold every year) or more is hyperinflation. Runaway inflation is conducive to rapid and violent social and political change stemming from four causes.

First, individuals and businesses develop an *inflation psychosis*, which causes them to buy quickly today in order to avoid paying even more tomorrow. The pressure is on everyone to spend earnings before their purchasing power deteriorates. No matter whether you are paid once, twice or any number of times per month, per week or even *per day* (yes, this has actually happened in some very extreme cases), you will be eager to spend it immediately.

Second, huge unanticipated inflation jeopardises debtor–lender contracts, such as credit cards, home mortgages, life insurance policies, pensions, bonds and other forms of savings. For example, if nominal interest rates rise unexpectedly in response to higher inflation, borrowers with variable interest rate contracts find it more difficult to make their monthly payments.

Wage–price spiral A situation that occurs when increases in nominal wage rates are passed on in higher prices, which in turn result in even higher nominal wage rates and prices.

Third, hyperinflation sets a vicious **wage–price spiral** in motion. A wage–price spiral can occur in quite normal economic circumstances but is deadly in terms of hyperinflation. It occurs in a series of steps when increases in nominal wage rates are passed on in higher prices, which in turn result in even higher nominal wage rates and prices. A wage–price spiral continues when management believes it can boost prices faster than the rise in labour costs. As the cost of living moves higher, however, labour must again demand even higher wage increases. Each round yields higher and higher prices as wages and prices chase each other in an upward spiral.

Fourth, because the future rate of inflation is difficult or impossible to anticipate, people turn to more speculative, but less economically productive, investments that might promise higher financial returns. In order to hedge against the high losses of purchasing power from hyperinflation, funds flow into gold, silver, stamps, jewels, art, antiques and other currencies, rather than new factories, machinery and technological research, which expand an economy's production possibilities frontier. This is an extreme case of the example mentioned above when we were discussing the costs of inflation.

History reveals numerous hyperinflation examples. One of the most famous occurred during the 1920s in the German Weimar Republic. Faced with huge World War I reparations payments, the Weimar government simply printed money to pay its bills. By late 1923, the annual inflation rate in Germany had reached *35 000 per cent per month*. Prices rose frequently, sometimes increasing in minutes, and German currency became so worthless that it was used as kindling for stoves. No one was willing to make new loans and credit markets collapsed. Wealth was redistributed, as those who were heavily in debt easily paid their debts and people's savings were wiped out.

When inflation rate is 116 000%, prices change by the hour

International focus

Applicable concept: hyperinflation

A 1985 *Wall Street Journal* article describes hyperinflation in La Paz, Bolivia:

> A courier stumbles into Banco Boliviano Americano, struggling under the weight of a huge bag of money he is carrying on his back. He announces that the sack contains 32 million pesos and a teller slaps on a notation to that effect. The courier pitches the bag into a corner. 'We don't bother counting the money any more,' explains Max Lowes Stah, a loan officer standing nearby. 'We take the client's word for what's in the bag.' Pointing to the courier's load, he says, 'That's a small deposit.' At that moment the 32 million pesos – enough bills to stuff a mail sack – were worth only $500. Today, less than two weeks later, they are worth at least $180 less. Life's like that with quadruple-digit inflation ...
>
> In 1984, prices zoomed 2,700 per cent, compared with a mere 329 per cent the year before. Experts are predicting the inflation rate could soar as high as 40,000 per cent this year [1985]. Even those estimates could prove conservative. The central bank last week announced January inflation of 80 per cent; if that pace continued all year, it would mean an annual rate of 116,000 per cent.
>
> Prices go up by the day, the hour or the customer. Julia Blanco Sirba, a vendor on this capital city's main street, sells a bar of chocolate for 35,000 pesos. Five minutes later, the next bar goes for 50,000 pesos. The two-inch stack of money needed to buy it far outweighs the chocolate ... The 1000-peso bill, the most commonly used, costs more to print than it purchases. It buys one bag of tea. To purchase an average-size television set with 1000-peso bills, customers have to haul money weighing more than 68 pounds into the showroom. (Inflation makes use of credit cards impossible here and merchants generally can't take checks, either.) To ease the strain, the government came out with a new 100,000-peso note, worth $1. But there aren't enough in circulation to satisfy demand.
>
> Three years ago, pharmacist Ruth Aranda says she bought a new luxury Toyota auto for what she now sells three boxes of aspirin. 'We're headed for the garbage can,' says Jorge von Bergen, an executive of La Papelera S.A., a large paper products company, who lugs his pocket-money around in a small suitcase ... [Brazilian restaurant owners often covered their menus with cellophane and changed prices several times daily using a dry-erase marker.][1]

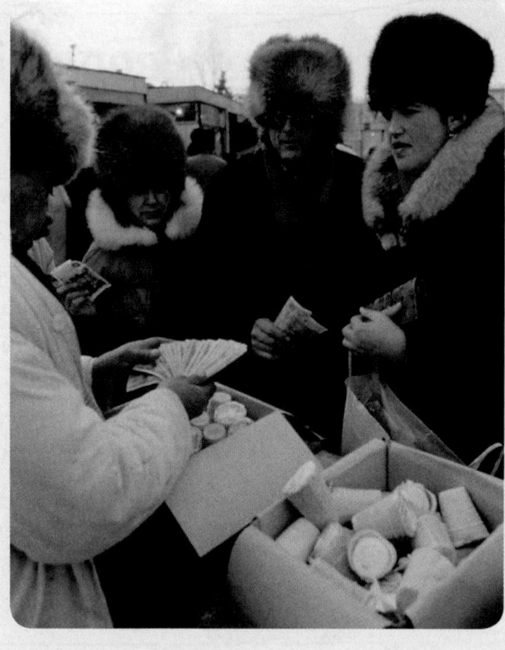

An Associated Press article reports a rate of inflation in the billions for Belgrade:

> The number on Wednesday was 286,125,293,792. It was not the day's winning lottery figures nor the number of miles to the Hubble space telescope. It was the latest calculation of Yugoslavia's nearly incalculable inflation rate ... To cover the costs of war and pay off the unemployed, the government has resorted to indiscriminately printing money. That has

PART 4

rendered the national currency, the dinar, practically worthless … 'Look at the prices,' Spomenka Magas, 39, a homemaker said in disgust. 'I cannot count all the zeroes any more.'[2]

A Dow Jones Newswire reported:

The Russian government is likely to try to solve the country's economic impasse by printing money and thus cause hyperinflation. If this happens, Russia's inflation rate will reach 450% to 500% this year, Gaidar, former Prime Minister, said. Even if the government rejects such measures, consumer prices will rise by 250% to 300% this year.[3]

---

1 Sonia L. Nazario, 'When inflation rate is 116 000%, prices change by the hour', 7 February 1985, p. 1. Reprinted by permission of the *Wall Street Journal*, © 1985 Dow Jones & Company, Inc. All Rights Reserved Worldwide.

2 Slobodan Lekic, 'Belgrade puts rate of inflation in billions', *Charlotte Observer*, 2 December 1993, p. 24A.

3 Paivi Munter, 'Russia's Gaidar: government to print money, trigger hyperinflation', *Dow Jones Newswire*, 2 October 1998.

Analyse the issue

1 Can you relate inflation psychosis to these excerpts? Give an example of a debtor–lender relationship that is jeopardised by hyperinflation.

2 Explain why the workers in Bolivia were striking, even though wages rose at an annual rate of 1500 per cent. Do you see any connection between hyperinflation and the political system?

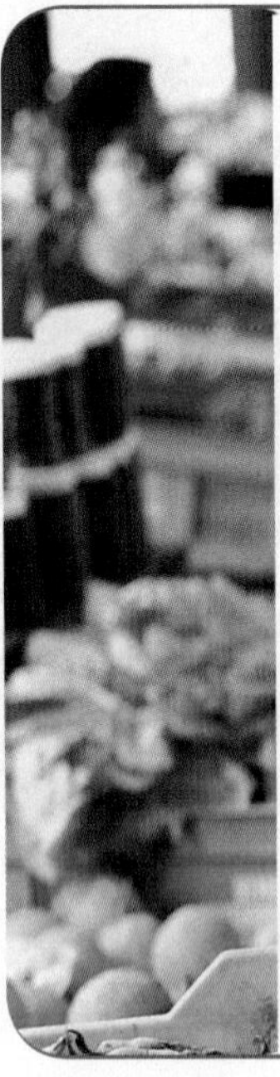

Economics and ethics

Hyperinflation is invariably the result of a government's ill-advised decision to increase dramatically a country's money supply to pay for government expenditure rather than raise taxes – or, of course, cut back on its own spending. Moreover, hyperinflation is not a historical relic, as we illustrated in our International Focus above. Again, referring back to our discussion on economics and ethics in Chapter 1, it can be argued that, to the extent that a government produces higher inflation by increasing a country's money supply to pay for its own purchases of goods and services, the government has, in effect, levied surreptitious taxes on the community. This follows because the resulting inflation reduces the real value of the stock of money held by the public. Therefore, effectively, there occurs a transfer of wealth from the private sector into the hands of the government – sounds quite a lot like a tax, doesn't it?

Unemployment

Since the abyss of the Great Depression, a major economic goal of Australia and most other developed countries around the world has been to achieve a high level of employment. For example, the Reserve Bank Act setting up Australia's Central Bank, the Reserve Bank of Australia (RBA), explicitly stipulates that one of the three goals of the RBA is to promote full employment in Australia. Of course, that raises the question: what is full employment?

The methods used in Australia to measure employment and unemployment are virtually identical to those used in most other developed nations. Each month the ABS conducts a survey of a random sample of households. Each member of the family who is 15 years of age or older is asked whether he or she is employed or unemployed. If a person works at least one hour per week for pay or at least 15 hours per week as an unpaid worker in a family business, that person is counted as employed. If the person is not employed, the question is then whether or not he or she has looked for work in the past month. If they have, the person is said to be unemployed. Using its survey data, the ABS publishes the **unemployment rate** and other employment-related statistics monthly.

The unemployment rate is the percentage of people in the **labour force** who are without jobs and are actively seeking jobs. But who is actually counted as an unemployed worker and which people belong to the labour force? Certainly, all people without jobs do not rank among the unemployed.

When workers lose their jobs they are eligible for unemployment compensation. For information on unemployment compensation, visit Centrelink (**www.centrelink.gov.au**).

unemployment rate

Unemployment rate The percentage of people in the labour force who are without jobs and are actively seeking jobs.

Civilian labour force The number of people 15 years of age and older who are employed or who are actively seeking a job, excluding those in the armed forces, home makers, students, discouraged workers and other persons not in the labour force.

PART 4

Exhibit 13.5 **Population, employment and unemployment**

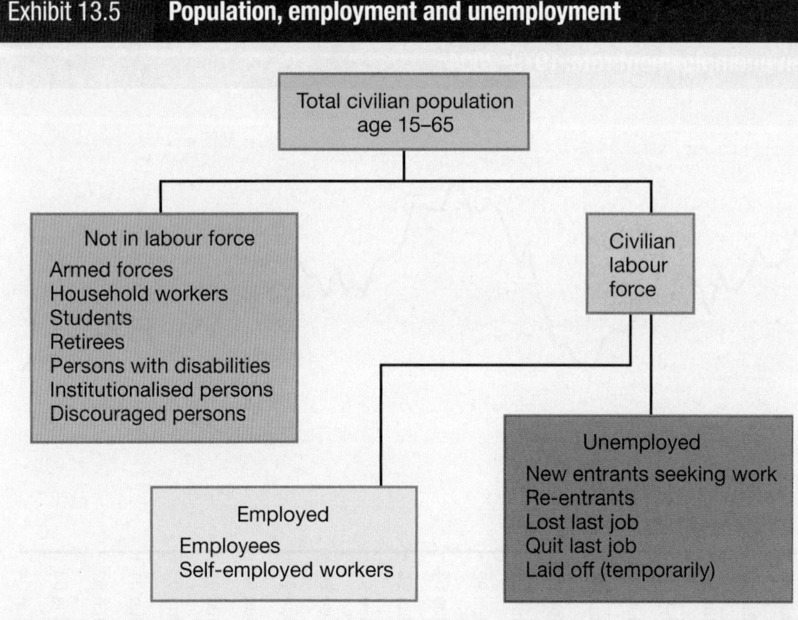

Babies, students and retired persons are not counted as unemployed. Likewise, workers who are ill or severely disabled are not included as unemployed.

Now we turn to Exhibit 13.5. The *civilian labour force* – which is usually what is reported and referred to in this text as simply the 'labour force' – is the number of people (excluding students) aged between 15 and 65 who are either employed or unemployed, excluding members of the armed forces and people in institutions such as prisons and mental hospitals. Based on survey data, the ABS computes the *civilian unemployment rate* – referred to in this text as simply the 'unemployment rate' – as the ratio of the number of unemployed to the labour force. In 2003–04, the unemployment rate averaged 5.8 per cent.

The Australian Bureau of Statistics provides data on consumer price indexes (**www.abs.gov.au**). Also, there are a variety of different price indexes from which inflation can be calculated. These indexes can be accessed through the Reserve Bank of Australia website (**www.rba.gov.au**). Select *Statistics*, then *Prices, then Bulletin Statistical Tables*.

The unemployment rate is widely reported and analysed and is always a very political issue. Indeed, governments can fall as a result of increased unemployment rates. Exhibit 13.6 charts the historical record of the Australian unemployment rate since the late 1970s. Note that the highest unemployment rate reached in the twentieth century was actually over 25 per cent during the years of the Great Depression (not charted). Since then, the highest rate of unemployment was experienced relatively recently, in 1992. At the other extreme, the lowest unemployment rate we have attained was below 2 per cent in some years during the 1960s.

The starkest feature of Exhibit 13.6 is the very dramatic effect that the early 1980s and early 1990s recessions had on Australia's unemployment rate. This is typical of the impact of recessions. Also notice the very long time it typically takes to get the unemployment rate back down after a recession.

Exhibit 13.6 **The Australian unemployment rate, 1978–2004**

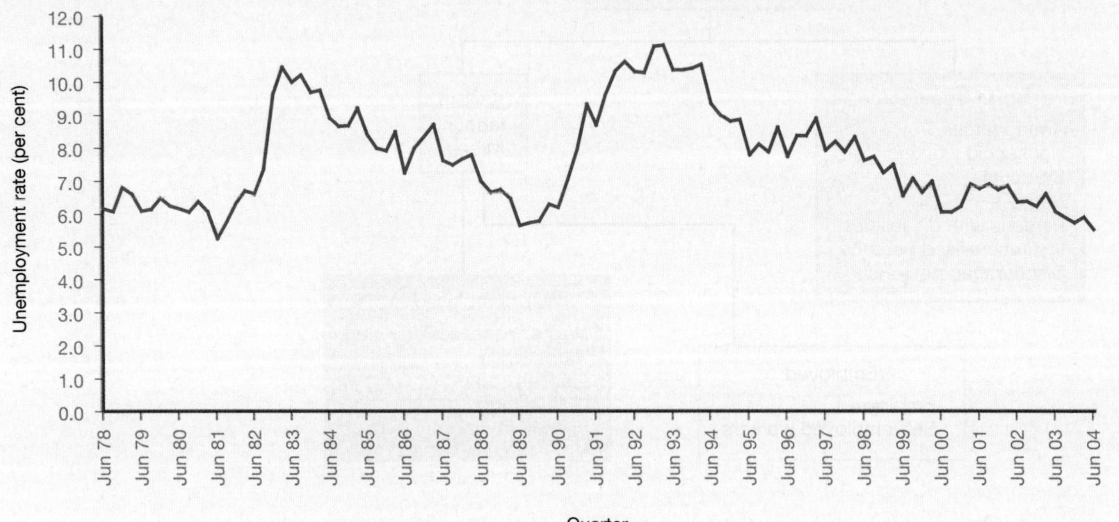

Source: Australian Bureau of Statistics, www.abs.gov.au, Cat. No. 6202.0.55.001, Table 3.

Unemployment in other countries

Exhibit 13.7 shows that, among developed countries, New Zealand had the lowest unemployment rate in 2003. The historically low rate in New Zealand during that year was the result of a number of consecutive years of very good economic growth. Australia also had a respectably low unemployment rate compared with other developed countries and continued to reduce its rate of unemployment down to 5.5 per cent by June 2004. Also note the very high unemployment rates in the European countries of France, Germany and Italy. Many economists argue that this is due to excess regulation and rigidity in the labour market systems of those countries. The United Kingdom also once had a very high unemployment rate until it significantly increased the flexibility of the operation of its labour markets in the 1980s and 1990s. By 2003, it registered one of the lowest unemployment rates in the developed world.

Exhibit 13.7 **Unemployment rates for selected nations, 2003**

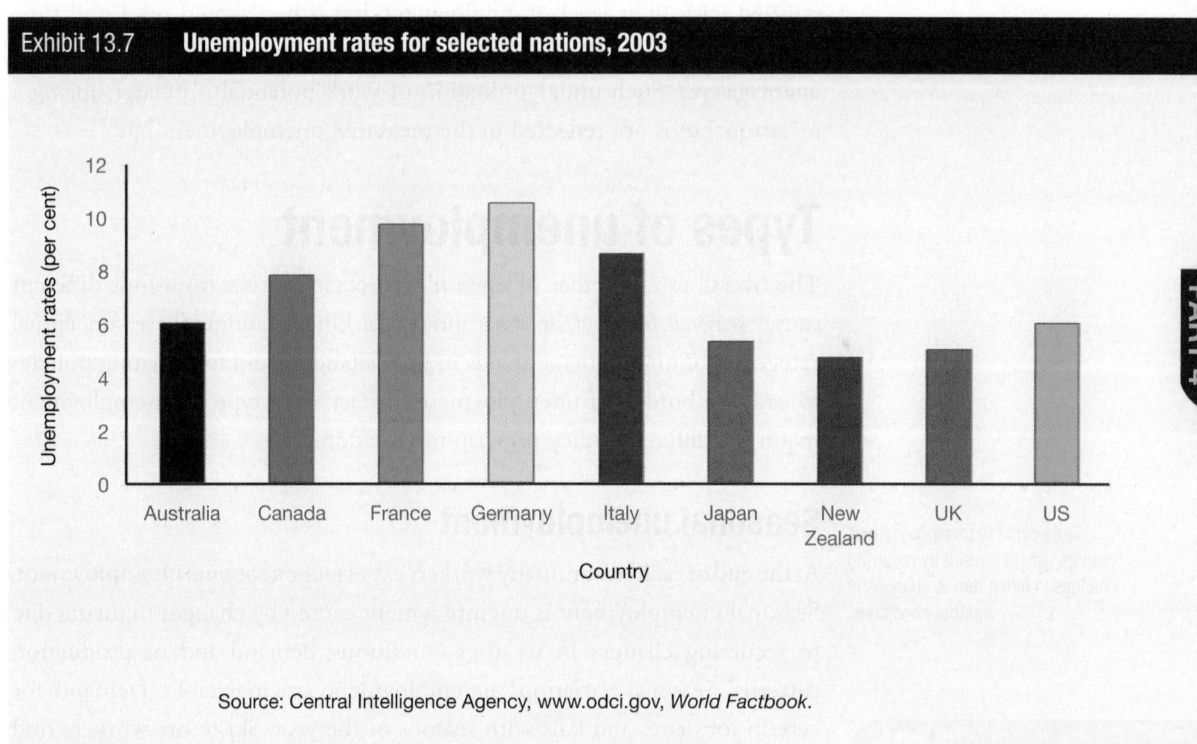

Source: Central Intelligence Agency, www.odci.gov, *World Factbook.*

Criticism of the unemployment rate

The unemployment rate is criticised for both understating and overstating the 'true' unemployment rate. An example of *overstating* the unemployment rate occurs when respondents to the ABS falsely report that they are seeking employment when they are not. The motivation may be that unemployment benefits depend on actively pursuing a job. Or an individual may be 'employed' in illegal activities.

PART 4

Discouraged worker
A person who wants to work, but who has given up searching for work because he or she believes there will be no job offers.

The other side of the coin is that the official definition of unemployment *understates* the unemployment rate by not counting so-called **discouraged workers**. A discouraged worker is a person who would really like to work, but who has given up searching for a job because he or she believes there will be no offers. After repeated rejections, discouraged workers often turn to their families, friends and possibly other forms of welfare for support. The ABS counts a discouraged worker as anyone who has looked for work within the last six months, but responds that he or she is no longer actively looking. The ABS simply includes discouraged workers in the 'not in labour force' category listed in Exhibit 13.5. Because the number of discouraged workers is likely to rise during a recession, the degree of underestimation of the official unemployment rate is thought to increase during a downturn.

Another example of *understating* the unemployment rate occurs because the official figure counts all part-time workers as equal to fully employed workers. These workers are actually partially employed. Many may be quite satisfied with their level of employment, but others would work full time if they could find full-time employment. These latter workers are, in effect, *underemployed*. Such under-utilisation of work potential is greater during a recession, but is not reflected in the measured unemployment rate.

Types of unemployment

The overall total number of unemployed persons arises from four different causes: *seasonal*, *frictional*, *structural* and *cyclical*. Understanding these conceptual categories of unemployment aids in understanding and formulating policies to ease the burden of unemployment. In fact, each type of unemployment requires a different policy prescription to address it.

Seasonal unemployment
Unemployment caused by recurring changes in hiring due to changes in weather conditions.

Seasonal unemployment

At the end of each season, many workers experience **seasonal unemployment**. Seasonal unemployment is unemployment caused by changes in hiring due to recurring changes in weather conditions, demand and/or production patterns. Seasonal variations in employment are inevitable. Demand for certain jobs rises and falls with seasons of the year. Ski resort workers find jobs at Australia's southern ski resorts during the winter, but not in the summer. The opposite is true for summer resort workers. Construction workers are sometimes seasonally unemployed – or laid off for short periods – during the wet season. When crops are harvested 'in season', farms hire many workers and when crops are 'out of season' these workers are seasonally unemployed. Some itinerant farm workers move from region to region to avoid being seasonally unemployed. As a final example, the Christmas season is generally a time of peak employment in the wholesale and retail trades areas.

For a useful perspective on real interest rates and other issues, see the Internet site maintained by Financial Pipeline (**www.finpipe.com/rintrate.htm**).

Frictional unemployment

For some unemployed workers, the absence of a job is only temporary. At any given time, some people with marketable skills lose their jobs and others voluntarily quit jobs to accept or look for new ones. And there are always young people who leave school and search for their first job. Workers in some industries, such as construction, experience short periods of unemployment between projects and temporary layoffs are common. Because jobs are available requiring their skills once the unemployed and the available jobs are matched, such workers are considered to be 'between jobs'.

This type of unemployment, called **frictional unemployment**, is usually quite short-term, and is therefore not of great concern from either a public policy or a social welfare perspective. Frictional unemployment is unemployment caused by the normal search time required by workers with marketable skills who are changing jobs, initially entering the labour force, or re-entering the labour force. The cause of frictional unemployment is either the transition time to a new job or the lack of immediate information required to match a job applicant immediately with a job vacancy. For this reason, frictional unemployment is sometimes called *transitional unemployment* or *search unemployment*.

Frictional unemployment Unemployment caused by the normal search time required by workers with marketable skills who are changing jobs, initially entering the labour force, or re-entering the labour force.

The fact that information about jobs is imperfect and sometimes difficult and costly to get influences the level of frictional unemployment in the economy at any time. Because it takes time to search for the information required to match employers and employees, there will always be some number of workers frictionally unemployed. Frictional unemployment is therefore simply a normal condition in an economic system that permits freedom of job choice. However, public policies can certainly affect the amount of frictional unemployment. Improved methods of distributing job information through a national data bank can help unemployed workers find jobs more quickly and reduce frictional unemployment. The introduction of the Job Network initiative by the Australian government in the late 1990s may be thought of as an example of trying to increase the efficiency of the job search and placement process.

Structural unemployment

Unlike frictional unemployment, **structural unemployment** is not a short-term situation. Instead it is long-term, or possibly permanent, unemployment resulting from the non-existence of jobs for some unemployed workers. Structural unemployment is unemployment caused by a mismatch of the skills of workers out of work and the skills required for existing job opportunities. While frictionally unemployed workers have marketable skills, structurally unemployed workers require additional education or retraining. Changes in the structure of the economy over time, resulting from changing tastes and demand conditions or from changed production processes, create the following three cases of structural unemployment.

Structural unemployment Unemployment caused by a mismatch of the skills of workers out of work and the skills required for existing job opportunities.

INFOTRAC®

structural unemployment

First, workers may face joblessness because they lack the education or the job-related skills to perform available jobs. This type of structural unemployment affects particularly teenagers and minority groups, but other groups of workers can be affected as well. For example, environmental concerns (resulting from changing community attitudes), such as protecting wildlife habitats, saving endangered forest areas or reducing the incidence of rising soil salinity may, by restricting tree cutting, reduce the overall number of jobs in the timber industry. To reduce such structural unemployment, timber industry workers would need to be retrained for entirely new jobs.

Second, the consuming public may change their pattern of demand. For example, they may increase the demand for imported cars and decrease the demand for domestically produced ones. This shift in demand could cause some local car workers to lose their jobs. If no other Australian car manufacturers needs workers, then such workers will become structurally unemployed. To regain employment, these unemployed car workers must retrain and find job openings in other industries (for example, manufacturing parts in the computer industry perhaps).

Third, implementation of the latest technology may also increase the pool of structural unemployment in a particular industry and region. For example, the Australian textile industry, located primarily in Victoria, can fight lower-priced foreign textile imports by installing modern machinery. This new capital may replace textile workers (and this has occurred). But suppose these unemployed textile workers do not wish to move to a new location where new types of jobs are available. The costs of moving, fear of the unknown and family ties are understandable reasons for reluctance to move and, instead, these workers become structurally unemployed.

There are many causes of structural unemployment, including poor educational levels, new products, new technology, foreign competition, geographic differences, restricted entry into jobs and shifts in government priorities. Because of the great dynamism of modern economies, with rapidly changing tastes and production techniques and the associated numerous sources of mismatching between skills and jobs, it is generally considered that a certain level of structural unemployment is inevitable. Public and private programs that retrain employees to fill existing job openings decrease structural unemployment.

Conversely, one of the concerns involved in minimum wage debates is that it may contribute to structural unemployment. This may happen if the regulated minimum wage is above the productivity of particular groups of unskilled workers. Rather than guarantee a minimum standard of living for the workers – the intention of the policy – it may, paradoxically, actually work against them by causing them to be unemployed. In Exhibit 4.5 in Chapter 4, we demonstrated that a minimum wage legislated above the equilibrium wage may cause unemployment. One approach intended to offset such undesirable effects of a minimum wage is a sub-minimum wage paid during a training period to give employers an incentive to hire unskilled workers. An alternative to this is to offer a separate financial incentive to the employer (thereby reducing the employment cost of the marginal worker) to hire workers who have been unemployed for a long time. Yet another alternative is to remove the minimum wage provisions entirely but ensure a reasonable minimum standard of living for the lowly paid through the tax and welfare system.

Cyclical unemployment

Cyclical unemployment is attributable directly to the lack of jobs caused by the business cycle. Cyclical unemployment is unemployment caused by the lack of jobs during a recession. When real GDP falls many companies cut back on production, other companies close altogether, jobs disappear and workers scramble for fewer available jobs. As in the game of musical chairs, there are not enough chairs (jobs) for the number of players (workers) in the game.

Cyclical unemployment Unemployment caused by the lack of jobs during a recession.

A dramatic example of cyclical unemployment was the Great Depression, when there was a sudden decline in consumption, investment, government consumption expenditures and net exports. As a result of this striking fall in real GDP, the unemployment rate rose to over 25 per cent. More recently, look what has happened to unemployment during each of Australia's recessions in the 1970s, 1980s and 1990s (see Exhibit 13.6). In each case unemployment rose dramatically and in a short time. Also notice that, after the recession is over, it seems to take a long time for enough jobs to be generated to get the unemployment rate back down again. For example, in the 1990s recession it took less than two years for the unemployment rate to rise from under 6 per cent to over 11 per cent but then took eight years to get back down to anything like 6 per cent. To smooth out these swings in unemployment, a focus of macroeconomic policy is to moderate cyclical unemployment.

The goal of full employment

In this section we take a closer look at the meaning of **full employment**. Because both frictional and structural unemployment are present in good and bad times, *full employment* does not mean 'zero per cent unemployment'. Full employment is the situation in which an economy operates at an unemployment rate equal to the sum of the seasonal, frictional and structural unemployment rates. Full employment therefore defines the rate of unemployment that exists without cyclical unemployment.

Full employment The situation in which an economy operates at an unemployment rate equal to the sum of the seasonal, frictional and structural unemployment rates.

Unfortunately, economists cannot state with certainty what percentage of the labour force is frictionally and structurally unemployed at any point in time. In practice, full employment is therefore difficult to define. Moreover, the full-employment rate of unemployment – sometimes referred to as the 'natural rate of unemployment' or the 'non-accelerating inflation rate of unemployment' (NAIRU) – quite clearly changes over time. In Australia in

full employment

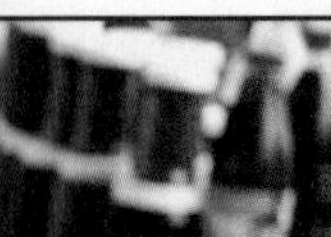

Analyse the issue

Applicable concept: types of unemployment

Is it a robot's world?

In the late 1980s, an article described the music industry:

People looking for job security have rarely chosen the music industry. But these days, musicians say, competition from machines has removed what little stability there was. Modern machines can effectively duplicate string sections, drummers and even horn sections, so with the exception of concerts, the jobs available to live musicians are growing fewer by the day …

It is not the first time that technology has thrown a wrench into musical careers. When talking pictures helped usher in the death of vaudeville and again, when recorded music replaced live music in radio station studios, the market for musicians took a beating from which it never fully recovered … The musicians' plight is not getting universal sympathy. Some industry insiders say that the current job problems are an inevitable price of progress and that musicians should update their skills to deal with the new instruments …

But others insist that more than musicians' livelihood is at stake. Mr Glasel, [Musicians' Union] Local 802's president, warns that unbridled computerization of music could eventually threaten the quality of music. Jobs for trumpet players, for instance, have dropped precipitously since the synthesiser managed a fair approximation of the trumpet. And without trumpet players, he asked, 'where is the next generation going to get its Dizzy Gillespie?'[1]

The following articles place the above in a global perspective by reporting on twenty-first century crystal ball gazing:

Will robots be stepping into the operating room? Research by the U.S. military is leading to a 'telemedicine' revolution that will someday see surgeons operating on patients hundreds or thousands of miles away across the globe by sending 'microrobots' inside patients' bodies to clamp and cut and sew and transferring medical information and images anywhere in seconds.[2]

And will the 21st century be the best of times and the worst of times? One best-of-times future has robots as concierges buying theater tickets. Automated workers taking care of messy, dangerous jobs such as disaster cleanup, mining and construction. 'Digital Docs' who help people live longer, more productive lives. 'Cybercountries' where people with like values will form their own virtual communities, dissolving political boundaries. People working anyplace, anytime via technology that beams pictures, sounds and information across time zones. A global workforce, raising the standard of living for Latin America, Africa and Asia.

The other worst-of-time future has an overpopulated world unable to sustain itself. Poor countries suffering from 'life system collapse' as sewers overflow, clean water dries up and the environment dies. Unemployment or lower wages as computers, robots and Latin American, African and Asian workers take over more jobs held by North Americans and Europeans. Less and less human contact as face-to-face socialization gives way to virtual work, virtual neighborhoods and virtual countries.[3]

A more recent article peeks at the American workplace just twenty years from now: fewer people will work at work sites like office buildings. Instead, many more will telecommute or work at satellite work centres in suburbs or rural areas. With sophisticated communications technology, virtual companies will become commonplace, operating globally. As a result, leadership styles will change to manage virtual employees.[4]

Using the above information, answer the following questions.

1 Are the musicians experiencing seasonal, frictional, structural, or cyclical unemployment? Explain.
2 What solution would you propose for the trumpet players mentioned above?

---

1 James S. Newton, 'A death knell sounds for musical jobs', *New York Times*, 1 March 1987, sec. 3, p. 9.

2 Richard Saltus, '"Telemedicine" foresees robots as surgeons', *Boston Globe*, 8 April 1996, sec. 3, p. 2.

3 Lini S. Kadaba, 'Futurists see more gizmos, fewer jobs', *Charlotte Observer*, 30 July 1995, p. 1A.

4 Toni Cardarella, 'Hold tight: futurists expect huge changes in workplace', *Kansas City Business Journal*, Vol. 16, No. 49, 21 August 1998, pp. 21–2.

the 1960s, 2 per cent unemployment was generally considered to represent full employment. During the 1970s it seemed to rise to around 4 per cent, in the 1980s and 1990s it was probably around 6 to 7 per cent, and in the 2000s up until the time of writing it was probably around 5 per cent.

Several reasons are given for why the full-employment rate of unemployment is not fixed. One reason may be that, during the period between the early 1960s and the early 1980s, the participation of women in the labour force increased significantly. This change in the labour force composition is thought to have increased the full-employment rate of unemployment because women typically experience higher unemployment rates than men. Another frequently cited, but not completely uncontroversial, explanation for the rise in the full-employment rate of unemployment since the 1960s is that larger relative unemployment benefits, welfare and the interaction of the tax and welfare systems have operated to make unemployment less painful and employment a less attractive option. In other words, it is argued that unemployment may now be a relatively more attractive economic alternative than in the 1950s and 1960s.

The ABS has a wealth of information relating to changing patterns of employment. For example, go to **www.abs.gov.au** and select *Australian Social Trends*, then *General information & Cumulative topic list*, then *Cumulative Topic List*, then *WORK*, then *Changing industries, changing jobs*.

You make the call

What kind of unemployment did the invention of the wheel cause?

But Egor, what about the effect on labor?

Would the invention of the wheel have caused frictional, structural or cyclical unemployment?

Hysteresis When the full-employment rate of unemployment increases (decreases) as the actual unemployment rate increases (decreases).

Finally, it is argued that the full-employment rate of unemployment is itself dependent on the recent path of actual measured unemployment. This is called unemployment **hysteresis**. Hysteresis occurs when the full-employment rate of unemployment increases (decreases) as the actual unemployment rate increases (decreases). There are a few explanations suggested as to why hysteresis might exist. First, if people become cyclically unemployed but stay unemployed for a long period, then their job skills can atrophy and their job readiness can reduce. The very fact that they have been unemployed for a long period of time can make them unattractive to prospective employers. As a result they can become structurally unemployed and almost unemployable. Another argument – referred to as the insider/outsider argument – is that, when demand again begins to take off at the end of a recession, those with jobs (insiders) will bid up market wage rates, thereby making the relatively unattractive recently unemployed (the outsiders) more expensive to hire and thereby increase the likelihood of their remaining unemployed.

Non-monetary and demographic consequences of unemployment

The burden of unemployment is more than the loss of potential output measured by the output that could have been produced by the unemployed. There are also non-monetary costs of unemployment. Some people endure it pretty well because they have substantial savings to draw on, but others sink into despair. Without work, many people lose their feeling of self-worth. A person's self-image suffers when they cannot support a family and be a 'valuable' member of society. It is generally agreed that people derive much more from their employment than simply their salary. Research has associated high unemployment with despair, family break-ups, suicides, crime, political unrest, mental illness, heart attacks and other health problems.

Various labour-market groups share the impact of unemployment unequally. Exhibit 13.8 presents the unemployment rates experienced by selected demographic groups. In 2003–04, the overall unemployment rate was on average about 5.8 per cent, but the figures in the exhibit reveal the unequal burden imposed by, among other things, age. First, it may surprise some that the unemployment rate for males was about the same as for females. Second, young people (15–19 year olds) experienced a relatively high unemployment rate because they are new entrants to the workforce who have little employment experience, high quit rates, and little job

Exhibit 13.8 Unemployment rates by selected groups, 2003–04

Demographic group	Unemployment rate (per cent)
Overall	5.8
Sex	
Male	5.6
Female	6.0
Age (years)	
15–19	15.7
20–24	8.9
25–34	5.4
35–54	4.1
55 and over	3.3
By unemployment duration (weeks)	**% of total unemployed**
Under 4	25.0
4 to under 13	24.7
13 to under 26	15.8
26 to under 52	13.5
52 and over	21.0

Source: Australian Bureau of Statistics, www.abs.gov.au, Cat. No. 6291.0.55.001, Table 1.

You make the call

Applicable concept: human costs of unemployment

Brother, can you spare a dime?

The unemployment rate does not measure the full impact of unemployment on individuals. Prolonged unemployment not only means lost wages, but also impairs health and social relationships. Developed nations around the world fought their toughest battle against unemployment during the Great Depression of the 1930s. In fact, it was precisely because of the Great Depression that nations around the world put in place the beginnings of today's modern welfare systems. As noted earlier, the unemployment rate reached a maximum of 25 per cent during the Depression and stayed in the 20 per cent plus region for several years during the 1930s. For comparison, at the low point of the 1990–92 recession – the worst since World War II – the unemployment rate in Australia 'only' reached a high of 11 per cent.

But these statistics tell only part of the horror story. Millions of workers were 'discouraged workers' who had simply given up looking for work because there was no work available, and these people were not counted. During the Great Depression people were standing in line at soup kitchens, selling produce on the street, or roaming the outback looking for whatever work they could find. The Australian movie *The Sundowners* told the story of the men who would arrive at a farm or station at dusk and try to get a meal and a place to sleep that night by doing some odd jobs. In America 'Brother, can you spare a dime?' was a common greeting; some people jumped out of windows and others roamed the country trying valiantly to survive. For example, John Steinbeck's great novel *The Grapes of Wrath* described millions of Midwesterners who drove in caravans to California after being wiped out by drought in what became known as the Dust Bowl.

A 1992 US study estimated the frightening impact of sustained unemployment not reflected in official unemployment data. Mary Merva, University of Utah economist, co-authored a study of unemployment in thirty selected big cities from 1976 to 1990. The finding of this research was that a 1 percentage point increase in the national unemployment rate resulted in

- 6.7 per cent more murders,
- 3.1 per cent more deaths from stroke,
- 5.6 per cent more fatal heart disease and
- a 3.9 per cent increase in suicides.[1]

Although these estimates are subject to statistical qualifications, they underscore the notion that prolonged unemployment poses a real danger to many individuals. As people change their behaviour in the face of layoffs, cutbacks or a sudden drop in net worth, more and more people find themselves at risk with respect to their mental health.

There is no question to analyse here, but it is important to understand the broad social and human cost of unemployment in addition to the direct economic cost.

1 Robert Davis, 'Recession's cost: lives', *USA Today*, 16 October 1992, News, p. 1A.

mobility. You will also see the quite low unemployment rates among the over-55s. This is because the vast majority of people in that age bracket either voluntarily leave the labour force or become discouraged in seeking work and subsequently leave the labour force.

Finally, comparison of the unemployment rates in 2003–04 by unemployment duration reveals that quite a large proportion (21 per cent) of the unemployed had been unemployed for over a year. This group is referred to as 'the long-term unemployed' and it is this group for whom it is most difficult to find new jobs. Encouragingly, however, at the time of writing the first edition of this book in 2001, the latest data then available for 1999–2000 indicated the unemployment rate among this group was then 29 per cent. Over the intervening four years till 2003–04, some progress had evidently been made in reducing the proportion of those suffering long-term unemployment to 21 per cent.

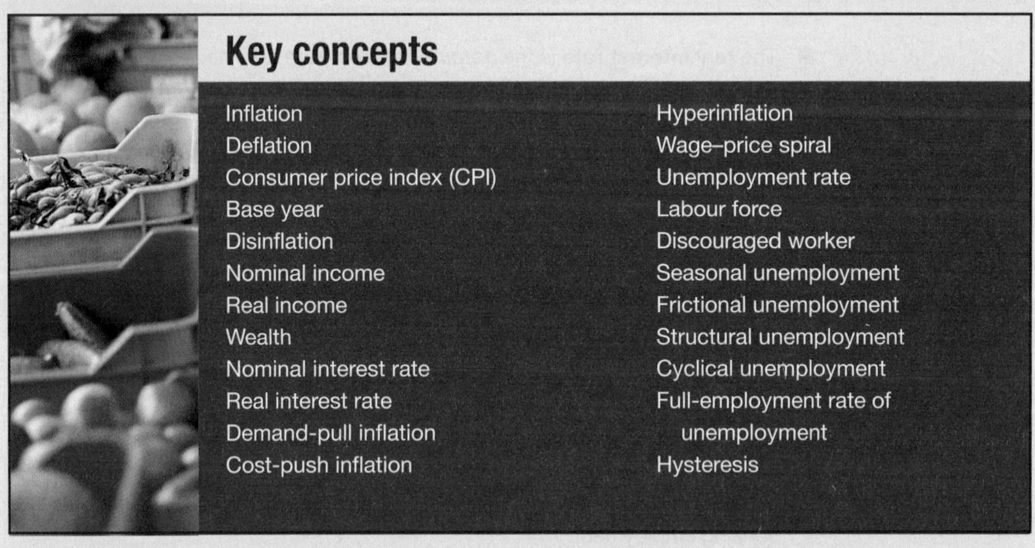

Key concepts

- Inflation
- Deflation
- Consumer price index (CPI)
- Base year
- Disinflation
- Nominal income
- Real income
- Wealth
- Nominal interest rate
- Real interest rate
- Demand-pull inflation
- Cost-push inflation
- Hyperinflation
- Wage–price spiral
- Unemployment rate
- Labour force
- Discouraged worker
- Seasonal unemployment
- Frictional unemployment
- Structural unemployment
- Cyclical unemployment
- Full-employment rate of unemployment
- Hysteresis

PART 4

Summary

- **Inflation** is an increase in the general (average) price level of goods and services in the economy.

- The **consumer price index (CPI)** is the most widely known price-level index. It measures the cost of purchasing a market basket of goods and services by a typical household during a time period relative to the cost of the same bundle during a base year. The annual rate of inflation is computed using the following formula:

$$\text{Annual rate of inflation} = \frac{\text{CPI in given year} - \text{CPI in previous year}}{\text{CPI in previous year}} \times 100$$

- **Deflation** is a decrease in the general level of prices. During the early years of the Great Depression, there was deflation and the CPI declined at a double-digit rate. More recently, in some quarters of 1997–2000 Australia experienced deflation and during the 1990s deflation was common in Japan.

- **Disinflation** is a reduction in the inflation rate. Between 1992 and 2000 there were a number of years of disinflation in Australia. This does not mean that prices were falling, but only that the inflation rate fell (for example from, say, +5 per cent to +3 per cent).

- The **CPI** is criticised because (1) it is not representative, (2) it incorrectly adjusts for quality changes and (3) it ignores the relationship between items' price changes and their relative importance in the market basket.

- **Nominal income** is income measured in actual money amounts. Measuring your purchasing power requires converting nominal income into **real income**, which is nominal income adjusted for inflation.

Percentage change in real income = Percentage change in nominal income – Percentage change in CPI

- The **real interest rate** is the *nominal interest rate* adjusted for inflation. If real interest rates are negative, lenders incur losses.

- **Demand-pull inflation** is caused by pressure on prices originating from the buyers' side of the market. On the other hand, **cost-push inflation** is caused by pressure on prices originating from the sellers' side of the market.

- **Hyperinflation** can seriously disrupt an economy by causing inflation psychosis, credit market collapses, a **wage–price spiral** and speculation. A wage–price spiral occurs when increases in nominal wages cause higher prices and, in turn, higher wages and prices.

- The **unemployment rate** is the ratio of the number of unemployed to the number in the labour force multiplied by 100. The nation's **labour force** consists of people who are employed plus those who are out of work but seeking employment.

- **Discouraged workers** are persons who want to work, but have given up looking for work. Critics say that the existence of discouraged workers means the unemployment rate is *understated*. Another criticism of the unemployment rate is that it *overstates* unemployment because respondents can falsely report that they are seeking a job.

- **Seasonal**, **frictional**, **structural** and **cyclical unemployment** are different types of unemployment. **Seasonal unemployment** is unemployment due to seasonal changes. **Frictional unemployment** results when workers are seeking new jobs that exist but imperfect information prevents matching of the applicants with the available jobs. **Structural unemployment** is unemployment caused by the changing structural features of an economy. Such structural changes include changing job skill needs in the

PART 4

economy, changes in product demand and technological change. **Cyclical unemployment** is unemployment resulting from recessions.

- **Full employment** occurs when the unemployment rate is equal to the total of the seasonal, frictional and structural unemployment rates. The actual rate can change through time and is considered to be at least partially a function of a community's labour market institutional arrangements. If it increases (decreases) with increases (decreases) in the actual measured unemployment rate this is known as **hysteresis**. Currently, the full-employment rate of unemployment in Australia is considered to be around 6 per cent. At this rate of unemployment, the economy would be producing at its current maximum potential.

Study questions and problems

1 Consider this statement: 'When the price of a good or service rises, the inflation rate rises.' Do you agree or disagree? Explain.

2 What are three criticisms of the CPI?

3 Suppose you earned $100 000 per year in 2004. Using 1996 as the base year, calculate your real 2004 income measured in 1996 dollars, assuming the CPI is 155 in 2004.

4 Who loses from inflation? Who wins from inflation?

5 Suppose the annual nominal rate of interest on a bank certificate of deposit is 12 per cent. What would be the effect of an inflation rate of 13 per cent?

6 When the economy approaches full employment, why does demand-pull inflation become a problem?

7 How does demand-pull inflation differ from cost-push inflation?

8 Explain this statement: 'If everyone expects inflation to occur, it will'.

9 Describe the relevant criteria that government statisticians use to determine whether a person is 'unemployed'.

10 How has the official unemployment rate been criticised for overestimating and underestimating unemployment?

11 Why is frictional unemployment inevitable in an economy characterised by imperfect job information?

12 How does structural unemployment differ from cyclical unemployment?

13 Is it reasonable to expect the unemployment rate to fall to zero for an economy? What is the relationship of frictional, structural and cyclical unemployment to the full-employment rate of unemployment, or the natural rate of unemployment?

Online exercises

Exercise 1

Visit the Reserve Bank of Australia website (**www.rba.gov.au**) and select **Statistics, Prices, Bulletin Statistical Tables, Prices and Output**, then **Labour Costs**.

1 Find the annual percentage changes in the 'wage cost index' since March 2000.

2 Similarly, calculate the annual inflation rates as measured by the percentage change in the CPI since March 2000. (After **Prices**, select **Consumer Price Index**.)

3 Compare the two patterns.

Exercise 2

Visit the ABS site (**www.abs.gov.au**) and Select **AusStats, Publications & Data, Time Series Spreadsheets, By Catalogue/Subject, OECD** and then **OECD – Consumer Prices**. Compare the Australian inflation rate in the 1970s, 1980s and 1990s with that for Japan, Germany, New Zealand, Canada, the United Kingdom and the United States. Over what time frame did inflation rise most rapidly for all of these countries? What could have caused this?

Exercise 3

Visit the Australian Bureau of Statistics site (**www.abs.gov.au**) and select **AusStats**, **Publications & Data**, **Time Series Spreadsheets**, **By Catalogue/Subject**, **62. Labour Force**, then find data on the Un Rates for Australia's regions.

1 Select your state unemployment rate series for the latest period.

2 Compare the Australia-wide unemployment rate with your state's unemployment rate for that period.

Exercise 4

Visit the UN website (**www.un.org/databases**). Select **Social Indicators** and then **Unemployment**, and compare Australia's unemployment rate with the unemployment rates of New Zealand, Singapore, Thailand, Canada, the United Kingdom, Germany, France and the United States.

Answers to 'You make the call'

The university education price index

If you said the price of a university education increased 9.8 per cent in 2004, YOU ARE CORRECT.

What kind of unemployment did the invention of the wheel cause?

The invention of the wheel represented a new technology for people in ancient times. Many workers who transported goods lost their jobs, even in the primitive era, to the more efficient cart with wheels. If you said the invention of the wheel caused structural unemployment, YOU ARE CORRECT.

Multiple-choice questions

1 Inflation is
- a an increase in the general price level.
- b not a concern during war.
- c a result of high unemployment.
- d an increase in the relative price level.

2 If the CPI in 2003 was 300 and 315 in 2004, the rate of inflation was
- a 5 per cent.
- b 15 per cent.
- c 25 per cent.
- d 315 per cent.

3 Consider an economy with only two goods: bread and wine. Let's say that, in 1990, the typical family bought 4 loaves of bread at 50 cents per loaf and 2 bottles of wine for $9 per bottle. In 2004, let's say bread cost 75 cents per loaf and wine cost $10 per bottle. The CPI for 2004 (using a 1990 base year) is
- a 100.
- b 115.
- c 126.
- d 130.

4 As shown in Exhibit 13.9, the rate of inflation for Year 2 is
- a 5 per cent.
- b 10 per cent.
- c 20 per cent.
- d 25 per cent.

Exhibit 13.9 **Consumer price index**

Year	Consumer price index
1	100
2	110
3	115
4	120
5	125

5 As shown in Exhibit 13.9, the rate of inflation from Year 3 to Year 5 is
- a 4.2 per cent.
- b 10 per cent.
- c 8.7 per cent.
- d 25 per cent.

6 Deflation is
- a an increase in most prices.
- b a decrease in the general price level.
- c a situation that has never occurred in Australian history.
- d a decrease in the inflation rate.

7 Which of the following would overstate the consumer price index?
- a substitution bias
- b improving quality of products
- c neither **a** nor **b**
- d both **a** and **b**

8 Suppose a typical automobile tyre cost $50 in 1991 and had a useful life of 40 000 km. In 2004, let's suppose the typical automobile tyre cost $75 and had a useful life of 75 000 km. If no adjustment is made for mileage, the CPI would
- **a** underestimate inflation between the two years.
- **b** overestimate inflation between the two years.
- **c** accurately measure inflation between the two years.
- **d** not measure inflation in this case.

9 When the inflation rate rises, the purchasing power of nominal income
- **a** remains unchanged.
- **b** decreases.
- **c** increases.
- **d** changes by the inflation rate minus one.

10 Last year the Harrison family earned $50 000. This year their income is $52 000. In an economy with an inflation rate of 5 per cent, which of the following is correct?
- **a** The Harrisons' nominal income and real income have both risen.
- **b** The Harrisons' nominal income and real income have both fallen.
- **c** The Harrisons' nominal income has fallen and their real income has risen.
- **d** The Harrisons' nominal income has risen and their real income has fallen.

11 The labour force consists of all persons
- **a** 21 years of age and older.
- **b** 21 years of age and older who are working.
- **c** 15 years of age and older.
- **d** 15 years of age and older who are working or actively seeking work.

12 People who are not working will be counted as out of the labour force if they are
- **a** on vacation.
- **b** a student.
- **c** both **a** and **b**.
- **d** neither **a** nor **b**.

13 Frictional unemployment applies to
- **a** workers with skills not required for existing jobs.
- **b** short periods of unemployment needed to match jobs and job seekers.
- **c** people who spend long periods of time out of work.
- **d** unemployment related to the ups and downs of the business cycle.

14 Structural unemployment is caused by
- **a** shifts in the economy that make certain job skills obsolete.
- **b** temporary layoffs in industries such as construction.
- **c** the impact of the business cycle on job opportunities.
- **d** short-term changes in the economy.

15 Unemployment due to a recession is
- **a** involuntary unemployment.
- **b** frictional unemployment.
- **c** structural unemployment.
- **d** cyclical unemployment.

16 Seasonal, frictional and structural unemployment is equal to
- **a** frictional unemployment.
- **b** structural unemployment.
- **c** cyclical unemployment.
- **d** full employment.

17 Which of the following statements is *true*?
- **a** Full employment by definition is when unemployment is zero.
- **b** When unemployment is rising, real GDP is rising.
- **c** The economic problem typically associated with a recovery is rising unemployment.
- **d** Full employment exists in an economy when the unemployment rate equals the sum of seasonal, frictional and structural unemployment rates.

18 Which of the following is *true*?
- **a** The GDP gap is the difference between full-employment real GDP and actual real GDP.
- **b** We desire economic growth because it increases the nation's real GDP.
- **c** Economic growth is conventionally measured by the annual percentage increase in a nation's real GDP.
- **d** Discouraged workers are a reason why critics say the unemployment rate is understated.
- **e** All of the above are true.

14 A simple model of the macro economy

In many countries around the world the 1920s are known as the 'Roaring 20s'. It was a time of optimism and prosperity. Between 1920 and 1929 real GDP rose rapidly. Australia had one of the highest levels of real GDP per capita in the world. Stock prices rose strongly year after year. As business boomed, companies invested in new factories and unemployment was low. It was a time when people bought fine clothes, had parties and danced the popular Charleston. Then, after October 1929, the business cycle took an abrupt downturn. Following the lead from New York, stock markets around the world crashed and the most severe world recession of the twentieth century began within a year. During this terrible economic contraction, which became known as the Great Depression, stock prices fell, wages fell, real output fell, banks failed, businesses closed their doors and the unemployment rate soared to 25 per cent. Men (at that time men comprised almost the entire workforce) would fight over a job, sell produce on the corner to survive and walk the streets and country in bewilderment.

The misery of the Great Depression created a revolution in economic thought. Prior to the Great Depression, economists had recognised that over the years business downturns would interrupt a nation's prosperity, but they believed these episodes were temporary and self-correcting. They argued that in a short time the price system would reliably and automatically restore an economy to full employment without government intervention.

Why – even after four years or more – didn't the economy self-correct back to its 1929 level of real output? What went wrong? The stage was set for some new ideas offered by the great British economist John Maynard Keynes (pronounced 'canes'). Keynes argued that the economy was not self-correcting and that unemployment could indeed continue indefinitely because of inadequate aggregate spending. Keynes's work not only explained the Depression, but also offered policy prescriptions requiring the government to play an active role in managing the economy. Whether or not modern economists agree with Keynes, his ideas still influence macroeconomics today.

This chapter begins with a discussion of classical economic theory before Keynes. Then you will learn more about what determines the various components of demand expenditures (C, I, G and $X - M$) and how these components are combined to form a simple demand-oriented Keynesian macroeconomic model. In particular, you will learn about one of the most powerful ideas in Keynesian theory, the spending multiplier. This simple Keynesian model offers an understanding of a cure for an economy in severe recession where inflation is not a problem. The policy prescription for such an economy is for government to expand aggregate demand (through its own spending or by cutting taxes), raise output and production, create jobs and restore full employment.

Later, this demand-oriented model is extended to incorporate issues relating to aggregate supply, and you will learn how aggregate demand and supply analysis can be used to understand more fully the forces that generate the business cycle. We will open with a presentation of the aggregate demand curve and then the aggregate supply curve. Once these concepts are developed, the analysis shows why modern macroeconomics teaches that shifts in aggregate supply or aggregate demand can influence the price level, the equilibrium level of real GDP and employment. You will probably return to this chapter often because it provides the basic tools with which to organise your thinking about the macro economy.

In this chapter, you will examine these economics questions:

- Why did classical economists believe the Great Depression was impossible?
- Why did Keynes reject the classical theory that 'supply creates its own demand'?
- Why did Keynes argue that the government should adopt active policies rather than allow the private market system to prevail?
- Why does the aggregate supply curve have three different segments?
- Would the greenhouse effect cause inflation, unemployment or both?
- Was John Maynard Keynes's prescription for the Great Depression right?

Introducing classical theory and the Keynesian revolution

To read more about Adam Smith, visit **www.blupete.com/Literature/Biographies/Philosophy/Smith.htm.**

Prior to the Great Depression, a group of economists known as the *classical economists* dominated economic thinking. The founder of the classical school of economics was the great Adam Smith. The classical economists believed that the forces of supply and demand, which you studied in Chapter 4, would naturally achieve full employment in the economy because flexible prices (including wages and interest rates) in competitive markets bring all markets to equilibrium. Markets – perhaps after a short adjustment period – always clear, enabling firms to sell all goods and services offered for sale.

CONCLUSION **The classical economists believed that a continuing depression is impossible because private markets eliminate persistent shortages or surpluses of products and labour.**

Say's Law The theory that supply creates its own demand. Say's Law was the cornerstone of classical economics as it applied to macroeconomics.

The simple idea known as **Say's Law**, developed in the early 1800s by Jean-Baptiste Say, convinced classical economists that a prolonged depression was impossible. Say's Law is the theory that supply creates its own demand. Say's Law was the cornerstone of classical economics as it applied to macroeconomics. Simply put, this theory states that the production of goods and services (supply) generates an equal amount of total spending (demand) for these goods and services.

In brief, their position can be explained as follows. Recall the circular flow model explained in Chapter 11 on GDP. Suppose a firm produces 100 000 loaves of bread that it intends to sell in the product markets for $1 each to consumers. This supply decision potentially creates $100 000 of income for the household sector to be paid through the factor markets (paid out, say, in wages and profits). The production thereby potentially creates just the right amount of income in the economy to purchase all the product produced without layoffs. If, after all, the bread could not be sold for $1, prices and wages would quickly drop to clear the bread market and maintain full employment (but at a lower wage). If unemployment were to occur, it would be the result of a short-lived adjustment period during which wages and prices declined in order to clear markets. Anyone unemployed after the short-run adjustment period had passed would have chosen that state voluntarily rather than work at the prevailing wage rates.

John Maynard Keynes

In 1936, *John Maynard Keynes* published *The General Theory of Employment, Interest and Money*.[1] In his book, Keynes challenged the classical thinking by turning Say's Law upside down. In effect, Keynesian theory placed great primacy on the demand side of the economy and, if you like, argued that 'demand creates its own supply.' Keynes argued that, over long enough

1 John Maynard Keynes, *The General Theory of Employment, Interest and Money*, Macmillan, London, 1936.

periods to be materially of concern, *aggregate expenditures* can be inadequate for an economy to achieve full employment.

Aggregate expenditures are the sum of consumption (*C*), investment (*I*), government spending (*G*) and net exports (*X* – *M*). Aggregate expenditures are also known as aggregate spending or aggregate demand. Recall from Chapter 11 on GDP that *C*, *I*, *G* and (*X* – *M*) are national accounting categories used to calculate GDP following the expenditure approach. The remainder of this section is devoted to outlining briefly the economic determinants of the consumption, investment, government and net exports expenditure components of aggregate demand.

Consumption demand (*C*)

What determines your family's spending for food, clothing, cars, education and other consumer goods and services? The most important factor is considered to be disposable income (personal income after taxes). It is widely accepted as a fundamental psychological premise that, if take-home pay increases, consumers can be expected to increase their spending – but not necessarily by the full amount of the extra income. The relationship between consumption and disposable income is represented by the so-called **consumption function**. The consumption function shows the amount households want to spend on goods and services at different levels of disposable income. Recall from Exhibit 11.3 in Chapter 11 that consumption (*C*) is the largest single component of aggregate expenditures. (In modern developed economies it now accounts for about 60 to 65 per cent of total production.)

Consumption function Shows the amount households want to spend on goods and services at different levels of disposable income.

Marginal propensities to consume and save

As income grows, so does consumption, but by less than income. This crucial concept is called the **marginal propensity to consume (MPC)**. The marginal propensity to consume is the change in consumption resulting from a given change in disposable income. For example, an MPC of 0.75 means that, for every dollar increase (decrease) in disposable income, consumption should increase (decrease) by 75 cents.

Marginal propensity to consume (MPC) The change in consumption resulting from a given change in disposable income.

In each model developed throughout this text, we assume that the MPC is constant for all income levels. This is admittedly an unrealistic assumption, as those on lower incomes will certainly have higher MPCs than those on higher incomes. Nevertheless, none of the fundamental ideas discussed in the text are changed by recognising that MPCs do in fact vary for different income groups. What do households do with extra disposable income if they do not spend it? They save it. The **marginal propensity to save (MPS)** is the change in savings resulting from a given change in disposable income; it is therefore 1 – MPC. In our example the MPS is 0.25.

Marginal propensity to save (MPS) The change in savings resulting from a given change in disposable income; that is, 1 – MPC.

You make the call

What's your MPC?

As your income increases over time, your marginal propensity to consume (MPC) can remain constant, or it can change. Would you expect your MPC to increase, decrease or remain constant as your income increases throughout your career?

Factors other than income affecting consumption behaviour

The current status of consumer confidence (or sentiment) is measured monthly in Australia by the Melbourne Institute. For more information visit (**www.melbourneinstitute.com**)and select *Publications, Economic and Indicators*, then *Westpac-Melbourne Institute Surveys of Consumer Sentiment*.

Expectations and consumption demand

Consumer expectations are subjective – optimistic or pessimistic – views of the future, which can change consumption spending in the present. Expectations may involve the future inflation rate, the likelihood of becoming unemployed, the likelihood of receiving higher income, or the future shortage of products resulting from, say, a war, strikes or drought, or many other matters. Suppose households believe prices will be much higher next year and buy now, rather than paying more in the future. The effect of such expectations would be to trigger current spending and increase consumption across income groups. The anticipation of a recession and fears about losing jobs would make families more tight-fisted in their current spending. This means a decrease in consumption across all income groups.

Wealth

Holding all other factors constant,[2] the more wealth households accumulate, the more they spend at any current level of disposable income. The dramatic stock market crash of 1929 sharply decreased the financial wealth of many and was a significant factor in the depressed consumption of the 1930s. Similarly and more recently, the surge in share prices in the late 1990s, particularly in the United States, is widely considered to have been an important cause of the very rapid growth in consumption in that country during that period. In the same way, the abrupt sharp downward adjustment in US and other share markets in early 2000 through to the end of 2002 was regarded as having a depressing effect on household consumption spending. Wealth owned by households includes both *real* assets such as, for example, homes, cars, televisions and DVD players, and *financial* assets including, for example, cash, savings accounts, shares, bonds, superannuation, managed funds and

2 This is a favourite phrase of economists. The words 'ceteris paribus', explained in Chapter 1, mean the same thing. Of course, in the real world, other things are never constant but are changing all the time. Economists realise this, but if you are to have any hope of understanding how changes in a whole host of things can be expected to affect others, then to grasp the fundamental causal mechanisms at work it is useful to isolate each separate determinant and analyse what its individual impact would be if nothing else were to change.

insurance policies. Changes in stock market prices, real estate prices and prices of other assets affect the value of wealth and, in turn, can change the willingness of the nation's consumers to spend.

The price level

Any change in the general price level shifts consumption demand by reducing or enlarging the *purchasing power* of financial assets (wealth) with fixed nominal value. Suppose you own a $100 000 government or corporate bond. If the price level increases by, say, 10 per cent, this same financial asset will buy approximately 10 per cent less when you sell it. If the real value of financial wealth falls, families are poorer and spend less at any level of current disposable income. The next section discusses this phenomenon in more detail.

The interest rate

Some consumption – for example, spending on big-ticket consumer durables like expensive kitchen appliances, electronic gear, boats and cars – often requires borrowing to finance the spending. A lower rate of interest on loans encourages consumers to borrow more and a higher interest rate discourages consumer indebtedness. If interest rates fall, households across the various income groups will be more inclined to use more credit to finance consumer purchases.

Investment demand (*I*)

It is widely accepted that changes in the private-sector components of aggregate expenditures (personal consumption and investment spending) are the major cause of the business cycle. And the more volatile of these two components is investment spending. Possibly the explanation for the relatively greater stability of consumption spending is that changes in determinants of personal consumption other than income tend to offset each other. Or maybe people are simply reluctant to change their personal consumption habits and, if necessary, they tend to draw on their accumulated savings to try to maintain their consumption. Whatever the reason, the stability of personal consumption has been widely observed in many countries over many different time periods. Recall from Chapter 11 that investment expenditures (gross private domestic investment) consist of spending on newly produced residential and non-residential structures, plant and equipment and on changes in inventories.

The current status of business expectations is measured quarterly by the Australian Chamber of Commerce and Industry. Visit **www.acci.asn.au** and select *Surveys*, then *National Survey of Business Expectations*, then whatever quarter you want to look at.

There are two major determinants of investment spending, namely expectations of future returns from a potential investment and the interest rate, which is the financing cost of any investment proposal. Using a microeconomic example to illustrate the investment decision-making process, suppose a consulting firm plans to purchase a new computer program for $1000 that will be obsolete in a year. It is expected that the new software will increase the firm's revenue by $1100. Thus, assuming no taxes

The Reserve Bank of Australia publishes current and historical data on interest rates (www.rba.gov.au).

and other expenses exist, the expected rate of return is 10 per cent from this investment.

Now consider the impact of the cost of borrowing funds to finance the software investment. If the interest rate is less than 10 per cent the business will expect to earn a positive return from the investment, so it will be inclined to buy the computer program. On the other hand, a rate of interest higher than 10 per cent means the software investment will result in a loss, so this project would not be undertaken. In other words, businesses will undertake all planned investment projects for which the expected rate of return equals or exceeds the interest rate. In aggregate, and ignoring other determinants of investment demand, this suggests that aggregate investment spending in the economy will increase as interest rates drop.

Why then is investment demand so unstable? The reason is that there are also many volatile determinants influencing investment demand other than interest rates. In short, any factor that decreases the expected rate of return may be expected to lower the investment component of real GDP. For quite understandable reasons, businesspeople are susceptible to moods of optimism and pessimism concerning economic conditions. Their *expectations* (or, as Keynes defined it, their 'animal spirits') about the future translate into estimates of future sales, future costs and future profitability of investment projects. These forecasts involve a clouded crystal ball, requiring a high degree of intuition or normative analysis. There are always so many ever-changing factors, such as consumer sentiment, government spending and tax policies, monetary policy changes by central banks, national and world events, population growth and stock market conditions, that forecasting is extremely difficult.

When a wave of pessimism becomes pervasive, businesspeople reduce their expectations of profitability at any available interest rate. Such a pessimistic attitude can become contagious and reduce investment spending in the entire economy. This was the case during the Great Depression, when the outlook was very bleak. There were also elements of this at work during 2001 and into 2002. During this time the world's major economies entered a synchronised economic downturn (but Australia did not) and business expectations about the immediate future became quite pessimistic. At other times, businesspeople can become very optimistic and quickly revise upward their expected rate of profit from investment at any interest rate. Thus, changes in business confidence (expectations) are a major cause of fluctuations in investment spending.

Other factors affecting investment behaviour

Technological progress includes the introduction of new products and new ways of doing things. Robots, personal computers, fax machines, cellular phones, the Internet and similar new inventions provide less costly means of production. New technologies create a flurry of investment spending as firms buy the latest innovations in order to improve their production capabilities, causing investment demand to rise.

Capacity utilisation is also a factor. During a recession, many businesses operate well below their maximum productive capacity. Since much of the nation's capital stock stands idle during such a time, firms have little incentive to invest in more. Conversely, firms may be operating their plants at a high rate of capacity utilisation and the outlook for sales growth is optimistic. In this case, there is pressure on firms to invest in new investment projects to meet sales demand, and investment spending increases.

Business taxes can shift investment demand. Business decisions in reality depend on the expected *after-tax* rate of profit. An increase in business taxes therefore would lower profitability and reduce investment for any interest rate. On the other hand, the government may wish to encourage investment by allowing, say, a *tax credit* of some form for new investment. A 10 per cent *investment tax credit* means that, if Shell decides to invest $10 million in a new plant, then in addition to the usual allowance for depreciation the corporation's tax bill to the Australian Taxation Office will be cut by $1 million. The effect of this tax policy is that the government increases the after-tax profitability of new investment projects, and investment demand could be expected to increase.

In summary, then, **investment demand** by businesses increases as rates of interest drop. Shifts in investment demand result from changes in profit expectations, technological change, capacity utilisation and business taxes.

Investment demand
Investment demand by businesses increases as rates of interest drop or as profit expectations increase. Shifts in investment demand result from changes in expectations, technological change, capacity utilisation and business taxes.

Government demand (*G*)

Government consumption and investment expenditures comprise the second-largest component of aggregate expenditures in most modern developed countries. Government spending can be considered an **autonomous expenditure**. Expenditures that do not respond in any systematic way to such determinants as interest rate changes or income changes are said to be autonomous. The reasoning is that government spending is primarily the result of a political decision made independent of the level of national output or interest rates.

Autonomous expenditure
Any spending that does not vary in any systematic way to such determinants as the current level of disposable income or interest rates.

This category was crucial to Keynes's policy prescription for dealing with severely recessed economies. In such situations Keynes thought that the private sector would be very reluctant to expand its consumption and investment spending, due to negative sentiment about the future. What would be needed would be a 'kick start' from new spending by the government to stimulate the economy, improve sentiment about the future and thereby get private-sector activity going. More on this below.

Net export demand (*X* – *M*)

Like government spending, exports can be treated – at least as a first approximation – as autonomous expenditures unaffected by a nation's domestic level of real GDP. Economic conditions in the countries that buy

Australian products affect the level of our exports. On the other hand, the level of imports purchased by Australian residents is significantly influenced by economic conditions in Australia. As Australian real GDP increases then – other things being equal – we can expect imports to increase and net exports ($X - M$) to reduce. Of course, for a given level of Australian real GDP (thereby determining a certain level of import demand in Australia), we can expect net export demand to increase if world economic activity increases.

Other important determinants of net export demand are changes in exchange rates and the terms of trade. More will be said on this in Chapter 18 on international trade and finance. For the time being, however, it is useful to sketch out the main points.

For current international trade data, visit the Australian Bureau of Statistics website (**www.abs.gov.au**) and select *AusStats, Publications & Data, Time Series Spreadsheets, By Catalogue/Subject*, then *54. International Trade*.

As the international price of a country's currency – its exchange rate – reduces, the nation's exports become more affordable in other countries. This can stimulate demand for such exports. At the same time, imports into the country become more expensive in domestic currency terms, thereby discouraging spending on imports. Thus, in this situation, other things being equal, net export demand can be expected to increase. The opposite can be expected when the international price of a country's currency increases.

The terms of trade are defined as the ratio of a country's export prices to the prices of its imports. As the terms of trade increase it means that the country's exports are becoming relatively more valuable internationally. This encourages exporters to expand production, with the result that net exports can be expected to increase. The opposite result could be expected when the terms of trade deteriorate.

The aggregate demand–output model

Aggregate demand–output model (also called the **Keynesian model**) The model that determines the equilibrium level of real GDP by equating output produced to aggregate demand.

Aggregate demand The sum total of the four categories of demand, namely $C + I + G + (X - M)$.

Aggregate demand (AD) is simply the sum total of the above categories of demand, namely $C + I + G + (X - M)$. This is exactly the same way we defined GDP in Chapter 11, but do not be confused. There, we were simply defining the accounting identity: that GDP was the sum of all the various types of expenditures in the economy in any given period. Any discrepancy between what was produced and what people actually bought was accounted for by intended or unintended accumulation or decumulation in inventories.

Now we are using these same categories, but here we are talking about them as categories of demand. And it is quite possible that, in a given period, the total aggregate demand by households (C), businesses (I), government agencies (G) and foreigners ($X - M$) will not be exactly equal to the total production that firms had expected to sell. This is because the factors feeding into the spending decisions of all the various economic players are quite different from those factors influencing those who are making the production decisions. Keynes persuasively argued that aggregate demand might not necessarily equal total production, thereby debunking the prevailing classical view as embodied in Say's Law.

It is perhaps worth repeating once more. At any given time, as a result of expectations about likely demand for their product, firms will be offering a quantity of their output for sale on the market at prices they suppose will be acceptable to buyers and which will yield a suitable return over and above all explicit costs (including the cost of borrowing). We refer to this total, newly produced output in the economy as aggregate production or aggregate supply.

At the same time buyers, which will include households, government, other firms and foreigners, will be in the market offering to take up this output. The extent to which they will be willing to purchase the output of the firms will depend upon their needs, their expectations about the future, the prices of the goods in relation to their income and to the prices of close substitutes and, in the case of large purchases, the cost of borrowing. We refer to the total of this 'willingness to purchase' goods and services as aggregate demand.

In any given period these two aggregates will not necessarily be equal. Any divergence between them will be accounted for in that period by an unintended change in firms' inventories and will precipitate adjustments in subsequent periods. Adjustments can take the form of production or price changes or both. For the moment, in the simple **Keynesian model**, we assume that the response is an output one only.

Keynesian model

To fix our ideas, let's consider a specific hypothetical situation. Imagine an economy operating at a particular point in time at its full-employment productive capacity of, say, $450 billion dollars. What would happen if, in the next period, households were not willing to purchase all the output at the prices offered? Suppose aggregate demand turned out to be only $440 billion dollars (perhaps because of emerging consumer pessimism, for example)? Firms will find goods left on their shelves and in their warehouses and will have to make an *unplanned inventory investment* of $10 billion. They may be expected to respond to this unhappy state of affairs by subsequently laying off staff and reducing output. As a result of this process, the economy moves below its full employment equilibrium.

In the above hypothetical example, it is reasonable to ask why the adjustment to the disequilibrium would be by way of reduced output and employment. Why not a price adjustment? This is what the classical economists believed would happen. In the classical world, prices and wages would drop so as to clear the product markets and, given the lower wages, firms would be able to continue to employ the same numbers of people.

Keynes simply argued that this type of adjustment was just not the way he believed the real world worked. In reality, he believed prices – particularly the price of labour (wages) – tended to be resistant to downward adjustments. Thus the adjustment could be expected to be on the output side rather than the price side. Furthermore, once output was cut, people laid off and expectations about the future curtailed, aggregate demand in subsequent periods may well be stuck for long periods at a level below the economy's full-employment production level, thereby resulting in continuing involuntary unemployment.

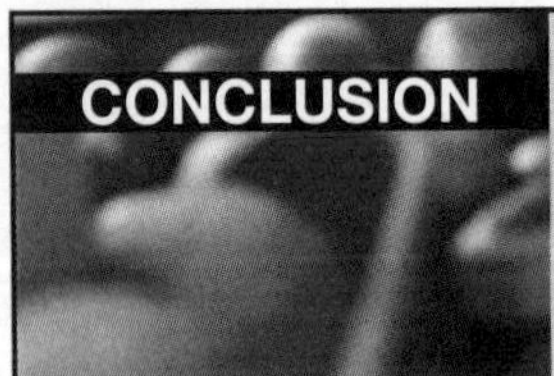

Aggregate demand in Keynesian economics can pull aggregate output away from full-employment equilibrium in the economy. The economy can remain at levels of production below those required to maintain full employment for long periods, resulting in involuntary unemployment. This is in stark contrast with the classical view.

Now it's time to pause, take a breath, and appreciate what you have been studying so diligently. It's a powerful idea! The basic explanation offered by Keynes for the Great Depression is as follows: *Once an equilibrium is established between aggregate demand and aggregate output, in contrast to what pre-Keynesian economists had believed, there may well be no tendency for the economy to change, even when that equilibrium is well below the full-employment output level.* The solution Keynes offered Western economies facing the Great Depression was to increase aggregate demand through government spending until the full-employment equilibrium was reached. Otherwise, prolonged unemployment might persist indefinitely and the economy might never self-correct. We now turn to a key idea behind changes in aggregate spending to stabilise the macro economy.

The spending multiplier effect

Changes in aggregate demand in the Keynesian model make things happen. The simple demand-oriented Keynesian model assumes that there is sufficient excess capacity in the economy to allow any increase in aggregate demand to be met by an increase in production. The existence of such excess capacity would certainly have been a reasonable assumption in the severely recessed economy of the Great Depression that Keynes was witnessing in the 1930s, but would also be quite a reasonable assumption for any modern-day economy significantly below its full-employment level of economic activity. The crux of Keynesian macroeconomic policy depends on a change in aggregate government expenditures or taxation, which is then multiplied or amplified by rounds of spending and re-spending throughout the economy. To understand this, you should note that the categories of aggregate demand outlined above (C, I, G and $(X - M)$ are not independent of each other.

For example, a stimulus to consumption demand (brought about perhaps by a generally more optimistic view of future economic conditions) could lead firms to expand production, increase their expenditure on plant and equipment (thereby increasing investment demand and providing a stimulus to those firms producing capital equipment) and hire more staff. These expenditures in turn would further stimulate consumption expenditure by virtue of the increased employment and income of the employees of the consumption-producing and capital-goods-producing firms. This would further stimulate investment, and so the process would continue.

Thus the original consumption demand stimulus would have a 'ripple effect' throughout the economy. The induced rounds of expenditure are often collectively referred to as the **spending multiplier**. The fact that the initial expenditure increases (or decreases, for that matter) are multiplied in their macroeconomic effect provides a critical insight into Keynes's prescription for a severely recessed economy. In such an economy, private-sector demand needs to be stimulated. By increasing its own spending on goods and services, the government can provide this stimulus, with the final stimulatory impact on the economy being much greater than the initial increase in government spending.

Spending multiplier The induced rounds of spending that occur in an economy after some initial stimulus to spending.

spending multiplier

Any initial change in spending by the government, households or firms creates a chain reaction of further spending, which causes a greater cumulative change in aggregate demand.

The multiplier is important in the Keynesian model because it means that the initial change in aggregate expenditures results in an amplified change in the equilibrium level of real GDP. This is both good and bad news for an economy. The bad news occurs, for example, when the multiplier amplifies small declines in total spending from, say, consumer and business pessimism, into downturns in national output, income and employment. The good news is that, at least in theory, macroeconomic policy can manage, or manipulate, the economy's performance by a relatively small initial change in aggregate expenditures.

The appendix to this chapter provides a more detailed presentation of the Keynesian aggregate demand–output model. Further insights into some of its workings can also be provided within the context of the now widely used *AD–AS* model described below.

The aggregate demand–aggregate supply model

As explained in the previous section, classical economists before Keynes argued that the economy would bounce back to full employment as long as prices and wages were flexible. As the unemployment rate soared and persisted during the Great Depression, Keynes formulated a new theory with new policy implications. Instead of a policy of waiting until markets would self-correct the economy, Keynes argued that policy makers had to take action to influence aggregate spending through changes in government spending.

The prescription for the Great Depression was simple: increase government spending and jobs will be created. Although Keynes was not concerned with the problem of inflation, his theory has implications for fighting demand-pull inflation. In this case, the government would cut spending or increase taxes to reduce aggregate demand. However, Keynes placed little or no analytical emphasis on aggregate supply considerations. To properly understand modern business cycles, the simple demand-oriented Keynesian framework outlined in the previous section needs to be augmented.

In this section you will use aggregate demand and supply analysis to study the business cycle. The section opens with a presentation of the aggregate demand curve and then the aggregate supply curve. Once these concepts are developed, the analysis shows why modern macroeconomics teaches that shifts in aggregate supply or aggregate demand can influence the price level, the equilibrium level of real GDP and employment.

The aggregate demand curve

Here we are considering the collective economy-wide demand for *all* goods and services, rather than the *market* demand for a particular good or service. Exhibit 14.1 shows the **aggregate demand (AD) curve**, which slopes downward and to the right for a given period. The aggregate demand curve shows the level of total real GDP that households, businesses, government and foreigners (net exports) would be willing to purchase at different possible average price levels during the time period, ceteris paribus. Just as we have seen with the demand curve for an individual product, other factors remaining constant, the lower the economy-wide price level, the greater the aggregate quantity demanded of real goods and services.

Aggregate demand curve Curve showing the level of total real GDP that households, businesses, government and foreigners (net exports) would be willing to purchase at different possible average price levels during a time period, ceteris paribus.

aggregate demand curve

The downward slope of the aggregate demand curve shows that people are willing to buy more goods and services at a lower average price level. While the horizontal axis in an individual market supply and demand model measures *physical* units, such as a tonne of wheat, the horizontal axis used in the aggregate demand and supply model measures the value of all *final* goods and services included in real GDP. The horizontal axis therefore represents the quantity of aggregate production demanded, measured in some base year's dollars. The vertical axis is an *index* of the overall price level, such as the GDP deflator or the CPI rather than, say, the price per tonne of wheat. As shown in Exhibit 14.1, if the price level measured by the CPI is 150 at point *A*, a real GDP of $400 billion would be demanded in, say, the year 2004. If the price level is 100 at point *B*, a real GDP of $600 billion would be demanded.

Although the aggregate demand curve looks like an individual product demand curve, these concepts are very different. As we move along a product demand curve, the price of related goods is assumed to be unchanging. But when we deal with changes in the general or average price level in an economy, this assumption is meaningless because we are using a market basket measure for *all* goods and services.

Was John Maynard Keynes right?

Analyse the issue

Applicable concept: aggregate demand and aggregate supply analysis

In *The General Theory of Employment, Interest and Money*, Keynes wrote:

> The ideas of economists and political philosophers, both when they are right and when they are wrong, are more powerful than is commonly understood. Indeed the world is ruled by little else. Practical men, who believe themselves to be quite exempt from any intellectual influences, are usually the slaves of some defunct economist. Madmen in authority, who hear voices in the air, are distilling their frenzy from some academic scribbler of a few years back … There are not many who are influenced by new theories after they are twenty-five or thirty years of age, so that the ideas which civil servants and politicians and even agitators apply to current events are not likely to be the newest.[1]

John Maynard Keynes (1883–1946) is regarded as the father of modern macroeconomics. He was the son of an eminent English economist, John Neville Keynes, who was a lecturer in economics and logic at Cambridge University. Keynes was educated at Eton and Cambridge in mathematics and probability theory, but ultimately selected the field of economics and accepted a lectureship in economics at Cambridge.

Keynes was a many-faceted man. He was an honoured and supremely successful member of the British academic, financial and political upper class. For example, Keynes amassed a $2 million personal fortune by speculating in stocks, international currencies and commodities. (Use CPI index numbers to compute the equivalent amount in 2004 dollars.) In addition to making a huge fortune for himself, Keynes served as a trustee of King's College and built its endowment from 30 000 to 380 000 pounds.

Keynes was a prolific scholar who is best remembered for *The General Theory*, published in 1936. This work made a convincing attack on the classical theory that, left alone, markets would self-correct and bring an economy out of a severe recession without intervention. Keynes based his model on the belief that increasing aggregate demand would achieve full employment, while prices and wages remain inflexible. Moreover, his bold policy prescription was that the government raise its spending and/or reduce taxes in order to increase the economy's aggregate demand curve and put the unemployed back to work.

Was Keynes correct? Based on the following data for the United States, use the aggregate demand–aggregate supply model to explain Keynes's theory that increases in aggregate demand propel an economy towards full employment.

Price level, real GDP and unemployment rate, 1933–41

Year	CPI (1982–84 = 100)	Real GDP (billions of 1992 $)	Unemployment rate (per cent)
1933	13.0	577	24.9%
1939	13.9	867	17.2
1940	14.0	941	14.6
1941	14.7	1102	9.9

Sources: US Department of Labor, CPI Detailed Report: October 1998, Table 24; Survey of Current Business, www.bea.doc.gov/bea/dn1.htm, Table 2A; and Economic Report of the President, 1999, www.gpo.ucop.edu/catalog/erp99.html, Table B-31.

1 J. M. Keynes, *The General Theory of Employment, Interest and Money*, Macmillan, London, 1936, p. 383.

PART 5

Exhibit 14.1 **The aggregate demand curve**

For current and historical data on consumer and other prices, visit the Australian Bureau of Statistics website (**www.abs.gov.au**) and select *AusStats, Publications & Data, Time Series Spreadsheets, By Catalogue/Subject*, then *64. Prices*.

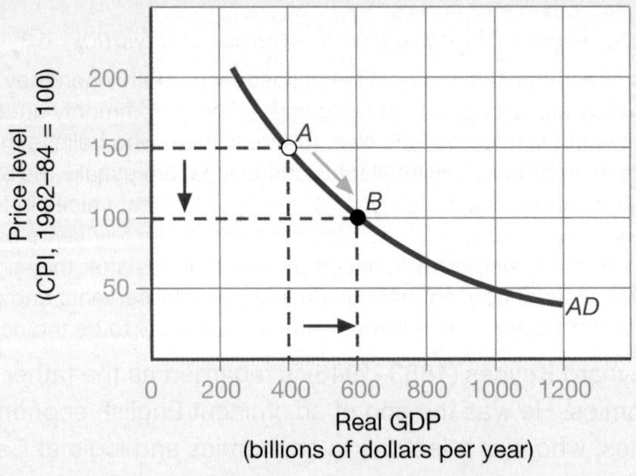

CAUSATION CHAIN

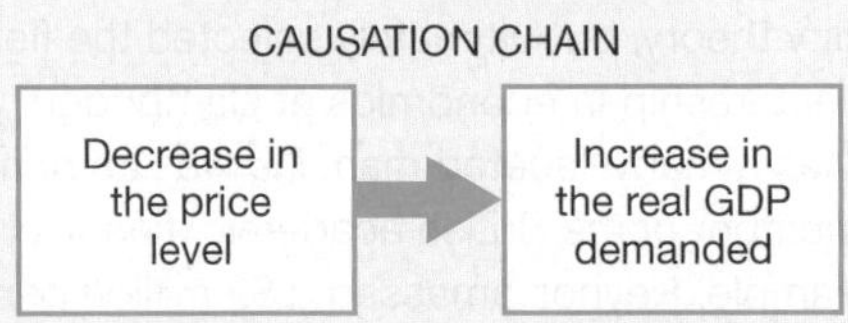

The aggregate demand curve shows the relationship between the price index level and the level of real GDP, other things being equal. The lower the price level, the larger the GDP demanded by households, businesses, government and foreigners. If the price index level is 150 at point *A*, a real GDP of $400 billion would be demanded. If the price index level is 100 at point *B*, the real GDP demanded increases to $600 billion.

The aggregate demand curve and the demand curve for an individual product are not the same concepts.

Reasons for the aggregate demand curve's shape

As you will recall from Chapter 3, in the case of the demand curve for an individual product, the reason the demand curve slopes downwards is that it is assumed that the prices of the product's close substitutes remain unchanged. Thus, as the price of the product reduces, it becomes relatively cheaper compared with other similar products and we therefore expect that, ceteris paribus, more of it will be demanded.

The reasons for the downward slope of an aggregate demand curve are very different and include *the real balances* or *wealth effect, the interest-rate effect* and *the net exports effect*. Furthermore, the key to the real balances or wealth effect and the interest-rate effect is that, for the time period in question to which an *AD* curve relates, the total nominal quantity of liquid financial assets in the economy is assumed to be fixed. A liquid financial asset is one that can be converted easily – with little or no loss of nominal value – into a form that can be used to buy goods and services. Cash in your pocket is the most liquid, while a fixed-term deposit you have in your bank or some shares you may have in a company are much less liquid.

Real balances or wealth effect

Cash and bank deposits are just a couple of examples of financial assets whose real value (in terms of purchasing power) changes with the price level. If prices are falling, households are more willing and able to spend. Suppose you have $1000 in a cheque account with which to buy 10 weeks' worth of groceries. If prices fall by 20 per cent, $1000 will now buy enough groceries for 12 weeks. This rise in real wealth may make you more willing and able to purchase a new DVD player out of current income.

Consumers spend more on goods and services because lower prices make their dollars more valuable. Therefore, the real value of money and other liquid financial assets is measured by the quantity of goods and services each dollar buys.

When inflation reduces the real value of the nominal stock of financial assets held by households, the result is lower consumption and real GDP falls. The effect of a change in the price level on real consumption spending is called the **real balances or wealth effect**. The real balances or wealth effect is the impact on total spending (real GDP) caused by the inverse relationship between the price level and the real value of financial assets with fixed nominal value.

Real balances or wealth effect The impact on total spending (real GDP) of the inverse relationship between the price level and the real value of financial assets with fixed nominal value.

Interest-rate effect

A second reason that the aggregate demand curve is downward-sloping involves the **interest-rate effect**. The interest-rate effect is the impact on total spending (real GDP) caused by the direct relationship between the price level and the interest rate. Again, remember that a key assumption of the aggregate demand curve is that the supply of money available for borrowing in the time period relevant to the *AD* curve remains fixed. A high price level means people must take more dollars from their wallets and cheque accounts in order to purchase goods and services. At a higher price level, the demand for borrowed money to buy products will also increase and, given a fixed supply, will push up the cost of borrowing; that is, nominal interest rates will rise. Rising interest rates discourage households from borrowing to purchase homes, cars, electronic equipment and other big-ticket consumer products. Similarly, at higher interest rates, businesses cut investment projects because the higher cost of borrowing diminishes the

Interest-rate effect The impact on total spending (real GDP) of the direct relationship between the price level and the interest rate.

likely profitability of these investments. Thus, assuming fixed nominal credit availability, an increase in the price level translates through higher interest rates into a reduced aggregate demand for real GDP.

Net exports effect

Whether Australian-made goods have lower prices than foreign goods is another important factor that determines the aggregate demand curve. A higher domestic price level tends to make Australian goods more expensive compared with foreign goods and the quantity of imports rises because consumers substitute imported goods for domestic goods. An increase in the price of Australian goods in foreign markets also causes Australian exports to decline. Consequently, a rise in the domestic price level in an economy tends to increase imports, decrease exports and thereby reduce the net exports component of the aggregate demand for real GDP. This condition is the **net exports effect**.

Net exports effect The impact on total spending (real GDP) of the inverse relationship between the price level and the net exports of an economy.

The net exports effect is the impact on total aggregate demand (for real GDP) caused by the inverse relationship between the price level and the net exports of an economy. Note that here we are assuming that the foreign exchange rate remains unchanged (the ceteris paribus assumption again!). Thus a particular *AD* curve is drawn not only with a fixed stock of available nominal liquid financial assets in mind but also with a particular exchange rate in mind.

Exhibit 14.2 summarises the three effects that explain why the aggregate demand curve in Exhibit 14.1 is downward-sloping.

Exhibit 14.2 Why the aggregate demand curve is downward-sloping

Effect	Causation chain
Real balances or wealth effect	Price level decreases → Purchasing power rises → Wealth rises → Consumers buy more goods → Real GDP demanded increases
Interest-rate effect	Price level decreases → Increase in the real value of the fixed nominal supply of credit → Nominal interest rates fall → Businesses and households borrow and buy more goods → Real GDP demanded increases
Net exports effect	Price level decreases → Home country's goods become less expensive than foreign goods → Domestic residents and foreigners buy more home country goods → Exports rise and imports fall → Real GDP demanded increases

Non-price-level determinants of aggregate demand

As was the case with individual demand curves, we must distinguish between *changes in real GDP demanded,* caused by changes in the price level, and *changes in aggregate demand*, caused by changes in one or more of the *non-price-level determinants*. Once the ceteris paribus assumption is relaxed, changes in variables other than the price level cause a change in the location of the aggregate demand curve. Non-price-level determinants include changes in the consumption (*C*), investment (*I*), government spending (*G*) and net exports (*X* – *M*) components of aggregate expenditures explained earlier.

Any change in aggregate expenditures shifts the aggregate demand curve. **CONCLUSION**

Exhibit 14.3 illustrates the link between an increase in expenditures and an increase in aggregate demand. Begin at point *A* on aggregate demand curve AD_1, with a price level of 100 and a real GDP of $600 billion. Assume that the price level remains constant at 100 and that there is then an increase in aggregate demand from AD_1 to AD_2. Consequently, the level of real GDP demanded rises from $600 billion (point *A*) to $800 billion (point *B*) at the price level of 100. What might be the cause of such a shift in one or more of the components of aggregate demand?

The cause might be that consumers have become more optimistic about the future and their consumption expenditures (*C*) have risen. Another factor bringing about an increase in consumer demand would be an increase in the wealth of consumers unrelated to the general price level. This may happen for instance as a result of increases in house prices or significant rises in stock markets. More generally, any increase in the value of assets held by consumers can be expected to have a positive effect on their spending. Or possibly an increase in business optimism has increased profit expectations and the level of investment (*I*) has risen because businesses are spending more for plant and equipment. The same increase in aggregate demand could also have been caused by a boost in autonomous government spending (*G*).

Finally, a rise in net exports (*X* – *M*) may have been responsible. This is particularly relevant to an economy like Australia's, which is based on a great deal of international trade. In this case the cause may be due to a boost to the economic activity of a country's trading partners, resulting in higher export demand from those countries. Alternatively, such an increase in net exports can arise from a reduction in the international price of the country's

Exhibit 14.3 **A shift in the aggregate demand curve**

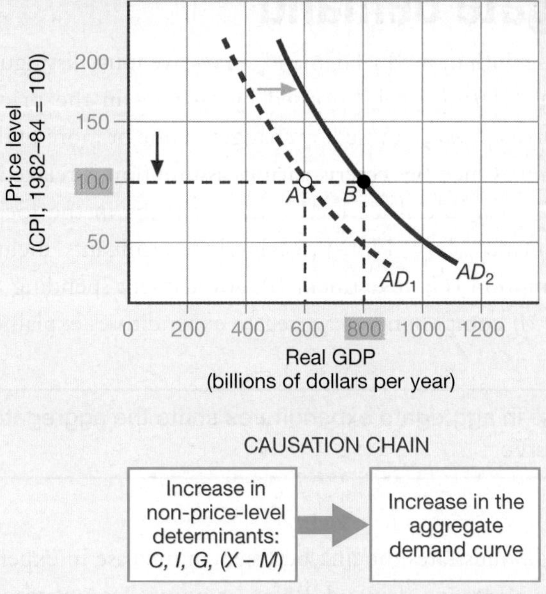

At the price level of 100, the real GDP level is $600 billion at point *A* on AD_1. An increase in one of the non-price-level determinants of consumption (*C*), investment (*I*), government spending (*G*) or net exports (*X* – *M*) causes the level of real GDP to rise to $800 billion at point *B* on AD_2. Because this effect occurs at any price level, an increase in aggregate expenditures shifts the *AD* curve rightward. Conversely, a decrease in aggregate expenditures shifts the *AD* curve leftward.

currency (that is, a depreciation in its exchange rate). The reduced value of the currency means that domestic prices are lower in foreign currency terms, leading to increases in foreign demand for exports at any domestic price level. Thus, a fall in the exchange rate can lead to an outward shift in the *AD* curve.

Similar factors are also responsible for inward shifts in the *AD* curve. A swing to pessimistic expectations by consumers or firms will cause the aggregate demand curve to shift leftward. A leftward shift in the aggregate demand curve may also be caused by a decrease in government spending or investment pessimism, or by declines in net exports. Again, the latter case is particularly important for countries engaged in a great deal of international trade. An inward shift on this score could be the result of reduced overseas demand for exports on account of reduced international economic activity. Alternatively, such a reduction in net exports could result from an increase in the international price of the country's currency (an appreciation in its exchange rate).

The determinants and economic effects of changes in a country's exchange rate are discussed in greater detail in Chapter 18.

The aggregate supply curve

As you will soon see, the aggregate supply curve – at least in the short run – is, just like the individual product supply curve, also considered to be upward-sloping. However, as in the case of the *aggregate demand* and *market demand* curves, the theory for a *market supply* curve does not at all apply directly to the *aggregate supply* curve. The supply curve for an individual product is upward-sloping because profit-maximising firms with fixed and variable production costs will be induced to bring more product to the market if the market price rises. The same mechanism cannot be at work in the case of the aggregate supply curve because, as the general price level rises along the curve, all prices in the economy are assumed to be rising. This would include not only product selling prices but also the prices of inputs into the production process (including the cost of labour).

Keeping this in mind for the time being, we can define the **aggregate supply (*AS*) curve**. The aggregate supply curve shows the level of real GDP that firms would be willing to produce at different possible price levels during a time period, ceteris paribus. Stated simply, the aggregate supply curve shows the total dollar amount of goods and services that firms would seek to produce in an economy at various price levels. Given this general definition, we must pause to discuss two polar characterisations of the nature of the *AS* curve – the Keynesian horizontal aggregate supply curve and the classical vertical aggregate supply curve.

Aggregate supply curve
The curve that shows the level of real GDP that firms would be willing to produce at different possible price levels during a time period, ceteris paribus.

The Keynesian view of aggregate supply

As previously explained, Keynes argued that price and wage inflexibility meant that unemployment could be a prolonged affair. Unless an economy trapped in a depression or severe recession is rescued by an increase in aggregate demand, full employment may not be achieved for many years. This Keynesian prediction calls for active aggregate demand management policies by government in order to avoid depression or recession.

Again, why did Keynes assume very sticky product prices and wages? During a deep recession or depression, there are many idle resources in the economy. Consequently, producers are willing to sell additional output at current prices. Moreover, the supply of unemployed workers willing to work for the prevailing wage rate diminishes the power of workers to increase their wages. Furthermore, other cost pressures affecting firms from the actions of other firms are likely to be minimal given the widespread excess capacity in the economy. Given the Keynesian assumption of fixed or very sticky product prices and wages – particularly in the downward direction – changes in the aggregate demand curve result in changes in the quantity of real GDP produced rather than increased prices; that is, the Keynesian model outlined in the preceding section assumes a horizontal aggregate supply curve. In short, Keynesian theory argues that, in a severely recessed economy, increases in aggregate demand will boost production rather than prices.

Exhibit 14.4 portrays the core of Keynesian theory. We begin at equilibrium E_1, with the fixed price level of 100. Given aggregate demand schedule AD_1, the equilibrium level of real GDP is \$300 billion. Now government spending (*G*) increases, causing aggregate demand to rise from AD_1 to AD_2 and equilibrium to shift from E_1 to E_2 along the horizontal aggregate supply curve, *AS*. At E_2 the economy moves to \$400 billion, which is closer to the full-employment GDP of \$500 billion.

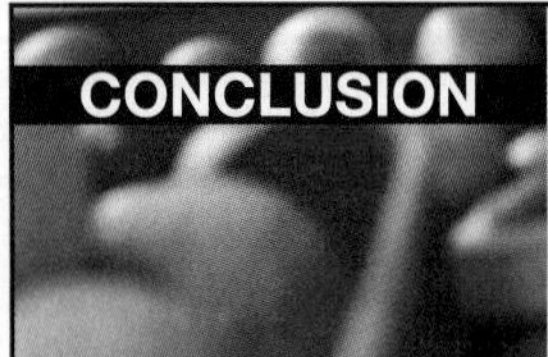

When the aggregate supply curve is horizontal and an economy is below full employment, the only effects of an increase in aggregate demand are increases in real GDP and employment, while the price level does not change. Stated simply, the Keynesian view is that 'demand creates its own supply.'

The classical view of aggregate supply

Exhibit 14.5 uses the aggregate demand and supply model to illustrate the classical view that the aggregate supply curve, *AS*, is vertical at the full-employment output of \$10 trillion. The vertical shape of the classical aggregate supply curve is based on two assumptions. First, the economy

Exhibit 14.4 The Keynesian horizontal aggregate supply curve

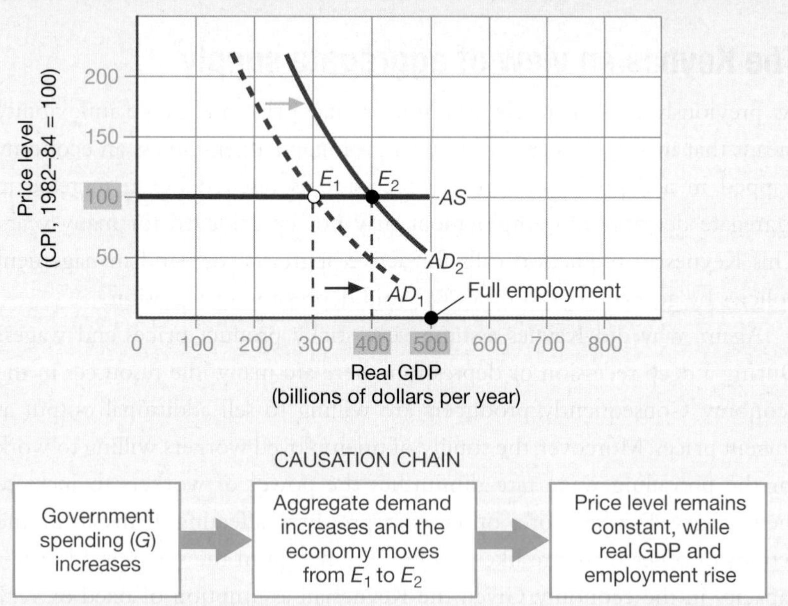

The increase in aggregate demand from AD_1 to AD_2 causes a new equilibrium at E_2. Given the Keynesian assumption of a fixed price level, changes in aggregate demand cause changes in real GDP along the horizontal portion of the aggregate supply curve, *AS*. Keynesian theory argues that only shifts in aggregate demand possess the ability to restore a depressed economy to the full-employment output of \$500 billion.

normally operates at its full-employment output level. Second, the selling prices of products and production costs are flexible and change rapidly in order to maintain a full-employment level of output. This classical theory of flexible prices and wages is at odds with the Keynesian concept of sticky (inflexible) prices and wages.

Exhibit 14.5 illustrates why classical economists believed a market economy self-corrects. Consider the following classical scenario in which a market economy automatically self-corrects to full employment. Initially, the economy is in equilibrium at E_1, the price level is 150, real output is at its full-employment level of $500 billion and aggregate demand curve AD_1 traces total spending. Now suppose private spending falls because households and businesses are pessimistic about economic conditions. This condition causes AD_1 to shift leftward to AD_2. At a price level of 150, the immediate effect is that aggregate output exceeds aggregate spending by $100 billion ($E_1$ to E') and unexpected inventory accumulation occurs. To eliminate unsold inventories resulting from the decrease in aggregate demand, business firms temporarily cut back on production and reduce their prices.

Exhibit 14.5 The classical vertical aggregate supply curve

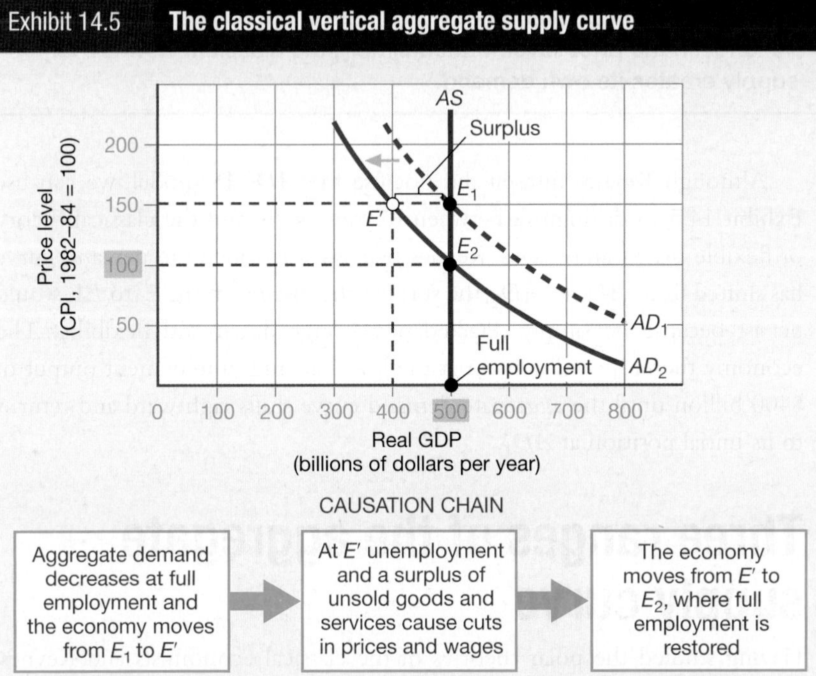

Classical theory posits that prices and wages quickly adjust to keep the economy operating at its full-employment output of $500 billion. A decline in aggregate demand from AD_1 to AD_2 will temporarily cause a surplus of $100 billion, the distance from E_1 to E'. Businesses respond by cutting the price level from 150 to 100. As a result, consumers increase their purchases because of the real balances or wealth effect and wages adjust downward. Thus, classical economists predict that the economy is self-correcting and will restore full employment at point E_2. E_1 and E_2 therefore represent points along a classical vertical aggregate supply curve, *AS*.

At E', the decline in aggregate output in response to the surplus also affects prices in the factor markets. The result of the economy moving from point E_1 to E' is a decrease in the demand for labour, raw materials and other inputs used to produce products. This surplus condition in the factor markets, assuming prices can adjust reasonably freely, means that prices will be bidden down – including the price of labour (that is, wages). Why would workers be willing to accept reduced wages? If prices generally are coming down, it is argued that the real purchasing power of the reduced nominal wages will be maintained. Workers will be aware of this and so the reduced nominal wage offers will remain attractive to them. Owners of other production inputs and capital will likewise accept lower prices.

Exhibit 14.5 represents this economy-wide fall in prices and wages by the movement downward along AD_2 from E' to a new equilibrium at E_2. At E_2, the economy self-corrects – through downwardly flexible prices and wages – back to its full-employment level of $500 billion worth of real GDP at the lower price level of 100. E_1 and E_2 therefore represent points along a classical vertical aggregate supply curve, *AS*.

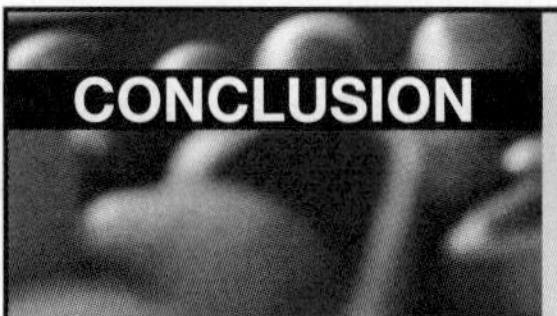

When the aggregate supply curve is vertical at the full-employment GDP, the only effect over time of a change in aggregate demand is a change in the price level. Stated simply, the classical view is that 'supply creates its own demand.'

Although Keynes himself did not use the *AD–AS* model, we can use Exhibit 14.5 to distinguish between Keynes's view and the classical theory of flexible prices and wages. Keynes believed that once the demand curve has shifted from AD_1 to AD_2, the surplus, the distance from E' to E1, would persist because he simply rejected price–wage downward flexibility. The economy therefore will remain at the less-than-full-employment output of $400 billion until the aggregate demand curve shifts rightward and returns to its initial position at AD_1.

Keynesian range The horizontal segment of the aggregate supply curve, which represents an economy in a severe recession.

Intermediate range The rising segment of the aggregate supply curve, which represents an economy as it approaches full-employment output.

Classical range The vertical segment of the aggregate supply curve, which represents an economy at full-employment output.

Three ranges of the aggregate supply curve

Having studied the polar theories of the classical economists and Keynes, we will now discuss an eclectic or general view of how the shape of the aggregate supply curve varies as real GDP expands or contracts. This eclectic view is sometimes referred to as the 'Keynesian-Neoclassical Synthesis'. The aggregate supply curve, *AS*, in Exhibit 14.6 has three distinct ranges or segments, labelled (1) **Keynesian range**, (2) **intermediate range** and (3) **classical range**.

Exhibit 14.6 **The three ranges of the aggregate supply curve**

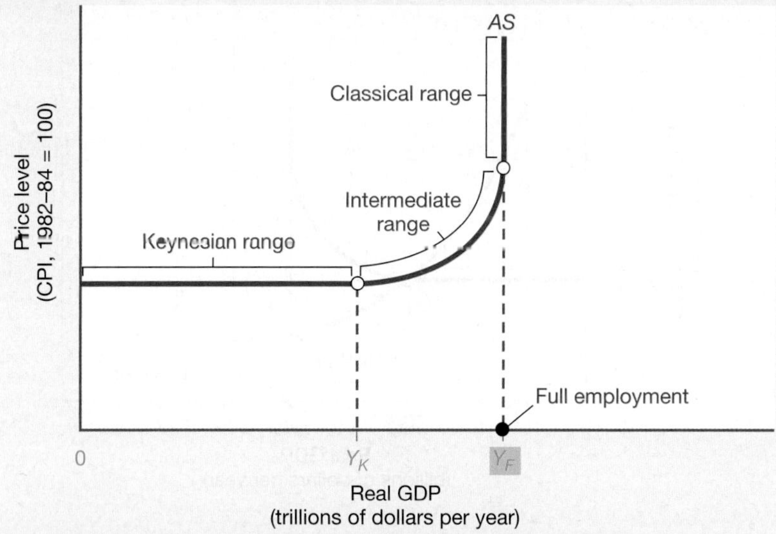

The aggregate supply curve shows the relationship between the price level and the level of real GDP supplied. It consists of three distinct ranges: (1) a Keynesian range up to *YK* wherein the price level is constant for an economy in severe recession; (2) an intermediate range between *YK* and *YF* wherein both the price level and the level of real GDP vary as an economy approaches full-employment demand; and (3) a classical range wherein the price level can vary, while the level of real GDP remains constant at the full-employment level of output, *YF*.

The Keynesian range is the horizontal segment of the aggregate supply curve, which represents an economy in a severe recession. In Exhibit 14.6, below real GDP *YK*, the price level remains constant as the level of demand for real GDP rises. Between *YK* and the full-employment output of *YF*, the price level rises moderately as demand for real GDP level rises. The intermediate range is the rising segment of the aggregate supply curve, which represents an economy as it approaches full-employment output. Finally, at *YF*, the level of real GDP remains constant and only the price level rises with further increases in aggregate demand. The classical range is the vertical segment of the aggregate supply curve, which represents an economy at full-employment output.

Aggregate demand and aggregate supply macroeconomic equilibrium

In Exhibit 14.7, the *macroeconomic equilibrium* level of real GDP corresponding to the point of equality, *E*, is $300 billion and the equilibrium price level is 100. This is the unique combination of price level and output level that equates how much people want to buy with the amount businesses want to produce

Exhibit 14.7 **The aggregate demand and aggregate supply model**

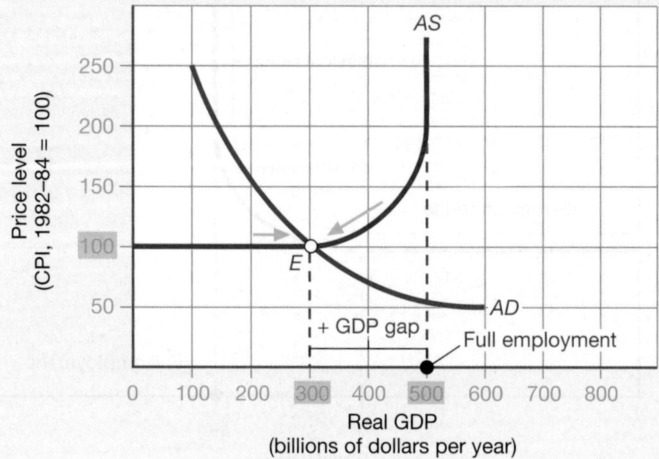

Macroeconomic equilibrium occurs where the aggregate demand curve, *AD*, and the aggregate supply curve, *AS*, intersect. In this case, equilibrium, *E*, is located at the far end of the Keynesian range, where the price level is 100 and the equilibrium output is $300 billion. In macroeconomic equilibrium, businesses neither overestimate nor underestimate the real GDP demanded at the prevailing price level.

and sell. Because the entire real GDP value of final products is bought and sold at the price level of 100, there is no upward or downward pressure for the macroeconomic equilibrium to change. Note that the economy shown in Exhibit 14.7 is operating on the edge of the Keynesian range, with a GDP shortfall of $200 billion compared with full-employment output.

Suppose for a moment that the level of production in the economy happens to be below $300 billion and that the *AD* curve remains unchanged, as in Exhibit 14.7. At a price level of 100, the real GDP demanded exceeds the real GDP supplied. Under such circumstances, businesses cannot fill orders quickly enough and inventories are drawn down unexpectedly. Business managers react by hiring more workers and producing more output. Because the economy is operating in the Keynesian range, the price level remains constant at 100. The opposite scenario occurs if the level of real GDP supplied is in the intermediate range between $300 billion and $500 billion on the *AS* curve and therefore exceeds the level of real GDP demanded. In this output segment the price level is between 100 and 200 and businesses face sales that are less than expected. In this case, unintended inventories of unsold goods pile up on the shelves and management will lay off workers, cut back on production and reduce prices.

This adjustment process continues until the equilibrium price level and output level are reached at point *E* and there is no upward or downward pressure for the price level to change. Here the production decisions of sellers in the economy equal the total spending decisions of buyers during the given period of time.

At macroeconomic equilibrium, sellers neither overestimate nor underestimate the real GDP demanded at the prevailing price level.

Changes in the *AD–AS* macroeconomic equilibrium

The National Bureau of Economic Research (NBER) (www.nber.org/) measures US business cycle expansions and contractions (www.nber.org/cycles.html). The Melbourne Institute of Applied Economic and Social Research maintains the dates for Australian business cycle turns (www.ecom.unimelb.edu.au/iaesrwww/bcf/bdates5197.html).

Equilibrium shifts arising from aggregate demand shifts

One explanation of the business cycle is that the aggregate demand curve moves along a stationary aggregate supply curve. The next step in our analysis is therefore to *shift* the aggregate demand curve along the three ranges of the aggregate supply curve and observe the impact on the real GDP and the price level. As the macroeconomic equilibrium changes, the economy experiences more or fewer problems with inflation and unemployment.

Keynesian range

Keynes's macroeconomic theory offered a powerful solution to the Great Depression. Keynes perceived the economy as driven by aggregate demand and Exhibit 14.8(a) demonstrates this theory. The range of real GDP below \$300 billion is consistent with Keynesian price and wage stickiness. Assume the economy is in equilibrium at E_1, with a price level of 100 and a real GDP of \$200 billion. In this case, the economy is in recession far below the full-employment GDP of \$500 billion. The Keynesian prescription for a recession is to increase aggregate demand until the economy achieves full employment. Because the aggregate supply curve is horizontal in the Keynesian range, 'demand creates its own supply.' Suppose demand shifts rightward from AD_1 to AD_2 and a new equilibrium is established at E_2. Even at the higher real GDP level of \$300 billion, the price level remains at 100. Stated differently, aggregate output can expand throughout this range without raising prices. This is because, in the Keynesian range, substantial idle production capacity (including plant and unemployed workers competing for available jobs) can be put to work at existing prices.

As aggregate demand increases in the Keynesian range, the price level remains constant as real GDP expands.

Exhibit 14.8 **Effects of increases in aggregate demand**

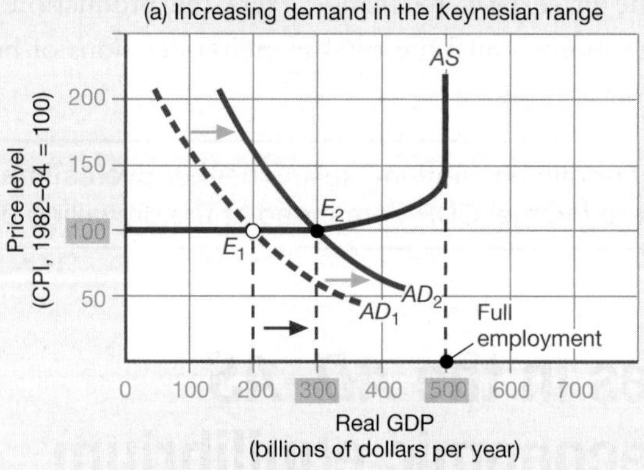

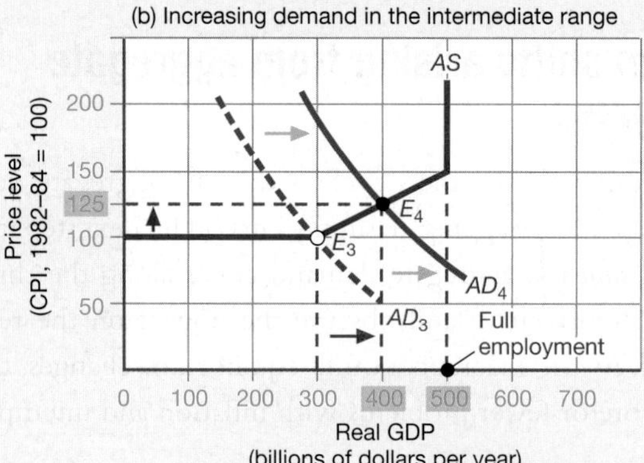

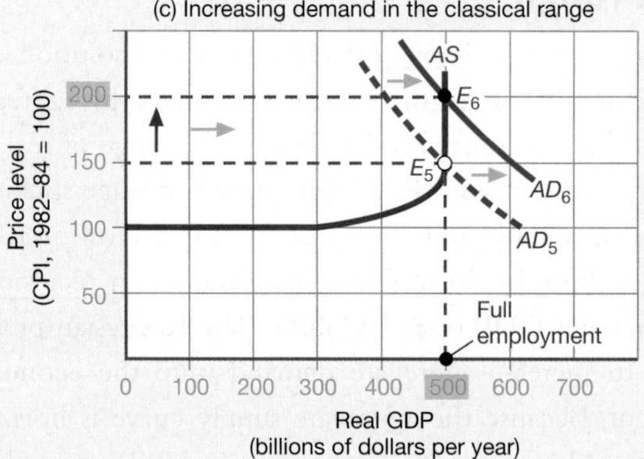

The effect of a rightward shift in the aggregate demand curve on the price and output levels depends on the range of the aggregate supply curve in which it occurs. In part (a), an increase in aggregate demand causing the equilibrium to change from E_1 to E_2 in the Keynesian range will increase the real GDP from $200 billion to $300 billion, but the price level will remain unchanged at 100.

In part (b), an increase in aggregate demand causing the equilibrium to change from E_3 to E_4 in the intermediate range will increase the real GDP from $300 billion to $400 billion and the price level will rise from 100 to 125.

In part (c), an increase in aggregate demand causing the equilibrium to change from E_5 to E_6 in the classical range will increase the price level from 150 to 200, but the real GDP will not increase beyond the full-employment level of $500 billion.

PART 5

Intermediate range

The intermediate range in Exhibit 14.8(b) is between $300 billion and $500 billion worth of real GDP. As output increases in the range of the *AS* curve near the full-employment level of output, the considerable slack in the economy disappears. Assume an economy is initially in equilibrium at E_3 and aggregate demand increases from AD_3 to AD_4. As a result, the level of real GDP rises from $300 billion to $400 billion and the price level rises from 100 to 125. In this output range, several factors contribute to inflating prices.

First, *bottlenecks* (obstacles to output flow) develop when some firms have no unused capacity and other firms operate below full capacity. Suppose the steel industry is operating at full capacity and cannot fill all its orders for steel. An inadequate supply of one resource, such as steel, can hold up car production even when the car-making industry is well below capacity. Consequently, the bottleneck causes firms to raise the price of steel and, in turn, cars.

Second, a shortage of certain labour skills while firms are earning higher profits may lead labour to exert its market power to obtain sizeable wage increases, so businesses raise prices to offset these production cost increases. Wage demands are more difficult to reject when the economy is prospering, because businesses will want to hold on to good employees who may consider leaving because of attractive alternative employment opportunities. Besides, businesses believe higher prices can be passed on quite easily because consumers will be experiencing rising incomes as output expands to near full capacity.

Third, as the economy approaches full employment, firms must use less productive employees and less efficient productive capacity. This less efficient operation creates higher production costs, which may also be passed on to consumers in the form of higher prices.

In the intermediate range, increases in aggregate demand increase both the price level and real GDP.

PART 5

Classical range

While inflating prices resulting from an outward shift in aggregate demand was no problem in the Keynesian range and only a minor problem in the intermediate range, it becomes a serious problem in the classical or vertical range.

Once the economy reaches full-employment output in the classical range, additional increases in aggregate demand merely cause inflation, rather than more real GDP.

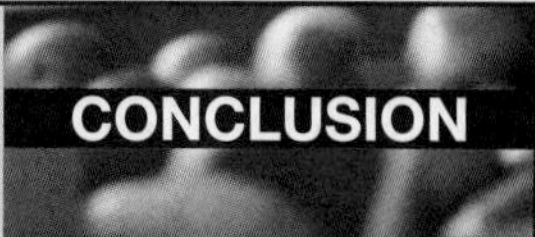

Assume the economy shown in Exhibit 14.8(c) is in equilibrium at E_5, which intersects *AS* at the full-capacity output. Now suppose aggregate demand shifts rightward from AD_5 to AD_6 as a result perhaps of excessively easy monetary policy on the part of the central bank (more later). Because *AS* is vertical at $500 billion, this increase in the aggregate demand boosts the price level from 150 to 200, but fails to expand real GDP. The explanation is that, once the economy operates at capacity, businesses raise their prices in order to ration fully employed productive capacity to those willing to pay the highest prices.

In summary, the *AD–AS* model presented in this chapter is a combination of the contrasting assumptions of the Keynesian and the classical views separated by an intermediate range, which fits neither extreme precisely. Be forewarned that a controversy continues over the shape of the aggregate supply curve. Modern-day classical economists – called New Classicists – believe the entire aggregate supply curve is very steep. On the other hand, New Keynesian economists contend that the aggregate supply curve is much flatter.

Equilibrium shifts arising from aggregate supply shifts

Our discussion so far has explained changes in real GDP supplied resulting from changes in the aggregate demand curve, given a stationary aggregate supply curve. Now we consider a stationary aggregate demand curve and changes in the aggregate supply curve caused by changes in one or more determinants. Such factors affecting aggregate supply include resource costs (domestic and imported), technological change, taxes, subsidies and regulations.

Note that each of these factors affects production costs. At a given price index level, the profit businesses make at any level of real GDP depends on production costs. If costs change, firms respond by changing their output or prices (or both). Lower production costs shift the aggregate supply curve rightward, indicating that greater real GDP will be supplied by firms at all different possible price levels. Conversely, higher production costs shift the aggregate supply curve leftward, meaning that less real GDP will be supplied at any particular price level.

Exhibit 14.9 represents a supply-side explanation of the business cycle, in contrast to the demand-side case presented in Exhibit 14.8. (Note that for simplicity the supply curve is drawn using only the intermediate segment.) The economy begins in equilibrium at point E_1, with the real GDP at $350 billion and the price level at 175. Then suppose better employer–employee industrial relations causes increased labour productivity. This reduces the labour costs of producing output. With lower labour costs per unit of output, businesses seek to increase profits by expanding production at any price

Does a stock market crash affect the economy?

International focus

Applicable concept: aggregate expenditure function

World stock markets soared during the 'Roaring 20s' and then, on 29 October 1929, the US market crashed. The Dow Jones average of industrial stock prices fell 37 points, a 12.7 per cent drop. Over the years, much debate has taken place over whether the 1929 crash was merely a symptom or a major cause of the downturn. Evidence exists that the 1929 crash only reflected an economic decline already in progress. Between August and October 1929, production fell at an annual rate of 20 per cent and personal income fell at an annual rate of 5 per cent.

The argument over the impact of a stock market crash on the economy was renewed on 19 October 1987, when America's stock exchanges suffered their worst single-day loss ever. The Dow Jones Industrial Average fell 23 per cent for a whopping loss of $500 billion in the value of outstanding stocks in a single day. Economists, stock analysts and government officials are still debating the causes and consequences of 'Black Monday'. As a result of the September 11 attack on the United States in 2001, the US stock market suffered its worst one-week loss since the Great Depression. In the immediate aftermath, equities losses were an extraordinary $1.2 trillion in value.

Stock market plunges are often widely reported in the news. People feel poorer because of the threat to their life savings. In only a few hours, spectacular paper losses reduce the wealth that people are counting on to purchase homes, automobiles, college tuition or retirement. Although only one in five US households owns shares – in Australia the percentage is much higher – everyone fears that the share market roller coaster will affect their jobs and income. If a stock market crash led to a recession, it would cause layoffs or cut profit-sharing and adversely affect superannuation funds. Businesses fear that many families will postpone buying major consumer items for fear they may need their cash to tide them over the difficult economic times ahead. Reluctance of consumers to spend would lower demand and, in turn, prices and profits would fall. Falling sales and anxiety about a recession may lead many executives to postpone modernisation plans. Rather than buying new factories and equipment, which help reduce costs, businesses would continue with used plants and machinery. This would mean less private investment spending and lower employment, output and income for the overall economy.

Analyse the issue

Immediately following the attack on the US on 11 September 2001, the stock market plunged and many observers expected a recession in the US (and possibly elsewhere). Using the *AD–AS* model, explain their prediction.

Exhibit 14.9 **A rightward shift in the aggregate supply curve**

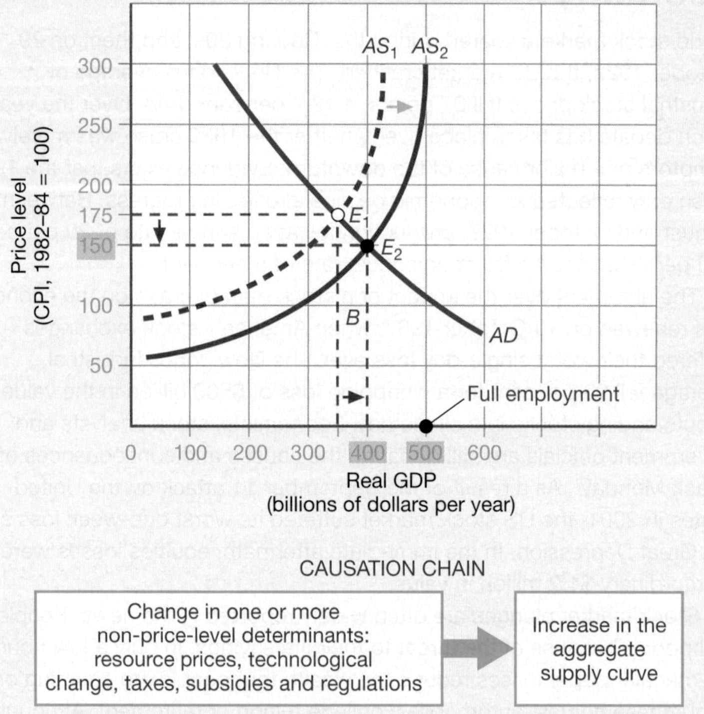

Holding the aggregate demand curve constant, the impact on the price level and the real GDP depends on whether the aggregate supply curve shifts to the right or the left. A rightward shift of aggregate supply from AS_1 to AS_2 will increase the real GDP from $350 billion to $400 billion and reduce the price level from 175 to 150.

level. Hence, the aggregate supply curve shifts rightward from AS_1 to AS_2 and equilibrium changes from E_1 to E_2. As a result, the real GDP increases $50 billion and the price level decreases from 175 to 150.

Changes in many other things can also cause an increase in aggregate supply. Lower oil prices, better management practices, improvements in basic infrastructure inputs into the production process (microeconomic reform), lower taxes and reduced government regulation are just a few other examples of conditions that lower production costs and therefore cause a rightward shift of the aggregate supply curve.

What kinds of events might raise production costs and shift the aggregate supply curve leftward? Perhaps there is war in the Middle East or OPEC restricts supplies of oil and higher energy prices spread throughout the economy. Under such a 'supply shock', businesses decrease their output at any price level in response to higher production costs per unit. Similarly, larger-than-expected wage increases, higher taxes to protect the environment (see

Exhibit 4.7 in Chapter 4), or greater unnecessary government regulation might increase production costs and therefore shift the aggregate supply curve leftward. A leftward shift in the aggregate supply curve is discussed further in the next section.

Cost-push and demand-pull inflation revisited

We now apply the aggregate demand and aggregate supply model to the two types of inflation introduced in the previous chapter. This section begins with a historical example of **cost-push inflation** caused by an inward shift of the aggregate supply curve. Next, another historical example illustrates **demand-pull inflation**, caused by outward shifts in the aggregate demand curve.

Cost-push inflation A rise in the price level resulting from an inward shift in the aggregate supply curve while the aggregate demand curve remains unchanged.

Demand-pull inflation A rise in the price level resulting from an increase in the aggregate demand curve while the aggregate supply curve remains unchanged.

Stagflation The condition that occurs when an economy experiences the twin maladies of high unemployment and rapid inflation simultaneously.

INFOTRAC®
stagflation

From the mid-1970s to the early 1980s, many developed economies experienced **stagflation**. Stagflation occurs when an economy experiences the twin maladies of high unemployment and rapidly rising prices simultaneously. How could this happen? It has been argued that the dramatic increase in the price of oil in 1973–74 was a significant factor in a *cost-push inflation* scenario in many countries around the world at the time. Cost-push inflation is defined in terms of our macro model as a rise in the price level resulting from an inward shift in the aggregate supply curve while the aggregate demand curve remains unchanged. As a result of cost-push inflation, our *AD–AS* supply model predicts real output and employment decrease; this is consistent with the mid-1970s experience resulting from the oil price shock.

Exhibit 14.10(a) uses actual data to show how a leftward shift in the supply curve can cause stagflation. In this exhibit, aggregate demand curve $AD_{73/74}$ and aggregate supply curve $AS_{73/74}$ represent the Australian economy in 1973–74. Equilibrium was at point E_1, with the price index level (CPI) in December 1973 at 22.7, annual inflation at 12.9 per cent and the real GDP at $68 billion for the quarter. However, during late 1973 and into 1974 and 1975, as a result of a huge push by unions for higher wages that were very significantly in excess of labour productivity increases, production costs increased dramatically. Thus this wage push in Australia represented a major supply shock, which had a similar impact in Australia to the effect that the oil price shock mentioned above had on other developed nations around the world.

In the Australian case this supply shock can be represented in our analysis by a shifting inwards of the aggregate supply curve leftward from $AS_{73/74}$ to $AS_{74/75}$. Assuming a stable aggregate demand between 1973–74 and 1974–75, the impact of the wage shock resulted in a new equilibrium at point E_2, with the June 1974 CPI at 24.3. The inflation rate for that period therefore increased to an annualised rate of 14.6 per cent. At the same time, real GDP

Exhibit 14.10 Cost-push and demand-pull inflation

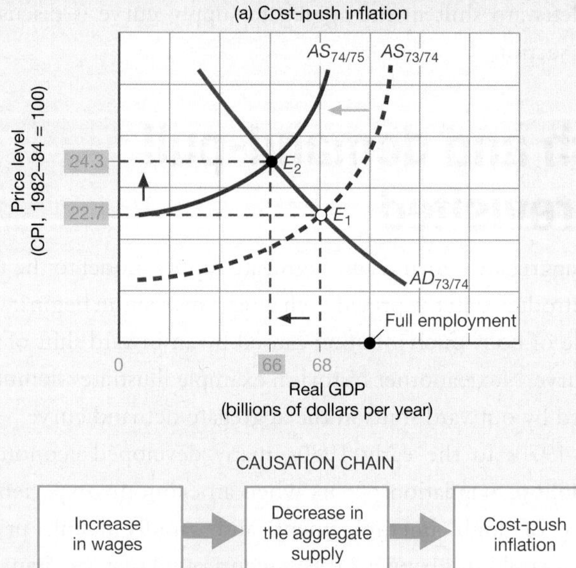

CAUSATION CHAIN

Increase in wages → Decrease in the aggregate supply → Cost-push inflation

Parts (a) and (b) show the distinction between cost-push inflation and demand-pull inflation. Cost-push inflation is inflation that results from a decrease in the aggregate supply. In part (a), a 1974–75 wage surge in Australia can be represented by an inward shift in the aggregate supply curve from $AS_{73/74}$ to $AS_{74/75}$. As a result, real GDP fell from $68 billion in December 1973 to $66 billion in June 1974 and the price level (CPI) rose from 22.7 to 24.3, implying that the underlying inflation rate had increased to 14.6%. This combination of higher inflation and lower real output is called stagflation.

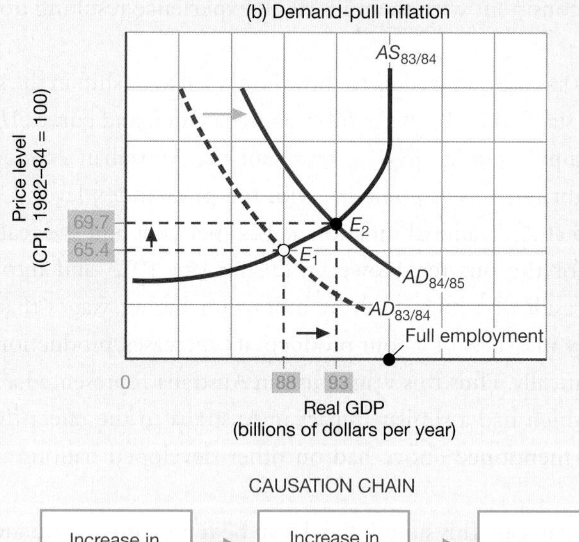

CAUSATION CHAIN

Increase in government spending → Increase in the aggregate demand → Demand-pull inflation

As shown in part (b), demand-pull inflation is inflation that results from an increase in aggregate demand beyond the Keynesian range of output represented in the exhibit in moving from $AD_{83/84}$ to $AD_{84/85}$. Consequently, real GDP rose from $88 billion to $93 billion and the price level (CPI) rose from 65.4 to 69.7, implying an increase in the rate of inflation from 4% to 6.6%.

fell from $68 billion in December 1973 to $66 billion by June 1974. In other words, the economy contracted at the same time as inflation increased. Australia experienced stagflation around this time for the first time since World War II. The cause was a shift in aggregate supply.

On the other hand, an outward shift in the aggregate demand curve can result in *demand-pull inflation*. Demand-pull inflation in terms of our macro model is a rise in the price level resulting from an increase in the aggregate demand curve while the aggregate supply curve remains unchanged. Again, we can use aggregate demand and supply analysis and actual data to explain a demand-pull inflation episode in recent Australian history.

Exhibit 14.10(b) illustrates what happened to the economy in the 1984–85 period. In 1982–83 Australia experienced a recession. As a result, a Keynesian expansionary macroeconomic policy was set in place by the authorities to try to 'kick start' private-sector demand. In other words, in terms of our aggregate demand/aggregate supply analysis, the authorities' actions can be represented by a shifting out of the aggregate demand curve. The initial equilibrium is represented by E_1 at the intersection of $AD_{83/84}$ and $AS_{83/84}$. Here, in June 1984, for example, real GDP was $88 billion, the CPI was 65.4 and the annual inflation rate at the time was 4 per cent.

The aggregate demand stimulus occurred during 1983 and into 1984 and early 1985 and is represented in the exhibit by a movement of the aggregate demand curve out to $AD_{84/85}$. The aggregate supply curve is assumed unchanged at $AS_{83/84}$. The resulting equilibrium point for the period is represented by E_2. At this point, which represents the economy at, say, June 1985, real GDP had accelerated to $93 billion – a very strong annual economic growth rate of almost 6 per cent; but at the same time the CPI had increased to 69.7, representing an annual inflation rate of 6.6 per cent. Thus the *AD* stimulus accelerated real output growth but also served to produce a demand-pull acceleration in inflation from an underlying rate of 4 per cent to 6.6 per cent.

In summary, the aggregate supply and aggregate demand curves shift in different directions for various reasons over different time periods. These shifts in the aggregate supply and aggregate demand curves may be used to understand upswings and downswings in real GDP and the rate of inflation – that is, the business cycle. A leftward shift in the aggregate demand curve or aggregate supply curve, for example, can cause a recession. On the other hand, a rightward shift of the aggregate demand curve or aggregate supply curve can cause real GDP and employment to rise and the economy recovers.

The business cycle may be understood as the result of shifts over time in the aggregate demand and aggregate supply curves.

Exhibit 14.11 summarises the shift factors of aggregate demand and supply for further study and review. In Chapter 17 on fiscal policy you will learn in more detail how changes in the taxation and spending policies of government can affect the economy. The *AD–AS* framework you have learned about here will be used again there. Also, in Chapter 16 on monetary policy, you will learn how the *AD–AS* model can help you understand how changing the supply of financial liquidity in the economy can affect the business cycle.

Exhibit 14.11 Summary of the shift factors of aggregate demand and aggregate supply

Shift factors of aggregate demand (total spending)	Shift factors of aggregate supply (total production)
1 Consumption (*C*)	1 Resource prices (domestic and imported)
2 Investment (*I*)	2 Taxes
3 Government spending (*G*)	3 Technological change
4 Net exports (*X* – *M*)	4 Subsidies
	5 Regulation

You make the call

Would the greenhouse effect cause inflation, unemployment or both?

You are the head of the Federal Treasury. There has been an extremely hot and dry summer due to the climatic change known as the greenhouse effect. As a result, crop production has fallen drastically. The Prime Minister calls you to the Lodge to discuss the impact on the economy. Would you explain to the Prime Minister that a sharp drop in Australian crop production would cause inflation, unemployment or both?

Key concepts

- Say's Law
- Consumption function
- Marginal propensity to consume (MPC)
- Marginal propensity to save (MPS)
- Investment demand
- Government demand
- Net export demand
- Spending multiplier
- Aggregate demand (AD)
- Real balances or wealth effect
- Interest-rate effect
- Net exports effect
- Aggregate supply (AS)
- Keynesian range
- Intermediate range
- Classical range
- Stagflation
- Demand-pull and cost-push inflation

Summary

- **Say's Law** is the classical theory that states that 'supply creates its own demand' and that therefore the Great Depression was impossible. Say's Law is the belief that the value of production generates an equal amount of income and, in turn, total spending. The classical economists rejected the challenge that under-consumption is possible because they believed that flexible prices, wages and interest rates soon correct any imbalance between supply and demand.

- **John Maynard Keynes** rejected the classical theory that the economy self-corrects in the long run to full employment. The key in Keynesian theory is aggregate demand, rather than the classicals' focus on aggregate supply. Unless aggregate spending is adequate, the economy can experience prolonged and severe unemployment.

- The **consumption function** (*C*) is determined by changes in the level of disposable income. Changes in such non-income determinants as expectations, wealth, the price level, interest rates and the stock of durable goods can cause shifts in consumption demand.

- The **marginal propensity to consume** (MPC) is the change in consumption associated with a given change in disposable income. The MPC tells how much of an additional dollar of disposable income households will spend for consumption.

- The **marginal propensity to save** (MPS) is the change in saving associated with a given change in disposable income. The MPS measures how much of an additional dollar of disposable income households will save.

- **Investment demand** (*I*) by businesses increases along the demand curve as rates of interest drop. Shifts in investment demand result from changes in expectations, technological change, capacity utilisation and business taxes.

- **Autonomous expenditure** is spending that does not vary with the current level of disposable income or interest rates.

- The **aggregate demand curve** shows the level of demand in the economy for real GDP purchased at different price levels during a period of time.

- **Stagflation** exists when an economy experiences inflation and unemployment simultaneously. Holding aggregate demand constant, a decrease in aggregate supply results in the unhealthy condition of a rise in the price level and a fall in real GDP and employment.

- **Reasons why the aggregate demand curve is downward-sloping** include the following three effects: (1) The **real balances** or **wealth effect** is the impact on demand for real GDP caused by the inverse relationship between the purchasing power of a fixed nominal stock of financial assets and rising prices and which causes a shift in consumption demand. (2) The **interest-rate effect** occurs as a result of rising prices increasing the demand for borrowed funds. As the demand for borrowed funds increases, interest rates rise, causing consumption and investment spending to fall. (3) The **net exports effect** is the impact on real GDP caused by the inverse relationship between net exports and rising prices. An increase in domestic price level tends to reduce domestic exports and increase imports and vice-versa.

Shift in the aggregate demand curve

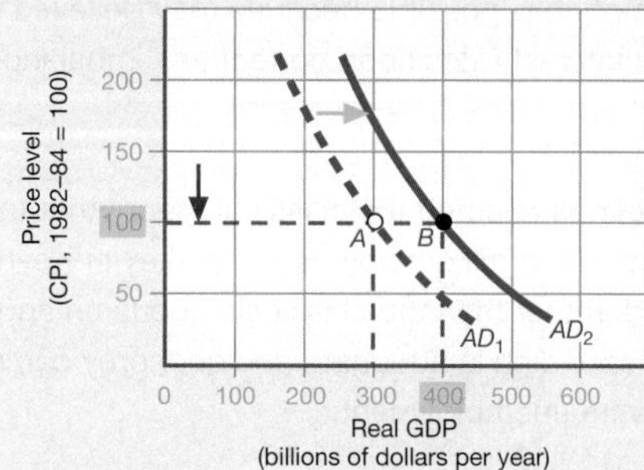

- The **aggregate supply curve** shows the level of real GDP that an economy will produce at different possible price levels. The shape of the aggregate supply curve depends on the flexibility of prices and wages as real GDP expands and contracts. The aggregate supply curve has three ranges: (1) The **Keynesian range** of the curve is horizontal because neither the price level nor production costs will increase when there is substantial unemployment in the economy. (2) In the **intermediate range**, both prices and costs rise as real GDP rises towards full employment. Prices and production costs rise because of bottlenecks, the stronger bargaining power of labour and the utilisation of less-productive workers and capital. (3) The **classical range** is the vertical segment of the aggregate supply curve. It coincides with the full-employment output. Because output is at its maximum, increases in aggregate demand will only cause a rise in the price level.

Aggregate supply curve

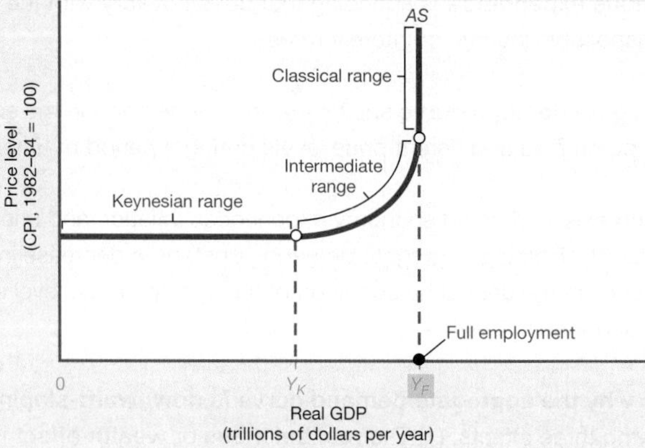

PART 5

- **Aggregate demand and aggregate supply analysis** determines the equilibrium price level and the equilibrium real GDP by the intersection of the aggregate demand and the aggregate supply curves. In macroeconomic equilibrium, businesses neither overestimate nor underestimate the real GDP demanded at the prevailing price level.

- **Cost-push inflation** is inflation that results from an inward shift in the aggregate supply curve while the aggregate demand curve remains unchanged.

Cost-push inflation

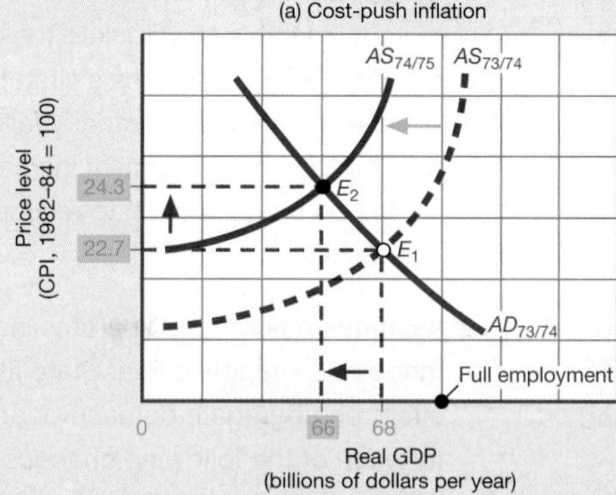

- **Demand-pull inflation** is inflation that results from an increase in the aggregate demand curve in both the classical and the intermediate ranges of the aggregate supply curve while the aggregate supply curve is fixed.

Demand-pull inflation

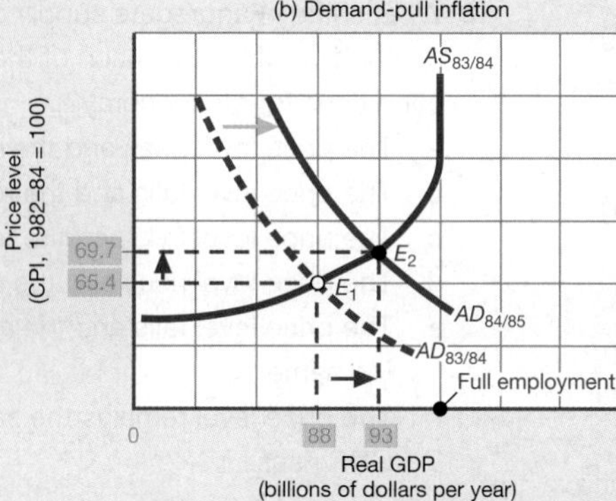

Study questions and problems

1 Explain how the classical economists concluded that Say's Law is valid and long-term unemployment impossible.

2 Explain why the MPC and the MPS must always add up to one.

3 Explain how each of the following affects consumption demand.
   a The expectation is that a prolonged recession will occur in the next year.
   b Stock prices rise sharply.
   c The price level rises by 10 per cent.
   d The interest rate on consumer loans rises sharply.
   e Income taxes increase.

4 Why would investment demand be less stable than consumption demand? What are the basic determinants that can shift investment demand?

5 Suppose most business executives expect a slow-down in the economy. How might this situation affect the economy?

6 Explain why the aggregate demand curve is downward-sloping. How does your explanation differ from the reasons behind the downward-sloping demand curve for an individual product?

7 Explain the theory of the classical economists that flexible prices and wages ensure that the economy operates at full employment.

8 In which direction would each of the following changes in conditions cause the aggregate demand curve to shift? Explain your answers.
   a Consumers expect an economic downturn.
   b A new government is elected and the profit expectations of business executives rise.
   c The federal government increases spending for highways, bridges and other infrastructure.
   d Australia increases exports of wheat and other crops to Russia.

9 Identify the three ranges of the aggregate supply curve. Explain the impact of an increase in aggregate demand in each segment.

10 Consider this statement: 'Equilibrium GDP is the same as full employment.' Do you agree or disagree? Explain.

11 In which direction would each of the following changes in conditions cause the aggregate supply curve to shift? Explain your answers.
   a The price of petrol increases because of an OPEC decision to reduce oil production.
   b Labour unions and all other workers agree to a cut in wages to stimulate the economy.
   c Electricity companies switch to solar power and the price of electricity falls.
   d The federal government increases the excise tax on petrol in order to reduce the budget deficit.

12 Assume an economy operates in the intermediate range of its supply curve. State the direction of effect on aggregate demand or aggregate supply for each of the following changes in conditions. What is the effect on the price level? On real GDP? On employment?
   a The price of crude oil rises significantly.
   b Spending on national defence doubles.
   c The costs of imported goods increase.
   d An improvement in technology raises labour productivity.

13 What shifts in aggregate supply or aggregate demand would cause each of the following conditions for an economy?
   a The price level rises and the real GDP rises.
   b The price level falls and the real GDP rises.
   c The price level falls and the real GDP falls.
   d The price level rises and the real GDP falls.
   e The price level falls and the real GDP remains the same.
   f The price level remains the same and the real GDP rises.

14 Explain cost-push inflation verbally and graphically, using aggregate demand and aggregate supply analysis. Assess the impact on the price level, the real GDP and employment.

15 Explain demand-pull inflation graphically using aggregate demand and supply analysis. Assess

the impact on the price level, the real GDP and employment.

Online exercises

Exercise 1

Go to **cepa.newschool.edu/het/index.htm** and select **Alphabetical Index** and then **John Maynard Keynes**. Selectively read about Keynes's contributions to macroeconomics as highlighted there.

Exercise 2

Visit the Australian Bureau of Statistics **www.abs.gov.au** to find the latest consumer price index measurements and select **AusStats**, **Publications & Data**, **Time Series Spreadsheets**, **By Catalogue/ Subject**, **64. Prices**, then **6401.0 – Consumer Price Index, Australia**.

1 What has happened to the CPI level in the past two years?

2 Given your answer to Question 1, now what can you conclude has happened to aggregate demand and and/or aggregate supply in order to have created these changes in prices?

3 Is a change in aggregate demand or the change in aggregate supply more likely to be responsible for the change in the CPI? Why?

Exercise 3

Visit the OECD (**www.oecd.org/home**) and search for **"Quarterly National Accounts"**. Select **Quarterly National Accounts for OECD Member Countries**. Select six countries of interest and compare their economic growth (GDP) performance over the past few years. What changes in aggregate demand and/ or aggregate supply would be required to bring about desirable changes in these nations' economies?

Answers to 'You make the call'

What's your MPC?

Early in your career, when your income is relatively low, you are likely to spend your entire income and perhaps even dis-save, just to afford necessities. During this stage of your life, your MPC will be close to one. As your income increases and you have purchased the necessities, additional income can go to luxuries. If you become wealthier, you have a higher marginal propensity to save and consequently a lower marginal propensity to consume. If you said your MPC will probably decrease as your income increases, YOU ARE CORRECT.

Would the greenhouse effect cause inflation, unemployment or both?

A drop in food production reduces aggregate supply. The decrease in aggregate supply causes the economy to contract, while prices rise. In addition to the OPEC oil embargo between 1972 and 1974, worldwide weather conditions destroyed crops and contributed to the supply shock that caused stagflation in the US economy. If you said that a severe greenhouse effect would cause both higher unemployment and inflation, YOU ARE CORRECT.

Multiple-choice questions

1 The French classical economist Jean-Baptiste Say transformed the equality of production and spending into a law that can be expressed as follows:

a The invisible hand creates its own supply.
b Wages always fall to the subsistence level.
c Supply creates its own demand.
d Aggregate output does not always equal consumption.

2 Autonomous government expenditure is

a positively related to the level of taxes.
b negatively related to the level of consumption.
c positively related to the level of income.
d independent of the level of income.

3 John Maynard Keynes's proposition that a dollar increase in disposable income will increase consumption, but by less than the increase in disposable income, implies a marginal propensity to consume that is

a greater than or equal to one.
b equal to one.
c less than one, but greater than zero.
d negative.

4 Which of the following changes produces an upward shift in consumption demand?
   a an increase in consumer wealth.
   b a decrease in consumer wealth.
   c an increase in disposable income.
   d both **a** and **c**.

5 Which of the following changes produces a reduction in investment demand?
   a a wave of optimism about future profitability.
   b technological change.
   c high plant capacity utilisation.
   d an increase in business taxes.

6 The aggregate demand curve is defined as
   a the net national product.
   b the sum of wages, rent, interest and profits.
   c the real GDP purchased at different possible price levels.
   d the total dollar value of household expectations.

7 When the supply of nominal liquidity is fixed, an increase in the price level stimulates the demand for liquidity, which in turn reduces consumption and investment spending. This argument is called the
   a real balances effect.
   b interest-rate effect.
   c net exports effect.
   d substitution effect.

8 The real balances effect occurs because a higher price level will reduce the real value of people's
   a financial assets.
   b wages.
   c unpaid debt.
   d physical investments.

9 The net exports effect is the inverse relationship between net exports and the ______ of an economy.
   a real GDP.
   b GDP deflator.
   c price level.
   d consumption spending.

10 Which of the following will shift the aggregate demand curve to the left?
   a an increase in exports.
   b an increase in investment.
   c an increase in government spending.
   d a decrease in government spending.

11 Which of the following will *not* shift the aggregate demand curve to the left?
   a Consumers become more optimistic about the future.
   b Government spending decreases.
   c Business optimism decreases.
   d Consumers become pessimistic about the future.

12 The popular theory prior to the Great Depression that the economy will automatically adjust to achieve full employment was
   a supply-side economics.
   b Keynesian economics.
   c classical economics.
   d mercantilism.

13 Classical economists believed that the
   a price system was stable.
   b goal of full employment was impossible.
   c price system automatically adjusts the economy to full employment in the long run.
   d government should attempt to restore full employment.

14 Macroeconomic equilibrium occurs when
   a aggregate supply exceeds aggregate demand.
   b the economy is at full employment.
   c aggregate demand equals aggregate supply.
   d aggregate demand equals the average price level.

15 Along the classical or vertical range of the aggregate supply curve, a decrease in the aggregate demand curve will decrease
   a both the price level and real GDP.
   b only real GDP.
   c only the price level.
   d real GDP and the price level.

16 Other factors held constant, a decrease in the prices of raw materials will shift the aggregate
   a demand curve leftward.
   b demand curve rightward.
   c supply curve leftward.
   d supply curve rightward.

17 Assuming a fixed aggregate demand curve, a leftward shift in the aggregate supply curve causes
   a an increase in the price level and a decrease in real GDP.

b an increase in the price level and an increase in real GDP.
c a decrease in the price level and a decrease in real GDP.
d a decrease in the price level and an increase in real GDP.

18 An increase in the price level caused by a rightward shift of the aggregate demand curve is called
a cost-push inflation.
b supply shock inflation.
c demand shock inflation.
d demand-pull inflation.

19 Suppose workers become pessimistic about their future employment, which causes them to save more and spend less. If the economy is on the intermediate range of the aggregate supply curve, then
a both real GDP and the price level will fall.
b real GDP will fall and the price level will rise.
c real GDP will rise and the price level will fall.
d both real GDP and the price level will rise.

APPENDIX TO CHAPTER 14

Further on the aggregate demand–output model: the 'Keynesian Cross'

In the chapter we sketched out in brief what we call the 'aggregate demand–output model', also known as the Keynesian model. In this appendix we provide some additional details.

We have referred to the aggregate 'willingness to purchase' goods and services in some period as aggregate demand. As has also been mentioned, the largest component of aggregate demand is consumption and one of the most significant determinants of consumption demand is income.[1] What is expected is that, as income increases, other things being equal, consumption

Exhibit 14A.1 **The 'Keynesian Cross' in diagrammatic form**

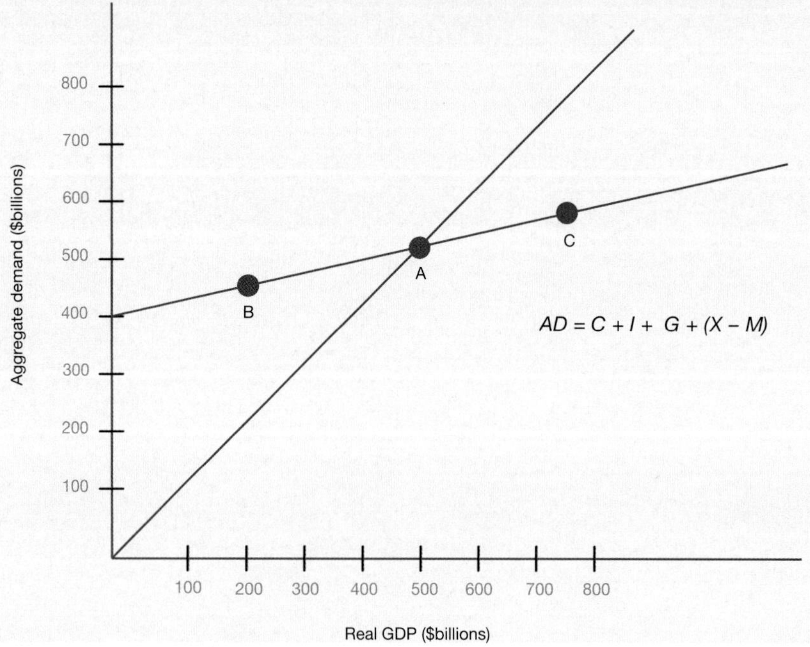

1 As mentioned in the text, other important determinants are wealth, expectations, the price level and interest rates.

spending can be expected also to increase. Therefore, given the significance of consumption spending in aggregate demand, an important determinant of overall aggregate demand is income.

In Exhibit 14A.1 this relationship between aggregate demand and income is presented in graphical form. It should also be noted that, given the theoretical equivalence of income and output (refer back to Chapter 11), real GDP is used in the exhibit instead of income.

In the exhibit, aggregate demand (measured on the vertical axis) is depicted as an upward-sloping line representing the relationship between aggregate demand and output (i.e. income). As output (and income) increases, aggregate demand can be expected to be higher because the higher income induces increased consumption expenditure, ceteris paribus.

The 45-degree line in the exhibit simply represents points where the value on the horizontal axis is equal to the value on the vertical axis. Point *A*, therefore, represents a point of equilibrium for the economy where aggregate demand is equal to total production. Point *B*, on the other hand, represents a disequilibrium situation where aggregate demand is greater than output. In this situation firms would find their inventories running down and so, in the next period, production would be increased – to production point *A*. The reverse situation would apply at point *C*.

Now, assuming the economy is currently in equilibrium in some period, what would happen if there were some change to aggregate demand? In

Exhibit 14A.2 Using the 'Keynesian Cross' to represent the effect of an increase in aggregate demand

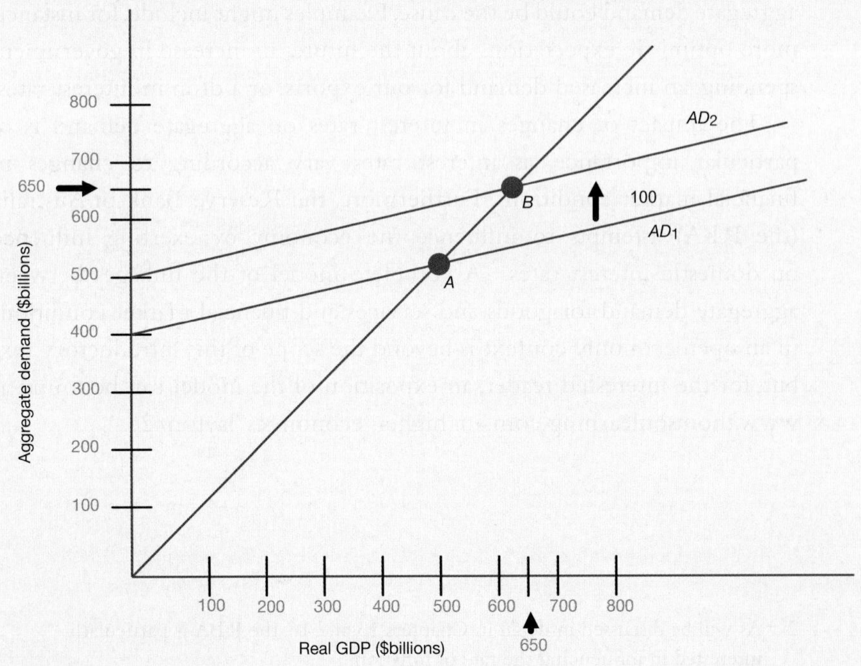

Exhibit 14A.2 the economy is assumed to be at equilibrium at point *A*. An increase in aggregate demand of $100 billion is depicted by a vertical shift of $100 billion in the aggregate demand schedule. The result of this upward shift in aggregate demand is a new equilibrium at point *B*. Here production has increased to meet the higher aggregate demand.

However, notice that the new equilibrium is more than $100 billion higher than the old. This is because of the impact of the spending multiplier discussed in the chapter. At point *A*, the initial increase in demand results in greater production. The higher production generates higher income, which in turn generates higher consumption spending. The higher consumption spending in turn will stimulate higher production and so on until the new equilibrium at point *B* is reached. These additional spending rounds result in a new equilibrium, which is higher than the original by more than the initial $100 billion stimulus.

Exhibit 14A.2 is sometimes referred to as a 'Keynesian Cross' diagram. It is simply a way of representing the notion that, in the Keynesian aggregate demand–output model, any change in aggregate demand results in a change in production without any change in prices. In the text, in the more general *AD–AS* model framework, a change in aggregate demand can have both an output and a price response, depending on where the economy is in relation to full employment production. In the Keynesian model it is assumed that there is sufficient excess capacity in the economy such that any change in aggregate demand is met by a change in output only.

What might cause such a shift in aggregate demand as depicted in Exhibit 14A.2? A change in any one of the non-income determinants of aggregate demand could be the cause. Examples might include, for instance, more optimistic expectations about the future, an increase in government spending, an increased demand for our exports, or a drop in interest rates.

The impact of changes in interest rates on aggregate demand is of particular importance, as interest rates vary according to changes in financial market conditions. Furthermore, the Reserve Bank of Australia (the RBA) attempts to influence the economy by exerting influence on domestic interest rates.[2] A complete model of the linkages between aggregate demand for goods and services and financial market conditions in an open economy context is beyond the scope of this introductory text but, for the interested reader, an exposition of the model can be found at www.thomsonlearning.com.au/higher/economics/layton/2e.

2 As will be discussed in detail in Chapters 15 and 16, the RBA is particularly interested in influencing the rate of inflation.

15 The monetary and financial system

As the lyrics of the old song go, 'Money makes the world go around, the world go around, the world go around ...'. Recall the circular flow model presented in Chapter 11 on GDP. Households exchange *money* for goods and services in the product markets and firms exchange *money* for resources in the factor markets. In short, money affects the way an economy works. In the previous chapter on aggregate demand and supply the *AD–AS* model was developed without explicitly discussing the role of money. In this chapter and the next, money takes centre stage.

Exactly what is money? The answer may surprise you. Imagine yourself on the small South Pacific island of Yap. You are surrounded by exotic fowl, crystal-clear lagoons, delicious fruits and sunny skies. Now suppose, while leisurely strolling along the beach one evening, you discover a beautiful bamboo hut for sale. It so happens that, to pay for your dream hut, you may well be asked to roll a five-foot-diameter stone to an area of the island designated as the 'bank'.

We begin our discussion of money with the three functions that money serves. We will also talk about what determines the demand for money. Next, we define the components of four different money supply definitions used in Australia. Although there will inevitably be some definitional differences across countries, these four definitions will have broad parallels in any country with a well-developed financial system. The remainder of the chapter describes the organisation and function of Australia's central bank, the Reserve Bank of Australia (RBA), the role of banks and some other important aspects of the financial system. Beginning in this chapter and continued in the next, you will learn how the RBA controls the stock of money in the economy. Then, using the *AD–AS* model, you will learn how variations in the stock of money in the economy affect total spending, output, unemployment and prices.

In this chapter, you will examine these economics questions:

- Why do nations use money?
- When is 'plastic money' really money?
- What does a central bank do?
- Exactly how is money created in the economy? That is, how does the money supply increase?
- Why do people wish to hold money balances?
- What is a monetary policy transmission mechanism?

What makes money '*money*'?

Barter The direct exchange of one good for another good, rather than for money.

Can exchange occur in an economy without money? It certainly can, using a trading system called **barter**. In fact, organised barter systems still exist for restricted ranges of goods and services, even in countries with very modern financial systems like Australia. Barter is the direct exchange of one good for another good, rather than for money. The problem with barter is that it requires a *coincidence of wants*. Imagine for a moment that dollars and coins are worthless and Farmer Tang needs shoes, so he takes his kilos of wheat to the shoe shop and offers to barter wheat for shoes. Unfortunately, the shop owner refuses to trade because she wants to trade shoes for pencils, toothpaste and coffee. Undaunted, Farmer Tang spends more time and effort to find Mr Jones, who has pencils, toothpaste and coffee that he will trade for kilos of wheat. Although Farmer Tang's luck has improved, he and Mr Jones must agree on the terms of exchange. Exactly how many kilos of coffee, for example, is a kilo of wheat worth? Assuming this exchange is worked out, Farmer Tang must spend more time returning to the shoe shop and negotiating the terms of an exchange of pencils, coffee and toothpaste for shoes.

The use of money simplifies and therefore facilitates an increase in market transactions. Money also prevents wasting time that could otherwise be devoted to production, thereby promoting economic efficiency and growth by increasing a nation's production possibilities.

The three functions of money

INFOTRAC®
three functions of money

Suppose the planet of Starcom and its citizens want to replace their barter system and must decide what to use for money. Assuming this planet is fortunate enough to have economists, they would explain that anything, regardless of its innate value, can serve as money if it conforms to the following definition of **money**. Money is anything that serves as a medium of exchange, unit of account and store of value. Money is not limited to five-cent coins, 20-cent coins and dollar bills. Anything that meets the three tests is a candidate to serve as money. This explains why money can be (and has been in different places and at different times) precious metals, beaver skins, wampum (shells strung in belts) or cigarettes. Let's discuss each of the three functions money serves.

Money Anything that serves as a medium of exchange, unit of account and store of value.

Money as a medium of exchange

In a simple society, barter is a way for participants to exchange goods and services in order to satisfy wants. Barter, however, requires wasting time in the process of exchange that people could use for productive activities. If the goal is to increase the volume of transactions and live in a modern economy, the most important function of money is to serve as a **medium of exchange**. This means that, to be 'money', something has to be very widely accepted in exchange for goods and services. Money removes the problem of coincidence of wants, because every person is willing to accept money in payment rather than goods and services. You give up a $20 note in exchange for a ticket to see a concert. This $20 note is accepted because the concert organiser has every confidence that she will be able to trade the $20 for the equivalent quantity of goods and services that she may want. Because money serves as generalised purchasing power, all in society know that no one will refuse to trade their products for money. In short, money increases trade by providing a much more convenient method of exchange than a cumbersome barter system.

Medium of exchange The primary function of money to be widely accepted in exchange for goods and services.

PART 5

For a look at the history of money, visit *History of Money from Ancient Times to the Present Day* (**www.ex.ac.uk/~RDavies/arian/llyfr.html**).

Money as a unit of account

How does a wheat farmer know whether a tonne of wheat is worth one, two or more pairs of shoes? How does a family compare its income to expenses, or a business know whether it is making a profit? Government must be able to measure tax revenues collected and its program expenditures. And GDP is the *money* value of final goods and services used to compare the national economic growth of Australia to, say, that of New Zealand. In each of these examples, money serves as a **unit of account**. Without money, we face the difficult task of, say, pricing sushi in terms of other goods. Unit of account is the function of money to provide a common measurement of the relative value of goods and services. Without dollars, there is no common denominator. We are obliged to decide if one sushi serving equals a box of pencils, 20 oranges or four litres of oil. Now let's compare the value of

Unit of account The function of money to provide a common measurement of the relative value of goods and services.

two items using money. If the price of a sushi serving is $10 and the price of a movie ticket is $5, then one sushi serving equals two movie tickets. In Australia the monetary unit is the dollar; but in other countries the monetary unit may have a different name; thus in Japan it is the yen, in Malaysia it is the ringgit, in Europe it is the euro, and so on.

Money as a store of value

Could you save fresh seafood for months and then exchange it for some product? You could, but not without the extra expense of freezing the seafood for an extended period. Money, on the other hand, serves as a cheap **store of value**. Store of value is the ability of money to hold value over time. You can bury money in your backyard or store it under your mattress for months or years and not worry about it spoiling. Stated differently, the durability of money allows us to synchronise our income more precisely with expenditures. However, recall from Chapter 13 that inflation can destroy the store-of-value function and, in turn, the medium-of-exchange function.

Store of value The ability of money to hold value over time.

CONCLUSION **Money is a useful mechanism for transforming income in the present into future purchases.**

The key property of money is that it is completely *liquid*. This means that money is immediately available to spend in exchange for goods and services without any additional expense. Money is more liquid than real assets (such as real estate, gold or jewellery) or some other types of paper assets (say stocks or bonds). These assets also serve as stores of value, but liquidating (selling) them often involves expenses, such as brokerage fees, time delays and loss of nominal value due to a possibly forced sale when their market value is low.

CONCLUSION **Money is the most liquid form of wealth because it can be spent directly in the marketplace.**

Are credit cards money?

It is an understandable misconception that credit cards, such as VISA, MasterCard and American Express, are 'plastic money'. Let's test credit cards for the three functions of money. First, because credit cards are widely accepted, they certainly serve as a means of payment in an exchange for goods or services. However, the reason for this is that there is a legal guarantee by the credit card company that, at a later stage, the required number of dollars will be transferred to the seller of the product.

Second, the credit card statement and not the card itself serves as the unit of account. One of the advantages of credit cards is that you receive a statement listing exactly the price in dollars paid for each item you charged. Your credit card statement clearly records the dollar amount you spent for petrol, a dinner or a trip.

Finally, credit cards clearly fail to meet the store-of-value criterion. The word *credit* means receiving money today to buy products in return for a promise to pay in the future. Credit cards represent only a prearranged short-term loan up to a certain limit. If the credit card company goes out of business or for any reason decides not to honour your card, it is worthless. Hence, credit cards do not store value and are *not* money. If credit cards were money, you would be indifferent about whether you received $1000 in cash or an equal dollar increase in your credit limit. Few people would be indifferent faced with these two alternatives.

Credit cards are really nothing more than a more modern way to conduct transactions compared with, say, cheques. A cheque is not money either. It is simply an instruction to a bank to transfer some number of dollars (which are money) from you to someone else in payment for services rendered or goods provided. Credit cards – and cheques – certainly improve the efficiency of our system of conducting transactions, but in themselves they do not constitute money. Similarly, the widespread use of EFTPOS facilities has greatly increased the convenience and efficiency of conducting transactions. However, these facilities merely increase the efficiency with which the underlying medium of exchange – bank deposits of dollars – can be used to purchase goods and services.

Are debit cards money?

Debit cards are used to pay for purchases and the funds are automatically deducted from the user's bank account at the time and place of purchase. Are debit cards therefore money?

Other desirable properties of money

Once something has passed the three basic requirements to serve as money, there are additional hurdles to clear. First, an important consideration is *scarcity*. Money must be scarce, but not too scarce. Sand, for example, could theoretically serve as money. But sand is a poor choice because people can easily gather a bucketful to pay their bills. Picasso paintings would also be undesirable as money. Because there are so few in circulation, people would have to resort to barter.

Counterfeiting threatens the scarcity of paper money. Advances in computer graphics, scanners and colour copiers have potentially allowed counterfeiters to gain an advantage over the monetary authorities. However, the introduction in Australia of plastic notes (this kind of 'plastic' really is money!) was motivated at least in part to reduce the possibility of counterfeiting. The other great advantage of plastic notes is that they have increased durability. For example, they dry very quickly – and do not shrink – even after you forgetfully leave them in your pants when you do your washing (the authors can vouch for this). Other countries are now adopting this style of note.

CONCLUSION **The supply of money must be great enough to meet ordinary transactions needs, but not be so plentiful that it becomes worthless.**

Second, money should be *portable* and *divisible*. That is, people should be able to reach into their pockets and make change to buy items at various prices. Miniature statues of some specified list of sporting greats might be attractive money to some, but they would be difficult to carry and make change with. Finally, money must be *uniform*. An ounce of gold is an ounce of gold. The quality differences of beaver skins and seashells, on the other hand, complicate using these items for money. Each exchange would involve the extra trouble of buyers and sellers arguing over which skins or shells were better or worse.

International focus

Dollar dethroned by the might of frequent-flyer miles

Applicable concept: functions of money

In a recent article, the business magazine *The Economist* drew attention to the incredibly large contingent liability of unredeemed frequent-flyer miles that airlines have worldwide. In a somewhat tongue-in-cheek – but nonetheless useful – way, the article drew some parallels with the stock of US-denominated currency.

In December, we warned that the dollar's role as the world's main currency was under threat if the US continued in its profligate ways. Yet the dollar has been dethroned even sooner than we expected!

It has been superseded not by the euro, nor by the yen or yuan, but by another increasingly popular global currency: frequent-flyer miles.

Calculations by *The Economist* suggest the total stock of unredeemed frequent-flyer miles is now worth more than all the dollar bills in circulation around the globe.

By the end of 2004 almost 14 trillion frequent-flyer miles had, by our estimate (updating figures from webflyer.com), been accumulated worldwide. ...

But what is a mile worth? Airlines sell them to credit card firms at an average of just under 2 cents a mile; their value, when used to buy a ticket or to upgrade to business class, can be anywhere between 1 cent and 10 cents per mile.

Using the mid-point of this range means the global stock of frequent-flyer miles is now worth over $700 billion, more than all the dollar notes and coins at large. Pedants will complain that we have ignored dollars sitting in bank accounts, but after a couple of free in-flight gin and tonics, most frequent-flyers care little about the difference between M0 (the narrowest measure of the supply of miles, or rather, money) and M3.

Frequent-flyer miles have long been a form of money, used as a means of exchange and a store of value. Mileage junkies check their statements monthly; divorce settlements often place a value on frequent-flyer miles; and corporate high-flyers look forward to spending their huge balances in retirement.

It has never been so easy to earn miles. Airlines offer special triple-mile bonuses at certain times of the year such as, in the northern hemisphere, January and February, and half of all miles are now earned not in the air, but on the ground, notably on credit card payments.

But as a result, airlines have been printing too much of their currency. The number of miles outstanding has risen by almost 20 per cent a year over the past decade. At current rates of redemption, even if no more miles were issued, it would take 25 years to use up the stock.

In 2002, *The Economist* predicted that such inflationary policies would inevitably lead to a devaluation of frequent-flyer miles.

This has indeed started to happen: several airlines have increased the number of miles required for a free flight, or made them harder to use at the time you want to travel.

But, making it harder to use frequent-flyer miles today merely raises airlines' future financial liabilities from unredeemed miles.

Were it to exist, the IMF (the International Mileage Fund) would by now repeatedly have warned that these growing external liabilities were unsustainable in exactly the same way that the US cannot keep borrowing from the rest of the world.

If the new global currency was left entirely to the market, the value of frequent-flyer miles would plummet in order to match the demand for and supply of free flights just as the dollar would be weaker if Asian central banks stopped intervening.

Frequent-flyer miles are no better as a[n international] reserve currency than the greenback. But this misses a crucial point. Central banks and finance ministries have a far greater interest in defending the value of frequent-flyer miles than in propping up the dollar.

After all, their officials are continually criss-crossing the globe to attend meetings, racking up miles in their personal accounts.

If their free first-class flight to the Caribbean is at risk, they are likely to fight to the death to stop a devaluation.

Against such competition, the dollar does not stand a chance.

Source: edited text of 'Dollar dethroned by the might of frequent-flyer miles', *The Australian*, 10 January 2005, p. 27 – a reprint of an article originally appearing in *The Economist*.

Analyse the issue

1 What functions of money do frequent-flyer miles possess?

2 Can you think of limitations and/or dangers that militate against the adoption of such a new form of money?

PART 5

What stands behind our money?

Commodity money Anything that serves as money while having market value in other uses.

Historically, early forms of money played two roles. If, for example, a ruler declared beans as money, you could spend them or sell them in the marketplace. Precious metals, cigarettes and tobacco, cows and other tangible durable goods are examples of **commodity money**. Commodity money is anything that serves as money while having market value in other uses. This means that a commodity money itself has intrinsic worth (the market value of the material). For example, money can be pure gold or silver, both of which are valuable for non-money uses, such as making jewellery and serving other industrial purposes.

The Reserve Bank of Australia publishes an online brochure about the history of Australia's currency note issue. To peruse it, go to **www.rba.gov.au**, click on *Search* and select *Currency Notes*, then *History of the Note Issue*.

Today, Australia's paper money and coins are no longer backed by gold or silver or any other physical commodity. Australia's money was at one time exchangeable for gold. So too were other countries' currencies. During this time such countries were on the so-called 'gold standard'. Today, if you go into your bank – or indeed into your country's central bank – and seek to exchange your old, fraying dollar bill or whatever is your currency, what you will get at best will be a new dollar bill. There is no intrinsically valuable commodity backing the world's currencies. They are **fiat money**. Fiat money is money issued by the central bank that is accepted by law, but not because of any redeemability or intrinsic value. A dollar bill contains only about three cents' worth of paper, printing inks and other materials. Pull out a note and look at it closely. Somewhere on it you should find something to the effect of its being 'legal tender' – it is therefore legally acceptable in the payment of all debts. In Australia, the wording is: 'This Australian Note is Legal Tender Throughout Australia and Its Territories.' Also notice that nowhere on your note does it say there is any promise to redeem it for gold, silver or anything else.

Fiat money Money accepted by law and not because of redeemability or intrinsic value.

CONCLUSION Whether or not an item will serve as money does not depend on its own market value or the backing of precious metal.

The demand for money

Why do people want to hold (demand) money – or more generally some quantity of highly liquid financial assets such as currency and cheque deposits – rather than putting their money to work in stocks, bonds, real estate or other non-money forms of wealth? Because money yields no (or very little) direct return, people (including businesses) who hold cash or cheque account balances incur an *opportunity cost* of forgone interest or profits on the amount of money held. So what are the benefits of holding money? Why would people hold money and thereby forgo earning interest payments? There are considered to be three important motives for doing so: transactions motive, precautionary motive and speculative motive.

Transactions motive for the demand for money

The first motive for holding money is the *transactions motive*. The **transactions motive for the demand for money** is the wish of people to hold a stock of money to pay everyday predictable expenses. The desire to have 'walking-around money' to make quick and easy purchases is the principal reason for holding money. Students, for example, have a good idea of how much money they will need to hold for rent, groceries, electricity, petrol and other routine purchases. A business can also predict its payroll, electricity bill, consumables bills, suppliers' bills and other routine expenses. Without enough cash, the public must suffer inconvenience and possibly withdrawal penalties as a result of converting their stocks, bonds or certificates of deposit into currency or cheque account deposits in order to make transactions. There is, however, a cost for holding this money, namely the interest rate you forgo instead of holding that quantity of your wealth in some form that earns good interest.

Transactions motive for the demand for money The explanation for the stock of money people hold to pay everyday predictable expenses.

Precautionary motive for the demand for money

In addition to holding money for routine expected purchases, people have a second motive for holding money, called the **precautionary motive**. The precautionary motive for the demand for money is the desire of people to hold a stock of money to pay unpredictable expenses. This is the 'mattress money' people hold to guard against those proverbial rainy days. For example, your car may break down or your income may drop unexpectedly. Similarly, a business may experience unexpected repair expenses or lower-than-anticipated cash receipts from sales. Because of unforeseen events that could prevent people from paying their bills on time, people hold precautionary balances. This affords them the peace of mind that goes with knowing that unexpected payments can be made without having to cash in interest-bearing financial assets or to borrow. Nevertheless, holding money balances for this reason again incurs the opportunity cost of the interest you forgo by not holding that amount of your wealth in some other form that earns interest.

Precautionary motive for the demand for money The explanation for the stock of money people hold to pay unpredictable expenses.

Speculative motive for the demand for money

The third motive for holding money is the **speculative motive**. As noted above, people will, in general, seek to economise on their holdings of money when interest rates are high because the opportunity cost of holding money is high. They would be better off if they held less of their wealth in the form of money and more of their wealth in other interest-bearing assets. However, there is another important aspect to people's decisions about how much of their wealth to hold as money when interest rates are high.

Speculative motive for the demand for money The explanation for the stock of money people hold to take advantage of expected future changes in the price of bonds, stocks or other non-money financial assets.

The speculative motive for the demand for money is the motive for holding money to take advantage of expected future changes in the price of bonds, stocks or other non-money financial assets. In addition to the transactions and the precautionary motives, individuals and businesses demand 'betting money' to speculate as to whether the prices of alternative assets will rise or fall. This desire to take advantage of profit-making opportunities when the prices of non-money assets fall (and therefore their implied rates of return rise) is the driving force behind the speculative demand. When the interest rate is high, people may believe that it is likely to fall in the future. Therefore they may be willing to 'park' some of their money in fixed interest bonds, because if interest rates do fall in the future, their bonds, which pay a higher interest rate, will experience an increase in value on the market.

Similarly, when the interest rate is low, people will want to hold more money because they may expect interest rates to rise in future. Any fixed interest bonds they may purchase when interest rates are low will lose market value if interest rates rise in the future. Suppose the interest rate on, say, two-year corporate bonds is low. If so, people may decide to hold more of their money in the bank and *speculate* that soon the interest rate on corporate bonds will climb higher. If it does rise at some later date, they will then transfer some of their money holdings into corporate bonds.

Overall demand for money

Demand for money Schedule representing the overall quantity of money that people wish to hold at different interest rates, ceteris paribus.

The three motives for holding money combine to create an overall **demand for money**. As is evident from the above discussion, the important factor determining all three types of demand is the prevailing level of interest rates. The demand for money is therefore a function of 'the' interest rate, ceteris paribus. As an aside, throughout the text we will usually just say 'the interest rate'. Of course, there is a vast array of interest rates in the real world. When we say 'the interest rate', this is a convenient shorthand for that array. It is also true that, in the real world, all interest rates will tend to vary over time in fairly systematic ways relative to one another and you could therefore think of 'the interest rate' as some average or representative rate of all of the available rates.

Other things being equal, people will increase their money balances when interest rates fall. The reason is that people will not feel it is so important to park their wealth in such places as money-market managed funds, fixed interest deposits and so on. Instead, they will be content with holding higher amounts of their wealth as money balances such as currency and cheque account deposits.

CONCLUSION

There is an inverse relationship between the quantity of money demanded and the interest rate. As interest rates fall, more financial assets will be held in the most liquid forms such as currency and cheque deposits; that is, as interest rates fall, the demand for money increases.

Note that another important determinant of the demand for money not explicitly highlighted here is income. Other things being equal, as individuals and firms experience higher levels of income they will tend to want (or need) to hold larger money balances to accommodate their higher dollar volumes of transactions. Any tendency for rises in income to increase money demand will, of course, be affected by movements in interest rates. For simplicity of exposition, we have chosen here to emphasise the role of interest rates in influencing the demand for money.

Four money-supply definitions

Now that you understand the basic definition of money and what determines the demand for holding money, we turn to the question of what exactly constitutes the money supply of modern economies. In the real world there is no hard and fast answer to this question, so central banks compile and monitor a range of measures. The following section presents four different definitions of the money supply in Australia, officially called monetary base, M1, M3 and Broad Money. Other countries may adopt slightly different definitions, but any country with an advanced financial system, such as Australia, will have very similar definitions.

- **Monetary base** This is the primary liquidity of the financial system. The assets in the Base are the most liquid of all financial assets and consist of all currency in circulation (notes and coins) plus the deposits of banks with the Reserve Bank of Australia (RBA). The Base is under the close control of the RBA and is important in understanding how monetary policy adjustments are made. More will be said about the Base shortly.
- **M1**. This is defined as the sum of currency in the hands of the non-bank public plus the stock of cheque account deposits at banks.
- **M3**. Defined as the sum of M1 plus all other bank deposits of the non-bank public.
- **Broad Money** Defined as the sum of M3 plus the public's deposits at non-bank financial intermediaries (NBFIs) less the currency and bank deposits held by these NBFIs.

Exhibit 15.1 shows the components of the four money-supply definitions based on daily averages during June 2004.

- **Currency** Currency includes coins and paper money. The first component of M1 is the cash the public holds for immediate spending. Currency comprises only about 20 per cent of the economy's M1 money supply. Thus, currency is indeed 'small change' when it comes to what we regard as 'money'. The purpose of currency is to permit us to make small purchases.
- **Cheque account deposits** Most 'big ticket' purchases are paid for with cheques, credit or debit cards rather than currency. As you have seen, credit and debit cards are not money. However, the money spent by customers in their use of these cards is often held as deposits in cheque accounts. Cheques and credit (and debit) cards simply dramatically

Monetary base The primary liquidity of the financial system. The assets in the Base are the most liquid of all financial assets and consist of currency in circulation (notes and coins) plus the deposits of banks and money market dealers with the RBA.

M1 The narrowest definition of the money supply. It includes currency in the hands of the non-bank public and cheque account deposits.

M3 The definition of the money supply that equals M1 plus all other deposits of the non-bank public at banks.

Broad Money The definition of the money supply that equals M3 plus net deposits of all non-bank financial intermediaries.

Currency Money, including coins and paper money.

Cheque account deposits The total of cheque account balances in banks convertible to currency 'on demand' by writing a cheque without advance notice.

reduce the need to make trips to the bank and they are safer than cash. If lost or stolen, cheques and credit cards can be replaced at little cost – money cannot. Exhibit 15.1 shows that the largest share of M1 consists of cheque account deposits. These are deposits in banks convertible to currency 'on demand' by writing a cheque without advance notice. A cheque account balance is an electronic bookkeeping entry at a bank, often called a *demand deposit* because it can be converted into cash 'on demand'. In June 2004, 80 per cent of M1 was in cheque deposits.

- **Savings deposits** As shown in Exhibit 15.1, M1 was only about 28 per cent of M3 in June 2004, with *savings deposits* constituting the other 72 per cent of M3. Savings deposits are interest-bearing accounts at banks that can be withdrawn easily. These deposits include passbook savings accounts and other types of interest-bearing deposits with commercial banks.
- **NBFI deposits** These are all deposits of all other deposit-taking institutions other than banks. Such institutions include, for example, building societies and credit unions. Exhibit 15.1 shows that NBFI deposits were only about 10 per cent of Broad Money in June 2004 and represent the remaining category of financial assets which are currently usually incorporated as constituting some form of 'money'.

CONCLUSION M1 is considered more liquid than M3 or Broad Money.

To simplify the discussion throughout the remainder of this text, we will be referring to the narrower definitions of money (say the Base or M1) when we discuss the money supply. However, one can argue that M3 or Broad Money or another measurement of the money supply may be the best definition. For example, in the various definitions above, all components have equal weights and this is conventional practice around the world. A dollar in circulation (in your pocket) and a dollar in a fixed term deposit in a bank both count as a dollar in M3, even though the latter dollar is a lot less liquid than the former. It has been suggested therefore that the different categories should be weighted somehow according to their relative degrees of 'moneyness'. Actually, the boundary lines for any definition of money are necessarily somewhat arbitrary.

The RBA (www.rba.gov.au) maintains current and historical data on MB, M1, M3 and Broad Money. Select *Statistics*, then *Statistics by Frequency of Publication*, then *Financial Aggregates*, then *Monetary Aggregates*.

Exhibit 15.1 **Components of Australia's money supply, June 2004 ($ million)**

Currency	Current deposits	M1	Other savings deposits at banks	M3	Net NBFI deposits	Broad Money	Monetary base
31 900	131 500	163 400	423 600	587 000	67 700	654 700	37 200

Source: Derived from September 2004 issue of *RBA Bulletin*, Table D3.

The equilibrium interest rate

We are now ready – at least conceptually – to consider the money market and the determination of the equilibrium interest rate by putting the demand for money and the supply of money together. Later in this chapter we will also give you the flavour of how the monetary system works in the real world. Here we will sketch out the basic principles of interest rate determination. In Exhibit 15.2, the money demand curve (*MD*) is a graphical representation of the discussion we had above with respect to the inverse relationship between the demand for money balances and the interest rate. The supply of money curve (*MS*) is drawn as a vertical line on the presumption that the $20 billion quantity of money in supply in the financial system does not respond to changes in the interest rate. The reason is that our model assumes the central bank has used its various tools to set the money supply at this quantity of money regardless of the interest rate. Given the critical role played by the central bank in a country's financial system, this is not an unrealistic assumption.

At point *E*, the equilibrium interest rate is 8 per cent at the intersection of the demand for money curve and the vertical supply of money curve. People wish to hold exactly the amount of money in circulation and, therefore, neither upward nor downward pressure on the interest rate exists.

Excess quantity of money demanded

Suppose the interest rate in Exhibit 15.2 is 4 per cent instead of 8 per cent. Such a low opportunity cost of money means that people desire to hold a greater quantity of money (from the exhibit you can see it is $30 billion) than the quantity supplied. To try to eliminate this shortage of $10 billion, individuals and businesses adjust their financial asset portfolios. They seek more money by selling their bonds or other non-money assets. When many people sell or try to sell their bonds, there is an increase in the supply of bonds relative to the demand for bonds. Consequently, the price of bonds falls and the interest rate rises. This rise in the interest rate ceases at the equilibrium interest rate of 8 per cent because people are content with their portfolio of money and bonds at point *E*.

Here we need to pause and look at an example to understand what is happening (see Exhibit 15.3). Suppose Shell pays 4 per cent on its $1000 two-year corporate bonds. This means it is guaranteeing to pay a bondholder $40 in interest each year and promises to repay the original $1000 (the bond's face value) at the end of two years. However, a holder of these bonds can sell these bonds before maturity at a market-determined price. If bondholders desire to hold more money, they will increase the supply of these bonds for sale in the market. As a result the increase in the supply of bonds causes the price of bonds to fall to, say, $500. At a price of $500 the implied interest rate rises to 8 per cent ($40/$500) and, at this interest rate, people in aggregate

Exhibit 15.2 **The equilibrium interest rate**

The Reserve Bank of Australia publishes current and historical data on interest rates (**www.rba.gov.au**). For example, to see the values of the three-year fixed bank housing loan rate, select *Statistics*, then *Bulletin Statistical Tables*, then *Financial Markets*, then *Indicator Lending Rates*.

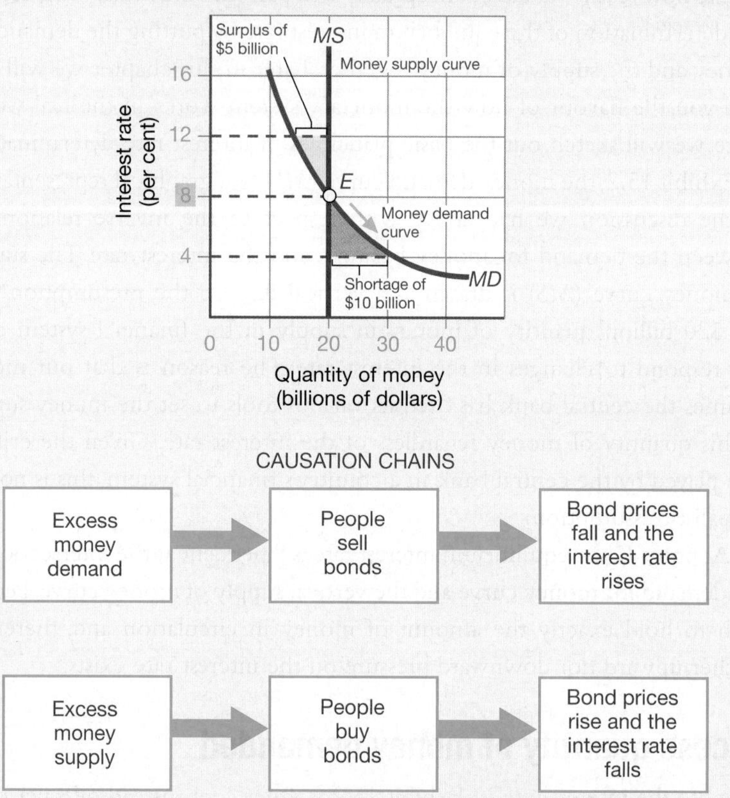

The money market consists of the demand for and the supply of money. The market demand curve represents the quantity of money people are willing to hold at various interest rates. The money supply is a vertical line at $20 billion, based on the assumption that this is the quantity of money supplied by the central bank. The equilibrium interest rate is 8 per cent and occurs at the intersection of the money demand and the money supply curves (point *E*). At any other interest rate – for example, 12 per cent or 4 per cent – the quantity of money people desire to hold does not equal the quantity available.

are satisfied to hold the existing stock of money in supply.[1] The money market would therefore be in equilibrium and, ceteris paribus, there would not be any pressure for the interest rate to move further.

Excess quantity of money supplied

The story reverses for any rate of interest above 8 per cent. Let's say the interest rate is 12 per cent. In this case, people are holding more money than they wish. In fact they wish to hold only $15 billion rather than the $20 billion in circulation. To correct this imbalance, people will try to move out

1 The situation is a little more complicated than this because of the time period over which the coupon payments and the face value are paid. Nevertheless, the essence of the inverse relationship between the price of a bond and its yield is reflected in the example.

Exhibit 15.3 **Illustrating the relationship between the market price of a fixed interest bond and its yield**

Market price of bond	Interest paid annually (4% of $1000)	Yield (Implied interest rate)
2 000	40	2%
1 000	40	4%
500	40	8%

of cash and cheque deposits by buying interest bearing bonds. This increase in the demand for bonds will drive up the price of bonds (say to $2000) and lower the implied interest rate (say to 2 per cent). As the interest rate falls, the quantity of money demanded increases as people become more willing to hold money. Finally, the money market reaches equilibrium at point *E* and people in aggregate are content with their mix of money and interest-bearing bonds.

There is an inverse relationship between bond prices and the interest rate that enables the money market to achieve equilibrium.

How monetary policy affects the interest rate

Assuming an unchanging demand for money schedule, the equilibrium rate of interest changes in response to changes in monetary policy. As you will learn in more detail in the next chapter, a nation's central bank – in Australia's case, the Reserve Bank of Australia – can alter the money supply through a number of means. For the present, though, simply accept that the central bank can and does alter the volume of money in the economy's financial system. What you will learn now is how the central bank's power to change the money supply can alter the equilibrium rates of interest in the economy and can therefore have subsequent effects on output, employment and prices. In other words you are about to learn the basics of **monetary policy**. Monetary policy is the term used to describe actions taken by the central bank to influence the monetary base, interest rates, economic activity and prices in the economy.

monetary piolicy

Monetary policy Actions taken by the central bank to influence the monetary base, interest rates, economic activity and prices in the economy.

The RBA must first determine the state of the economy before deciding what to do, if anything, to the monetary base and interest rates. It publishes a summary of economic conditions each quarter in its monthly bulletin. Visit **www.rba.gov.au** and select *Publications & Research*, then *Reserve Bank Bulletin*.

Increasing the money supply

Exhibit 15.4(a) shows how increasing the money supply – an expansionary monetary policy – will cause the equilibrium rate of interest to fall. Our analysis begins at point E_1, with the money supply at $20 billion and equal to the quantity of money demanded and with the equilibrium interest rate at 12 per cent. Now suppose the central bank increases the money supply to

PART 5

$30 billion. The impact of the central bank's expansionary monetary policy is to create a $10 billion surplus of money at the prevailing 12 per cent interest rate.

How will people react to this excess money in their pockets or cheque accounts? Money becomes a 'hot potato', and people buy interest-bearing bonds. The rush to purchase bonds drives the price of bonds higher and the interest rate lower. As the interest rate falls, people are *willing* to hold larger money balances. Or, stated differently, there is an increase in the quantity of money demanded until the new equilibrium at E_2 is reached. At the lower interest rate of 8 per cent, the opportunity cost of holding money is also lower and the imbalance between money demand and money supply disappears.

Decreasing the money supply

Exhibit 15.4(b) illustrates how the central bank can put upward pressure on the interest rate with contractionary monetary policy. Beginning at point E_1, the money market is in equilibrium at an interest rate of 8 per cent. This time the central bank shrinks the money supply. The result is that the money

Exhibit 15.4 The effect of changes in the money supply

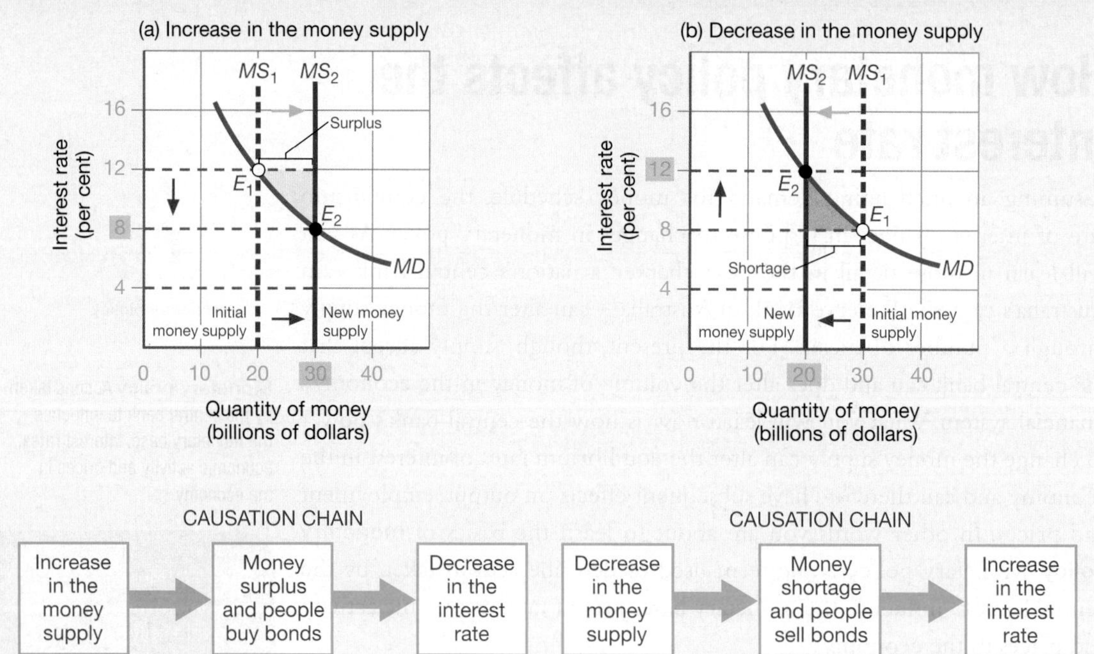

In part (a), the central bank increases the money supply from $20 billion ($MS_1$) to $30 billion ($MS_2$). At the initial interest rate of 12 per cent (point E_1), there is an excess of $10 billion beyond the amount people wish to hold. They react by buying bonds, and the interest rate falls until it reaches a new lower equilibrium interest rate at 8 per cent (point E_2).

The reverse happens in part (b). The central bank decreases the money supply from $30 billion ($MS_1$) to $20 billion ($MS_2$). Beginning at 8 per cent (point E_1), people wish to hold $10 billion more than is available. This imbalance disappears when people sell their bonds. As the price of bonds falls, the interest rate rises to the new higher equilibrium interest rate of 12 per cent at point E_2.

supply decreases from $30 billion to $20 billion. At the initial equilibrium interest rate of 8 per cent, this decrease in the money supply causes a shortage of $10 billion.

Individuals and businesses wish to hold more money than is available. How can the public try to put more money in their pockets and cheque accounts? They can sell their bonds for cash. This selling pressure lowers bond prices, causing the implied rate of interest to rise. At point E_2, the upward pressure on the interest rate stops. Once the equilibrium interest rate reaches 12 per cent, the $20 billion money supply is willingly held by people in the community.

Australian monetary policy adjustments

You make the call

From December 1999 Australian interest rates (as measured by the 'cash rate', discussed further in the next chapter) moved up from 5 per cent to 6.25 per cent by August 2000. At the same time, the monetary base contracted from $29.7 billion to $28.2 billion. In January 2001, interest rates moved from 6.25 per cent down to 4.25 per cent by December 2001. Over the same period, the Base expanded from $29.2 billion to $37.0 billion. In May 2002, interest rates moved from 4.25 per cent to 5.25 per cent by December 2003. However, over the same period, the Base *expanded* from $35.0 billion to $38.8 billion!

Interpret these data from the point of view of monetary policy adjustments at the time and the impact of the interaction of the demand and supply for money on interest rates.

How monetary policy affects prices, output and employment

INFOTRAC®

monetary policy transmission mechanism

The next step in our journey is to understand how monetary policy alters the macro economy. Here you should pause and study Exhibit 15.5. This exhibit illustrates the causation chain linking monetary policy and economic performance. This is often referred to as the **monetary policy transmission mechanism**. It is simply a description of how a monetary policy change might be transmitted through into the economy, thereby affecting output, prices and employment.

Monetary policy transmission mechanism A description of how a monetary policy change might be transmitted through into the economy, thereby affecting output, prices and employment.

Changes in the supply of money affect interest rates. In turn, interest rates affect investment spending, aggregate demand and, finally, real GDP, employment and prices.

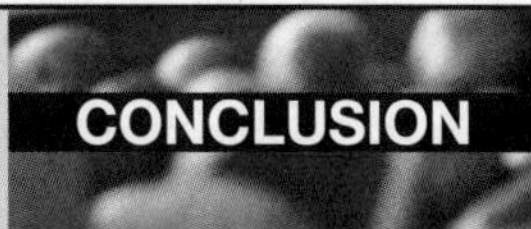

Exhibit 15.5 **The basics of the monetary policy transmission mechanism**

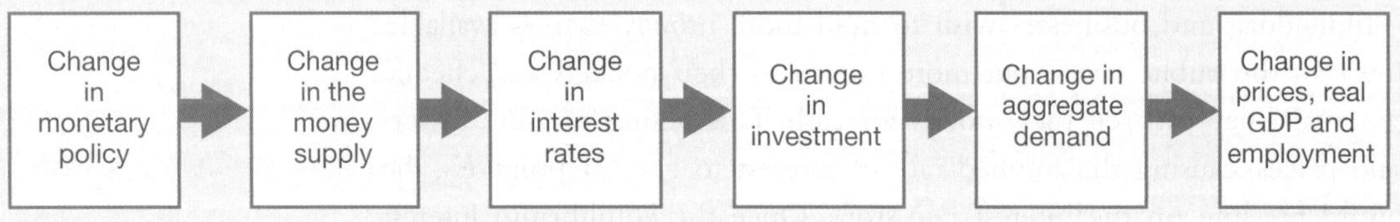

A widely accepted view of the transmission mechanism is that changes in monetary policy affect interest rates and investment spending. In turn, aggregate demand shifts and this affects prices, real GDP and employment.

The impact of monetary policy using the *AD–AS* model

So far we have sketched out how monetary policy can affect the level of interest rates prevailing in the economy. How do changes in the rate of interest affect aggregate demand? Begin with Exhibit 15.6(a), which is identical to Exhibit 15.4(a) and represents the money market. As explained earlier, we assume that the central bank increases the money supply from \$20 billion (MS_1) to \$30 billion (MS_2) and the equilibrium interest rate falls from 12 per cent to 8 per cent. We know from our discussion in the previous chapter that, with lower interest rates, ceteris paribus, firms will be more willing to spend on structures, plant and equipment. With lower interest rates, people may also be more willing to purchase newly constructed houses and apartments which, as you will recall from Chapter 11, are also regarded as investment.[2]

This is represented graphically in part (b), where you can see that the falling rate of interest causes an increase in the quantity of investment spending per year from \$100 billion to \$120 billion. Stated another way, there is an increase in investment demand (*I*), which, you will recall from the previous chapter, is a component of total spending or aggregate demand. The investment demand curve shows the amount businesses and households spend for investment goods at different possible rates of interest.

In Exhibit 15.6(c), we use the aggregate demand and aggregate supply analysis developed earlier. Begin at point E_1, with a real GDP per year of \$500 billion and a price level of 150. Now consider the link to the change in the money supply.

The increase in investment resulting from the fall in the interest rate works through the *spending multiplier* to increase aggregate demand by more than the initial increase in investment (refer back to the discussion in the

2 In reality, spending on components of consumption, such as big-ticket consumer durable items like white goods and motor cars, will also tend to rise if borrowing costs are down.

previous chapter on the multiplier). The aggregate demand curve therefore shifts rightward from AD_1 to AD_2. At the new equilibrium point, E_2, the level of real GDP rises from $500 billion to $540 billion (a $40 billion increase) and full employment is achieved. In addition, the price level rises from 150 to 155.

Exhibit 15.6 The effect of expansionary monetary policy on aggregate demand

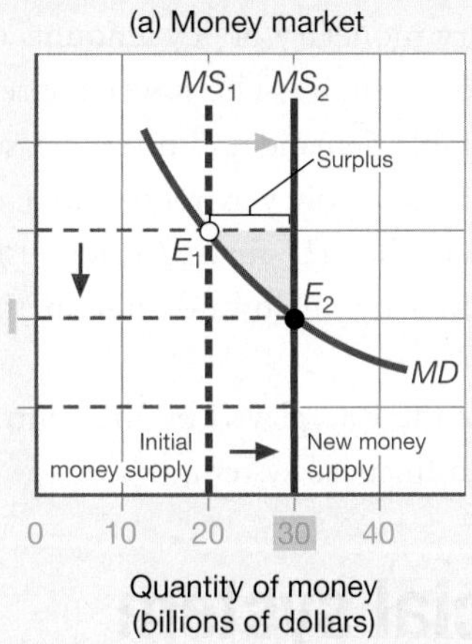

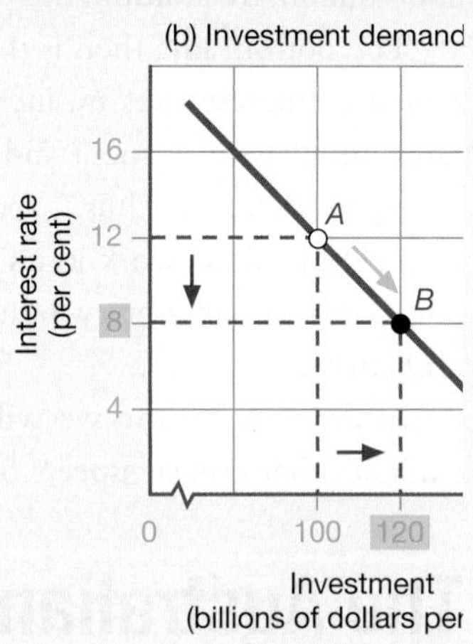

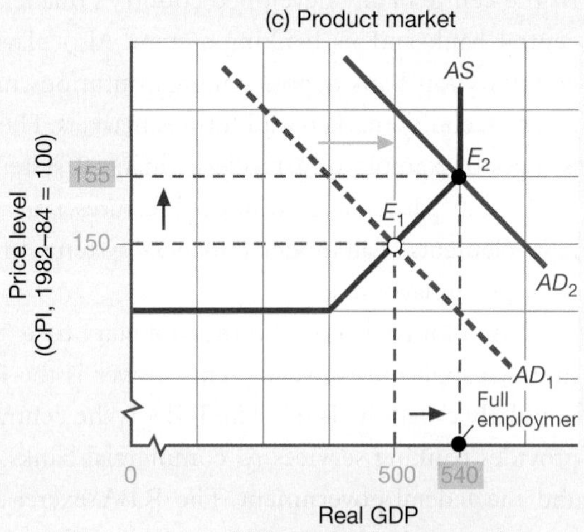

In part (a), the money supply is initially MS_1 and the equilibrium rate of interest is 12 per cent. The equilibrium point in the money market changes from E_1 to E_2 when the central bank increases the money supply to MS_2. This causes an increase in the quantity of money people wish to hold from $20 billion to $30 billion and a new lower equilibrium interest rate is established at 8 per cent.

The fall in the rate of interest shown in part (b) causes a movement downward along the investment–demand curve from point *A* to point *B*. Thus, the quantity of investment spending per year increases from $100 billion to $120 billion.

In part (c), the investment component of the aggregate demand curve increases, causing this curve to shift outward from AD_1 to AD_2. As a result, the aggregate demand and supply equilibrium in the product market changes from E_1 to E_2 and the real GDP gap is eliminated. The price level also changes from 150 to 155.

Exhibit 15.6 can also be used to understand how a contractionary monetary policy would work. In part (a), imagine the money supply started at MS_2. In the contractionary case, the money supply then shifts inward from MS_2 to MS_1, causing the equilibrium rate of interest to rise from 8 per cent to 12 per cent. The central bank's 'tight' monetary policy causes the level of investment spending to fall from $120 billion to $100 billion, which in turn decreases the equilibrium level of real GDP per year from $540 billion to $500 billion. In addition, the price level falls from 155 to 150.

The bottom line then is that expansionary monetary policy amounts to reducing interest rates by increasing the money supply. The lower interest rates stimulate investment and consumer durable demand and this increases aggregate demand. Thus, expansionary monetary policy is represented in the *AD–AS* framework as an outward shift in the *AD* curve. Analogously, contractionary monetary policy is represented by an inward shift in the *AD* curve.

In the next section we will look beyond the role played by the central bank at other crucial aspects of the Australian financial system.

The Australian financial system

INFOTRAC®
Reserve Bank of Australia

At the centre of any developed country's financial system stands the nation's central bank and its banking system. Also playing a key role will be the country's non-bank deposit-taking institutions, money markets, fixed interest markets, equity markets and futures markets. The Australian financial system is a good example of a modern financial system and so, in reading about some of its particular institutional features, you will gain an insight into the basic elements of all modern financial systems. In this book we will give only its essential flavour.

Reserve Bank of Australia (RBA) The central bank of Australia responsible for monetary policy, the payments system and financial system stability, which also provides banking services to the banks, other financial institutions and the federal government.

Who ultimately controls the monetary base (the foundation of Australia's money supply) in Australia? The answer is the **Reserve Bank of Australia**, popularly called the RBA. The RBA is the central banker for the nation and provides banking services to commercial banks, other financial institutions and the federal government. The RBA exercises close control of the size of the monetary base and can greatly influence market interest rates and thereby significantly influences the economy's performance.

Australia's financial system is made up of the Reserve Bank of Australia, the banking system and the major financial markets. Each will be briefly discussed in turn.

The Reserve Bank of Australia

The Reserve Bank of Australia (RBA) was created by an act of Parliament in 1959. Its powers and responsibilities were originally enunciated in the *Reserve Bank Act 1959*, the *Banking Act 1959* and the *Financial Corporations*

Act 1974. More recently, its powers and responsibilities have been amended as a result of the 1997 Financial System Inquiry, commonly known as the Wallis Inquiry.

The first of the above Acts outlined the duty that the RBA has to the Australian people to maintain the stability of the currency (fight inflation), to maintain full employment and to ensure the economic prosperity and welfare of the Australian people. The second Act required the RBA to uphold the integrity of the banking system. To this end it had the power to regulate trading and savings bank lending, interest rates and asset structures. The third Act gave the RBA the power to monitor and potentially control Australia's many non-bank financial intermediaries (NBFIs). NBFIs include, among others, building societies and credit unions.

The role of the RBA – as embodied in the above three Acts – was significantly changed as a result of the government's acceptance of a range of recommendations made in the Wallis Inquiry. For example, as a result of the Wallis Inquiry, the prudential supervision of all of Australia's deposit-taking institutions – including banks, building societies and credit unions – as well as the nation's superannuation and insurance companies now falls to the **Australian Prudential Regulation Authority**. The RBA still retains responsibility for overall financial system stability, for regulating and standing behind the nation's payments system and for determining and implementing monetary policy. Also, as a result of the Wallis Inquiry, a new body called the **Australian Securities and Investments Commission** was created to ensure proper financial disclosure, oversee financial market integrity and uphold consumer protection.

The RBA is governed by its board, the **Reserve Bank Board**, chaired by the Reserve Bank Governor. (In 2004 this was Mr Ian Macfarlane.) Also on the board are the Deputy Governor, the Secretary to the Commonwealth Treasury and six other members. In 1996, the RBA Governor and the Federal Treasurer co-signed the Statement on the Conduct of Monetary Policy, which commits the government to endorsing the RBA's freedom to implement – through the determinations of its board – whatever monetary policy it thinks is appropriate to ensure the achievement of the target inflation rate agreed with the government. That target, also stipulated in the Statement, is that the RBA operate to hold the underlying inflation rate (as defined by the CPI) to between 2 and 3 per cent per annum over the course of the business cycle.

Reserve Bank Board
RBA board that determines monetary policy in Australia; it consists of the Governor, the Deputy Governor, the Under Treasurer and six other members appointed by parliament.

Careful readers will notice that there was no mention in the 1996 Statement of anything to do with 'the maintenance of full employment and economic prosperity of Australia' – just an inflation target. This is because it is now fairly widely accepted by economists and policy makers – and is certainly strongly believed by the RBA – that the best way for a central bank to assist with the achievement of full employment and strong economic growth over the long term is for it to keep inflation low. By doing this, it prevents inflation from taking off and thereby avoids all the attendant

To read more about the role of the RBA (as described by the bank itself) visit **www. rba.gov. au** and select *About the RBA*, then *Overview of Functions and Operations*.

problems associated with high inflation outlined in Chapter 13. This way it is believed that, over the long term, economic growth will be higher and unemployment will be lower than if the RBA had in the short term let go of its inflation target to try to actively reduce unemployment. Note, though, that if there is ever an unresolvable disagreement between the RBA Board and the government as to the correct monetary policy course to pursue, the government's view will prevail. In this circumstance, however, there is a provision in the Reserve Bank Act that entitles the RBA to have its opinion made public.

commonwealth government securities

Commonwealth government securities Commonwealth government bonds (maturities of more than one year) and treasury notes (13- and 26-week). These are bought and sold by the RBA in the money markets to bring about changes to the monetary base and short-term interest rates.

The RBA acts as banker to the federal government, the banking system and other major financial organisations, as well as managing the government's debt. In its latter role, on behalf of the Treasury, it sells commonwealth government bonds (maturities of more than one year) and treasury notes (13- and 26-week) by tender to the public. Together these are commonly known as **commonwealth government securities**. The proceeds of these sales of securities are deposited – along with taxation receipts – into the government's account maintained at the RBA and are subsequently used by the government to pay for its expenditures. These securities are considered riskless by financial market participants and, once issued, trade freely in the financial markets. The prices at which they trade are therefore determined by, and will influence, market rates of interest.

The banking system

Banks occupy a crucial position in our community. As far as the public is concerned, the solvency of a bank is virtually guaranteed. This belief is reasonably well justified by virtue of the careful and comprehensive supervision of a bank's activities and the particular asset structure it is required to maintain. However, a common misperception is that a bank is as 'safe as houses' because it will not be allowed by the authorities to fail. In fact this is not true. No bank or any other financial institution is absolutely guaranteed to remain solvent. However, the RBA is obliged to act in such a way as to minimise the possibility of a systemic collapse. In addition, the vigilant supervision of each bank, along with the very strong liquidity and capital adequacy requirements demanded of them all, ensures that the public confidence, so crucial to the efficient operation of the financial system, is well placed.

Exchange settlement account Each bank maintains an exchange settlement account with the RBA. Any direct business it conducts with the central bank, other banks, the government and certain other financial organisations is settled through deposits to or withdrawals from this account. It is this direct RBA access that enables an organisation like a bank to offer cheque-writing facilities to its customers. Exchange settlement accounts must always have a positive balance by the end of each trading day.

We may define a bank as a lending institution, authorised by the RBA under the Banking Act, which therefore has direct access to the RBA and the payments clearance mechanism. Each bank maintains an **exchange settlement account** with the RBA and any direct business it conducts with the central bank, other banks, the government and certain other financial organisations is settled through deposits to or withdrawals from this account. It is this direct RBA access that enables a bank to offer cheque-writing facilities to its customers.

How does the RBA make its monetary policy decisions?

Analyse the issue

Applicable concept: monetary policy

The RBA Board meets twelve times a year at the RBA in Martin Place, Sydney. Prior to the meeting, Board members are provided with analyses of the economy and financial markets by the RBA staff (prepared by the Economic Analysis Department). Among these analyses are the Bank's forecasts of future inflation as well as the likely future path of economic growth overseas and domestically. These would be on the basis of 'no change' in monetary policy as well as a range of other assumptions. In addition, scenarios are provided as to likely macroeconomic outcomes if monetary policy were adjusted.

The meeting occurs on the first Tuesday of each month. After much discussion, a consensus decision is reached as to whether to leave interest rates unchanged or, if the decision is to adjust policy, then the quantum of the adjustment. The instrument the RBA uses is the cash rate and, if an adjustment is decided, it will be to adjust the cash rate by 0.25 per cent, 0.50 per cent or 1 per cent. The most common adjustments are 0.25 per cent and 0.50 per cent.

If a decision is made to adjust the cash rate, this will be enacted the next morning at 9.30 a.m. The RBA does not set this interest rate (as a commercial bank might set its mortgage rate), but it continuously influences the rate through its daily financial operations in the money markets. If the RBA *buys* treasury notes, the supply of excess reserves in the banking system increases and the cash rate falls. If the RBA *sells* T-notes, the supply of excess reserves in the banking system decreases and the cash rate increases. As a result of these changes in the cash rate, interest rates in general are influenced. The next chapter explains in more detail how this occurs and the link between changes in interest rates and changes in other key macro measures.

If the decision is taken to adjust monetary policy, a statement is issued on the Wednesday by the Governor providing a summary rationale for the adjustment. Unlike other jurisdictions (like the United States, for example), the RBA does not publish minutes of its Board meetings. However, considerable information is provided to the general public on the RBA's underlying analysis of the economy via a biannual appearance by the Governor before the parliament and the Bank's quarterly Statement on Monetary Policy.

Using the above information, answer the following questions.

1. What happened at the last RBA Board meeting?
2. If there was a change in monetary policy, what was the rationale provided by the Governor?
3. If there was no change, when was the last adjustment in monetary policy?
4. What would you conclude from the Bank's most recent quarterly statement on monetary policy?

To get help with these questions visit the RBA website, (**www.rba.gov.au**). To view the current composition of the RBA Board, visit this website and select *About the RBA*, *Structure of the RBA*, *Reserve Bank Board*, then *Composition of the Reserve Bank Board*

There are now some fifty banks authorised by the RBA to conduct business in Australia. Since the freeing up of the financial system in the 1980s, over half of these banks are foreign owned. Some well-known names of authorised banks include, for example, the 'big four' (CBA, Westpac, ANZ and NAB), Citibank, Macquarie Bank, Suncorp-Metway, St George Bank, Bank of Queensland, Bank West, Bank of New Zealand, Bank of America and Bank of Tokyo.

The day-to-day business of a bank is to act as financial intermediary for the general public, taking in deposits and making loans. In addition, banks are very active participants in bond and money markets and the foreign exchange markets (discussed below), and through these activities provide other services to their customers such as currency conversion. In conducting their business, banks are subject to three forms of regulation:

- A bank's exchange settlement account must have a positive balance at the end of each trading day.
- Each bank must maintain appropriate high standards of liquidity management.
- Each bank must satisfy certain prescribed capital adequacy requirements.

The first requires that exchange settlement accounts maintained with the RBA must always have a positive balance at the end of each day. The RBA pays interest on these accounts, but the rate is less than what could be obtained in the broader financial markets. Banks therefore monitor their level closely. Any funds considered excess to basic liquidity requirements are normally placed at 11 a.m. call (meaning they must be recalled, relent or be renegotiated by 11 the next morning) with a money market dealer.

Exchange settlement accounts are an integral part of the payments system in modern financial systems such as Australia's. The vast majority of payments for transactions these days consist of electronic payments rather than the exchange of hard currency. People write cheques, use credit cards, telephone transfer, EFTPOS, direct debit and so on rather than pay with currency. These transactions will ultimately involve the electronic transfer of funds held at one financial institution to another. During the course of the day many thousands of such non-cash transactions will occur, and it is necessary for the financial institutions to settle with one another on account of all of these transactions occurring among their many customers. These settlements occur through appropriate adjustments being made to their exchange settlement accounts at the RBA.

The second regulation requires each bank – and other financial institutions – to maintain appropriate high standards of liquidity management. In order to fulfil this prudential requirement, the financial institution must demonstrate that it has an acceptable set of management strategies in place to ensure it has adequate liquidity at all times. As an alternative to this, the financial institution may simply be required to maintain a **minimum liquidity requirement**. This requirement means that a bank must always maintain a certain minimal reserve level of highly liquid assets to cover any short-run demands from its many depositors and other creditors.

Minimum liquidity requirement Requirement that a bank must always maintain a certain minimal reserve level of highly liquid assets to cover any short-run demands from its many depositors and other creditors.

The third regulation is the so-called financial **capital adequacy** requirement. The financial capital adequacy regulation requires a supervised financial institution to maintain a certain minimum percentage of its risk-weighted assets in the form of shareholders' equity. In acquiring assets, like any other company, a bank raises funds by either selling shares (shareholders' equity) or borrowing (liabilities). By definition, assets = liabilities + shareholders' equity. If a bank needs to pay off creditors (like its depositors) it can liquidate some of its assets – hence the minimum liquidity requirement discussed above – but in an emergency situation the value of its assets may be uncertain. Thus a bank's solvency will ultimately depend on the extent of its financial capital base as represented by its shareholders' equity. This financial capital backing provides further reassurance to creditors and depositors that their funds remain safe.

Capital adequacy
Requirement that a supervised financial institution maintain a certain minimum percentage of its risk-weighted assets in the form of shareholders' equity.

The banking system and creating money

Money may make the world go round, but how exactly does money get created in the modern financial system? We begin with a history lesson. In the Middle Ages, gold was the money of choice in most European nations. One of the problems with gold is that it is a heavy commodity, which makes it difficult to use in transactions or to hide from thieves. The medieval solution was to keep it safely deposited with the people who worked with gold, the *goldsmiths*. This demand for their services inspired goldsmith entrepreneurs to become the founders of modern-day banking. The goldsmiths sat on their benches with ledgers close by and recorded gold placed in their vaults. In fact, the word *bank* is derived from the Italian word for bench, which is *banco*. After assessing the purity of the gold, a goldsmith issued a receipt to the customer for the amount of gold deposited. In return, the goldsmith collected a service charge, just as you pay today for services at your bank. Anyone who possessed the receipt and presented it to the goldsmith could make a withdrawal for the amount of gold written on the receipt.

With these gold receipts in circulation, people began using them to pay their debts, rather than actually exchanging gold. Thus, goldsmiths' receipts became paper money. At first, the goldsmiths were very conservative and issued receipts exactly equal to the amount of gold stored in their vaults. However, some shrewd goldsmiths observed that net withdrawals in any period were only a *fraction* of all the gold 'on reserve'. This observation produced a powerful idea. Goldsmiths discovered that they could make loans for more gold than the actual gold held in their vaults. As a result, goldsmiths made extra profit from interest on loans and borrowers had more money for spending in their hands. The medieval goldsmiths were the first to practise **fractional reserve banking**. Modern fractional reserve banking is a system in which banks keep only a percentage of their deposits on reserve as vault cash and deposits at the central bank. Holding less than 100 per cent on reserve allows banks to create money.

Fractional reserve banking
A system in which banks keep only a percentage of their deposits on reserve as vault cash and deposits at the central bank.

To see how this happens, suppose that in some mythical economy there is just one single financial institution – say, the BigFriendlyBank. BFB has just had $100 000 in cash deposited with it and it is considering the best use for it. One possibility among many would be for it simply to use the cash to buy some very secure government securities so that it could earn some interest on the money. However, another – and potentially much more profitable – possibility would be for it to extend loans to new or existing customers who need money for some business ventures.

Suppose the bank's management has agreed that, in order to satisfy its prudential liquidity management requirements, it needs to maintain a minimum liquidity requirement of at least 10 per cent (a nice round figure used here purely for expositional purposes) of its liabilities in the form of cash, deposits at the central bank, government securities and other highly liquid assets. Given its 10 per cent reserve requirement, it could use the $100 000 cash as its minimum liquidity requirement against it extending loans of $900 000 on which it could earn a market rate of interest. The advances augment its assets by $900 000 ($900 000 of new loans on its books), which are balanced by an increase in its outstanding liabilities as it credits the borrowers' bank accounts with deposits of $900 000.

Credit creation and the **money multiplier** Credit creation is the process by which money is created by banks extending new loans to their customers in the form of newly created bank deposits. Because bank deposits are regarded as money, this results in money being created. The extent to which banks can multiply an initial increase in their reserves in this credit creation process is given by the so-called money multiplier. In general, the money multiplier may be thought of as the reciprocal of whatever is the minimum reserve liquidity ratio banks maintain to satisfy regulatory requirements.

INFOTRAC®

money multiplier

This process is known as **credit creation**. Furthermore, since the bank's deposits are regarded as money by participants in the economy (recall the above definitions), the bank has – literally at the stroke of a pen – created an additional $900 000 of money in the economy! At the end of this process, the bank has on its balance sheet $1 000 000 of additional deposit liabilities – the original $100 000 deposit plus the ensuing created deposits of $900 000 – offset by assets of $100 000 in cash and $900 000 in new loans.

In this example the initial increase in the bank's reserves – the $100 000 – was associated with a ten-fold increase of $1 000 000 in bank deposits. The so-called **money multiplier** in this case is 10. In general the money multiplier may be thought of as the reciprocal of whatever is the required liquidity reserve ratio – here 0.10 (i.e. 10 per cent).

Of course, in a real-world economy with many financial institutions, not all of the $900 000 deposits created by BigFriendlyBank are likely to stay with that bank. The customers receiving the loans will use them to buy goods and services and some, or all, of it will be electronically transferred to other banks and financial institutions. Thus, in the real world, the initial $100 000 cash deposit and the additional $900 000 in created deposits will end up being distributed among many members of the banking system.

Also note that, in the real world, the extent to which the money supply will increase as a result of increased reserves at banks (i.e. the $100 000 cash deposit used in the above example) is not as precise as suggested by the simple multiplier as just defined. The actual increase will depend on many factors, among them the risks perceived by banks in extending loans. These risks will change over the course of the business cycle. Nevertheless, the concept of the money multiplier does capture an important aspect of the real-world money supply process.

In the next chapter you will learn how the monetary policy actions of the central bank work to alter the quantity of money and credit available in the economy and thereby the prevailing level of interest rates. For now, we will finish this chapter with some brief descriptions of other aspects of Australia's financial system.

The short-term money market

There are a number of financial markets in Australia that exist to allow the lending and borrowing of (very large amounts of) money for short periods of up to about a year, but often for periods as short as just a few hours or overnight. In some instances money itself is simply borrowed or lent and in other instances a financial instrument is exchanged in return for money. For convenience in this text we refer collectively to these interrelated markets by the term 'the short-term money market' (STMM).[3] We will look closely at these markets, because they are an integral part of the mechanism by which changes in monetary policy by the RBA are implemented and transmitted throughout the broader financial system.

Unlike the share market, where there is a physical location where trading is carried out, there is no particular physical location for the STMM. Deals are done using the telephone, fax and electronic trading screens and securities ownership transfer is accomplished electronically.

As you will see in the next chapter, the main instrument that the RBA uses in implementing monetary policy is the buying or selling of short-term government securities to banks and certain other participants in the STMM who have been granted the right to have exchange settlement accounts with the RBA. When the RBA pays for these securities it increases the monetary base (money supply) by creating and injecting new money into the financial system. When the RBA sells such securities, the money given up by market participants to the RBA in exchange for them is withdrawn from the financial system, thereby reducing the monetary base (money supply).

Participants in the STMM consist of banks, merchant banks, building societies, finance companies, insurance companies, large commercial and industrial companies, stockbrokers (and the like) and individuals with large sums to invest or borrow for short periods. (The smallest transaction is normally $100 000.)[4] As noted above, the commodity being traded on the markets is short-term funds. These funds can be transferred on the basis of a straight loan with an agreed interest rate for a fixed term or they can be used to buy a marketable security (instrument) with the advantage that it can either be held to maturity or, if necessary, on-sold to someone else to obtain funds. A couple of the most common instruments traded on the money market are treasury notes and bank-accepted bills.

3 This term was once in common usage in the financial system but has fallen out of fashion in recent years.

4 Not all STMM participants have been granted the right to maintain an exchange settlement account at the RBA.

Treasury note (T-note) A T-note is sold by the Treasury on behalf of the federal government and is considered riskless. Since payment at maturity is absolutely guaranteed, T-notes are traded freely in the financial markets.

- A **treasury note (T-note)** is sold by the Treasury on behalf of the federal government and is considered riskless. At maturity the holder presents the note and receives the face value (a dollar amount printed on the note, which is paid to the holder at maturity). When it is sold or traded on the market it sells at a discount to the face value, with the difference being the interest to the holder if held to maturity. Since payment at maturity is absolutely guaranteed, T-notes are traded freely in the financial markets.

Commercial bill A bill created when, as evidence of a loan, a borrower draws up a bill that stipulates a face value (say $100 000) and the time to maturity (usually 90 or 180 days). The lender then makes the loan by buying the bill from the borrower at a discount to the face value, with the difference representing the implied interest rate.

- A **commercial bill** is created when, as evidence of a loan, a borrower draws up a bill that stipulates a face value (say, $100 000) and the time to maturity (usually 90 or 180 days). The lender then makes the loan by buying the bill from the borrower at a discount to the face value, with the difference representing the interest. To remove the risk of default by the borrower, a bank may, for a fee, guarantee payment at maturity. The bank is referred to as the acceptor of the bill and the bill is thus called a bank-accepted bill. The bank's guarantee converts the bill into a safe and highly tradeable financial instrument.

Apart from the STMM, many other financial markets have evolved to satisfy people's financial needs. They all basically have at least one of two important roles: first, to distribute the community's savings to those uses expected to yield the highest returns; and second, to redistribute risk associated with various economic transactions to those most willing to bear them, thereby increasing the overall efficiency with which we use our scarce economic resources.

To go into these other markets in any detail would take us far beyond the purpose of this text. What follows is a brief introduction to some of them.

The Australian Stock Exchange

Australian Stock Exchange (ASX) Where shares in Australia's (and some foreign) publicly listed companies are floated and traded. It has an actual physical location.

The **Australian Stock Exchange (ASX)** is where shares in Australia's (and some foreign) publicly listed companies are floated and traded. Unlike the STMM, the ASX has an actual physical location.

Australian Stock Exchange

A company listed on the ASX is called a public company. A public company is one that is owned by a great many individuals (often thousands) whose financial liability in case of the company becoming insolvent is limited only to the value of their fully paid-up shares in it.

In 'going public' a company floats its shares on the stock exchange and in doing so is able to increase very considerably the amount of financial capital it has to expand its businesses. In addition, in going public, the company has to meet a range of financial and reporting conditions placed upon it by the Corporations Law and the rules of the ASX. The shares of listed companies are traded extensively on a daily basis. Such trading allows individuals to reduce or increase their ownership in a range of companies based on their estimates of the companies' likely future economic performance and their own individual appetites for risk.

The foreign exchange market

On any given day, for a multitude of reasons, thousands of individuals and companies want to exchange Australian dollars for foreign currencies or vice-versa. For example, exporters want to sell foreign currency for Australian dollars, importers need to buy foreign currency and companies need to buy foreign currency to make payments to overseas investors or to convert funds borrowed overseas into Australian dollars. The **foreign exchange (FOREX) market** has evolved to accommodate such transactions.

Foreign exchange (FOREX) market On any given day many thousands of individuals and companies want to exchange Australian dollars for foreign currencies or vice-versa. The foreign exchange (FOREX) market has evolved to accommodate such transactions.

As with the money market, the FOREX market is not confined to a physical location. Trading of currencies is carried out by the electronic transfer of bank deposits denominated in different currencies, with participants in communication via the telephone, fax and computer trading screen. The major players in the market are the banks but, in total, there are currently over eighty institutions authorised by the RBA to conduct FOREX operations in Australia.

Other key financial markets

This section is optional. It is provided for readers who are interested in knowing about some other very common and important modern financial markets.

The RBA (**www.rba.gov.au**) publishes current and historical data on money market interest rates. For example, to see the values of the cash rate (also called 11 a.m. call rate), treasury note rate and bank accepted bill rate, select *Statistics*, then *Bulletin Statistical Tables*, then *Financial Markets*, then *Interest Rates and Yields*.

PART 5

Financial futures markets

It is quite often the case that an individual or company will be aware that they will either require or receive foreign currency at some fixed date in the future. For instance, an exporter usually receives payment only upon safe receipt of their goods by the foreign importer. Thus the goods are shipped today but payment will not normally be received for, say, three months. Suppose further that the supply contract stipulates that the exporter will be paid in, say, $US and the exporter is concerned that the $A may increase in value (meaning they will receive fewer $A for the $US) over the next three months. To hedge this exchange rate risk so that the exporter has some certainty over the $A they will have at their disposal when the $US payment is received, futures markets have evolved.

financial futures markets

Another example of a financial futures contract is the 90-day bank-accepted bill contract, which may be used to hedge against future interest rate movements. To illustrate the use of this contract, imagine that a company knows it will need to borrow a quantity of money in six months for a period of three months and is concerned that interest rates may unexpectedly rise before it borrows the money. To remove this interest rate risk, it can use interest rate futures to hedge against such a rise in interest rates and thereby lock in now what its borrowing costs will be in six months' time.

Options markets

Options have become extremely popular in recent years because they offer people very great flexibility in managing their financial risk.

In general terms, an option is a contract in which the buyer of the option has the absolute right but not the obligation – until some specified future date – to either purchase or sell an underlying asset at an agreed fixed price. Thus the purchase of an option is a little like buying an insurance policy (except that you do not have to have an accident to benefit!) and in fact the price of an option for that reason is referred to as a premium.

For example, consider a company that knows it will receive a certain payment – say $100 000 – in six months' time and wants to invest it for three months at that time. Interest rates are currently high, but the company is concerned that, by the time it receives the money, they may drop significantly. One possibility would be for it to enter into a futures contract described above for some agreed interest rate on a 90-day bank-accepted bill due for settlement in six months. Since the futures contract is a legal obligation, the company could in this way lock in now the interest rate it will receive for its funds due to be received in six months.

Now, what if interest rates were to actually unexpectedly rise over the course of the next few months? This means the company may have been able to do better by simply waiting and investing in a 90-day bank-accepted bill in the market after receiving its funds in six months. By buying an option on a 90-day bank-accepted bill futures contract, the company can avoid this risk of forgone interest. If interest rates move lower, the company will simply exercise its option of entering into the futures contract as outlined above. If interest rates move higher, it will allow the option to lapse and invest its funds at the higher interest rate prevailing in the market in six months. Thus, for the price of the premium – paid regardless of whether the option is exercised – the company has removed its downside risk (an interest rate fall) but retained the possibility of making even greater gains should interest rates move favourably.

Key concepts

- Barter
- Money
- Medium of exchange
- Unit of account
- Store of value
- Commodity money
- Fiat money
- Monetary base, M1, M3, Broad Money
- Currency
- Cheque account deposits
- Reserve Bank of Australia
- Monetary policy transmission mechanism
- Short-term money market (STMM)
- Australian Prudential Regulation Authority
- Australian Securities and Investments Commission
- Statement on the Conduct of Monetary Policy
- Exchange settlement accounts
- Credit/money creation
- The money multiplier
- Australian Stock Exchange (ASX)
- FOREX market
- Futures and options

Summary

- **Money** can be anything that meets three tests. Money must serve as (1) a medium of exchange, (2) a unit of account and (3) a store of value. Money facilitates exchange more efficiently than barter. Other desirable properties of money include scarcity, portability, divisibility and uniformity.

- **Medium of exchange** is the most important function of money. This means that money is widely accepted in payment for goods and services.

- **Unit of account** is another important function of money. Money is used to measure relative values by serving as a common yardstick for valuing goods and services.

- **Store of value** is the property of money to hold its value over time. Money is said to be highly *liquid*, which means it is readily usable in exchange.

- **Credit cards** are not money. Credit cards merely facilitate the provision of short-term loans. Similarly, debit cards are not money either. They merely enable the more rapid transfer of bank deposits from buyer to seller.

- **Commodity money** is money that has a marketable value, such as gold and silver. Today, all modern economies use *fiat money*, which must be accepted by law but is not convertible into gold, silver or any commodity.

- **Monetary base** is the primary liquidity of the financial system. The assets in the Base are the most liquid of all financial assets and consist of currency in circulation (notes and coins) plus the deposits of banks and other money market participants with the RBA. **M1** equals currency in the hands of the non-bank public plus cheque account deposits. **M3** is a broader definition of money, which equals M1 plus other bank deposits. **Broad Money** is an even broader definition of money, which equals **M3** plus deposits of **NBFIs**.

- **Transactions motive for the demand for money** is the motive people have for holding money to pay everyday predictable expenses.
- **Precautionary motive for the demand for money** is the motive people have for holding money to pay unpredictable expenses. This is the 'mattress money' people hold to guard against proverbial rainy days.
- **Speculative motive for the demand for money** is the motive people have for holding money to take advantage of expected future falls in the prices of bonds, stocks or other non-money financial assets.
- **Monetary policy** is the term used to describe actions taken by the central bank to influence interest rates, economic activity and prices in the economy.
- **Monetary policy transmission mechanism** refers to the process by which changes in the money supply affect interest rates and investment spending, which in turn bring about aggregate demand shifts, thereby affecting prices, real GDP and employment.
- **The Reserve Bank of Australia** is Australia's central bank. It has responsibility for overall financial system stability, for regulating and standing behind the nation's payments system and for determining and implementing monetary policy. The RBA acts as banker to the federal government, the banking system, other major financial organisations (since 1999) and money market dealers, as well as managing the government's debt.
- **Fractional reserve banking** is a system in which banks keep only a percentage of their deposits on reserve as vault cash and deposits at the central bank. Holding less than 100 per cent on reserve allows banks to create money.
- **The money multiplier** is the multiple by which the money supply increases as the result of an increase in bank reserves. It is the reciprocal of the required liquidity reserve ratio.

Study questions and problems

1 Could each of the following items potentially serve as money? Consider each as (1) a medium of exchange, (2) a unit of account and (3) a store of value.

   a VISA credit card

   b a dollar note

   c cattle

   d beer mugs

2 Consider each of the items in Question 1 in terms of scarcity, portability, divisibility and uniformity.

3 What backs the Australian dollar? Include the distinction between commodity money and fiat money in your answer.

4 Distinguish between M1 and M3. Which is the narrower definition of money?

5 What are the major purposes of the Reserve Bank of Australia?

6 Relate Shakespeare's admonition 'Neither a borrower, nor a lender be' to the goldsmiths' evolutionary use of fractional reserve banking.

7 Consider this statement: 'Banks do not create money because this is the RBA's responsibility.' Do you agree or disagree? Explain.

8 Suppose you deposit your pay cheque drawn on another bank. Explain the impact on the overall money supply in the economy.

9 Suppose you remove $1000 from under your mattress and deposit it in the Westpac bank. If the required reserve ratio is 10 per cent, what is the maximum amount the bank can lend from this deposit?

10 How much money do you keep in cash or deposits on a typical day? Under the following conditions, would you decide to increase or decrease your demand for holding money balances? Also identify whether the condition affects your transactions motive, precautionary motive or speculative motive for holding money.
 a Your salary doubles.
 b The rate of interest on bonds and other assets falls.
 c An automatic teller machine (ATM) is installed next door and you have a card.
 d Bond prices are expected to rise.
 e You are paid each week, instead of monthly.

11 What are the three basic motives underlying people's demand for money? Explain how these three motives combine to yield the total demand for money.

12 Suppose a bond pays annual interest of $80. Compute the interest rate per year that a bondholder can earn if the bond has a market value of $800, $1000 and $2000. State the conclusion drawn from your calculations.

13 Using the demand and supply schedule for money shown below, do the following:
 a Graph the demand for and the supply of money curves.
 b Determine the equilibrium interest rate.
 c Suppose the RBA increases the money supply by $10 billion. Show the effect in your graph and describe the money market adjustment process to a new equilibrium interest rate. What is the new equilibrium rate of interest?

Money market

Interest rate (per cent)	Demand for money (billions of dollars)	Supply of money (billions of dollars)
8	10	20
6	20	20
4	30	20
2	40	20

Online exercises

Exercise 1

Visit the RBA website (**www.rba.gov.au**) and select **Speeches**. Review the most recent testimony to parliament by Ian Macfarlane as well as his most recent commentary on the economy and monetary policy.

Exercise 2

Think about the credit card application forms you receive in the mail or visit VISA (**www.visa.com**) or MasterCard (**www.mastercard.com**). Is it clear from these advertisements that credit cards are not money?

Exercise 3

Go to the RBA website (**www.rba.gov.au**) and select **Statistics**, then **Statistics by Frequency of Publication**, then **Financial Aggregates**, then **Monetary Aggregates**. What are the most recent measures of the monetary base, M1, M3 and Broad Money?

Exercise 4

Go to the RBA website (**www.rba.gov.au**) and select **Statistics**, then **Bulletin Statistical Tables**, then **Financial Markets** and then **Interest Rates and Yields**. What are the most recent values for the cash rate (also called 11 am call rate), treasury note rate and bank-accepted bill rate?

Answers to 'You make the call'

Are debit cards money?

Debit cards facilitate the exchange of goods and services and debit card statements serve as a useful summary of expenditures. Furthermore, unlike credit cards, debit cards do not represent an extension of credit. However, like cheques (which also facilitate exchange, do not represent an extension of credit, and whose bank statement provides a useful summary of expenditures) debit cards are themselves not money. What is money are the deposits in the accounts from which the card facilitates the withdrawal of funds to pay for transactions. If you said debit cards are not money because they do not satisfy any of the three functions required for money, YOU ARE CORRECT.

Australian monetary policy adjustments

The period from December 1999 to August 2000 was a period of monetary policy tightening in Australia. During this period interest rates were raised by the RBA by 1¼ per cent from 5 per cent to 6¼ per cent. To do this, the RBA reduced the monetary base. With demand for money either increasing over the period or remaining unchanged, this contraction in money supply put upward pressure on interest rates.

The period from January 2001 to December 2001 was a period of monetary policy easing. During this period interest rates were lowered by the RBA from 6¼ per cent to 4¼ per cent. To do this, the RBA increased the monetary base. With demand for money remaining relatively unchanged during this period, this expansion in money supply put downward pressure on interest rates.

The period from May 2002 to December 2003 was a period of monetary policy tightening. Nonetheless, the monetary base expanded over this period. Notwithstanding this, the demand for money was increasing more rapidly than supply during the period, with the result that overall financial market liquidity was tightened sufficiently by the RBA to result in the desired increases in the cash rate.

If you understood that these were periods of monetary tightening and easing respectively and that the interest rate movements were the result of the interaction of market demand for and the RBA-adjusted supply of money, YOU ARE CORRECT.

Multiple-choice questions

1 Which of the following is a problem with barter?
   - **a** Individuals will not exchange goods.
   - **b** Individuals' wants must coincide in order for there to be exchange.
   - **c** Goods can be exchanged, but services cannot.
   - **d** None of the above is a problem.

2 Which of the following is *not* a characteristic of money?
   - **a** It provides a way to measure the relative value of goods and services.
   - **b** It is always backed by something of high intrinsic value, such as gold or silver.
   - **c** It is generally acceptable as a medium of exchange.
   - **d** It allows for saving and borrowing.

3 Which of the following is a store of value?
   - **a** savings account.
   - **b** shares.
   - **c** a treasury note.
   - **d** all of the above.

4 The easier it is to convert an asset directly into goods and services without loss, the
   - **a** less secure it is.
   - **b** more secure it is.
   - **c** more liquid it is.
   - **d** less liquid it is.

5 The M1 definition of the money supply includes
   - **a** currency in circulation.
   - **b** currency in circulation held by the non-bank public and cheque account deposits.
   - **c** dollar notes, gold certificates and cheque account deposits.
   - **d** RBA notes and bank loans.

6 Which one of the following is part of the M3 definition of the money supply, but not part of M1?
   - **a** cheque account deposits.
   - **b** currency held in banks.
   - **c** currency in circulation in the hands of the non-bank public.
   - **d** deposits in building societies.

7 What will be the actual or likely effect on the money base, M1, M3 and Broad Money of each of the following?
   - **a** A building society converts to a savings bank.
   - **b** Holden pays its quarterly tax through its bank, the ANZ bank.
   - **c** A bank sells some government securities to the RBA.
   - **d** A money market participant buys some government securities from the

Commonwealth Bank and pays for them with exchange settlement funds.

- **e** The RBA pays interest to Suncorp-Metway bank on behalf of the federal government, on account of Suncorp-Metway bank's holdings of government securities.
- **f** The interest rate on cheque accounts increases relative to other deposit rates.
- **g** Economic activity picks up because of more optimistic expectations and this leads to a rise in the demand for loans for investment.
- **h** The public's demand for currency increases.

8 Which definition of the money supply includes credit cards or 'plastic money'?

- **a** M1.
- **b** M3.
- **c** Broad Money.
- **d** all of the above.
- **e** none of the above.

9 Which of these institutions has the responsibility to control the money supply?

- **a** commercial banks.
- **b** parliament.
- **c** the Treasury.
- **d** the Reserve Bank of Australia.

10 Which of the following is a function of the RBA?

- **a** clearing cheques.
- **b** supervising credit unions.
- **c** supervising and regulating banks.
- **d** controlling the money supply.
- **e** all of the above.

11 If a bank has total deposits of $100 000 with $10 000 set aside to meet reserve requirements, its reserve ratio is

- **a** $10 000.
- **b** 10 per cent.
- **c** 0.1 per cent.
- **d** 1 per cent.

PART 5

16 Macroeconomic policy I: monetary policy

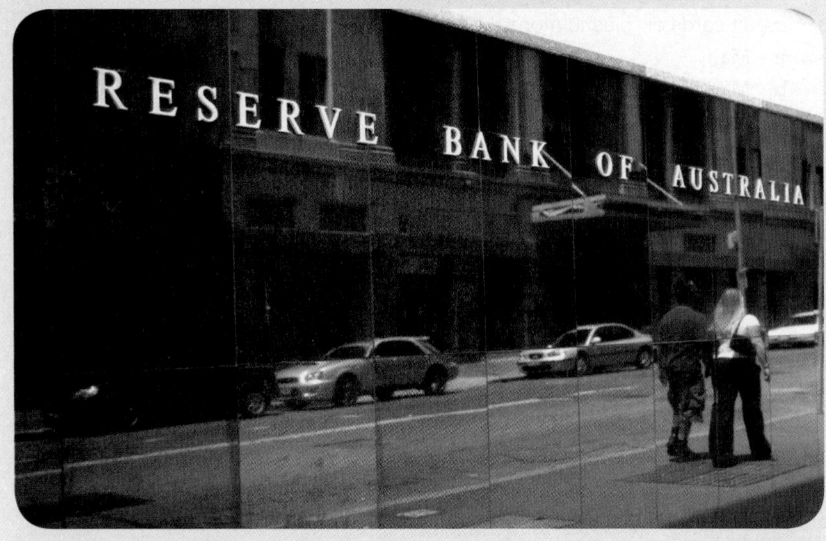

In this chapter and the next we will build on the material of the previous five chapters and provide you with an introduction to the two critical arms of macroeconomic policy. This chapter deals with monetary policy and the next deals with fiscal policy.

Vladimir Lenin, the first Communist leader of the Soviet Union, once said the best way to destroy a nation is to destroy its money. Adolf Hitler had the same idea. During World War II, he planned to counterfeit British currency and drop it from planes flying over England. Both cases illustrate that it matters how much money is in circulation. A sudden increase in the quantity of money can render a nation's currency valueless. As a consequence, people must resort to barter and waste time making direct exchanges of goods and services, rather than being productive.

The previous chapter provided the prerequisites for understanding the market for money and the basic characteristics of most modern financial systems. You have actually already learned a great deal about monetary matters. You have learned what makes money '*money*', several different definitions of the money supply, the determinants of the demand for money, how the demand and supply of money interact to determine interest rates, how changes in interest rates then influence aggregate demand, output, prices and employment in the economy, how the banking system creates money, and several other important features of the financial system.

In this chapter we add to this knowledge by elaborating upon the goals for monetary policy, alternative views as to the most appropriate role for it to play, reasons for a policy adjustment by the central bank and how it actually implements modern monetary policy. We will also discuss alternative views as to how monetary policy affects the macro economy, and provide some illustrations of recent developments and episodes in the conduct of monetary policy in Australia.

In this chapter, you will examine these economics questions:

- What is monetary policy?
- What reason would the central bank have for adjusting monetary policy?
- How does a monetary policy adjustment actually occur?
- Are there different views as to how monetary policy affects the economy?
- Why would a Nobel Laureate economist suggest replacing the US central bank with an intelligent horse?
- What are the major tools the central bank uses to implement monetary policy and control the supply of money?
- What is the 'cash rate' and when is 'cash' not really 'cash' at all?

The goals of monetary policy

As noted in the previous chapter, a nation's central bank has responsibility for the determination and implementation of monetary policy. There we also indicated that the **goal of monetary policy** – at least in Australia – is to keep inflation (as measured by the CPI) between 2 and 3 per cent over the course of the business cycle. Inflation targeting is not unique to Australia and is now a common approach of central banks around the world. Australia's inflation target has been given some extra clarity by the RBA Governor, Mr Ian Macfarlane. He has said that if, after a run of five years or so, the average annual inflation rate has a 2 before the decimal point, then the target may be said to have been achieved.

Goal of monetary policy
Since1996, in Australia, the formal goal of monetary policy has been to keep inflation between 2 and 3 per cent over the course of the business cycle.

As also noted in the previous chapter, the Reserve Bank Act of 1959 outlined that the RBA has a duty to the Australian people to maintain the stability of the currency (keep inflation low), to maintain full employment and to ensure the economic prosperity and welfare of the Australian people. This sounds as though the RBA's ongoing goals of monetary policy should number three, not one. However, the RBA believes that, by keeping inflation

Mr Ian Macfarlane became Governor of the RBA in 1996. You can browse speeches by Ian Macfarlane as well as other senior members of the RBA by going to **www.rba.gov.au** and following the instructions. You can also find out a little more about the membership of the RBA Board by visiting this site and selecting *About the RBA*, *Overview of Functions and Operations* and then *the Reserve Bank Board*.

low and steady, it can assist with the achievement of full employment and high economic growth over the medium to long term. By doing this it prevents inflation from taking off and thereby avoids all the attendant problems associated with high – and usually highly variable – inflation, which were outlined in Chapter 13.

With inflation low and stable, economic growth will be higher and unemployment will be lower over the longer term than if the RBA had, in the short term, let go of its inflation target to try to actively promote economic growth in order to reduce short-term unemployment. Thus, although it might seem counterintuitive, the RBA believes – and the government accepts – that the best way for it to contribute to the economic prosperity of Australia and keep unemployment low in the long run is to target inflation over both the short term and the long term. Thus, by achieving its inflation target, the RBA believes it will best achieve all three goals outlined in the original Act.

Given that the maintenance of average annual inflation at 2 to 3 per cent is the target of monetary policy, in the next section we will canvass two related but alternative views as to how changes in monetary policy actually affect inflation and the macro economy generally. This will be followed by a brief discussion of some views on how a central bank should approach the ongoing conduct of monetary policy.

Two views of the monetary policy transmission mechanism

The Keynesian view

In the previous chapter we described in some detail one view of the way monetary policy works. Although we didn't emphasise it there, that characterisation has its roots in Keynesianism. In brief, the Keynesian transmission mechanism is as follows.

Suppose the economy is operating above full employment and inflation has started to take off (from previously low and stable levels), which the central bank detects and wants to act upon. To do this it would tighten monetary policy. This means that it would reduce the supply of monetary base in the financial system and thereby raise interest rates in the economy. The higher interest rates would then act to reduce private-sector demand for investment goods and consumer durables. This reduced demand would also have multiplier effects through the rest of the economy so that aggregate demand would reduce. The reduction in aggregate demand would slow down economic activity and reduce the rate of inflation. In the Keynesian characterisation, interest rate changes are the key to the transmission process.

Exhibit 16.1 **The Keynesian and monetarist views of the monetary policy transmission mechanism**

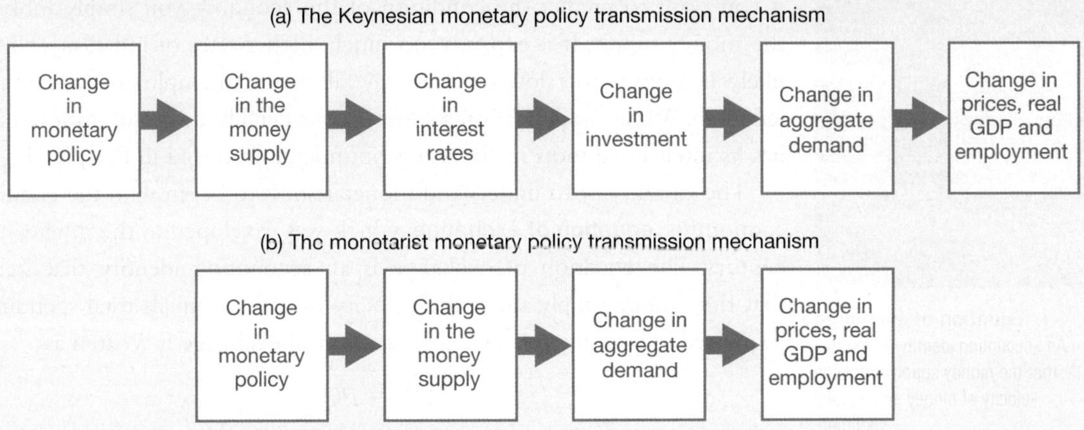

According to the Keynesian transmission mechanism shown in (a), changes in monetary policy first affect interest rates. Such interest rate changes affect investment and consumer durable demand and, through the spending multiplier, affect aggregate demand more generally, thereby resulting in changes to real output, employment and prices. Part (b) shows the monetarist monetary policy transmission mechanism. Monetarists emphasise that changes in the money supply directly cause changes in nominal aggregate demand and thereby changes in prices, real GDP and employment.

Exhibit 16.1 reproduces the Keynesian view of the monetary transmission mechanism. If you need a refresher on the details, have another look at the relevant section in the previous chapter.

The monetarist view

The monetarist school of thought has the view that monetary policy operates much more directly and widely than suggested in the above-described Keynesian description. In the Keynesian description, monetary policy acts indirectly, causing changes in interest rates first, before affecting investment and aggregate demand and then consequently affecting prices, real GDP and employment.

monetarism

An alternative view, called **monetarism**, challenges this characterisation. Monetarism argues that changes in the money supply directly determine changes in prices, real GDP and employment. Exhibit 16.1 also illustrates the monetarist transmission mechanism. Comparison of this with the Keynesian version of the transmission mechanism shows that the monetarist model de-emphasises the Keynesian interest rate–investment linkage.

Monetarism The theory that changes in the growth of the money supply directly determine changes in prices, real GDP and employment.

Read more about Adam Smith, the father of classical economics, John Maynard Keynes, the father of Keynesian economics and Milton Friedman, the father of monetarism, by visiting a website maintained by New School at **cepa.newschool.edu/het/index.htm.**

The equation of exchange

Monetarists put the spotlight firmly on the money supply. They argue that, if you want to predict the condition of the economy, you simply look at the money supply. If it expands too much, higher rates of inflation will be likely. If it grows too slowly, prices may fall or the unemployment line may lengthen. While modern monetarism is considerably more sophisticated, it has its intellectual roots in classical economics, introduced in Chapter 14.

The easiest way to understand monetarism is to begin with the classical economists' **equation of exchange**, which was developed in the nineteenth century. The equation of exchange is an accounting identity that states that the money supply times the velocity of money equals total spending. Expressed as a simple formula, the equation of exchange is written as

Equation of exchange An accounting identity that states that the money supply times the velocity of money equals total spending.

$$MV = PQ$$

Let's begin with the left-hand side of the equation (MV). M is the money supply (more precisely, let's say for argument's sake M1) in circulation and V represents the **velocity of money.** The velocity of money is the average number of times per time period (say, a year) a dollar of the money supply is spent on final goods and services. Assume you have one crisp \$20 note and this is the only money in an ultra-simple economy. Suppose you spend this money on a pizza and a drink at Zeno's Pizza Shop. Once Mr Zeno receives your money, he may decide to buy an economics book and learn about the difference between the views of Keynesians and monetarists. Assuming the price is exactly \$20, Mr Zeno buys the book at the local university bookstore, run by Ms Wise.

Velocity of money The average number of times per period a dollar of the money supply is spent on final goods and services.

At this point, both Mr Zeno and Ms Wise have sold \$20 worth of goods. Thus, a single \$20 bill has financed \$40 worth of total final spending. And as long as this \$20 bill passes from hand to hand during, say, one year, the value of final sales will increase. For example, assume the \$20 note in question travels from hand to hand five times. This means the velocity of money is five and the left-hand side of the equation of exchange is expressed as

$$\$20 \times 5 = \$100$$

The equation of exchange is an *identity* – true by definition – that expresses the fact that the value of what people spend is equal to, or exchanged for, what they buy. What people buy is nominal GDP or (PQ). Nominal GDP is equal to the average selling price during the year (P) multiplied by the quantity of actual output of final goods and services (Q). In our simple economy, total spending, or PQ, equals \$100. Note that the identity between MV and PQ only indicates what happens to the product of P and Q if MV increases. Although we know total spending (PQ) increases, we do not know whether the price level (P), the quantity of output (Q) or both, increase.

Consider a more realistic example. Suppose nominal GDP last year was \$400 billion and M1 was \$100 billion. How many times on average did each dollar of the M1 money supply have to be spent on final goods and services to generate this level of total spending in the economy? Using the equation of exchange,

$$MV = PQ$$
$$\$100 \text{ billion} \times V = \$400 \text{ billion}$$
$$V = 4$$

Thus, each dollar (in M1) is spent an average of four times per year in the purchase of final goods and services.

The quantity theory of money

The equation of exchange is converted from an *identity* to a *theory* by making certain assumptions. The classical economists became the forerunners of modern-day monetarists by arguing that the velocity of money (V) and real output (Q) are fairly constant. The classicists viewed V as constant because people's habits of holding a certain quantity of money, and therefore the number of times a dollar is spent during any given period, are slow to change (probably not a bad assumption in the nineteenth century). Also, recall from Chapter 14 that classical economists believed in price and wage flexibility. Hence, they believed the economy would automatically adjust very quickly to short-term shocks so as to remain close to long-run full-employment output (Q). Thus, they believed Q would be approximately constant at whatever was the full-employment level.

quantity theory of money

Because V and Q were considered approximately constant by the classical economists, we have one of the oldest theories of inflation, called the **quantity theory of money**. The quantity theory of money states that changes in the price level (inflation) are directly related to changes in the supply of money. Monetary policy based on the simple quantity theory of money therefore directly affects the price level. To illustrate, we will modify the equation of exchange by putting a bar (–) over V and over Q to indicate that they are fixed or constant in value:

Quantity theory of money The theory that changes in the price level (inflation) are directly related to changes in the money supply.

$$M \times \bar{V} = P \times \bar{Q}$$

Under these circumstances, what happens if the money supply doubles? The price level must also double. On this theory, if the central bank cuts the money supply in half, then the price level is also cut in half. Meanwhile, real output of goods and services, Q, remains unchanged.

According to the quantity theory of money, any change in the money supply must lead to a proportional change in the price level.

PART 5

In short, in the context of the quantity theory of money, the cause of inflation is described as 'too much money chasing too few goods'. Of course, the quantity theory of money was a very simple theory, which may have been a good approximation to the world of the nineteenth century. It may, however, be a less useful approximation to our present-day twenty-first-century world. For example, it abstracts from non-monetary factors – such as supply shocks from a hike in oil prices – that cause cost-push inflation (see Exhibits 14.9 and 14.10 in Chapter 14). Moreover, its predictions about the direct relationship between money growth and prices will tend to unravel if V does not remain fairly stable over time.

As far as the constancy of V is concerned, as noted above, the velocity of money will depend on the community's demand for money and, in times of very rapid financial innovation – such as, for example, occurred in the 1980s and 1990s – the demand for money could be changing very substantially. As just one example, the widespread introduction of EFTPOS facilities in Australia and elsewhere in the 1990s changed very dramatically the public's need and demand for 'walking around' currency.

Finally, we know that economies may at times be very far from full employment. (Recall discussions in previous chapters about recessions and the Great Depression.) In such circumstances, increases in money supply may mostly stimulate increases in output rather than price increases. Nevertheless, for economies at full employment and/or for economies experiencing extremely rapid money supply growth, the inflation predictions of the simple quantity theory may be realistic.

As mentioned previously, a very useful site for learning more about some of history's most famous and influential economists is that maintained by the New School. To read about any one of hundreds of economists, from Adam Smith right through to today's Nobel Laureates, go to **cepa.newschool.edu/het/index.htm** and use the alphabetical listing provided. This site is also very useful for descriptions of a number of influential schools of economic thought, including monetarism.

Modern monetarism

Of course, modern monetarists recognise the limitations of the overly simple original classical quantity theory of money for most economies in most circumstances in the world today. The empirical evidence indicates that velocity is not constant over time and that the economy does not always operate at full employment. Therefore, although M and P are reasonably highly correlated, they do not change exactly proportionally.

Monetarists argue that velocity is not unchanging, but is reasonably predictable. Suppose the *predicted* velocity of money ($\hat{V}$) in the next year is 5 and the money supply increases by $10 billion this year. Monetarists would predict that nominal GDP would increase next year by about $50 billion ($M \times \hat{V}$). Furthermore, modern monetarists would predict that, if the economy is far below full employment (say in a recession), most of the rise in total spending will be in real output rather than in rises in prices. If, on the other hand, the economy is near full employment, much of the increase in M will simply be in rising prices.

Monetarism and the Keynesian transmission mechanism compared

Although recognising that a changed availability of money is likely to affect interest rates, monetarists do not place the same critical emphasis as Keynesians do on the rate of interest in the transmission mechanism. Instead monetarists argue that, when people find themselves with larger quantities of money on their hands than they had intended or expected, they will go out and spend the money on a wide range of things and not just buy interest-bearing securities. This buying pressure will manifest not only in increased prices of bonds (i.e. lower interest rates) but also in increased prices and quantities of a wide range of goods and services. Instead of working just through the rate of interest to affect investment and the economy, changes in the money supply directly determine economic activity.

There is a famous thought experiment that illustrates the monetarist position. Suppose one morning a community's inhabitants wake up to find $50 notes lying all over their yards – perhaps as a result of a midnight helicopter drop from some mysterious benefactor. What do they do? Some will certainly rush out to buy some financial securities, let's say, thereby exerting downward pressure on interest rates with consequential effects on investment demand. But won't others race out to buy cars, washing machines, clothes, food and so on? This general increased buying pressure – as well as the lower nominal interest rates – could be expected to raise nominal GDP (and, in this parable, probably almost entirely as a result of rising prices rather than output).

To avoid inflation and unemployment, the monetarists' prescription is to be sure that the money supply growth rate is maintained at the proper level.

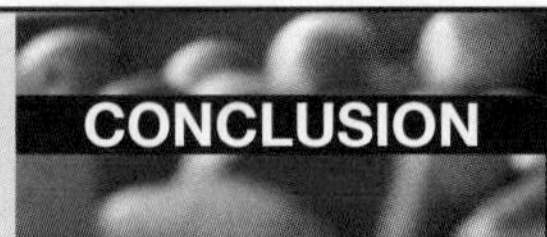

The appropriate role for monetary policy: the rules versus discretion debate

Although they have different views about the transmission mechanism of monetary policy, one thing Keynesians and monetarists agree on is that monetary policy has powerful effects on the macro economy. They even largely agree that the short-run effects – say from three to nine months – of a monetary change are likely to manifest mostly in changes in demand, production and employment, with changes in inflation taking somewhat longer – usually from about nine to eighteen months. Despite their agreement on the power of monetary policy to influence the course of the economy, their policy prescriptions for the proper role of monetary policy are in reality quite different.

Those economists who have a Keynesian predisposition favour the central bank retaining considerable discretion to adjust monetary policy as needed and as frequently as required to achieve its stated goals. Economists with a monetarist bent, on the other hand, are more likely to prescribe a policy whereby the central bank is required to adhere fairly closely to pre-announced and widely known monetary policy rules and not to have the discretion to adjust its policies as economic circumstances appear to change. The most common type of rules-based approach is one involving pre-set targets for money supply growth.

While the 'stick to your rules, sit on your hands and do nothing' approach in the face of constantly changing macroeconomic circumstances may at first sound counterintuitive, those who advocate such an approach to monetary policy do so with good reasons, which most Keynesians no doubt appreciate. As with many things in life, the view taken by anyone in a position to influence policy will not only be the result of one's best informed and most sound conceptual reasoning but also will involve a good helping of the 'lesser of two evils' philosophy thrown in for good measure.

In what follows we will try to give you the flavour of some of the core issues at stake in this debate.

Monetarism gained intellectual credibility among the academic economic community in the late 1950s and 1960s, led by Nobel Laureate Professor Milton Friedman, at the University of Chicago. It also consequently had a significant impact on the conduct of monetary policy around the world in the 1970s and early 1980s.

countercyclical macroeconomic policy

Countercyclical macroeconomic policy has the aim of smoothing out the fluctuations in the business cycle. Monetarists believe countercyclical macroeconomic policy may actually unintentionally make the business cycle worse rather than less pronounced on account of three policy lags: the information lag, the policy determination lag and the policy effectiveness lag. For these reasons monetarists advocate a rules-based approach to monetary policy rather than the discretionary approach favoured by Keynesians.

Consider Exhibit 16.2. Suppose the yellow line represents the course the economy would follow over time if left to its own accord without any policy intervention. In other words, the yellow line represents the economy's business cycle. **Countercyclical macroeconomic policy** has the aim of smoothing out the fluctuations in the business cycle. In terms of the exhibit, successful countercyclical monetary policy would have the central bank adjusting monetary policy in a timely way so that the impact of monetary policy adjustments would be felt in the macro economy at just the right time to dampen down the swings in the business cycle. The path followed by the economy with such successful policy intervention might follow something like the green line in the exhibit.

Friedman argued very persuasively that, due to information lags, policy determination lags and policy effectiveness lags, such discretionary countercyclical monetary policy can have the opposite effects on the macro economy to those intended by policy makers. These lags may well result in the monetary policy intervention affecting the economy at precisely the

Exhibit 16.2 A stylised depiction of the business cycle and countercyclical macroeconomic fine-tuning policy

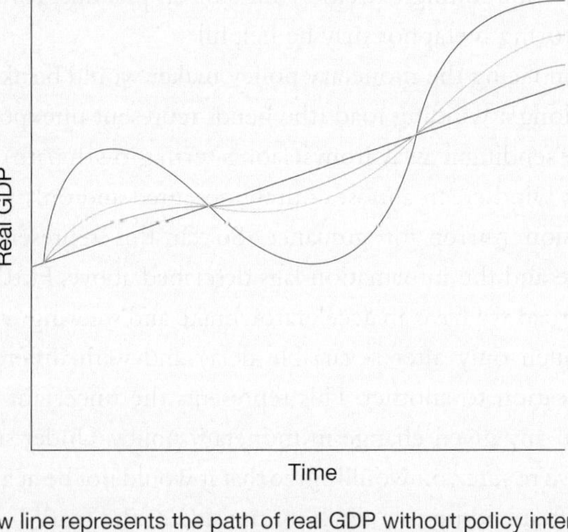

The yellow line represents the path of real GDP without policy intervention. The green line represents the path of real GDP under successful countercyclical macroeconomic fine-tuning policy. The red line represents the path of real GDP under the effects of inappropriate policy that exacerbates the business cycle rather than dampening it.

wrong time, exacerbating the business cycle rather than dampening it. Such an undesirable result is represented in the exhibit by the red line. Let's spend a little time discussing these lags.

Information about the current phase of economic activity in the real world is imperfect and partial, and becomes available only after a lag of some months. This time delay constitutes the **information lag**. It then takes more time for the authorities to decide on the appropriate policy response. This can involve protracted deliberations, particularly in light of the partial and sometimes conflicting messages being distilled from the various monthly and quarterly macroeconomic indicators as they become available. The time taken to decide on an apparently appropriate policy response may amount to several months and is known as the **policy determination lag**.

Once a policy is initiated there will be a further lag before it begins to take effect on economic activity. This lag is referred to as the **policy effectiveness lag** and is likely to be quite long for monetary policy, particularly if one accepts the Keynesian version of the transmission mechanism. As has already been mentioned, the channel of influence in the Keynesian case is indirect, operating through the cost of credit, and therefore a change in monetary policy can take a long time to have a discernible impact on the macro economy. Most economists agree that, from the moment any given monetary policy change is implemented, this time is most likely to be at least three months and could be up to over a year.

Information lag The time delay (of some months) before information about the current phase of economic activity in the real world becomes available.

Policy determination lag The time taken to decide on an apparently appropriate policy response; this may be several months.

Policy effectiveness lag The delay between the time when a policy is initiated and the time when it begins to take effect on economic activity.

If the abovementioned lags were nicely stable over time the situation would not be so bad, but unfortunately they have been and can be expected to be not only long but also highly variable. This makes active countercyclical monetary policy fine tuning extremely difficult in practice. To illustrate the difficulty, a motoring metaphor may be helpful.

The situation facing the monetary policy maker would be akin to trying to drive a car along a winding road (the bends represent unexpected shocks to the economy sending it away from its long-term growth path) with vision out of the front windscreen almost entirely obscured and only an imperfect (fuzzy) rear-vision mirror for guidance. So far this represents the very uncertain future and the information lags described above. Furthermore, to keep us on the road we have an accelerator, brake and steering wheel, which react to our touch only after a variable delay and with differential effect from one application to another. This represents the uncertain response of the economy to any given change in monetary policy. Under such adverse circumstances we're sure you would agree that it would not be at all surprising for the car to often end up in a ditch on the side of the road!

The monetarists have an answer to the above problems and to how we can try to make sure the economy grows at about the right rate over the longer term. Instead of running the risks of policy errors, the answer is to forget about policy activism and instead follow steady, predictable monetary policy. In particular, given the very important role they ascribe to money supply growth, monetarists argue that the central bank should announce a target for money growth (in, say, the monetary base, M1 or M3, for example) for, say, the year ahead and the reasons for that target in the context of its overall goals (as agreed with the government).

The bank should then use its various tools to try to meet the announced money supply target, with the target itself subjected to annual review. The central bank would continue to seek to meet the pre-announced money supply target, irrespective of what happens economically over the course of the year in question. Monetarists argue that such an approach would deliver more certainty to economic decision makers and, in the longer term, deliver better macroeconomic outcomes – for inflation, growth and employment – than following a discretionary approach.

Monetarists would advise that the central bank should be prevented from tinkering with the money supply, missing the target and making the economy worse rather than better. Instead, the money supply should expand at the same rate as what is considered to be the potential growth rate in real GDP (say 3 per cent) plus some desired inflation rate (say 2–3 per cent); that is, it should increase somewhere between 5 and 6 per cent per year. The central bank should pick a rate and stick to it, even if unexpected changes in velocity cause short periods of inflation or low-output growth.

Monetarists argue that their 'straitjacket' approach would reduce the average intensity and duration of unemployment and inflation by eliminating the monetarists' public enemy number one – the central bank's discretion to change the growth rate of the money supply. Needless to say, this view is not necessarily endorsed by all economists. A Keynesian-type proponent of the discretionary approach might quip that the rules-based money supply growth approach is best summed up by a significant variation on a well-known expression: 'Don't do something, just stand there'.

Monetarists advocate that the central bank should follow a publicly known rules-based approach to setting the growth in the money supply each year.

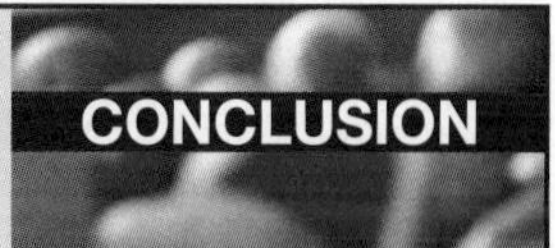

A horse of which colour?

A famous Nobel Prize-winning economist once proposed replacing the United States Fed – the central bank of the United States – with an intelligent horse. Each New Year's day, the horse would stand in front of Fed headquarters to answer monetary policy questions. Reporters would ask, 'What is going to happen to the money supply this year?' The horse would tap its hoof four times and the next day headlines would read 'Fed to Once Again Increase the Money Supply 4 Per Cent.'

Is this famous economist a Keynesian or a monetarist?

How stable is velocity?

How stable or predictable is the velocity of money? This is a critical question in the debate as to whether money supply growth targeting is the appropriate approach to monetary policy or whether a discretionary approach is preferable. All economists would agree that velocity may be variable over the short run. Any differences in opinion occur in terms of the behaviour of velocity over the longer term.

Keynesians do not accept the monetarists' argument that, over long periods of time, velocity evolves in a fairly stable and predictable way. Given that velocity is determined by the community's demand for holding money balances, this is equivalent to Keynesians arguing that the demand for money is unstable both in the short and the longer term. If this were the case and V was unstable and unpredictable, a change in the money supply could lead to a much larger or smaller change in nominal GDP than the monetarists would predict.

Keynesians further argue that, even if changes in velocity are fairly stable and reasonably predictable in the longer term, the focus should be on its short-run variations, and in the short run it is known to be volatile. They therefore argue that following a monetary rule is folly. Suppose the money supply increases at a constant rate, but the velocity is greater than expected.

This means that total spending will be greater than predicted, causing inflation. Lower-than-predicted velocity results in unemployment because the economy expands too little. Keynesians believe that the central bank must be free to change the money supply to offset unexpected changes in velocity.

Monetarists counter that the central bank *cannot* predict short-run variations in V, so its 'quick-fix' changes in the money supply will often be wrong. This is why monetarists advocate the central bank following a monetary rule. Keynesians are willing to accept occasional policy errors and reject this idea in favour of maintaining central bank flexibility to change the money supply in order to affect interest rates, aggregate demand and the economy.

A case study in monetary targeting: Australia 1976–85

While the monetarist view started to gain support in academic circles in the late 1950s and enjoyed its strongest academic support in the late 1960s, it made its policy impact around the world in the mid-1970s. Incidentally, the 1960s was the decade in which Keynesian ideas had their greatest policy impact, while they had their strongest academic support in the 1940s and 1950s.

These are two good examples of the time it usually takes – about 10 to 15 years – for new economic theories originating from universities to make their impact in policy-making circles. This is no accident, as this is about how long it takes for revolutionary new theories to gain the widespread intellectual support they need – within both universities and policy agencies – to become viable real-world policy alternatives. This is also about how long it takes for new graduates to reach sufficiently senior positions in the various major economic policy-making agencies to start to have significant internal influence on government policy determination!

Conditional projection The implementation of monetary policy in Australia during the period 1976–85 consisted of a form of monetary targeting – a monetarist-type policy recommendation adopted by many countries in the 1970s. Each year a 'conditional projection' for the growth of the monetary aggregate, M3, was announced in the Federal Budget by the Treasurer. The projections were conditional in the sense that, if world or domestic economic conditions changed unexpectedly, the government allowed itself room to vary the targets over the course of the year.

Australia was just one of many countries around the world that experimented with policy based on the monetarist policy prescription of monetary targeting. In this section we provide a discussion of this very important macroeconomic episode. In the next section we will describe how monetary policy has been conducted in Australia from the late 1980s until the present.

Because of the historically very high rates of inflation in the early 1970s in Australia and the worldwide intellectual influence of monetarism, the implementation of monetary policy in Australia during 1976–85 consisted of a form of monetary targeting. Each year a '**conditional projection**' for the growth of the monetary aggregate, M3, was announced in the Federal Budget by the Treasurer. These projections were in the nature of bands within which the RBA was expected to keep the growth of M3. The projections were

Monetary policy during the Great Depression

International focus

Applicable concept: Keynesians versus monetarists

Monetarists and Keynesians still debate the causes of the Great Depression. Monetarists Milton Friedman and Anna Schwartz, in their book *A Monetary History of the United States*,[1] argued that the Great Depression was caused by the decline in the money supply, as shown in Exhibit 16.3(a). The accompanying parts (b), (c) and (d) present changes in the price level, real GDP and unemployment rate.

During the 1920s, the money supply expanded steadily and prices were generally stable. In response to the great stock market crash of 1929, bank failures, falling real GDP and rising unemployment, the US central bank, the Fed, changed its monetary policy. Through the Great Depression years from 1929 to 1933, M1 declined by 27 per cent. And assuming velocity is relatively constant, how will a sharp reduction in the quantity of money in circulation affect the economy? Monetarists predict a reduction in prices, output and employment. As Exhibit 16.3(b) shows, the price level declined by 24 per cent between 1929 and 1933. In addition to deflation, Exhibit 16.3(c) shows that real GDP was 30 per cent lower in 1933 than in 1929. Unemployment rose from 3.2 per cent in 1929 to 24.9 per cent in 1933.

Friedman and Schwartz argued that it was the ineptness of the Fed's monetary policy during the Great Depression that caused the trough in the business cycle to be more severe and sustained. As proof, let's look at the period after 1933. The money supply grew and was followed closely by an increase in prices, real GDP and employment.

The Great Depression was indeed not the Fed's finest hour. In the initial phase of the contraction, fearful foreign banks made large withdrawals of their gold from US banks. To stop the outflow of gold to other countries, the Fed raised the interest rate on its loans to banks in 1931. As a result, banks borrowed less from the Fed and the money supply fell dramatically. Later the Fed lowered the interest rate it was charging banks, but only after the economy was deeper into the Great Depression.

What should the Fed have done? Friedman and Schwartz argued that the Fed should not have waited until 1931 to use open-market operations to increase the money supply. Thus, the conclusion is that the Fed is to blame for not pursuing an expansionary policy, which would have reduced the severity and duration of the contraction.

Finally, although the emphasis here is on monetary policy, it should be noted that both monetary and fiscal policies worsened the situation. President Hoover was attempting to balance the budget, rather than using expansionary fiscal policy.

---

1 Milton Friedman & Anna J. Schwartz, *A Monetary History of the United States, 1867–1960*, Princeton University Press, Princeton, NJ, 1963.

Analyse the issue

1 Explain why monetarists believe the Fed should have expanded the money supply during the Great Depression.

2 The Keynesians challenge the Friedman–Schwartz monetarists' monetary policy cure for the Great Depression. Use the aggregate demand and aggregate supply model to explain the Keynesian view. (Hint: Your answer must include the investment demand curve.)

Exhibit 16.3 The Great Depression economic data, 1929–34

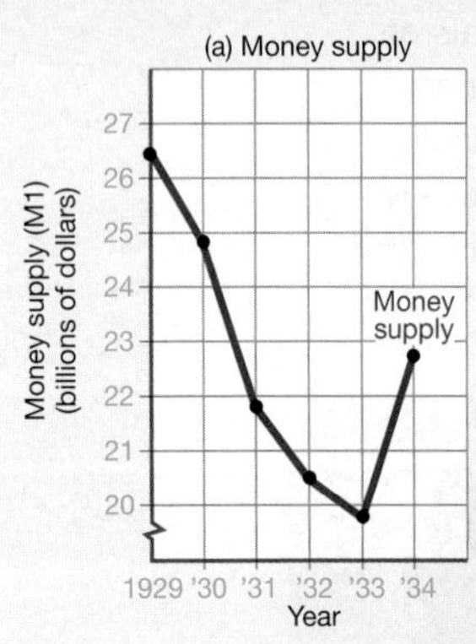

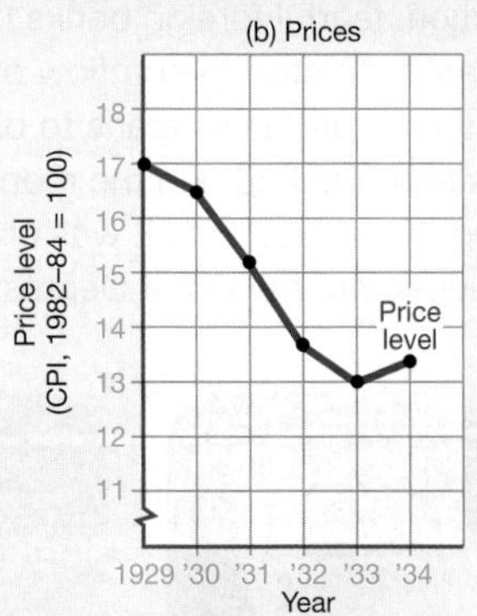

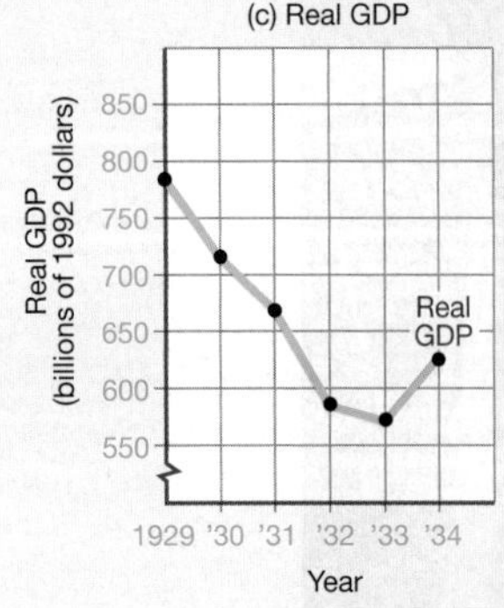

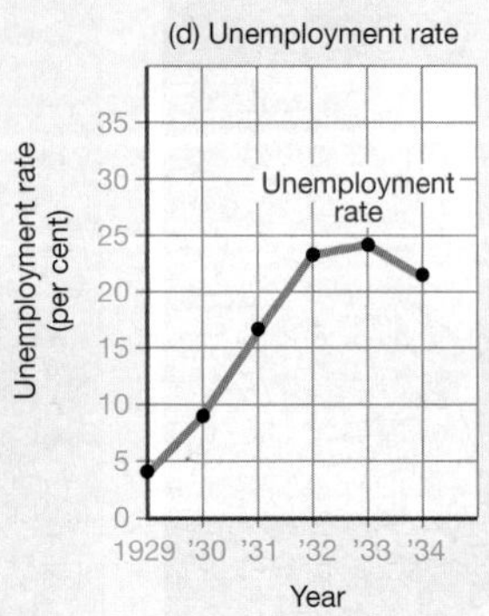

conditional in the sense that, if world or domestic economic conditions changed unexpectedly, the government allowed itself the room to vary the targets over the course of the year. This era of monetary targeting continued from late 1976 until early 1985.

The RBA had varying degrees of success in achieving these targets, mainly because the financial institutional framework in place at the time severely hampered its ability to control money growth. Nevertheless, the policy presumably had some impact on inflation. Refer to Exhibit 16.4. From a peak of 19 per cent in 1974–75 (yes, 19 per cent per year!), inflation had dropped to about 8 to 9 per cent by the middle of the 1980s. At the same time unemployment, unfortunately, had also increased from about 5 per cent to about 8 per cent by the mid-1980s.

Exhibit 16.4 Australian inflation and unemployment in the 1970s and 1980s

Year	Inflation[1]	Unemployment[2]
1970–71	6.1	1.4
1971–72	6.7	1.9
1972–73	5.6	2.7
1973–74	12.1	2.2
1974–75	19.0	4.1
1975–76	16.8	4.9
1976–77	11.4	5.2
1977–78	9.2	6.2
1978–79	9.1	6.3
1979–80	10.3	6.1
1980–81	9.8	5.9
1981–82	9.4	6.2
1982–83	10.9	9.0
1983–84	7.4	9.6
1984–85	6.0	8.6
1985–86	8.4	7.9
1986–87	8.7	8.3
1987–88	7.2	7.8
1988–89	7.0	6.6
1989–90	6.5	6.2
1990–91	5.4	8.4
1991–92	2.5	10.4

1 Source: 1970–71 to 1974–75: R. Foster & S.E. Stewart, 'Australian economic statistics', *Occasional Paper No. 8*, Reserve Bank of Australia, 1991; 1974–75 to 1991–92: ABS Cat. No. 5206.0.

2 Source: M. Parkin & R. Bade, *Macroeconomics and the Australian Economy*, 2nd edn, Allen & Unwin, Sydney, 1990, pp. 39–41; *Reserve Bank of Australia Bulletin*, December 1991 and November 1992, Table G.4.

PART 5

The financial institutional issues that hampered the RBA in meeting its announced monetary targets were rectified by 1985, giving the RBA greater ability than it had had during the previous eight years to achieve the agreed annual targets for M3. Yet it was precisely at this time that the government and the RBA decided to abandon monetary targeting as a means of conducting monetary policy. Why was this, and was the decision a correct one?

The justification for abandoning the targets stemmed from the correct perception by the authorities that the demand for M3 – and for the other monetary aggregates – was shifting around unpredictably due to the substantial financial deregulation and rapid financial innovations that were occurring at the time. In other words, it was precisely at this time that the velocity of money (*V*) had become very unstable and unpredictable both in the short run and in the longer term. Thus, the conditions for a monetarist approach being a sensible one – namely that the demand for money balances and therefore the velocity of money be stable – ceased to apply. Exhibit 16.5 presents the velocity of money in Australia (as defined by M3) from 1976 to 2001. As you can see it was around 1984–85 that the velocity began to change significantly.

To elaborate on this point a little more, as you have now learned, it is the interaction of the demand and supply of money that determines interest rates. Controlling the growth of the supply of money (in this case M3) will only have predictable effects on interest rates if the growth in

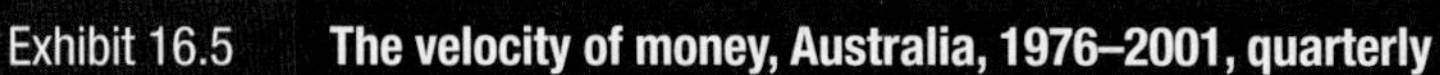

Exhibit 16.5 The velocity of money, Australia, 1976–2001, quarterly

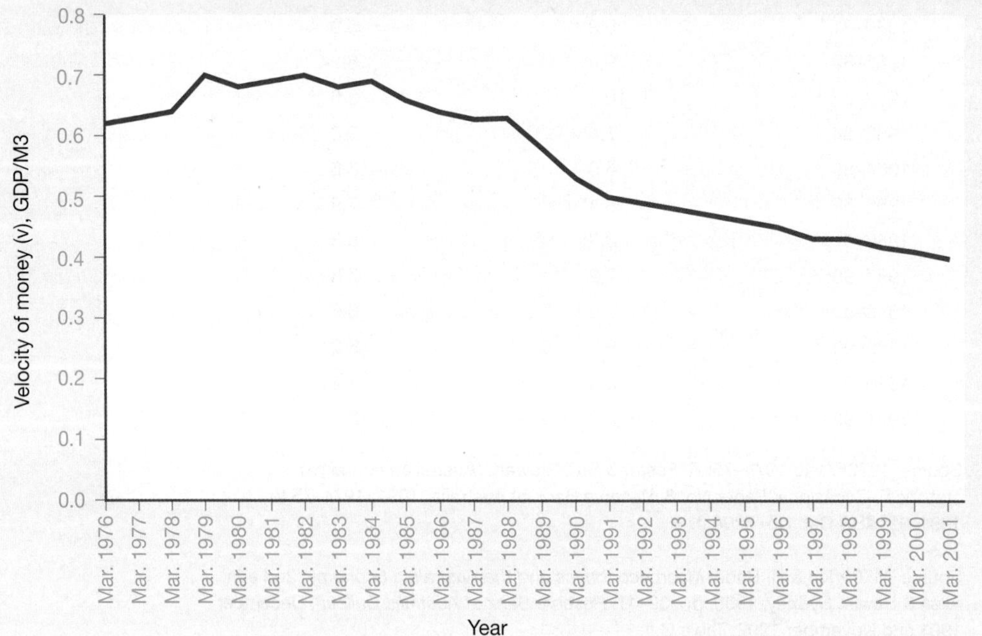

the demand for money can be predicted fairly accurately. It may turn out in fact that interest rates become unnecessarily volatile simply because the supply of money is being controlled while the demand is fluctuating. Such interest rate volatility could prove detrimental to economic growth. In such circumstances it would be better to directly target interest rates at whatever level is desired to maintain the appropriate level of aggregate demand rather than target money growth. Money growth would simply increase or decrease as necessary to curb any market pressure for interest rates to change from their desired levels. In fact, this simple idea led to the approach the RBA now uses in its operation of monetary policy.

Statement on the Conduct of Monetary Policy

Modern monetary policy implementation in Australia

To view a recent history of cash rate movements, go to the RBA website (**www.rba.gov.au**) and select *Statistics*, then *Alphabetical Index of Statistics*, then *Cash Rate Target.*

Since the abandonment by Australia of monetary targeting in 1985, the approach to monetary policy implementation has evolved through a couple of stages, which we won't dwell upon here. The important thing is for you to understand how monetary policy has been conducted since the early 1990s. As we mentioned earlier, the RBA unofficially adopted an inflation target of 2 to 3 per cent around 1993 and in 1996 this was made official with the co-signing by the Treasurer and the RBA Governor of the **Statement on the Conduct of Monetary Policy**. What we need to do here is to give you an understanding of just how the RBA goes about trying to achieve this target.

Modern monetary policy in Australia is implemented by the RBA seeking to maintain the **overnight cash rate** at a pre-announced level. The overnight cash rate (or just 'cash rate' for short) is the interest rate that borrowers in the money markets must pay to borrow funds for as short a period as overnight. In particular, this is the interest rate that banks charge one another for borrowing funds from one another to cover their short-term needs. As such, its value influences bank wholesale and retail interest rates and all other interest rates in the money markets. The value of the cash rate thereby influences all interest rates throughout the economy. It is by this influence on the interest rates in the wider economy that the RBA seeks to affect aggregate demand and influence the rate of inflation.

To influence the cash rate the RBA carries out **open-market operations** in the money markets to alter the supply of primary liquidity (referred to as 'cash') available to the financial system. Open-market operations consist of the RBA buying and selling commonwealth government securities from the private sector – usually banks – for cash.[1] In so doing, it increases or reduces the

Statement on the conduct of monetary policy was signed by the RBA Governor and the Federal Treasurer in 1996. It encapsulates the Australian government's agreement that the RBA should have the goal of keeping inflation on average at 2 to 3 per cent p.a. and be free to implement monetary policy as it sees fit to achieve that goal.

Overnight cash rate ('cash rate') The interest rate that borrowers in the money markets must pay to borrow funds overnight. Its value influences all other interest rates in the money markets and thereby its value influences all interest rates throughout the economy. It is by this influence on interest rates in the wider economy that the RBA seeks to affect aggregate demand and the inflation rate.

Open-market operations The buying and selling of government securities by the central bank to the private-sector financial markets to bring about changes to the monetary base and the 'cash rate'.

1 In settling any transaction between itself and a buyer or seller of securities, the RBA simply electronically credits or debits their exchange settlement account (refer to previous chapter). Funds in these accounts are called 'exchange settlement money' or simply 'cash'. The use of the word 'cash' in the money markets has nothing to do with the everyday meaning of the word, namely notes and coins.

To view current interest rates or selected interest rates on commonwealth government securities, go to the RBA website (**www.rba.gov.au**) and select *Statistics*, then *Statistics by Frequency of Publication*, then *Indicative Mid Rates of Selected Commonwealth Government Securities and Interbank Overnight Cash Rate*.

financial system's liquidity (and the money supply) and thereby changes short-term interest rates prevailing in the money market (for example, the interest rate on bank accepted bills, introduced briefly in the previous chapter).

If the pressure is maintained, the changes to short-term money market interest rates will filter through to other interest rates such as the home mortgage rate, the prime lending rate (the rate banks charge their best corporate borrowers), credit card rates, personal loan rates and so on. Changes in these latter rates, if maintained, will affect consumption, investment activity and aggregate demand, as has been described above and in the previous chapter. The schematic in Exhibit 16.6 may help you visualise how open-market operations by the central bank affect the monetary base, broader definitions of money supply and interest rates.

To illustrate an open-market operation, suppose the RBA has evidence that the underlying inflation rate is – or soon will be – creeping up towards the top end of its acceptable range (3 per cent). What will it do? If the RBA Board feels that this higher rate of inflation is likely to persist into the future, it will most likely decide that it is necessary to reduce the monetary base, tighten financial conditions, increase the cash rate and raise interest rates generally. The extent to which it will seek to raise the cash rate is a matter of judgement, but in reality it does so in a series of small steps as more and more information on current and likely future economic conditions comes to hand.

To accomplish the monetary policy tightening, the RBA will offer to sell government securities from its portfolio to banks and other money market participants at prices implying an attractive rate of interest. Suppose a bank buys some of the securities on offer. In payment for them, the RBA will immediately debit the bank's exchange settlement account and, by doing this, will immediately reduce the monetary base in the financial system.

To see this, suppose the funds needed to pay for the securities amount to \$100 million. As soon as the RBA debits the \$100 million from the exchange settlement account of the purchasing bank, these funds have been taken out of the private-sector financial system and are no longer part of its liquidity base. Since the bank's deposits with the RBA are part of the monetary base and since the deposits are extinguished in payment for the securities, the monetary base of the economy is reduced by \$100 million. Since the base has been reduced we can also expect that, through the action of the credit multiplier (refer to the previous chapter), M1 and the other broader monetary aggregates will also reduce.

The RBA must first determine the state of the economy before deciding what to do, if anything, to the monetary base and interest rates. It publishes a summary of economic conditions each quarter in its monthly bulletin. Visit **www.rba.gov.au**. and select *Publications and Research*, then *Reserve Bank Bulletin*.

In this monetary policy tightening example, as the cash rate rises, to remain competitive other short-term deposit rates in the rest of the money market and wider financial markets will have to rise. The higher short-term interest rates available in the financial system will induce investors to start shifting their funds out of longer-maturity securities with the result that their interest rates will – other things being equal – also tend to rise along with the rises in the short-term rates. And so the entire spectrum of interest rates in the economy is affected by the RBA's actions.

Exhibit 16.6 **Open-market operations**

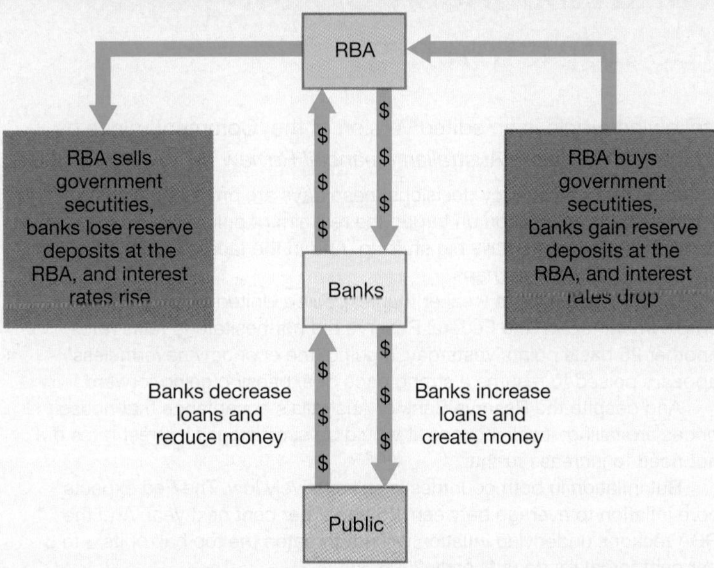

When the RBA buys government securities, it also increases the reserve deposits of the banks. The increase in monetary base lowers interest rates. Banks also use these extra reserve deposits to make loans, which operate through the money multiplier to expand the money supply. When the RBA sells government securities, it decreases the reserve deposits of the banks. The reduction in monetary base increases interest rates. The banks' capacity to lend also diminishes and, as a consequence, the money supply decreases.

The money supply curve when the RBA targets an interest rate

In the previous chapter you learned that it is the interaction of the demand and supply of money that determines interest rates. As you learned above, in implementing monetary policy today the cash rate is the interest rate that the RBA focuses on controlling at some desired target level. Just as with any market interest rate, the value of the cash rate is determined by the interaction of the demand and supply of the relevant funds.

Assume a downward-sloping money demand curve and imagine that money demand in financial markets is fluctuating, as it would be from period to period. You would represent this shifting demand by shifts (inward and outward) in the demand curve. In these circumstances, if the RBA is seeking to control the cash rate at some target level, what would be the effective shape of the money supply curve?

Analyse the issue

Error avoidance now the key to rates adjustments

Applicable concept: monetary policy implementation

The following article is an edited version of the 'Comment' piece by David Bassanese in the *Australian Financial Review* on 12 August 2004.

Although monetary policy decisions these days are often explained in terms of keeping inflation on target, the real aim of policy is probably far humbler – avoiding a really big stuff-up. And in the face of uncertainty, it's not such a bad aim, perhaps.

Despite last Friday's weaker than expected United States July employment report, the Federal Reserve did not hesitate to raise rates another 25 basis points yesterday, arguing 'the economy nevertheless appears poised to resume a strong pace of expansion going forward.'

And despite the Reserve Bank of Australia's acceptance that house prices are falling, it still reckons 'it would be surprising' if interest rates did not need to increase further.

But inflation in both countries is still relatively low. The Fed expects core inflation to average between 1.5 and 2 per cent next year. And the RBA reckons underlying inflation will not threaten the top half of its 2 to 3 per cent target range until early 2006.

So why the angst about raising interest rates?

It's not about targeting inflation per se, but rather applying decision-making theory in the face of long-run economic uncertainty.

Rather than trying to wring every bit of growth out of an economy subject to keeping inflation within target, central banks these days simply strive to minimise the chances of being caught out by a really big policy error.

It is really big errors that can cause recessions, and really big losses in output and employment.

US Fed funds and Australian cash rates: monthly, 1998–2004

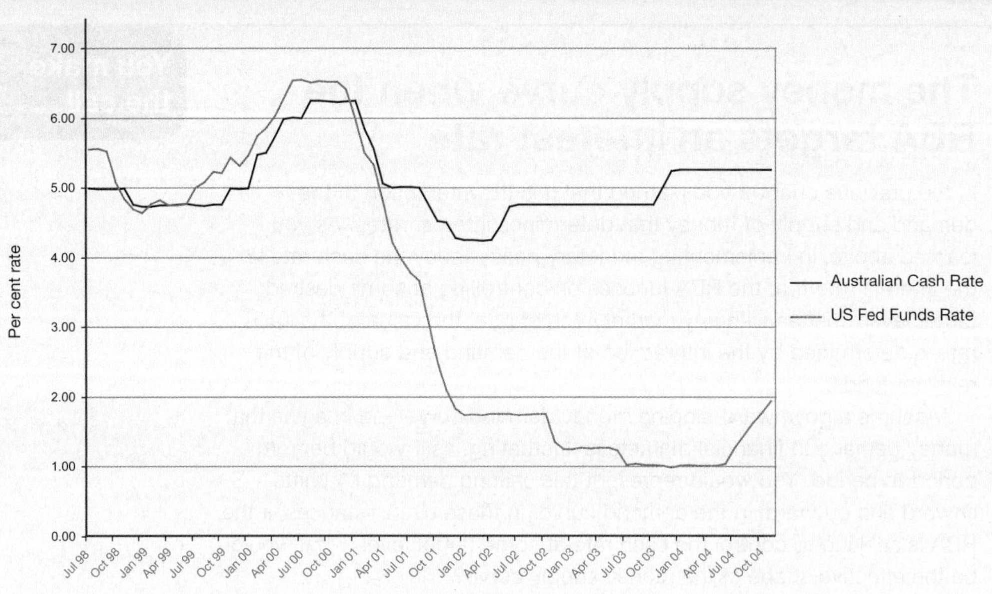

So when economies are operating normally (around average rates of economic growth), central banks reckon it's prudent to be moving interest rates closer to normal and keep them there. That way, policy has maximum leeway to respond to upside or downside economic shocks.

It's for this reason the Fed is 'reloading the cannon' by raising interest rates from near-record lows while the US economy is expanding briskly and best able to cope.

Similarly, having interest rates closer to 'normal' levels will reduce the chances of a normal economy overheating – and reduce the chances of a large, disorderly change in rates being required should it do so.

This seems to be driving RBA thinking at present – the economy is operating normally, but interest rates are still a touch below normal.

Discuss the writer's views in the context of monetary policy implementation and the chapter's discussion of the difficulties of countercyclical macroeconomic fine tuning.

Linking the RBA operation of monetary policy to the *AD–AS* framework

To link the above process back to the *AD–AS* framework you learned about in Chapter 14, consider Exhibit 16.7. Suppose that, prior to the RBA monetary policy tightening, the economy is represented by point *A*. The tightening is represented by an inward shift of the *AD* curve. Why? As mentioned above, in tightening, the RBA sells government securities to the private sector and thereby reduces the volume of nominal money supply.

Therefore, for any particular price level in the economy, the quantity of real money balances in supply will be reduced. This will increase interest rates in the economy, which will tend to reduce demand for investment and consumer durables. This reduced demand will have a ripple effect through the rest of the economy (remember the multiplier discussion in Chapter 14), producing a further reduction in aggregate demand. This overall reduction in *AD* is represented in the exhibit by the inward shift of the *AD* curve. With unchanged conditions on the supply side of the economy, the *AS* curve remains unchanged. The macroeconomic result of the RBA tightening therefore is represented by point *B* in the exhibit where demand, economic activity, production and the price level are all lower.

Note that, in reality, the price level is unlikely to actually drop (as implied in Exhibit 16.7 on p. 493) as a result of such a monetary tightening. What will happen is that the rate of increase in the price level (the rate of inflation) will fall back to an acceptable level (say, from +3 per cent to +2 per cent). The *AD–AS* analysis of Exhibit 16.7 nevertheless captures quite well the flavour of the economic adjustments involved.

PART 5

Economics and ethics

A noteworthy feature of monetary policy is that it may be regarded as quite a 'blunt' policy instrument. In this context, 'blunt' means that the policy instrument cannot be used to impact very narrowly on particular sections of the community or sectors of the economy. If interest rates are engineered up by the RBA because it is concerned about current and future inflation, the higher borrowing costs will impact equally on all who either have existing loans or who wish to take out new loans.

In particular, for those who have existing loans – and variable interest rate commitments – such interest rate rises can have very substantial impacts on their cash flows, causing some households to experience extreme hardships and some businesses perhaps to even go into bankruptcy. It could well be that many of those who experience financial stress may not in fact have contributed to whatever may have been the root causes of the inflationary circumstances that lead to the central bank's monetary tightening.

For example asset price booms, particularly if the price rises seem out of step with underlying economic fundamentals (and therefore are probably unsustainable) and if they lead to very large increases in aggregate debt levels in a community, can sometimes factor in a central bank's considerations in setting monetary policy.[1] To the extent that such developments may contribute to a particular monetary tightening, everyone will be affected by the higher interest rates irrespective of whether they were direct participants in the asset price boom. Thus, while it's not the case that any ethical considerations are at play in this case, some may well question the 'social justice' of such outcomes.

1 Such asset price booms can become a concern to a central bank for several reasons. If the associated wealth increases lead to increased aggregate demand and price rises for goods and services, eventually general inflation may be affected. Related to this, if the asset price rises turn out to be largely speculative and lead eventually to a correction, this can have very serious damaging effects on economic activity and employment. The central bank may consider it in the best interests of the community to act pre-emptively to stave off such an outcome. In practice most central banks, including the RBA, monitor such developments very carefully but are equally very careful and reticent about intervening in asset price booms.

Foreign exchange market operations

The floating of the Australian dollar in December 1983 has also had important implications for the conduct of monetary policy. Before Australia moved to the current system of floating exchange rates, any discrepancy between the demand and supply of $A for sale in the foreign exchange (FOREX) market had to be met by the RBA in order to maintain the foreign exchange value of the $A fixed.

Thus, if there was an excess supply of $A for sale the RBA would have to purchase the excess $A, selling some of its holdings of foreign exchange

Exhibit 16.7 A monetary policy tightening by the RBA

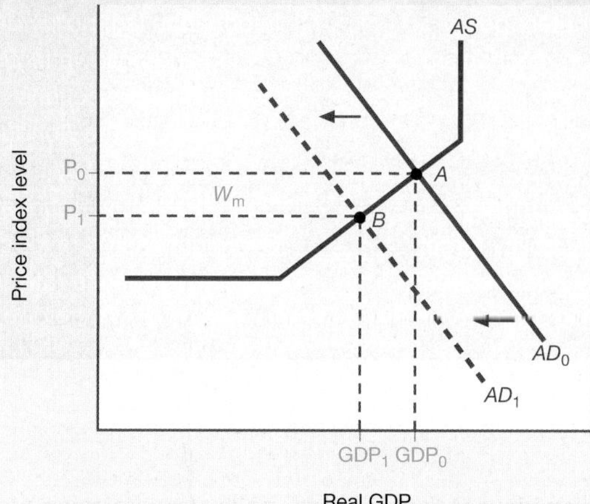

in return. This sale of RBA assets would reduce the liquidity of the financial system, since the monetary base would decline because the $A purchased by the RBA would no longer be available for use by the private sector. This tighter liquidity would have the further undesirable effect of tending to push up domestic interest rates and hinder economic growth.

To view recent exchange rates for the $A, go to the RBA website (**www.rba.gov.au**) and select *Statistics*, then *Statistics by Frequency of Publication*, then *Exchange Rates*.

Such action by the RBA is no longer necessary. Since Australia now does not maintain a fixed exchange rate, the RBA need not involve itself in the FOREX market to ensure that the demand and supply of the $A is equal at some predetermined price for the $A. Instead, Australia now has a **floating exchange rate**. With a floating exchange rate, if sellers of the $A cannot find buyers, they simply have to reduce the price of the $A until buyers are forthcoming. Of course, the RBA still regularly operates in the market if it considers the $A is coming under undue short-run speculative pressure or if FOREX market conditions are excessively volatile. The latter activity is termed 'smoothing' while the former is referred to as 'testing'.

Floating exchange rate In a floating exchange rate, market demand and supply determine the foreign price of the currency. If sellers of the $A cannot find buyers they have to reduce the price of the $A until buyers are forthcoming.

'**Smoothing**' operations by the RBA are intended to be only very short-term, sometimes over the course of a day and rarely for more than a few days. '**Testing**' by the RBA, also referred to as 'leaning against the wind', is intended to test the market's resolve in moving away from what the RBA might consider to be the current equilibrium value for the $A. However, given sustained market pressure to shift the exchange rate, the RBA will (by necessity) follow the market.

Smoothing and **testing** Even though Australia now allows its exchange rate to float, the RBA still regularly operates in the market if it considers the $A is coming under undue short-run speculative pressure or if FOREX market conditions are excessively volatile. The latter activity is termed 'smoothing' while the former is referred to as 'testing'.

When the value of the $A reached historic lows against the $US in early 2001 (as low as $US0.47) the RBA considered the fundamentals of the Australian economy to be such that it was oversold. On several occasions, therefore, it entered the FOREX market to buy $A to lend support to it. As it turned out, by mid-2001 it had returned to around $US0.52. By late 2003 it had rebounded very strongly to $US0.80 before retracing to under $US0.70 in the first half of 2004. At the time of writing it was around $US0.75.

floating exchange rate

Key concepts

Keynesian monetary policy transmission mechanism
Monetarism
Equation of exchange
Velocity of money
Quantity theory of money
RBA's monetary policy target
Countercyclical macroeconomic policy
Information lag, policy determination lag and policy effectiveness lag
Conditional projections
Statement on the Conduct of Monetary Policy
Open-market operations
Overnight cash rate (or cash rate)
Floating exchange rate

Summary

- The **Keynesian view of the monetary policy transmission mechanism** operates as follows. First, the central bank uses its policy tools to change the money supply and equilibrium interest rates. These in turn affect investment (and consumer durable) spending. Finally, the change in investment shifts aggregate demand and influences the price level, real GDP and employment.

- **Monetarism** is the view that changes in monetary policy not only influence interest rates and thereby investment demand, but also have more direct effects on aggregate demand and thereby prices, real GDP and employment. Monetarists focus more on the money supply itself than on rates of interest.

- The **equation of exchange** is an accounting identity. The equation $MV = PQ$ states that the money supply multiplied by the velocity of money (V) is equal to the price level multiplied by real output. The **velocity of money** is the number of times each dollar is spent during a year. Keynesians view velocity as volatile and unstable both in the short run and the longer term. Monetarists believe that, over the longer term, V is stable and predictable.

- The **quantity theory of money** is a classical economics argument that the velocity of money (V) and the output (Q) variables in the equation of exchange are relatively constant. Given this assumption, changes in the money supply yield proportionate changes in the price level.

- **Countercyclical macroeconomic policy** has the aim of smoothing out fluctuations in the business cycle.

- Monetarists believe countercyclical macroeconomic policy may actually unintentionally make the business cycle worse rather than less pronounced on account of three policy lags. The **information lag** arises because information about the current phase of economic activity in the real world becomes available only after a lag of some months. The time taken to decide on an apparently appropriate policy response may amount to several months and is known as the **policy determination lag**. Once a policy is initiated, there will be a further lag before it takes effect on economic activity. This lag is referred to as the **policy effectiveness lag**. For these reasons monetarists advocate a **rules-based** approach to monetary policy rather than the **discretionary approach** favoured by Keynesians.

- The implementation of monetary policy in Australia during 1976–85 consisted of a form of monetary targeting. Each year a '**conditional projection**' for the growth of the monetary aggregate, M3, was announced in the Federal Budget by the Treasurer. The projections were conditional in the sense that, if world or domestic economic conditions changed unexpectedly, the government allowed itself the room to vary the targets over the course of the year.

- The **overnight cash rate** (or 'cash rate' for short) is the interest rate that borrowers in the money markets must pay to borrow funds overnight. Its value influences all other interest rates in the money markets and thereby it influences all interest rates throughout the entire economy. It is by this influence on the interest rates in the wider economy that the RBA can affect aggregate demand and influence the rate of inflation.

- The **Statement on the Conduct of Monetary Policy** was signed by the RBA Governor and the Federal Treasurer in 1996. It encapsulates the Australian government's agreement that the RBA should have the goal of holding inflation on average to between 2 and 3 per cent per annum and that the RBA be free to implement monetary policy as it sees fit to achieve that goal.

- To influence the cash rate the RBA carries out **open-market operations** in the private-sector money markets to alter the supply of primary liquidity available to the financial system. Open-market operations consist of the RBA buying and selling commonwealth government securities in the private-sector money markets.

Open-market operations

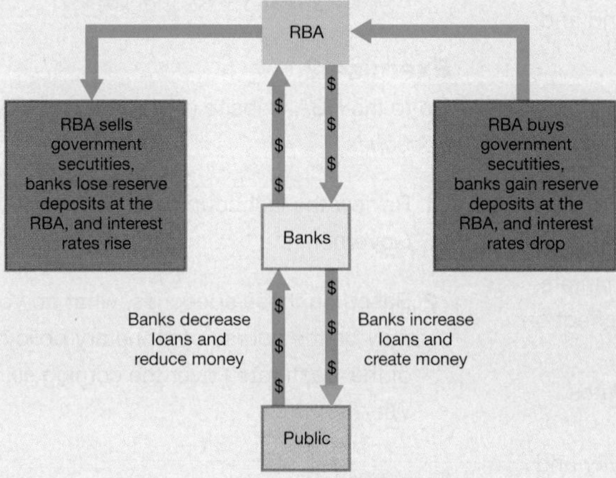

- With a **floating exchange rate**, demand and supply determine the foreign price of the currency. If sellers of the $A cannot find buyers they simply have to reduce the price of the $A until buyers are forthcoming.

- Even though Australia now allows its exchange rate to float, the RBA still regularly operates in the market if it considers the $A is coming under undue short-run speculative pressure or if FOREX market conditions are excessively volatile. The latter activity is termed '**smoothing**' while the former is referred to as '**testing**'.

Study questions and problems

1 Using diagrams analogous to those in Exhibit 15.5 in Chapter 15, trace out the likely effects of a decision by the RBA to sell commonwealth government securities to the money market.

2 What is the equation of exchange and what does each term in the equation represent?

3 A sewerage investigator might say that the sewer flow of 8000 litres an hour consisted of an average of 400 litres in the sewer at any one time, with a complete turnover of the water 20 times every hour. Interpret this statement using the equation of exchange.

4 Explain the difference between the Keynesian and monetarist views on how an increase in the money supply causes inflation.

5 Based on the simple quantity theory of money, what would be the impact of increasing the money supply by 25 per cent?

6 Suppose the investment demand curve is almost a vertical line (refer to Exhibit 15.5). Given this condition, would the Keynesian or the monetarist view of the impact of monetary policy on investment spending, aggregate demand and economic activity be more correct?

7 Why is the shape of the aggregate supply curve important to the Keynesian–monetarist controversy?

8 If the RBA bought $100 million of government securities from private-sector money markets, other things equal, what would be the effect on:
   a the economy's monetary base.
   b short-term money market interest rates.
   c longer maturity interest rates.
   d aggregate demand, economic activity and inflation.

9 For Question 8, answer **a–d** if Westpac bought the $100 million government securities from Macquarie Bank because it needed to cover its minimum liquidity requirements. The RBA was not involved in this transaction.

10 What, if anything, happens to the economy's monetary base if the RBA buys $100 million in foreign currency from the ANZ Bank? Explain.

11 In Exhibit 16.2 the money supply curve, *MS*, was drawn as vertical. Imagine that the money demand curve was shifting around due to fluctuating financial market demand for funds. What do you think would be the shape of the money supply curve if the RBA targeted a particular level of interest rates rather than set the volume of money supply at a particular level? Explain.

Online exercises

Exercise 1

To see how the RBA implements monetary policy, go to the RBA website (**www.rba.gov.au**) and select **Education**.

1 Open and read the document 'Monetary Policy'.

2 Determine the different values of the 'cash rate' over the last three years.

3 What do you conclude about changes in monetary policy over that period?

Exercise 2

Go to the RBA website (**www.rba.gov.au**) and select *Speeches*.

1 Review the last couple of speeches by the RBA Governor.

2 Based on these speeches, what do you think may be the course of monetary policy (the course of the 'cash rate') over the coming six months? Why?

Exercise 3

In the United States, the central bank is called the Fed and monetary policy is determined by the Fed's Open Market Committee. Experience a Fed OMC meeting through a simulation created by the New York Fed. Visit the NY Fed website at **www.ny.frb.org** and search for **FOMC Simulation**.

PART 5

Answers to 'You make the call'

A horse of which colour?

The famous economist was Milton Friedman, who favoured a monetary rule for the Fed. The story of the horse is a sarcastic way of rejecting Keynesian activist policies that destabilise the economy. Friedman has even argued that the Board of Governors of the Federal Reserve System should announce the growth rate for the money supply each year and should resign if the target is missed. If you said this famous economist is a monetarist, YOU ARE CORRECT.

The money supply curve when the RBA targets an interest rate

When the RBA targets a particular value for the cash rate, it must adjust the supply of liquidity to the money markets in such a way as to equate the supply to whatever is the particular demand for liquidity at the desired target value for the cash rate. Consider Exhibit 16.8. Suppose the RBA wants to keep the cash rate at 10 per cent and demand is represented by MD_1. The RBA would therefore need to ensure it supplied $30 billion of funds to the money markets to bring about a cash rate of 10 per cent. Now suppose that for some reason money market demand increased, represented in the exhibit as a shift from MD_1 to MD_2. If there were no increase in the supply, there would be pressure for the cash rate to increase. To offset this pressure, the RBA would therefore need to respond to this increase in demand by increasing the available supply of liquidity to the money markets from $30 to $40 billion.

Exhibit 16.8

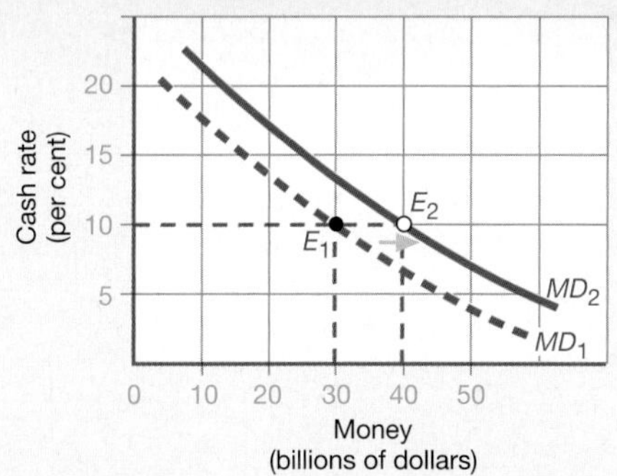

Effectively, then, the RBA has to supply whatever funds are demanded by the markets at the desired cash rate of 10 per cent. If you said that when the RBA targets the cash rate the money supply curve must be horizontal at the targeted rate, YOU ARE CORRECT.

Multiple-choice questions

1 Keynes gave which of the following as a motive for people holding money?

- **a** transactions motive.
- **b** speculative motive.
- **c** precautionary motive.
- **d** all of the above.

2 A decrease in the interest rate, other things being equal, causes

- **a** an upward movement along the demand curve for money.
- **b** a downward movement along the demand curve for money.
- **c** a rightward shift of the demand curve for money.
- **d** a leftward shift of the demand curve for money.

3 Assume the demand for money curve is stationary and the RBA increases the money supply. The result is that people

- **a** increase the supply of bonds, thus driving up the interest rate.
- **b** increase the supply of bonds, thus driving down the interest rate.
- **c** increase the demand for bonds, thus driving up the interest rate.
- **d** increase the demand for bonds, thus driving down the interest rate.

4 Assume the demand for money curve is fixed and the RBA decreases the money supply. The result is a temporary

- **a** excess quantity of money demanded.
- **b** excess quantity of money supplied.
- **c** increase in the price of bonds.
- **d** increase in the demand for bonds.

5 Assume the demand for money curve is fixed and the RBA increases the money supply. The result is that

- **a** the price of bonds rises.

b the price of bonds remains unchanged.
c the price of bonds falls.
d none of the above occurs.

6 Using the aggregate supply and demand model, assume the economy is in equilibrium on the intermediate portion of the aggregate supply curve. A decrease in the money supply will decrease the price level and
a lower both the interest rate and real GDP.
b raise both the interest rate and real GDP.
c lower the interest rate and raise real GDP.
d raise the interest rate and lower real GDP.

7 Based on the equation of exchange, the money supply in the economy is calculated as
a $M = V/PQ$.
b $M = V(PQ)$.
c $M = PQ/V$.
d $M = PQ - V$.

8 The *V* in the equation of exchange represents the
a variation in the GDP.
b variation in the CPI.
c variation in real GDP.
d average number of times per year a dollar is spent on final goods and services.

Macroeconomic policy II: fiscal policy

17

In Australia in the early 1990s the federal government increased government expenditures relative to revenue in a bid to expand aggregate demand. Its objective was to boost national output and employment in order to assist in ending the recession of 1990–91. This also occurred in late 2000 and into 2001, when the economy began to experience an economic growth slowdown in the wake of the introduction of Australia's new goods and services tax (GST) and with the prospect of an international economic slowdown.

During the Australian federal election year of 2001 both sides of politics made promises about assisting Australia's near-term and long-term economic growth prospects by boosting government spending and making adjustments to various taxes. The spending program included such areas as education, health and much-needed enhancements to the nation's physical infrastructure such as roads, rail, ports, bridges and telecommunications networks. Taxation promises ranged from cuts to personal income taxes through to adjustments to the range of products attracting GST. Another raft of spending promises was made by both the Coalition and Labor in the lead up to the October 2004 federal election.

Fiscal policy The use of government spending and taxes to influence the nation's output, employment and price level.

A major issue then that touches everyone's life is **fiscal policy**. Fiscal policy is the use of government spending and taxes to influence the nation's output, employment and price level. Federal government spending policies potentially affect all areas of the economy and the community more generally. Government spending initiatives directly affect specific sectors of the economy but also have indirect flow-on effects into other sectors. Changes to social welfare provisions directly affect welfare recipients, but also again have flow-on effects to others in the community via changes to the spending levels of such recipients. Changes in tax policies can change the amount of all of our pay packets and therefore directly influence our spending and saving decisions.

Using fiscal policy to influence the performance of the economy has been an important idea since the Great Depression of the 1930s. This chapter looks at fiscal policy from the perspective of two opposing economic viewpoints. First, you will study Keynesian demand-side fiscal policies that 'fine tune' aggregate demand so the economy achieves full employment, albeit possibly with a higher price level. Second, you will study supply-side fiscal policy, which gained prominence during the early 1980s. Supply-siders view aggregate supply as far more important than aggregate demand. Their fiscal policy prescription is to adjust policies to increase aggregate supply so the economy grows and achieves full employment with a lower price level.

In addition, you will learn how and why the government might run a budget deficit, its macroeconomic importance, how it can be financed, the impact the deficit may have on a country's national debt and whether and when such increases in national debt can prove a problem.

In this chapter, you will examine these economics questions:

- Does an increase in government spending or a tax cut of equal amount give the greater stimulus to economic activity?
- Can the government fight a recession without taking any action?
- Why might it be possible to increase tax revenues by cutting taxes?
- How can the government spend more than it raises in revenues without having to increase its borrowing from the public?
- Why might the 'burden' of the national debt not really be a burden at all?
- What does 'crowding out' mean in macroeconomics?

Discretionary fiscal policy

Here we begin where Chapter 14 left off – that is, discussing the use of **discretionary fiscal policy**, as Keynes advocated, to influence the economy's performance. Discretionary fiscal policy is defined as the deliberate use of changes in government spending and/or taxes to alter aggregate demand in an attempt to stabilise the economy in some desirable way. As you will see later, the national government's approach to fiscal policy is enunciated each year in the federal government's annual budget.

Discretionary fiscal policy
The deliberate use of changes in government spending and/or taxes to alter aggregate demand and stabilise the economy's business cycle.

INFOTRAC®
discretionary fiscal policy

Exhibit 17.1 lists two basic types of discretionary fiscal policies and some of the corresponding ways in which the government can pursue each of these options. The first column of the table shows that the government can choose to increase aggregate demand by following an *expansionary* fiscal policy. The second column lists *contractionary* fiscal policy options the government can use to restrain aggregate demand.

Exhibit 17.1 Discretionary fiscal policies

Expansionary fiscal policy	Contractionary fiscal policy
Increase government spending	Decrease government spending
Decrease taxes	Increase taxes
Increase government spending and also decrease taxes	Decrease government spending and also increase taxes
Increase government spending and *increase* taxes equally*	Decrease government spending and *decrease* taxes equally*

*This last alternative relates to the 'balanced budget multiplier' discussion in the text.

PART 5

Increasing government spending to combat a recession

Suppose the economy represented in Exhibit 17.2 has fallen into recession at equilibrium point E_1, where aggregate demand curve AD_1 intersects the aggregate supply curve AS in the near-full-employment range. (Note that for simplicity the aggregate demand and aggregate supply curves are drawn here as straight lines.) The price level measured by the CPI is 150 and the real GDP gap happens to be $20 billion below the full-employment output of $520 billion real GDP. As explained in Chapter 14, one approach on the part of the authorities is provided by classical theory: namely, do nothing and wait until the economy self-corrects to full employment by adjustments in AS and AD – as a result of price and wage adjustments – so that equilibrium is re-established at the full-employment level of output. Alternatively, policy makers may instead elect to follow Keynesian economics and act to try to

Exhibit 17.2 **Using government spending to combat a recession**

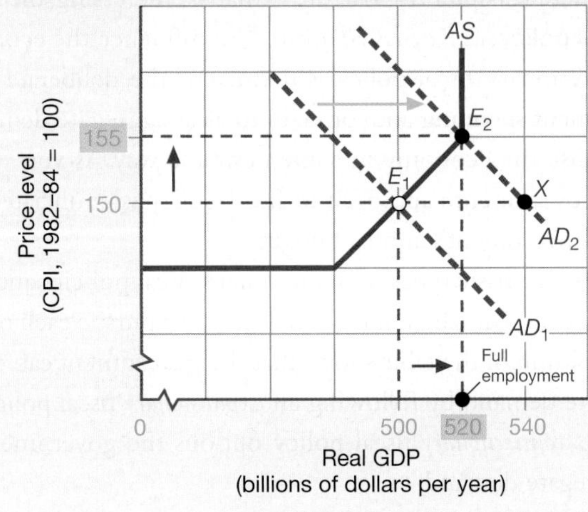

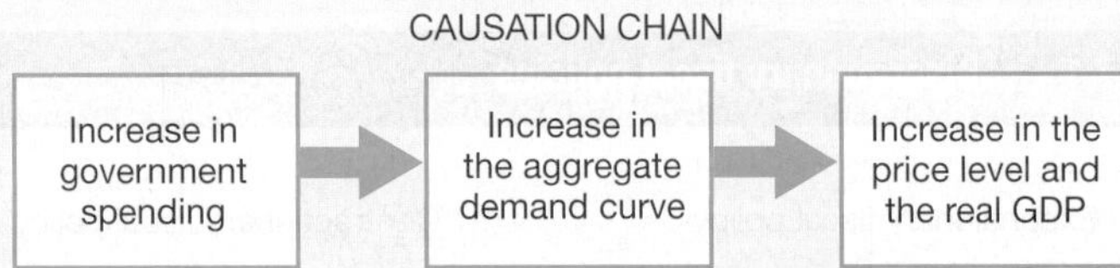

The economy in this exhibit is in recession at equilibrium point E_1 on the intermediate range of the aggregate supply curve, *AS*. The price level is 150, with an output level of $500 billion real GDP. To reach the full-employment output of $520 billion in real GDP, the aggregate demand curve must be shifted to the right by $40 billion real GDP, measured by the horizontal distance between point E_1 on curve AD_1 and point *X* on curve AD_2. The necessary increase in aggregate demand from AD_1 to AD_2 can be accomplished by increased government spending. Given a spending multiplier of 4, a $10 billion increase in government spending brings about the required $40 billion rightward shift in the aggregate demand curve and equilibrium in the economy changes from E_1 to E_2. Note that the equilibrium real GDP changes by $20 billion and not the full amount by which the aggregate demand curve shifts horizontally.

Information on Australia's economic growth, inflation and unemployment can be obtained from the ABS (**www.abs.gov.au**) or the RBA (**www.rba.gov.au**).

shift the aggregate demand curve rightward from AD_1 to AD_2, thereby bringing about an end to the recession but in the process also producing a higher price level.

How can the government do this? Remember that, in theory, any increase in private-sector demand, namely consumption (*C*), investment (*I*) or net exports (*X* – *M*), can spur aggregate demand. But these spending boosts are not directly under the government's control, whereas government spending (*G*) is. After all, there is always a long wish list of spending proposals for national, state and local roads, health care, education, other transport infrastructure, environmental programs and so on. Therefore, rather than waiting for the private sector to increase its demand for and production of consumption and investment goods and services, suppose the government chooses to increase government spending to boost employment in the short term.

But just how much new government spending is required? Suppose the government increases its spending on transport infrastructure by $10 billion. How much will aggregate demand increase as a result? The answer is by considerably more than the initial $10 billion! This is through the action of the spending multiplier. (If you need to, refer back to Chapter 14 for details.) However, in brief, the initial spending by the government is amplified as some of it is in turn spent by those receiving the money as income and some of that money spent again by those who received it as income from the second induced spending round and so on.

The original spending causes a ripple effect throughout the entire economy. The extent of the ripples depends on the marginal propensity to consume (MPC) of the recipients of the income. In the exhibit it is assumed that the MPC is 0.75 which, as will be shown below, implies a spending multiplier of four. Thus, the *AD* curve is depicted as shifting out horizontally by $40 billion (and not by the initial increase in spending of $10 billion by the government).

Why does an MPC of 0.75 imply a multiplier of 4? Consider $1 of initial spending. This will give rise to an induced second round of spending of $0.75 (with the other $0.25 saved). This second round of spending will give rise to a third round of spending of $0.56 (0.75 × 0.75), a fourth round of spending of $0.42 (0.56 × 0.75), a fifth round of spending of $0.32 (0.42 × 0.75) and so on. Each round the induced spending gets smaller. Total spending will eventually be 1 + 0.75 + 0.56 + 0.42 + 0.32 + … . After a very large number of spending rounds, the induced spending in the next round will be almost zero and subsequent spending could be ignored. After such a large number of spending rounds the resulting sum will be approximately 4, meaning the MPC of 0.75 results in a spending multiplier of 4.[1]

Rather than write down all the spending rounds until further induced spending gets very small, a much quicker way of calculating a spending multiplier from a given MPC is to recognise that the above sum converges in the limit to 1/(1 – MPC). Thus, for an MPC of 0.75 the multiplier would be 1/(1 – 0.75), which equals 4. With a larger MPC – meaning a greater proportion of any income received is spent – each round of induced spending will be greater and so the multiplier will be larger. For example, for an MPC of 0.8, the multiplier would be 5, while for an MPC of 0.50 the multiplier would be 2.

Now, as described in Chapter 14, bottlenecks, labour shortages and diminishing returns to labour productivity occur throughout the upward-sloping range of the *AS* curve. This means that costs of production rise as production increases in response to the greater aggregate demand. In times of buoyant demand these cost increases are likely to be passed on as higher prices. Returning to Exhibit 17.2, you can see that $10 billion worth of new government spending shifts aggregate demand from AD_1 to AD_2. As a

1 The spending multiplier discussion in this chapter abstracts from the issue of taxes and so the calculated multipliers make no allowance for tax rates.

result, the equilibrium in the economy changes from point E_1 to point E_2 and full employment is achieved. In the process, the economy experiences *demand-pull inflation* (refer back to Chapter 14) and the CPI rises from 150 to 155. Note that, although the aggregate demand curve shifted to the right by $40 billion, total output rose by only $20 billion between points E_1 and E_2. The other effect of the extra aggregate demand was to raise prices in the economy.

In the intermediate segment of the aggregate supply curve, the equilibrium real GDP changes by less than the change in government spending times the spending multiplier.

Calculating the size of the spending multiplier

Suppose the MPC for a community is 0.6 and suppose there is an initial stimulus to spending of $100 million. Calculate the total stimulus to spending after five rounds of induced spending. Now calculate the total spending stimulus after eight and then twelve rounds of induced spending.

What does the total spending stimulus appear to be approaching? What do you conclude about the size of the spending multiplier in this case?

PART 5

Visit the Melbourne Institute (**www.ecom.unimelb.edu.au**) and the National Bureau of Economic Research (**www.nber.org/cycles.html**) for a history of Australian and US business cycles.

Cutting taxes to combat a recession

Another type of expansionary fiscal policy intended to increase aggregate demand and restore full employment calls for the government to cut taxes. Let's return to point E_1 in Exhibit 17.2. As before, the task is to shift the aggregate demand curve to the right. But this time, instead of a $10 billion increase in government spending, assume parliament votes a $10 billion tax cut. How does this cut in taxes affect aggregate demand? First, *personal disposable income* (take-home pay) increases by $10 billion – the amount of the tax reduction. Second, once again, assuming the MPC is 0.75, the increase in personal disposable income induces new consumption spending of $7.5 billion (0.75 × $10 billion).

Notice that the initial stimulus of $7.5 billion to aggregate demand here is less than the $10 billion cut in taxes. The reason is that some of the tax cut will be saved rather than spent. After this initial round of new consumption spending of $7.5 billion, the spending multiplier process as described above and in Chapter 14 will again produce further rounds of spending. However, because the initial stimulus is less than before ($7.5 billion versus $10 billion), an important thing to note here is that the tax cut produces a smaller overall increase in aggregate demand than does the impact of the same-sized increase in government spending. In this case, with an MPC of 0.75, the total stimulus from the $10 billion tax cut will be $30 billion (4 ×

$7.5 billion) and this would be represented by an outward horizontal shift of the *AD* schedule by $30 billion.

In passing, it is worth pointing out that the same is true in principle of an increase in welfare payments, since the recipients can be expected to save some portion of their payment. Again, say their MPC is 0.75, and the government increases welfare payments by $10 billion. Their spending would thus increase by $7.5 billion only and the final stimulus to overall aggregate demand would therefore again be $30 billion, rather than the $40 billion resulting from increased government spending of $10 billion.

A warning about the above analysis: first, in reality, different income groups will have different MPCs and so the actual spending impact of cuts in taxes will depend very much on where they are targeted. It is also highly likely that, as far as welfare payments are concerned, their recipients are almost certain to have a higher MPC than others in the community. Also, it is likely that the MPC for any group over time may change and so the spending impact of any given change in tax policy may be quite difficult to predict. If people – for one reason or another – decide to save much of any given tax cut rather than spending it, then the hoped-for impact on aggregate demand may be very much reduced.

Calculating the required tax cut

Suppose you are an economic adviser in the Federal Treasury and you believe the economy needs a real GDP increase of $20 billion to reach full-employment equilibrium. If the marginal propensity to consume (MPC) is 0.80 and you are a Keynesian, by how much do you believe the government must cut taxes in order to restore the economy to full employment?

Using fiscal policy to combat inflation

So far, Keynesian expansionary fiscal policy, born of the Great Depression, has been presented as the cure for an economic downturn. Contractionary fiscal policy, on the other hand, can assist in the fight against inflation, particularly demand-pull inflation. Exhibit 17.3 shows an economy operating at point E_1 on the classical range of the aggregate supply curve, *AS*. This economy is producing the full-employment output of $520 billion real GDP and the price level is 160. In this situation, any increase in aggregate demand only causes inflation, while real GDP remains unchanged.

Suppose the government decides to use fiscal policy to reduce the CPI from 160 to 155 because it wants to reduce the rate of inflation in the economy. One possible way of doing this is by cutting government spending. Given a marginal propensity to consume of 0.75, the spending multiplier is 4. Cutting government spending by $5 billion will therefore reduce aggregate demand by $20 billion (4 × $5 billion). As shown in Exhibit 17.3, such a reduction in *AD* (note that the horizontal distance between point E_1 on

AD_1 and point E' on AD_2 is \$20 billion) from AD_1 to AD_2 is enough to establish equilibrium at E_2, with a price level of 155.

What is happening here is that the \$5 billion cut in government spending produces a total decrease in the aggregate demand curve of \$20 billion (from AD_1 to AD_2). The result is a temporary excess aggregate supply of \$20 billion, measured by the distance from E' to E_1. This excess supply creates pressure on firms to reduce prices and so inflation consequently cools, with the final new equilibrium being E_2.

The level of the CPI would rarely drop in real-world modern economies. In a real-life situation the government might want to reduce the CPI rate of growth – that is, reduce the inflation rate from, say, 5 per cent back down

Exhibit 17.3 Using fiscal policy to combat inflation

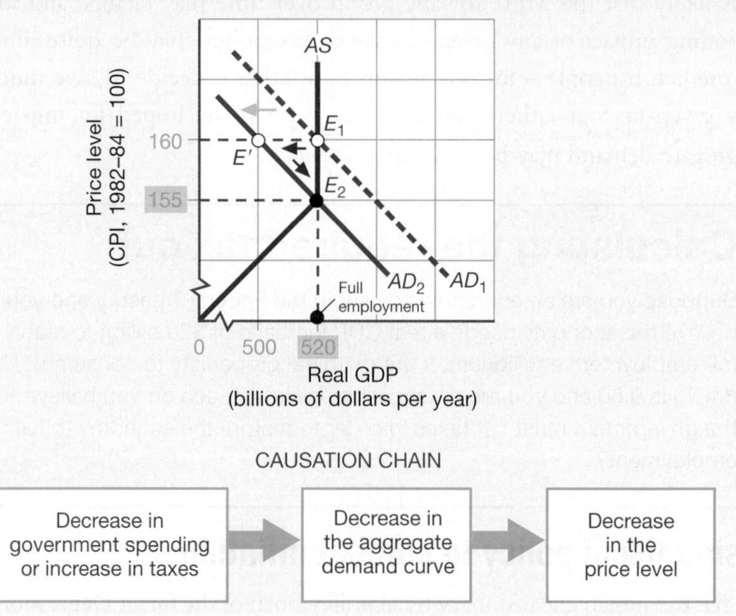

The economy in this exhibit is in equilibrium at point E_1 on the classical range of the aggregate supply curve, *AS*. The price level is 160 and the economy is operating at the full-employment output of \$520 billion real GDP. To reduce the price level to 155, the aggregate demand curve must be shifted to the left by \$20 billion, measured by the horizontal distance between point E_1 on curve AD_1 and point E on curve AD_2. One way this can be done is by decreasing government spending. With MPC equal to 0.75 and therefore a spending multiplier of 4, a \$5 billion decrease in government spending results in the needed \$20 billion leftward shift in the aggregate demand curve. As a result, equilibrium in the economy reaches point E_2 and the price level falls from 160 to 155, while real output remains unchanged at full capacity.

An identical decrease in the aggregate demand curve can be obtained by a hike in taxes. A \$6.67 billion tax increase would reduce disposable income by this amount and, with an MPC of 0.75, would result in an initial reduction in spending of \$5 billion and thereby, through the spending multiplier (of 4 with an MPC of 0.75), work to bring about the needed \$20 billion decrease in the aggregate demand curve from AD_1 to AD_2.

to, say, 3 per cent. As you learned in the previous chapter, one way to try to accomplish this would be for the central bank to tighten monetary policy. An alternative approach would be to use fiscal policy as just described. The essential mechanism is as above but the outcome, if successful, would be a reduction in the rate of inflation rather than an absolute reduction in the CPI level.

Another approach to the inflation problem would be for the government to raise taxes (a brave move!). Although this approach is often considered political suicide, let's calculate the amount of the tax hike required to reduce aggregate demand by $20 billion. To see this, think about how much the government would need to cut taxes if it were trying to increase aggregate demand by $20 billion! The amount we calculate will also be the same amount by which the government would need to raise taxes to reduce demand by the same amount.

With a spending multiplier of 4 we know that an initial increase in spending of $5 billion will produce an increase in aggregate demand of $20 billion. In order to bring about an initial spending increase of $5 billion, the government would need to reduce taxes by $6.67 billion if the MPC was 0.75 ($5 billion = 0.75 × $6.67 billion). In other words, if disposable income were to rise by $6.67 billion, people would only spend 75 per cent of this amount, namely $5 billion. Alternatively, if the government wanted to *reduce* *AD* by $20 billion, taxes would need to be *raised* by $6.67 billion.

Although theoretically fiscal policy could be used to try to curb an inflationary situation as illustrated in Exhibit 17.3, in reality the job of trying to control inflation these days falls to the country's central bank and its appropriate use of monetary policy.

PART 5

The balanced budget multiplier

The analysis of Keynesian discretionary fiscal policy presented in the previous section supposes that the federal government selects a change in *either* government spending or taxes as a remedy for recession or inflation. However, one approach to fiscal policy that gained support during the 1980s and 1990s is the idea that the government be required to match or 'balance' any new spending with new taxes; in other words, a requirement that new spending initiatives should have – in the first instance – a neutral effect on government finances. The proponents of this type of approach argue that it represents a more prudent way of financing government.

balanced budget multiplier

Understanding the impact on the economy of this type of fiscal policy requires consideration of the so-called **balanced budget multiplier**. In the discussion so far we have seen that, for a change in either taxes or government spending, the size of the spending multiplier depends on the size of the MPC. What would be the size of the multiplier if a spending increase by government was at the same time exactly offset by an increase in taxes? It turns out that the multiplier in this instance – the so-called balanced

Balanced budget multiplier
An equal change in government spending and taxes, which changes aggregate demand by the amount of the change in government spending.

budget multiplier – is one! This means that, for a simultaneous equal change in government spending and taxes, the overall final impact on aggregate demand will be equal to the amount of the initial change in government spending. In other words, the overall spending multiplier of these fiscal policy actions is one. Furthermore, this will be the case irrespective of the MPC of the community.

To see how the balanced budget multiplier works, suppose the government enacts a $1 billion increase in government spending for highways and simultaneously finances this spending with a $1 billion increase in petrol excise taxes. Let's look at what the impact of this will be on the economy. As outlined above, with an MPC of 0.75, the $1 billion increase in direct government spending will, with a spending multiplier of 4, generate an overall increase in aggregate demand of $4 billion.

The increase in petrol tax will reduce disposable income by $1 billion. However, given that some (25 per cent) of this income would have been saved had it not been taxed away, means that the direct reduction in consumption spending will only be $0.75 billion. Again, this initial spending reduction of $0.75 billion will have a multiplied impact on overall demand and, given the same spending multiplier of 4, will result in a reduction in aggregate demand of $3 billion. Thus, the net addition to total aggregate demand of this balanced budget increase in government spending is just $1 billion ($4 billion – $3 billion).

Notice that the discussion in the previous two paragraphs would still have produced exactly the same outcome if the MPC had instead been 0.8 or 0.6, or anything else for that matter. In other words, the balanced budget multiplier is always equal to one and the cumulative change in aggregate demand is always the amount of the initial change in government spending.

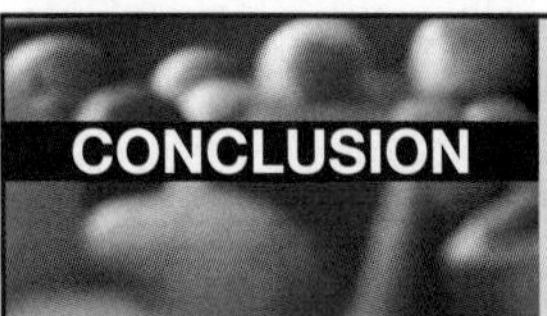

Regardless of the MPC, the net effect on the economy of an equal initial increase (decrease) in government spending and taxes is an increase (decrease) in aggregate demand equal to the initial increase (decrease) in government spending.

Automatic stabilisers

Automatic stabilisers Federal expenditures and tax revenues that automatically change over the course of the business cycle in such a way as to help stabilise an economic expansion or contraction.

Unlike discretionary fiscal policy, **automatic stabilisers** are mechanisms built into the federal budget that automatically help fight unemployment and inflation without there being any need to alter spending and tax laws. Automatic stabilisers are federal expenditures and tax revenues that automatically change over the course of the business cycle in such a way as to help stabilise an economic expansion or contraction.

Exhibit 17.4 illustrates the influence of automatic stabilisers on the economy. The downward-sloping line *G* represents federal government expenditures, including such *transfer payments* as unemployment benefits and other forms of social welfare payments. This line falls as real GDP rises. To understand this, consider that when the economy expands, unemployment for example falls and government spending on unemployment benefits therefore also falls. During a downturn, people lose their jobs and government spending automatically increases because unemployed individuals become eligible for unemployment benefits and other transfer payments. The direct relationship between tax revenues and GDP is shown by the upward-sloping line *T*. During an expansion, jobs are created, unemployment falls, workers and companies earn more income and therefore pay more taxes. Thus, income tax collections automatically vary directly with the growth in real GDP.

We will illustrate the importance of automatic stabilisers by looking at a case in which the federal budget is initially in balance. Federal spending, *G*, is equal to tax collection, *T*, and the economy is in equilibrium at $500 billion GDP. Now assume consumer optimism soars and a spending spree

Exhibit 17.4 Automatic stabilisers

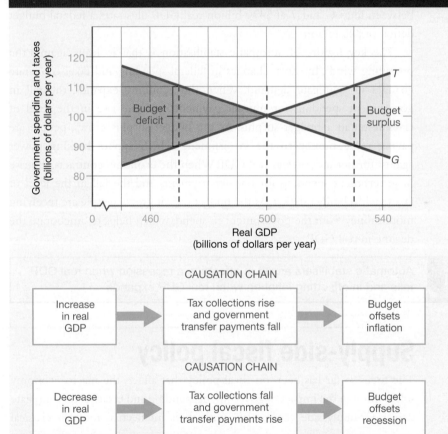

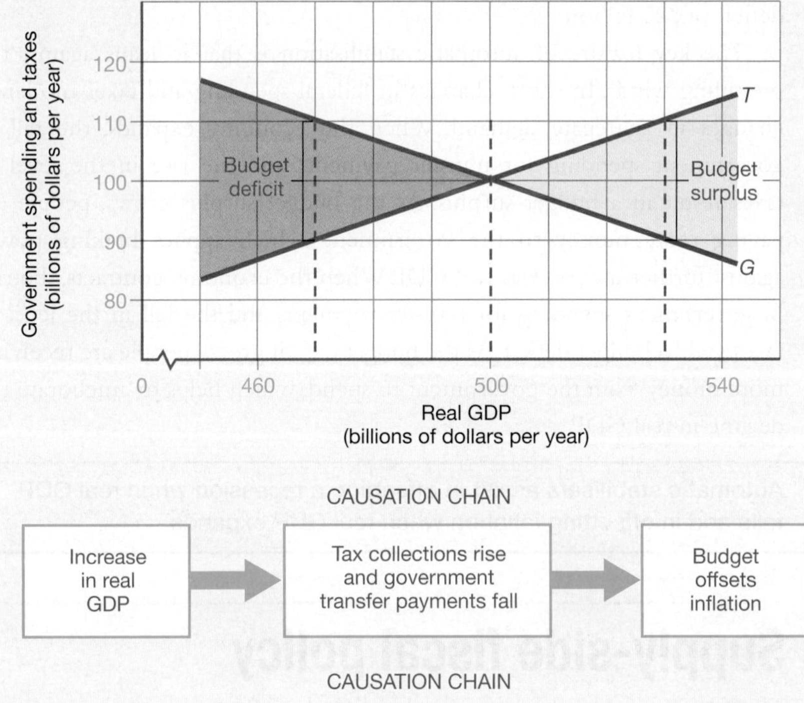

Federal government spending is represented by the downward-sloping line *G*. Taxes, on the other hand, vary directly with real GDP. This means government spending for welfare and other transfer payments declines as real GDP rises. Thus, if the real GDP falls below $500 billion, the budget deficit rises automatically. The size of the budget deficit is shown by the vertical distance between lines *G* and *T*. This budget deficit assists in offsetting a recession because it stimulates aggregate demand. Conversely, when the real GDP rises above $500 billion, a federal budget surplus increases automatically and assists in offsetting inflation.

increases the consumption component (*C*) of total spending. As a result, the economy moves to a new equilibrium at $530 billion GDP. The rise in GDP creates more jobs and generates higher tax collections. Consequently, taxes rise to $110 billion on line *T* and the vertical distance between lines *T* and *G* represents a federal **budget surplus** of $20 billion. A budget surplus occurs when government revenues exceed government expenditures in a given time period.

Budget surplus A budget situation in which government revenues exceed government expenditures in a given time period.

Now begin again with the economy at $500 billion in Exhibit 17.4 and let's change the scenario. Assume that business managers lower their profit expectations, so they cut investment spending (*I*), causing aggregate demand to decline. The corresponding decline in GDP from $500 billion to $470 billion causes tax revenues to fall from $100 billion to $90 billion on line *T*. The combined effect of the fall in spending and taxes creates a **budget deficit**. A budget deficit occurs when government expenditures exceed government revenues in a given time period. The vertical distance between lines *G* and *T* at $470 billion real GDP illustrates a federal budget deficit of $20 billion.

Budget deficit A budget situation in which government expenditures exceed government revenues in a given time period.

The key feature of automatic stabilisation is that it 'leans against the prevailing wind'. In short, changes in federal spending and taxes moderate changes in aggregate demand. When the economy expands, the fall in government spending for transfer payments and the rise in the level of taxes result in a budget surplus. As the budget surplus grows, people are paying more money to the government, which applies braking power against further increases in real GDP. When the economy contracts, the rise in government spending for transfer payments and the fall in the level of taxes yield a budget deficit. As the budget deficit grows, people are receiving more money from the government to spend, which helps to ameliorate the decline in real GDP.

Automatic stabilisers assist in offsetting a recession when real GDP falls and in offsetting inflation when real GDP expands.

Supply-side fiscal policy

INFOTRAC®
supply-side fiscal policy

The focus so far has been on fiscal policy that affects the macro economy solely through the impact of government spending and taxation on aggregate demand. Supply-side economists, with their intellectual roots in classical economics, argue that *stagflation* in the 1970s was the result of the federal government's failure to follow the theories of **supply-side fiscal policy**. Supply-side fiscal policy emphasises government policies that increase aggregate supply in order to achieve long-run growth in real output, full employment and a lower price level.

Supply-side fiscal policy A fiscal policy that emphasises government policies that increase aggregate supply in order to achieve long-run growth in real output, full employment and a lower price level.

Supply-side policies became an active economic idea in the early 1980s. As discussed in Chapter 13, many economies in the 1970s experienced high rates of both inflation and unemployment. Stagflation caused concern about the ability of economies to generate long-term advances in the standard of living. This set the stage for a new approach to macroeconomic policy.

Suppose the economy is initially at E_1 in Exhibit 17.5(a), with a CPI of 150 and an output of $480 billion real GDP. The economy is experiencing high unemployment, so the goal is to achieve full employment by increasing real GDP to $500 billion. As described earlier in this chapter, the federal government might follow a Keynesian expansionary fiscal policy and move to increase the aggregate demand curve from AD_1 to AD_2. Higher government spending or lower taxes operate through the multiplier effect and cause this increase in aggregate demand. The good news from such a demand-side fiscal policy prescription is that the economy moves towards full employment, but the bad news is that the price level rises. In this case, *demand-pull inflation* would cause the price level to rise from 150 to 200.

Exhibit 17.5(b) represents the supply-siders' alternative to Keynesian fiscal policy. Again, suppose the economy is initially in equilibrium at E_1. Supply-side economists argue that the federal government should adopt policies that shift the aggregate supply curve rightward from AS_1 to AS_2. An increase in aggregate supply would move the economy to E_2 and achieve the full-employment level of real GDP. Under supply-side theory, there is an additional bonus to full employment. Instead of the price level rising, as in (a), the price level in Exhibit 17.5(b) falls from 150 to 100. Comparing the two graphs in Exhibit 17.5, you can see that supply-siders seem to provide a better policy prescription than proponents of demand-side fiscal policy when both inflation and unemployment are concerns.

Note the causation chain under each graph in Exhibit 17.5. The demand-side fiscal policy options are from column 1 of Exhibit 17.1 and the supply-side policy alternatives are reproduced from Exhibit 14.11 in Chapter 14. For supply-side economics to be effective, the government must implement policies that increase the total output that firms want to produce at each and every price level. A shift in aggregate supply can be accomplished by some combination of cuts in resource prices (by, for example, enacting various economic reform policies aimed at increasing the efficiency with which such resources are produced), technological advances, government subsidies and/or reductions in taxes and reductions in government regulation.

Two examples of recent supply-side fiscal policy initiatives

Microeconomic reform in Australia

Much of the microeconomic policy reforms pursued in Australia from the middle of the 1980s into the 1990s may be viewed as having a strong supply-side flavour to them. Major policy reforms over this time included: the reduction of tariffs; deregulation of the Australian financial system and the

Exhibit 17.5 Keynesian demand-side versus supply-side effects

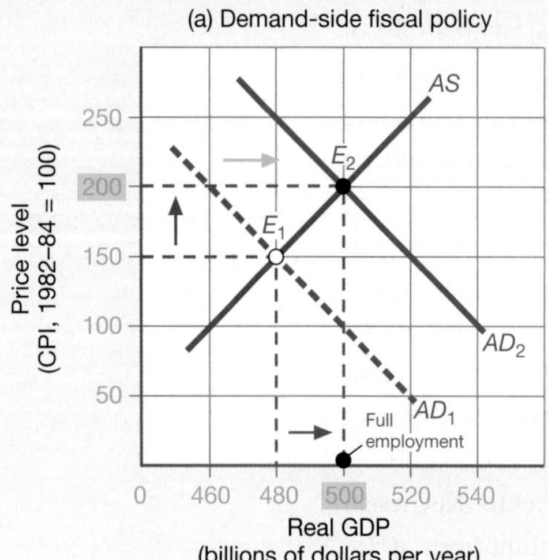

In part (a), assume an economy begins in equilibrium at point E_1, with a price level of 150 and a real GDP of $480 billion. To boost real output and employment, Keynesian economists prescribe that the federal government raise government spending or cut taxes. By following such demand-side policies, the policy makers work through the multiplier effect and increase the aggregate demand curve from AD_1 to AD_2. As a result, the equilibrium changes to E_2, where the real GDP rises to $500 billion, but the price level also rises to 200. Hence, full employment has been achieved at the expense of higher inflation.

CAUSATION CHAIN

Increase in government spending; decrease in net taxes → Increase in the aggregate demand curve

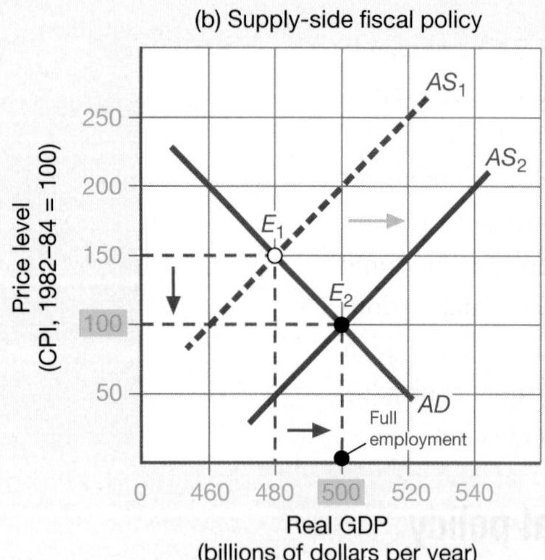

The initial situation for the economy at point E_1 in part (b) is identical to that shown in part (a). However, supply-siders offer a different fiscal policy prescription than the Keynesians. Using some combination of cuts in resource prices, technological advances, tax cuts, subsidies and regulation reduction, supply-side fiscal policy shifts the aggregate supply curve from AS_1 to AS_2. As a result, the equilibrium in the economy changes to E_2 and the real GDP increases to $500 billion, just as in part (a). The advantage of the supply-side versus the demand-side stimulus is that the price level falls to 100, rather than rising to 200.

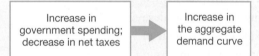

CAUSATION CHAIN

Decrease in resource prices; technological advances; decrease in taxes; subsidies; decrease in regulations → Increase in the aggregate supply curve removal of interest rate controls; the floating of the Australian dollar and the removal of foreign exchange controls; foreign bank entry; the introduction of a range of competition policy reforms; labour market reforms to allow greater flexibility in work practices; and taxation reform with the introduction of the goods and services tax along with a number of income tax changes.

Many of the reforms had the aim of increasing the efficiency of production processes in Australia, thereby reducing the costs associated with any given level of supply of goods and services. In other words, in the context of the *AD–AS* framework, such policies were supply-side in nature and aimed at shifting the aggregate supply curve out and down. (You might want to refer back to Chapter 10 for a refresher on microeconomic reform matters.)

The ABS has a wealth of information relating to changing patterns of employment. For example, go to **www.abs.gov.au** and select *Australia Now*, *Australian Social Trends*, *General information & Cumulative topic list*, *Cumulative Topic List*, *WORK* and then *Changing Industries, Changing Jobs*.

The Reagan tax cuts in the United States

Another well-known recent large-scale implementation of what is regarded as supply-side economics was the very significant income tax cuts implemented in 1981 in the United States. By reducing tax rates on wages and profits, the Reagan administration sought to increase the aggregate supply of goods and services at any price level. As has been illustrated above, however, tax cuts may also be regarded as a Keynesian-type policy intended to increase aggregate demand. But supply-siders have quite a different view of the impact of tax cuts on the economy.

Income tax cuts increase disposable income. In Keynesian economics, this boost in disposable personal income works through the *spending multiplier* to increase aggregate demand, as discussed earlier. Supply-side economists argue, instead, that changes in disposable income affect the incentives of people to supply labour, to save and to invest. On this view the income tax cuts would work to increase the amount of labour supplied and thereby increase overall aggregate supply.

Consider how a supply-side tax cut influences the labour market. Suppose supply and demand in the labour market are initially in equilibrium. At equilibrium there will be a set of wage rates at which people will be supplying quantities of labour just equal to the quantities of labour being demanded by firms. When tax rates are cut, supply-side theory predicts that labour supply will increase, since an increase in the after-tax wage rate being received by people increases their incentive to work more hours per year. Those in the labour force will want to work longer hours. And because the government takes a smaller bite out of workers' pay cheques, many of those not already in the labour force will now supply their labour. As a result of the increase in labour supply, while after-tax wages increase due to the tax cuts, pre-tax wages may actually fall and the equilibrium number of hours worked increases. (You might want to brush up on how labour markets work by looking again at Chapter 10.)

Supply-side tax cuts of the early 1980s in the United States also provided tax breaks that subsidised business investment. There were tax credits for new equipment and plant and for research and development to encourage

The Laffer curve

Applicable concept: supply-side fiscal policy

Laffer curve Representation of the relationship between the income tax rate and the amount of income tax revenue collected by the government.

Supply-side economics became popular during the early 1980s. The fiscal policy prescription of income tax cuts came to be associated with the supply-side economist Arthur Laffer. The basic idea is easily explained using the so-called Laffer curve. The **Laffer curve** is a graph depicting the relationship between tax rates and total tax revenues.

As shown in the graph, the hypothetical Laffer curve can be drawn with the income tax rate on the horizontal axis and tax revenue on the vertical axis. The idea behind this curve is that the income tax rate affects the incentive for people to work, save, invest and produce, which in turn influences tax revenue. As the tax rate climbs, Laffer and other supply-siders argue that the erosion of incentives shrinks national income and total tax collections.

Suppose the federal government sets the federal income tax rate at zero (point *A*). Here people have the maximum incentive to produce and optimum national output will be produced. But there is zero income tax revenue for the government. Now assume the federal government sets the income tax rate at the opposite extreme of 100 per cent (point *D*). At a 100 per cent income tax rate, people have no reason to work, produce and earn income. People seek ways to reduce their tax liabilities by engaging in unreported or underground transactions or by not working at all. As a result, again no income tax revenue is collected by the authorities. Because the government confiscates all reported income, the incentive to work and produce is much less at a 100 per cent tax rate than at a zero per cent tax rate.

Because the federal government wishes to collect some income tax revenue, it sets the income tax rate between zero and 100 per cent. Assuming there is the tax-rate/tax-revenue relationship depicted in the graph, maximum tax revenue, *Rmax*, is collected at a tax rate of *Tmax* (point *B*). Laffer argued that the federal income tax rate of *T* (point *C*) in 1981 exceeded *Tmax* and the resulting tax revenue of *R* was below *Rmax*.

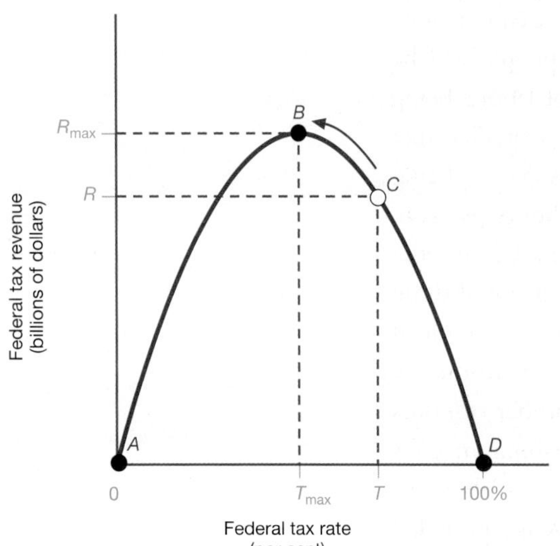

In Laffer's view, reduction of the income tax rate would lead to an increase in tax revenue because people would increase their work effort, saving and investment, and would reduce their attempts to avoid paying taxes. Thus, the Laffer curve policy argued that a cut in federal income tax rates would unleash reported economic activity and boost tax revenues to such an extent that the federal government would actually raise more revenue with the lower tax rates than with the higher rates.

The Laffer curve remains a controversial part of supply-side economics. There is still considerable uncertainty about the shape of the Laffer curve and at what point, *B*, *C* or otherwise, the economy is operating. Thus, the practical usefulness of the Laffer curve is a matter of debate.

Based on what you have just read, compare the common perception of how a tax rate cut affects tax revenues with Laffer's theory.

technological advances. The idea here was to increase the nation's productive capacity by increasing the quantity and quality of capital. Consequently, aggregate supply would shift rightward because production processes would be more efficient and businesses would therefore be able to produce more at each price level.

The idea of using tax cuts to shift the aggregate supply curve outward is not without controversy. Despite its logic, Keynesians argue that the magnitude of any rightward shift in aggregate supply is likely to be small and occur only in the longer run. For example, they argue that it may take many years before tax cuts for business generate any change in actual plant and equipment or technological advances. Thus, as a short-term countercyclical macroeconomic policy tool it may not be as useful as policies directed more at shifting aggregate demand.

Notwithstanding this, supply-siders may well argue that the very long US economic expansion of the 1990s was at least partially the result of the earlier supply-side tax inducements to encourage firms to invest in research and development. It is certainly widely acknowledged that the very rapid growth in productivity in the second half of the 1990s in the United States was driven by technological advances, particularly in computing and communications, and it could well be argued that these ICT technological advances were significantly stimulated by the earlier R&D investment tax incentives.

The federal budget

The federal budget is the principal fiscal policy statement by the federal government each year; in Australia it is delivered by the Treasurer each May. As well as presenting estimated final figures for government revenues and expenditures for the current financial year (ending in June) it also contains all-important forecasts of the government's financial situation for the coming year. Budget speech night is a big media event and the budget is closely scrutinised by economic analysts. Any changes to federal taxation policies and/or expenditure policies are announced in the Budget. Also tabled are the Federal Treasury Department's forecasts for the coming year for such macroeconomic variables as inflation, wages growth, unemployment, GDP growth, the current account deficit and so on.

The Australian federal government budget papers and budget-related information are available on the central budget website at **www.budget.gov.au**.

Of particular interest to analysts is the size of the budget deficit/surplus which is, as noted above, the difference between total federal government outlays and receipts. Federal budget outcomes (as a percentage of GDP) for the past thirty years or so are provided in Exhibit 17.6. The budget outcome has been both positive and negative over this period, but note in particular the very long run of deficits (negative outcomes) from 1975–76 until 1986–87. This 12-year period was considered too long for the budget to be in deficit and this was part of the motivation for the government seeking to produce the budget surpluses of the years 1987–88 to 1990–91. The string of deficits until 1996–97 similarly provided strong motivation for the government to deliver the subsequent surpluses beginning in 1997–98. More will be said about these surpluses, particularly the government's motivation for achieving those in the 1987–88 to 1990–91 period, in the next chapter.

Exhibit 17.6 **Australian general government sector cash revenue, outlays and surplus**

	Revenue (per cent of GDP)	Outlays (per cent of GDP)	Cash surplus (per cent of GDP)
1970–71	20.9	18.7	2.1
1971–72	20.9	18.9	2.0
1972–73	19.8	19.2	0.6
1973–74	20.6	18.8	1.8
1974–75	22.6	22.5	0.1
1975–76	23.0	25.0	–2.0
1976–77	23.3	24.7	–1.4
1977–78	23.4	25.4	–2.0
1978–79	22.6	24.5	–1.8
1979–80	23.1	24.1	–1.0
1980–81	24.1	24.2	–0.1
1981–82	24.3	24.0	0.3
1982–83	24.7	26.5	–1.8
1983–84	24.0	27.4	–3.4
1984–85	25.6	28.2	–2.6
1985–86	26.1	28.1	–2.0
1986–87	26.9	27.7	–0.8
1987–88	26.1	25.6	0.6
1988–89	25.1	23.4	1.8
1989–90	24.8	23.1	1.7
1990–91	24.6	24.5	0.1
1991–92	22.9	25.7	–2.8
1992–93	22.2	26.2	–4.0
1993–94	22.4	26.2	–3.8
1994–95	23.3	26.1	–2.8
1995–96	24.1	26.1	–2.0
1996–97	24.5	25.5	–1.0
1997–98	24.2	24.0	0.2
1998–99	24.7	24.0	0.7
1999–00	26.5	24.4	2.1
2000–01	24.0	23.1	0.9
2001–02	22.8	22.9	–0.1
2002–03	23.4	22.4	1.0
2003–04	22.8	22.3	0.6
2004–05(e)	**22.6**	**22.3**	**0.3**
2005–06(p)	22.3	22.1	0.2
2006–07(p)	22.1	21.8	0.4
2007–08(p)	22.1	21.6	0.4

(e) estimates, (p) projections

Source: From Budget Paper No. 1, 2004–05, Statement 13, Table 1, pp. 13–14

PART 5

The overall budget outcome is of interest for a couple of reasons. First, federal outlays as a percentage of GDP represent the size and influence of the federal government in the economy. Those in favour of a reduced role for government look for reductions in this percentage over time. Second, the size of the deficit/surplus is interpreted in many quarters as a summary overall measure of the government's **fiscal stance** – that is, the extent to which the authorities are actively trying to expand or retard the activity in the national economy through the settings of government revenue-raising and spending policies. A larger deficit, because it means the government is spending more than it is receiving, is interpreted as expansionary, with the prospect of there being a stimulus to economic activity with a concomitant increased risk of higher inflation and higher interest rates. On the other hand, a larger surplus is interpreted as a brake on economic activity along with the expectation of lower future inflation and interest rates.

Fiscal stance The term used to represent the extent to which the authorities are actively trying to expand or retard the growth of the national economy through the settings of government revenue-raising and spending policies.

The macroeconomic significance of the budget

The countercyclical role of fiscal policy

As described earlier in this chapter, the Keynesian view of the role of fiscal policy is that manipulation of aggregate demand by the authorities in order to stabilise the business cycle is appropriate. This is termed 'discretionary fiscal policy activism' and means, for example, that government should respond to unacceptably high unemployment levels by temporarily supplementing private-sector demand with increases in its own expenditure so as to reflate the economy. Such a countercyclical role for fiscal policy implies large deficits in recessionary times offset by surpluses (reduced government spending and increased taxation revenue from the higher levels of activity) in growth periods.

While there has certainly long been a strong Keynesian element in Australia's approach to the conduct of fiscal policy, in his 1997 budget speech the Treasurer indicated that there would henceforth be a greater fiscal discipline exercised by the government in future years 'to ensure that the federal budget would remain in balance, on average, over the course of the business cycle.' This approach would still allow fiscal policy to be appropriately stimulatory (that is, to run deficits if necessary) during times of economic slowdown or recession, but would then require it to be tightened again once economic recovery was under way.

Consider again Exhibit 17.6 in the context of the 1990–91 recession. This recession was well and truly over by the end of 1992, yet the federal budget remained in deficit right through the 1990s until 1996–97. Given this, many economic commentators argued that fiscal policy had been allowed to be inappropriately stimulatory for too many years into the ensuing long economic expansion. Indeed, the continuation of budget deficits for so long into the expansion provided the motivation for the incoming government in 1996 to embark on a period of significant fiscal consolidation.

Other roles of fiscal policy

A great deal of useful economic and fiscal information may be found on the Federal Treasury's website: (**www.treasury.gov.au**). Treasury's current view of the state of the macro economy can be found in its publication 'Economic Roundup' and its assessments of the government's fiscal position is available in the '2003–04 Mid-Year Economic and Fiscal Outlook' and the 'National Fiscal Outlook'. All of these can be accessed from the site by selecting *Publications*.

Apart from its short-term business cycle stabilisation role, fiscal policy is also used more generally to try to achieve desirable medium-to-long-term economic and social goals. The introduction of the GST in Australia in July 2000 is an example of a fiscal policy initiative with medium-to-long-term economic objectives. Briefly, these objectives were to:

- broaden the range of goods and services attracting tax, thereby removing a lot of hitherto tax-induced distortions to consumption patterns and allowing the burden of taxation to be spread more widely and evenly across the economy
- reduce the reliance on income taxation in government revenue-raising
- reduce the ability of individuals to avoid paying their legally obliged taxes
- encourage increased rates of community saving by taxing income when it was spent rather than when it was earned.

Another example of recent fiscal policy changes in Australia with a clear medium-term focus has been a range of policy initiatives focusing on reducing Australia's unemployment rate. Of course, the best and most sustainable way of reducing unemployment is to employ appropriate macroeconomic policies to keep the nation's rate of economic growth as strong as possible. However, it is also important to ensure there are the right micro incentives in place to encourage the appropriate responses from the unemployed and from prospective employers. Recent policy initiatives in these areas include:

- the creation of a publicly funded private-sector job network
- mutual obligation initiatives whereby, in return for unemployment benefits, the unemployed are required to actively seek employment, to either engage in training and/or education to improve their job-readiness, or otherwise to work in a wide range of part-time volunteer community-oriented projects
- limited employment subsidies provided to employers to encourage the hiring of long-term unemployed
- the removal of financial disincentives that discourage people from accepting work offers. These disincentives arise from the sometimes unhelpful interactions between the welfare and taxation systems, which result in some people on welfare support facing very high effective marginal tax rates on small amounts of earned income.

Some words of caution

As noted above, while the overall size of the deficit/surplus is widely interpreted as a summary measure of the extent to which government fiscal policy is meant to be expansionary, several important caveats are worth noting.

First, in determining the macroeconomic impact of a given budget, we need also to consider the actual pattern of expenditure and revenue in addition to the bottom line deficit/surplus figure. A simple example will clarify the importance of this. Imagine that the government wants to provide an expansionary stimulus to the economy. There are many alternatives open to it to try to accomplish this.

On the revenue side it could reduce taxes, but which taxes? It can choose from company taxes, payroll taxes, import taxes, excise taxes or personal income taxes, to name just a few. Since these taxes initially affect different sections of the community we can expect them to have varying macroeconomic outcomes. For instance, cutting the personal marginal income tax rate of high-income earners could be expected to have a different impact on consumption than cutting the taxes of low-income earners because of their different marginal propensities to save. Alternatively, the government can alter the extent of income tax concessions accruing to various classes of expenditures. For example, it could alter the tax treatment of business investment – such as changing depreciation allowances – which would have its direct impact on aggregate investment rather than consumption.

On the expenditure side, the government can choose broadly from either increasing its own purchases of goods and services or increasing its transfer payments. The purchases decision can be further broken down into a choice between spending to increase the nation's capital stock (building more roads, for example) and spending on current consumption (holding more parliament house functions, for example). On the other hand, the impact on the economy of increased transfer payments will depend on the socioeconomic characteristics of the recipients of the increased welfare payments.

A second caveat involves the importance of distinguishing between the domestic budget deficit and the overall deficit. While the federal government's receipts are almost entirely derived from domestic sources, a significant percentage of its spending is on foreign production (for example, spending on defence equipment). The **domestic deficit** is the difference between domestically derived revenue and domestic government expenditure. Hence, the overall deficit may increase due to additional government spending on imports without any increase in the domestic component at all, and this spending will not have any expansionary impact on the economy whatsoever. Therefore it is important to look at the domestic deficit as well as the overall deficit in analysing the likely expansionary impact of the budget.

Domestic deficit The difference between domestically derived revenue and domestic government expenditure.

Cyclically adjusted budget deficit The actual recorded budget deficit for some period adjusted for the stage of the economy's business cycle during the period.

INFOTRAC®

cyclically adjusted budget deficit.

A third caveat involves the so-called **cyclically adjusted budget deficit**. It is important to recognise that, as an economy moves through a business cycle over time, the government's finances are automatically affected by the varying levels of economic activity occurring at the different stages of the cycle. The cyclically adjusted budget deficit is the actual recorded budget deficit for some period adjusted for the stage of the economy's business cycle during the period.

As mentioned earlier in the discussion of automatic stabilisers, during periods of slow economic activity government expenditure on unemployment benefits will increase, while government receipts will decline due to lower taxation revenue. Thus, even without any conscious government fiscal policy decision to try to reflate the economy, the budget deficit will increase as a result of the cyclical impact of the slowdown. Similarly, the budget deficit will automatically reduce and move into surplus as economic activity accelerates during the cyclical upturn.

Although such changes in the budget outcome provide some useful information about broad macroeconomic effects of government activities, they occur passively. They therefore give little indication of whether the government is actively trying to use fiscal policy to expand or retard economic activity; that is, they give little indication of the government's active fiscal policy stance.

To more precisely gauge the active stance of fiscal policy, economic analysts often adjust the actual deficit to account for such passive cyclical effects. For example, consider two periods, the first of which was characterised by cyclically high unemployment and the second by cyclically low unemployment. The actual measured budget outcomes would be converted into cyclically adjusted budget outcomes by appropriately reducing the size of the actual deficit in the first period and increasing it appropriately in the second. The resulting adjusted budget outcomes may then give a more precise indication of what the government's active fiscal stance was in the two different business cycle periods.

Economics and ethics

This is an appropriate point to refer back to our discussion in the previous chapter about the 'bluntness' of monetary policy as a policy instrument. It is certainly the case – as the above discussion about the range of options available to the government when it adjusts fiscal policy should illustrate – that fiscal policy may be regarded as an instrument that can be used to impact more precisely on some sections of the community and/or sectors of the economy than on others.

Of course, through the spending multiplier effects, any change in taxation or spending policies by the government is likely eventually to spread throughout the economy and community. Nonetheless, it will certainly be true that some will feel the effects much more directly and significantly than others.

This fact inevitably leads to considerations that reach far beyond the realm of straight economics. It may be, for example, that most analysts agree that a fiscal easing (extra spending or/and reduced taxation) is in order. However, there may well be – and usually is – very great disagreement as to which group(s) should have their taxes reduced or, alternatively, whether some welfare payments should be increased (again, to which groups?); whether increased spending should be on better public housing, health and medical services, or whether it should rather be on much-needed physical infrastructure, and where in the country this spending should occur.

Thus – again, while ethical considerations are not necessarily in question here – all of these issues will inevitably involve ideological and political dimensions with the result that some in the community may be led to question the 'fairness' and appropriateness of the enacted policy changes.

Implications of the budget outcome for government debt levels

Budget deficits and Australia's national debt

Every time the government runs a budget deficit, the national debt is increased by the government issuing securities to pay for its expenditures in excess of its tax receipts. A useful statistical definition of Australia's **national debt** therefore is the total value of outstanding commonwealth government securities; it represents the extent of previous borrowing by the federal government. Using this perspective, the national debt has fallen steadily from 57 per cent of annual GDP in 1960 to just over 5 per cent by the end of the 1990s. Exhibit 17.7 also provides an international comparison of various countries' general government debt levels. As is evident from the exhibit, Australia's debt levels are really quite modest when compared internationally.

National debt The total value of outstanding commonwealth government securities; it represents the extent of previous borrowing by the federal government.

A portion of a country's national debt will be held by the central bank and corresponds to that part of the debt that has been monetised. This is because the bank, in purchasing the government securities, pays for them by simply creating money. Therefore, this part of the government's outstanding debt is transformed into increases in the country's money stock. The rest of the debt will be held by the general public in the form of interest-bearing liabilities of the government.

The Reserve Bank of Australia publishes data on Australia's national debt levels. Go to the website (**www.rba.gov.au**), select *Statistics*, then *Bulletin Statistical Tables*, then *Government Finance*, and peruse the series on *Commonwealth Government Securities on Issue*.

Exhibit 17.7 General government net debt levels in selected countries (decade from 1996 to 2005)

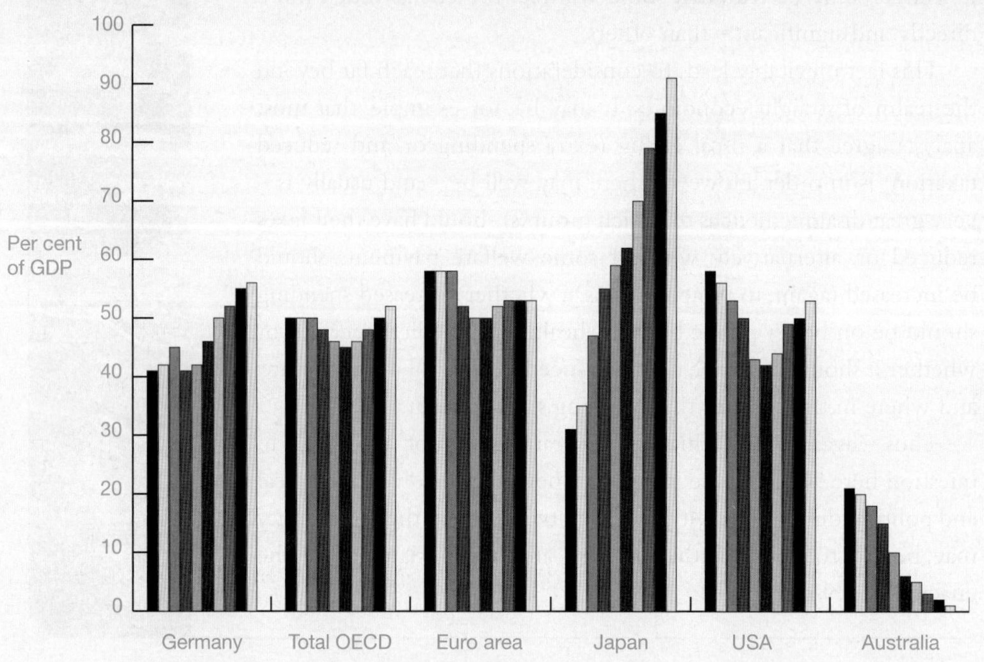

Source: Federal Government Budget Paper No. 1, 2004–05, pp. 1–6, Chart 3.

Money financing The financing of a budget deficit by the central bank purchasing the securities issued by the government to fund its deficit. This part of the deficit is monetised in that the government has financed its spending by virtue of the central bank expanding the money supply.

Debt financing The financing of a budget deficit by selling government securities to the general public – that is, by the government borrowing from the public to fund its expenditure.

Thus, to finance a budget deficit, the government must sell securities. If any of these securities are purchased by the central bank, then part of the deficit is monetised; financing a deficit in this way is known as **money financing**. The government pays for its expenditures by using this newly created money. The rest of the deficit is financed by the government selling the securities to the general public; that is, by the government borrowing from the public. Financing a deficit in this way is known as **debt financing**.

Until the 1970s it was quite common in Australia for budget deficits to be financed at least partially through money financing. However, since the early 1980s, budget deficits in Australia have been financed virtually entirely through debt financing.

The burden of the debt

Burden of the debt The possibility that existing national debt may represent a burden on current and future generations, namely to pay the future interest payments on it and to eventually repay the principal. In fact, to the extent that the national debt is internal – that is, not owed to foreigners – such debt is not likely to represent a net burden.

This borrowing by the government from the private sector leads to the question of the so-called **burden of the debt**. When the government borrows, the lenders can either be residents or foreigners. If we view the national debt as the collective debt of the Australian people, this debt is currently about $3000 per person. Is this a burden?

For the moment let's just consider the portion of the national debt that is domestically held. In this case, the answer is almost certainly no. It is an internal debt that we owe to ourselves. It's like one family member borrowing from another to finance some kind of spending. Although one family member now has a debt obligation to another, the net increase in debt of the family in total is zero. Just as with the family, as far as the nation is concerned, there may certainly be future redistributive effects as the debt matures and the holders of the securities (who may be the original lenders, their heirs or someone else who has subsequently bought the securities) are paid from government tax revenue or from new government borrowing. Of course, this redistribution is perfectly reasonable, since those who previously had lent to the government sacrificed some of their current income and consumption so that the wider community might benefit from the subsequent government expenditure.

INFOTRAC®
money financing
burden of the debt

It's also very important to keep in mind that the national debt is only one side of the nation's balance sheet. On the other side is the nation's stock of publicly owned capital assets. If the government borrows to fund capital spending on the construction of additional public infrastructure, such spending will increase the nation's productive capacity in a similar way to increases in the capital stock of firms. However, if the government borrows to finance its own current consumption spending rather than to augment the country's national capital stock, it is possible that such debt may become a burden on future generations. This is an appropriate point at which to introduce the notion of crowding out.

The crowding-out issue

Critics of Keynesian fiscal policy believe that increased government spending – designed to boost aggregate demand – that gives rise to federal budget deficits has little if any effect on real GDP. The reason is that crowding-out effects may dampen down the stimulus to aggregate demand arising from the increased federal government spending. The **crowding-out effect** is a reduction in private-sector spending as a result of federal budget deficits financed by government borrowing. How does this occur?

Crowding-out effect
A reduction in private-sector spending as a result of federal budget deficits financed by government borrowing. The mechanism for this crowding out would be through higher interest rates in the financial markets resulting from the increased demand for loan funds from the private sector by the government.

The reasoning is as follows. Since the federal government competes with other borrowers for available saving, interest rates experience upward pressure as the government seeks to borrow funds from the financial markets. The result of this rise in interest rates may be lower consumption and business investment, which would act to offset the boost in aggregate demand from the increased government spending. If so, some private-sector demand would be said to be crowded out by the public-sector spending.

If significant, the crowding-out effect provides a possible avenue through which future generations may bear a burden for the current generation's accumulation of national debt. Recall from Chapters 2 and 12 that present investment spending increases living standards in the future by increasing the country's capital stock, thereby shifting the production possibilities curve outward. (See Exhibit 2.4 in Chapter 2.) If federal deficits crowd out private investment in plant and equipment, future generations will not have this additional private-sector productive capacity available to them.

INFOTRAC®
crowding-out
effect

PART 5

The crowding-out effect is not uncontroversial. Keynesian economists argue that any private-sector crowding-out effects may be unimportant when viewed in comparison to the increases in public-sector capital stock arising from the government spending. Of course, this argument relies on the implicit assumption that the government spending in question is of a capital nature. For example, government capital spending for highways, dams, hospitals, schools, universities and rail and ports infrastructure financed by borrowing may well offset any decline in private-sector investment. On the other hand, this argument does not have as much force if the government spending is of a current consumption nature (say, financing a lavish visit from a group of foreign diplomats).

Another Keynesian argument is that consumers and businesspeople may believe the federal deficit spending is 'just what the doctor ordered' for an ailing economy. For instance, federal budget deficits may be incurred to increase aggregate demand during a period of severely subdued private-sector demand. This deficit spending by the government may in fact subsequently provide much-needed increases in private-sector consumption and business investment. The extra government spending may significantly stimulate increased consumption spending through the spending multiplier. This in turn may also raise the profit expectations of businesses, thereby stimulating additional investment spending. The effect of such increased private-sector spending could nullify some or all of the crowding-out effect that would otherwise have offset the boost in aggregate demand from the increased government spending.

Regardless of these arguments about the existence and significance of private-sector investment crowding out, one thing remains reasonably uncontroversial. While borrowing by the government reduces the immediate pool of saving available to finance private investment – and even if this does put upward pressure on interest rates – this should not prove to be a burden on future generations if the government spending is directed into the provision of public infrastructure. Such expenditure is likely to increase the nation's future income-generating potential and, as such, should not be a problem. Again, it is important to remember that, when considering the national debt, we should never forget the publicly owned national capital stock that this debt will have financed.

The external component of national debt

The portion of a country's national debt that is owed to foreigners is a different matter. In Australia at the time of writing this was only a very small component of national debt. This is an external debt that should increase the quantity of output from future production but will also involve repayment with interest to foreigners. Thus this type of debt is not a debt 'owed to ourselves'. As such, in this case, it is important to carefully weigh the potential future income-generating benefits of the capital accumulation financed by the debt against the future obligations the increased debt places on the nation. Of course, foreign borrowing by governments to finance current government consumption is a dubious practice.

International focus

How real is the US federal budget deficit?

Applicable concepts: national debt; real versus nominal; capital budgeting

Perhaps federal budget deficits and the national debt are really not as large as we think. At least this is the case presented by Professor Robert Eisner, past president of the American Economic Association. He says:

> With all the deficits, the general trend of real federal debt – the debt adjusted for inflation – has been downward. On a per capita basis it has indeed gone down very sharply over most of the last forty years.[1]

Eisner and other economists argue that we should use real, rather than nominal, increases in the national debt. Suppose the national debt is $4 trillion and the price level increases by 5 per cent in a given year. The real value of the national debt therefore falls by $200 billion. According to Eisner, this $200 billion real-value inflation adjustment of the national debt should be subtracted from the actual federal budget deficit for the year. Let's say the deficit as reported by government statisticians is $225 billion. Using Eisner's 'new accounting', the real deficit is only $25 billion ($225 billion official deficit – $200 billion inflation adjustment). In effect, the $200 billion inflation adjustment is as much a receipt for the federal government as an equal amount of tax revenue. Recall from the chapter on inflation that increases in the price level redistribute buying power from creditors to debtors.

Eisner warns that a federal budget balanced by current federal rules of accounting is an economic disaster. Private businesses, as well as state and local governments, use two budgets. One is the operating budget, which includes salaries, interest payments and other current expenses. The second type of budget is called a *capital budget*. The US federal government does not use a capital budget. Capital budgeting allows for spreading the cost of long-lasting assets over future years. For example, the federal budget makes no distinction between the cost of maintaining a federal office building and the cost of building a new federal office building to replace rented office space. In the latter case, reduced rent payments offset interest payments on the borrowing. If a capital budgeting system were utilised, Eisner believes that we would see that most of the deficit really finances assets yielding long-term benefits.

Finally, some economists argue for other numerical adjustments that show the federal deficit is not really as large as it seems. They say it is not the federal deficit that really matters, but the combined deficit of federal, state and local governments. When state and local governments run budget surpluses, these surpluses are a source of saving into financial markets that offsets federal borrowing to finance its deficit. Also recall the adjustment for the *cyclical component of the deficit* explained earlier in the chapter. The measured budget deficit reflects the state of the economy, rather than discretionary fiscal policy. Subtracting the cyclical component from the actual budget deficit yields the cyclically adjusted – or full-employment – budget deficit, which has been smaller in recent years in the United States than the actual budget deficit.

1 Robert Eisner, *How Real is the Federal Deficit?* Free Press, New York, 1986, p. 4.

Analyse the issue

1 Do households make a distinction between spending for current expenses and spending for capital expenses? Compare borrowing $5000 to take a vacation in Hawaii to borrowing $180 000 to buy an apartment and move out of your rented apartment.

2 Critics of 'new accounting' for federal budget deficits argue that it does not matter what the government spends the money on. What matters is the total amount that the government spends minus taxes collected. Explain this viewpoint.

Key concepts

Fiscal policy
Discretionary fiscal policy
Balanced budget multiplier
Automatic stabilisers
Budget surplus
Budget deficit
Supply-side fiscal policy
Laffer curve
Fiscal stance
Domestic deficit
Cyclically adjusted budget deficit
National debt
Money financing of the deficit
Debt financing of the deficit
Burden of the debt
Crowding-out effect

Summary

- **Fiscal policy** is the use of government spending, taxes and transfer payments for the purpose of stabilising the economy.

- **Discretionary fiscal policy activism** follows the Keynesian argument that the federal government should manipulate aggregate demand in order to influence the output, employment and price levels in the economy. Discretionary fiscal policy requires the government to vary its spending or taxes in order to stabilise the economy's business cycle.
- **Expansionary fiscal policy** is a deliberate increase in government spending, a deliberate decrease in taxes or some combination of these two options.
- **Contractionary fiscal policy** is a deliberate decrease in government spending, a deliberate increase in taxes or some combination of these two options. Using either expansionary or contractionary fiscal policy, the government can shift the aggregate demand curve in order to combat recession, cool inflation or achieve other macroeconomic goals.
- The **spending multiplier** is the multiplier by which an initial change in spending changes aggregate demand (total spending) after an infinite number of spending cycles. Expressed as a formula (and abstracting from taxes), the spending multiplier = 1/(1 – MPC).
- A **balanced budget multiplier** is the net impact on the economy of an equal increase in government spending and taxation. A balanced budget adjustment to government spending is the situation where the government offsets a spending increase (or decrease) with an equal change to tax collected. However, other things equal, a dollar of government spending increases real GDP more than a dollar cut in taxes. Thus, even though the one dollar increase in government spending is offset by an increase in tax collected, it is still able to stimulate the economy. The balanced budget multiplier is one.
- A **budget surplus** occurs when government revenues exceed government expenditures. A **budget deficit** occurs when government expenditures exceed government revenues.
- **Automatic stabilisers** are changes in tax revenue and government spending that occur automatically in response to changes in the level of real GDP. The business cycle therefore creates – at least partially – its own braking/accelerating adjustment. A *budget surplus* tends to slow down an expanding economy. A *budget deficit* tends to mitigate a downturn in the economy.

Automatic stabilisers

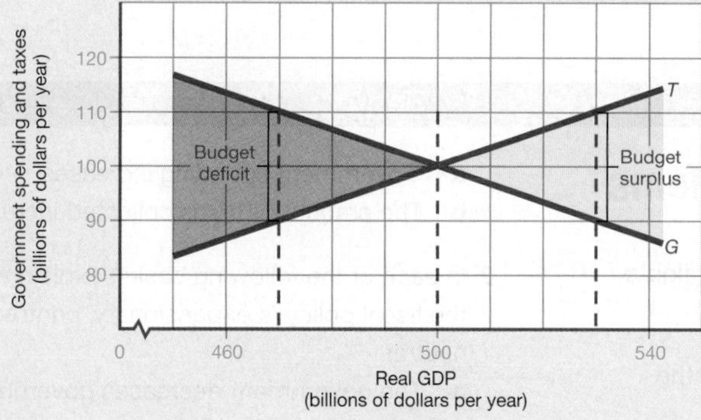

- According to **supply-side fiscal policy**, lower taxes encourage work, saving and investment, which shift the aggregate supply curve rightward. As a result, output and employment increase without inflation.
- The **Laffer curve** represents the relationship between the income tax rate and the amount of income tax revenue collected by the government.
- **Fiscal stance** is the term used to represent the extent to which the authorities are actively trying to expand or retard activity in the national economy through the settings of government revenue raising and spending policies.
- **Domestic deficit** is the difference between domestically derived revenue and domestic government expenditure.
- **Cyclically adjusted budget deficit** is the actual recorded budget deficit for some period adjusted for the stage of the economy's business cycle during the period.
- **National debt** is the total value of outstanding commonwealth government securities; it represents the extent of previous borrowing by the federal government.
- **Money financing** occurs when a budget deficit is financed by the central bank purchasing the securities issued by the government to fund its deficit. This part of the deficit is monetised in that the government has financed its spending by virtue of the central bank expanding the money supply.
- **Debt financing** occurs when a budget deficit is financed by selling government securities to the general public – that is, by the government borrowing from the public to fund its expenditure.
- **Burden of the debt** This refers to the possibility that existing national debt may represent a burden on future generations, namely to pay the future interest payments on it and to eventually repay it. To the extent that the national debt is internal – that is, not owed to foreigners – such debt is not likely to represent a net burden.
- The **crowding-out effect** is a reduction in private-sector spending as a result of federal budget deficits financed by government borrowing. The mechanism for this crowding out would be through higher interest rates brought about by the increased government borrowing from the private sector.

Study questions and problems

1 Explain how discretionary fiscal policy fights recession and inflation.

2 How does each of the following affect the aggregate demand curve?

a Government spending increases.

b The amount of taxes collected increases.

3 In each of the following cases, explain whether the fiscal policy is expansionary, contractionary or neutral.

a The government decreases government spending.

b The government increases taxes.
c The government increases spending and taxes by an equal amount.

4 Why is the multiplier effect of a reduction in taxes less than the multiplier effect of an increase in government spending by an equal amount? Which policy is more expansionary: a $100 billion increase in government spending for goods and services or a $100 billion cut in taxes?

5 Consider an economy that is operating at well below the full-employment level of real GDP. Assuming the MPC is 0.90, predict the effect on the economy of a $50 billion increase in government spending balanced by a $50 billion increase in taxes. What would be your answer if the MPC had instead been 0.75? What would have been your answer had the economy been operating at full employment?

6 What is the difference between discretionary fiscal policy and automatic stabilisers? How are federal budget surpluses and deficits affected by the business cycle?

7 Assume you are a supply-side economist who is an adviser to the government. If the economy is in recession, what would your fiscal policy prescription be?

8 Suppose federal parliament enacts a tax reform law and the average income tax rate drops from 40 per cent to 30 per cent (as it did in 2000). Researchers subsequently investigate the impact of the tax cut and find that income tax revenue increases from $600 billion to $800 billion. The theoretical explanation is that workers have increased their work effort in response to the incentive of lower taxes. Is this a movement along the downward-sloping or the upward-sloping portion of the Laffer curve?

9 Indicate the change in either the aggregate demand curve or the aggregate supply curve for each of the following:
a expansionary fiscal policy
b contractionary fiscal policy
c supply-side policies
d demand-pull inflation
e cost-push inflation

10 Explain the relationship between budget deficits and the national debt.

11 Explain this statement: 'The national debt is like taking money out of your left pocket and putting it into your right pocket.'

12 Suppose the percentage of the federal debt owned by foreigners increases sharply. Would this trend concern you? Why?

13 Explain the theory that crowding out can weaken or nullify the effect of expansionary fiscal policy financed by federal government borrowing.

14 Suppose the federal government has no national debt and spends $100 billion, while raising only $50 billion in taxes.
a What amount of government bonds will the government issue to finance the deficit?
b Next year, assume tax revenues remain at $50 billion and the government again wants to spend $100 billion. If the government pays a 10 per cent rate of interest, add the debt-servicing interest payment to the government's $100 billion expenditure for goods and services the second year.
c For the second year, compute the deficit, the amount of new debt issued and the new national debt.

15 Consider this statement: 'Our grandchildren may not suffer the entire burden of a federal deficit.' Do you agree or disagree? Explain.

Online exercises

Use the Federal Treasury's website at **www.treasury.gov.au** to do the first two exercises. For both exercises, first select **Business**, then **Economic**.

Exercise 1

Peruse the latest edition of the Treasury's 'Economic Roundup' and summarise the department's current view of the macro economy. In particular, what is its view of prospects for employment growth, unemployment and Australia's economic growth for the year?

Exercise 2

Find the data on competitiveness measures and look at the data on nominal unit labour costs (ULC). ULC is an estimate of the labour cost involved in producing a unit of output expressed in index form; the numbers represent ULC for any year relative to some particular base year (the base is denoted by 100). Using this, answer the following questions.

a Interpret the data provided for the year 1983–84.

b What was the percentage rise in ULC from 1983–84 to 1988–89?

c What was the percentage rise in ULC from 1998–99 to 2003–04?

d What does this suggest to you in terms of the impact that microeconomic reform policies (introduced from the mid-to-late 1980s) may have had on the efficiency of labour use in production?

Exercise 3

Go to the Federal Budget website (**www.budget.gov.au**). Go to **Budget Overview** and determine what the estimate of the federal budget underlying cash surplus is for the current fiscal year (ending in June) – in billions of dollars and as a percentage of GDP – as well as the previous year and the forecast for the following year. Interpret these data in terms of the relative impact on the economy of government spending and revenue activities in the three years. Does this represent the fiscal stance of the federal government across the three years? Why or why not?

Answers to 'You make the call'

Calculating the size of the spending multiplier

For an MPC of 0.6 and $1 of initial spending, the total spending stimulus after five rounds of induced spending will be 1 + 0.6 + 0.36 + 0.216 + 0.1296 + 0.0778 = $2.38. The next three rounds of induced spending would amount to 0.0467 + 0.028 + 0.0167 (i.e. 0.0914). Thus the total stimulus from eight rounds of induced spending would be $2.47. The next four rounds of induced spending would add only a further $0.0218 spending stimulus, to give a total spending stimulus after 12 rounds of induced spending of $2.49.

The total spending stimulus thus appears to be approaching $2.50. You could further check this for yourself by going through the above process for, say, three or four further rounds. Thus, for an initial spending stimulus of $100 million, the total spending stimulus to the economy would be $250 million. If you said the spending multiplier for an MPC of 0.6 is 2.5, YOU ARE CORRECT.

Calculating the required tax cut

A Keynesian would argue that, to increase real GDP by $20 billion, what would be required would be to increase aggregate demand by $20 billion. This assumes that all the increased *AD* results in increased output rather than any increases in the price level.

To increase *AD* by $20 billion means that the initial spending stimulus plus all induced spending must equal $20 billion. This means the initial spending stimulus would need to be $4 billion if the MPC was 0.8. This follows because $20 billion = (initial spending stimulus)/(1 – 0.8). Now, given the MPC of 0.8, this means that 20 per cent (i.e. 0.2) of any tax cut by the government will be saved by the recipients. Therefore, to get the initial spending stimulus of $4 billion, the government would need to cut taxes by $5 billion ($5 billion × 0.8 = $4 billion). If you said the tax cut needed would be $5 billion, YOU ARE CORRECT.

Multiple-choice questions

1 Contractionary fiscal policy is deliberate government action to influence aggregate demand and the level of real GDP through
- **a** expanding the money supply.
- **b** encouraging business to expand investment.
- **c** regulating net exports.
- **d** decreasing government spending or increasing taxes.

2 The spending multiplier is defined as
- **a** 1/(1 – marginal propensity to consume).
- **b** 1/(marginal propensity to consume).
- **c** 1/(–marginal propensity to save).
- **d** 1/(marginal propensity to consume + marginal propensity to save).

3 If the marginal propensity to consume is 0.60, the value of the spending multiplier is
- **a** 0.4.
- **b** 0.6.
- **c** 1.5.
- **d** 2.5.

4 Assume the economy is in recession and real GDP is well below full employment, the marginal propensity to consume is 0.80 and the government increases spending by $50 billion. As a result, aggregate demand will rise by
- **a** zero.
- **b** $250 billion.
- **c** more than $250 billion.
- **d** less than $250 billion.

5 Assume the marginal propensity to consume (MPC) is 0.75 and the government increases taxes by $25 billion. The aggregate demand curve will shift to the
   a left by $100 billion.
   b right by $100 billion.
   c left by $75 billion.
   d right by $75 billion.

6 Suppose that, in the absence of any fiscal policy changes, the aggregate demand curve in the next period will exceed the current aggregate demand curve by $50 billion at any level of prices. Assuming the marginal propensity to consume is 0.80, this increase in aggregate demand could be prevented by
   a increasing government spending by $50 billion.
   b increasing government spending by $40 billion.
   c increasing taxes by $40 billion.
   d increasing taxes by $12.5 billion.

7 Suppose inflation is anticipated to be a threat because the current aggregate demand curve is expected to increase next period by $60 billion at any price level. If the marginal propensity to consume is 0.75, federal policy makers could follow Keynesian-type fiscal policy and restrain inflation by
   a decreasing taxes by $60 billion.
   b decreasing transfer payments by $20 billion.
   c decreasing government spending by $20 billion.
   d increasing government spending by $15 billion.

8 Which of the following is *not* an automatic stabiliser?
   a defence spending.
   b unemployment compensation benefits.
   c personal income taxes.
   d welfare payments.

9 Which of the following statements is true?
   a A reduction in tax rates along the downward-sloping portion of the Laffer curve would increase tax revenues.
   b According to supply-side fiscal policy, lower tax rates would shift the aggregate demand curve to the right, expanding the economy and creating some inflation.
   c The presence of the automatic stabilisers tends to destabilise the economy.
   d To combat inflation, Keynesians recommend lower taxes and greater government.

10 Since the 1980s the federal government has financed the federal deficit by
   a taxing businesses and households
   b selling treasury securities.
   c printing more money.
   d reducing its purchases of goods and services.

11 Which of the following owns a proportion of the national debt?
   a private Australian citizens.
   b banks.
   c foreigners.
   d all of the above.

12 The portion of a country's national debt held by foreigners
   a may represent a burden because it transfers some future income from the country's citizens to other countries.
   b is an accounting entry that represents no real burden.
   c is no real problem because the country can simply refuse to pay the debt back.
   d should be eliminated as soon as possible because it is not good for governments to borrow from foreigners.

13 Which of the following statements about crowding out is *true*?
   a It is caused by a budget surplus.
   b It is not caused by a budget deficit.
   c It cannot completely offset the multiplier effect of deficit government spending.
   d It affects interest rates and, in turn, consumption and investment spending.

18 International trade and finance

Just imagine your life without world trade. For openers, you would not be able to buy music CDs by overseas artists, nor would you be able to hire videos or see movies made in other countries, enjoy foreign beers, sip French wine, drink Colombian coffee or have a cup of Indian tea. Also forget about driving foreign-made motorcycles or cars. In addition, you could not buy Italian or French clothing, or most DVD players, televisions, fax machines and personal computers because many are foreign made. Taking your holiday in Paris, New York or London would also be ruled out if there were no world trade. And the list goes on, so the point is clear. World trade is important because it increases world production and gives consumers more power by expanding their choices. Today, the speed of transportation and communication means producers must compete on a global basis for the spending dollars of consumers.

The first part of this chapter explains why countries should specialise in producing certain goods and then trade them for imports. Then we will consider the issue of 'fair trade' and whether it should be preferable to 'free trade'. Is there a need for protection for Australian firms from the 'unfair' trade practices of other countries? You will learn how nations

pay each other for world trade and be introduced to issues relating to a country's current account balance and its levels of foreign debt. You will also discover why (at the time of writing in late 2004), for example, one Australian dollar was worth about 80 yen, US$0.75, euro 0.59, NZ$1.08 and 795 Korean won.

In this chapter, you will examine these economics questions:

- How do Don Bradman's decision to concentrate on batting and Richard Hadlee's decision to concentrate on bowling provide a useful analogy for an important principle in international trade?
- Why do most economists prefer free trade to 'fair trade'?
- Is there ever a valid argument for trade protectionism?
- Are current account deficits and foreign debt things to be avoided?
- Should Australia ever return to a fixed exchange rate system instead of its current floating exchange rate system?

Why nations need trade

Exhibit 18.1 below reveals which regions are Australia's major trading partners in merchandise trade (i.e. trade in goods only). About 21 per cent of Australia's merchandise exports go to the European Union (EU) and the United States and about 31 per cent of its merchandise imports come from these areas. However, when exports and imports of services are taken into account, the relative importance of the EU and the USA is increased considerably, particularly in respect of imports. The composition of Australia's exports is also quite different from its imports. Over 50 per cent of its total exports are commodities, while virtually all of its imports are manufactured goods and services. Leading Australian exports are: commodities – such as coal, iron ore, bauxite, gold, wool, beef, cotton, sugar, cereal grains and other agricultural products; services – such as tourism, medical and health services and education; and manufactures – such as steel and various metal products, aluminium and a range of food-related products. Major imports include cars and trucks, heavy machinery, petroleum, electrical and electronic equipment, and clothing.

Why does a nation even bother to trade with the rest of the world? Does it seem strange for Australia to import goods it could probably produce for itself? Indeed, why doesn't Australia become self-sufficient by growing all its own food, making all its own cars, machinery and other manufactured goods and prohibiting sales of all foreign products? This section explains why specialisation and trade are a nation's keys to unlocking a higher standard of living for its citizens.

Exhibit 18.1 **Australia's merchandise trade trading partners, 2003–04**

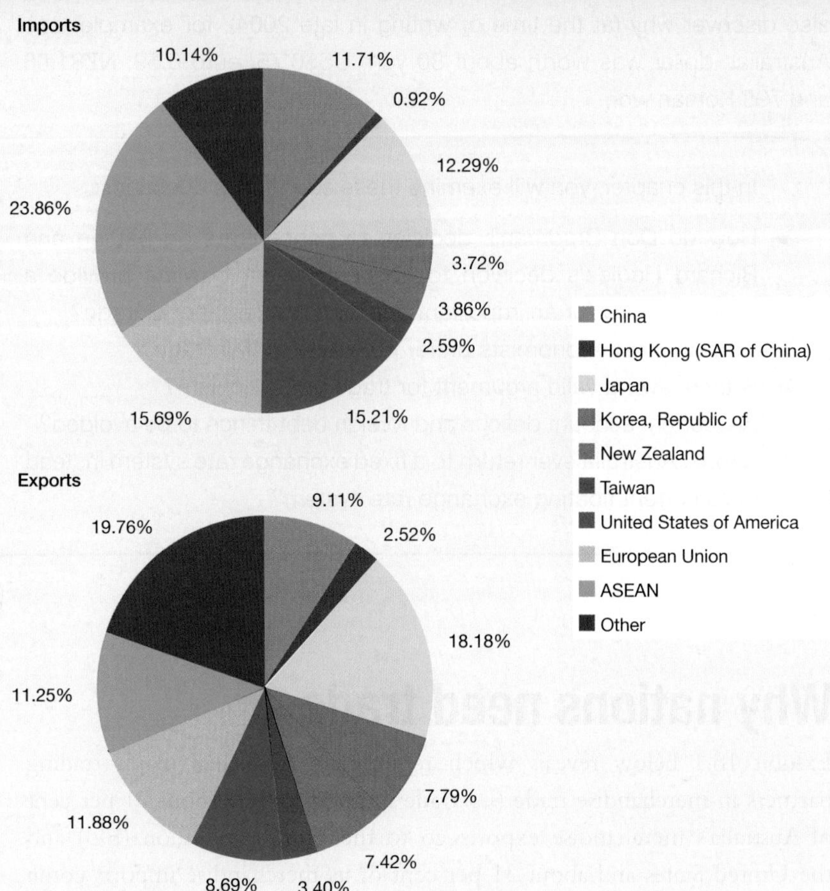

In 2003–04, Asian countries accounted for about 52 per cent of Australian merchandise exports, while the EU and the United States accounted for 21 per cent. On the other hand, 55 per cent of Australia's merchandise imports were sourced from Asia, with 31 per cent coming from the EU and the United States.

Source: Australian Bureau of Statistics, 'International Trade in Goods and Services', December 2004, Cat. No. 5368.0, Table 10.

The production possibilities frontier revisited

Consider a world with only two countries – Australia and Malaysia. To keep the illustration simple, also assume both countries produce only two generic 'goods' – agricultural products and electronic equipment. Accordingly, we can construct in Exhibit 18.2 a *production possibilities frontier* for each country. We will also – for the purposes of this discussion – set aside the *law of increasing opportunity costs* (explained in Chapter 2) and assume workers are equally suited to producing agricultural products or electronic equipment. This assumption does not alter the essential validity of the discussion to follow, but simplifies things by transforming the bowed-out shape of the production possibilities frontier of Chapter 2 into a straight line.

Exhibit 18.2 **The benefits of trade**

(a) Australian production and consumption

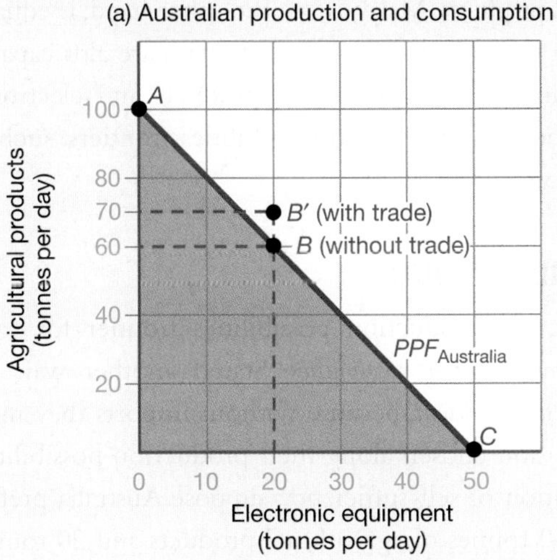

(b) Malaysian production and consumption

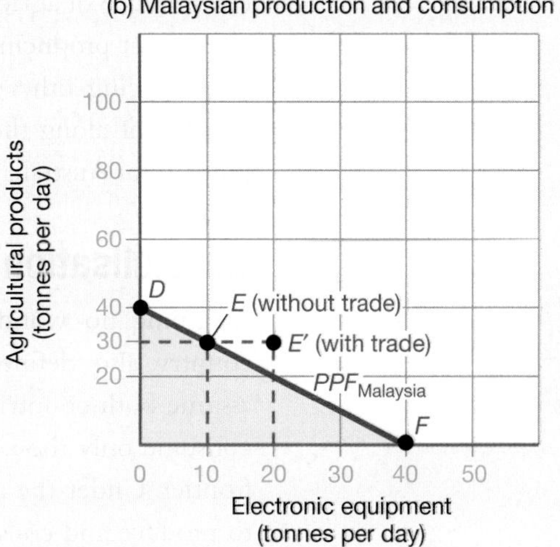

As shown in part (a), assume Australia chooses point *B* on its production possibilities frontier, $PPF_{Australia}$. Without trade, Australia produces and consumes 60 tonnes of agricultural products and 20 tonnes of electronic equipment. In part (b), assume Malaysia also operates along its production possibilities frontier, $PPF_{Malaysia}$, at point *E*. Without trade, Malaysia produces and consumes 30 tonnes of agricultural products and 10 tonnes of electronic equipment.

Now assume Australia specialises in producing agricultural products at point *A* and imports 20 tonnes of Malaysian electronic equipment in exchange for 30 tonnes of agricultural products. Through specialisation and trade, Australia moves to consumption possibility point *B′*, outside its production possibilities frontier. Malaysia also specialises in producing electronic equipment (point *F*) and moves to a higher standard of living at consumption possibility point *E′*, outside its production possibilities frontier.

By comparing parts (a) and (b) of Exhibit 18.2 we see that Australia can produce more agricultural products than Malaysia. If Australia devotes all its resources of land, labour and capital to this purpose, 100 tonnes of agricultural products may be produced per day, represented by point *A* in Exhibit 18.2(a). The maximum agricultural products production of Malaysia, on the other hand, is 40 tonnes per day because Malaysia has less labour, arable land and other factors of production than Australia. This capability is represented by point *D* in Exhibit 18.2(b).

Now consider the capacities of the two countries for production of electronic equipment. If all their respective resources are devoted to this output, Australia produces 50 tonnes per day (point *C*) and Malaysia produces 40 tonnes per day (point *F*). Again, the greater potential maximum electronic equipment output of Australia reflects its greater resources.

However, you should notice in passing that Australia is relatively less efficient at producing electronic equipment than agricultural products – using all its resources it can only produce half as much electronic equipment as it can produce of agricultural products. Malaysia, on the other hand, is equally efficient at producing both types of goods. Both countries are also capable of producing other combinations of agricultural products and electronic equipment along their respective production possibilities frontiers, such as point *B* for Australia and point *E* for Malaysia.

Specialisation without trade

Assuming no world trade, the production possibilities frontier for each country also defines its *consumption possibilities*. Stated another way, we assume both countries are *self-sufficient*, because without imports they must consume only the combination chosen along their production possibilities frontier. Under the assumption of self-sufficiency, suppose Australia prefers to produce and consume 60 tonnes of agricultural products and 20 tonnes of electronic equipment per day (point *B*). Also assume Malaysia chooses to produce and consume 30 tonnes of agricultural products and 10 tonnes of electronic equipment (point *E*). Exhibit 18.3 lists data corresponding to points *B* and *E* and shows that the total two-country world output is 90 tonnes of agricultural products and 30 tonnes of electronic equipment.

Now suppose Australia specialises by producing and consuming at point *A*, rather than point *B*. Suppose also that Malaysia specialises by producing and consuming at point *F*, rather than point *E*. As shown in Exhibit 18.3, specialisation in each country increases total world output per day by 10

Exhibit 18.3 **Effect of specialisation on world output**

	Agricultural products production (tonnes per day)	Electronic equipment production (tonnes per day)
Before specialisation		
Australia (at point *B*)	60	20
Malaysia (at point *E*)	30	10
Total world output	90	30
After specialisation		
Australia (at point *A*)	100	0
Malaysia (at point *F*)	0	40
Total world output	100	40

tonnes of agricultural products and 10 tonnes of electronic equipment. Because this extra world output has the potential for making both countries better off, why wouldn't Australia and Malaysia specialise and produce at points *A* and *F*, respectively? The reason is that, although production at these points is clearly possible, neither country wants to consume these combinations of output. Australia prefers to consume fewer agricultural products and some electronic equipment at point *B* compared to point *A*. Malaysia, on the other hand, prefers to consume some agricultural products and less electronic equipment at point *E*, rather than point *F*.

When countries specialise, total world output increases and, therefore, the potential for greater total world consumption also increases.

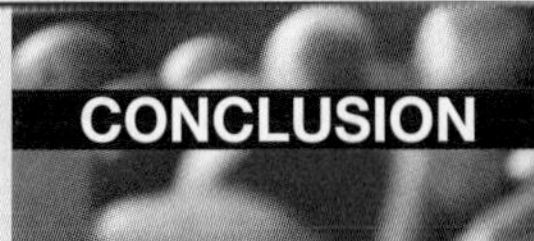

Specialisation with trade

Now we return to Exhibit 18.2 and demonstrate how world trade benefits countries. Suppose Australia agrees to specialise in agricultural products production at point *A* and to import 20 tonnes of Malaysian electronic equipment in exchange for 30 tonnes of its agricultural products output. Does Australia gain from trade? The answer is yes. At point *A*, Australia produces 100 tonnes of agricultural products per day. Subtracting the 30 tonnes traded to Malaysia leaves Australia with 70 tonnes for its own consumption. In return for the agricultural products, Malaysia trades 20 tonnes of electronic equipment to Australia. Hence, specialisation and trade allow Australia to move from point *A* to point *B*′, which is a consumption possibility outside its production possibilities frontier in Exhibit 18.2(a). At point *B*′, Australia consumes the same amount of electronic equipment and 10 more tonnes of agricultural products compared to point *B* (without trade).

The World Trade Organization (WTO) (**www.wto.org**) is an international body addressing trade among nations. It provides data and analysis on international trade.

Malaysia also has an incentive to specialise by moving its production mix from point *E* to point *F*. With trade, Malaysia's consumption would be at point *E*′. At point *E*′, Malaysia has as much agricultural production to consume as it had at point *E*, plus 10 more tonnes of electronic equipment. After trading 20 tonnes of the 40 tonnes of electronic equipment produced at point *F* for agricultural products, Malaysia can still consume 20 tonnes of electronic equipment from its production, rather than only 10 tonnes of electronic equipment at point *E*. Thus, point *E*′ is a consumption possibility that lies *outside* Malaysia's production possibilities frontier also.

International trade allows a country to consume a combination of goods that lies outside its production possibilities frontier.

To learn more about any country and its economy – including trade information – visit the World Factbook, a comprehensive publication of the US Central Intelligence Agency (CIA) (**www.cia.gov/cia/publications/factbook/index.html**). Select the country of your choice.

Comparative and absolute advantage

In the above analysis it was shown that Australia would be economically better off by producing and exporting agricultural products and importing electronic equipment. Similarly, Malaysia was better off by producing and exporting electronic equipment and importing agricultural products. Here you will study the economic principle that determines specialisation and trade. It is one of the most fundamental and important principles of economics.

Comparative advantage

comparative advantage

Comparative advantage The ability of a country to produce a good at a lower opportunity cost than another country.

Engaging in world trade permits countries to escape the consumption prison of their own production possibilities frontiers and produce iron ore, cars or whatever goods they make best, while using that production to trade with other countries to acquire other goods and services they wish to consume. Australia's decision to specialise in and export agricultural products and the decision of Malaysia to specialise in and export electronic equipment are based on **comparative advantage**. Comparative advantage is the ability of a country to produce a good at a lower opportunity cost than another country.

Returning to our earlier example, we can calculate opportunity costs for the two countries and use comparative advantage to determine which countries should specialise in agricultural products or electronic equipment. For Australia, the opportunity cost of producing 50 tonnes of electronic equipment is 100 tonnes of agricultural products not produced, or 1 tonne of electronic equipment costs 2 tonnes of agricultural products forgone. For Malaysia, the opportunity cost of producing 40 tonnes of electronic equipment is 40 tonnes of agricultural products, or 1 tonne of electronic equipment costs 1 tonne of agricultural products forgone.

Malaysia's electronic equipment is therefore cheaper than Australia's in terms of agricultural products forgone. This means Malaysia has a comparative advantage over Australia in electronic equipment production, because less agricultural production has to be given up to produce electronic equipment in Malaysia than in Australia.

Conversely, we could measure the cost of agricultural products in terms of electronic equipment. For Australia, one tonne of agricultural products costs half a tonne of electronic equipment. For Malaysia, one tonne of agricultural products costs one tonne of electronic equipment forgone. Australia has a comparative advantage over Malaysia in agricultural products because its opportunity cost in terms of electronic equipment forgone is lower. Thus, Australia should specialise in agricultural products because it is more efficient in their production. Malaysia, on the other hand, is relatively more efficient at producing electronic equipment and should specialise in this product.

Comparative advantage refers to the relative opportunity costs between countries of producing the same goods. World output and consumption are maximised when each country specialises in producing goods for which it has a comparative advantage and trading them for those for which it does not have a comparative advantage.

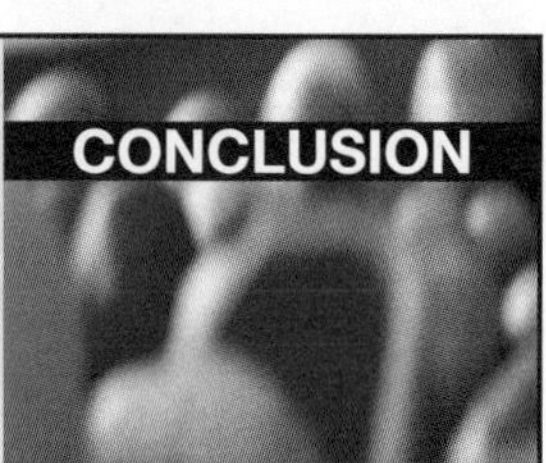

Absolute advantage

So far, it has been shown that a country's production and international trade decisions depend on comparing what a country gives up to produce more of a good. It is important to note that comparative advantage is based on opportunity costs, regardless of the absolute costs of resources used in production. In the above analysis we did not consider how much labour, land or capital either Australia or Malaysia uses to produce a tonne of agricultural products or electronic equipment. **Absolute advantage** is the ability of a country to produce a good using fewer resources than another country.

Absolute advantage The ability of a country to produce a good using fewer resources than another country.

For instance, suppose, purely for argument's sake, that Malaysia might have an absolute advantage in producing both agricultural products and electronic equipment. If this were the case it would need to use fewer resources per tonne to produce agricultural products and electronic equipment than Australia. However, such an absolute advantage on the part of Malaysia does not matter at all in specialisation and world trade decisions.

Having such an absolute advantage in both goods does not mean that Malaysia should produce both types of goods. If Australia has a comparative advantage in agricultural production compared to Malaysia, it would improve world economic output if it were to specialise in agricultural production, even if Malaysia could produce both agricultural products and electronic equipment with fewer resources.

Comparative and absolute advantage compared

A few examples will help to further clarify the difference between absolute advantage and comparative advantage.

As mentioned in Chapter 2, when Babe Ruth played baseball for the New York Yankees in the 1930s he was the best hitter and the best pitcher on the team. In other words, he had an absolute advantage in both hitting and throwing the baseball. For example, he could produce the same number of home runs as any other team-mate with fewer times at bat, and he had the best pitching figures of anyone in the team.

The problem was that, if he pitched, he would bat fewer times because pitchers need rest after pitching. The coaches decided that, even though he was both the best hitter and the best pitcher on the team, the Babe had a comparative advantage in hitting. Other pitchers on the team could pitch almost as well as the Babe, but no one could come close to his hitting. In terms of opportunity costs, the Yankees would get more runs and lose fewer games if the Babe specialised in hitting.

A similar argument explains why, in cricket, Don Bradman specialised in batting even though he was quite handy with the ball, while Richard Hadlee allowed others to bat while he specialised in bowling. The well-known US basketballer, Michael Jordan, tried baseball for a while and proved to be better than most. However, his comparative advantage was on the basketball court and his baseball career was short-lived.

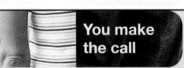

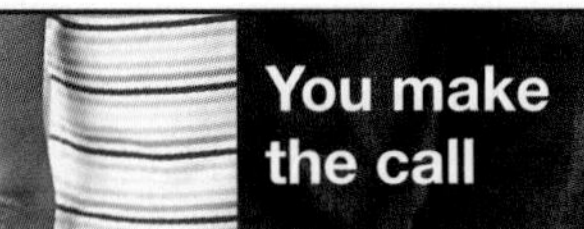

Do nations with an absolute advantage gain from trade?

Comparing labour productivity, suppose, for the sake of argument, that Australia has an absolute advantage over Indonesia in the production of both calculators and towels. In Australia, a worker can produce four calculators or 400 towels in 10 hours. In Indonesia, a worker can produce one calculator or 50 towels in the same time. Under these conditions, would Australia benefit economically by trading with Indonesia?

The same argument explains why most of us specialise in some particular thing as our livelihood rather than becoming 'jacks of all trades'. By specialising and then trading our output we are able to expand our consumption possibilities. For example, theoretically a person could grow their own food, make their own clothes, educate their children, build their own house, do all their own mechanical repairs, and so on. However, individuals typically choose to specialise in a small number of things in which they have a comparative advantage compared with others in their communities. They then trade their production (through spending their earned income) for that of others who have similarly specialised in other activities. In this way the whole community achieves higher levels of consumption and economic welfare than would otherwise have been the case had they all tried to do everything for themselves. What makes obvious sense for the individual and domestic communities is equally sensible for entire countries.

Free trade, fair trade and protectionism

Free trade The flow of goods between countries without restrictions or special taxes.

Protectionism The government's use of embargoes, tariffs, quotas and other restrictions to protect domestic producers from foreign competition.

In theory, economists argue that international trade should be based on comparative advantage and **free trade**. Free trade is the flow of goods and services between countries without restrictions or special taxes on their flow. In practice, despite the advice of economists, every nation protects its own domestic producers from foreign competition to some degree. **Protectionism** is the government's use of embargoes, tariffs, quotas and other restrictions to protect domestic producers from foreign competition.

Embargo

Embargoes are the strongest limit on trade. An embargo is a law that bars trade with another country. For example, the United States and other nations in the world imposed an arms embargo on Iraq in response to Iraq's invasion of Kuwait in 1990.

Embargo A law that bars trade with another country.

Tariff

Tariffs are the most common and visible measures used to discourage trade. A tariff is a tax on an import. Tariffs are also called customs duties. A tariff can be based on weight, volume or number of units or it can be *ad valorem* (figured as a percentage of the price). The average Australian tariff is now less than 5 per cent, but remains quite high on motor vehicles and textiles. However, the high level of protection afforded to motor vehicle and textile production in Australia is being progressively wound back over the course of the early twenty-first century, beginning in 2005. The purpose of tariffs is to reduce imports by raising their selling prices compared with similar domestic goods. The tax revenue raised from their sale also adds to government revenues.

Tariff A tax on an import.

In Australia, the Department of Foreign Affairs and Trade (**www.dfat.gov.au**) provides commentary on a wide range of trade-related issues as well as international trade statistics.

During the worldwide Great Depression of the 1930s some nations decided to try to protect their own industries and workers from foreign competition by erecting high tariffs on imported goods. It was thought that imports meant domestic jobs lost. Unfortunately, as one nation raised its tariffs to protect its industries and jobs, other nations retaliated by raising their tariffs. In the end, all that these so-called 'beggar-thy-neighbour' policies achieved was a worldwide reduction in demand and production, thereby actually bringing about the higher unemployment such ill-conceived policies were aimed at avoiding!

In 1947, most of the world's industrialised nations mutually agreed to gradually bring down the tariff walls by signing the General Agreement on Tariffs and Trade (GATT). Since then, GATT nations – now members of the World Trade Organization (WTO) – have met periodically to negotiate multilateral reductions in tariff rates around the world with the aim of stimulating world trade and output.

For example, the 1994 Uruguay round achieved substantial reductions in tariffs on a range of goods, with some progress also being made in the area of services. In particular, tariff reductions in the agricultural area were of considerable benefit to Australia as well as to many poor, struggling, developing countries whose economies are still largely agriculturally based. A new round of talks was due to commence in September 2000 in Seattle, but was disrupted by demonstrations and eventually cancelled. This was a great pity, since further reductions in trade barriers by the developed nations would potentially provide many new job opportunities to people in the less developed, poorer nations of the world – people about whom the demonstrators purported to be concerned!

Fortunately, in November 2001 at Doha, Qatar, the trade ministers of the 144 WTO member nations agreed to initiate a new trade negotiation round. It had been scheduled to take three years, but at the time of writing in late 2004 virtually no solid progress had yet been made. However, it is to be hoped, one way or the other, either through this latest WTO-sponsored multilateral round of trade negotiations or through a range of emerging bilateral agreements between various pairs of countries around the world, reductions in international trade barriers will be achieved in coming years. This will further enrich the world through greater trade, economic activity and employment opportunities, particularly for those suffering severe economic hardships in less-developed countries.

Quota

Quota A limit on the quantity of a good that may be imported in a given time period.

Another way to limit foreign competition is to impose a **quota**. A quota is a limit on the quantity of a good that may be imported into a country in a given time period. For example, a country may allow 10 million tonnes of sugar to be imported over a one-year period. Once this quantity is reached, no more sugar can be imported for the year. Quotas can limit imports from all foreign suppliers or from specific countries. For example, in 2000 the United States imposed quotas on the importation of Australian lamb and this restriction created tension between the two countries until the quotas were lifted in late 2001.

Quotas, like all barriers to trade, invite other nations to retaliate with more measures to restrict trade, the end result being that all nations use their scarce resources in sub-optimal ways and thereby become worse off than they otherwise could be.

In addition to embargoes, tariffs and quotas, some nations use more subtle measures to discourage trade. For example, some countries set up an overwhelming number of bureaucratic steps that must be taken in order to import a product. Australia, for example, has been accused from time to time of using quarantine and health regulations to restrict unnecessarily the importation of various agricultural products from other nations.

Fair trade and strategic trade

Free trade was defined above as the free flow of goods and services between countries without restrictions or special taxes on their flow. In recent years much has been made of the notion of fair trade, particularly by those opposed to allowing international trade to flow unencumbered by nationally imposed import restrictions of the types listed above. The term has a nice ring to it, so it is important to understand what exactly is meant by it, in what sense the word 'fair' is used, and whether it is or isn't desirable.

Fair trade The term used to represent the view that a country should only reduce its barriers to imports from another country if the other country does not have some sort of 'unfair' competitive advantage over it and provided the other country is also willing to reduce its import barriers reciprocally.

Fair trade is the term used to represent the view that a country should only reduce its barriers to imports from another country if the other country does not have some sort of 'unfair' competitive advantage over it and provided the other country is also willing to reduce its import barriers reciprocally. The notion of fair trade has popular appeal, so it is important to spend a little time thinking critically about it.

First and foremost, how should one define 'unfair' competitive advantage? For example, is it unfair if another country has a lot more rainfall and easily accessible fertile and arable land to use in its production of agricultural products than does the home country? If this means the foreign country can produce a range of such products at 50 per cent of the cost of the home country, is that a reason for the home country to claim 'unfair competition', impose high tariffs on agricultural imports from it and thereby deny itself this source of high-quality, cheap products? Another common example of supposed 'unfair' advantages is differential wage rates between developing and developed nations. On this, see the discussion that follows.

Second, you also need to ask who is being hurt when a country imposes high tariffs on the importation of another country's products. The foreign country is most likely being hurt because it probably can't sell as much as it could into the home country's markets. But, very importantly, the home country is also being hurt by its own actions. The tariffs will result in people having to pay higher prices for such products than they need to and too much of the home country's scarce resources will be used up in inefficient production rather than being freed up and redirected into more productive areas. As a well-known Australian economist once remarked, imposing tariffs in such situations is like shooting yourself in the foot with a shotgun in the hope that a few of the pellets will also hit your competitors!

The moral that should be drawn and remembered here is that the prime motivation for a country to lower its tariffs is not to give a helping hand to firms in other countries. Other countries will certainly benefit from such action since the international markets for their products will be expanded. However, the most important reason – and prime motivation – for reducing import barriers at home is that the home country will itself derive very significant benefits from such action! Furthermore, this will happen irrespective of whether another country lowers its tariffs in return for such action. In fact, a recent study by Australia's Department of Foreign Affairs and Trade estimated that, while the greatest benefits to Australia – in terms of a net increase in GDP and employment – would result if there occurred a multilateral reduction in tariffs, there would nevertheless be significant net output and employment benefits to Australia if it unilaterally reduced its tariffs without any of its trading partners following suit.

We have already seen the explanation for this. If another country's firms can produce a good or service at a smaller opportunity cost than can be achieved in the home country – that is, if the foreign firms have a comparative advantage in the production of that good or service – then isn't this precisely why it is in the best interests of the home country to allow the importation of quantities of the good or service in question? This frees up scarce resources in the home country that can then be used in the production of goods and services in which it does have an international comparative advantage. These products can then be traded in return for imported products in which it doesn't enjoy comparative advantages. By doing so it incurs lower opportunity costs in the use of its scarce resources than it would if it produced such products itself. The home country can therefore enjoy the benefits of more goods and services and a higher standard of living than it otherwise could.

Strategic trade theory The idea that governments should seek to be strategic in their use of their spending and taxing powers in order to actively facilitate some sectors of the economy that they may feel have the potential to be strong export earners for their nations.

strategic trade theory

Strategic trade theory is the term used for the idea that governments should seek to be strategic in the use of their spending and taxing powers in order to actively facilitate some sectors of the economy that they may feel have the potential to be strong export earners for their nations. Proponents argue that a country's comparative advantages are not static. On the contrary, they would argue that nations can develop comparative advantages over other nations by careful and selective support for some industries over others. They point to a country like Singapore, for example, which had little in the way of natural comparative advantages (in mining, agriculture, manufacturing and so on) but which, through careful and successful government policies, has become one of the powerhouses of the East Asia region.

This approach to trade is not without its critics, who argue that the private sector is better placed – and better skilled – to develop export opportunities. They point to the equally successful performance of Hong Kong over recent decades. Hong Kong followed a market-based approach to developing its export markets with little strategic direction – critics would say 'interference' – from the government. They also argue that there are many counter-examples to the case of Singapore that bear out how wasteful and counterproductive such interventionist government policies can often be when they go wrong.

Be that as it may, on one thing there is agreement: it is certainly true that comparative advantages are dynamic. Just as an individual person's comparative advantages can – and usually do – evolve over time, so too do those of an entire country. Thus, rather than remaining static, a nation's comparative advantages evolve over time as technology and international tastes change. What is not agreed upon is the appropriate role for government to play in such circumstances.

The political economy of reducing barriers to trade

If trade is apparently so obviously beneficial to the economic prosperity of countries, why is free trade strongly opposed by some and why do some countries severely restrict trade? As you will see, the reason essentially stems from the political influence of narrow special-interest groups that are likely to be negatively affected by any reductions in a country's trade restrictions.

Free trade provides consumers with lower prices and larger quantities of products from which to choose. Thus, removing or lowering import barriers – by, for example, reducing tariffs – might take a few hundred dollars a year off the cost of living for an individual family. When added up across the entire community these savings are considerable, but for each family it might not be a huge amount and, furthermore, the families in question are unlikely to link their reduced cost of living directly back to the tariff reductions anyway.

Another benefit of the reduced tariffs would be that the resultant extra buying power of consumers is likely also to stimulate other areas of domestic production, with concomitant increases in employment. However, again, the firms who experience the extra demand would not necessarily make the link back to this being a benefit of the reduced tariffs and neither would the people who receive the additional jobs that those firms are then able to offer.

Finally, many firms use imported components and machinery in the production of their goods and services. Reduced import prices arising from the lower tariffs will therefore lower the costs of production of firms generally. This will be of great benefit to exporting firms in particular. It will enable them to be more competitive, sell more output into international markets, earn greater income for their owners and provide greater numbers of jobs. However, again, such firms and employees are unlikely to appreciate the link between the reduced tariffs and their increased good fortunes and extra opportunities.

On the other hand, the problem is that – particularly in the short term – the cheaper imports resulting from the reduced tariffs may significantly reduce the incomes of the owners of the firms competing directly with the cheaper imports. Furthermore, some employees in such firms may lose their jobs, resulting in considerable short-term hardship for them.

Thus, the benefits of the tariff reduction are dispersed across a wide cross-section of the community, often come after some time lag, and are enjoyed by many who do not necessarily even make the link back to the tariff reductions anyway. However, the costs of the tariff reductions are felt by a small, easily identified group who are usually very much aware of the reason for their reduced fortunes.

It is no wonder then that, in spite of the great total benefits to the community in the wide, trade barriers continue to exist in most countries. The employees and owners of import-competing firms have a great deal at stake and their plight often makes for good sensationalist news and current affairs shows. They are therefore also likely to find a sympathetic hearing from politicians – particularly those in regions most negatively affected by the tariff reductions, who have at least one eye fixed firmly on the next election.

Some common (but specious) arguments for protection

The following are some of the most popular rationalisations used by those seeking protection. These arguments have strong political or emotional appeal, but weak support from most economists.

Infant industry argument

INFOTRAC®
infant industry argument

The infant industry argument, as the name suggests, is that a new domestic industry needs protection because it is not yet ready to compete with established foreign competitors. An infant industry is in a formative stage and must bear high start-up costs. These high costs result from the need to train an entire workforce, develop new technology, establish marketing channels and reach economies of scale. With time to grow and with protection, an infant industry can reduce costs and 'catch up' with established foreign firms.

While this may all sound quite reasonable, there are very considerable real-world practical problems associated with it. For example, economists ask where one draws the arbitrary line between an 'infant' and a 'grown-up' industry. It is also difficult to make a convincing case for protecting an infant industry in a developed country where industries that are consistent with the country's natural comparative advantage should be well established.

The infant industry argument may have some validity for less-developed countries. However, even for these countries, there is a danger. Once protection is granted, the new industry will not necessarily feel the competitive pressures necessary to encourage the adoption of the most efficient production technologies and best management and work practices and so on to achieve reasonably quick growth and participation in world trade. Also, once an industry is given protection, it can prove extremely difficult to take away that protection, for all the reasons already mentioned.

National security argument

Another common argument is that defence-related industries must be protected with embargoes, tariffs or quotas to ensure national security. By protecting critical defence industries, a nation will not be dependent on foreign countries for the essential defence-related goods it needs to defend itself in wartime. The national defence argument has been used from time to time to protect a long list of industries, including petrochemicals, munitions, steel and rubber.

In today's highly interlinked world of the twenty-first century, where countries have a multiplicity of interwoven military, diplomatic and economic ties with many other countries, this argument makes little sense in most cases. Of course, a country must make a sensible investment in the necessary military assets and personnel to provide for its own security. However, again, rather than trying to be self-sufficient in the actual production of all such things, the much more sensible approach is to purchase through trade those military assets for which the country does not have a comparative advantage in their production.

Employment argument

The employment argument suggests that restricting imports increases domestic jobs in the protected industries. According to this protectionist argument, the sale of an imported good comes at the expense of its domestically produced counterpart. Lower domestic output therefore leads to higher domestic unemployment than would otherwise be the case.

It is true that protectionism may increase output and save jobs in some domestic industries. What is ignored, however, are all the other employment-reducing effects that were covered earlier. The net outcome could well be that the tariffs actually act to reduce the total number of domestic jobs available in the country compared with what would have been the case in the absence of the tariffs. In fact, one of the most important arguments for the significant tariff reductions in Australia in the 1970s and 1980s was that, in aggregate terms, they would be output- and employment-augmenting! As it turned out, this was indeed what happened.

As a concrete example, suppose higher tariff protection is given to domestically produced motor vehicles in Australia and this results in cars and trucks being, say, $5000 per unit dearer in Australia than they would be otherwise. This may well protect a few hundred jobs in the domestic motor vehicle production industry. However, another effect of this is that consumers will have that much less to spend on other products and this may cost jobs in those firms whose demand is reduced on account of the reduced consumer buying power. The higher-cost cars and trucks also increase the production costs of all firms who use vehicles in some way in the production of their goods or services. This again may cost jobs in those firms, particularly those export-oriented firms that need to compete in international markets to sell their products. In short, while protection for one industry may well protect some jobs in that industry, it may actually cause a net reduction in the nation's total employment. In fact, most thorough, economy-wide analyses of the output and employment impacts of protection find just this outcome.

Cheap foreign labour argument

Another popular claim is the cheap foreign labour argument. It goes something like this: 'How can we compete with such unfair competition? Labour costs a minimum of around $15 an hour in Australia and firms in many developing countries pay only $1 an hour. Without protection, Australian wages will be driven down and our standard of living will fall.'

A major flaw in this argument is that it neglects the essential reason for the difference in the wage rates between countries. Australian workers have

International focus

Applicable concept: protectionism

World trade slips on banana peel

Until the end of the 1980s growing bananas for European markets was a multi-billion-dollar bright spot for Latin America's struggling economies. In fact, about half of this region's banana exports traditionally were sold to Europe. Then in 1993 the fifteen-nation European Union (EU) adopted a package of quotas and tariffs aimed at cutting Europe's banana imports from Latin America. The purpose of these restrictions was to give trade preference to 66 former banana-growing colonies of European nations in Africa, the Caribbean and the Pacific. Ignored is the fact that Latin American growers grow higher-quality bananas at half the cost of EU-favoured growers because of their low labour cost and flat tropical land near port cities.[1]

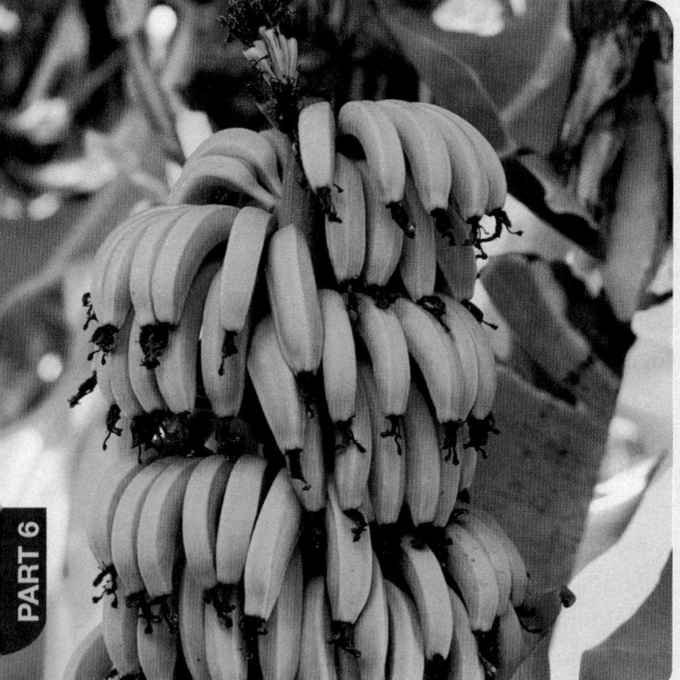

In September 1997, the World Trade Organization (WTO) ruled that the EU rules covering bananas unfairly discriminated against Latin American-grown bananas. The EU modified its banana rules, but the United States contended that these changes were merely cosmetic and announced that punitive tariffs of 100 per cent would be imposed in 1999 on millions of dollars of European imports, including items ranging from cashmere sweaters and Italian handbags to sheep's milk cheese, British biscuits and German coffee-makers. Denmark and the Netherlands were to be exempt from the US tariffs because they were the only nations voting against the EU banana rules.

An official of the EU immediately denounced the US threat of sanctions and said a case would be filed before the WTO challenging the validity of these US tariffs. It should also be noted that the United States may actually have been motivated to push the case because American companies, including Chiquita Brands International Inc. and Dole Food Co., grew their bananas mostly in Latin America.

1 James Brooke, 'Forbidden fruit in Europe: Latin bananas face hurdles', *New York Times*, 5 April 1993, p. A1.

Analyse the issue

Analyse this issue in international trade from the point of view of the arguments outlined in the text. What would you recommend as the most desirable economic outcome for the United States, Latin America and Europe?

PART 6

more education, training, capital and access to more advanced technology. They are therefore able to produce more output per hour than workers in less-developed countries with lower wage rates. Therefore, if Australian workers produce more output per hour than workers in another country then, even with the higher wages per worker, the labour costs per unit of production should remain internationally competitive.

A counter-example may clarify this point further. The reason why Australian motor vehicle production is currently receiving protection against foreign producers in Germany, Japan and the United States is not the cheaper wages in those countries compared with Australia. On the contrary, wages in those countries are similar to (if not higher than) those in Australia. No, the reason is that, in this industry, Australia has never been able to combine its labour and capital at a sufficiently large scale of production to achieve the production efficiencies needed to produce motor vehicle output at an internationally competitive per unit cost. Furthermore, many would argue that it has been precisely the very large protection afforded the industry during the past fifty years or more that has resulted in such efficiencies never being reached.

Free trade agreements

Free trade agreements In a free trade agreement, parties to a free trade area agree to eliminate tariffs and other trade barriers among themselves. However, each individual country maintains its own tariff policy against non-parties to the agreement.

free trade agreements

The trend in recent years has been for nations to negotiate reductions in trade barriers on bilateral bases. For instance, Australia has had a free trade agreement (FTA) with New Zealand since the 1980s (called Closer Economic Relations or CER). More recently it has also signed such agreements with Singapore and Thailand and there have been some embryonic steps taken towards some sort of future agreements with China, Malaysia and ASEAN. Most significantly, at the time of writing (in late 2004) it had also just formally accepted a comprehensive FTA with the United States. An FTA is an agreement whereby participating members eliminate all (or most) trade barriers among themselves. Other important FTAs around the world are as follows.

In Europe, fifteen nations joined together in 1958 to form a customs union called the European Economic Community (EEC) which, over time, evolved into an FTA known as the European Union (EU). The EU has removed virtually all trade barriers among its members, thereby creating, by the 1990s, a single European economy comparable in size to the US economy. In addition, a new currency, the euro, has now replaced the individual currencies of a twelve-country subset of the EU countries. For example, German marks, French francs and Italian lire – along with the individual currencies of the other nine countries – were all progressively taken out of circulation from 1 January 2002. These twelve euro-currency countries now all have the same currency and are all subject to the same monetary policy controlled by the European Central Bank (the ECB).

In 1993, the United States entered into an FTA with Canada and

Read more about NAFTA at **www.fas.usda.gov/itp/policy/nafta/nafta.html.** Similarly, more information can also be obtained on the FTA between Australia and NZ (CER) from the Department of Foreign Affairs and Trade website (**www.dfat.gov.au/trade/negotiations/anzcer.html**). Information on the Asian Pacific Economic Co-operation (APEC) forum can be found at **www.dfat.gov.au/trade/apec_int_reg_fora.html.**

Mexico called the North American Free Trade Agreement (NAFTA). Under NAFTA, effective 1 January 1994, tariffs and other impediments to trade among the three nations were to be progressively phased out over fifteen years. The Asia-Pacific Economic Cooperation group (APEC) was formed in 1994 by the leaders of eighteen Asian nations (Australia is included in APEC). This organisation is based on a non-binding agreement to reduce trade barriers over time among member nations. South American nations also have entered into a limited FTA known as Mercosur. Finally, the agreed FTA between Australia and the US, formally ratified by both countries in late 2004 with implementation from January 2005, immediately eliminates or significantly reduces tariffs across a wide range of manufacturing, allows for the timed reduction of trade barriers across most of agriculture (notably, however, sugar was excluded from the agreement), puts in place agreements in respect of intellectual property and services, and allows for much freer financial investment and tendering for government contracts across the two countries. For Australia the FTA offers the exciting prospect of being intimately and intricately linked economically to the largest and most dynamic economy in the world.

Critics of bilateral and/or regional FTAs fear they may largely result in trade diversion rather than net trade creation and that they will make global, multilateral agreements increasingly difficult to achieve in the future. They therefore fear that, over time, trading blocs may emerge that will erect new trade barriers across blocs, thereby creating 'Fortress North America', 'Fortress Europe', 'Fortress Asia' and similar impediments to the worldwide reduction of trade barriers.

Economics and ethics

Despite the incredible income and wealth available in developed countries at the start of the twenty-first century, very significant poverty continues to exist in quite a large number of less-developed, third-world countries, particularly in Africa. This poverty continues to plague generation after generation in such countries with the result that the quality of life is extremely poor, child mortality is shamefully high, and life expectancy is low.

Each year, the developed countries of the world dutifully contribute aid to such countries – usually around one per cent or so of their annual GDP. However, the aid never seems to permanently improve the economic lot of the people in the recipient countries and the poverty cycle just goes on. What else can be done?

A number of commentators are increasingly arguing that freer international trade, particularly in agricultural products – in tandem with better internal governance and anti-corruption measures in some of the poor countries concerned – may be the best way forward. It is unfortunately true that a number of richer developed countries, despite their wealth, nonetheless continue to maintain significant trade barriers such as import tariffs, quotas and embargoes, and inappropriate quarantine laws, as well as various forms of government subsidies to their own exporters and so on.

The existence of these trade barriers means that poor countries may have little opportunity to use their comparative advantage – low labour cost – to trade their way to a better life. Thus, as is often the case, allowing markets to operate without undue government interference can well provide a superior outcome from many perspectives, including in relation to ethical concerns.

The balance of payments

When trade occurs between Australia and other nations, many types of financial transactions occur and the net results of all these transactions are recorded in summary form in the so-called **balance of payments**. The balance of payments is a bookkeeping record of the international transactions between a country and other countries during a given period of time. This summary records the value of a nation's spending inflows and outflows made by individuals, firms and governments.

Balance of payments A summary record of the international transactions between a country and other countries during a given period of time.

balance of payments

The concept of a nation's balance of payments was introduced briefly in Chapter 11. Here we go into its various aspects in more detail. (If necessary, go back to Chapter 11 and re-read the relevant material.) Exhibit 18.4 reproduces Exhibit 11.7 from that chapter. The exhibit is a simplified balance of payments for Australia for 2003–04. Note the pluses and minuses in the table. A transaction that results in a dollar flow to Australia is entered as a positive amount, while a payment by Australia to another country is entered with a minus sign. As our discussion unfolds, you will learn that the balance of payments provides much useful information.

Current account

The first section of the balance of payments is the current account which includes, as the name implies, trade in currently produced goods and services. The most widely reported and largest part of the current account is the **current account balance on merchandise trade** (line 3 in Exhibit 18.4). The current account balance on merchandise trade is the value of a nation's merchandise imports subtracted from its merchandise exports. As shown in Exhibit 18.4, Australia had a merchandise trade deficit of $23.7 billion in

Current account balance on merchandise trade The value of a nation's merchandise imports subtracted from its merchandise exports.

Exhibit 18.4 **Australia's balance of payments, 2003–04**

Current account transactions	Amount (billions of dollars)
Goods	
1 Exports (credits)	109.2
2 Imports (debits)	–132.9
3 Balance on merchandise trade (1 + 2)	–23.7
Services	
4 Exports (credits)	34.0
5 Imports (debits)	–34.4
6 Net services (4 + 5)	–0.4
7 **Balance on goods and services (3 + 6)**	**–24.1**
Foreign income	
8 Credits	15.8
9 Debits	–39.1
10 Net income paid overseas (8 + 9)	–23.3
Transfers	
11 Credits	4.3
12 Debits	–4.3
13 Net transfers (11+12)	0.0
Balance on current account (7 + 10 + 13)	**–47.4**
Capital and financial account transactions	
14 Capital account	1.2
Financial account	
Direct investment	
15 Abroad	–24.4
16 In Australia	9.6
17 Portfolio investment	77.4
18 Financial derivatives	0.9
19 Other investment	–11.3
20 Change in official reserve assets	–5.1
21 **Balance on capital account (14 + … + 20)**	**48.3**
Balancing item	–0.9

Source: Australian Bureau of Statistics, www.abs.gov.au, Cat. No. 5302, Table 1.

2003–04. A merchandise trade deficit occurs when the value of a country's imports of goods exceeds the value of its exports of goods.

Of course, a nation's trade consists of more than just goods. For example, each year Australia enjoys many visits from tourists, and many international students come here for education. Their spending in Australia is counted as services exports. On the other hand, Australians enjoy, for example, going to movies made overseas and making trips overseas. Such spending is recorded as services imports. When services exports and imports are added to the balance of merchandise trade we have the so-called **current account balance on goods and services** (item 7 in Exhibit 18.4). In 2003–04 Australia's balance on goods and services was a deficit of \$24.1 billion.

Current account balance on goods and services This represents the nation's net position in respect of its exports and imports of both goods and services.

You should recall at this point the fundamental national income identity of GDP = $C + I + G + (X - M)$, which was first introduced in Chapter 11. The current account balance on goods and services is the $(X - M)$ component in this identity. In 2003–04 this amounted to a deficit of \$24.1 billion; that is, $(X - M) = -\$24.1$ billion. This means, therefore, that Australia's total spending that year by consumers, business and governments $(C + I + G)$ exceeded its total production of goods and services (GDP) by \$24.1 billion. This excess of domestic demand over domestic production was met by a net inflow of goods and services into Australia from abroad.

Items 10 and 13 of the current account in Exhibit 18.4 list ways other than direct trade in goods and services that result in flows of dollars into and out of Australia in a particular reporting period on account of current period activity.

Income flowing into Australia from the investments abroad of Australian residents – such as shares in foreign companies, real estate owned abroad and loans made to offshore residents – are payments for the services of this Australian investment abroad. These income flows would include interest payments on the loans, rent on the property and dividends on the shares. Analogously, residents of foreign countries also receive income flowing from the application of their investments in Australia. The difference between these flows in aggregate is known as **net foreign income**.

Net foreign income The difference between aggregate investment income flows into and out of a country. Such income includes interest payments on loans, rent on property and dividends on shares. Foreign income credits for Australia, for example, represent income flowing into Australia from the investments of Australian residents abroad, while foreign income debits represent income flowing out of Australia to foreigners on account of the application of their investment capital in Australia.

Item 10 of Exhibit 18.4 reports a net flow of such investment income out of Australia of \$23.3 billion in 2003–04. This is actually almost as large as the goods and services trade deficit of \$24.1 billion! This is not unusual for Australia and arises on account of the very significant foreign investment in the country over the past century. More will be said on this below.

Finally, we consider item 13, net transfers abroad. This category includes gifts made by the Australian government, charitable organisations or private individuals to other governments or private parties elsewhere in the world. For example, this item includes Australian foreign aid to other nations. Also included here would be pensions paid to Australian residents living abroad, for example. These are two examples of transfer debits. Similar transfers into Australia (credits) must be added to determine net transfers. Net transfers for Australia in 2003–04 were, purely by chance, estimated to be approximately zero.

In Australia, monthly data on the current account of the balance of payments are published by the Australian Bureau of Statistics at **www.abs.gov.au**.

Adding items 7, 10 and 13 gives the current account balance for 2003–04, a deficit of \$47.4 billion. A current account deficit is normal for Australia and means that, in aggregate net terms, Australians were undertaking a higher level of current payments to foreigners than foreigners were making

Exhibit 18.5 **Australia's current account balance, percentage of GDP, 1960–61 to 2003–04**

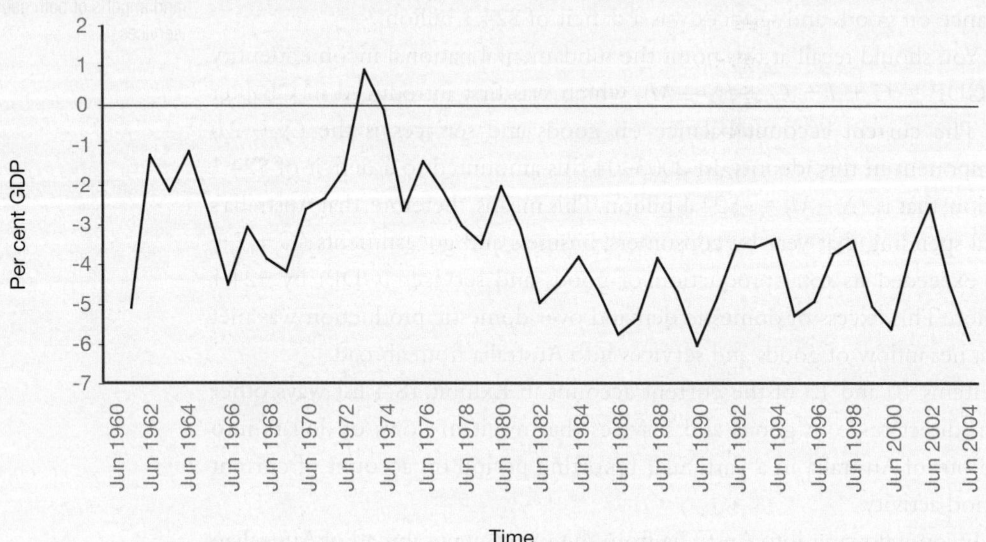

Since 1960–61 Australia has experienced current account deficits in every year except 1972–73. In fact, this has been the case in almost every year over the past century.

Source: Australian Bureau of Statistics, www.abs.gov.au, Cat. No. 5302, Table 40.

to Australians. Australia's current account balance – as a percentage of GDP – since 1960–61 is provided in Exhibit 18.5. As can be seen from the exhibit, Australia has registered a current account deficit in every year except 1972–73. More will be said on this shortly.

Capital account

The second section of the balance of payments is the capital account, which records the dollar payment flows on account of the purchases of foreign assets by Australians or Australian assets by foreigners. Examples include purchasing shares or bonds, extending loans, buying government securities or directly purchasing property. For example, when Taiwanese investors buy Australian Treasury bonds or AMP debentures, some coastal property in Queensland, shares in Telstra or a mine or a cattle station in Western Australia, there is an inflow of dollars into Australia. Such investments in Australia by foreigners will show up as a capital account credit. Similar investments by Australians overseas are recorded as capital account debits.

You should be sure to recognise that what are recorded on the capital account are the purchases (or sales) of investment assets, whereas what are recorded on the current account (in the net foreign income section) are the dividends, rent and interest payments that flow over time from these asset purchases. As Exhibit 18.4 shows, in 2003–04 it was estimated that Australia experienced a capital account surplus of $48.3 billion (item 21). This means that, in aggregate net terms, foreigners made investments in Australia $48.3 billion in excess of Australian residents' investments abroad.

The capital and current accounts exactly offset

You will also notice that included in Exhibit 18.4 is a line titled 'balancing item' with a value of –$0.9 billion which, when added to the estimated capital account surplus of $48.3 billion, exactly equals the estimated current account deficit for the year of $47.4 billion. This illustrates a very important aspect of a country's balance of payments, namely that in principle the two accounts – the current and the capital accounts – should balance and that any difference is simply due to measurement errors involved in trying to account for all of a country's many millions (or even billions) of transactions. Why must Australia's current account deficit of $47.4 billion in 2003–04 be matched with an exactly offsetting capital account surplus for the same year?

The reason is very simple. The current account deficit represents the extent to which a nation's spending in a particular period exceeded its income. In Australia's case, in 2003–04 the nation's residents in aggregate spent an estimated $47.4 billion more on imported goods and services and on payments of investment income to foreigners than they received from exports of goods and services and from inflows of investment income. The shortfall of $47.4 billion was provided to Australia by foreigners and something needed to be provided to them in return to induce them to do this. What were provided were claims to Australian-based assets. These assets were either loans made to Australians, property purchases by foreigners or purchases by foreigners of shares in Australian companies. In effect, foreigners were willing to accommodate the additional expenditure by Australians by becoming investors in the country.

An analogy may clarify this important point even further. Imagine that in a particular year you earned $50 000 after running costs from your small photocopying business. Of this, you spent $40 000 on your own personal consumption but also invested in some new photocopiers to the value of $20 000. Your total spending was $60 000 but your income was only $50 000. Where did the other $10 000 come from? One possibility is that it was provided by a bank in the form of a loan, on which you will need to pay interest over coming years and eventually pay it back. In this example, your spending was greater than your income by $10 000 and so your 'current account deficit' was $10 000. This current account deficit was exactly offset by a 'capital account surplus' of $10 000 in the form of the loan from the bank. You now have a liability to the bank.

CONCLUSION

A current account deficit is financed by a capital account surplus.

You make the call

Should everyone keep a balance of payments?

Nations keep balances of payments and calculate accounts such as their merchandise trade deficit or surplus. If nations need these accounts, should Australia's eight states and territories also maintain balance of payments accounts to properly manage their economies? What about cities? Why or why not?

Are current account deficits a bad thing?

In Exhibit 18.5 you saw that Australia has experienced current account deficits in every year bar one since 1960. In fact, over the entire twentieth century Australia ran up a current account deficit in just about every year. We also now know that a current account deficit means that as a nation we are spending more than the income we generate and, as you saw earlier, a result of this is that foreigners are continually accumulating Australian assets. Surely this must be a bad thing and cannot possibly be sustained for much longer!

Let's look a little more closely at this question, using the photocopy business example again. In that example, your spending consisted of consumption, C, of $40 000 plus investment, I, of $20 000 for a total spending ($C + I$) of $60 000, which exceeded your income (your GDP if you like) of $50 000. However, notice that out of your income of $50 000 you spent only $40 000 on consumption; the rest you saved. In this case your saving of $10 000 took the form of investment back into your business.

The reason for your 'current account deficit' was therefore that your desired investment of $20 000 exceeded your saving of $10 000. To fund the other $10 000 of desired investment, which you couldn't fund from your own saving, you approached a bank. The bank would have looked at your recent earnings from your business, your future business prospects and your other assets and made a business decision that it was likely to be in its commercial interests to lend you the money.

Given that the bank was willing to give you the loan, its judgement would have been that you were very likely to pay the interest on the loan as well as be able to repay the principal in the future. For your part, you would have judged that your business prospects with the extra photocopiers were such that you would not only be able to pay the interest on the loan as well as pay back the principal, but that you would also be able to generate some additional net economic benefits for yourself over and above these payments.

The same is true for a nation's current account deficit. Provided it is being incurred to fund additional investment beyond the nation's available saving, it is unlikely to prove a problem. As a result of the current account deficit there will certainly be additional liabilities to foreigners being accumulated. However, the resulting dividends, interest and rent payments payable overseas on account of the extra foreign liabilities should be able to be made out of the additional future production made possible from the extra capital stock. Furthermore, there is also likely to be a net residual benefit remaining that will accrue to Australian residents so that their standard of living will be higher than it otherwise would have been without the use of the foreign investment.

This has certainly been the case for Australia. Over the past two centuries Australia has had an abundance of investment opportunities, but has been short of both labour and capital. To solve this it has had a long tradition of importing both. Its available workforce has been increased much more rapidly by having a significant immigration program. This started in earnest with the gold rush days of the 1850s and continues today.

At the same time, it has also needed more capital investment than could be provided by its small population's saving. Therefore, it has also imported foreign capital. The alternative to using the foreign capital would have been to let the available investment opportunities go untapped and for Australia's economic growth to have been slower.

The financial manifestation of this capital importation is accumulated foreign liabilities in the form of debt and/or foreign participation in the ownership of Australian assets. The physical manifestation has been large quantities of imported equipment as well as extra factories, offices and other buildings. The result has been that Australia's economy has been able to grow much more rapidly than it would have in the absence of the larger stock of capital. Given that the provision of this capital stock has been shared between residents and foreigners, the benefits of this more rapid economic growth have also quite properly been shared by both Australian and foreign residents.

Australia's foreign liabilities – should we be concerned?

As noted above, every time Australia runs a current account deficit, foreigners – banks, businesses and individuals – either purchase Australian assets or grant loans to Australians equivalent to the current account deficit. A loan to an Australian by a foreigner adds to our foreign debt liabilities,

INFOTRAC®

total foreign liabilities

while the purchase of a share in an Australian asset by a foreigner adds to Australia's foreign equity liabilities. The sum of these two types of liabilities is referred to as Australia's total foreign liabilities.

From time to time commentators and analysts have become excited about the composition of Australia's total foreign liabilities or their overall size. For example, in the 1970s there was much debate about how 'Australia was selling off the farm', implying a concern over the extent to which foreign liabilities were in the form of equity ownership of Australian assets. Then, in the mid to late 1980s, the concern shifted to 'Australia's dangerously high and unsustainable foreign debt'. Certain commentators were then concerned about the country's vulnerability and its ability to make interest payments on the debt in case of an economic downturn. It was sometimes even suggested that it would be far better if foreign investment had been in the form of 'more committed' – or 'patient' – equity investment rather than debt. The argument was that, in times of economic downturn, the dividends accruing to foreigners on their equity investments would automatically reduce, whereas interest payments on debt liabilities would not. This line of argument was, of course, quite at odds with the concerns about foreign equity investment that had been expressed by some in the previous decade.

The World Bank (**www.worldbank.org**) maintains data on the international foreign liabilities of nations.

Exhibit 18.6 provides a graphical representation of both Australia's net foreign debt liabilities and its total net foreign liabilities (debt and equity) expressed as a percentage of Australia's annual GDP. The gap between the two line graphs represents net foreign equity in Australia. It is important to compare such data with something like GDP to get a meaningful perspective on their changing values over time.

As can be seen, there has been a rise in both total foreign liabilities and the debt component over the past 25 years. The net equity component has also increased, but not by very much. In 1976 foreign debt was about 5 per cent of GDP and total foreign liabilities were about 10 per cent of GDP. By 2004 these stood at around 48 per cent and 61 per cent respectively. Net foreign equity therefore increased from about 5 per cent (10–5) to 13 per cent (61–48) over the 28-year period.

On the face of it, these increases in foreign liabilities are significant and it is reasonable to ask whether the current levels are too large and will prove to be a problem. Of course, an alternative question might be: were the ratios in evidence in the 1960s and early 1970s too small? Remember that in the 1960s and 1970s the world – Australia included – had a very restricted international financial system that severely constrained international investment. A country's capital accumulation was therefore much more constrained to be commensurate with the saving of its own residents. This may have resulted in lower foreign liabilities in some countries, but it also meant slower capital stock accumulation and economic growth than might otherwise have been the case.

Starting in the early 1980s, Australia and many other countries progressively relaxed controls on the international flow of capital and saving

Exhibit 18.6 Australia's foreign debt and total foreign liabilities, 1976–2004, per cent of GDP

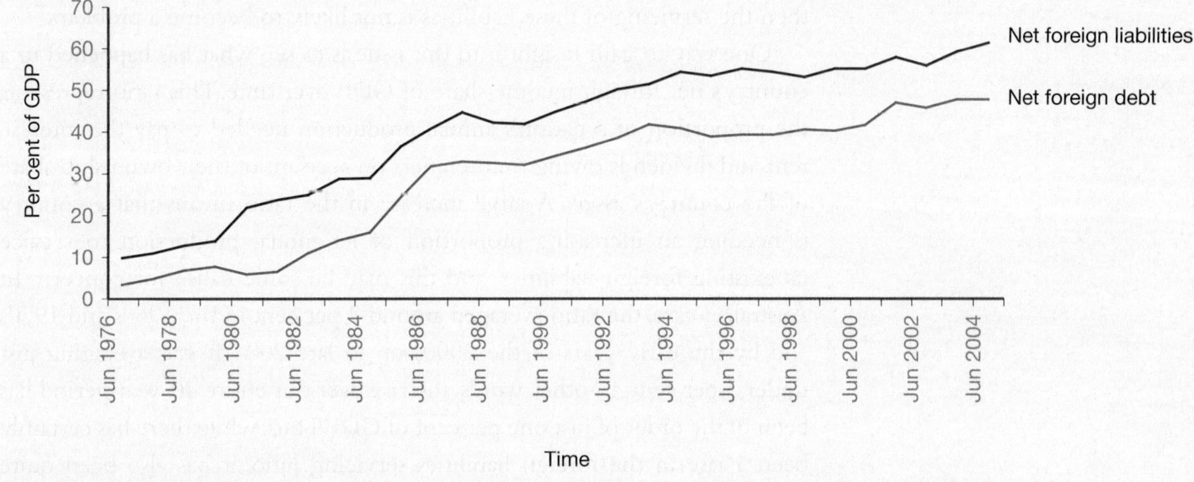

Source: Australian Bureau of Statistics, www.abs.gov.au, Cat. No. 5302, Table 40.

across their borders. This allowed saving – wherever it was sourced (perhaps in, say, Japan) – to flow to wherever its likely maximum rate of return was located (perhaps in, say, Australia). The increase in Australia's foreign liabilities is most likely simply a reflection of the more deregulated international financial system of the past couple of decades.

While the freeing up of international financial markets may explain the increase in Australia's foreign liabilities, one can still ask: is the level of Australia's foreign liabilities now becoming a problem? Asking this is really very similar to asking yourself whether your own level of liabilities is a problem. It really depends on how big those liabilities are, how big the servicing payments (like interest payments) are on it in relation to your income and what you have used the funds for.

Most of us who own a house and have a nice big mortgage with a bank would probably have a debt to annual income ratio well in excess of 100 per cent, and yet this doesn't seem to keep most of us up every night worrying over it. The reason for this is that we also know that we have a very valuable asset offsetting our debt. For the same reason, the bank is not too worried either because, in the event of some serious unforeseen eventuality, it always has the house as collateral.

Thus, there is really no reason to think that a foreign debt to GDP ratio of 48 per cent or total foreign liabilities to GDP ratio of 61 per cent – or, for that matter 75 per cent, 85 per cent or something else – is anything to be worried about in and of itself. The foreign liabilities will only become a problem if a country begins to have difficulty in servicing them. The important issue, therefore, is what the foreign liabilities have been used to finance. If they have been incurred to fund income-generating capital assets, then the servicing of these liabilities is not likely to become a problem.

One way to gain insight into this issue is to see what has happened to a country's net foreign income share of GDP over time. This ratio represents the proportion of a nation's annual production needed to pay the interest, rent and dividends owing to foreigners on account of their ownership share of the country's assets. A large increase in the ratio means that a country is needing an increasing proportion of its annual production to service its existing foreign liabilities, and this may be some cause for concern. In Australia's case, the ratio averaged around 2 per cent in the 1960s and 1970s and by the early years of the 2000s up to late 2004 it was averaging just under 3 per cent. In other words, the rise over this entire 40-year period has been of the order of just one per cent of GDP. Thus, while there has certainly been a rise in the foreign liabilities servicing ratio, it has also been quite modest. It is therefore unlikely that the current level of foreign liabilities in Australia is problematic.

The Reserve Bank of Australia (www.rba.gov.au) maintains extensive data on the value over time of the Australian dollar in terms of many foreign currencies. Also, the Pacific Exchange Rate Service (**pacific.commerce.ubc.ca/xr**) provides a list of all the currencies of the world and the countries' exchange rate arrangements.

How is a country's exchange rate determined?

In the discussion above, no mention was made about currencies and exchange rates. And yet, different countries have different currencies and when investors want to channel some of their funds into another country they need to exchange their currency for that of the foreign country. How is the price of another country's currency in terms of the home country's currency determined? It is to this issue that we now turn.

Each transaction recorded in the balance of payments requires an exchange of one country's currency for that of another. Suppose an Australian buys a Japanese car made in Japan – say a Mazda. Mazda wants to be paid in yen, not dollars, so dollars must be traded for yen. On the other hand, suppose a Japanese meat processing company wants to pay for the Australian beef it has just imported. It earns revenue from its Japanese customers in yen but must make its payments to Australian beef suppliers in dollars, and so it has to convert some yen into dollars.

exchange rate

Exchange rate The number of units of one nation's currency that equals one unit of another nation's currency.

The critical question for these businesses and everyone involved in world trade is: what is the exchange rate at which these currency conversions take place? The **exchange rate** is the number of units of one nation's currency that equals one unit of another nation's currency. For example, assume NZ\$1.25 is exchangeable for one Australian dollar. This means the exchange rate is AUD\$1 = NZ\$1.25. Alternatively, the exchange rate can be expressed as a reciprocal. Dividing 1 AUD by 1.25 NZ\$ gives AUD\$0.80 per NZ\$1.

Now suppose you are visiting New Zealand and you want to buy a T-shirt with a price tag of NZ$20. Knowing the exchange rate tells you the T-shirt costs AUD$16 (NZ$20 × AUD$0.80 per NZ$).

An exchange rate can be expressed in one of two ways, depending on which currency is being used to express the value of the other.

We now turn to how an exchange rate is determined.

Supply and demand for foreign exchange

The exchange rate for dollars or any nation's currency is determined by international forces of supply and demand. For example, consider the exchange rate for yen and dollars shown in Exhibit 18.7. Like the price and the quantity of any good traded in markets, the quantity of dollars exchanged is measured on the horizontal axis and the price per unit is measured on the vertical axis. In this case, the price per unit is the value of the AUD expressed as the number of yen per dollar.

The demand for dollars in the world currency market (from holders of yen) comes from Japanese individuals, corporations and governments that want to buy Australian exports and assets. Because the Japanese buyers must pay for the Australian exports and assets with dollars, they seek to exchange their yen for dollars. As expected, the demand curve for dollars or any foreign currency is downward-sloping. A decline in the number of yen per dollar means that one yen buys a larger portion of a dollar. This

Exhibit 18.7 The supply of and demand for Australian dollars

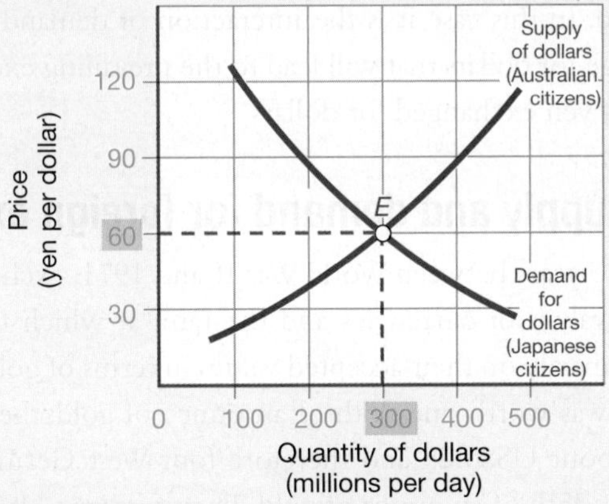

The number of Japanese yen per Australian dollar in the foreign exchange market is determined by the demand for dollars by Japanese citizens and the supply of dollars by Australian citizens. The equilibrium exchange rate is 60 yen per dollar and the equilibrium quantity is AUD$300 million per day.

means Australian goods and investment opportunities are less expensive to Japanese buyers because they must pay fewer yen for each dollar. Thus, as the yen price of dollars decreases, the quantity of dollars demanded by the Japanese to purchase beef, shares, land and other Australian products and investments increases.

For example, suppose a BHP Billiton share has an AUD$13 price tag. If the exchange rate is 76 yen to the dollar, a Japanese investor would pay 988 yen. If the price of dollars falls to 66 yen each, the same $13 share will cost Japanese investors only 858 yen. This lower price will encourage Japanese investors to increase their purchases of shares and other goods and services, which in turn increases the quantity of dollars demanded.

The supply curve of dollars is upward-sloping. This curve shows the amount of dollars offered for exchange at various yen prices per dollar in the world currency exchange market. Similar to the demand curve, the supply of dollars in this market flows from individuals, corporations and governments in Australia that want to buy Japanese goods and services, shares and land and make other investments in Japan.

Because Australian citizens must pay for the Japanese goods and services in yen, they must exchange dollars for yen. For example, suppose a Nikon camera sells for 100 000 yen in Tokyo and the exchange rate is 60 yen per dollar. This means the camera costs an Australian tourist AUD$1666.67. Now assume the exchange rate rises to 100 yen per dollar. The camera will now cost the Australian buyer only AUD$1000. Because the prices of the Nikon camera and other Japanese products fall when the number of yen per dollar rises, Australians respond by seeking to purchase more Japanese goods, services and assets, which in turn increases the quantity of dollars supplied.

The foreign exchange market in Exhibit 18.7 is in equilibrium at an exchange rate of 60 yen for $1. As you learned in Chapter 3, it is the interaction of demand and supply for a product that determines its price and quantity traded. In this case it is the interaction of demand and supply for yen in exchange for dollars that will lead to the prevailing exchange rate and the quantity of yen exchanged for dollars.

Shifts in supply and demand for foreign exchange

For most of the years between World War II and 1971, exchange rates were fixed and the values of currencies and the rates at which they exchanged were based primarily on their accepted values in terms of gold. For example, the US dollar was worth one-35th of an ounce of gold, the German mark was fixed at about US$0.25 and therefore four West German marks were also worth one-35th of an ounce of gold. Therefore one US dollar equalled four marks, or US$0.25 equalled one mark.

In 1971, most Western nations agreed to stop fixing their exchange rates and to allow their currencies to adjust continuously according to the forces of supply and demand. This type of system is known as a **flexible exchange rate system**. Australia continued to fix the value of its currency in one way or another until December 1983, at which time the authorities decided that the AUD should also be allowed to adjust flexibly in response to fluctuations in demand and supply.

Flexible exchange rate system A system in which countries allow their currencies to adjust continuously according to the forces of supply and demand. Most developed countries in the world today employ this type of exchange rate system.

Exhibit 18.8 illustrates that the exchange rate can and does fluctuate widely. For example, in 1984 one AUD was worth about 210 Japanese yen and US$0.88. After fluctuating during the 1980s and 1990s – but essentially trending downwards – the AUD hit post-war lows of about 60 yen per dollar and US$0.50 in 2001. At the time of writing in late 2004 the AUD was worth about 80 yen and US$0.75 respectively.

flexible exchange rate system

Recall from Chapter 4 that the equilibrium price for products changes in response to shifts in the supply and demand curves. The same supply and demand analysis applies to equilibrium exchange rates for foreign currency. There are four important sources of shifts in the supply and demand curves for foreign exchange. Let's briefly consider each in turn.

Exhibit 18.8 Changes in the Yen/AUD and US$/AUD exchange rates, 1984–2004

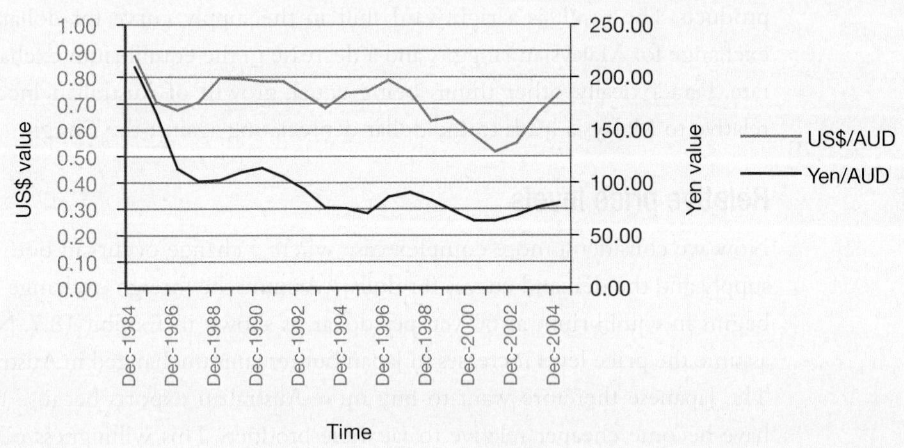

Today, most economies are on a system of flexible exchange rates. As demand and supply curves for currencies change, exchange rates also change. In 1984, one AUD was worth about 210 Japanese yen and US$0.88. By 2001, the AUD had dropped to lows of 60 yen and US$0.50 but subsequently rebounded.

Source: Reserve Bank of Australia, www.rba.gov.au, Table 40. Annual data compiled by authors from monthly data.

Tastes and preferences

Suppose the Japanese lose their 'taste' for a range of Australian exports. This decline in the popularity of Australian products in Japan decreases the demand for dollars at each possible exchange rate and the demand curve in Exhibit 18.7 would shift inward. This change would cause the equilibrium exchange rate to fall. Because the number of yen to the dollar declines, the AUD is said to **depreciate**. Depreciation of a currency is a fall in the value of one currency relative to another.

Depreciation of currency
A fall in the price of one currency relative to another.

What happens to the exchange rate if the 'buy Australian-made' idea changes our tastes and the demand for Japanese imports decreases? In this case, Australian citizens supply fewer dollars in exchange for Japanese yen at any possible exchange rate and the supply curve in Exhibit 18.7 would shift up and leftward. As a result, the equilibrium exchange rate would rise. Because the number of yen per dollar rises, the dollar is said to **appreciate**. Appreciation of currency is a rise in the value of one currency relative to another.

Appreciation of currency
A rise in the price of one currency relative to another.

Relative incomes

Assume income in Australia rises, while income in Malaysia remains unchanged. As a result, Australian citizens will tend to buy relatively more Malaysian imports than the residents of Malaysia will be buying of Australian products. The result is a rightward shift in the supply curve for dollars in exchange for Malaysian ringgits and a decrease in the equilibrium exchange rate. Paradoxically, other things being equal, growth of Australian income relative to Malaysia leads to the dollar depreciating against the ringgit.

Relative price levels

Now we consider a more complex case where a change occurs in both the supply and the demand curves for dollars. Assume the foreign exchange rate begins in equilibrium at 60 yen per dollar, as shown in Exhibit 18.7. Now assume the price level increases in Japan but remains unchanged in Australia. The Japanese therefore want to buy more Australian exports because they have become cheaper relative to Japanese products. This willingness of the Japanese to buy Australian goods and services shifts the demand curve for dollars outward. In addition, Australian products are cheaper for Australian citizens compared to Japanese imports. As a result, the willingness to import from Japan is reduced at each value of the exchange rate, which means the supply curve of dollars also shifts upward. The result of the shifts in both the demand and the supply curves for dollars is to establish a new equilibrium where the exchange rate is at a higher level (at, say, 70 yen); that is, the AUD will appreciate against the yen.

Relative real interest rates

Changes in relative real (inflation-adjusted) interest rates can have an important effect on the exchange rate. Suppose real interest rates in Australia rise, while those in New Zealand remain constant. To take advantage of more attractive yields, New Zealand investors buy an increased amount of bonds and other interest-bearing securities issued by private and government borrowers in Australia. This change increases the demand for Australian dollars, which increases the equilibrium exchange rate of NZ$ to the AUD, causing the Australian dollar to appreciate (or the NZ$ to depreciate).

There can also be an effect on the supply curve for dollars in this instance. When real interest rates rise in Australia, its residents purchase fewer NZ securities. Hence, they offer fewer dollars at each possible value of the exchange rate and the supply curve for Australian dollars shifts leftward. As a result, the equilibrium exchange rate increases and the Australian dollar appreciates from changes in both the demand for and the supply of dollars.

The economic impact of exchange rate fluctuations

Now it is time to stop a minute, take a breath and draw some important conclusions. As you have just learned, exchange rates between most major currencies are flexible. Instead of being pegged to gold or another fixed standard, their value is determined by the laws of supply and demand. Consequently, shifts in supply and demand result in a lower or higher exchange rate for the AUD.

However, it should be understood that exchange rates do not fluctuate without any influence from the monetary authorities. Central banks like the Reserve Bank of Australia will often buy and sell currencies to prevent wide swings in exchange rates. Notwithstanding this, it needs to be emphasised that its objective is not to try to reverse a change in a currency's value resulting from changes to its fundamental determinants. Rather, its actions are an attempt to smooth out excessive fluctuations in the exchange rate and to bring about an orderly market adjustment of the currency's value to whatever is its apparent new equilibrium level.

You also need to understand that the international price of any nation's currency has a profound impact on its economy.

A lower value for the AUD enhances the international competitiveness of Australian producers. For example, suppose an Australian exporter's production cost is AUD$20 per unit and the exchange rate is AUD$1 = US$1. This means the exporter's production cost is also US$20 per unit. If the AUD depreciates to, say, AUD$1 = US$0.80, the exporter's US$ production cost is only US$16 (AUD$20 × 0.8). This enables the exporter to be more price-competitive in US markets. Such a depreciation also means import-competing firms are better able to compete with imported goods and services because the AUD prices of imports goes up. Thus, Australian economic activity is likely to be stimulated by a depreciated dollar with a commensurate increase in jobs.

The downside is that it also means that those Australians who like to consume imports, travel overseas or need to use imported goods in their production processes face higher AUD costs. A lower value for the AUD also carries the risk that domestic inflation may increase as a result of the higher AUD prices of imported goods and services.

When the dollar is low or depreciates, Australian goods and services cost foreign consumers less, so they will buy more Australian exports. At the same time, a low dollar means foreign goods and services cost Australian consumers more, so they will buy fewer imports.

A higher value for the AUD, on the other hand, has the opposite effects to those described above. It reduces the international competitiveness of Australian producers. Because the Australian dollar equivalent of the international prices of goods and services reduces, this means the AUD earnings of Australia's exporters declines. It also means import-competing firms are less able to compete with imported goods and services because the AUD prices of imports goes down. Thus, Australian economic activity is likely to be retarded by an appreciated dollar, with a commensurate loss of jobs.

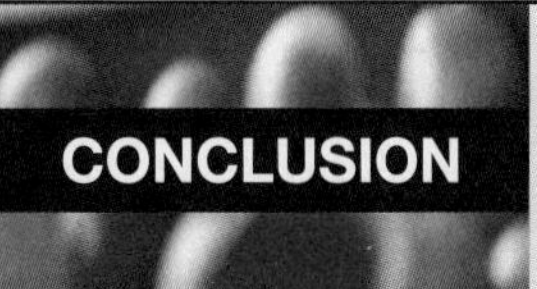

When the dollar is high or appreciates, AUD revenues from exports reduce. At the same time, a high dollar means foreign goods and services cost Australian consumers less in dollars so they will buy more foreign imports.

Analyse the issue

External shocks and the role of the exchange rate

Applicable concept: the advantages of a flexible exchange rate

As already mentioned, Australia adopted a flexible exchange rate system in December 1983. Since then the value of the AUD has fluctuated considerably, and a large part of the reason for this is that Australia is a very open economy, which engages in a great deal of international trade with the rest of the world.

As explained earlier in this chapter, this openness to international trade has great advantages in terms of the higher standard of living that such trade delivers. However, it does mean that international shocks can potentially affect the Australian economy significantly. This is where a flexible exchange rate can be very advantageous.

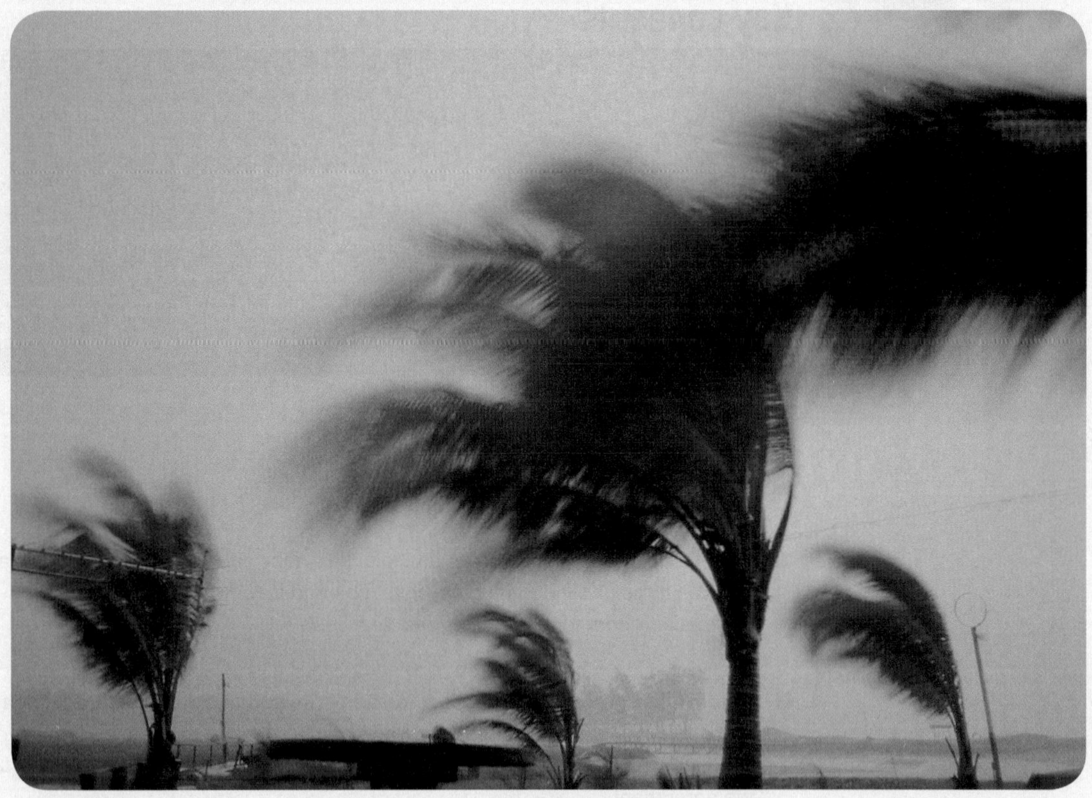

Consider the financial and economic crisis that hit East Asia in late 1997 and into 1998. This crisis started in Thailand but eventually affected virtually all the economies in the East Asian region. The currencies of many of these countries depreciated dramatically over this period and most of the economies in question went into recession.

Given that a significant percentage of Australia's export markets are located in these countries and given that over 20 per cent of Australia's total production is exported, this was potentially a very serious situation for Australia. In fact, at the time many analysts were convinced that Australia would not be able to avoid a recession.

As it turned out, Australia recorded very robust economic growth in excess of 4 per cent in each of 1997–98, 1998–99 and 1999–2000. This outcome so surprised the well-known international economist Paul Krugman that he referred to the Australian economy as a 'miracle economy'.

How was this outcome to be explained? There were certainly a number of factors at work, but one important one was what happened to the value of the AUD as a result of the financial crisis in Asia. During 1998 the AUD depreciated by about 15 per cent! It is now widely recognised that the flexible exchange rate provided Australia with a very important buffer against the economic turmoil occurring at the time in Asia.

Can you explain the economics of how the flexible exchange rate helped Australia through the 1997–98 Asian financial and economic crises? Outline the consequences of what might have happened if Australia had at the time been maintaining a fixed exchange rate.

Key concepts

Comparative advantage
Absolute advantage
Free trade
Fair trade
Strategic trade theory
Protectionism
Embargo
Tariff
Quota
Balance of payments
Balance of merchandise trade
Balance on goods and services
Net foreign income
Exchange rate
Flexible exchange rate system
Depreciation of currency
Appreciation of currency

Summary

- **Free trade** benefits a nation as a whole, but in the short term some individuals in some firms and industries may lose jobs and incomes because of the competition from foreign goods and services.

- **Free trade agreement** In a free trade agreement, parties to a free trade area agree to eliminate tariffs and other trade barriers among themselves. However, each individual country maintains its own tariff policy against non-parties to the agreement.

- **Protectionism** is a government's use of embargoes, tariffs, quotas and other methods to impose barriers intended to both reduce imports and protect particular domestic industries. Embargoes prohibit the import of particular goods. Tariffs (taxes on imports) discourage imports by making them more expensive to buy. Quotas limit the quantity of imports of certain goods. These trade barriers often result primarily from domestic special-interest groups that exert political pressure in order to gain from these barriers.

- **Fair trade** is the term used to represent the view that a country should only reduce its barriers to imports from another country if the other country does not have some sort of 'unfair' competitive advantage over it and provided the other country is also willing to reduce its import barriers reciprocally.

- **Comparative advantage** is a principle that explains why nations gain from trade. Comparative advantage suggests that each nation should specialise in products in which its opportunity costs – in terms of the forgone production of other products – are lower. Each nation should then engage in trade to acquire those products in which it does not have a comparative advantage. When nations follow this principle, they gain. The reason is that world output increases and each nation ends up with a higher standard of living by consuming more goods and services than would be possible without specialisation and trade.

Comparative advantage

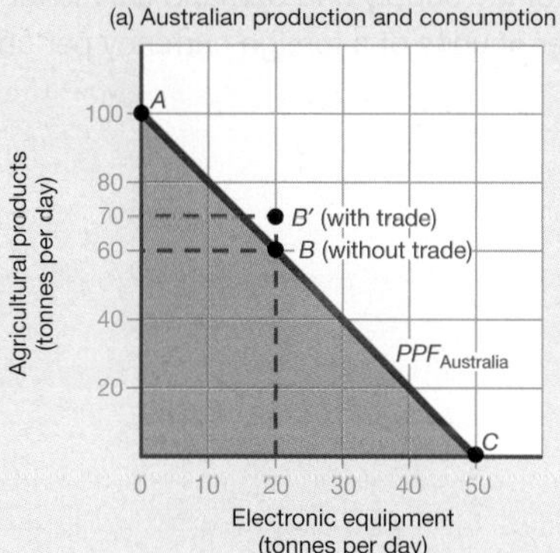

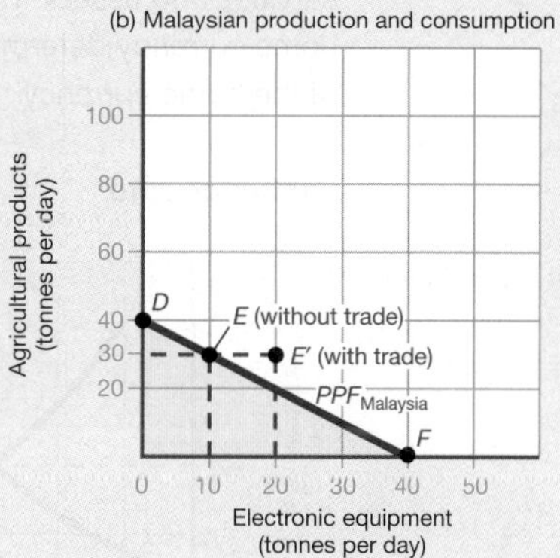

- **Strategic trade theory** is the term used to refer to the idea that governments should seek to be strategic in their use of their spending and taxing powers in order to actively facilitate some sectors of the economy that they may feel have the potential to be strong export earners for their nations.

- The **balance of payments** is a summary bookkeeping record of the international transactions a country makes during a year. It is divided into two accounts: the current account and the capital account. The current account summarises all transactions in currently produced goods and services. The capital account summarises the net accumulation of assets in Australia by foreigners. The overall balance of payments is conceptually zero and is made so in practice by the addition of a balancing item.

- The **balance of merchandise trade** measures only goods (not services) that a nation exports and imports. A balance of merchandise trade can be in deficit or in surplus. The balance of trade is the most widely reported and largest part of the current account.

- The **balance on goods and services** represents the nation's net position in respect of its exports and imports of both goods and services.

- **Net foreign income** is the difference between aggregate investment income flows into and out of a country. Income flowing into Australia from the investments of Australian residents abroad – such as shares in foreign companies, real estate owned abroad and loans made to offshore residents – are payments for the services of this Australian investment capital. These income flows (foreign income credits) would include interest payments on the loans, rent on the property and dividends on the shares. Analogously, residents of foreign countries also receive income flowing from the application of their investment capital in Australia (foreign income debits).

- An **exchange rate** is the price of one nation's currency in terms of another nation's currency. Foreigners who wish to purchase domestic goods, services and assets have a demand for the home currency. The supply of home currency reflects the desire of domestic citizens to purchase foreign goods, services and assets. The intersection of the supply and demand curves for the home currency determines the number of units of a foreign currency per unit of the home currency.

Exchange rate

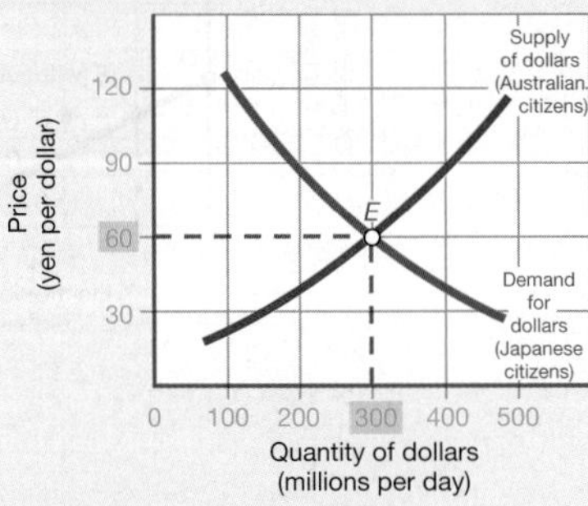

- A **flexible exchange rate system** is one in which countries allow their currencies to adjust continuously according to the forces of supply and demand. Most developed countries in the world today employ this type of exchange rate system.

- **Shifts in supply and demand for foreign exchange** result from changes in such factors as tastes, relative price levels, relative real interest rates and relative income levels.

- **Depreciation of currency** occurs when one currency becomes worth fewer units of another currency. Depreciation of a nation's currency increases its exports and decreases its imports.

- **Appreciation of currency** occurs when one currency becomes worth more units of another currency. Appreciation of a nation's currency decreases its exports and increases its imports.

Study questions and problems

1 The countries of Alpha and Beta produce diamonds and pearls. The production possibilities schedule shown here describes their potential output in tonnes per year.

	Alpha		Beta	
Points on PPF	Diamonds Tonnes	Pearls Tonnes	Diamonds Tonnes	Pearls Tonnes
A	150	0	90	0
B	100	25	60	60
C	50	50	30	120
D	0	75	0	180

Using the data in the table, answer the following questions.

a What is the opportunity cost of diamonds for each country?

b What is the opportunity cost of pearls for each country?

c In which good does Alpha have a comparative advantage?

d In which good does Beta have a comparative advantage?

e Suppose Alpha is producing and consuming at point *B* on its production possibilities frontier and Beta is producing and consuming at point *C* on its production possibilities frontier. Use a table such as Exhibit 18.3 to explain why both nations would benefit if they specialised.

f Draw a graph and use it to explain how Alpha and Beta benefit if they specialise and Alpha agrees to trade 50 tonnes of diamonds to Beta and Alpha receives 50 tonnes of pearls in exchange.

2 Bill can paint either two walls or one window frame in one hour. In the same time, Frank can paint either three walls or two window frames. If there are three windows and four walls to be painted, to minimise the total time each of them spends painting, who should specialise in painting walls and who should specialise in painting window frames, or should they each do both?

3 Consider this statement: 'The principles of specialisation and trade according to comparative advantage among nations also apply to states in Australia.' Do you agree or disagree? Explain.

4 Would there be any advantage to the Australian government in using tariffs or quotas to restrict imports?

5 If Australia passed a law stating that it would not purchase imports from any country that imposed any trade restrictions on Australia's exports, who would benefit directly and who would lose directly from such retaliation?

6 Now consider Question 5 in terms of the impact on domestic exporters. Does this policy adversely affect them in some way?

7 Consider this statement: 'Unrestricted foreign trade costs domestic jobs.' Do you agree or disagree? Explain.

8 Discuss this statement: 'Because each nation's balance of payments equals zero, it follows that there is actually no significance to a balance of payments deficit or surplus.'

9 For each of the following situations, indicate the direction of the shift in the supply or the demand curve for domestic currency, the factor causing the change and the resulting movement of the equilibrium exchange rate for the domestic currency in terms of foreign currency.

a The domestic country's exports become more popular overseas.

b The domestic country experiences a recession, while other nations enjoy economic growth.

c Inflation rates accelerate in the domestic country, while inflation rates remain constant in other nations.

d Real interest rates in the domestic country rise, while real interest rates abroad remain constant.

e Tourism from the domestic country increases sharply because of a fare war among airlines.

10 The following table summarises supply and demand for the euro.

	Euros per AUD			
	E0.45	E0.55	E0.60	E0.65
Quantity of AUD demanded (per day)	500	400	200	100
Quantity of AUD supplied (per day)	100	200	400	500

Using the above table:

a Graph the supply and demand curves for AUD.

b Determine the equilibrium exchange rate.

c Determine what the effect of a fixed exchange rate at E0.50 per AUD would be.

Online exercises

Exercise 1

Visit the ABS website (**www.abs.gov.au**) and select **Statistics, Publications & Data, Time Series Spreadsheets, By Catalogue/Subject** and then **53. Balance of payments and international investment**.

1 For the most recent quarter available, what were Australia's current account balance and its balance on goods and services?

2 What accounts for the difference between these two balances?

3 What was Australia's measured capital account balance?

4 What was the value of the balancing item for this period?

5 What is the role of this balancing item?

Exercise 2

Visit the ABS website (**www.abs.gov.au**) and select **Statistics, Publications & Data, Time**

Series Spreadsheets, By Catalogue/Subject, 54. International Trade, then **5432.0.65.001 International Merchandise Exports, Electronic Delivery**.

1 Which region (or country) is Australia's largest export market?

2 What are the four largest?

3 Which region (or country) is Australia's largest import supplier?

4 What are the four largest?

5 Looking at these four, what differences are evident compared with the set of four largest export markets?

6 What else do you need to add to the merchandise trade balance to arrive at the current account balance?

Exercise 3

Visit the ABS website (**www.abs.gov.au**) and select **Statistics, Publications & Data, Time Series Spreadsheets, By Catalogue/Subject, 53. Balance of payments and international investment**, then **Table 40**.

1 In the most recent period available, what was Australia's net foreign debt liabilities as a ratio to GDP?

2 What was its total foreign liabilities as a ratio to GDP?

3 What is the other component of Australia's foreign liabilities and what therefore must its value be as a ratio to GDP?

4 Are these ratios larger or smaller than the most recent ratios available in the text?

Exercise 4

Visit the Reserve Bank of Australia's website (**www.rba.gov.au**) and select **Statistics, Bulletin Statistical Tables**, then **Financial markets, Exchange Rates**.

1 What are the most recent values of the Australian dollar in: US$, yen, euros, Korean won, NZ dollars, Taiwan dollars, Singapore dollars, Indonesian rupiah, Malaysian ringgits and HK dollars?

2 What is its value in trade weighted index (TWI) terms?

3 What has been the recent trend in the TWI?

4 What would this trend mean for changes in the competitiveness of Australia's exporters?

Answers to 'You make the call'

Do nations with an absolute advantage gain from trade?

In Australia, the opportunity cost of producing one calculator is 100 towels. In Indonesia, the opportunity cost of producing one calculator is 50 towels and is therefore lower in Indonesia than in Australia. Due to this difference in opportunity costs between the two countries, Indonesia has a comparative advantage in calculator production and Australia has a comparative advantage in towel production.

If Australia diverted 10 existing hours of labour from calculator to towel production, 400 more towels would be produced at a cost of four calculators. If Indonesia diverted 40 existing hours of labour from towel to calculator production, four more calculators would be produced at a cost of 200 fewer towels. Australia could export 200 of its additional towels to Indonesia in return for Indonesia's four additional calculators. This leaves Indonesia no worse off for the same labour input and Australia better off by an extra 200 towels for the same level of labour input.

If you said that, even though it has an absolute advantage in both goods, Australia can benefit by trade with Indonesia because it has a comparative advantage in one good compared with Indonesia, YOU ARE CORRECT.

Should everyone keep a balance of payments?

The principal purpose of the balance of payments is to keep track of payments of national currencies. Because states and cities within the same nation use the same national currency, payments for goods and services traded between these parties do not represent an outflow or inflow of foreign currencies. If you said only nations need to use the balance of payments to account for flows of foreign currency across national boundaries, YOU ARE CORRECT.

Multiple-choice questions

1 With trade, the production possibilities for two nations lie
   a outside their consumption possibilities.
   b inside their consumption possibilities.
   c at a point equal to the world production possibilities frontier.
   d at none of the above points.

2 Free trade theory suggests that when trade takes place,
   a both nations will be worse off.
   b one nation must gain at the other nation's expense.
   c both nations will be better off.
   d one nation will gain and the other nation will be neither better nor worse off.

3 Which of the following is true when two countries specialise according to their comparative advantage?
   a It is possible to increase their total output of all goods.
   b It is possible to increase their total output of some goods only if both countries are industrialised.
   c One country is likely to gain from trade, while the other loses.
   d None of the above are true.

4 According to the theory of comparative advantage, a country should produce and
   a import goods in which it has an absolute advantage.
   b export goods in which it has an absolute advantage.
   c import goods in which it has a comparative advantage.
   d export goods in which it has a comparative advantage.

5 In the table shown here, which country has the comparative advantage in the production of potatoes?

Potatoes and wheat output (tonnes per hour)		
Country	Potatoes	Wheat
Australia	1	3
Ireland	1	2

   a Australia because it requires fewer resources to produce potatoes.
   b Australia because it has the lower opportunity cost of potatoes.
   c Ireland because it requires fewer resources to produce potatoes.
   d Ireland because it has the lower opportunity cost of potatoes.

6 In the previous table, the opportunity cost of wheat is
   a 1/3 tonne of potatoes in Australia and $\frac{1}{2}$ tonne of potatoes in Ireland.
   b 2 tonnes of potatoes in Australia and 1 $\frac{1}{2}$ tonnes of potatoes in Ireland.
   c 8 tonnes of potatoes in Australia and 4 tonnes of potatoes in Ireland.
   d $\frac{1}{2}$ tonne of potatoes in Australia and $\frac{2}{3}$ tonne of potatoes in Ireland.

7 In the table in Question 5, the opportunity cost of potatoes is
   a $\frac{1}{2}$ tonne of wheat in Australia and $\frac{2}{3}$ tonne of wheat in Ireland.
   b 2 tonnes of wheat in Australia and 1 $\frac{1}{2}$ tonnes of wheat in Ireland.
   c 16 tonnes of wheat in Australia and 6 tonnes of wheat in Ireland.
   d 3 tonnes of wheat in Australia and 2 tonnes of wheat in Ireland.

8 If the countries in the table in Question 5 follow the principle of comparative advantage, Australia should
   a buy all its potatoes from Ireland.
   b buy all its wheat from Ireland.
   c buy all its potatoes and wheat from Ireland.
   d produce both potatoes and wheat and not trade with Ireland.

9 A tariff increases
   a the quantity of imports.
   b the ability of foreign goods to compete with domestic goods.
   c the prices of imports to domestic buyers.
   d all of the above.

10 The infant industry argument for protectionism is based on which of the following views?
   a Foreign buyers will absorb all the output of domestic producers in a new industry.
   b The growth of an industry that is new to a nation will be too rapid unless trade restrictions are imposed.

c Firms in a newly developing domestic industry will have difficulty growing if they face strong competition from established foreign firms.

d It is based on none of the above.

11 The figure that results when merchandise imports are subtracted from merchandise exports is

a the capital account balance.

b the balance of merchandise trade.

c the current account balance.

d always less than zero.

12 Which of the following international accounts records payments for exports and imports of goods, military transactions, foreign travel, investment income and foreign gifts?

a the capital account

b the merchandise account

c the current account

d the official reserve account

13 Which of the following international accounts records the purchase and sale of financial assets and real estate between Australia and other nations?

a the balance of trade account

b the current account

c the capital account

d the balance of payments account

14 If a Japanese radio priced at 2000 yen can be purchased for AUD$40, the exchange rate is

a 50 yen per dollar.

b 20 yen per dollar.

c 50 dollars per yen.

d none of the above.

15 Australia

a was on a fixed exchange rate system prior to December 1983, but now is on a flexible exchange rate system.

b has been on a fixed exchange rate system since 1945.

c has been on a flexible exchange rate system since 1945.

d was on a flexible exchange rate system prior to late 1983, but now is on a fixed exchange rate system.

16 Suppose the exchange rate changes so that fewer New Zealand dollars are required to buy an AUD. We would conclude that

a the New Zealand dollar has depreciated in value.

b Australian citizens will buy fewer New Zealand imports.

c New Zealanders will demand fewer Australian exports.

d none of the above is correct.

17 Which of the following would cause a decrease in the demand for euros by those holding Australian dollars?

a inflation in Europe, but not in Australia.

b inflation in Australia, but not in Europe.

c an increase in the real rate of interest on investments in Europe above the real rate of interest on investments in Australia.

d none of the above.

18 An increase in the foreign equilibrium price of a nation's currency could be caused by

a a decrease in the supply of the nation's currency.

b a decrease in the demand for the nation's currency.

c an increase in the supply of the nation's currency.

d an increase in the demand for the nation's currency.

19 If the Australian dollar appreciates, this causes

a the relative price of Australian goods to increase for foreigners.

c Australian exports to fall and Australian imports to rise.

d a balance of trade deficit for Australia.

e all of the above to occur.

20 Which of the following would cause the Australian dollar to depreciate against the Malaysian ringgit?

a greater popularity of Australian exports in Malaysia.

b a higher price level in Malaysia.

c higher real interest rates in Australia.

d higher incomes in Australia.

Glossary

absolute advantage The ability of a country to produce a good using fewer resources than another country. (Chapter 18)

aggregate demand The sum total of the four categories of demand, namely $C + I + G + (X - M)$. (Chapter 14)

aggregate demand curve Curve showing the level of total real GDP that households, businesses, government and foreigners (net exports) would be willing to purchase at different possible average price levels during a time period, ceteris paribus. (Chapter 14)

aggregate demand–output model (also called the Keynesian model) The model that determines the equilibrium level of real GDP by equating output produced to aggregate demand. (Chapter 14)

aggregate supply curve The curve that shows the level of real GDP that firms would be willing to produce at different possible price levels during a time period, ceteris paribus. (Chapter 14)

appreciation of currency A rise in the price of one currency relative to another. (Chapter 18)

arbitrage The practice of earning a profit by buying a good at a low price and reselling the good at a higher price. (Chapter 8)

Australian Stock Exchange (ASX) Where shares in Australia's (and some foreign) publicly listed companies are floated and traded. It has an actual physical location. A company listed on the ASX is called a public company, which is one owned by a great many individuals (often thousands) whose financial liability in case of the company becoming insolvent is limited only to the value of their fully paid-up shares in it. (Chapter 15)

automatic stabilisers Federal expenditures and tax revenues that automatically change over the course of the business cycle in such a way as to help stabilise an economic expansion or contraction. (Chapter 17)

autonomous expenditure Any spending that does not vary with the current level of disposable income or interest rates. (Chapter 14)

average fixed cost Total fixed cost divided by the quantity of output produced. (Chapter 6)

average total cost Total cost divided by the quantity of output produced. (Chapter 6)

average variable cost Total variable cost divided by the quantity of output produced. (Chapter 6)

balance of payments A summary record of the international transactions between a country and other countries during a given period of time. (Chapter 18)

balanced budget multiplier An equal change in government spending and taxes, which changes aggregate demand by the amount of the change in government spending. (Chapter 17)

barter The direct exchange of one good for another good, rather than for money. (Chapter 15)

base year A year chosen as a reference point for comparison with some earlier or later year. (Chapter 13)

Broad Money The definition of the money supply that equals M3 plus net deposits of all non-bank financial intermediaries. (Chapter 15)

budget deficit A budget situation in which government expenditures exceed government revenues in a given time period. (Chapter 17)

budget surplus A budget situation in which government revenues exceed government expenditures in a given time period. (Chapter 17)

burden of debt The possibility that existing national debt may represent a burden on current and future generations, namely to pay the future interest payments on it and to eventually repay the principal. In fact, to the extent that the national debt is internal – that is, not owed to foreigners – such debt is not likely to represent a net burden. (Chapter 17)

business cycle Alternating periods of economic growth and contraction, which can be dated by changes in output, income, sales and employment measures. (Chapter 12)

capital The physical plant, machinery and equipment used to produce other goods. Capital goods are human-made goods that do not directly satisfy human wants. (Chapter 1)

capital adequacy Requirement that a supervised financial institution maintain a certain minimum percentage of its risk-weighted assets in the form of shareholders' equity. (Chapter 15)

cartel A group of firms formally agreeing to control the price and the output of a product. (Chapter 9)

ceteris paribus A Latin phrase that means that, while certain variables change, 'all other things remain unchanged.' (Chapter 1)

change in demand An increase or decrease in the demand at each possible price. An increase in demand is a rightward shift in the entire demand curve. A decrease in demand is a leftward shift in the entire demand curve. (Chapter 3)

change in quantity demanded A movement between points along a stationary demand curve, ceteris paribus. (Chapter 3)

change in quantity supplied A movement between points along a stationary supply curve, ceteris paribus. (Chapter 3)

change in supply An increase or decrease in the supply at each possible price. An increase in supply is a rightward shift in the entire supply curve. A decrease in supply is a leftward shift in the entire supply curve. (Chapter 3)

cheque account deposits The total of cheque account balances in banks convertible to currency 'on demand' by writing a cheque without advance notice. (Chapter 15)

circular flow model A diagram showing the flow of products from businesses to households and the flow of resources from households to businesses. In exchange for these resources, money payments flow between businesses and households. (Chapter 11)

civilian labour force The number of people fifteen years of age and older who are employed or who are actively seeking a job, excluding those in the armed forces, home makers, students, discouraged workers and other persons not in the labour force. (Chapter 13)

classical range The vertical segment of the aggregate supply curve, which represents an economy at full-employment output. (Chapter 14)

coincident indicators Variables that change at about the same time as the economy shifts from one business cycle phase into another. (Chapter 12)

commercial bill Bill created when, as evidence of a loan, a borrower draws up a bill that stipulates a face value (say $100 000) and the time to maturity (usually 90 or 180 days). The lender then makes the loan by buying the bill from the borrower at a discount to the face value, with the difference representing the implied interest rate. To remove the risk of default by the borrower, a bank may, for a fee, guarantee payment at maturity. The bank is referred to as the acceptor of the bill and the bill is called a bank-accepted bill. The bank's guarantee converts the bill into a safe and highly tradeable financial instrument. (Chapter 15)

commodity money Anything that serves as money while having market value in other uses. (Chapter 15)

commonwealth government securities Commonwealth government bonds (maturities of more than one year) and treasury notes (13- and 26-week). They are bought and sold by the RBA in the money markets to bring about changes to the monetary base and short-term interest rates. (Chapter 15)

comparative advantage The ability of a country to produce a good at a lower opportunity cost than another country. (Chapter 18)

competition policy Government policy that has the objective of increasing competition in the economy, or of encouraging firms that are not competitive to behave as if they were. (Chapter 7)

complementary good A good that is jointly consumed with another good. As a result, there is an inverse relationship between a price change for one good and the demand for its 'complementary' good. (Chapter 3)

concentration ratio A measure that indicates the percentage of total sales in the industry generated by its largest firms. (Chapter 9)

conditional projection The implementation of monetary policy in Australia during the period 1976–85 consisted of a form of monetary targeting – a monetarist-type policy recommendation adopted by many countries in the 1970s. Each year a 'conditional projection' for the growth of the monetary aggregate, M3, was announced in the Federal Budget by the Treasurer. The projections were conditional in the sense that, if world or domestic economic conditions changed unexpectedly, the government allowed itself the room to vary the targets over the course of the year. (Chapter 16)

constant-cost industry An industry in which the expansion of industry output by the entry of new firms has no effect on the firms' cost curves. (Chapter 7)

constant returns to scale A situation in which the long-run average cost curve is horizontal as the firm increases output. (Chapter 6)

consumer price index (CPI) An index that measures changes in the average prices of consumer goods and services. (Chapter 13)

consumer sovereignty The freedom of consumers to make their own choices about which goods and services to buy. (Chapter 3)

consumption function Shows the amount households want to spend on goods and services at different levels of disposable income. (Chapter 14)

cost-push inflation A rise in the general price level resulting from an increase in the cost of production, irrespective of demand conditions. (Chapter 13) A rise in the price level resulting from an inward shift in the aggregate supply curve while the aggregate demand curve remains unchanged. (Chapter 14)

countercyclical macroeconomic policy Policy that aims to smooth out the fluctuations in the business cycle. Monetarists believe countercyclical macroeconomic policy may actually unintentionally make the business cycle worse rather than less pronounced on account of three policy lags: the information lag, the policy determination lag and the policy effectiveness lag. For these reasons monetarists advocate a rules-based approach to monetary policy rather than the discretionary approach favoured by Keynesians. (Chapter 16)

credit creation and the money multiplier Credit creation is the process by which money is created by banks extending new loans to their customers in the form of newly created bank deposits. Because bank deposits are regarded as money, this results in money being created. The extent to which banks can multiply an initial increase in their reserves in this credit creation process is given by the so-called money multiplier. In general, the money multiplier may be thought of as the reciprocal of whatever is the minimum reserve liquidity ratio that banks maintain to satisfy regularity requirements. (Chapter 15)

cross-elasticity of demand The ratio of the percentage change in the quantity demanded of a good or service to a given percentage change in the price of a related good or service. (Chapter 5)

crowding-out effect A reduction in private-sector spending as a result of federal budget deficits financed by government borrowing. The mechanism for this crowding out would be through higher interest rates in the financial markets resulting from the increased demand for loan funds from the private sector by the government. (Chapter 17)

currency Money, including coins and paper money. (Chapter 15)

current account balance The total value of a country's exports of goods and services less its imports of goods and services and less its net income (interest and dividends) paid overseas. (Chapter 11)

current account balance on goods and services This represents the nation's net position in respect of its exports and imports of both goods and services. (Chapter 18)

current account balance on merchandise trade The value of a nation's merchandise imports subtracted from its merchandise exports. (Chapter 18)

cyclical unemployment Unemployment caused by the lack of jobs during a recession. (Chapter 13)

cyclically adjusted budget deficit The actual recorded budget deficit for some period adjusted for the stage of the economy's business cycle during the period. (Chapter 17)

debt financing When a budget deficit is financed by selling government securities to the general public – that is, by the government borrowing from the public to fund its expenditure. (Chapter 17)

decreasing-cost industry An industry in which the expansion of industry output by the entry of new firms decreases the firms' cost curves. (Chapter 7)

deflation A decrease in the general (average) price level of goods and services in the economy. (Chapter 13)

demand curve for labour A curve showing the different quantities of labour employers are willing to hire at different wage rates in a given time period, ceteris paribus. It is equal to the marginal revenue product of labour. (Chapter 10)

demand for money Schedule representing the overall quantity of money that people wish to hold at different interest rates, ceteris paribus. (Chapter 15)

demand-pull inflation A rise in the general price level resulting from an excess of total spending (demand) over supply. (Chapter 13) A rise in the price level resulting from an increase in the aggregate demand curve while the aggregate supply curve remains unchanged. (Chapter 14)

depreciation of currency A fall in the price of one currency relative to another. (Chapter 18)

derived demand The derived demand for labour – and other factors of production – depends on the demand for the goods and services the factor produces. (Chapter 10)

direct relationship A positive association between two variables. When one variable increases, the other variable increases, and when one variable decreases, the other variable decreases. (Chapter 1 Appendix)

direct taxes Taxes levied on income. (Chapter 10)

discouraged worker A person who wants to work, but who has given up searching for work because he or she believes there will be no job offers. (Chapter 13)

discretionary fiscal policy The deliberate use of changes in government spending and/or taxes to alter aggregate demand and stabilise the economy's business cycle. (Chapter 17)

diseconomies of scale	A situation in which the long-run average cost curve rises as the firm increases output. (Chapter 6)
disinflation	A reduction in the rate of inflation. (Chapter 13)
domestic deficit	The difference between domestically derived government revenue and domestic government expenditure. (Chapter 17)
domestic factor income (DFI)	The total income earned by domestic resource owners, including wages, rents, interest and profits (after depreciation); conceptually also equal to net domestic product less indirect taxes. (Chapter 11)
economic growth	The ability of an economy to produce greater levels of output, represented by an outward shift of its production possibilities frontier. (Chapter 2) An expansion in national output measured by the annual percentage increase in a nation's real GDP. (Chapter 12)
economic profit	Total revenue minus explicit and implicit costs. (Chapter 6)
economics	The study of how society chooses to allocate its scarce resources to the production of goods and services in order to satisfy unlimited wants. (Chapter 1)
economies of scale	A situation in which the long-run average cost curve declines as the firm increases output. (Chapter 6)
efficiency	An efficient outcome is one in which society maximises the benefits it obtains from the use of its scarce resources. (Chapter 3)
elastic demand	A condition in which the percentage change in quantity demanded is greater than the percentage change in price. (Chapter 5)
embargo	A law that bars trade with another country. (Chapter 18)
endogenous growth	Modern explanations of the economic growth process argue that the process of technological change is endogenous to economic growth rather than being treated as exogenous, as in the earlier Solow growth model. (Chapter 12)
enlightened self-interest	This involves members of the community respecting the laws and social mores of society while they pursue their own individual goals. (Chapter 1)
enterprise bargaining	Process typically involving unions in each workplace undertaking direct bargaining as a group with their employer to determine terms and conditions of employment for a period of up to five years. (Chapter 10)
entrepreneurship	The creative ability of individuals to seek profits by combining resources to produce new or existing products. (Chapter 1)
equation of exchange	An accounting identity that states that the money supply times the velocity of money equals total spending. (Chapter 16)
equilibrium	A market condition that occurs at any price for which the quantity demanded and the quantity supplied are equal. (Chapter 3)
exchange rate	The number of units of one nation's currency that equals one unit of another nation's currency. (Chapter 18)
exchange settlement account	Each bank maintains an exchange settlement account with the RBA, and any direct business it conducts with the central bank, other banks, the government and certain other financial organisations is settled through deposits to or withdrawals from this account. It is this direct RBA access that enables an organisation like a bank to offer cheque-writing facilities to its customers. Exchange settlement accounts must always have a positive balance by the end of each trading day. (Chapter 15)
expansion	An upturn in the business cycle during which real GDP, employment and other measures of aggregate economic activity rise. (Chapter 12)

expenditure approach The national income accounting method that measures GDP by adding all the spending for final products during a period of time. (Chapter 11)

explicit costs Payments to non-owners of a firm for their resources. (Chapter 6)

externality A cost or benefit imposed on people other than the consumers and producers of a good or service. (Chapter 4)

fair trade Term used to represent the view that a country should only reduce its barriers to imports from another country if the other country does not have some sort of 'unfair' competitive advantage over it and provided the other country is also willing to reduce its import barriers reciprocally. (Chapter 18)

fiat money Money accepted by law and not because of redeemability or intrinsic value. (Chapter 15)

final products Finished goods and services produced for the ultimate user. (Chapter 11)

fiscal policy The use of government spending and taxes to influence the nation's output, employment and price level. (Chapter 17)

fiscal stance The term used to represent the extent to which the authorities are actively trying to expand or retard the growth of the economy through the settings of government revenue-raising and spending policies. (Chapter 17)

fixed input Any resource for which the quantity cannot change during the period of time under consideration. (Chapter 6)

floating exchange rate In a floating exchange rate, market demand and supply determine the foreign price of the currency. If sellers of the $A cannot find buyers they have to reduce the price of the $A until buyers are forthcoming. (Chapter 16)

flexible (or floating) exchange rate system A system in which countries allow their currencies to adjust continuously according to the forces of supply and demand. Most developed countries in the world today employ this type of exchange rate system. (Chapter 18)

flow A rate of change in a quantity during a given time period, measured in units per time period, such as dollars per year. For example, income and consumption are flows that occur per week, per month or per year. (Chapter 11)

foreign exchange (FOREX) market On any given day many thousands of individuals and companies want to exchange Australian dollars for foreign currencies or vice-versa. The foreign exchange (FOREX) market has evolved to accommodate such transactions. (Chapter 15)

fractional reserve banking A system in which banks keep only a small percentage of their deposits on reserve as vault cash and deposits at the central bank. (Chapter 15)

free trade The flow of goods and services between countries without restrictions or special taxes. (Chapter 18)

free trade agreement (FTA) In a free trade agreement, parties to a free trade area agree to eliminate tariffs and other trade barriers among themselves. However, each individual country maintains its own tariff policy against non-parties to the agreement. (Chapter 18)

frictional unemployment Unemployment caused by the normal search time required by workers with marketable skills who are changing jobs, initially entering the labour force or re-entering the labour force. (Chapter 13)

full employment The situation in which an economy operates at an unemployment rate equal to the sum of the seasonal, frictional and structural unemployment rates. (Chapter 13)

game theory Analyses the strategic decisions of players when the outcome for each is dependent on the behaviour of others. (Chapter 9)

GDP at factor cost A measure of GDP arrived at by adding all the incomes of all factors of production (including, labour, land and capital). (Chapter 11)

GDP at market prices A measure of GDP arrived at by valuing GDP produced at the prices at which the goods and services sell. The difference between this and GDP at factor cost is the existence of indirect taxes less subsidies. (Chapter 11)

GDP chain price index A measure that compares changes in the prices of all final goods during a given period to the prices of those goods in a base year. (Chapter 11)

GDP gap The difference between full-employment real GDP and actual real GDP. (Chapter 12)

goal of monetary policy Since 1996, in Australia the formal goal of monetary policy has been to keep inflation between 2 and 3 per cent over the course of the business cycle. (Chapter 16)

goals of macroeconomic policy These are to reduce the severity of the ups and downs of the business cycle and to assist with the achievement of the highest possible sustainable economic growth trajectory consistent with the economic social and cultural aspirations of the community. (Chapter 12)

'Golden Rule' steady-state level of capital stock per capita The rate of capital stock per capita – and associated saving rate – that results in the maximum level of consumption per capita in the long-run steady state. (Chapter 12)

gross domestic product (GDP) The market value of all final goods and services produced in a nation during a period of time, usually a quarter or a year. (Chapter 11)

gross investment Any spending that maintains or increases the capital stock in the country. (Chapter 11)

gross national expenditure (GNE) The sum of consumption, investment and government spending in the economy in a quarter or a year ($= C + I + G$) irrespective of whether the spending was on domestic production or on imports. (Chapter 11)

gross national product (GNP) The income accruing to a country's residents from the production of all final goods and services during a period of time, no matter where in the world the goods and services are produced. (Chapter 11)

human capital The accumulation of education, training, experience and health status that help a worker be productive in an occupation. (Chapter 10) A term used to distinguish spending on physical capital – that is, spending on physical goods and services to improve the productive process – from spending that has the purpose of enhancing the productivity of the human input into production. (Chapter 11)

hyperinflation An extremely rapid rise in the general price level. (Chapter 13)

hysteresis Occurs when the full employment rate of unemployment increases (decreases) as the actual unemployment rate increases (decreases). (Chapter 13)

implicit costs The opportunity costs of using resources owned by a firm. (Chapter 6)

income approach The national income accounting method that measures GDP by adding all incomes including compensation of employees, rents, net interest and profits. (Chapter 11)

income elasticity of demand The ratio of the percentage change in the quantity demanded of a good or service to a given percentage change in income. (Chapter 5)

increasing-cost industry An industry in which the expansion of industry output by the entry of new firms increases the firm's cost curves. (Chapter 7)

independent relationship No association between two variables. When one variable changes, the other variable remains unchanged. (Chapter 1 Appendix)

indirect taxes Taxes levied on the sale of goods and services. (Chapter 10)

indirect taxes less subsidies Government taxes levied on the production and/or sale of goods and services sold, less any subsidies paid to business from government. Examples include general sales taxes, excise taxes and customs duties. (Chapter 11)

inelastic demand A condition in which the percentage change in quantity demanded is smaller than the percentage change in price. (Chapter 5)

inferior good Any good or service for which there is an inverse relationship between changes in income and its demand curve. (Chapter 3)

inflation An increase in the general (average) price level of goods and services in the economy. (Chapter 13)

information lag The delay (months) before information about the current phase of economic activity in the real world becomes available. (Chapter 16)

interest-rate effect The impact on total spending (real GDP) of the direct relationship between the price level and the interest rate. (Chapter 14)

intermediate goods Goods and services used as inputs for the production of final goods. (Chapter 11)

intermediate range The rising segment of the aggregate supply curve, which represents an economy as it approaches full-employment output. (Chapter 14)

inverse relationship A negative association between two variables. When one variable increases, the other variable decreases, and when one variable decreases, the other variable increases. (Chapter 1 Appendix)

investment The process of producing capital, such as factories, machines and inventories. (Chapter 2)

investment demand Investment demand by businesses increases as rates of interest drop or as profit expectations increase. Shifts in investment demand result from changes in expectations, technological change, capacity utilisation and business taxes. (Chapter 14)

Keynesian range The horizontal segment of the aggregate supply curve, which represents an economy in a severe recession. (Chapter 14)

kinked demand curve A demand curve faced by an oligopolist who assumes that rivals will match a price decrease but ignore a price increase. (Chapter 9)

labour The mental and physical capacity of workers to produce goods and services. (Chapter 1)

Laffer curve Representation of the relationship between the income tax rate and the amount of income tax revenue collected by the government. (Chapter 17)

lagging indicators Variables that change direction after a phase change in the economy has occurred, thereby confirming it. (Chapter 12)

land A shorthand expression for any resource provided by nature. (Chapter 1)

law of demand The principle that there is an inverse relationship between the price of a good or service and the quantity buyers are willing to purchase in a defined time period, ceteris paribus. (Chapter 3)

law of diminishing returns The principle that, beyond some point, the marginal product decreases as additional units of a variable factor are added to a fixed factor. (Chapter 6)

law of increasing opportunity costs The principle that the opportunity cost increases as the production of one output expands. (Chapter 2)

law of supply The principle that there is a direct relationship between the price of a good and the quantity sellers are willing to offer for sale in a defined time period, ceteris paribus. (Chapter 3)

leading indicators	Variables that change direction before the economy shifts from one business cycle phase into another. (Chapter 12)
long run	A sufficient period of time to allow all inputs to be varied. (Chapter 6)
long-run average cost curve	The curve that traces the lowest cost per unit at which a firm can produce any level of output when the firm can build any desired plant size. (Chapter 6)
M1	The narrowest definition of the money supply. It includes currency in the hands of the non-bank public and cheque account deposits. (Chapter 15)
M3	The definition of the money supply that equals M1 plus all other deposits of the non bank public at banks. (Chapter 15)
macroeconomics	The branch of economics that studies decision-making for the economy as a whole. (Chapter 1)
marginal analysis	An examination of the effects of additions to or subtractions from a current situation. (Chapter 2)
marginal-average rule	When applied to cost relationships, the rule stating that, when marginal cost is below average cost, average cost falls. When marginal cost is above average cost, average cost rises. When marginal cost equals average cost, average cost is at its minimum point. (Chapter 6)
marginal cost	The change in total cost when one additional unit of output is produced. (Chapter 6)
marginal product	The change in total output produced by adding one unit of a variable input, with all other inputs used being held constant. (Chapter 6)
marginal propensity to consume (MPC)	The change in consumption resulting from a given change in disposable income. (Chapter 14)
marginal propensity to save (MPS)	The change in savings resulting from a given change in disposable income, namely 1 – MPC. (Chapter 14)
marginal revenue	The change in total revenue from the sale of one additional unit of output. (Chapter 7)
marginal revenue product (MRP)	The increase in total revenue to a firm resulting from hiring an additional unit of labour or other variable resource. (Chapter 10)
market	Any arrangement in which the interaction of buyers and sellers determines the price and quantity of goods and services exchanged. (Chapter 3)
market failure	A situation in which the price system fails to operate efficiently, creating a problem for society. (Chapter 4)
market structure	A classification system for the key characteristics of a market, including the number of firms, the similarity of the products they sell, and the ease of entry into and exit from the market. (Chapter 7)
medium of exchange	The primary function of money, which is to be widely accepted in exchange for goods and services. (Chapter 15)
microeconomic reform	Government policies that deregulate or re-regulate markets for goods, services or factors of production so as to increase competition and raise economic efficiency. (Chapter 10)
microeconomics	The branch of economics that studies decision-making by a single individual, household, firm or industry. (Chapter 1)
minimum liquidity requirement	Requirement that a bank must always maintain a certain minimal reserve level of highly liquid assets to cover any short-run demands from its many depositors and other creditors. (Chapter 15)
model	A simplified description of reality used to understand and predict the relationship between variables. (Chapter 1)

monetarism The theory that changes in the growth of the money supply directly determine changes in prices, real GDP and employment. (Chapter 16)

monetary base The primary liquidity of the financial system. The assets in the Base are the most liquid of all financial assets and consist of currency in circulation (notes and coins) plus the deposits of banks and money market dealers with the RBA. (Chapter 15)

monetary policy Actions taken by the central bank to influence the monetary base, interest rates, economic activity and prices in the economy. (Chapter 15) The central bank's use of open market operations to bring about changes in the monetary base and interest rates. (Chapter 16)

monetary policy transmission mechanism A description of how it is thought that a monetary policy change is transmitted through into the economy, thereby affecting output, prices and employment. (Chapter 16)

money Anything that serves as a medium of exchange, unit of account, and store of value. (Chapter 15)

money financing When a budget deficit is financed by the central bank purchasing the securities issued by the government to fund its deficit. This part of the deficit is monetised, in that the government has financed its spending by virtue of the central bank expanding the money supply. (Chapter 17)

money multiplier See *credit creation and the money multiplier*

monopolistic competition A market structure characterised by (1) many small sellers, (2) a differentiated product and (3) easy market entry and exit. (Chapter 9)

monopoly A market structure characterised by (1) a single seller, (2) a unique product and (3) extremely difficult or impossible entry into the market. (Chapter 8)

mutual interdependence A condition in which an action by one firm may cause a reaction on the part of other firms. (Chapter 9)

national debt The total value of outstanding commonwealth government securities; it represents the extent of previous borrowing by the federal government. (Chapter 17)

national disposable income (NDI) Obtained after subtracting net transfers overseas (mainly foreign aid and pensions paid to recipients living abroad) from net national product. (Chapter 11)

national investment A country's total spending on capital goods by the private sector and government. If national investment is greater than national saving, then the country will have a current account deficit.

national saving A country's total income accruing to its residents less its consumption.

natural monopoly An industry in which the long-run average cost of production declines throughout the entire range of output. As a result, a single firm can supply the entire market demand at a lower cost than two or more smaller firms. (Chapter 8)

net domestic product (NDP) Gross domestic product minus depreciation of the capital worn out in producing output. (Chapter 11)

net exports effect The impact on total spending (real GDP) of the inverse relationship between the price level and the net exports of an economy. (Chapter 14)

net foreign income The difference between aggregate investment income flows into and out of a country. Such income includes interest payments on loans, rent on property and dividends on shares. Foreign income credits for Australia, for example, represent income flowing into Australia from the investments of Australian residents abroad, while foreign income debits represent income flowing out of Australia to foreigners on account of the application of their investment capital in Australia. (Chapter 18)

net investment Only that spending that actually increases the nation's capital stock. (Chapter 11)

net national product (NNP) The income accruing to a nation's residents from the production of all final goods and services during a period, no matter where the production of goods and services is located, after an allowance for depreciation is subtracted. (Chapter 11)

nominal GDP The value of all final goods based on the prices existing during the time period of production. (Chapter 11)

nominal income The actual number of dollars received over a period of time. (Chapter 13)

nominal interest rate The actual rate of interest earned over a period of time. (Chapter 13)

non-price competition The situation in which a firm competes using differences in advertising, packaging, product development, quality and service, rather than lower prices. (Chapter 9)

normal good Any good or service for which there is a direct relationship between changes in income and its demand. (Chapter 3)

normal profit The minimum profit necessary to keep a firm in operation. A firm that earns normal profit earns total revenue equal to its total opportunity cost (total explicit and implicit costs). (Chapter 6)

normative economics An analysis based on value judgements. (Chapter 1)

oligopoly A market structure characterised by (1) few sellers, (2) either a homogeneous or a differentiated product and (3) barriers to market entry. (Chapter 9)

open-market operations The buying and selling of government securities by the central bank to the private-sector financial markets to bring about changes to the monetary base and the 'cash rate'. (Chapter 16)

opportunity cost The best alternative sacrificed for a chosen alternative. (Chapter 2)

overnight cash rate 'Cash rate' for short. The interest rate that borrowers in the money markets must pay to borrow funds overnight. Its value influences all other interest rates in the money markets and thereby its value influences all interest rates throughout the entire economy. It is by this influence on the interest rates in the wider economy that the RBA seeks to affect aggregate demand and influence the rate of inflation. (Chapter 16)

peak The phase of the business cycle in which the economy reaches its maximum after rising during an expansion. (Chapter 12)

perfect competition A market structure characterised by (1) a large number of small firms, (2) a homogeneous product and (3) very easy entry into or exit from the market. (Chapter 7)

perfectly competitive firm's short-run supply curve The firm's marginal cost curve above the minimum point on its average variable cost curve. (Chapter 7)

perfectly competitive industry's long-run supply curve The curve that shows the quantities supplied by the industry at different equilibrium prices after firms complete their entry and exit. (Chapter 7)

perfectly competitive industry's short-run market supply curve The supply curve derived from the horizontal summation of the short run supply curves of all firms in the industry. (Chapter 7)

perfectly elastic demand A condition in which a small percentage change in price brings about an infinite percentage change in quantity demanded. (Chapter 5)

perfectly inelastic demand A condition in which the quantity demanded does not change as the price changes. (Chapter 5)

policy determination lag The time taken to decide on an apparently appropriate policy response; may be several months. (Chapter 16)

policy effectiveness lag The delay between the time when a policy is initiated and the time when it begins to take effect on economic activity. (Chapter 16)

positive economics	An analysis limited to statements that are verifiable. (Chapter 1)
precautionary motive for the demand for money	The explanation for the stock of money people hold to pay unpredictable expenses. (Chapter 15)
price ceiling	A legally established maximum price a seller can charge. (Chapter 4)
price discrimination	This occurs when, for the same product, a seller charges different customers different prices not justified by cost differences. (Chapter 8)
price elasticity of demand	The ratio of the percentage change in the quantity demanded of a product to a percentage change in its price. (Chapter 5)
price elasticity of supply	The ratio of the percentage change in the quantity supplied of a product to the percentage change in its price. (Chapter 5)
price floor	A legally established minimum price a seller can be paid. (Chapter 4)
price leadership	A pricing strategy in which a dominant firm sets the price for an industry and the other firms follow. (Chapter 9)
price maker	A firm that faces a downward-sloping demand curve and can therefore choose among price and output combinations along the demand curve. (Chapter 8)
price system	A mechanism that uses the forces of supply and demand to create an equilibrium through rising and falling prices. (Chapter 3)
price taker	A seller with no control over the price of its product. (Chapter 7)
product differentiation	The process of creating real or apparent differences between goods and services. (Chapter 9)
production function	The relationship between the maximum amounts of output a firm can produce and various quantities of inputs. (Chapter 6)
production possibilities frontier	Shows the maximum combinations of two outputs that an economy can produce, given its available resources and technology. (Chapter 2)
protectionism	The government's use of embargoes, tariffs, quotas and other restrictions to protect domestic producers from foreign competition. (Chapter 18)
public good	A good or service that, once produced, has two special properties: (1) users collectively consume benefits and (2) there is no way to prevent people who do not pay (free riders) from consuming the good or service. (Chapter 4)
quantity theory of money	The theory that changes in the price level (inflation) are directly related to changes in the growth of the money supply. (Chapter 16)
quota	A limit on the quantity of a good that may be imported in a given time period. (Chapter 18)
real balances or wealth effect	The impact on total spending (real GDP) of the inverse relationship between the price level and the real value of financial assets with fixed nominal value. (Chapter 14).
real GDP	The value of all final goods and services produced during a given time period based on the prices existing in a selected base year. (Chapter 11)
real income	The actual number of dollars received (nominal income) adjusted for changes in the CPI. (Chapter 13)
real interest rate	The nominal rate of interest minus the inflation rate. (Chapter 13)
recession	A downturn in the business cycle in which output, sales and employment decline. (Chapter 12)
Reserve Bank Board	RBA board that determines monetary policy in Australia; it consists of the Governor, the Deputy Governor, the Under Treasurer and six other members appointed by parliament. (Chapter 15)
Reserve Bank of Australia (RBA)	The central bank of Australia, responsible for monetary policy, the payments system and financial system stability, and providing banking

services to the banks, other financial institutions and the federal government. (Chapter 15)

resources The basic categories of inputs used to produce goods and services. Resources are also called factors of production. Economists divide resources into three categories: land, labour and capital. (Chapter 1)

Say's Law The theory that supply creates its own demand; the cornerstone of classical economics as it applied to macroeconomics. (Chapter 14)

scarcity The condition in which human wants are forever greater than the available supply of time, goods and resources. (Chapter 1)

seasonal unemployment Unemployment caused by recurring changes in hiring due to recurring changes in weather conditions, demand and/or production patterns. (Chapter 13)

short run A period of time during which there is at least one fixed input. (Chapter 6)

shortage A market condition existing at any price where the quantity supplied is less than the quantity demanded. (Chapter 3)

slope The ratio of the changes in the variable on the vertical axis (the rise or fall) to the change in the variable on the horizontal axis (the run). (Chapter 1 Appendix)

smoothing and testing Even though Australia now allows its exchange rate to float, the RBA still regularly operates in the market if it considers the AUD is coming under undue short-run speculative pressure or if FOREX market conditions are excessively volatile. The latter activity is termed 'smoothing', while the former is referred to as 'testing'. (Chapter 16)

Solow growth model An early growth model that sought to explain how consumption, saving, capital, labour and technological change combine in the longer term to determine a nation's economic growth. In the Solow model, technological change is assumed to be exogenous. (Chapter 12)

speculative motive for the demand for money The explanation for the stock of money people hold to take advantage of expected future changes in the price of bonds, stocks or other non-money financial assets. (Chapter 15)

spending multiplier The induced rounds of spending that occur in an economy after some initial stimulus to spending. (Chapter 14)

stagflation The condition that occurs when an economy experiences the twin maladies of high unemployment and rapid inflation simultaneously. (Chapter 14)

Statement on the Conduct of Monetary Policy Policy signed by the RBA Governor and the Federal Treasurer in 1996. It encapsulates the Australian government's agreement that the RBA should have the goal of keeping inflation on average to between 2 and 3 per cent per annum and that the RBA be free to implement monetary policy as it sees fit to achieve that goal. (Chapter 16)

stock A quantity measured at one point in time, such as an inventory of goods or the amount of money in a cheque account. (Chapter 11)

store of value The ability of money to hold value over time. (Chapter 15)

strategic trade theory The idea that governments should seek to be strategic in their use of their spending and taxing powers in order to actively facilitate some sectors of the economy that they may feel have the potential to be strong export earners for their nations. (Chapter 18)

structural unemployment Unemployment caused by a mismatch of the skills of workers out of work and the skills required for existing job opportunities. (Chapter 13)

substitute good A good that competes with another good for consumer purchases. As a result, there is a direct relationship between a price change for one good and the demand for its 'competitor' good. (Chapter 3)

supply curve of labour A curve showing the different quantities of labour workers are willing to offer employers at different wage rates in a given time period, ceteris paribus. (Chapter 10)

supply-side fiscal policy A fiscal policy that emphasises government policies that increase aggregate supply in order to achieve long-run growth in real output, full employment, and a lower price level. (Chapter 17)

surplus A market condition existing at any price where the quantity supplied is greater than the quantity demanded. (Chapter 3)

tariff A tax on an import. (Chapter 18)

tax incidence The share of a tax ultimately paid by consumers or by sellers. (Chapter 5)

technology The body of knowledge applied to how goods and services are produced. (Chapter 2)

testing See *smoothing and testing*.

total cost The sum of total fixed cost and total variable cost at each level of output. (Chapter 6)

total fixed cost Costs that do not vary as output varies and that must be paid even if output is zero. These are payments that the firm must make in the short run, regardless of the level of output. (Chapter 6)

total revenue The total number of dollars a firm earns from sales of a good or service; it is equal to its price multiplied by the quantity demanded. (Chapter 5)

total variable cost Costs that are zero when output is zero and vary as output varies. (Chapter 6)

transactions motive for the demand for money The explanation for the stock of money people hold to pay everyday predictable expenses. (Chapter 15)

transfer payment A government payment to individuals not in exchange for goods or services currently produced. (Chapter 11)

treasury note (T-note) A T-note is sold by the Treasury on behalf of the federal government and is considered riskless. Since payment at maturity is absolutely guaranteed, T-notes are traded freely in the financial markets. (Chapter 15)

trough The phase of the business cycle in which the economy reaches its minimum after falling during a recession. (Chapter 12)

unemployment rate The percentage of people in the labour force who are without jobs and are actively seeking jobs. (Chapter 13)

unit of account The function of money to provide a common measurement of the relative value of goods and services. (Chapter 15)

unitary elastic demand A condition in which the percentage change in quantity demanded is equal to the percentage change in price. (Chapter 5)

variable input Any resource for which the quantity can change during the period of time under consideration. (Chapter 6)

velocity of money The average number of times per period a dollar of the money supply is spent on final goods and services. (Chapter 16)

wage–price spiral A situation that occurs when increases in nominal wage rates are passed on in higher prices, which in turn result in even higher nominal wage rates and prices. (Chapter 13)

wealth The value of the stock of assets owned at some point in time. (Chapter 13)

Index